Seventh Edition

THE SOCIOLOGY OF EDUCATION

A SYSTEMATIC ANALYSIS

Jeanne H. Ballantine
Wright State University

Floyd M. Hammack
New York University

PEARSON

Boston   Columbus   Indianapolis   New York   San Francisco   Upper Saddle River
Amsterdam   Cape Town   Dubai   London   Madrid   Milan   Munich   Paris   Montreal   Toronto
Delhi   Mexico City   Sao Paulo   Sydney   Hong Kong   Seoul   Singapore   Taipei   Tokyo

Publisher: Karen Hanson
Project Manager: Elizabeth Gale Napolitano
Editorial Assistant: Christine Dore
Executive Marketing Manager: Kelly May
Marketing Assistant: Janeli Bitor
Production Manager: Meghan DeMaio
Creative Director: Jayne Conte
Cover Designer: Karen Salzbach
Cover Image: © Yuri Arcurs / Fotolia
Editorial Production and Composition Service: Moganambigai Sundaramurthy, Integra Software Services
Printer/Binder/Cover Printer: R. R. Donnelley & Sons

Photo Credits
p. 20: © spirit of america/Shutterstock; p. 32: © Charles Tasnadi/AP Images; p. 82: © Myrleen Pearson/Alamy;
p. 100: © PCN Black/PCN Photography/Alamy; p. 132: © ZUMA Press, Inc./Alamy; p. 163: © Golden Pixels
LLC/Shutterstock; p. 181: © Pressmaster/Shutterstock.com; p. 214: © Sonya Etchison/Shutterstock.com;
p. 244: © Marmaduke St. John/Alamy; p. 262: © hxdbzxy/Alamy.com; p. 299: © Leila Cutler/Alamy; p. 328: © John
Brown/Alamy; p. 367: © Stockbroker/Purestock/SuperStock

Library of Congress Cataloging-in-Publication Data
Ballantine, Jeanne H.
    The sociology of education : a systematic analysis / Jeanne H. Ballantine, Floyd M. Hammack.—7th ed.
        p. cm.
    Includes bibliographical references and index.
    ISBN-13: 978-0-205-80091-9 (alk. paper)
    ISBN-10: 0-205-80091-2 (alk. paper)
    1. Educational sociology.   I. Hammack, Floyd M.   II. Title.
    LC191.B254 2011
    306.43—dc22

                                                                                    2011015889

10 9 8 7 6 5 4 3 2—DOH—15 14

ISBN-10: 0-205-80091-2
ISBN-13: 978-0-205-80091-9

BRIEF CONTENTS

CONTENTS

v

PREFACE

Integrating the important and diverse topics in the field of sociology of education by showing how they are related is the main goal of this text. It emphasizes the diversity of theoretical approaches and issues in the field and the application of this knowledge to the understanding of education and schooling. Education is changing rapidly; it is no easy task to present the excitement of a dynamic field with diverse and disparate topics. To present the material to students in a meaningful way, a unifying framework—an open systems approach—is used. It is meant to provide coherent structure, not to detract from the theory and empirical content of sociology of education. In the seventh edition of the text, several changes are noted. The first chapter has been updated to provide an overview of education in the twenty-first century. In addition, extensive updating of findings on educational data and problems, plus current issues in education, has been included.

After teaching sociology of education to many undergraduate and graduate students and using a variety of materials, we were concerned that the materials available, though excellent in quality, were not reaching undergraduate students who were from sociology, education, and other majors. The level of many texts is quite advanced, the themes of some books make their coverage or approach limited, and the books present research in such depth that they are beyond the grasp of undergraduate and beginning graduate students, and therefore difficult for them to apply to their work in educational settings. During work with the Project on Teaching Undergraduate Sociology, the authors developed a guide for teaching sociology of education and focused on presentation of materials to undergraduates. These materials and ideas have been incorporated into this text. The book is best suited for sociology of education and social foundations/cultural context of education courses at the undergraduate or beginning graduate level.

Several goals guided the writing of this book:

1. *To make the book comprehensible and useful to students.* Realizing that most students are interested in how the field can help them deal with issues they will face, we emphasize the usefulness of research findings. Choices had to be made concerning which studies and topics to cover. Those chosen should have high interest for students and help them as they work in and interact with school systems.

2. *To present material in a coherent framework.* The authors present key ideas in the sociology of education by utilizing a systems framework. The instructor has leeway within the open systems approach to add topics, exclude sections of the text, and rearrange the order of topics without losing the continuity and integration present in this framework.

3. *To present diverse theoretical approaches in sociology of education.* Several valuable perspectives in the field are influential today; the book gives examples throughout of traditional and new theories and how they approach issues in the field.

4. *To include topics that have not been singled out by many authors, but are important current or emerging topics that are of interest to students.* Separate chapters are devoted to higher education, organization of schools and roles in schools, informal education ("climate" and the "hidden curriculum"), the school environment, education around the world, and educational movements and alternatives.

5. *To indicate how change takes place and what role sociologists play in both understanding and bringing about change.* With the increasing emphasis on applied sociology, more

courses are including information on applied aspects of topics covered. This is the focus of the final chapter but is covered throughout the text.

6. *To stimulate students to become involved with educational systems where they can use the knowledge available in this and other textbooks.* This text can be used to stimulate discussion and encourage other topics of interest to be introduced into the course in a logical way. Useful features of the book to enhance teaching effectiveness include projects at the end of each chapter; the coverage of issues; and the Instructor's Manual, complete with classroom teaching aids, techniques, and test questions.

The book does not attempt to use one theoretical approach to the exclusion of others. Rather, it focuses on the value of several different approaches and their emphases in dealing with the same issue. Because the book is meant as an overview, it surveys the field rather than providing comprehensive coverage of a few topics. This allows instructors the flexibility to expand where desired.

SUPPLEMENTARY MATERIALS

Instructor's Manual and Test Bank (ISBN 0205842356): The Instructor's Manual and Test Bank has been prepared to assist teachers in their efforts to prepare lectures and evaluate student learning. For each chapter of the text, the Instructor's Manual offers different types of resources, including detailed chapter summaries and outlines, learning objectives, discussion questions, classroom activities and much more.

Also included in this manual is a test bank offering multiple-choice, true/false, fill-in-the-blank, and/or essay questions for each chapter. The Instructor's Manual and Test Bank is available to adopters at www.pearsonhighered.com <http://www.pearsonhighered.com/>.

MyTest (ISBN 0205020674): The Test Bank is also available online through Pearson's computerized testing system, MyTest. MyTest allows instructors to create their own personalized exams, to edit any of the existing test questions, and to add new questions. Other special features of this program include random generation of test questions, creation of alternative versions of the same test, scrambling question sequence, and test preview before printing. Search and sort features allow you to locate questions quickly and to arrange them in whatever order you prefer. The test bank can be accessed from anywhere with a free MyTest user account. There is no need to download a program or file to your computer.

PowerPoint Presentations (ISBN 020502064X): Lecture PowerPoints are available for this text. The Lecture PowerPoint slides outline each chapter to help you convey sociological principles in a visual and exciting way. They are available to adopters at www.pearsonhighered.com <http://www.pearsonhighered.com/>.

MySearchLab: MySearchLab provides a host of tools for students to master a writing or research project, it provides online access to reliable content for internet research projects, including thousands of full articles from the EBSCO ContentSelect database a complete online handbook for grammar and usage support. A tutorial on understanding and avoiding plagiarism, and AutoCite, which helps students correctly cite sources.

Thanks go to many people for suggestions on early drafts: for reviews of the manuscript for the seventh edition, we are grateful to Carol Ward, Brigham Young University; Beth Duckles, University of Arizona; Robert A. Ibarra, University of New Mexico; Theodore C. Wagenaar,

Miami University; Sheying Chen, University of Guam; J. Russell, Tarleton State University; Paula B. Moore, Eastern Kentucky University; and William A. Mirola, Marian College. For providing the materials and atmosphere for producing the end product, thanks go to Antioch University Library, University of Reading (England) Library, and the University of London and Bodleian libraries. A special thanks go to the supportive group at Pearson, especially Publisher Karen Hanson, who provided expert editorial guidance.

Finally, our interest in this field is constantly stimulated by the diverse and ever-changing experiences of our children as they have passed through the stages of schooling and share their experiences, and, for Jeanne, by Hardy, whose knowledge and creative ideas in the field of education gave original impetus and continuing support and encouragement to this work. Floyd thanks Nancy for her usual attention to detail and to her continuing interest in his work.

Jeanne H. Ballantine
and Floyd M. Hammack

1

Sociology of Education

A Unique Perspective for Understanding Schools

"Joyce Irvine vs. millions. You can buy a lot of help for children with that money," commented the principal of Wheeler Elementary School in Vermont (Winerip, 2010). She had just been fired from her position. Why? The district superintendent commented that they had to fire her in order to follow the government mandates and requirements for receiving $3 million in government support—and "we need every bit of support we can get!" The superintendent lamented the loss of one of her best employees. Wheeler Elementary School had students mostly from immigrant families, many of them who had recently arrived, and with few English skills. In the fifth grade alone, 37 of the 39 students were refugees or students with special-education needs—or both. This hard working, talented, compassionate principal had made great strides with these children. However, it was not enough to satisfy well-intentioned government requirements and definitions of failing schools, based on testing that was inappropriate for these children. This example sets the stage for a look at the sometimes conflicting interrelationships that make up the educational system in the United States. While we attempt to meet the needs of all children, some "need" more than others.

As we explore the many issues facing education in the United States and around the world, we must ask if we are failing to educate our children for their—and our—futures? Some of the issues are as follows: How can we increase academic achievement? Do schools simply perpetuate the country's stratification system? What moral or religious impact should schools have on young people? Are children who have access to technology in schools better prepared for the future? In addition, moral, political, and religious questions pervade the educational landscape around the world.

Education is a lifelong process. It begins the day we are born and ends the day we die. It is found in every society and comes in many forms, ranging from the "school of hard knocks," or learning by experience, to formal institutional learning—from postindustrial to nonindustrial communities, from rural to urban settings, and from youth to older persons. Sociologists of education look into questions such as what is being done about these issues, how policies regarding these and other questions affect schools, and what seems to be working to educate young people. While sociologists do not try to answer questions of right and wrong, good and bad, they do consider the state of education and the outcomes of certain policies and practices.

SOCIOLOGY AND EDUCATION

Sociologists study people who are in interacting and in small to large group situations. Within this broad general framework are many specialties; these can be divided into studies of institutions in societies (established aspects of society that address common needs of people), studies of processes, and studies of interactions between individuals and groups. The structure of society (recurring patterns of behavior and ordered interrelationships to achieve the needs of people) is represented by six major institutions that constitute some of the major subject areas in sociology: family, religion, education, politics, economics, and health. Formal, complex organizations, such as schools, are part of the institutional *structures* that carry out the work of societies.

Processes, the action part of society, bring the structures alive. Through the process of socialization, people learn how to fit into society and what roles are expected of them. The process of *stratification* determines where people fit into the social structure and their resultant lifestyle. *Change* is an ever-present process that constantly forces schools and other organizations to adjust to new demands. *Learning* takes place both formally in school settings and informally by our family, peers, media, and other influences in our lives. Not all children in the world receive a formal school education, but they all experience processes that prepare them for adult roles.

The institution of education interacts and is interdependent with each of the other institutions. For instance, the family's involvement in education will affect the child's achievement in school. Other examples throughout the book will make these connections apparent, as will the open systems model diagrammed later in this chapter.

Sociology of education as a field is devoted to understanding educational systems; the subject matter includes questions ranging from teacher and student interactions to large educational systems of countries. By studying education systematically, sociologists offer insights to help guide policies for schools. Research on educational systems is guided by sociological theories and studied using sociological methods. Although sociology provides a unique and powerful set of tools to objectively explore the educational systems of societies, it may disappoint those who have an axe to grind or whose goal is to proselytize rather than objectively understand or explore. Sometimes simply raising certain questions is ideologically uncomfortable for those who "know the right answer," but where there is a controversy about educational policy, several different views emerge and proponents feel their view is the right answer. The goal of sociology of education is to objectively consider educational practices, sometimes controversial topics, and even unpopular beliefs to gain understanding of a system that affects us all.

Please approach this book and its subject matter with an open mind. Ask questions. Challenge ideas. Explore findings—but do so with the intent of opening new avenues for thought, discussion, and research. The purpose of this introductory chapter is to acquaint you with the unique perspective of the sociology of education: the questions it addresses, the theoretical approaches it uses, the methods used to study educational systems, and the open systems approach used in this book. We begin our discussion with an overview of sociology of education.

Why Study Sociology of Education?

There are several answers to this question. Someday you may be a professional in the field of education or in a related field; you will be a taxpayer, if you aren't already; or you may be a parent with children in the school system. Right now you are a student involved in higher or continuing education. Why are you taking this class? If you are a sociology major, you are studying education as one of the major institutions of society; if you are an education major, sociology may give you a new or different perspective on your field. You may be at college in pursuit of knowledge; or this course may be required, you may need the credit, perhaps the teacher is supposed to be good, or it simply may fit into your schedule. Let's consider some of these reasons for studying sociology of education.

TEACHERS AND OTHER PROFESSIONALS.   Study findings indicate that between 2008 and 2018, the most job openings, 597,000, for those with a bachelor's degree will be in elementary education (The College Board, 2010). In the United States in 2003–2004, more than 106,000 college students graduated with majors in the field of education, and many went on to hold teaching positions. An estimated 3.5 million teachers are involved in public school education (Bureau of Labor Statistics, 2010–2011). Other college graduates teach in their respective academic fields or become involved with policy matters in the schools. Professionals in such fields as social work and business have regular contact with schools when dealing with clients and employees.

TAXPAYERS.   Taxpayers play a major role in financing schools at the elementary-, secondary-, and higher-education levels. Almost 100 percent of the money used to pay for physical plants, materials, salaries, and other essentials in the U. S. public educational system comes from taxes. Revenues for schools come from three main sources: local, state, and federal funds from sales, income, and property taxes. Considering variations in U.S. school districts with high and low parental incomes, and differences among states and districts, the local district contribution ranges from 28 to 56 percent, and the federal contribution from 3 to 12 percent. In 2008, the total education budget in the United States was $581.1 billion, with local contributions making up 43.7 percent, state 48.3 percent, and federal 8.1 percent of the total (U.S. Census Bureau, 2010). Average per pupil expenditures in K–12 public schools increased from $7,365 in 1990 to $10,041 in 2006–2007 (in constant dollars) (NCES, 2010), with low-income areas receiving significantly less than high-income areas. Sociology helps taxpayers understand the school system for which they are paying.

PARENTS.   A large percentage of adults in the United States are parents; the average size of a household in 2006 was 2.6 members (Whipps, 2006). According to the Gallup polls on adult attitudes toward education, adults expect schools to teach basic skills, discipline children, and instill values and a sense of responsibility. The concerns of the American public regarding schools have shown a high level of consistency from year to year (See Table 1.1) (Bushaw and McNee, 2009). Lack of financial support and lack of discipline topped the list of problems seen by the public in 2009, with overcrowding being the third. Drugs and violence were number 4 and 5 on the list.

Table 1.1 What Do You Think Are the Biggest Problems that the Public Schools of Your Community Must Deal With?

	National Totals			Public School Parents		
	2009 (%)	2008 (%)	2007 (%)	2009 (%)	2008 (%)	2007 (%)
Lack of funding	32	17	22	30	19	26
Lack of discipline	10	10	10	8	3	5
Overcrowding	9	6	7	10	11	9
Drugs	5	4	4	5	4	3
Fighting	4	6	6	6	8	8
Lack of standards	3	3	4	2	2	4
Lack of good teachers	3	4	5	2	3	4

Parents' rankings differed somewhat, in part because they need to make decisions regarding their children's education.

STUDENTS.   Grade school education is mandatory in most countries. High school level education is mandatory in developed countries, and available in some developing countries. According to a new study by Harvard University and the Asian Development Bank, only 6.7 percent of the world's population has a college degree (The Huffington Post, 2010). In the United States, 27.2 percent have college degrees, 8.9 percent masters degrees, and 3 percent PhDs (U.S. Census Bureau, 2002).

College attracts a wide variety of students with numerous incentives and goals for their educational experience. Understanding your own and others' goals will help you get the most from your education. For sociology majors, sociology of education provides a unique look at educational systems and their interdependence among other major institutions in society. For education majors, new insights can be gained by looking into the dynamic interactions both within educational settings and between the institution of education and other institutions in society. These insights should give education majors the ability to deal with complex organizational and interpersonal issues that confront teachers and administrators.

OTHER REASONS.   Being an informed citizen, understanding how tax dollars are spent, and gaining knowledge for the sake of knowledge—learning what there is to learn—are among the other reasons to study sociology of education.

Questions Asked by Sociologists of Education

As students, parents, and members of a community, we face educational issues constantly. Consider the following examples.

ARE OUR CHILDREN SAFE IN SCHOOLS?   Among the most serious school problems according to surveys of the American public are lack of discipline; use of drugs; and fighting, violence, and gangs in schools (Bushaw and McNee, 2009). Yet, even with the recent school shootings, 90 percent of the public believe school discipline is satisfactory. National studies indicate that most students do not experience criminal victimization, and those that do are more likely to experience property crimes. Students in schools with gang members present express more concern about safety. In addition, one-third of students indicate that drugs are available and one-fifth that alcohol is available at their school (Addington et al., 2002). Are our students safer in schools than out of school? Most studies conclude that schools are safe.

SHOULD MINIMUM COMPETENCY IN KEY SUBJECTS SUCH AS READING AND MATH BE REQUIRED FOR HIGH SCHOOL GRADUATION?   In many countries and in some parts of the United States, students are required to take reading and math exams in order to enter high school and be graduated from it. The "No Child Left Behind" and "Race to the Top" federal policies in the United States require all students be tested at various times throughout their school years. Increasingly, states hold schools and teachers responsible for the academic competence of students who move through the system (Borman and Cotner, 2011). This is what got Joyce in Vermont (opening scenario) fired. Thus, tests are viewed by many as one way to hold schools accountable for students' progress. Yet, some educators and researchers question the value of requiring competency tests because they have little benefit for students who pass them and can harm students who do not pass (Warren and Grodsky, 2009). What are some implications of requiring tests? This question will be discussed in later chapters.

HOW SHOULD EDUCATION BE FUNDED?   Many countries have centralized governmental educational funding and decision making. Across the United States, however, local taxpayers vote on local school levies, and some schools are being forced to curtail programs and cut the number of teachers because there is no money. The federal government has allotted funds from the stimulus money to help districts retain some teachers whose jobs are threatened. Is failure of school levies a protest against the job schools are doing? Is it a demand for the development of other funding sources? Is it a bid for more community control? Is it rebellion against any higher taxes? Some aspects of these difficult issues will be addressed.

WHAT TYPE OF TEACHERS AND CLASSROOM ENVIRONMENTS PROVIDE THE BEST LEARNING EXPERIENCE FOR CHILDREN?   Educators debate lecture versus experiential learning, and cooperative learning versus individualized instruction. Studies (e.g., Pescosolido and Aminzade, 1999) of effective teaching strategies provide information to help educators carry out their roles effectively. For example, research on the most effective size of classes and schools attempts to provide policy makers with data to inform decision making (Darling-Hammond, 2010). What other classroom factors influence teaching and learning?

A review of the titles of articles in the premiere journal, *Sociology of Education,* provides an overview of current topics being studied in the field. For example, in 2009 and 2010 researchers explored immigrant education, causes of academic failure and dropping out, social class differences in college expectations and entrance, interracial friendships, racial segregation in schools, educational attainment and attitudes toward schooling, higher education aspirations and enrollments, and females and males in different academic fields. Look through this book and other sociology of education resources to add to the list of questions asked by sociologists of education; they cover a fascinating array of topics. Sociological research knowledge sheds light on educational issues, and thus helps teachers, citizens, and policy makers with the decision-making process. Multitudes of questions arise, and many of them are being studied around the world.

Applying Sociology to Education: *From what you have read so far, what topics in sociology of education interest you?*

BOX 1.1

Current Research in the Sociology of Education

The following sampling of current research questions gives an idea of the wide range of subject matter:

1. If parents are involved in their children's schooling, are children more successful in school?
2. How effective are different teaching techniques, styles of learning, classroom organizations, and school and classroom size in teaching students of various types and abilities?
3. What are some community influences on the school, and how do these affect decision making in schools, especially as it relates to the school curriculum and socialization of the young?
4. Do teacher proficiency exams increase teaching quality?
5. Can minority students learn better or more in an integrated school?
6. Do schools perpetuate inequality?
7. Should religion be allowed in schools? What are the practices around the world?
8. Does tracking (ability grouping) help or hurt student learning?
9. Is the U.S. government policy "No Child Left Behind" and "Race to the Top" having a positive or negative effect overall?
10. Do schools prepare students for the transition to work?
11. Who are the world's most prepared students according to international tests, and why?
12. Are some students overeducated for the employment opportunities that are available to them?
13. How does education affect income potential?

U.S. SCHOOLS IN THE EARLY TWENTY-FIRST CENTURY

When several prominent sociologists of education were asked about their predictions for the field in the years ahead, most predicted that the problems facing American schools would see little improvement in the near future. The problems facing our schools reflect the problems in our society. They suggested that sociological theories and methods will make a major contribution to understanding the societal forces and the school dynamics that underlie the problems schools will face; this knowledge is essential to tackle the problems of the twenty-first century. The number of children living in poverty and "at risk" educationally is increasing, especially in urban areas. Books such as Kozol's *Savage Inequalities* (1991) and MacLeod's *Ain't No Makin' It* (2009) document the inequalities between rich and poor school districts and life in poor neighborhoods and schools.

An example of information collected by sociologists, other social scientists, and educators provides an overview of schools in the twenty-first century and samples of predictions for the future based on research data. Planning for change assumes knowledge of educational systems and future trends. Demographers provide us with relevant information: population projections, migration patterns, and social trends. Other social scientists also study educational systems. Proposals for reform and innovation come both from within the educational organization and from its environment—political, economic, and technological dimensions as well as national and world trends. In this section, we provide examples of some trends and projections that affect education, and some policy implications to lead us into the study of education.

Demographic Trends

The rapid growth of education through the 1960s in the United States and many other countries created a boom mentality: There was an expansion of teacher training programs in public schools and universities; new facilities were built; and when monies became available, innovations were

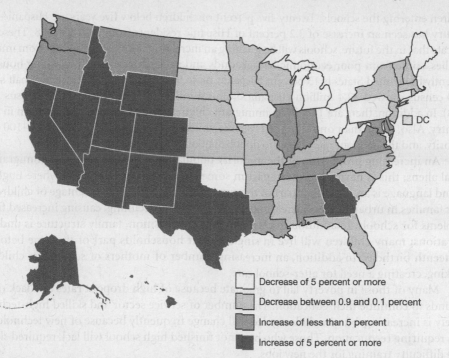

FIGURE 1.1 Percent change in grades K-12 enrollment in public schools, by stage: Fall 1999 to Fall 2010. *Source:* U.S. Department of Education, National Center for Education Statistics, Common Core of Data (CCD), "Early Estimates of Public Elementary/Secondary Education Survey," 1999–2000 and State Public Elementary and Secondary Enrollment Model. (Originally published as figure 7 on p. 9 of the complete report from which this article is excerpted.)

Legend:
- Decrease of 5 percent or more
- Decrease between 0.9 and 0.1 percent
- Increase of less than 5 percent
- Increase of 5 percent or more

implemented. With the end of the boom came the prophets of doom, loss of jobs, boarded-up schools, and dropping financial support.

Rising immigration and a 25 percent increase in the annual births peaked in 1990, but served to increase enrollments. Public school K-12 enrollments in 2004 topped 48 million, and are predicted to top 50 million by 2014, with the largest increases in the western United States. Figure 1.1 shows projected percentage changes in K-12 public school enrollments to the year 2010.

Family and Social Trends

Change in the social class composition of the school-age population is taking place because minority groups, many of whom fall disproportionately at the lower end of the educational achievement scale, are the fastest-growing populations in the United States. They also have the highest percentage of children living in poverty. More than one in five U.S. children live in poverty today, with 22 percent being the highest in two decades (Szabo, 2010). Over 50 percent of children living in poverty live in female single-parent homes, 8.6 percent in male single-parent homes, and 40.5 percent in homes with married parents (Child Health USA, 2003). Twenty-seven percent of mothers and 12.9 percent of fathers and their children live in poverty (U.S. Census Bureau, 2007).

Consider the Hispanic population, the fastest-growing ethnic group in the United States. Hispanics surpassed African Americans as the largest minority in 2005. By 2050, Hispanics are predicted to be 25 percent of the U.S. population; thus, the rise in enrollments is due in part to Hispanic children entering the schools. Twenty-five percent of children below five years are Hispanic and the country has seen an increase of 3.2 percent of Hispanic residents from 2007 to 2008. These figures indicate that in the future, schools will be teaching an increasing number of children from immigrant families, some from poor economic backgrounds and non-native-English-speaking households. Presently the United States is 15 percent Hispanic, or 46.9 million (an increase of over half since the 1990 census showed 22.4 million Hispanics), plus 4 million Puerto Ricans (U.S. Census Bureau, 2008). In addition, there are 14 million immigrant children with at least one parent born in another country. Also, more than one-third of Hispanic children attend schools that are 90–100 percent minority, and the dropout rate is close to double that of other groups.

An increasing proportion of the minority population are Asian refugees, immigrants, and illegal aliens; this is having a great impact in some states, such as California, where English as a second language is an important part of the curriculum. Because the percentage of children from poor families in urban areas is increasing, city tax bases are declining, causing increased financial problems for schools. In addition to class and race composition, family structure is undergoing alterations; many children will live in single-parent households part of the time before their eighteenth birthday. In addition, an increasing number of mothers of school-age children are working, creating a need for after-school care.

Many of those in poverty fail to graduate because of high dropout rates and lack of access or funds to continue their education. The number of service sector and skilled high-tech jobs in society is increasing, but the skills needed will change frequently because of new technologies, in turn requiring reeducation. Those who have not finished high school will lack required skills and have difficulty training for the new jobs.

As our society moves into the postindustrial information age, knowledge creation and processing becomes a primary commodity. Service sector jobs in health, education, and other service areas are growing rapidly, and white-collar jobs are outstripping blue-collar jobs. Jobs in primary sectors of fishing, forestry, agriculture, and manufacturing are declining. Although private sector jobs are increasing slowly since the recession (Bureau of Labor Statistics, 2010), many have been lost to outsourcing. The growth sectors will require information-processing skills, especially the ability to use computers and related technologies. Thus, job growth will be in areas requiring high levels of education and technological knowledge. High school dropouts and less educated citizens will have increasing difficulty competing, with some being left behind.

Schools in the New Century

Predictions are always problematic. Technologies are changing at such a rapid rate that tomorrow is uncertain. However, a number of futurologists have attempted to draw scenarios of the schools of tomorrow using knowledge of socioeconomic conditions, predicted new technologies, recommendations from more than 30 commission and task force reports, knowledge of demographics, and other sources. Predictions of possible changes for schools of the future include school choice, small neighborhood schools, reduced class sizes, more technology in schools, changed missions including curricula, reconfigured classrooms, 24/7 schools, less use of paper, changes in grade distributions, mainstreamed special education, more early childhood education, and more home schooling using computer technology (Stevenson, 2007).

Futurologists predict that technology will play an increasing role in the educational process both in classrooms and in information retrieval out of classrooms. If economic difficulties do not turn trends around, teachers are likely to become more involved with their students, adding a human touch to education; more class time will be devoted to group discussions; field trips will become more frequent; demonstrations, investigative projects, and hands-on lab experiences will increase; and education will become more individualized. Lifelong learning will be a regular part of the adult experience and will take place in many settings. Structures of schools may also change, including smaller schools; more private schools, especially if a voucher system is enacted; and more hours of operation including after-school and evening programs.

Most of these plans sound plausible, but we must keep several factors in mind. First, money. Most of the suggestions for school changes require money, and at a time when many districts are struggling to hold on to the programs and teachers they have without making major cutbacks, this appears problematic. So far the public record on passage of levies for additional monies has not been promising.

In addition, some poorer socioeconomic groups in American society may not be prepared to participate in the new educational and economic state. The knowledge and skill gap that exists today is likely to widen the gap between socioeconomic groups and leave an even more pronounced underclass.

Reform and Policy in Educational Systems

Throughout this book we discuss issues facing education today. In some cases, policies have been formulated and programs implemented to deal with problems. In other existing and emerging areas, such as world systems of education and inequalities between boys and girls education, problems are just beginning to receive attention.

In the United States, the Bush administration's "No Child Left Behind" policy, passed in 2001, called for increased accountability, more choice for parents and students, greater flexibility for educational systems, putting reading first, and other mandates aimed at improving educational performance (U.S. Department of Education, 2005). The Obama administration's "Race to the Top" has been transforming many areas of education including how teachers are promoted and compensated. These reform plans will be discussed throughout your text.

Sociologists have a role to play in research, policy making, and the change process. Every organization needs to have built-in, ongoing data-collection mechanisms to determine whether it is meeting goals. For example, sociologists are studying the impact of government policies on achievement. Programs often require evaluation to determine whether goals are being met, and sociologists are frequently called on to provide these program evaluations and develop procedures for collecting and analyzing data. Sociologists contribute to our understanding of educational systems by studying how systems work and how the parts fit together.

Sources of tension, strain, and change from both inside and outside the organization provide impetus for change; yet many reformers are pessimistic about changing the self-preserving educational system in more than a superficial way. We will see that educational systems are vulnerable to pressures from within the system and from outside. If those who implement change take into consideration the educational system, reform is possible. To bring about reform, one should have an understanding of individuals, organizations, and environments that make up the total educational system.

Sociology of Education in the United States

In the early development of sociology of education in the United States the motivation was to reform society. Lester Frank Ward, one of the six founding fathers of American sociology and the first president of the American Sociological Association, argued in 1883 that education is a principal source of human progress and an agent of change that can foster moral commitment and cognitive development to better society (Bidwell, 1979). The field was referred to as *educational sociology*, and it focused on practical issues and the formulation of policy and recommendations. The name *sociology of education* was introduced in the late 1920s by Robert Angell (1928). Angell and others believed educational institutions were sources for scientific data; they felt that sociology could not and should not promise to produce answers or suggest changes to solve school problems. Today, however, there is a need for sociologists with both emphases: one group to carry out objective research and one to work with schools in interpreting and implementing scientific findings. The latter group needs to have special training in scientific methodology, as well as practical knowledge of how schools work in order to apply sociological findings.

This book deals both with theoretical studies of schools and with the practical application of theory in schools and classrooms. The latter aspect is important because most of you will be using this knowledge in your roles as parents or professionals. Sociology has practical applications and an impact on policy in addition to its abstract and theoretical side. We turn next to the role of theory in studying education.

THEORETICAL APPROACHES IN THE SOCIOLOGY OF EDUCATION

So many questions, so many topics for research, so much important information for schools! To guide research studies into the many questions posed, sociologists use theories, *statements regarding how and why facts are related to each other and the connections between these facts.* This section provides an overview of the major theories used in the sociology of education.

Sociology of education is a fairly new field of inquiry, but with roots in classical sociological theory. In the past century, emphasis has been given to education as a unique institution and an objective field of study. During this period, research has focused on the many social issues already discussed in which education plays a part.

In the twenty-first century, work in the sociology of education can be divided into different *levels of analysis*, from the large-scale *macro-level* studies that consider education systems of countries and world trends to the small-scale *micro-level* studies of classroom interactions. Scientists use theoretical perspectives to provide logical explanations for why things happen the way they do. Starting the study of a subject with a theoretical perspective provides a guide, or a particular conception of how the social world works.

A theoretical point of view also influences what the researcher sees and how it is interpreted. Just as our individual experiences influence our interpretations of events in our everyday lives, sociologists have several theoretical perspectives to help explain why things happen the way they do in society. Just as each individual interprets situations differently depending on his or her background, theorists focus on different key aspects of a research problem. A theoretical approach helps to determine the questions to be asked by researchers and the way to organize research in order to get answers.

In this section we discuss several important theories. Sociologists using each theory have made major contributions in the field of sociology of education, and we will discuss many of them throughout the text. The first two approaches concern differing views of the way societies work—the macro-level. The next two deal with interactions in social situations—the micro-level. The functional and conflict approaches tend to deal with macro-level (large-scale) institutions of education in societies, whereas the interaction approaches focus on micro-level (small-scale) interaction between individuals and small groups. The open systems approach, which provides the model or framework for this book, is explained at the end of this chapter.

Functionalist Theory

Just as the heart and brain are necessary for the survival of a human being, an educational system is necessary for the survival of society. One major theoretical approach in sociology is *functionalism* (also referred to as structural-functionalism, consensus, or equilibrium theory). This theory is sometimes compared to the biological functioning of the human body: Each part of the society's system—family, education, religion, politics and economics, health care—plays a role in the total working society, and all parts are dependent on each other for survival, just as all organs of the body work together to keep us functioning. A sociologist using this approach starts with the assumption that society and institutions within society, such as education, are made up of interdependent parts all working together, each contributing some necessary activity to the functioning of the whole society to maintain order and consensus among individuals in the group. The assumed fit between the educational system and society guides functionalists' research and policy recommendations. Functionalists see change in systems as helping the system continually adapt to new circumstances; change is generally viewed as a slow evolutionary process that does not disrupt the ongoing system. As you read about functionalism, think about how and when this theory could be useful in understanding educational systems.

Reviewing past work of functional theorists in sociology of education helps us understand the theoretical and practical base on which the field was built; it also helps provide an historical perspective on the field. Although many philosophers, educators, and social scientists contributed their insights on education to sociological knowledge, early sociologists provided the first scientific treatments of education as a social institution.

DURKHEIM'S CONTRIBUTIONS TO FUNCTIONALISM AND EDUCATION. Émile Durkheim (1858–1917) set the stage for the functional approach to education. As professor of pedagogy at the Sorbonne in Paris before sociology was "admitted" as a major field, he was the first person to recommend that a sociological approach be used in the study of education. He was awarded the Sorbonne's professorship of sociology combined with education in 1906 and held that post for most of the following years until his death. Thus, sociology came into France as a part of education. Because Durkheim taught all students graduating in education, many were exposed to his ideas.

Durkheim was employed to lecture primarily in education, but his sociological approach was his unique contribution. The ideas centered on the relationship between society and its institutions, all of which he believed were interdependent and therefore resulted in social cohesion. He was concerned with the breakdown of community, and with the maintenance of solidarity and cohesion in the move from traditional to modern societies. Many of the issues about which Durkheim spoke in the late 1800s are as real today as they were then: the needs of different segments of society in relation to education, discipline in the schools, and the role of schools in preparing young people for society. Most importantly, Durkheim attempted to understand why education took the forms it did, rather than judging those forms as good or bad, as had been done so often.

Durkheim's major works in the field of sociology of education were published in collections titled *Moral Education* (1961), *The Evolution of Educational Thought* (1977), and *Education and Sociology* (1956). In these works, he outlined a definition of education and the concerns of sociology as he saw them, the importance of education in creating moral values as the foundation of society, and a definition of the field for future sociologists. He wrote

> Education is the influence exercised by adult generations on those that are not yet
> ready for social life. Its object is to arouse and to develop in the child a certain number

of physical, intellectual and moral states which are demanded of him by both the political society as a whole and the special milieu for which he is specifically destined. (1956, p. 28)

Education takes different forms at different times and places; we cannot separate the educational system from the society for they reflect each other. In *The Evolution of Educational Thought*, he described the history of education in France, combining ideas from some of his other works in a historical, sociological analysis of the institution of education. Always he stressed that in every time and place education is closely related to other institutions and to current values and beliefs of the society.

In *Moral Education*, Durkheim outlined his beliefs about the function of schools and their relationship to society. Moral values are, for Durkheim, the foundation of the social order, and society is perpetuated through its educational institutions, which help instill values in children. Any change in society reflects a change in education and vice versa. In fact, education is an active part of the process of change; he analyzed classrooms as "small societies," or agents of socialization. The school serves as an intermediary between the emotional ties and affective morality of the family and the rigorous morality of life in society. Discipline, he contended, is the morality of the classroom, and without it the class is like a mob.

Durkheim was concerned primarily with rituals that provide meaning, cohesion, and value transmission for stability of society; he did not consider the possible conflict between this stable view and the values and skills necessary for changing, emerging industrial societies. He did, however, recognize that new forms of social control emerge as societies modernize; education should be under the control of the state, free from special-interest groups. Yet today we recognize that most governments are subject to influence from interest groups and to trends and pressures affecting society. Pressures from the school's environment in the areas of curriculum content, for instance, are very real. Some aspects of education that are of great concern today—the function of selection and allocation of adult roles and the gap between societal expectations of schools and actual school performance—were not dealt with by Durkheim.

Durkheim outlined certain areas that he believed were important for sociologists as researchers to address, including the functions of education, the relationships of education to societal change, cross-cultural research, and the social system of the school and classroom (Brookover and Erickson, 1975, pp. 4–5). His writings and guidelines for further research provided an important and useful beginning for the field; they also serve as a measuring stick for how far we have come. Durkheim set the stage for the current functionalist theoretical approach to education. Themes of his general writing are reflected in his concerns about consensus, conflict, and structure in education.

FUNCTIONAL THEORY TODAY   Schools are one part of an interdependent system in which each part contributes to the whole. These parts include groups, organizations, and institutions of society—family, religion, politics, economics, health care, sports, military, and other institutions that make up society. The consensus and common bond between members of society, taught and reinforced in schools through socialization into shared norms, unites groups working toward common goals and keeps groups from disintegrating (Cookson and Sadovnik, 2002, p. 267). The degree of interdependence among parts in the system relates to the degree of *integration* among these parts; all parts complement each other, and the assumption is that a smooth-running, stable system is well integrated. Shared values, or consensus, among members are important components of the system, as these help keep it in balance.

Functional theorists conceive of institutions as parts of total societies or social systems. The parts of the system are discussed in terms of their *functions*, or purposes, in the whole system. A primary function of schools, according to Talcott Parsons (1937), is the passing on of the knowledge and behaviors necessary to maintain order in society. Because children learn to be social beings and develop appropriate social values through contact with others, schools are an important training ground. Following Durkheim, modern sociologists see the transmission of moral and occupational education, discipline, and values as necessary for the survival of society, and education plays a major role in this transmission.

The focus of functional research is on questions concerning the structure and functioning of organizations. For instance, sociologists using this theoretical approach to study educational systems would be likely to focus attention on the structural parts of the organization, such as sub-systems (schools and classrooms) and positions within the structure (teachers, administrators, and students), and on how they are functioning to achieve certain goals. Functionalist Robert Dreeben (1968) considered the workings of the school as a social organization, while James Coleman, et al. (1982) conducted national studies of student backgrounds and their achievement. Another important functionalist research topic has been how schools sort students into groups based on merit, and the *status attainment* of students as a key factor in occupational mobility (Blau and Duncan, 1967). Key reports based on studies, such as the famous "A Nation at Risk," assumed a connection between education, occupational mobility, and the economic state of the nation.

A major problem, according to critics of the functionalist approach, is that it fails to recognize divergent interests, ideologies, and conflicting group values. Instead, these critics assert that functionalists view schools as supporting the interests of the dominant groups. In addition, the relationships among schooling, skills, and jobs are not necessarily rational or fair, according to critics (Hurn, 1993, pp. 50–55). In heterogeneous societies, each subgroup may have its own agenda for the schools—an agenda to further its own interests. Functionalists do not adequately deal with conflicting goals held by different groups in society.

A second problem is the difficulty of analyzing interactions, such as the classroom dynamics of teacher–student or student–student relationships, from this perspective. A related criticism is that the functionalist approach does not deal with the "content" of the educational process (Karabel and Halsey, 1977, p. 11), what is taught and how it is taught. Individuals do not perform roles only within the structure; they create and modify the roles and dynamics not focused on by functional studies.

A third problem is a built-in assumption in functional theory that change, when it does occur, is slow and deliberate, planned, and does not upset the balance of the system—which simply is not true in all situations. The assumption of change as an evolutionary "chain reaction" is implied, but it does not necessarily reflect the reality of rapidly changing societies.

In a classic analysis, Jean Floud and A. H. Halsey (1958) suggest that little progress has been made in the field since the studies of Durkheim and Max Weber (whose theories are discussed in the next section). They argue that functionalism has not been capable of moving the field ahead because of its status quo orientation, when societies are faced with constant change. "The structural-functionalist is preoccupied with social integration based on shared values . . . therefore education is a means of motivating individuals to behave in ways appropriate to maintain society in a state of equilibrium. This preoccupation tends to play down problems of (conflict, inequality, and) social change, and is therefore . . . unsuitable for the analysis of modern industrial societies" (Floud and Halsey, 1958, p. 171). In part as a reaction to these shortcomings of structural-functionalism, conflict theory began to play a prominent role in the field. It is important to keep in mind that both functional and conflict theories attempt to explain how education contributes to the maintenance of the status quo in society.

Conflict Theory

In contrast to functional theory, *conflict theory* assumes a tension in society and its parts created by the competing interests of individuals and groups. Variations within this approach stem from the writings of Karl Marx and Max Weber. Marx (1818–1883) laid down the foundations for conflict theory based on his outrage over the social conditions of the exploited workers in the class system resulting from capitalism (Marx, 1946). He contended that society's competing groups, the "haves" and the "have-nots," were in a constant state of tension, which could lead to the possibility of conflict and struggle. The "haves" control power, wealth, material goods, privilege (including access to the best education), and influence; the "have-nots" present a constant challenge as they seek a larger share of society's wealth. This struggle for power between groups and individuals helps determine the structure and functioning of organizations and the hierarchy that evolves as a result of power relations. The "haves" often use coercive power and manipulation to hold society together to their benefit, but this theory recognizes that change is inevitable and sometimes rapid, as the conflicts of interest lead to the overthrow of existing power structures.

WEBER'S CONTRIBUTIONS TO THE SOCIOLOGY OF EDUCATION.   Max Weber (1864–1920) presented a particular brand of conflict theory. He believed that power relationships between groups form the basic structure of societies and that a person's status identifies his or her position in the group. He is noted for his work on bureaucracy and for the concept of *status group relationships*. In fact, he writes that the primary activity of schools is to teach particular "status cultures." Power relationships and the conflicting interests of individuals and groups in society influence educational systems, for it is the interests and purposes of the dominant groups in society that shape the schools. Weber's unique approach combined the study of the macro-level school organization with an interpretive micro-level view of what brings about a situation and how individuals interpret or define that situation.

Within the school there are "insiders" whose status culture is reinforced through the school experience, and "outsiders," who face barriers to success in school. Transfer these ideas to school systems today as they deal with poor and minority students and the relevance of Weber's brand of conflict theory becomes evident. His theory deals with conflict; domination; and groups struggling for wealth, power, and status in society. These groups differ in property ownership; cultural status, such as ethnic group; or power derived from positions in government or other organizations. Education is used as one means to attain desired ends. Relating this to Karl Marx's writings on conflict theory, education produces a disciplined labor force for military, political, or other areas of control and exploitation by the elite.

Weber's writings, using cross-cultural examples and exploring preindustrial and modern times, shed light on the role of education in different societies at various time periods (Weber, 1958). In preindustrial times, education served the primary purpose of a differentiating agency that trained people to fit into a way of life and a particular "station" in society. With industrialism, however, new pressures faced education from upwardly mobile members of society vying for higher positions in the economic system. Educational institutions became increasingly important in training people for new roles in society.

Weber described a trend toward the rational organization of bureaucracy in modern society, noting that one characteristic of modern bureaucratic organization is its rational-expert leadership. The leaders are selected on the basis of examinations that single out those who best fit jobs at different levels of the bureaucracy. Today, charismatic leaders and those born into positions of power are less dominant in many institutions, including educational institutions, than are competent, professional experts whose merit is measured by examination (Weber, 1961).

In his essay, "The Rationalization of Education and Training" (Gerth and Mills, 1946), Weber points out that rational education develops the "specialist type of man" versus the older type of "cultivated man," described in his discussion of educational systems in early China. Again we see the relevance of Weber's writings: Today's institutions of higher education are debating the value of vocationally oriented education versus education for the well-rounded person, or comprehensive schools versus college preparatory courses. Weber contributed less directly than Durkheim to the sociology of education and provided a less systematic treatment of education. His work in related fields of sociology, however, has contributed to our understanding of many aspects of education.

CONFLICT THEORY TODAY.   Weber and Marx set the stage for branches of conflict theory held by theorists today. Research from the conflict theorists' perspective tends to focus on those tensions created by power and conflict that ultimately cause change. Some conflict theorists see mass education as a tool of capitalist society, controlling the entrance into higher levels of education through the selection and allocation function and manipulating the public. Following a Marxist perspective, Samuel Bowles and Herbert Gintis (1976) wrote about the link between education and society. Their conclusion was that until society is radically changed, schools will continue to reinforce societal stratification patterns. Schools reinforce inequality between students rather than encouraging students to achieve according to their merits.

Another conflict theorist who followed in Weber's tradition is Randall Collins. Weber described "the growing 'tyranny' of educational credentials as a prerequisite for high-status positions" (Hurn, 2002). Collins expands on "credentialism," a technique of increased requirements for higher-level positions used by more advantaged individuals to further their status (Collins, 1978). Many conflict theorists believe that until society's economic and political systems are changed, school reforms that attempt to provide equal access will be impossible (Bowles and Gintis, 1976).

Applying conflict theory to the school and classroom level of analysis, Willard Waller believes that schools are in a state of constant potential disequilibrium; teachers are threatened with the loss of their jobs because of lack of student discipline; academic authority is constantly threatened by students, parents, school boards, and alumni who represent other, often competing, interest groups in the system; and students are forced to go to schools, which they may consider oppressive and demeaning (Waller, 1965, pp. 8–9).

Another branch of conflict theory called *cultural reproduction and resistance theories* argues, very generally, that those who dominate capitalistic systems mold individuals to suit their own purposes. Beginning in the 1960s in Europe, these theorists considered how forms of culture are passed on by families and schools (Bourdieu and Passeron, 1977). The amount of "cultural capital" one has is an indicator of one's status, and families and schools differ in the amount of cultural capital they provide to children. For instance, an elite, preparatory school provides more cultural capital than a poor, urban school (MacLeod, 2009). Reproduction theorists study the cultural processes by which students learn knowledge and what knowledge is transmitted. Resistance to school control has also been the topic of many recent studies. These theories are discussed in later chapters.

The conflict theory approach implies a volatile system and the ever-present possibility of major disruption because of the unequal distribution of status, power, cultural capital, opportunity, and other resources. The approach can be useful in attempting to explain situations where conflict exists (Anyon, 1981); however, critics argue that the connection between curriculum to perpetuate status of the "haves" and capitalism has not been laid out clearly and that little empirical data has been presented to substantiate these claims. Also, this theory does not offer useful explanations concerning the balance or equilibrium that does exist between segments of a system or the interactions between members of the system. Neither conflict theory nor functional theory focuses on the individual, the individual's "definition of the situation," or interactions in the educational system, as does the third theory, discussed in the next section.

Interaction and Interpretive Theories

Interaction theorists look at what teachers and students "do" in school; they question even the most commonplace, taken-for-granted actions and interactions, things most people do not question. This third theoretical approach in sociology, a micro-level theory, focuses on individuals in interaction with each other. Individuals sharing a culture are likely to interpret and define many social situations in similar ways because of their similar socialization, experiences, expectations, and culture. Hence, common norms evolve to guide behavior, and these commonly understood "interaction rituals" in turn hold societies together (Goffman, 1967). Differences in interpretations of events also occur, however, based on individual experiences, social class, and status. This theory stems from the work of G. H. Mead and C. H. Cooley on the development of self through social interaction, whether in school or other situations.

Interaction theories grew from reactions to the macro-level of structural-functional and conflict theories, which focused on large-scale structure and process of organizations. These micro-level theories have been used increasingly since World War II. Macro-level approaches can miss the dynamics of everyday school life that shape children's futures. Interactionists ask social-psychological questions about the most common, ordinary interactions between school participants. Sociologists of education using this approach are likely to focus on interactions between groups of peers, between teachers and students, or between teachers and principals; they consider student attitudes, values, and achievements; students' self-concepts and their effect on aspirations; socioeconomic status as it relates to student achievement; and many other questions. From this approach have come studies on the effects of teacher expectations of student performance and achievement; studies of the results of ability grouping of students; and studies of schools as total institutions, among others (e.g., Mehan, 2001).

Two interaction theories useful in sociology of education are labeling theory and rational choice (exchange) theory. If Johnny is told repeatedly that he is dumb and will amount to little, he may incorporate this label—"a self-fulfilling prophesy"—as part of his self-concept and behave as the label suggests. With labeling theory, we can better "understand how micro-level interactions in the school contribute to individuals' formulations of their sense of 'self.' Young people from 6 to 18 years old spend much of their time in school or school-related activities; . . . interaction with others in school affects the student's sense of self. The image that is reflected back to someone . . . can begin to mold one's sense of competence, intelligence, and likeability" (Ballantine and Spade, 2011).

Consider the example of student behavior. Whether students behave well or badly depends in part on teacher expectations. Ray Rist "demonstrated how teacher expectations of students based on categories such as race, class, ethnicity, and gender affect student perceptions of themselves and their achievements" (Rist, 1970, 1977). *Labeling theory* is discussed further in other sections of the book.

Rational choice (exchange) theory is based on the assumption that there are costs and rewards involved in our interactions. If benefits outweigh costs, the individual will likely make the decision to act in order to continue receiving benefits. If the costs outweigh the benefits, the individual will choose to move in a different direction. This theory has relevance to education in school choices made by students, teachers, and administrators (Hatcher, 1998). *Reciprocal interactions,* that is interactions that bind individuals and groups with obligations, play into the situation; for example, teachers are rewarded when students learn and rewarded behavior is likely to continue. However, the problem of teacher burnout occurs when the rewards are outstripped by the costs of the teaching situation (Dworkin, 2008).

Recent Theories in the Sociology of Education: Critical, "New," Postmodern, and Feminist Theories

Paulo Freire's book, *Pedagogy of the Oppressed* (1970), was a landmark treatise on the inequality in education; it helped establish the *Critical Pedagogy* movement. Freire's efforts to educate Brazilian sugar cane workers and other oppressed people around the world drew attention to the struggle for justice and equity in the education system. He spoke of the colonizers and colonized, and argued throughout his life that the oppressed should be educated to give them a voice. Several contemporary theorists have followed Freire's lead (Davies, 1995; Giroux, 1981).

A "NEW" SOCIOLOGY OF EDUCATION.   This theoretical approach developed in England around the same time as the critical pedagogy movement, the late 1960s and early 1970s, and has followers in the United States and elsewhere (Apple, 1978; Wexler, 1987). Known as "new" because it broke ranks with structural functional theories that had dominated the theoretical scene in sociology of education, it critiqued and suggested an alternative approach to "macrocosmic" approaches, which put little emphasis on understanding and interpreting the meaning of interactions and of the curriculum, known as "school knowledge," in schools (Wexler, 2002, p. 593). Some "new" sociologists of education argued that the field should be seen as a subfield of the sociology of knowledge, the idea that all knowledge is "socially created" and a product of humans. Thus what we teach in schools is created by people, often those with the most power.

Curricula are not necessarily objective (Young, 1971). These sociologists stress the need to understand and examine our commonsense views of reality—how we come to view the events and situations around us and react to them as we do. They base their ideas on symbolic interaction, ethnomethodology, and phenomenology, arguing that an alternative approach to sociology of education is needed if we are to understand micro-level aspects of educational systems. As applied to education, these "new" theories have taken the form of studying interaction processes in classrooms, the management and use of knowledge, the question of what it is to be "educated" in different societies, curriculum content, and so forth. Some examples of work using this approach are cited in Chapter 6.

Some theorists have attempted to synthesize micro- and macro-level theories, arguing that both must be considered if we are to understand educational systems (Bernstein, 1990), which is a view that is consistent with the open systems approach that underlies this book.

The works of two European sociologists argue for a holistic approach to education, looking at both macro-level class analysis and micro-level interaction analysis, and considering how Durkheim's functional approach and Marx's conflict approach might be used together. Basil Bernstein and Pierre Bourdieu (Karabel and Halsey, 1977, p. 60) have attempted to show a synthesis of macro- and micro-level approaches rather than developing a totally new approach (Bernstein, 1975; Bourdieu, 1973).

Bernstein's goal for his life work was to "prevent the wastage of working-class educational potential" (Bernstein, 1961, p. 308). He provided an analysis of the relations among society, schools, and the individual, and explained how these reproduce social inequality. Bernstein argued that the class and power relations of educational systems (the macro-levels of analysis) and the interactional educational processes of the school (the micro-levels) need to be integrated in order to gain an understanding of educational systems (Bernstein, 1974). One effort at integration is seen in his work on the speech patterns that, he argued, perpetuate one's social class. The family class position of students determines speech patterns, which, in turn, affect one's position in society, as exemplified by the poorer academic performance of working-class children. He also pointed out the need to evaluate the effect of class bias in teaching and educational ideology on students' performance.

Bernstein's later work focused on curriculum and the pedagogy used to transmit knowledge. Curriculum—what is taught—defines "valid knowledge," that which is defined, approved, and transmitted to students. How it is transmitted has consequences for different groups of students based on social class and power relations. His attempts to link the societal, institutional, interactional, and intrapsychic realms have moved the field closer to integration. However, more empirical testing of his theories is necessary, and applicability to educational practice and policy needs to be shown (Bernstein, 1990).

The central concept in Pierre Bourdieu's work is *cultural capital*. Children from higher social classes have more cultural capital (e.g., proper language; knowledge of art, music, theater, and literature; and knowledge of ideas important in the world), a commodity that can be traded in for higher status in school and later in the workforce. Thus, cultural capital allows students to reproduce their social class through family and schooling. In later chapters we discuss not only cultural capital, but also social and human capital.

Today "critical pedagogy" and the "new" sociology are no longer "new," but much of their content has been absorbed into yet newer theoretical branches. Equity in race, class, and gender has been adopted as a common theme today, and "cultural studies" affirm the importance of taking these differences into account in educational research. Even resistance and reproduction theories have been incorporated into new trends in sociology of education. We now move to a discussion of modern and postmodern theories.

MODERNISM AND POSTMODERNISM.   Several recent proposals for reform of schools have been based on educational theories. *Modernism*, largely a Western perspective on education, includes "modern" ideas of rational thought, progress through science and technology, humanism, democracy (equality, justice, and liberty), and the primacy of individualism over established authority (Elkind, 1994, p. 6). It replaced the idea of the divine right of kings and the church with the ideas of progress, universality, and regularity, which led to modern education. Many of the proposed systemic changes in education, such as government goals for uniform national standards (as in *Goals 2000, No Child Left Behind, and Race to the Top*) and reforms of teacher education training, fall into the modernism category (Darling-Hammond and McLaughlin, 1995).

Postmodernism moves beyond the modernist thought that was more relevant in the industrial era than in the current postindustrial era, according to these scholars. While modernism attempted all-encompassing explanations of the world and progress based on science and technology, postmodernists stress the importance of theories relevant to local situations; the connection between theory and practice; and democratic, antitotalitarian, and antiracist ideas. They call for respect and understanding of human differences. Sometimes postmodernism is called "critical education theory" and some recent postmodernist writers that you may encounter include Baudrillard (1984), Cherryholmes (1988), Derrida (1982), Freire (1970, 1987), Giroux (1991), Lyotard (1984), and McLaren (1991), to name a few.

Postmodernism honors human diversity, including the variations and ambiguity in the way different people learn and see the world. It also recognizes the political setting in which education occurs. Schools are seen as often being racist and sexist (Giroux, 1991). Thus, postmodern theory is linked to feminist theory (human diversity) and cultural theory (recognizing differences). Giroux attempts to "synthesize the contributions of modernism, postmodernism, and feminism" (Giroux, 1991). Education results from choices that cannot be made without reference to sets of values and interests in the community, which are entangled in power structures (Cherryholmes, 1988). "Postmodernism is not a rejection of regularity, just a demand that irregularity be accepted as well" (Elkind, 1994, p. 12). This means that curricula should be interdisciplinary and represent diverse interests, that universal skills such as critical thinking should be stressed, and that individual children can reach a common goal by different paths. The locus of control in this model is at the individual school level, and children's achievements can be measured in many ways: tests, portfolios, performances, and projects—whatever works best for the children in that school (Bernstein, 1993; Sizer, 1992).

Feminist Theories in Sociology of Education

In line with postmodern theorists, feminist theorists argue for more attention to the condition of women. For most of history, the human condition has been explained through the eyes of white European men. Feminists argue that these men cannot accurately portray the experiences of women around the world. Feminist theory has developed along several lines, sometimes paralleling the theories that we have discussed. Here we outline some major themes in this large body of literature; these are expanded upon in the chapters of this book.

Feminist theorists have pointed out the injustices and differential treatment faced by many girls and women in schools around the world. They attribute these differences to many factors including differential access to education, preference for male education, patriarchy and exploitation, and male dominance. One direction of research has been to study the effect of educational policies on girls and their future opportunities. These interests parallel those of postmodernists (Ballantine and Spade, 2011).

Unfortunately, despite improvements in some areas, research shows inequalities in others. Girls are treated differently in classrooms (Sadker and Sadker, 1994), especially in math and science, and these differences can result in males receiving better, higher paying jobs. In addition, in many countries girls barely see classrooms due to lack of access and opportunity. Boys around the world have a much better chance of completing levels of education from grade school on. Today feminist theorists are increasingly aware of the differences in experiences of women around the world and attempt to address these differences (Dillabough and Arnot, 2002).

We have made the point that a number of approaches are useful in the sociology of education, depending on the questions one is asking. These theories help us understand and work with educational systems.

> **Applying Sociology to Education:** *Select an educational topic of interest to you. Which of these theoretical approaches would be useful in studying this topic?*

THE OPEN SYSTEMS APPROACH

By now it is clear that a number of theoretical approaches are used to study the institution of education. Each provides valuable insights into a complex system. How can we order this complexity and make it understandable? Some sociologists favor one theoretical approach for all of their work; others select an approach to fit the problem. Our goal is to understand the

A one-room schoolhouse.

educational system and the contribution that each approach can make to that understanding. For this reason, this book is organized around an open systems model, or framework, of education. Using this model, we can break this complex system into its component parts for study. One theoretical approach is more applicable than another for the study of certain parts of the system or of educational problems that arise in the system. The model enables us to see the interconnections between parts and theories and helps us determine which theory and research methods are most appropriate for our study. Let us now move to an explanation of the model.

If we want to understand an educational system as a whole, integrated, and dynamic entity, we are faced with a problem. Most research studies focus on parts of the whole system, and most theoretical approaches have specific foci. An open systems model can help us conceptualize a whole system, understand how the small pieces fit together, and see which pieces do not fit. A model provides a useful way of visualizing the many elements in the system; it helps order observations and data and represents a generalized picture of complex interacting elements and sets of relationships (Griffiths, 1965, p. 24). The following model does not refer to one particular educational system or theoretical approach or one type of school. Rather, it gives us a framework to consider the common characteristics of many educational settings. Any school system or theory can be placed in the framework, and parts of the system become the focus of a research study—within the context of the larger system.

Although this model shows the component parts of a total system, it does not imply that one part or theory is better or more important than another for explaining situations or events in the system. Neither does it suggest which is the best methodology to use in studying any part of the system. It does allow us to visualize the parts we may read about or study in relation to the whole system to see where they fit and what relationship they bear to the whole. Then we can better select the most appropriate theory and methods for our problem or study.

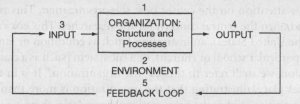

FIGURE 1.2 Systems model. *Source:* Adapted from
Ludwig Von Bertalantly, "General Systems Theory—A
Critical Review," *General Systems* Vol. 7, 1962, pp. 1–20.

Consider the following description of an open systems model:

> It is not a particular kind of social organization. It is an analytical model that can be
> applied to any instance of the process of social organization, from families to nation.
> . . . Nor is [it] a substantive theory—though it is sometimes spoken of as a theory in
> sociological literature. This model is a highly general, content-free conceptual frame-
> work within which any number of different substantive theories of social organization
> can be constructed. (Olsen, 1978, p. 228)

Figure 1.2 shows the basic components of any social system.
We discuss the five parts in a five-step process. An example for each step, taken from an educational
organization (see Figure 1.3), is included to help clarify the content of each part of the system.

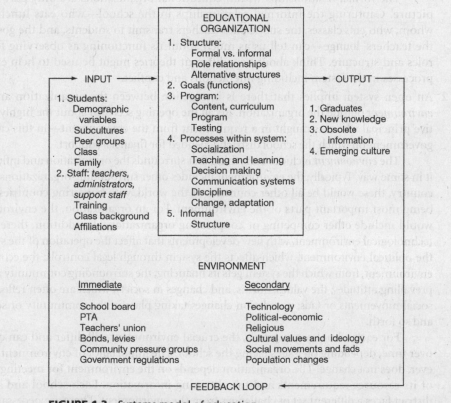

FIGURE 1.3 Systems model of education.

Step 1   Focus your attention on the center box, the *organization*. This refers to the center of activity and often the central concern for the researcher. This box can represent a society (such as the United States), an institution (such as education or family), an organization (such as a particular school or church), or a subsystem (such as a classroom). For purposes of discussion, we shall refer to this as "the organization." It is in the organization that action takes place, illustrating that the organization is more than structure, positions, roles, and activities. Within the organizational boundaries there is a structure consisting of parts and subparts, positions and roles. Although we speak of the organization as though it were a living entity, we are really referring to the purposes for the structure and hierarchical structure of the personnel who carry out the activities of the organization and make decisions about organizational action. The processes in the system bring the organization alive. Decision making by key personnel, communication among members of the organization, and socialization into positions in the organization are among the many activities that are constantly taking place, carrying out the purposes of the organization.

Some theoretical approaches emphasize only this internal organization analysis, a *closed system*, but these processes do not take place in a vacuum. The decision makers holding positions and performing roles in the organization are constantly responding to demands from both inside and outside the organization. The boundaries of the organization are not solid, but remain flexible and pliable in most systems to allow system needs to be met. We call this "open boundaries" or an *open system*.

The formal relationships within educational organizations are only part of the picture. Capturing the informal relationships in the school—who eats lunch with whom, who cuts classes, the subtle cues teachers transmit to students, and the gossip in the teachers' lounge—can tell us as much about its functioning as observing formal roles and structure. Think about how different theories might be used to help explain processes in the system including interactions and conflict.

Step 2   An open system implies that there is interaction between the organization and the *environment* outside the organization. Recall the opening scenario about the highly effective principal who was caught in a requirement from the environment—in this case the government on which the school district depended for financial support.

The *environment* includes everything that surrounds the organization and influences it in some way. Typically, the environment includes other surrounding organizations. For a country, these would be all other countries of the world, with bordering countries often being most important parts of the environment. For an organization, the environment would include other competing or cooperating organizations. In addition, there is the technological environment, with new developments that affect the operation of the system; the political environment, which affects the system through legal controls; the economic environment, from which the system gets its financing; the surrounding community and its prevailing attitudes; the values, norms, and changes in society, which are often reflected in social movements or fads; population changes taking place in the community or society; and so forth.

For each school organization, the crucial environment will differ and can change over time, depending on issues facing the school. The importance of environment, however, does not change. The organization depends on the environment for meeting many of its resource requirements and for obtaining information. Each school and school district faces a different set of challenges from the environment. There are necessary and desired interactions with the environment, and some interactions are not so pleasant. The interaction of the school with the environment takes place in our systems model in the form of *inputs* and *outputs*.

Step 3   The organization receives *inputs* from the environment in such forms as information, raw materials, students, personnel, finances, government mandates, and new ideas. Furthermore, the persons who are members of an organization belong to other organizations in the environment and bring into the organization influences from the outside environment.

Some of the environmental inputs are mandatory for the organization's survival (finances, human resources, and technology). Other inputs vary in degree of importance. For most organizations, some inputs are undesirable, but unavoidable, such as new legal restrictions, competition, or financial pressures. Usually the organization can exert some control over the inputs. For instance, schools have selection processes for new teachers, textbooks, and other curricular materials. Certain positions in the organization are held by personnel who act as *buffers* or liaisons between the organization and its environment. The secretary who answers the phone, for example, has a major protecting and controlling function, and the social worker, school nurse, special education teacher, and counselor are additional links with the environment.

Step 4   *Output* refers to the material items and the nonmaterial ideas that leave the organization— for example, completed products such as research findings, graduates, wastes, information, evolving culture, and new technology. There may be personnel in boundary-spanning positions bridging the gap between the organization and the environment. Personnel with responsibility for selling the organization's product, whether they work in a manufacturing organization or in a placement office for college graduates, serve this function.

Step 5   A key aspect of a systems model is the process of *feedback*. This step implies that an organization constantly adapts to changes and demands in the environment as a result of new information it receives. For instance, the organizational personnel compare the current state of affairs with desired goals and environmental feedback to determine new courses of action. The positive or negative feedback requires different responses. The basic model (Figure 1.2) can serve us in many ways. It is used as a framework for organizing content in this book. But, as conceived by some of its early proponents, it is more inclusive and flexible, and it can help promote interdisciplinary study. Consider, for example, Kenneth Boulding's (1956) statement:

> [A]n interdisciplinary movement has been abroad for some time. The first signs of this are usually the development of hybrid disciplines. . . . It is one of the main objectives of General Systems Theory to develop these generalized areas, and by developing a framework of general theory to enable one specialist to catch relevant communications from others. (p. 197)

Sociology of education cannot be discussed only within the fields of education and sociology. Examples of related fields are numerous: economics and school financing; political science, power, and policy issues; the family and the child; church–state separation controversies; health fields and medical care for children; psychology and children's motivation and aspirations; humanities and the arts; and the school's role in early childhood training.

Several social scientists have pointed to the value of an open systems approach in organizational analysis. David Easton, for example, writes: "A systems analysis promises a more expansive, more inclusive, and more flexible theoretical structure than is available even in a thoroughly self-conscious and well-developed equilibrium approach" (Easton, 1965, p. 20). For our book, this approach not only serves the purposes noted but also helps give unity to a complex field. Each chapter in this book describes some part or process in the educational system. If you get lost, check out the model to see where you are.

RESEARCH METHODS IN SOCIOLOGY OF EDUCATION

A theory is used to give direction to research studies, determine data and materials to be collected, and guide interpretations of data. However, a theory is only a framework. Content must be added. Using scientific and objective techniques, data must be collected in order to test the usefulness and accuracy of theoretical explanations of events.

A sociologist is a scientist and, therefore, employs the scientific method in studying issues and problems. Some sociologists focus their attention on the institution of education and issues related to it. Their research techniques are essentially the same as those used by sociologists studying other areas.

Prior to 1950, few studies of education used objective standards and measures. Most frequently, anecdotes and value judgments were used to illustrate and support arguments. Gradually, the emphasis in published literature moved to empirical studies. Several research methods are now used in sociology of education: participant observation, surveys, secondary analysis, controlled laboratory studies, and case studies. To decide which technique to use, the researcher must define the problem to be studied and determine the level of analysis and possible sources of information related to the problem. Then the researcher selects the population or group to be studied and determines whether to study all or part of the population. The researcher may want to talk directly with the persons in the group to be studied, observe them at some task, obtain statistical information such as test scores, or use a combination of these and other techniques.

Several well-known works rely heavily on *observation* in schools (Jackson, 1968; Lubeck, 1985; McFarland, 2001; Metz, 1978; Willis, 1981;). In each, observation in schools and classrooms produced data to study research questions. For instance, in a study of similarities and differences among American high schools based on social class differences of students served, Mary Haywood Metz studied teachers' work by observing their classrooms, interviewing them, and reviewing documents about each school. What Metz found was a "common script." The roles and plots were similar; however, the setting and actors' lines were recognizable but different based on the social class composition of the school (Metz, 1990).

Another famous study used *controlled classroom settings*. Robert Rosenthal and Lenore Jacobson studied the effects of teacher expectations on student performance by manipulating the classroom situation. They assigned some children to a special treatment group, and others remained in the regular classroom (Rosenthal and Jacobson, 1968). This experiment comes close to being a controlled laboratory experiment with a minimum of influence from external sources, yet it is difficult to rule out all of the influences from outside the classroom that might have affected the study results.

In yet another well-known study, James Coleman and others (1966) used *surveys* of approximately 5 percent of the schools in the United States to ascertain the degree of equality of educational opportunity. In this massive study, students at five grade levels were given standardized tests. Additional information about the students and schools was collected by survey and secondary analysis. These are several examples of different data collection methods. Other examples of research techniques are considered as we discuss various studies throughout the book.

At times it is useful to *combine methodological techniques* in order to obtain the most accurate picture of what we are studying. Coleman, for instance, was criticized for not using observation or other techniques to describe the day-to-day life that went on in the schools he surveyed. Using multiple methods to collect data is called *triangulation*; this technique helps researchers overcome weaknesses of any one method.

ORGANIZATION OF THE BOOK

Each chapter in this book describes some part of the open system of education. As you read, be aware of which part is being discussed, and by the end of the book you should have a fairly complete picture of the total educational system. The chapters can be studied out of order and still present the total model. Theoretical approaches discussed in this chapter are related to practical issues throughout the book. In addition, you can enhance your effectiveness in dealing with schools by learning to "do" sociology, learning about the methodology used, and becoming knowledgeable producers and consumers. At the end of each chapter you will find a chapter summary and suggested projects related to each topic. You are encouraged to try to make the subject more useful to yourself by doing these projects. For instance, after reading this chapter, ask yourself what questions you feel sociologist of education should address. Keep these in mind as you read. You might also consider doing further research on the questions you raise.

We are now ready to enter the school. The scene is an active, dynamic one. Let us take a close look at some of the processes taking place to accomplish the purposes or functions of education.

Summary

In this chapter we have discussed the perspective of sociology of education.

I. SOCIOLOGY AND EDUCATION

Sociologists study group life. One of the social institutions that makes up society is education; as a part of group life, it is of interest to sociologists. All of us are involved in educational systems during our lives, and education interacts with and is interdependent with other institutions in society. We study sociology of education because it is or will be relevant to roles we play as taxpayers, parents, professionals, and students.

Researchers in sociology of education have focused on numerous areas of study: the socialization process, the relationship between education and stratification, control of education, and so forth. Many examples of questions sociologists of education ask are presented in this chapter.

II. THEORETICAL APPROACHES AND THE DEVELOPMENT OF SOCIOLOGY OF EDUCATION

Sociology of education is a fairly new field; much of the literature has been developed in the past 60 years. It has its roots, however, in the works of early European sociologists including Durkheim, Marx, and Weber.

In recent years, the field has moved from practical to more theoretical emphases, although both approaches are still used. Three types of theory and research dominate sociology of education: large systems, specific institutions, and interaction in educational settings. Each theory focuses on a different level of analysis and uses different methods for research:

Functionalist theory views the educational system as an integral, interrelated part of the whole societal system, carrying out certain necessary functions for the survival of society. Systems are held together by shared values. Durkheim first applied the sociological perspective and methods to the study of education. The functions or purposes of education are the same in each society but are carried out differently. These functions are not always carried out smoothly and may be points of conflict in school policies.

> *Conflict theory* assumes that tension exists in society because of competing interest groups. The "haves" control the power and resources, and thus the educational systems including access to higher levels of education. There is the ever-present possibility of struggle. Weber's contributions, less directly in the field of education than Durkheim's, were in the areas of organization and training members for society.

> *Interaction theory* focuses on individuals and how they form interpretations of the world around them. Labeling and rational choice (exchange) theories are two examples of interaction theory.

> *Recent perspectives* include critical theory, the "new" sociology of education, modernism and postmodernism, and feminist theory.

These theories attempt to move educational theory to be more inclusive of all race, class and gender groups. In addition, some recent theories attempt to synthesize interaction theory and macro-level theories.

III. THE OPEN SYSTEMS APPROACH

This book is organized around the open systems model presented in Figures 1.2 and 1.3. Each part of the educational system is discussed: the organization, its environment, inputs and outputs, and feedback. Using this approach allows us to visualize the whole system, each subpart in relation to the whole, and the environment surrounding the system. Models help us visualize the relationship between parts.

IV. RESEARCH METHODS IN SOCIOLOGY OF EDUCATION

Sociological methods used to study educational systems include observations, surveys, the use of existing data such as test scores, controlled laboratory experiments, and case studies (among others). Any of these methods, or a combination of methods, can be used—depending on the theory and level of analysis used—to collect data to help answer questions within a theoretical framework.

Sample Research Questions in Sociology of Education

The following are examples of research questions that have been asked in recent studies:

- Is college a route for getting ahead in society?
- How are social class and school achievement related?
- Why do girls take fewer math and science courses than boys?
- Do schools make a difference in our earning power?

- To what extent should religion enter the classroom?
- What teaching styles are most effective?
- Should non-native-language speakers learn in their own language or in English?
- What differences do teacher expectations of students make in students' performance?
- What effects does TV watching have on educational achievement?

Putting Sociology to Work

1. Evaluate your own motive for going to college and for taking this course. Understanding your goals can help you get the most from this course and help you meet your educational needs (refer to pp. 3 and 4).

2. Write down some questions you have concerning schools and relate them to questions asked by functionalists (indicated on pp. 11–13).
3. From the brief descriptions of contributions made by Emile Durkheim and Max Weber, describe those

issues facing education today that relate to aspects of their writings.

4. What are some questions concerning education that come to mind when using functional theory? conflict theory? interaction theory? critical and postmodern theory? feminist theory?

5. View the film *High School*. Diagram this school using the elements of a systems model. Indicate roles people play and processes being performed. Compare this with your own high school experience (refer to p. 21).

6. Use an example to explain how the open systems approach can help us conceptualize a whole working educational organization.

7. Consider the questions asked above in relation to each theoretical perspective (project 4). What method(s) could be used to help you answer each question?

8. The projects in this chapter give you the framework for developing a research project of your own: a theoretical perspective, a research question, or a methodology. Plan a research project based on a question of interest to you.

Conflicting Functions and Processes in Education

What Makes the System Work?

Texas and California have a lock on the market—the K-12 public school textbook market that is! Because their state boards of education select textbooks for all state districts and these are very large states, what they demand to be covered in textbooks determines the content for the textbooks of the rest of the country. Few textbook publishers can opt out of the competition for these two huge markets, so they adapt to the desires of these state boards of education. Changes of topics, phrases, what knowledge is—or isn't—covered, and how topics are covered are all fair game for the state boards of education in these powerful states.

In spring 2010, Texas began an every-10-year review process of its history textbooks (Texas Textbook Controversy, 2010). The 15-member board consists of 10 Republicans and 5 Democrats. Those in power call the shots when it comes to what revisions they want. Some of the suggested changes were to cut references to Thomas Jefferson, change the work "capitalism" to "free enterprise system" (seen as less derogatory), change from "imperialism" to "expansionism," eliminate most mention of Mexican Americans in the history of Texas, exonerate McCarthy and the House UnAmerican Activities Committee which accused many people of being Communists, and indicate that the United States was founded based on Christianity and belief in God (some critics argue this is a challenge to the separation of church and state). Over 60 amendments were made by one member of the board, and other members added greatly to that number. Advocates for the changes indicate that they want a less "liberal bias" in texts and a more conservative, God and country-friendly presentation of history. Critics argue, among other things, that politicians (school board members) are changing the way history is presented, and in many cases distorting it (Texas Textbook Controversy, 2010; Religion and Ethics Newsweekly, 2010).

What is the issue here? One of the functions of education is the transmission of knowledge to students—but what and whose knowledge? In a country with a very diverse population and views, this is a controversial issue as we shall see. In history, science, English, social studies, and other subject areas, textbook content will remain a flashpoint between different groups in society. This chapter is about controversies in schools.

Surrounding each function, or purpose, of education are debates about power, access, whose knowledge, and knowledge for whom. Schools exist within a larger framework of society. The economic, political, and cultural spheres influence everyday activities in schools (Apple and Weis, 1986). Therefore, controversies in society at large become controversies within schools. After a general introduction to the conflicting nature of educational functions and the importance of processes in educational systems, we examine selected issues and controversies related to each major function of education.

CONFLICTING FUNCTIONS OF EDUCATION

Each society educates its children in the ways of the group and skills necessary to prosper in that society. The basic functions, or purposes, of education are the same in most societies, but the importance of these functions and the means of achieving them vary greatly across societies and even among groups or social classes within each society. For instance, the level of development of a society will affect the content and the form of the educational process. The type of the political system will affect the content and control of the educational process. The expectations of the family in socializing the child to be a productive member of the society will affect the type of educational content. Politics, family, and education provide an example of the interdependence of parts in society. The following are five major functions of education:

Function 1 *Socialization: Learning to Be Productive Members of Society through the Passing On of Culture.* New generations of children learn the rights and wrongs, values, and role expectations of the society into which they are born. In learning their role, children are socialized, or taught, how to meet the expectations placed on them. Educational systems socialize students to become members of society, to play meaningful roles in the complex network of interdependent positions. Research evidence, however, indicates that students have different experiences in the school system depending on their gender, social class, racial or ethnic background, neighborhood in which they live, and other variables that influence their education.

Function 2 *Transmission of Culture.* Similarly, the transmission of culture is often controversial, with each interest group wanting its programs, curricula, or values to take precedence. Different groups of students—rich, poor, religious—are taught different norms, skills, values, and knowledge. Thus, a student destined for a leadership or elite position may acquire a different set of skills and knowledge base than one who will enter the blue-collar workforce.

Function 3 *Social Control and Personal Development.* In preparing young people to enter society as responsible adults, schools teach not only subject areas such as English and math but also how to be a responsible, law-abiding adult. Yet even how to enforce discipline and social control in schools is controversial. Discipline methods differ by social class, racial–ethnic group, and sex, even though the offense may be the same. Controversies, for instance, surround search and seizure, free speech, and constitutional rights of students (Zirkel, 2009). Do school officials have the right to "protect all students" by testing for drugs or searching for weapons or drugs, especially when these searches may affect some groups of students disproportionately? Supreme Court cases such as *Tinker v. Des Moines* (1969), *Goss v. Lopez* (1975), *Hazelwood School District v. Kuhlmeier* (1988), *Vernonia School District 47 v. Acton* (1995), and *Morse v. Frederick* (2007) have answered some questions and left others up in the air.

Function 4 *Selection, Training, and Placement of Individuals in Society.* Probably the most controversial function of schools is the selection, training, and placement of individuals in society. Conflict theorists argue that schools are "reproducing" the social classes from which students come rather than providing opportunities for their advancement. This includes maintaining the social hierarchy with educational policies and practices that select some students for higher tracks. Yet some policies, such as testing, give the "appearance" of equality and success based on merit.

Consider the example of technology. The access that students have to technology influences their chances to compete for jobs in the information society of the future. Experience with computers and other high-tech machines gives some students an edge on leadership positions because these students will gain the skills needed for high-tech jobs. This issue raises questions of balance between ascribed characteristics (what students are born with—gender and ethnicity) and achieved characteristics (skills and knowledge students learn) in the determination of one's future educational and occupational success (Apple and Weis, 1986, p. 14; Darling-Hammond, 2010). Chapters 3 and 4 focus on this function.

Function 5 *Change and Innovation.* New knowledge and technologies challenge students and teachers of all ages as they advance knowledge and change the way work is done. Yet, workers in organizations, including the institution of education, often resist changes that affect their comfortable routine work tasks. Through education and research institutions we develop new innovations, but some innovations take time to become part of the fabric of society.

Conflicting aspects of each of these five functions, discussed in the following sections, show that carrying out the purposes of schools is a constant negotiation between various segments of society.

Unanticipated Consequences of Functions

Each of the functions noted may have both positive and negative outcomes; the intended purpose is not always the only result or even the main result of the process of education. For instance, schools bring age peers together in the classroom and for other school-related activities. This bringing together enables friendship groups or cliques to develop and the youth subculture to flourish; these groups in turn may profoundly influence the school, as we shall see in Chapter 7. Delaying young people's entry into the job market may serve the purpose of keeping more adults employed while the students receive more education, but it may also cause strain when overeducated, unemployed young people are ready to join the job market.

THE IMPORTANCE OF PROCESSES IN EDUCATIONAL SYSTEMS

Have you ever tried to describe your day using action verbs? Today I *got up, dressed, ate* my breakfast, *put on* my coat, *walked* to school, *entered* the classroom, *sat* at my desk, *opened* my book, *read* it, *took* notes as the teacher *lectured*, and *learned* about educational systems. The italicized verbs describe *processes*, the action part of your day. Learning, teaching, socializing, disciplining, selecting, innovating, decision making, and changing are only a few of the processes that make up the action part of education. *Processes* are the action part: what is happening in schools. Nothing is ever fixed or final. People, things, and organizations are always becoming something new through the process of change. Always we grow older, learn new behaviors, and adjust to changes in the world around us. Educational systems affect our change process, and, in turn, are affected by processes in their environment, or surroundings.

The educational system's *structure* is stable and relatively permanent. *Structure* refers to parts of the educational system that can be described and diagrammed: roles of administrators, teachers, students, and others who work in school systems; social classes from upper to lower; organizations including individual schools and administrative offices; institutions and their interaction with each other, such as schools and families; and societies, each with its own unique educational needs and system.

People who hold roles in the structure carry out "actions"—or *processes*. Teachers, students, parents, and others concerned with schools bring the structure alive. People bring their own personalities and interpretations to their actions. Structure and action (processes) cannot be separated; there would be no processes without structure, and structure would be meaningless without processes. We are not simply social statuses or roles; we are what results from those structural parts, their functions or purposes, and the processes that make them work.

Thus, a key part of an open systems approach to education is the processes that make any system a dynamic, working unit. Some processes are found in almost every organization—interaction, decision making, conflict, and cooperation. Others dominate in particular systems such as teaching and learning in educational systems. In addition to making the system work and giving it life, processes can produce controversy, as we shall see.

Processes also provide links between the organization and other parts, such as between an educational system and its environment. The process of communication, for instance, links the school with parents, community leaders, and state legislators. Let us now explore five functions of education and some controversies that arise in carrying out these functions.

THE FUNCTION OF SOCIALIZATION: WHAT WE LEARN AND HOW WE LEARN IT

According to functional theory, in order to prosper a society must train its members to be productive and to perform required roles. However, there is disagreement on how, when, and for whom training should take place. Criticisms of the process of socialization include a range of topics. Here we focus on two: early childhood education and the role of technology and media in socialization.

The Early Childhood Education Controversy

From the moment we are born, the socialization process becomes a lifelong part of our lives. Its influence is felt through the family, school, religious institution, and workplace. Learning to become a member of society has both formal, planned components and informal aspects.

Early childhood education takes on special significance because children are in the beginning processes of developing their self-concept and social awareness. From studies of mental development, we learn that 50 percent of general intelligence develops between birth and age four (Begley, 1996). Issues that surround early socialization include where early cognitive development should take place (at home or school), at what age children should begin formal schooling, whether there are benefits of preschool for children of working parents or for those living in poverty, and the role preschool and kindergarten programs should play in the socialization of children.

Variations in the process of early childhood socialization are tremendous; they depend on society, social class, and family background. As children grow, they come into contact with socialization agents outside the home: relatives, neighbors, church, nursery school, and playmates.

"Ready to Learn" initiatives prepare many young children for school.

But there is little preparation for the major transition to the formal institution of the school. More than half the nations of the world have some formal center-based early childhood education for young children under five to help socialize children and allow parents to work. In some countries, such as China and Israel, care begins shortly after birth and is sometimes mandatory, and in others, such as Sweden and the United Kingdom, legislation addresses the need and funding for day care and nursery schools. In the United States, 24 percent of children with employed mothers were in center-based programs, 20 percent were in other nonrelative settings such as home day care, and more than 32 percent were cared for by a relative (ChildStats.gov, 2009). In 2007, 57 percent of all three- to five-year-olds were enrolled in early childhood education programs. Poverty also affected enrollments: 60 percent of children above the poverty line were enrolled compared to 47 percent below (Child Trends Data Bank, 2007).

The family provides the primary context for initial socialization. The movement against day care comes mainly from those who consider it a threat to the family and to the maternal role. The argument is that children should receive education in the formative early years in the home. In addition, early childhood education is distrusted by some because many programs are aimed at particular ethnic and minority groups such as African Americans and Native Americans. Although stated intentions are to give these children advantages, this "special attention" has been interpreted by some conflict theorists and policy analysts as a technique to manipulate learning, perpetuate a class structure, and train compliant minority members of society.

Those for early childhood education argue that the greatest return on investment in terms of children's achievement in schools comes from providing preschool education for three- and four-year-olds from low-income families. These children are more likely to be at special risk of failure because they enter school at a significant disadvantage. Children from disadvantaged homes begin school with a disadvantage in cognitive ability, and often attend low-resource schools, compounding the gap (Early et al., 2007; Lee and Burkam, 2002). Risk factors cited for children include low household income, minority group status, non-English-speaking homes, single parents, large households, a disabling condition, a mother who became pregnant as a teen and who did not finish high school, and those behind in language and intellectual development by the time they start nursery school. In the United States, bills have been introduced in the U.S. Congress for years, proposing legislation to support early childhood education, reflecting pressure on government and work institutions from women's groups and others advocating for children.

The federal government has developed several programs that include provisions for early childhood education. Although the government does fund "model" programs such as Head Start, so far much of the past legislation for early childhood education has been defeated, despite the growing number of working mothers with children under age five needing day care. In 2004–2005, over 800,000 or 17 percent of the nation's four-year-olds attended state-funded preschools (Barnett et al., 2005), with 19 percent of three- to four-year-olds from poor neighborhoods attending Head Start programs (Child Trends Databank, 2005). Approximately 500,000 four-year-olds were in federally supported Head Start programs (Early et al., 2007; U.S. Department of Health and Human Services, 2006).

Those favoring early childhood education pose several arguments:

1. Early childhood education provides valuable learning experiences not always available at home.
2. Young children need to interact with children and with adults other than their parents.
3. Parents and siblings are not always the best or most capable handlers of children.
4. For many families, day care is necessary because both parents must work; in the case of single-parent families, the only alternative may be child care.
5. A good day care center is often preferable to leaving a child with relatives or neighbors.

Studies show that disadvantaged children are behind at the "starting gate"; they begin their education with lower cognitive skills than those children from higher socioeconomic levels and often end up in the worst schools (Lee and Burkam, 2002). Evidence from evaluations of preschool programs in the United States shows that preschool experiences help brain development, especially for at-risk children, and provide a foundation for later school success (Early et al., 2007, p. 558; NICHD, 2005).

Studies of access to and quality of preschool programs for at-risk children indicate that the quality of preschool programs such as Head Start and Early Head Start (for children from birth to three-year-olds) is comparable with that for children from high-income families, but not all qualified children have access to Head Start programs, usually due to lack of funding. Infant and Toddler Early Head Start programs help to overcome problems such as lack of prenatal care, parent isolation, substandard child care, poverty, inadequate health care, and lack of crucial brain development (National Research Council, 2000). Consider the following summary of findings for Head Start children compared with those not attending Head Start:

Cognitive benefits: Less grade repetition in later schooling; reduced need for special education; higher high school graduation rates and college attendance than those not attending Head Start; more Head Start parents reading to their children; less absenteeism; and higher skills in numbers, language, physical development, and social conduct—that is higher readiness to learn.

Economic benefits: Society receives nearly $9 in benefits for every $1 invested in Head Start children (earnings, employment, family stability, decreased welfare dependency, crime costs, grade repetition, and special education).

Health benefits: Children receive health care screenings, dental exams, and other family services not readily available to non-Head Start counterparts; children are more likely to have all immunizations; and children are in excellent or very good health.

Social benefits: Less involved in crime and fewer arrests, fewer young and out-of-wedlock births, more cooperative behavior and less behavior problems, and higher achievement motivation and self-esteem (National Head Start Association, 2007).

This positive report card for Head Start programs has resulted in many advocates for providing funding to enroll all young children who qualify.

Early childhood education is not a substitute for many home care situations, but it can provide children with experiences that go beyond those received at home. The goal of these programs is to provide developmental experiences that will help children in later schooling. Although the debate over whether early childhood education should take place primarily at home or in preschool is likely to continue, the need for care will not diminish as more parents work outside the home.

> **Applying Sociology to Education:** *What impact might early childhood education have on children from different backgrounds? Should some or all children be removed from home for part of the day to attend preschool?*

Role of Technology and the Media in Socialization

Kids these days text in class, spend hours on social networking sites such as Facebook and MySpace, and play computer games during school hours. The impact of technology on today's students is increasing faster than the teacher can say, "stop Tweeting in class." New technologies and other media such as television complement and compete with schools for the attention of students. The question for teachers and schools is whether to fight the technology brought to schools or go with the flow. Some schools are accepting, if not requiring, students to bring cell phones, iPhones, iPads, or other portable technologies to help them with their work. They argue that this serves multiple purposes: students become proficient in the use of new technologies and they learn how to access information. One proponent says that textbooks become dated, but the iPhone is always up-to-date. The challenge for schools, according to proponents, is to teach students how to access information and how to judge its validity or accuracy. Since these technologies will be the tools of workers in the future, students need to become familiar with ways they can be used to solve problems (Chen, 2009).

Other educators and researchers question the use of technology in classrooms (Cherniavsky and Vanderputten, 2003; Fletcher, 2003). Cuban, an education professor at Stanford University, has pointed out in his well-researched book that since classrooms do not change much, technology is not relevant to the way teachers teach (Cuban, 2001). However, there is "no clear and substantial evidence of students increasing their academic achievement as a result of using information technologies" (Cuban, 2001, p. 133). While some point to the reluctance of teachers to learn and use new technologies, Cuban argues that is not the issue. Teachers are willing, but they do not integrate technology into their classrooms in a way that changes learning. This is partly because they are concerned about the reliability and complexity of the equipment when teaching and trying to adapt it to the context in which they are teaching, and partly because of demands for accountability as measured by tests of specific content.

In addition to new electronic devices, television is also an agent of socialization. "Most children plug into the world of television long before they enter school: 70 percent of child-care centers use TV during a typical day. In a year, the average child spends 900 hours in school and nearly 1,023 hours in front of a TV" (Gavin and Dowshen, 2005, p. 1)—that is on average 2.8 hours of watching TV a day. The controversy is over the impact of TV on learning opportunities. During the first two years of life, watching TV reduces the child's ability to explore, learn, interact, play, and develop important skills. Children who watch TV for more than four hours a day are more likely to be overweight, an increasingly alarming trend; believe the world is scary (from watching violent shows); and have gender and racial stereotypes reinforced (Gavin and Dowshen, 2005). The average child sees 200,000 violent acts on TV by age 18, and the list of effects from excessive TV watching goes on.

The evidence for the relationship between TV watching and school achievement is mixed; more TV means less time for other activities, such as reading and homework. On average, excessive amount of TV watching lowers achievement. The highest achievement has been found among those who watch up to ten hours of TV per week, and the lowest among those watching 30–40 hours a week. Thus, limited TV watching, depending on the type of shows watched, can positively affect the way we think and learn.

When TV first became widespread in the 1950s, many thought that it would solve educational problems and bring education to millions around the world. To some extent this has been realized. TV satellites and distance education beam a variety of programs to many nations and rural areas, ranging from basic literacy training to advanced college courses. Satellite transmission has made education accessible to a worldwide population. However, the controversy is this: Do the educational benefits of TV outweigh the negative outcomes? Concerns focus on school achievement and the amount of TV watched; TV's possible distortion of information; and TV's effects on negative behaviors, such as aggression and suicidal tendencies.

Although TV viewing may be satisfying different needs than those satisfied by reading and other activities, reading for pleasure is more beneficial to achievement. Yet according to a survey, "Reading at Risk," literary reading declined 10 percent from 1982 to 2002, with 18- to 24-year-olds showing the steepest declines. Less than half of the adult population in the United States read literature, and other types of reading such as newspaper reading are declining as well (Whelan, 2004). With this has come a decline in vocabulary. Interestingly, a survey of students indicates that 40 percent prefer reading to TV, yet most spend twice as much time watching TV as they do reading.

Why this decline in reading, especially among younger groups? Some experts point to the Internet, e-mail, cell phones, iPhones, iPods, and Blackberries (Whelan, 2004). Education level and family income in addition to other variables such as race, sex, parental education level, educational resources, and intelligence also play a role in TV and reading behaviors. For those concerned about the amount of viewing, it may be encouraging to know that the national poll on "TV watching as the favorite pastime of Americans" was down from 46 percent in 1966 and 1974 to 33 percent in 1986, and 31 percent in 1999. Reading was the favorite evening recreation for 18 percent of adults (Newport, 1999a).

Teachers complain that the TV generation expects to be entertained in school or they "turn off." There is some support for the "distraction hypothesis," which contends that exposure to TV leads to intolerance for the "slow" pace of schooling. The concern that we become mesmerized by the tube has led some critics to question whether we are critical enough in our TV watching. Perhaps the most serious controversy centers on the behavioral effects of TV watching. The concern is that TV socializes children into antisocial, aggressive behaviors. What kind of teacher is TV? Violence for entertainment teaches that violence is "legitimate, justified, rewarded, effective, clean, heroic, manly" (Slaby, 1994, p. 81). The sights and sounds on video games, films, and TV cartoons can also influence children negatively.

Clear evidence regarding the impact of TV on socialization and learning comes from two areas. First, parental involvement in children's TV watching has a powerful effect on its impact. Concerning elementary school children, the child's cognitive and behavioral tendencies are correlated with several aspects of family patterns, two of which are especially relevant to TV watching: parents who play an active role in helping children understand the world around them, including what they see on TV, and parents who watch a limited amount of television. The second source of evidence comes from studies of children's educational television, such as *Sesame Street*, which generally show positive outcomes for children (Biagi, 1998; Freepress, 2010).

In 1990, Congress passed the Children's Television Act with the goal of making TV programming more educational and discouraging commercial TV. Pressure from lobbying groups, such as Action for Children's Television, has resulted in less inappropriate advertising on children's television. Advertisements on children's TV are limited to 10.5 minutes an hour on weekends and 12 minutes per hour on weekdays, and no advertising is allowed in programming (Brown, 2004). Some schools offer programs to educate children about the effects of TV and about how to be sophisticated viewers. The Children's Television Workshop (the producers of *Sesame Street*) and CNN Newsroom are making specific episodes available to teachers through an index system, and educational computer and video games have been developed. The bottom line is that children are constantly bombarded by new exciting stimuli that may or may not enhance positive learning. Consider the case of Channel One.

Channel One, started in the spring of 1990 by Whittle Communications, promised to bring video technology and innovative news programming to U.S. classrooms for grades 6–12. "They provide schools with television and video equipment on the condition that the schools agree to have their students watch 12 to 13 minutes of Channel One programming a day" (Brighouse, 2005, p. 529). In exchange, the broadcasts have two minutes of this time for commercials, reaching an attractive target group for many companies. More than 12,000 schools, or 350,000 classrooms, across the United States and 8 million teens—that is, 40 percent of 12- to 18-year-olds in the United States—receive the 10-minute news programs and two minutes of commercials every school day (Brighouse, 2005).

Those two minutes of advertising for such products as snack foods, personal care products, movies, clothes, and electronics have created controversy in many school districts. Although the advertisements help pay for the equipment given to each school—satellite dish, TV in every classroom, DVD players, instructional videos, and public service announcements to stay in school and stay off drugs—some argue that it is inappropriate for schools to be involved in influencing students to buy certain products. This is especially important with the "fat" epidemic of overweight children.

Evaluation studies of Channel One programming showed that students liked the news stories and that they had already seen most of the advertisements on TV. Teachers approve of the programs, rating them A–/B+, and 61 percent of principals believe their schools are better because of Channel One (Johnston, 1995). Yet not everyone agrees! Some critics point out that this private commercial corporation shapes the social and institutional context of public schools and their administrators and school boards (Blokhuis, 2008). Channel One promotes commercialism, wastes class time, and ultimately costs taxpayers $1.8 billion in lost teaching time (Brighouse, 2005).

Schools and technology have not yet found a balance that can benefit both. Thus, the battle in this arena for the minds of children will continue.

Applying Sociology to Education: *How can schools and new technologies find ways to benefit children in schools—or can they?*

THE FUNCTION OF CULTURAL TRANSMISSION AND PROCESS OF PASSING ON CULTURE

"The educational foundations of our society are presently being eroded by a rising tide of mediocrity that threatens our very future as a Nation and a people. What was unimaginable a generation ago has begun to occur—others are matching and surpassing our educational attainments. . . . [W]e have, in effect, been committing an act of unthinking, unilateral educational disarmament" (Bell, 1983, p. 5). This statement from the 1983 U.S. report *A Nation at Risk* opened a floodgate of questioning and self-criticism that continues today.

With these hard words to the American people came concern about the "cultural literacy" and illiteracy of the United States. Are young people learning the very core of knowledge that holds a nation together with a common thread—information that is understood and shared by all? Some argue that this knowledge core has slipped in several ways (Hirsch, 1987, p. 152). For instance, we no longer teach many of the classics in Western literature that they argue form the core. Others argue that the "core" has changed and a multicultural curriculum is relevant to today's society. Conflicts occur over why educational attainment is low and illiteracy is high among certain groups, how to raise literacy levels, how to fund the special programs, and what content to teach. In this section we explore literacy, learning, and what should be taught and how.

Literacy, Science, Math—and Cultural Transmission

Imagine going into a store and not being able to read the labels on the cans. Illiteracy among young people and adults is a problem that many of those affected try to hide, yet 14 percent (30 million) of U.S. adults aged 16 years and above have "Below Basic" skills ("no more than the most simple and concrete literacy skills") and 29 percent (63 million) have "Basic" skills ("can perform simple and everyday literacy activities") (National Assessment of Adult Literacy—NAAL, 2003). Figure 2.1 shows literacy rates (from NAAL: Key Findings, 2003).

In the "Below Basics" group, 55 percent are not high school graduates; 44 percent had no English skills before starting school; 39 percent were Hispanic and 20 percent African American; 26 percent were aged above 65; and 21 percent had multiple disabilities. Immigrants and family mobility account for a large percentage of those with poor literacy skills (NAAL, 2003). There has been no change in the literacy rates between 1992 and 2003, although quantitative skills have risen slightly. The low level of scientific literacy is also of concern, and 80 percent of the public feel that supporting basic scientific research is important (Center for Science and Technology Policy Research, 2004).

Educational researchers are examining why 9 out of 10 children who start 1st grade in the bottom reading group stay there throughout elementary school. Currently, there is a hodgepodge of programs for teaching reading. For some children, new and coordinated approaches to reading may be key. Some advocate a return to phonics-based reading for low-income children instead of the whole-language approach, which works better with at-home support of reading. Others argue that the money spent on intensive, personalized education early in a child's education more than pays off later. For older students, educators are trying everything from tying drivers' licenses to academic performance and staying in school to offering literacy training in alternative locations such as work settings.

Prose Literacy

- Below Basic:
  - o no more than the most *simple* and *concrete* literacy skills

- Basic:
  - o can perform simple and everyday literacy activities

- Intermediate:
  - o can perform moderately challenging literacy activities

- Proficient
  - o can perform complex and challenging literacy activities

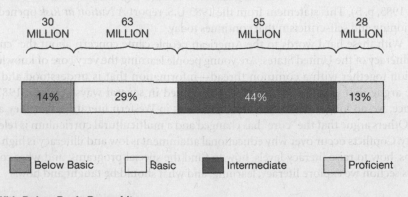

Adults With *Below Basic* Prose Literacy
Performance in 2003

- Several population groups are overrepresented in the *Below Basic* level. For example, 55 percent of adults with *Below Basic* prose literacy did not graduate from high school, compared to 15 percent of adults in the general population.

	Percent in Prose *Below Basic* Population	Percent in Total NAAL Population
Did not graduate from high school	55	15
No English spoken before starting school	44	13
Hispanic adults	39	12
Black adults	20	12
Age 65+	26	15
Multiple disabilities	21	9

FIGURE 2.1   Number of adults in each prose literacy level.   *Source:* National Assessment of Adult Literacy (NAAL), National Center for Education Statistics, 2003. Available: http://nces.ed.gov/naal/kf_demographics.asp (Retrieved July 21, 2007.)

The number of first-year college students who are unprepared for college-level work is also alarming. American high schools are not adequately preparing students for later success in college (The Education Trust, 2005). "Only 32 percent of 18 year olds in U.S. public high schools possess the minimum qualifications needed to attend a four-year college; for African-American students, the percentage of college-ready students falls to 20 percent, while only 16 percent of Hispanic students are at least minimally prepared" (Stewart, 2004). Data show that 13 percent of college students are in remedial reading, 17 percent are in remedial writing, and 24 percent are in remedial mathematics courses. Studies also show that scientific illiteracy is widespread (NCES, *Condition*, 1999).

Worldwide the number of literate citizens is increasing; the number of illiterate adults fell from 22.4 percent in 1995 to 20.3 percent in 2000, and if the current trends continue it was expected to drop to 15 percent by 2015. Asia and Africa saw the greatest gains in literacy. Although women make up two-thirds of the world's illiterate adult population, their rates of literacy are increasing faster than men. In Africa, for example, now just under half of the women are illiterate. The countries that have the highest illiteracy rates are also the poorest countries in the world (UNESCO Press, 2002; Wedgeworth, 2003). Literacy rates have a major impact on what people can learn.

Learning as a process is influenced not only by the teacher, the techniques used, the classroom setting, and the formal or informal material being taught, but also by the child's ability, motivation, interest in the subject matter, readiness to learn, retentiveness, values and attitudes, relationship with the teacher, feelings about self and ability, relationships with peers, background experiences, home life, encouragement from home—and literacy. Also of importance are the environmental pressures for learning, the time allotted for learning, family support for learning, and the atmosphere of the school and classroom. Children's learning experiences differ as a result of such variables as race, gender, and class. Thus, it is superficial to explain learning differences among children by one primary factor, such as intelligence.

Because of the *No Child Left Behind* and *Race to the Top* accountability movements, the back-to-basics movement, and concerns about declining achievement test scores, high school curricula have undergone significant changes. There has been particular emphasis in the areas of math and science, where educators believed that the United States was losing whatever competitive edge it may have had, especially in high-tech areas. "The low level of scientific and technological literacy in our society is deplorable, and the trickle of talent flowing into careers in engineering, mathematics, and the sciences . . . is deeply disturbing" (National Science Foundation, 1992, p. 1). So begins a National Science Foundation evaluation of science and math curricula in the United States.

As a result of tougher high school requirements, high school graduates are taking more academic courses, especially in math and science. Achievement results have also risen, with proficiency scores on the National Assessment of Educational Progress (NAEP) and Trends in International Mathematics and Science Study (TIMSS, to be conducted again in spring 2011) math and science tests average being somewhat above other participating countries (NCES, 2007).

The concern about math and science has resulted in the National Science Foundation funding many projects to support high schools, colleges, and graduate schools' efforts to encourage more women and minorities to enter related fields. The Science, Technology, Engineering and Math initiative (STEM) supports many women and minorities in pursuing science fields (STEM is discussed further in Chapter 4). Some educational policy makers suggest tighter control over curriculum and requirements, and changes in teacher education so that more teachers specialize in an area of teaching expertise rather than a general curriculum (The Center for Comprehensive School Reform and Improvement, 2005; School Matters, 2006). These efforts are beginning to show positive results in the United States. For instance, the achievement levels of students are rising to where they were in the 1950s and 1960s, and the majority–minority disparities are declining and the gap is becoming much narrower than in previous decades (Alexander, 1997).

How to Pass On Culture

The debate over *how* to pass on culture covers issues from what materials, textbooks, and technology to use to what philosophy of education should govern decision making. This section focuses on two issues related to passing on culture: what teaching techniques are most effective in producing learning outcomes and what role critical thinking plays in education.

Arguments about philosophy of education pit the "back-to-basics" and accountability advocates, who stress basic skills and testing, against the "progressive" educators, who argue that education must be relevant to the surrounding environment and future social civic participation of students. For much of the history of formal education, children have been taught those things that were regarded as important for the community and for the children's prosperity in it. John Dewey (1916) made a great impact on education with the idea that learning could be more effective if it were relevant to the lives of children. Dewey's progressivism contended that schools were irrelevant to the daily lives of most children, and, therefore, an alienating experience; techniques of memorization and authoritarian atmospheres were not conducive to learning. He proposed using the children's experience and involving them actively in the learning process. His extensive writings have been interpreted, misinterpreted, and modified, but they have influenced all movements in education since the turn of the twentieth century, including current postmodern and constructivist movements. Going beyond Dewey's ideas are child-centered curricula that focus on learner needs and interests, are highly flexible, provide many options to the learner, and involve learners in planning their own curricula around their needs. Some free, alternative, and charter schools have adopted these ideas.

Recent movements to improve the passing on of culture have included "writing-across-the-curriculum," technology in the classroom, accountability and assessment, stricter discipline and increased homework assignments, and critical thinking and deep learning—that is, reflective and reasonable thinking that is focused on deciding what to believe or do. Some of these ideas result from social forces such as achievement test scores, criticisms of schools, and the lack of correspondence between demands to think more maturely and what the school program teaches. For example, the ideas of critical thinking and deep learning contrasts with educational styles that concentrate only on facts. Related to Bloom's (1976) taxonomy and "higher order thinking skills," critical thinking and deep learning require one to evaluate evidence and support conclusions before making decisions.

Some teachers do include elements of critical thinking and deep learning in their teaching, but it is more often found in classrooms of college-bound or brighter students, not in classrooms for children who are most likely to hold working-class jobs. Conflict theorists argue that these children are taught differently because those who learn critical thinking would challenge the social system. All students need to be able to express their thoughts cogently in oral and written form, and to evaluate their value stances on issues. Training in critical thinking aids in these processes, but it is not equally available to all.

Recent reports on the status of education in the United States have made many recommendations, among them smaller classes, longer school days and year-round school (Darling-Hammond, 2010; Stedron, 2007), tougher graduation standards, stronger curriculum and instruction (Craig and Dillon, 2007), proficiency exams for promotion, intensive work with bilingual students (Komoski, 2007), smaller schools and classes, and more homework. As a result, changes are taking place in districts across the country.

What Culture to Pass On

Another debate related to cultural transmission focuses on *what is taught* in schools. What culture is transmitted and what should be transmitted? Who should decide these difficult questions? What should be the goals of the curriculum? In every society there are expectations, usually unwritten, concerning what a successful adult should be able to do, and related ideas about the "products" or "outputs" of schools. An assumption built into the curriculum is that there are desired changes to be made in the students' existing knowledge by the introduction of new ideas, by the correction of misconceptions, or by additions to existing knowledge. The curriculum provides for instruction in areas seen as desirable through "planned experiences."

WHO SHOULD MAKE DECISIONS CONCERNING CURRICULUM CONTENT?   We have mentioned environmental influences on curricular decisions. Many groups vie for decision-making responsibility, and many have an influence on decisions. Because educators have been professionally trained to deal with matters related to education and the curriculum, they naturally prefer to keep decision making in the schools, removed from external politics and other pressures. Educators have used various techniques to maintain control of educational decisions and to keep schools independent of external influences; controlling information about what is going on within the school, releasing selected positive information, and assigning sympathetic community members to committees are examples.

"Academic freedom" refers to attempts by schools and colleges to minimize control and influence on teachers and curricula, primarily from the external environment. Schools can maintain this autonomy to the extent that their program and staff remain independent and uncontroversial. Should controversy arise over issues of curriculum content (e.g., sex education or prayer in schools), school and teacher autonomy may be threatened. Education is an open system and, therefore, subject to pressures and scrutiny from the environment.

In heterogeneous societies without centrally run educational systems, curriculum planners face pressures from many diverse individuals and groups. In centrally run state systems, decisions are more protected from public scrutiny and challenges. The United States is an example of a heterogeneous society and a federally decentralized system.

WHAT SHOULD BE TAUGHT?   What is being taught in the formal curriculum can be fairly easily and accurately determined, though the range of findings is great. Examining curriculum plans and textbooks provides a start. Generally, curriculum plans in primary schools focus on developing basic skills; secondary schools refine these skills and add content. Math, language skills, science, art and music, social science, physical education, and history are common components of secondary school curricula.

Functional theorists see schools as transmitting those parts of the culture necessary to perform successfully in the adult world. Schools provide a transition from the warm, protective, accepting environment of the home to the competitive, performance-oriented atmosphere of the work world. Children learn that in school the same rules are supposed to apply to all. In this way schools serve the crucial function of preparing young people for society (Dreeben, 1968; Parsons, 1959).

Conflict theorists view the cultural transmission of these values and norms as serving the needs of a capitalist society rather than those of individuals who are dehumanized and alienated by the process (Bowles and Gintis, 1976). Schools are seldom completely effective in transmitting these cultural values, however, as exemplified by the disruptions and student rebellions in some schools. Jackson, Boostrom, and Hansen (1993) evaluate the many ways, formal and informal, that values are taught in schools; some of these values become part of the hidden curriculum, discussed in Chapter 8. What is controversial in many communities is the transmission of specific content, such as religious or sex education, because questions of responsibility and control of knowledge by family versus educational systems or religious groups are raised.

Consider the Scopes trial in Dayton, Tennessee, 1925, in which a public school teacher was convicted of violating a state law that prohibited the teaching of evolution in public school. This battle over content continued with the *Bryan v. Darrow* case over *what* religion to teach. The issue continues with the 1999–2006 Kansas Board of Education's challenges to the teaching of evolution and promotion of teaching intelligent design in science classes. In 2005, the Dover, PA board of education tried to require science teachers to read a statement on intelligent design, but the U.S. District Court judge called the mandate unconstitutional ("Exploring Constitutional Conflicts," 2006). Conflicts over teaching of evolution and intelligent design/creationism continue with Livingston Parish in Louisiana trying to include teaching of creationism in science classes (National Center for Science Education, 2010).

In the 1960s, the Supreme Court banned teacher-led prayers and Bible readings. Battles over religious and political content in curricula are still being waged today in communities from Pennsylvania to Missouri, reflecting the diverse populations that make up the United States and their desires to have their positions heard, respected, and reflected (see Box 2.1) (Zirkel, 2009).

BOX 2.1

"School Law All Stars"

The Supreme Court has made many decisions regarding schools, school districts, and education. This box describes briefly 10 of the most important decisions in the past 20 years. They were selected by a panel of experts who considered the impact of the decisions on the educational system.

Top 10 Education Decisions 1986–Present

1. *Hazelwood School District v. Kuhlmeier* (1988). This decision furthered the trend toward student rights that began in *Bethel School District v. Fraser* (1986). *Hazelwood* established a new category for student expression under the First Amendment—school-sponsored expression. The Court ruled that school-sponsored expression can be limited. Thus significantly reducing, without entirely reversing, *Tinker*

2. *Missouri v. Jenkins II* (1990) and *Missouri v. Jenkins III* (1995). This pair of decisions qualified for the list merely as illustrations of a long line of Supreme Court decisions that gradually moved from the lofty spirit of *Brown* integration down to the harsh reality of post *Brown* *implementation*. After trying to address the de facto segregation in communities, the courts lacked the capacity, or at least the commitment, to resolve more than de jure segregation in schools.

3. Americans with Disabilities Act (ADA) of 1990 and ADA Amendments (2008). These congressional re-actions reflected a continuing and expanding societal commitment to protect individuals—including students and employees—with disabilities from discrimination. The ADA effectively extended Section 504 to private schools and other such organizations that do not receive federal financial assistance but are larger than the mom-and-pop operation that is too small to engage in interstate commerce. The ADA amendments reversed the Supreme Court's restrictive interpretations of the meaning of "disability" under Section 504 and the ADA, including the Court's decisions in *Sutton v. United Airlines* (1999) and *Toyota Motor Manufacturingv. Williams* (2002).

4. *Lee v. Weisman* (1992) and *Santa Fe Independent School District v. Doe* (2000). These successive Supreme Court decisions rather remarkably concluded that clergy-led devotionals at public school commencement ceremonies and student-led devotionals at high school football games, respectively, violated the Establishment Clause. Nevertheless, the underlying criteria and the outer boundaries of these decisions are more fluid than fixed.

5. *Vernonia School District 47 J v. Action* (1986) and *Board of Education v. Earls* (2002). These two successive decisions marked the continuing erosion of students' rights under the Fourth Amendment since the Supreme Court's transitional decision in International Labor Organization (ILO). In these cases, the Court said the individualized responsible suspicion stan-dard did not apply to drug testing as a prerequisite for participating in interscholastic athletics specifically and in extracurricular activities generally.

6. *Gebser v. Lago Vista School District* (1998) and *Davis v. Monroe County Board of Education* (1998). In *Franklin v. Gwinnett County Public Schools* (1992), the Supreme Court established the standards for liability under the Title IX for teacher-on-student and student-on-student sexual harassment, in these two successive decisions. This multistep test has proven to be difficult in all but the most fragrant cases.

7. No Child Left Behind Act of 2001. Although the most comprehensive and controversial funding legislation for elementary and secondary education, NCLB introduced the school accountability standards of disaggregation, Adequate Yearly Progress, and highly qualified teachers. In addition, its more than 1,000 pages of legislation and regulation also addressed such varied topics as mili-tary recruitment, Boy Scouts, homeless children, persistently dangerous schools, gifted education, student surveys, school-prayer guidelines, and teacher liability protections.

8. *Zelman v. Simmons-Harris* (2002). In this decision, the Supreme Court held that a school voucher statute that provides parents a choice among private schools—both secular and religious—and public schools does not violate the First Amendment's Establishment Clause. This ruling moved the controversy concerning school vouchers to litigation under state constitutions and the political process in state legislatures.

9. *Morse v. Frederick* (2007). In this decision, the Supreme Court revised the map of First Amendment student speech to marginalize Tinker, thus continuing the constitutional trend away from the students' rights era. More specifically, the Court concluded that First Amendment protection did not extend to prodrug student speech. As Cambron-McCabe's article explains, a variety of other student freedom of expression cases have already surfaced in the lower courts.

10. *Parents Involved in Community Schools v. Seattle School District No. 1* (2007). This decision serves as the latest counterpoint to *Brown* with regard to applying the Fourteenth Amendment's Equal Protection Clause in favor of racial minority students. Here, the Court concluded that a public school assignment plan that accords preferences to racial minority students is unconstitutional in the absence of preponderant proof that it is necessary to achieve racial diversity.

Source: Zirkel, Perry A. "School Law All Stars: Two Successive Constellations" (using ONLY excerpt: "Top 10 Education Decisions 1986–Present"), *Phi Delta Kappan* Vol. 90, 2009. Available: www.pdkintl.org/kappan/k_v90/k0906zir.htm (Retrieved June 1, 2010). Used by Permission of the author.

What is being taught reflects forces both inside and outside the school. Internal educational forces are those that have a direct influence on the curriculum and processes of the school. For example, teachers and principals may express preferences for certain materials and classroom organization and reject others, and the structure, composition, hierarchy, philosophy, and architecture of any one school influence the curriculum content within that school. In addition to the internal educational forces affecting curricula, there are many environmental factors outside the school. Recall that in the systems model, the environment includes all those factors outside the school that influence what happens within it. Consider the following factors that affect what is taught:

1. Local, state, and federal regulations stipulate certain curricular requirements. For instance, a state board of education may require that a certain amount of state history be taken before students can graduate.
2. Accrediting agencies reflect state or regional decision making concerning school standards, and they may specify required content in the curriculum.
3. Testing services that develop achievement tests for different grade levels and for college entrance do much to influence knowledge that is taught. Many states require skills tests for graduation from high school.
4. National studies, reports, and reform plans include recommendations for change in the curriculum (Borman and Cotner, 2011).

Curriculum content is influenced by certain concerns and trends in society. Women's studies, minority studies (African American, Chicano, Native American, Appalachian, Chinese), multicultural and bilingual education, environmental studies, urban studies, drug and sex education, technology literacy, school-to-work curriculum, community service, and service learning are among the subjects that have been introduced into curricula as a result of societal trends.

The call for curricula that fairly represent the history and current status of minorities in the United States has led to the multicultural educational movement. Teaching race, class, and gender issues is receiving increasing attention (King, 1990, 1999). Some advocate courses and programs on specific minorities; others push for an accurate portrayal within the existing curriculum of minority history and contributions. Still others advocate global studies to familiarize students with the world issues that affect them. Sociologists are uniquely qualified to develop cross-cultural models for curricula that take into consideration micro- and macro-level explanations of societies and change.

Adopting multicultural curricula has met with criticism from those who oppose reducing or eliminating traditional Western culture, which has been at the core of most courses of study in U.S. high schools and colleges. They feel that altering this core reduces the common learning experience that holds the United States together. Recommendations to change minority education stress the need for inclusiveness and understanding of minorities from preschool to graduate school (The Carnegie Corporation, 1990). These subject areas may prove passing fads, they may be permanently integrated into the curriculum, or they may remain distinct fields of study.

We now discuss briefly two areas of curriculum decision making that have created heated controversy in many communities and that reflect the diversity in U.S. society: sex and drug education, and censorship of textbooks.

Applying Sociology to Education: What should be taught in schools, and who should make the decision(s)? What factors are you taking into account in answering these questions?

SEX AND DRUG ABUSE EDUCATION. Schools as condom dispensaries? A few years ago this idea was unthinkable, but with the threat of acquired immunodeficiency syndrome (AIDS) and other venereal diseases confronting more and more teens, "condom sense is common sense." School boards across the country debate the issue of "what culture should be taught," while a growing number of urban school systems, including New York, Philadelphia, and Los Angeles, are making condoms available in attempts to prevent teen pregnancy, venereal disease, and AIDS. The former surgeon general of the United States, Dr. Jocelyn Elders, was dismissed because of her controversial frank speech on the topic of teenage sex, and the 2002–2006 surgeon general, Dr. Richard H. Carmona, testified that he was muzzled when talking about sex education policies. These are controversial topics that many believe should be left to families.

Sex and AIDS education are increasing, despite objections from some parents and community groups. They feel schools should discourage sexual activity, not "encourage" it through classes and the distribution of condoms. Yet recent studies indicate that "making condoms available in high schools does not increase sexual activity among students, but does raise condom use by those already sexually active . . ." (Loughrey, 2003; Poppen, 2005). Others argue that if sex and AIDS education are part of the curriculum, moral education should be as well.

Three main approaches to sex education have been debated: abstinence-only programs, sex education programs, and making condoms available along with sex education in schools (Kirby, 2000). Fifteen percent of Americans surveyed believe in abstinence-only education, 46 percent believe in "abstinence-plus" (teaching about condoms and contraception while advocating abstinence), and 36 percent believe education should be about how students can make responsible decisions about sex ("Sex Education in America," 2004). The fact is that American teens are sexually active at increasingly younger ages. The number of women between ages 15 and 19 having sexual intercourse now equals that of men, both between 46.8 and 48 percent (Eaton, 2006, p. 19; National Survey of Family Growth, 2006). Women who see little future opportunity in school or work tend to become sexually active earlier than those who feel in control of their futures. Other high-risk activities such as using drugs, participating in criminal activities, and engaging with multiple partners are associated with early sex. Despite the general increase in contraceptive use, studies show that teenage girls are less likely than older partners to be protected.

Schools and family provide only part of the sex education children receive. Children are bombarded with sexual messages: pornography in magazines and on the Internet, music videos with 93 sexual situations (some hard core) per hour, and 83 percent of the top 20 shows watched by teens include sexual content. Watching more than 14 hours of rap music videos per week is correlated with teens having multiple sex partners. On the contrary, later onset of sexual intercourse was found in students aged 15–19 in the following situations: parents were more educated, supportive family relations, parental supervision, sexual abstinent friends, good grades, and church attendance (National Survey of Family Growth, 2006).

One of the U.S. public's top concerns about schools, rated number 4 in a nationwide poll in 2009 and high in the rankings for several years before that, is drug use. This concern is understandable considering the attention given to drug use among teens. However, according to the

National Institute on Drug Abuse (2010), there has been a decade-long drop in illicit drugs and alcohol use. The 2009 survey indicates decreases among 8th, 10th, and 12th graders in use of alcohol, hallucinogens, and methamphetamines. However, use of marijuana has held steady but that of Vicodin and OxyContin has increased.

Messages are passed on from parents, advertising, and peers about usage, with many underage drinkers being children of alcoholic parents. Factors that increase the probability of drug use include a history of family crime, drug use, or alcoholism; poor child-rearing patterns; low investment in education, delinquent behavior, or academic failure; and early use of drugs. These children are at higher risk for being abused, attempting suicide, running away, delinquency, and poor school achievement.

The most successful rehabilitation programs are those that begin before middle school and deal with both life skills and social influences. Thus, the most promising strategies are comprehensive—encompassing peer groups, families, schools, media, community organizations, and a wide variety of approaches that provide information, develop life skills, use peer facilitators, and change community policies and norms (Menehan, 2007). Drug Abuse Resistance Education (DARE) is one such program; it begins in elementary school and ends with a pledge by students to stay off drugs. In fact, DARE has become an international movement.

Substance abuse and other problems point again to the controversy—the role of schools versus families in educating students. Should the schools offer drug and alcohol counseling and rehabilitation, sex and AIDS education, pregnancy counseling and testing, contraceptives, and suicide-prevention programs? Or should these "personal and moral matters" be left to families?

> **Applying Sociology to Education:** *What should be the school's role in teaching about moral issues? Who should make these decisions?*

CENSORSHIP OF TEXTBOOKS AND LIBRARY BOOKS.   Obscenity, sex, nudity, political or economic "bias," profanity, slang or questionable English, racism or racial hatred, and antireligious or anti-American ideas—all have been cited as reasons for censoring text and library books in schools. Censorship refers to "the removal, suppression, or restricted circulation of literary, artistic or educational materials . . . on the grounds that these are morally or otherwise objectionable in light of the standards applied by the censor" (Cromwell, 2005). Such books as *Rumpelstiltskin*, *Madame Bovary*, *Soul on Ice*, *The Grapes of Wrath*, Shakespeare's *Hamlet*, Chaucer's *The Miller's Tale*, and Aristophanes's *Lysistrata* have been on the "hit list" of community organizations attempting to ban books. Some of the books that have been controversial and most frequently censored in recent years include books often assigned in high school English classes: Sophocles's *Antigone*, Huxley's *Brave New World*, Salinger's *The Catcher in the Rye*, Heller's *Catch-22*, Steinbeck's *The Grapes of Wrath*, Shakespeare's *The Merchant of Venice*, Orwell's *1984*, Vonnegut's *Slaughterhouse-Five*, and Lee's *To Kill a Mockingbird*. The most frequently mentioned reasons for objection to these books are their vulgar language, profanity, and sexual content. Other targeted books and the reasons given for the challenge include *The Diary of Anne Frank* (a passage suggests that all religions are equally valuable); *The Lion, Witch and Wardrobe*, *Harry Potter* books, *Cinderella*, *The Wizard of Oz*, and *Macbeth* (depictions of good witches and witchcraft, and references to the occult); *Romeo and Juliet* (romanticization of suicide); *Ordinary People* by Judith Guest (depressing and obscene); Alice Walker's *The Color Purple* (troubling ideas about race relations and human sexuality); and *Adventures of Huckleberry Finn* (for offensive

BOX 2.2

ALA American Library Association

Top 10 most frequently challenged books of 2009 out of 460 challenges as reported to the Office for Intellectual Freedom

1. *TTYL; TTFN; L8R, G8R* (series), by Lauren Myracle
   Reasons: nudity, sexually explicit, offensive language, unsuited to age group, drugs
2. *And Tango Makes Three*, by Peter Parnell and Justin Richardson
   Reasons: homosexuality
3. *The Perks of Being a Wallflower*, by Stephen Chbosky
   Reasons: homosexuality, sexually explicit, anti-family, offensive language, religious viewpoint, unsuited to age group, drugs, suicide
4. *To Kill A Mockingbird*, by Harper Lee
   Reasons: racism, offensive language, unsuited to age group
5. *Twilight* (series), by Stephenie Meyer
   Reasons: sexually explicit, religious viewpoint, unsuited to age group
6. *Catcher in the Rye*, by J.D. Salinger
   Reasons: sexually explicit, offensive language, unsuited to age group
7. *My Sister's Keeper*, by Jodi Picoult
   Reasons: sexism, homosexuality, sexually explicit, offensive language, religious viewpoint, unsuited to age group, drugs, suicide, violence
8. *The Earth, My Butt, and Other Big, Round Things*, by Carolyn Mackler
   Reasons: sexually explicit, offensive language, unsuited to age group
9. *The Color Purple*, Alice Walker
   Reasons: sexually explicit, offensive language, unsuited to age group
10. *The Chocolate War*, by Robert Cormier
    Reasons: nudity, sexually explicit, offensive language, unsuited to age group

Source: Used with permission from the American Library Association.

language and the portrayal of African Americans) (American Library Association, 2006, 2010). In 2009, books by Lauren Myracle, *TTYL; TTFN; L8R, G8R* (series), won the top place on most frequently challenged books. (See Box 2.2.)

The issue is whether concerned parents and groups have the right to have certain material removed from classes and school libraries, especially if they represent only a small percentage of the parents but are organized and supported by national groups giving them influence in their communities. The Supreme Court ruled in *Island Trees School District v. Pico* (1982) that "local school boards may not remove books from school library shelves simply because they dislike the ideas contained in these books." Rather, they must ensure that the books are not being removed in order to deny students access to ideas with which the party disagrees because this is a violation of the First Amendment (*Board of Education v. Pico*, 1982). However, this has not stopped districts from banning many of the above mentioned books for the reasons mentioned.

Controversies over library books and class texts have torn communities apart; no community is immune from censorship (Brinkley, 1999). Groups that feel disenfranchised or lack power find a legal way to express their beliefs and vent their frustrations through book banning. For example, the ultrafundamentalists (fundamentalists with a political agenda) "seek to have prayer included in the curriculum of the public schools, because it is a symbolic reaffirmation of their religious values and belief system" (Provenzo, 1990, p. 88). Banned books provide symbolic victories in status politics and in the struggle to regain what was lost in the social revolution of the 1960s. As the religious right has gained political power, censorship cases have risen in public schools and libraries. There were 460 book challenges reported in 2009 (American Library Association, 2010). The point is that decision making about curriculum content represents broader issues about power and control of people's lives, what happens to their children, threats to belief systems, and changes in their communities. Much of the impetus for resisting change in curricula comes from rural and small-town areas, where residents feel pressure from a rapidly changing, urbanized world threatening many of their long-held beliefs and values.

Most educators argue that censorship threatens academic freedom; groups calling for removal argue that they are protecting their children from secularism, obscenity, racial issues, "damaging" lifestyles, blasphemous dialog, sexual situations or dialog, excessive violence, and other negative influences (American Library Association, 2007). Court rulings have varied, but the balance of cases has come down on the side of academic freedom and First Amendment rights. Some districts are retaining controversial books but providing alternatives to children whose parents disapprove.

> **Applying Sociology to Education:** *How can school districts deal with the competing demands from interest groups?*

THE FUNCTION OF SOCIAL CONTROL AND PERSONAL DEVELOPMENT

According to some educators and sociologists, the biggest crisis in American schooling is the erosion of moral authority. This is a crisis because one of the major functions or purposes of schools is to socialize children into their roles as citizens. In order to create an environment for learning, schools must ensure safety of students and staff. Yet some schools are so dysfunctional and chaotic that they may actually produce crime rather than socialize children for their future lives (Arum, 2003). Threats, intimidation, and actual incidents of violence on school grounds "created an atmosphere of disorder that disrupted the educational process, particularly in urban settings where poverty was rife. Disorder in schools coupled with much publicized shootings also undermined individuals' sense of school safety" (Arum, 2003, p. 3). Public opinion polls for the last decade show that lack of discipline in schools is at or near the top of concerns most years (Gallup Poll, 2009).

Functional theory argues that community members expect students to learn the skills and values—obedience, punctuality, perseverance, respect, and others—necessary to become productive, law-abiding citizens. Through formal or informal means, schools are expected to instill values related to social control and personal development believed to be essential to survival in the workforce and in school. In this way, society's problems can be reduced because individuals will be trained to fit into society in acceptable ways.

In recent years, courts have been more involved in school conflicts. Questions revolve around individual rights versus school needs to maintain order (Arum, 2003). Whereas school personnel had the main power to make decisions about discipline, today courts enter into the decision making when cases are appealed, reducing the role of educators to make decisions regarding discipline. For some this means educators have lost the ability to pass on cultural values including civil and moral order. School discipline has become a constitutional and legal issue in many cases (Hymowitz, 2000). Conflict theorists have a different view of social control, however.

They contend that schools are the tools of capitalist societies—controlling training, sorting human beings for places in the societal system, and perpetuating unequal class systems. Keep these theoretical views in mind as we discuss social control and personal development in schools.

Schools have varying ways of passing on the skills of social control, ranging from authoritarian to humanistic methods. The process of discipline is the major method of enforcing control in schools. The means for achieving social control within the school and for preparing disciplined workers creates dilemmas and controversies for schools as well as for society. Two interrelated issues illustrate this point: violence and discipline in schools.

Violence and Discipline in Schools

Consider the following facts: 3,184 children and teens died from gunfire in the United States in 2006 (Children's Defense Fund, 2010). The chance that a white male between the ages of 15 and 19 will die from a gunshot wound now surpasses the chance of dying from natural causes, and over 50 percent of the deaths of African-American teen males are caused by firearms (Addington et al., 2002). About 6 percent of students carry weapons to school (10 percent of males and 3 percent of females) (NCES, *Indicators*, 2006d). Three percent of students report being victims of theft at school and two percent victims of violent crime (Bauer et al., 2009). A recent study indicates that school culture may actually influence the level of deviance and victimization in schools. If a "culture of futility" rather than optimism develops among students and teachers, school violence is more likely to occur. This is especially true if students attending ethnically mixed schools experienced more peer violence than those attending schools with ethnic concentration (Demanet and Van Houtte 2011; Agirdag, Demanet, Van Houtte, and Van Avermaet 2010).

One discipline problem is bullying. The incidence of bullying at school has increased, with 13 percent of 6th–10th graders bullying other students, while between 10 and 29 percent (depending on the school) are victims. Some children are both victims and bullies (Sampson, 2009). Between 7 and 9 percent of students reported being threatened or injured with a weapon such as a gun, knife, or club on school property (NCES, 2001). Even so, schools are fairly safe compared with some other settings in society. Nonetheless, violence at school directly affects educators and students by reducing school effectiveness and harming students' learning. Unsafe school environments cause fear in students, reducing achievement, and may place students who are already at risk of school failure for other reasons in further jeopardy.

Although incidents of violence have decreased over the past few years, perhaps it is the more serious incidents that lead the public to perceive "lack of discipline," "fighting, violence, and gangs," and "drug abuse" as among the most serious problems facing schools in the United States, locally and nationally (Bushaw and Lopez, 2010). Students' perceptions of school safety relate to their neighborhoods, community safety, and school climate. If students are to perceive schools as safe, they need to perceive neighborhoods as safe. The message is that schools and neighborhoods need to work together to ensure student safety at school and while going to and from school (Kitsantas, Ware, and Martinez-Arias, 2004).

Although the total number of crimes committed against students has decreased, the number of street gangs present in schools has not (NCES, *Indicators*, 2005). Twenty-seven percent of students reported gang presence at their schools (National Center on Addiction and Substance Abuse, 2010), with 31 percent in urban schools reporting street gangs. Hispanic (37 percent) and African-American students (29 percent) reported the most gang activity (Figure 2.2) (NCES, *Indicators*, 2005). This presence raises questions concerning the rights of students to wear gang insignia or colors to school, and the security of all students in schools with gang members present.

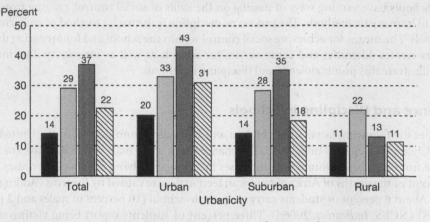

Percentage of students ages 12–18 who reported that street gangs were present at school during the previous 6 months, by urbanicity and race/ethinicity: 2003

FIGURE 2.2 Students' reports of gangs at school. *Source:* U.S. Department of Justice, Bureau of Justice Statistics, School Crime Supplement (SCS) to the National Crime Victimization Survey, 2003. Available: http://nces.ed.gov/programs/crimeindicators/zcrimeindicators2005/Indicators.asp? (Retrieved April 20, 2007.)

[a]Other includes Asians, Pacific Islanders, American Indians (including Alaska Natives), and students who indicated they were more than one race. For this report, non-Hispanic students who identified themselves as more than one race in 2003 (1 percent of all respondents) were included in the other category. Respondents who identified themselves as being of Hispanic origin are classified as Hispanic, regardless of their race.

Note: "At school" was defined as in the school building, on school property, on a school bus, or going to and from school.

Applying Sociology to Education: *Should the schools become guarded fortresses, or less coercive and punitive? Should potential troublemakers be removed to more secure environments, or can they be taught to behave according to school rules?*

This brings up the controversial issue of what type of discipline should be used in schools. Students can be expelled or suspended in many states for carrying a dangerous weapon, possessing illegal drugs, or assaulting a school employee, or if charged with a felony (Children's Law Center of Massachusetts, 2002). From 1960 to 1975, one study shows that suspension was the most common form of school discipline, used for up to 65 percent of cases. Suspensions dropped to 40 percent between 1976 and 1992. Expulsion, the next most common form of discipline, followed with from one-quarter to one-third of cases falling into this category (Arum, 2003, pp. 55–56).

Courts have tended to uphold school rulings in discipline cases, although more challenges to school discipline have been seen in recent years. Student rights advocates have brought cases against schools related to First Amendment rights and search and seizure. Yet some student rights court rulings have weakened educators' ability to control schools, and some research indicates that strict discipline is important for achievement, especially in low-income city schools. However, some schools have become repressive, hierarchical places with strict discipline and guards in the halls, at times resembling armed camps, and students in high schools and middle schools in some localities are angry and defiant in this atmosphere.

Contrary to authoritarian techniques and atmospheres, others argue that a positive school climate is necessary for students' personal development and achievement. In an ethnographical study of inner-city high schools using participant observation techniques, researchers delved into the lives of adolescents to understand how violence becomes normalized, an everyday part of attending school. "Security guards, high-tech devices for weapons searches, and use of police tactics for corridor surveillance" are an everyday part of school for some students. But some educators argue that this control does not allow teachers and administrators to understand what is going on in the lives of inner-city students. Administrators may be creating a culture of violence within which students must define their reality (Devine, 1996, p. 1). "Insufficient attention is paid to the alienation experienced by disliked and lonely students. Mental health nurses could play a pivotal role in fostering change in the social climate of schools . . ." (Thomas, 2004).

Some sociologists believe discipline problems represent power struggles between students and adults in a system where students are powerless and often rebel against the authoritarian rules restricting their thoughts and behaviors. These sociologists contend that unless the coercive, alienating power structure surrounding students is radically altered, discipline will always remain a problem. School actions may encourage a culture of violence. Punishment, critics claim, not only discourages students from making an effort to succeed but also labels them negatively among teachers. The point is that teachers and schools can teach violence by condoning and using physical force, or they can create a culture and climate to reduce violence (see Box 2.3).

BOX 2.3

Low-Level Violence in Schools

The pervasiveness of low-level school violence in the forms of bullying, peer sexual harassment, victimization based on sexual orientation, and the psychological maltreatment of students by teachers must be acknowledged and addressed in a more preventive and proactive manner. School personnel must assume a leadership role in conceiving and implementing interventions designed to change the culture and climate of schools to reduce low-level violence.

Recommendations

To prevent or reduce low-level, underlying violence in schools, we recommend that school personnel focus on changing a school's culture and climate by implementing interventions based on the following assumptions:

- Every individual should have the right to be spared oppression and repeated, intentional humiliation in school as well as in society at large. Schools must send a strong message to students and staff that all forms of low-level violence are inappropriate and that adults will actively intervene in all instances of low-level violence and that those who fail to recognize and stop low-level forms of violence as they occur actually promote violence.

- Because many school personnel do not acknowledge that low-level violence is a serious problem, it is essential that a needs assessment be conducted and all school personnel be informed about the extent of bullying, peer sexual harassment, victimization based on known or presumed gay or lesbian sexual

(Continued)

(Continued)

orientation in their school, and the psychological maltreatment of students by teachers and other school staff. If ignored, low-level violence in schools can jeopardize students' academic achievement, undermine their physical and emotional well-being, and may provoke retaliatory violence.

- The best way to reduce low-level forms of school violence is to create a school culture and climate characterized by warmth; tolerance; positive responses to diversity; sensitivity to others' views; cooperative interactions among students, teachers, and school staff; and an environment that expects and reinforces appropriate behavior. In cases of violations of limits and rules, nonhostile, nonphysical sanctions should be consistently applied.

- Homophobia makes schools unsafe for all students, not only for those who are gay and lesbian. Antigay prejudice and homophobia can make any student who defies the narrowly defined gender roles a target for violence and harassment. A concerted effort is required to address homophobic attitudes among school personnel.

- Rather than focusing on the perpetrators or victims alone, effective interventions must happen at multiple levels, concurrently. These multiple levels include school-level interventions (e.g., conflict resolution and diversity training workshops for teachers and school staff), classroom-level interventions (e.g., regularly scheduled classroom meetings during which students and teachers engage in discussion, role-playing, and creative activities related to preventing all forms of low-level violence), and individual-level interventions (e.g., formation of discussion groups for victims of low-level violence).

The middle and junior high grades (6 through 8) are a critical time for intervention and should receive highest priority.

Source: Dupper, David. R., and N. Meyer-Adams, "Low-Level Violence: A Neglected Aspect of School Culture," *Urban Education* Vol. 37, No. 3, pp. 350–364. (Using last print page in article—pp. 362–368). Copyright © 2002 by SAGE Publications. Reprinted by permission of SAGE Publications.

Schools have turned to a number of alternative techniques to deal with problems, some of which will be discussed in later chapters. Approaches include smaller schools, single-sex classes, required parental involvement, alternative and charter schools, vocational education programs, or weekday evening and weekend schools, to name a few. Evaluation of one policy, school suspension, shows that African-American male students in the United States are in many cases disproportionately suspended. Although suspension may solve the immediate goals of removing the problem and punishing the students, it can create long-term problems that cost society, for example, by reducing suspended students' chances for productive lives, limiting educational opportunities, increasing dropout rates, causing reliance on welfare services, future incarceration in prisons, and being committed to mental hospitals. An alternative used in many districts is in-school suspension, restricting students but allowing them to continue with their academic programs under strict supervision.

All human beings have certain basic needs—food, shelter, love and affection, respect, trust, knowledge, and truth (Maslow, 1962). If basic underlying needs are not met, children may exhibit disruptive behavior. For instance, if children come to school hungry or lacking affection at home, they are likely to be disruptive in school. Teachers do not always have the time, energy, or interest to deal with these problems directly and instead resort to techniques of discipline or control such as corporal punishment, expulsion (10 days or more) or suspension (10 days or less), detention, transfer to another class or school, loss of privileges, drugs to calm children, or special education classes. There are no easy answers to problems in schools, especially because they reflect problems in the society at large.

Applying Sociology to Education: *In what situations might strict authoritarian discipline be most effective? More humanistic discipline? Should suspensions be used, and if so, under what circumstances?*

THE FUNCTION OF SELECTION AND ALLOCATION: THE SORTING PROCESS

How should a society or school determine whether you or the person sitting next to you gets the best college placement, admission into your desired academic program, and the highest-paying and most prestigious job? Although this issue is discussed in detail in Chapters 3 and 4, here we consider one method used by most of the industrial countries to sort students—testing. The controversy lies in the role that exams play in placement and whether they are fair to all students.

The Testing Game

Many modern industrial societies emphasize achievement and merit. In these test-oriented societies, it is beneficial to be skilled at test-taking. Most of us are faced with intelligence quotient (IQ) tests, aptitude tests, achievement tests, career-interest inventories, psychological tests, civil service tests, Scholastic Aptitude Tests (SATs), American College Tests (ACTs), Miller's Analogy test, Graduate Record Examination, professional school exams, job-aptitude tests, and so on. Schools use exams at various checkpoints to track or stream students and to ensure that students are achieving at grade level, because schools are held accountable by the community for student achievement. Many states now require students to pass examinations in order to graduate from high school, and students must take the SAT or ACT for college entrance. Tests are a part of our lives, helping educators and others to select and allocate applicants according to their ability. Do some groups have an advantage in the testing process?

The use of IQ test scores has been controversial for years. Alfred Binet first developed intelligence tests in France to diagnose mental retardation and areas of individual difficulty or weakness. Binet felt that an individual's intelligence was not a fixed attribute but could be increased with expert training. It was not his idea to use the test for mass placements, but this soon became common. U.S. Army recruits were given intelligence tests and were classified as alpha (literate) or beta (illiterate) in order to sort and select them for various roles in the armed service. Concerns about IQ testing intensified when schools also began to use the tests for sorting purposes. This practice has come under attack, but many school districts still use IQ tests to help with general placement of children. Since the 1970s, debate intensified with the publication of several books and articles on the nature and use of IQ tests, and concerns have been raised about the nature of intelligence tests:

1. What are we really measuring?
2. To what extent do genetic or environmental factors influence test results?
3. Can we develop an unbiased culture-free test?

> **Applying Sociology to Education:** *Jot down some characteristics that make someone you know seem intelligent. Compare your ideas of intelligence with someone else's. Probably you have some overlap and some differences in your definitions. How would you develop test questions to measure these characteristics? Why?*

The first problem deals with the nature of intelligence. Social scientists try to pinpoint what we really mean by intelligence; but there is not complete agreement on what innate qualities to look for or how to find them and to what extent environmental factors influence intelligence. As many as 23 different mental abilities have been included in definitions of intelligence—including verbal fluency, spatial perception, analogical reasoning, series and sequence manipulation, memory, and creativity. In attempting to define intelligence, we are not referring to a simple quantity but to a complex system of reasoning. Howard Gardner (1987) refers to the many areas of human functioning as "multiple intelligences"—including practical, social, musical, spatial abilities, and others. Since he proposed the concept of multiple intelligences in 1983, Gardner has added to the list of intelligences, most recently "naturalist intelligence, a person's ability to identify plants and animals in the surrounding environment" (Gardner, 1999). Others believe intelligence is an information processing framework, which involves the processing of information from the time we perceive it until the time we act on it. The implication is that some people are more adept at processing certain kinds of information than others.

The second problem deals with the controversy over genetic and environmental determinants of intelligence. In 1969, Arthur Jensen stated that what IQ tests measure is 80 percent inherited and 20 percent cultural factors. Jensen and others, such as Richard J. Herrnstein (1980), theorized that IQ differences between socioeconomic, social, and ethnic groups are caused primarily by genetic factors. This statement and the general content of his article in the *Harvard Educational Review* generated a controversy that continues to this day.

Herrnstein and Murray (1994) created a firestorm in the scientific community with their book *The Bell Curve*, arguing that there is a direct link between low IQ, inherited genes, social class placement, and social ills. They implied that race, IQ, and social hierarchy fit together, and that the poor can be blamed for their position. Their thesis assumes that intelligence is understood, definable, and testable, and that we have a test that can measure intelligence accurately. If one could assume IQ tests to be valid and intelligence to be inherited (assumptions that are challenged by most researchers in the scientific community), some policy makers feel that the distribution of positions in society could be justified on the basis of intelligence groups—the argument being that some are more capable than others. Some individuals indeed may be more capable, but we must be sure that we can determine this accurately before pigeonholing the population on the basis of a test. Accuracy of a test presuming to measure intelligence is questionable and has not held up under scrutiny, yet some policy makers still use these measures for selection and allocation in schools and jobs.

Scientists have critiqued *The Bell Curve* on the basis of everything from its underlying assumptions to its methodology. One major critique uses alternative explanations of data, showing that economic success depends more on social class than on IQ, and that we must look beyond individual characteristics to the structure of society to find causes of inequality. Factors ranging from the wealth of individuals' parents to national policies on labor laws, education, and tax deductions serve to distribute rewards unequally. Racial inequalities are a result of, not a cause of, social inequalities.

Another problem with using intelligence tests to classify members of society deals with whether it is possible to devise tests that are free of cultural bias—class, ethnicity, regionalism, and the other variables that make our nation and school systems so diverse. Consider the following question: Children are asked to draw a horse. Who do you think would draw the "best" horse? The answer is Native American children living in rural areas do best at this task because of their familiarity with the subject. This is a culturally sensitive and biased question. The Native American child on a reservation asked about the role of the violin in an orchestra would be equally disadvantaged on a test.

Another environmental factor that affects intelligence tests is the region of the country from which a person comes. In IQ tests administered to army recruits after World War I, researchers noted that army recruits did not follow the stereotypic pattern of African Americans scoring lower than whites, but that region made a significant difference in their scores. Northern whites scored highest, followed in descending order by northern African Americans, southern whites, and southern African Americans. Studies showing the rise in IQ scores of children placed in enrichment programs also point to the importance of environmental factors in IQ. Several other variables affect test scores: the race of the person in charge of the testing situation, the sex of the test-taker, the motivation of the test-taker, how the test-taker feels on the day of the test—even whether the individual had a good breakfast. You probably remember feeling nervous on test days. Some children do better under stress, some do worse, and some just give up in the face of a threatening or difficult situation. Individual factors of this type can affect test scores significantly.

All of the studies point to the problem of ranking or classifying people on the basis of scores that are unreliable or changeable and that are influenced by environmental circumstances. For example, intelligence scores of young children exposed to lead may be adversely affected ("Challenging Assumptions about Lead and IQ," 2005). They also suggest that intelligence—as typically measured—is not a fixed, inherited attribute but a variable depending on stimulation and on cultural and environmental factors.

Achievement Tests

The scene of a student waiting by the mailbox in anticipation, dreading to open "the envelope," is familiar around the world. That envelope holds the key to the future of many young people—scores on achievement tests. Because of limited space in university systems, most countries rely on entrance examinations for placement in universities. Those test scores determine for many students their entrance to or rejection by universities. The scores are important—and controversial—because they tap the core of how we evaluate and place people in society.

In the United States, two national achievement tests are given to college-bound high school students: the ACT and the SAT. As of fall 2010, most higher education institutions accept either test; about 730 colleges make the test scores optional for at least some students (Marklein, 2007). In some states, all juniors take one of these exams as part of the state accountability system (Olson, 2006).

From 2000 to 2009, SAT and ACT scores stayed relatively constant (NCES, 2000, 2009) (see Table 2.1). However, scores of African-American students are still significantly lower than those of whites and of some other minorities. Some educators criticize the tests, arguing that they do not test classroom reality, but that they tend to shape what happens in the classroom. The Educational Testing Service, authors of the SAT and achievement tests, have developed revised tests that they say are more closely tied to classroom experiences.

With the government's testing and accountability requirements and state testing requirements, all students face multiple testing situations in reading, writing, math, and science. Whether the requirements are fair and whether they improve education levels or actually leave some children behind are conflicts in the debate over use of tests. In a nutshell, those in favor of minimum skills tests point to several factors: "1. It improves the accountability of students and schools; 2. It motivates students to really learn the material rather than just memorize for tests; 3. Knowledge is cumulative, so a student doing poor early can end up behind indefinitely." The tests allow schools to track students who are falling behind, and proponents argue that it is through testing that students can excel (Samuelsen, 2001).

On the flip side, those opposed to minimum skills testing argue, "1. Standardized tests can be biased or unfair; 2. Students in failing school districts will be punished; 3. It lessens the flexibility of teachers; 4. Learning material for tests means other material receives less emphasis" (Messerli, 2003). Parents, educators, and policy makers raise questions about the unintended consequences of exams on students and schools. For example, students from different backgrounds do not enter schools with the same resources and opportunities, and basing their futures on one or several high stakes exams may leave behind the very students the system says it is trying to help (Samuelsen, 2001).

Test-makers will continue to improve the validity of their tests; educators will continue to question the relationship between curricular materials and test items; parents and students will

Table 2.1A SAT Mean Scores of College-Bound Seniors, by Race/Ethnicity: Selected Years, 2000–2001 through 2008–2009

Race/ethnicity	2000–2001	2008–2009
SAT-Critical reading		
All students	506	501
White	529	528
Black	433	429
Mexican American	451	453
Puerto Rican	457	452
Other Hispanic	460	455
Asian/Pacific Islander	501	516
American Indian/Alaska Native	481	486
Other	503	494
SAT-Mathematics		
All students	514	515
White	531	536
Black	426	426
Mexican American	458	453
Puerto Rican	451	450
Other Hispanic	465	461
Asian/Pacific Islander	566	587
American Indian/Alaska Native	479	493
Other	512	514

Note: Data are for seniors who took the SAT any time during their high school years through March of the senior year. If a student took a test more than once, the most recent score was used. The SAT was formerly known as the Scholastic Assessment Test and the Scholastic Aptitude Test. Possible scores on each part of the SAT range from 200 to 800. The critical reading section was formerly known as the verbal section. The writing section was introduced in March 2005.

Source: U.S. Department of Education, National Center for Education Statistics, *Digest of Education Statistics, 2009* (NCES 2010-013), 2010, Chapter 2, Table 143.

Table 2.1B ACT Score Averages by Race/Ethnicity

Race/ethnicity	Year	
	2000	2009
White	22.7	22.2
Black	17.8	16.9
Mexican American	19.5	—
Other Hispanic	20.5	—
Hispanic	—	18.7
Asian American/Pacific Islander	22.4	23.2
American Indian/Alaska Native	20.4	18.9

share concerns about the meaning of tests for life chances; educators will continue to be concerned about the meaning of low scores for their schools and salaries (Morse et al., 2000); and minority advocates will keep a watchful eye on tests for bias. However, in meritocracies some forms of testing are likely to continue. This is the controversial function of selection and allocation.

THE FUNCTION OF CHANGE AND INNOVATION: LOOKING TO THE FUTURE

Schools provide a link with the future; it is through research and teaching the next generation new knowledge that societies move forward. Universities are generally on the cutting edge of research, passing this knowledge on to students. Although few deny the inevitability of change, questions arise as to how change takes place and who controls change. One thing we know is that those who possess technological skills and knowledge in the twenty-first century, and who know how to get information important to functioning in the future, will rise in the hierarchy. Can schools teach and implement new technology? Are these tools equally available to all?

The proliferation of computer technology is dramatically changing the process by which educators at all levels disseminate information to students. Whereas students in "traditional classrooms" listen to lectures, instructors in "postmodern classrooms" enhance their lectures with high-resolution computer graphics, video clips such as YouTube; virtual sounds; popular multimedia platforms; and Web-based class organizers such as PowerPoint, WebCT, Course Studio, and Blackboard. Students in traditional classrooms learn about remote cultures by reading a text, but some students in postmodern classrooms interact and communicate with people of different cultural backgrounds via the Internet.

In postindustrial societies, access to technology at all educational levels is increasingly important. By fall of 2003, nearly 100 percent of the public schools in the United States and 93 percent of classrooms had access to the Internet; the ratio of students to computers with Internet was 4.4 to 1. Many schools have a full-time school technology director (Kleiner and Lewis, 2003; Parsad and Jones, 2005). This is an amazing transformation since 1994 when only 3 percent of schools had Internet to today with 100 percent! The bottom line is that the postmodern classroom is quickly replacing the traditional classroom.

Reliance on computer technology is equally prevalent in institutions of higher education. Especially prominent is distance learning, a low-cost method of educating large numbers of students. Via two-way interactive video connections and the Internet, students can earn credit for online courses. Seventy-three percent of post-secondary institutions offering distance learning report increased demand for their existing online offerings, and requests for more offerings. Public institutions are more likely to offer distance learning courses, with more than 90 percent of two-year colleges offering distance learning courses. Of four-year public colleges, 89 percent were offering distance education classes in 2001, and those numbers have increased rapidly (NCES, 2003; Askov et al., 2003). In fall 2008, one in four students was taking one or more online courses. That is, the number of online students increased to 4.6 million, up from 3.9 million in 2007; 82 percent of online courses are undergraduate (Parry, 2010).

Supporters of distance learning point to the opportunities it provides to students who do not have access to colleges, and the flexibility for those with time constraints. Critics point to the potential for watered-down and entertainment courses, and the lack of interaction with professors and other students (Greenwald and Rosner, 2003). Many professors are critical for these reasons (Parry, 2010). Yet as distance learning courses become more established, more students will be reached through this medium.

Disparities between "high-minority-enrollment schools" (defined as 50 percent or more minority enrollment) and "low-minority-enrollment schools" in instructional rooms with Internet access were significant in 1994 (NCES, 1999), but today the differences between high- and low-poverty or minority schools are minimal except in the area of wireless connections. Internet connection is greater in wealthier schools; nearly 100 percent of public schools in the United States have some access to the Internet (Kleiner and Lewis, 2003), but the number of students per computer and with access to Internet varies greatly.

How computers are used in the classroom is key to determining the effectiveness of technology and the extent of a continuing "digital divide" between schools. Research suggests that many teachers in high-poverty schools are less proficient in technology and use computers for less sophisticated educational purposes (Peters, 2002). Moreover, computer and Internet access at home is limited to students whose parents can afford it. "The Web has grown from 130 sites in 1993 to nearly 450 million sites as of July 2006" (Hiemstra and Poley, 2007). Students with access to the Internet at home may be found doing homework by surfing the net while multitasking with their iPods, iPads, iPhones, Blackberries, and other technology—and new technologies enter the picture at a pace faster than students, or their parents and teachers, can keep up (Hiemstra and Poley, 2007). Around the world, the number of Internet users is expanding rapidly—16 million in 1995, 500 million in 2001, 1.3 billion in 2007—and growing (Drori, 2006; Miniwatts Marketing Group, 2008). Most growth is taking place in developed countries, causing the digital divide to increase between rich and poor countries.

Educators and policy makers face a formidable challenge in the twenty-first century. In a society dominated by computer technology, they must decide how to make effective use of computers and the Internet in classrooms and how to equitably distribute technological expertise. If such issues are not addressed, some students may be left in the twentieth-century digital divide.

Applying Sociology to Education: *How can educators best teach and prepare students for the future?*

Any educational issue we choose to investigate is likely to fall under one of the functions of education. Those discussed here provide a few examples. We move now to a discussion of the school function of selection and allocation, which takes place through the process of stratification (see Chapter 3).

Summary

In this chapter, we considered five primary functions of education and processes that make the system function.

I. CONFLICTING FUNCTIONS OF EDUCATION

To illustrate the dynamic nature of educational systems, we discussed examples of controversies surrounding each function.

II. THE IMPORTANCE OF PROCESSES IN EDUCATIONAL SYSTEMS

Processes are the action part of systems. They link the system parts and the system with the environment. Each function discussed involves processes of education.

III. THE FUNCTION OF SOCIALIZATION: WHAT WE LEARN AND HOW WE LEARN IT

Two controversies are discussed:

1. *The early childhood education controversy.* Controversies surround who should provide early care and the long-term results of early care. Research finds that there are some long-term positive effects of programs on poor children, especially if the efforts continue, and no deleterious effects of early childhood education on other children.
2. *Role of technology and the media in socialization.* Controversies surround the role of media in education or entertaining, and the possible negative results of television watching.

Excessive TV watching lowers achievement, and TV violence may increase aggression. There is clear evidence regarding the effects of parental involvement in TV decisions and the positive effects of educational TV for children.

IV. THE FUNCTION OF CULTURAL TRANSMISSION AND PROCESS OF PASSING ON CULTURE

Concern has risen over poor skills of students, as shown by low standardized test scores. Some advocate a strict core curriculum to correct deficiencies. What to teach and who should decide are also controversial questions, especially in heterogeneous societies. Two areas exemplify the controversies: (1) drug and sex education and (2) censorship of textbooks and library books, especially concerning issues such as evolution versus creationism.

V. THE FUNCTION OF SOCIAL CONTROL AND PERSONAL DEVELOPMENT

Two issues that point to the conflicting attempts by schools to maintain social control are violence and discipline. Controversies center on what type of discipline to use, the role of gangs in competing for students' attention, and how to deal with gangs and violence in schools.

VI. THE FUNCTION OF SELECTION AND ALLOCATION: THE SORTING PROCESS

How individuals are placed in society is the key controversy here. Because testing is used extensively for placement in schooling and jobs, the fairness of this procedure is discussed. (This function is discussed further in Chapters 3 and 4.)

VII. THE FUNCTION OF CHANGE AND INNOVATION: THE PROCESS OF LOOKING TO THE FUTURE

Who has access to the technological training necessary to advance in society is one issue raised here. To the extent that certain students have more access than others, they may have an edge in future placements and success, resulting in a "digital divide" for those left behind.

Putting Sociology to Work

1. Discuss the main processes involved in your role as a student.
2. What controversy over curriculum content has been present in a town with which you are familiar? What sociological factors underlie this controversy?
3. Visit a nursery school and observe. What types of socialization experiences are the children having that might differ from home experiences?
4. Discuss with some parents and teachers of young children their feelings about early childhood education.
5. Interview fundamentalist religious leaders about their views concerning the school curriculum. What changes or additions, if any, would they like to see? If there are fundamentalist church schools in your area, try to visit, observe, and learn about their programs.
6. Discuss with school board members and school administrators the pressure groups that influence their decision making, on what issues, and using what tactics.
7. Discuss with several teachers the techniques they feel are most effective in helping children learn and the discipline techniques they use in the classroom.
8. What are the biggest discipline problems facing schools in your area? Visit a school in a different type of community and find out the same information. What are the reasons for the similarities or differences in discipline problems? This may involve learning how the school deals with discipline.
9. Interview students of different ages to learn their views about discipline and students' rights.
10. Learn about the computer and Internet access in schools in your area. How are computers being used in the schools? Is there a difference in student access to computers between schools?

Education and the Process of Stratification

THE CRISIS IN SCHOOLING

Stay in School and Get Ahead. This mantra is repeated in one form or another countless times as parents, teachers, and others exhort students to achieve in school which will improve their chances of adult success. Educational attainment in the United States has represented a pathway to economic opportunity. However, one of our most vexing problems is that not all students are able to take advantage of the potential schools present. Reforming failing schools, the main educational policy objective of the Obama administration, is the latest in a long series of efforts to fulfill the promise of education for all students.

Within the schools lie the keys to our futures—we hope; most people believe that schooling is directly linked to occupational and financial success. Because "failing" public schools are accessible targets for criticism, anger, and hostility, parents, educators, students, and policy makers voice their concerns in public forums and at the ballot box.

There is general agreement that schools should produce individuals who can function in society, but how and why is controversial. Schools still carry out their tasks of transmitting basic skills, but most people around the world have higher expectations of what schools can and should do. In this chapter, we consider several issues related to selection and placement of students and to the process of stratification. One of those issues is the very meaning of the phrase *equality of educational opportunity*. Other issues relate to variables that cause different school outcomes for children and adults, public or private schools, ability grouping, home and community environments, teacher and student expectations, and other variables.

Education and Stratification in America

There is a crisis in education, according to our current president, who, in his 2010 State of the Union address, stated that we must invest in "reform that raises students' achievement, inspires students in math and science, and turns around failing schools that steal the future from too many young Americans . . . " (http://www.whitehouse.gov/photos-and-video/photogallery/state-union-0). Until recently, Americans believed that with education a person could do anything. Immigrants could come from societies where poverty and caste were inherited, rise in the social structure, and have a chance to reach their full potential. In 1848, Horace Mann, father of public education in the United States, wrote: "Education, beyond all other devices of human origin, is the great equalizer of the conditions of men—the balance wheel of the social machinery" (Mann, 1891). But things have not worked out quite that way.

In the early history of the United States, essential skills were passed from generation to generation through the family. With the growth of industry, new and more formal mechanisms to transmit knowledge were necessary, and this function was gradually transferred from family to school. Schools had the responsibility of preparing workers for industry and assimilating immigrant subcultures into the mainstream. Some early schools, including those for children working in factories, used the "monitorial system"; minimal learning was provided in reading, writing, math, and citizenship by monitors trained under teachers. Discipline was often very harsh, both physically and psychologically (Finkelstein, 1989). These schools gave way to the "common schools," espoused by Mann, in an attempt to create a common identity and unifying force in the United States. At first they were open to all white children; later, segregated schools were provided for African Americans. Some children rose in the social structure as a result of education, but others, including Native Americans and freed slaves, fell further behind. Some immigrant groups, not satisfied with the public school education, formed their own schools to serve their own needs (Rury, 2008). As industry and formal schooling expanded, the division of labor between those who controlled capital and decision making and those who were controlled began to be formalized and to result in inequalities. Private schools were established for elites, ensuring a continuation of their privileged positions. Mass education was encouraged to provide workers with necessary skills, including punctuality, obedience to authority, and accountability. Many felt that education for factory workers provided hope for a better life, and indeed that hope was realized for many. However, education also served to perpetuate class distinctions between the capitalists and the working class. Such practices as tracking generally favored advantaged students.

Society requires a cadre of trained workers to "keep the wheels of industry turning." Many levels and types of training are necessary, requiring a selection and allocation process that begins at school. The school system is thus expected to raise everyone's chances for a better life, to provide equality of opportunity, and to identify those who are most qualified for the most powerful and prestigious positions in society. The inherent contradiction inevitably leads to some dissatisfaction. Schooling helps some children move up; it locks others into low-level positions in society (Kozol, 1991; *Learning to Fail*, 1991).

Many subcultural groups today wish to maintain their ethnic identities and orientations; minority-group pressures have changed the emphasis over time from assimilationist goals to respect for and preservation of minority identities while providing access to social, economic, and political institutions. As we shall see, this model has met with mixed results and the controversies over access continue.

Education and Stratification around the World

Some argue that improvements in the educational standing of various groups in the United States would lead to social equality; in fact, there has been a reduction in equality of income even though most groups are completing more schooling. In 2008, 18.5 percent, or 13.5 million, children in the United States lived in poverty—34.4 percent of African-American children,

30.3 percent of Hispanics, 14.3 percent of Asians, and 14.3 percent of whites (http://www.census.gov/hhes/www/cpstables/032009/pov/new02_100.htm).

Mass education has spread around the world in the past two centuries; today, over 70 percent of primary-age children in least-developed countries are enrolled in some type of formal schooling (UNICEF, 2007, Table 5, p. 121), yet many others are excluded. In 2001–2002, UNESCO estimated that 115 million children were excluded from a primary education, with most living in sub-Saharan Africa (45 million) and South Asia (43 million) (UNESCO, 2005). Worldwide access to secondary education has also increased, but worldwide, less than 50 percent attend (UNICEF, 2007, p. 121). Similarities in the curricula at both the primary and secondary levels show standard world models, though some countries are providing specialized tracks at the secondary level (Benavot and Braslavsky, 2006).

Around the world, demographic factors such as sex, race, and family status affect individuals' chances for an education and have substantial effects on their future occupations, incomes, and prospects for poverty. Whether these ascribed factors, beyond a person's ability to change, are most responsible for their fate or whether their own actions are also influential are two sides of a long-standing debate. The degree to which individuals are personally responsible for what happens to them as adults is illustrated by a controversial thesis presented by Herrnstein and Murray in *The Bell Curve* (1994). This book essentially argues that individual placements in society are largely genetically determined. According to this idea, money for education or policies such as affirmative action will have little effect on people's place in society. Social scientists have criticized the book on many grounds, including manipulation of data, limited definitions of terms such as *IQ*, and faulty assumptions. Most point out that social factors in the United States and around the world are the root causes of inequality, and it is these factors that we need to understand and correct (Fraser, 1995; Hauser, 1995). Others argue that individuals' ability to act on their environment for their personal achievements should be emphasized (Gambetta, 2009).

In order to deal with the complex relationships between the process of stratification and education, we need to address a number of interrelated topics. Several key questions will provide the underlying framework for this chapter and Chapter 4:

1. What role does stratification play in the societal system?
2. What role does education play in social stratification?
3. What are some key variables, both in and outside the schools, that affect stratification?
4. Can education lead to equal opportunity for members of society?

THE PROCESS OF STRATIFICATION: IS INEQUALITY INEVITABLE?

Most of us have a general idea about the meaning of stratification: It refers to a position in society's hierarchy. In the United States, many think an "open class" system predominates. The majority of us would probably say that where we have ended up in society is at least in part due to our own actions. If asked about their social position, most would answer in the "middle class." "Middle class" implies an "average" lifestyle—a house, a car, a white-collar wage earner. There are extremely rich and poor people, but most individuals think of themselves as in a wide middle group.

This contrasts with caste or estate systems, in which structured inequality is built into the society—individuals are born into their permanent, ascribed positions and stay there throughout their lives. Such societies have little social mobility within or across generations. There is little reason to try to alter one's station in life as nothing one can do will change it. In the United States, there is a strong belief that our society offers opportunity to individuals to "better themselves."

We have long seen educational achievement as one of the routes to better life chances, and as a result we have expanded opportunities for more education to more people. In fact, expansion of education took place in the United States well ahead of European countries (Fischel, 2009). Yet deep concern has arisen about whether this opportunity remains available for many today. For example, according to a recent report, the United States has an unusually low level of intergenerational mobility, lower than most of Europe. Our parents' income is highly predictive of our incomes as adults (Hertz, 2006).

From our open class system perspective, stratification is perceived as an interwoven part of the whole societal fabric or system. We cannot isolate one institution, such as education, from the whole system and understand the phenomenon of stratification. Although our focus will be on education, we will bring aspects of family, politics, and economics into our discussion. Figure 3.1 indicates the interrelationships between the process of stratification and the educational system.

Determinants of Social Class

Sociologists study stratification, defining the meaning of *social class* and discussing its significance and implications for individuals in society. *Class* has been described by Weber (Gerth and Mills, 1946) as a multidimensional concept that is determined by three major variables: wealth, power, and prestige. *Wealth* refers to one's property, capital, and income. The striking fact about the United States is that 80 percent of the wealth is owned by one-twentieth of the population, and the top 1 percent owns 35 percent of the total, leaving a tremendous gulf between the rich and the poor. Most segments of society have raised their standard of living in recent years, but the proportion of wealth controlled by top segments has increased (Keister and Moller, 2000). The small group at the top of the hierarchy generally perpetuates itself through inherited wealth or high-paying positions.

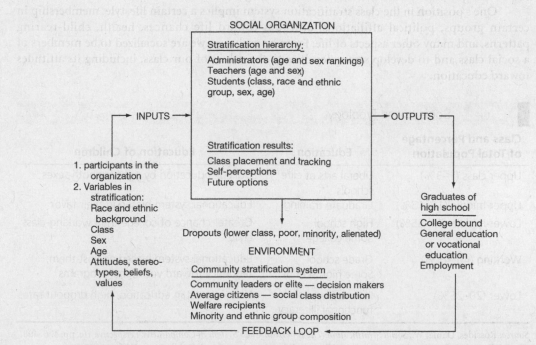

FIGURE 3.1 Stratification and the educational system.

Power implies the ability to make major decisions or to influence others to act on behalf of one's benefit. Much power has become concentrated in the upper levels of government and business. C. Wright Mills (1959) argues that the "power elite" that dominates society and controls decision making is composed of members of the economic, political, and military elite. Others argue that interest groups such as unions vie with each other for power (e.g., Dye and Zeigler, 1997). In either case, the average person has little power in decision making. In any case, this dimension of class directs our attention to the importance of politics and of political influence.

Occupation is a main factor in one's *prestige*. Education affects occupational status, and income is closely associated with one's occupation. Various occupations have different amounts of prestige, including the ability to influence others.

The class system in the United States has been described by many different sociologists. In the 1920s, the Lynds (1929) were among the first to study the relationship between social class and educational achievement. Through an in-depth analysis of a small Midwestern city in the United States referred to as "Middletown," the Lynds concluded that working-class children do not have many of the verbal and behavioral skills and traits that are prerequisite to success in the classroom. In a number of community studies conducted by Warner, Havighurst, and Loeb (1944) in the United States, schools sorted students based on their potential for upward mobility. Lower-class children are often regarded as not capable. Other studies have replicated the social class–educational achievement relationship and confirmed these findings.

Table 3.1 shows one of the many typologies of social class in the United States, indicating the relationship between class and education. Thus, educational achievement is highly correlated with social class; students from lower classes have a much lower likelihood of going on to college than those of higher classes, even though they may have high ability. This fact questions the role that educational achievement plays in determining where one is ultimately placed in the social structure, a point to which we return in the following section.

One's position in the class stratification system implies a certain lifestyle, membership in certain groups, political affiliations, attitudes toward life chances, health, child-rearing patterns, and many other aspects of life. From an early age, we are socialized to be members of a social class and to develop strong loyalties to the values of our class, including its attitudes toward education.

Table 3.1 Social Class Typology

Class and Percentage of Total Population	Education	Education of Children
Upper class (1–3%)	Liberal arts at elite schools	College education by right for both sexes
Upper-middle (10–15%)	Graduate training	Educational system biased in their favor
Lower-middle (30–35%)	High school Some college	Greater chance of college than working-class child
Working (40–45%)	Grade school Some high school	Educational system biased against them; tendency toward vocational programs
Lower (20–25%)	Illiteracy, especially functional illiteracy	Little interest in education, high dropout rates

Source: Rossides, Daniel W., *Social Stratification: The American Class System in Comparative Perspective* 1/e, pp. 406–408. Copyright ©1990. Reprinted by permission of Pearson Education, Inc., Upper Saddle River, NJ.

In the United States, the expectation is that we can improve our life position with good education and hard work, and that all members of society have an equal opportunity to experience upward mobility. Those with higher levels of education have more chances at better jobs and salaries, but the question remains: Who gets the higher levels of education?

The median earnings of wage and salary workers vary dramatically by amount of schooling completed. In constant dollars, men more than 25 years old with 9 years or less of education received approximate median earnings of $20,970 a year; women received approximately $13,590. With a high school diploma, these figures jumped to $33,940 for men and $22,300 for women. With a bachelor's degree the figures were $60,290 for men and $40,230 for women (*Digest of Educational Statistics*, 2009, Table 385).

Additional degrees command higher incomes. Those males over 25 who had a master's degree earned a median income of $71,880, and females earned $50,840. With a professional degree (law, medicine, and the like), the earnings for males were $100,000 and for females, $62,120 (*Digest of Educational Statistics*, 2009, Table 385). Education plays a role in sorting people into occupational categories. Many less tangible factors, however, enter into this sorting process, including the following:

1. Differences in the level and quality of education available in the country, region, or community in which one lives
2. Differential access to educational facilities according to one's social class status, religion, race, and ethnic origins
3. Differences in one's motivations, values, and attitudes; differences in the willingness and ability of one's parents and significant others to provide the financial and psychological supports necessary for the maximization of talent potentials.

The status attainment model (see Figure 3.2) shows six major ascribed and achieved variables that affect one's educational and occupational positions:

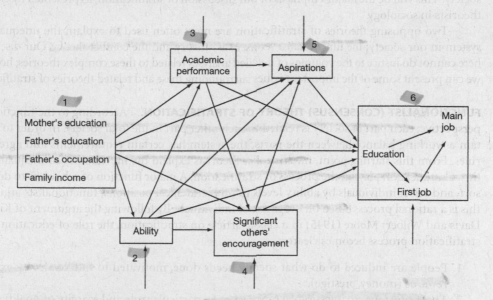

FIGURE 3.2 The process of status attainment in the United States. *Source:* Beeghley, Leonard, *The Structure of Social Stratification in the United States*, 2/e. Copyright © 1996 by Pearson Education. Reprinted by permission of Pearson Education, Inc., Upper Saddle River, NJ.

1. Father's and mother's education, father's occupation, family income
2. Ability, measured by achievement or IQ test (academic aptitude)
3. Academic performance
4. Significant others' encouragement
5. Educational/occupational aspirations
6. Educational attainment's direct influence on occupational attainment.

As the arrows imply, these factors with additional influences from external sources interact to determine one's position in society.

If we do not have other favorable factors in our lives, schooling alone is likely to make little difference to our economic and social success in society, though some recent programs in schools that involve one-on-one tutoring, more academic classes, and high expectations have proven successful in increasing the academic achievement of students.

Applying Sociology to Education: *Think of cases in which the positions of individuals in the stratification system have influenced their educational attainment.*

Major Explanations of Stratification

We all have ideas about how society should work and why some people succeed in society whereas others do not. Social scientists have explanations as well. From our systems perspective, we get a general framework for viewing stratification. Schools alone cannot cause or cure problems resulting from the stratification system, because they are but one part of a total, integrated system. Thus, to understand the role of schools in the process of stratification one must view interrelationships among schools, family, politics, religion, economics, and other integral parts of society. This will be the major emphasis of our discussion of stratification, as presented by classical theorists in sociology.

Two opposing theories of stratification are most often used to explain the unequal class system in our society: the functionalist (consensus) theory and the conflict theory. Our discussion here cannot do justice to the volumes of detailed analyses related to these complex theories; however, we can present some of the important issues surrounding these and related theories of stratification.

FUNCTIONALIST (CONSENSUS) THEORY OF STRATIFICATION.   According to the functionalist perspective, each part of society is related to each other part in the total society. In order to maintain a working balance between the parts, the system has certain requirements and agreed-on rules. From this starting point, functionalist theorists explain the inevitability of inequality and the role education plays in the process of stratification. A major function of schools is to develop, sort, and select individuals by ability levels to fill hierarchical positions; functionalists argue that this is a rational process based on the merit of individuals. By following the argument of Kingsley Davis and Wilbert Moore (1945) in a classic article on stratification, the role of education in the stratification process becomes clearer:

1. People are induced to do what society needs done, motivated to fulfill roles by extrinsic rewards (money, prestige).
2. The importance to the survival of society of a particular role and scarcity of qualified persons to fill the role determine the prestige ranking of positions. For instance, doctors are believed to be more important than bartenders and have more prestige and higher pay.

3. Those positions that are most complex and important and require the most talent and training—that is, education—are the most highly rewarded.

Presumably, then, the more schooling one has completed, the more productive and valuable one is to society. Hence, a stratification system evolves, with some inevitably attaining more education and higher positions than others.

Another well-known theorist, Talcott Parsons, has laid the groundwork for much of functionalist theory. Parsons argues that society has shared norms and values by which to judge or evaluate its members. Those who come closest to meeting the established needs and values of society are likely to have higher status and occupational prestige (Parsons, 1970). Inequality, then, is inevitable, according to Parsons. Some will always be at the top because of their value to society; others will fall to the bottom. The question for Parsons becomes not whether inequality needs to exist, but rather how much inequality is justifiable. There is no easy answer to such a question, although he contends that some inequality is useful in motivating members of society to work hard, get ahead, and fill the positions necessary to keep society running. How "value to society" is measured, of course, is not self-evident. Is a first-grade teacher less valuable to society than a center playing for a team in the National Basketball Association? Certainly, if we look at their salary or at their prestige among other citizens, there is little question. Is market value the same as value to society? Can value be manipulated or is it somehow "naturally" determined?

The selection process that will eventually determine occupational status begins in school, where functionalists argue that students are placed more according to individual performance than to group differences such as race and sex. Some functionalists point out opportunities that exist for working-class students to achieve mobility through school achievement. They argue that the system is flexible, allowing opportunity for most American students to attend college. They stress the improvements in educational achievement levels of the poor, minorities, and women as evidence that abilities are taking precedence over race and sex. Robert Hauser and David Featherman (1976) in a classic analysis of male students found that members of minority groups were completing more years of schooling; this, they believe, indicates that inequality in education is declining. While parents pass along their advantages and disadvantages to their children, education is a place where youth are more objectively evaluated—the further one goes in school, the less one's social origins matter.

The functionalist view of society has not only many proponents but also many critics. Criticisms fall into several categories, but of primary concern to us are the ideological critiques:

1. Functional or consensus theory presents a conservative view; many argue that it supports existing systems and the dominant power group, whether good or bad, and preserves the social order. Rather than finding a way out of wars, inequality, and scarcity, it is committed to making things work within existing systems (Gouldner, 1971; Hurn, 1993).
2. The implication that people must meet the needs of the system, rather than vice versa, is believed by some critics to be false and misleading. Similarly, functions of education may represent powerful individuals or groups pursuing their own interests (Hurn, 1993; Levitas, 1974, p. 165).
3. To assume that we can locate the most talented and motivated individuals through the schools or other institutions is questionable, especially when we look at statistics as to who is successful in society. The socioeconomic status of the student is an important determinant of college graduation. Consistently, higher-status students complete college at a greater rate than lower-status students (Bowen, Chingos, and McPherson, 2009).

4. To assume that extrinsic rewards, such as wealth and prestige, are primary motivators for individuals to train for certain occupations may be false. Individuals may have other motivations, such as humanitarian goals, for entering certain occupations. In addition, not all talented individuals who wish to become doctors or lawyers may have the opportunity to pursue those careers.

We turn now to contrasting views of the education system.

CONFLICT, NEO-MARXIST, AND REPRODUCTION THEORIES OF STRATIFICATION.   Conflict theorists see the stratification system and equality of opportunity from a different perspective. They believe that problems in the educational system stem from the conflicts in the society as a whole. Education is but one part of a system that is based on "haves" and "have-nots." Karl Marx, the father of conflict theory, believed that educational systems, like all social institutions, perpetuate the existing class structure. When the type of education and knowledge available to various groups of people is controlled, their access to positions in society is controlled. Thus, the educational system is doing its part to perpetuate the existing class system—to prepare children for their roles in the capitalistic, technological society, controlled by the dominant groups in society. As Marx put it, the ruling ideas of any period are the ideas of the ruling class.

Members of social classes share socialization, which leads to traits such as common language, values, lifestyle, manners, and interests. These "status groups" distinguish themselves from others in terms of categories of moral evaluation—honor, taste, breeding, respectability, propriety, cultivation, good fellows, and plain folk. Each group struggles for a greater share of those parts of society that make up "the good life"—wealth, power, and prestige—and it is because of this competition that conflicts exist. Some look to education to reduce inequalities, but according to conflict theorists, education, in fact, serves to reproduce the inequalities based on power, income, and social status (Carnoy, 1974). The values, rules, and institutions of society reflect the interests of the dominant groups, the ruling class; this is evident in the institution of education in the way resources are distributed (Scheurich and Imber, 1991). Thus, education is no exception.

Samuel Bowles, outlining the role of education from the conflict perspective, contends

(1) that schools have evolved in the U.S. not as part of a pursuit of equality, but rather to meet the needs of capitalist employers for a disciplined and skilled labor force, and to provide a mechanism for social control in the interests of political stability; (2) that as the economic importance of skilled and well-educated labor has grown, inequalities in the school system have become increasingly important in reproducing the class structure from one generation to the next; (3) that the U.S. school system is pervaded by class inequalities, which have shown little sign of diminishing over the last half-century; and (4) that the evidently unequal control over school boards and other decision-making bodies in education does not provide a sufficient explanation of the persistence and pervasiveness of inequalities in the school system. (Bowles, 1977, p. 137)

Origins of inequality are found in the class structure, capitalism, and modernity, and education reflects this. Inequality is part of the capitalist system, likely to persist as long as capitalism itself persists. Conflict theorists argue that although statistics show a narrowing of the educational gap between groups, this has not been translated into a more equal sharing of society's wealth. The characteristics of workers, such as their age, gender, race, and social class, influence the dollar value attached to education. The characteristics of the particular urban community and the economic structure in which individuals live, however, also affect their job opportunities and, thus, the value of their education. For instance, white male college graduates benefit in types of economic sectors that disadvantage equally educated females.

Schools have come under increasing attack by frustrated minority groups hoping to improve their lot. A great variety of new approaches and special programs to improve opportunities have been initiated through educational systems. Conflict theorists argue that more extensive alterations in the fabric of societal order will be necessary to attack the underlying causes of inequality (Anyon, 2005).

A group of scholars called "critical theorists" question the availability of chances for low-status individuals to find opportunities. Reproductionists, revisionists, and neo-Marxists have developed explanations of stratification stemming from the idea that the upper-middle class "conspires" to perpetuate their own class interests by limiting access to educational opportunities for other groups. These theorists argue that the underclasses are channeled into poor secondary schools, community colleges, vocational schools, and lower-level jobs. In the process, schools give knowledge to poor and minority children that make them accept failure in school, poor occupational status, and the dominant culture (Apple, 1993a, p. 215; Giroux, 1994). In this way, schools "reproduce" class inequality over generations. Scholars who share this view have "revised" the more positive view of education and opportunity in the United States.

Bowles and Gintis (1976) argue that schools are agencies for "reproducing" the social relations of production necessary to keep capitalistic systems working. Schooling and family are like economic production; some students gain more "cultural capital" for success, while others do not, thus reproducing the social class structure. This is referred to as the *correspondence principle.*

There is some empirical evidence to support the idea that classes are reproduced. In a study of American educational structures and reproduction of the "mental-manual" division of labor (or intellectual, white-collar class versus the working class), Colclough and Beck (1986) found that between 56 and 76 percent of male students reproduced their class status when looking at three key determinants of reproduction: public versus private schooling, socioeconomic community of the schools, and curriculum tracking within the schools. "Curriculum tracking was shown to be the critical determinant of reproduction." The authors found that "students from manual class backgrounds are over twice as likely to be placed in a vocational track" and from there are channeled into manual class jobs (Colclough and Beck, 1986, p. 172). In the recent return to the arguments in their *Schooling in Capitalist America* book, Bowles and Gintis (2002) review evidence for high correlations between parent's and children's income and the role schools play in abetting this transmission of status. They assert that their original arguments have largely been substantiated by research over the past 25 years since their book's original publication.

In the late 1960s and early 1970s, sociologists in Europe were exploring the effect that the cultural form and content inside schools had on stratification and reproduction. Young's *Knowledge and Control* (1971), followed by works of Bernstein, Bourdieu, Passeron, and others, argued that "the organization of knowledge, the form of its transmission, and the assessment of its acquisition are crucial factors in the cultural reproduction of class relationships in industrial societies" (Apple and Weis, 1986, pp. 19–20).

Some lower-class students do resist the tendencies toward class reproduction and learn to think independently, even to recognize their disadvantages. Willis describes the school counter-culture of working-class boys in England, who rejected the dominant values and norms of the educational process (Willis, 1981). In their rejection, they embraced the attitudes, behaviors, and values of their parents—and did not seek to become allies with other groups that also rejected the dominant institutions. Their understanding of their oppression was limited. Also, Willis's counterculture boys are only a few; many working-class students conform to the norms and try to make the system work for them. Some scholars have sought to identify other groups that resist the inducements of middle-class life, including women, sexual-identity minorities, and others (Davies, 1995). These "resistance theorists" seek to find those who may be the vanguard of broader social change in society. Even finding replicas of Willis's lads has not been easy, however (Davies, 1995). The lower and upper extremes of the stratification system are mostly locked into class positions; some individuals in the middle classes are mobile. Providing students with the knowledge needed to get ahead in a way they understand could help provide opportunities (Giroux, 1994).

Viewed from an international perspective, some have argued that schooling in the United States has a limited degree of stratification compared with other countries, especially in Europe. Rubinson points out that political forces in the United States have acted to limit the extent to which class-based decisions influence schools. Thus, according to this view, and contrary to Bowles and Gintis, class analysis is important but does not necessarily determine schooling (Rubinson, 1986).

Lower-class, minority, and female students in the United States fall disproportionately at the bottom of the economic hierarchy. These three groups—based on class, race, and sex—are those on which we focus throughout our discussion of equal educational opportunity here and in the next chapter. Sex and race are discussed extensively in Chapter 4.

Social-class background can aid or hinder students. Schools have a middle-class "bias" and are more closely aligned with the values and behavior patterns of middle-class children. A student's social class is determined by the home environment and is reflected in school grades, achievement, intelligence test scores, course failure, truancy, suspension, the high school curriculum pursued, and future educational plans. Class is not the only variable affecting achievement, and within each class there is wide variation, but there is definitely a significant relationship between class and achievement.

The sex difference favors girls initially, but this reverses later. Girls achieve grades as high as and higher than those of boys throughout high school. On standardized achievement tests, boys score higher than girls in some areas, such as math and science, and girls score higher in reading and writing. More girls graduate from high school, their enrollment in colleges and universities passed men in 1978, and the gap has continued to grow to the point that women are now over 57 percent of all undergraduate students (*Chronicle of Higher Education*, http://chronicle.com/article/United-States-Almanac-2009/48134/). As we will discuss in greater detail in Chapter 10, while women have achieved parity with men in many respects, and have surpassed them in others, there are still differences in majors and earning advanced degrees that remain to disadvantage them.

Other discussions of inequalities in education and society concern who has *access* to education, the *content* of education, and the *outcomes* of the educational process in terms of power, prestige, and income. These "new left" conflict theorists argue that it is the long-term results of education that in part determine class structure. Other modern theorists argue that *power* and *coercion* are more important determinants of inequality than economics and social class. An altogether different approach to inequality, phenomenology, is concerned with the *content* of the educational process and the passing on of information that can perpetuate the class system. Clearly, many factors contribute to the stratification into unequal class systems. One's theoretical perspective influences policy decisions, which in turn affect school reforms and allocation of resources, benefiting students unequally whether they are gifted, at risk, require special education, belong to a low- or high-socioeconomic level, are minority, or live in an urban or rural community. Our task in the remainder of this chapter is to explore in more detail the role of education in the stratification process.

> **Applying Sociology to Education:** *Consider students who are at the bottom of the school achievement hierarchy. What factors do you think contribute to their position in the system?*

STRATIFICATION AND EQUALITY OF EDUCATIONAL OPPORTUNITY

Equal opportunity exists when all people, even those without high status, wealth, or membership in a privileged group, have an equal chance of achieving a high-socioeconomic status in society regardless of their sex, minority status, or social class. This requires removing obstacles to individual achievement, such as prejudice, ignorance, and treatable impairments (Gardner, 1984, p. 46).

The Meaning of "Equality of Educational Opportunity"

James Coleman (1990) explored the concepts of equality and inequality, considering two opposing theories. One states that inequalities are justified only if they provide advantage to the unprivileged in society or if they benefit all. The other states that each person is entitled to what she or he has justly earned. Contrasting these two extremes reveals the dilemma of two sets of values in American society—equal access or individual freedom, and the state's right to impose equality versus the individual's right to choose his or her own school. There are many aspects of education where views are shaped by these opposing ideas. For example, in an effort to serve a diverse student body, many school systems differentiate their curriculum, creating pathways to rather different educational destinations—for example, immediate employment after high school or college. High achieving students and their parents want schools to offer what they think they have earned—access to Advanced Placement courses and the like. At the same time, evidence shows that the classes taken by the non-high achieving students are likely to move more slowly, cover much less material, and employ passive teaching methods (Oakes and Wells, 2004). A number of school systems have attempted to "detrack" their curriculum to avoid the inequalities that tracking creates (Wells and Serna, 1996). The "tracking wars" that result reflect these two theories have raged in many communities (Loveless, 1999). Over time, in part due to conflicts such as those just described, the concept of equality of educational opportunity has varied in meaning from equal school resources (inputs) to equal outputs (levels of academic achievement).

In our era of increasingly strict state standards for educational credentials, especially high school diplomas, another concept, "opportunity to learn," has come into use. It refers to whether students have been given the chance to learn material covered on mandatory state tests. Because schools may vary widely in the material they present to students, or spend very different amounts of time presenting material, the authenticity of the results of the tests have been challenged (Grodsky, Warren, and Felts, 2008).

In practice, each society places before its children the opportunities deemed appropriate and valuable in that society, and, if motivated by democratic values, it attempts to give children an equal chance to compete within that framework. Some children's talents may go unappreciated in any particular society. In the United States and other heterogeneous societies, there are many competing value systems; those who feel underrepresented argue that the schools are not giving them a fair shot at success within their framework of values. Some societies with high average levels of student achievement are very homogeneous, such as Japan with about 90 percent of its population sharing Japanese heritage, the same language, and same religion (Royko, 2004). The United States is incredibly more diverse, with many communities being made up of high propor- tions of immigrants speaking a different language, and with very different cultural resources.

Conflicts arise over differential treatment in school and unequal outcomes of the educa- tional process in terms of wealth, occupational status, and opportunities. Given that students have different abilities and needs, can some type of equality of outcome be expected? What if unequal outcomes break down along racial, ethnic, social class, or gender lines? Even more controversial are proposals that argue that life chances are unfair to some, and that to ensure "equality of results," society should control the distribution of jobs and wealth. These proposals range from progressive income taxes to curb extreme poverty and wealth to total restructuring of the economic system of society (Apple, 1993b). Coleman (1990) concludes that equal treatment of students alone cannot produce equal outcomes.

Social Class Reproduction: The Debate over Public versus Private Schools

Students who get the best educations are more likely to be selected for the preferred jobs in society. What are the "best" educations and how to get them are the questions. Those who can afford to go to elite private schools pay for the special "status rights" and social networks that allow for the "passage of privilege," and hope that this will maintain their children's privileged position or help them obtain a better position. Studies of women's elite boarding schools, for instance, show higher education attainment and major differences in postsecondary outcomes (Persell and Cookson, 1985; Persell, Catsambis, and Cookson, 1992). Elite secondary schools socialize students into elite peer groups that form their adult primary groups and perpetuate status (Cookson and Persell, 1985). Howard's recent book, *Learning Privilege* (2007), explores the lessons students learn in elite schools about their place in the world, their relationship with others, and who they are. Howard argues that these lessons reinforce and regenerate privilege. While all private schools charge tuition, not all serve elites; the selection of single-sex or religious private schooling is based largely on family tradition and preference (Lee and Marks, 1992).

A major research question, and one that has caused heated debate, is whether private schools produce significantly higher achieving students than public schools. If so, questions arise about the role of public schools, funding for private schools through vouchers, and char- ter schools. In 1982, James Coleman and colleagues published a controversial study, *Public and Private Schools* (Coleman, Hoffer, and Kilgore, 1981). In the study, 58,728 sophomores and seniors in 1,016 public, private, and parochial high schools around the country were tested. Major findings, which have stimulated controversies surrounding the study, indicated that, controlling for family background, students in private schools (mostly Catholic) achieved at a higher level than those in public schools; private schools tended to have smaller classes and a more limited academic curriculum, with fewer choices, and more student involvement; private schools provided more disciplined, orderly, and safe environments and have school climates more conducive to achievement; more homework is required in private schools, and they have better attendance records. All of these findings combine to produce higher academic achieve- ment (Hoffer, Greeley, and Coleman, 1985).

Coleman states, "The evidence is strong that the Catholic schools function much closer to the American ideal of the 'common school,' educating children from different backgrounds alike, than do the public schools" (Coleman, 1990, p. 242). Additional findings show that Catholic schools produce positive effects on verbal and math achievement from grades 10 to 12 in high school, with an advantage of one-half to one year over other students. These findings are greatest for minority and low-socioeconomic-group students. One of the reasons Catholic schools are more effective, Coleman argued, is that generally they don't track students. Usually smaller than public schools, these schools have only one class per subject and are necessarily fairly heterogeneous in student composition. All students are expected to take and succeed in the school's less differentiated curriculum.

Catholic schools do well in the inner city: Students there achieve higher test scores than do students in public inner-city high schools, have less gang involvement and fewer discipline and dropout problems, take more advanced courses, receive more value training and character building (MacFarlane, 1994, pp. 10–12), and have more parental involvement. Students in private schools for African Americans receive more college preparatory courses and achieve better test scores (Walsh, 1991). The contraction of urban Catholic school systems, however, is threatening their ability to offer an alternative to public schools for working-class families (Zehr, 2005).

The main criticisms of Coleman's study fall into three categories: methodological problems, accuracy of interpretations and alternative findings, and policy implications of the findings. Reanalysis of data by a number of researchers has challenged the major finding—that Catholic private schools are superior. Controlling for background variables such as class and race, and considering curriculum and teacher qualifications, critics argue that there is not a significant difference between good public schools and Catholic or other private schools in academic achievement (Topolnicki, 1994). An important attribute of all private schools is that parents have to select them, pay for them, and make sure that their children behave well enough so as to be allowed to stay in the school. None of these actions are required of public school parents. The difference between parents who select private schools and those who prefer public schools are potentially very important in affecting the achievement behavior of their children. Without being able to control for these differences, any conclusion about the superiority of private over public schools is suspect. To the degree that performance differences between public and private schools are found, they may be due to differences in the students and parents, not to the teachers or the schools they attend.

Just what is a significant difference in achievement is also in question. Some argue that findings that show a one-half-year to one-year difference are not large enough to claim that private schools are significantly superior (Alexander and Pallas, 1983, 1984, 1985).

Advocates of federal support for private education in the form of vouchers, tuition tax credits, or other federal aid are using Coleman's findings and recommendations to bolster their claims. Others, however, contend that federal support would increase religious and racial segregation of schools.

Alternative interpretations suggest other policies. James McPartland and Edward McDill (1982, pp. 77–78), arguing that student body composition accounts for school effectiveness, suggest that policy should be concerned with "allocation practices determining student body enrollments"; busing has been one such practice. This position is elaborated in Kahlenberg's book, *All Together Now* (2001), which argues that all children should have access to middle-class schools; that is he makes the case for social class desegregation, not racial desegregation.

Despite the controversies over Coleman's findings on academic achievement and access to the best educations, research reveals the characteristics that make for effective schools, public or private. Some of these characteristics are high standards and achievement expectations, committed staff, high self-concept in students, effective leadership, appropriate rewards, and flexible heterogeneous grouping (Brookover, Erickson, and McEvoy, 1996). The debate over how to provide all students equal opportunity will continue. But we need to be alert to factors that can affect school performance that are not due to characteristics of the schools, but to characteristics of the students. As with the research on private schools, some public schools have student selection criteria that influence their performance. For example, some charter schools begin their day at 7 AM and go until 5:30 PM and hold mandatory classes on Saturdays and during the summer. Some of these schools require parents and students to sign a contract to maintain this schedule or forfeit their eligibility for attendance. This requirement alone introduces selection effects that assure that the children (and parents) who attend the school are not typical of their communities (Hammack, 2010).

The Controversial Issue of "Choice"

If public schools are found to be wanting, or if private schools receive federal funding, are we undermining a basic institution in society, the mass public school? In response to arguments that we weaken public schools, some politicians and educational leaders are advocating "choice"—allowing parents to select from among schools. Choice is a strategy for reform and restructuring. The logic here is that parents are consumers of education and should have different schools from which to choose. Like any market, this thinking goes, competition among those offering education should improve it. Part of the problem of public education has been its monopoly over the provision of educational services, choice proponents argue. Since private schools are often expensive, only the affluent have a choice. In fact, school choice has largely been determined by place of residence since most children attend neighborhood schools. One driving force for the expansion of suburbs in the latter half of the twentieth century has been parental desire for alternatives to urban schools. Thus, choice plans have been adopted in many urban areas to provide parents with public school choice without requiring them to move. Choice presumes variety in the characteristics of schools. Challenging the historic idea of "common schools," choice plans involve developing schools with different themes, curricula, or other variation, such as size. District 4 in New York City was an early example of this plan; it offered several schools from which parents of elementary students could choose. Other plans involve giving families a voucher for each student and allowing them to select from among schools, including private schools. Of course, if there are meaningful differences among schools, parents need to have information about these differences so as to make informed choices for their children. Getting access to this information is not always easy; New York City publishes an annual high school directory that rivals the Manhattan phone directory in size and complexity, which advantages highly literate parents and those with insider knowledge (copies in Arabic, Bengali, Chinese, Haitian Creole, Korean, Russian, Spanish, and Urdu are available at the Department of Education's website).

Proponents argue that competition among schools for students will improve school quality. Choice helps increase accountability and gives parents and students more sense of ownership over schools. In fact, choice seems to have worked in some districts, and several states such as Massachusetts (Viadero, 1995), Minnesota, and Texas; and cities such as Milwaukee, White Plains, and parts of Harlem in New York City are experimenting with choice plans. More than half the states have forms of choice plans (Cookson, 1994).

In a controversial discussion of the choice issue, Chubb and Moe question whether school systems should be subjected to individual choice and market forces. The researchers focused on school practices and achievement differences between public and private school students, and their results support the side of choice (Chubb and Moe, 1990). They argue that most school systems have become so politically and bureaucratically complex that elements that encourage high achievement, including autonomy and professionalism of school staff, are limited. Under a free market system, educators could design any programs they think could compete successfully for students. This, in fact, is the idea behind many charter or community schools. Some momentum has been gained by the movement as it has proposed that vouchers be made available for students in "failing schools" as identified by the federal No Child Left Behind Act.

Opponents of choice decry the potential decline in numbers and quality of the common school, or public school, pointing out that only the least capable students will be left, accentuating the problem for ill-prepared students, and the best teachers will go to the better schools. School choice would likely increase religious and social segregation along race and class lines, though some studies show that African-American and Hispanic parents, even those with lower levels of education, were more likely than white and Asian Americans to take advantage of school choice options (Schneider et al., 1996). Critics also point out disparities between public and private school students now and argue that little will change without fundamental restructuring of the system. The percentage of children enrolled at each level of schooling by family income is shown in Figure 3.3. Note the differences in the high- and low-income categories (National Center for Education Statistics, *Condition*, 1999).

In an analysis that examined the debate across the political spectrum and did case studies of cities and states with choice programs, Cookson (1994) argues that student achievement and school improvement and equity cannot be better than the reforms put in place by districts to achieve equality and excellence. For instance, there is little evidence at this time that the Milwaukee or Harlem experiments are improving school achievement (Tashman, 1992). The General Accounting Office conducted a review of the evidence on the Cleveland and Milwaukee plans and agreed that the data did not provide a clear conclusion (General Accounting Office, 2001).

Recent court rulings in Florida, Maine, Vermont, Ohio, and Pennsylvania against school vouchers raise questions about the constitutionality of voucher systems. For instance, Florida courts threw out the nation's first statewide school voucher system, ruling that the Florida

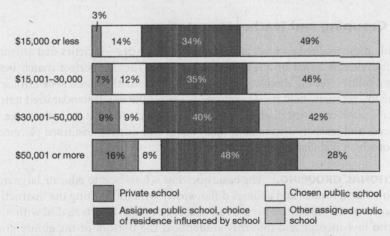

FIGURE 3.3 Distribution of public and private elementary and secondary students, by family income, October 1990. *Source:* U.S. Department of Commerce, Bureau of the Census. Reprinted in National Center for Education Statistics, *The Condition of Education 1994*, p. 3.

Constitution forbids public money to be spent on private education. In 2002, the U.S. Supreme Court, in a 5–4 decision, ruled that the Milwaukee voucher plan was legal, setting the stage for a potential expansion of the plans (*Simmons-Harris v. Zelman*). The Court determined that since the public funds represented by the vouchers went to a broad class of citizens who could decide whether to seek to attend religious schools or secular private schools, the support to religion offered by vouchers did not violate the constitutional prohibition of public support for religious activity. While there have been new laws passed in several states in support of voucher programs, there has not been the big expansion of them that proponents had hoped for. Provisions in many state constitutions prohibit state funding of religious activities (Walsh, 2002). Research has not supported the argument that all schools are improved by the option of school choice (Arum, 1996, pp. 29–46); rather it appears that when the private sector is large, states increase their support for public schools. The better educational outcomes in these states derive not from competition so much as the higher levels of public expenditures for public education.

When a 1999 Gallup poll asked for public attitudes toward public school choice, it found "support for public funding for attendance at private schools has slipped slightly, but the public remains divided on the issue." Asked, "Do you favor or oppose allowing students and parents to choose a private school to attend at public expense?" 55 percent oppose making such choice available, up from 50 percent in 1998. Even Catholic and other private school parents were not in favor of public funds paying for private schooling (Rose and Gallup, 1999). By 2002, after the Court's ruling in favor of vouchers, public sentiment was more in favor of them, up 12 points from 34 percent in 2001 to 46 percent in 2002. Yet many are still not in favor of the idea, and the issue remains one on which the public is deeply divided (Jacobson, 2002). One interesting point is that suburban parents are mostly not in favor of the idea as they are largely satisfied with their schools and don't want to lose control of the funding that would go with the vouchers (D'entremont and Huerta, 2007).

Applying Sociology to Education: *What are some advantages and disadvantages of school choice programs for your district?*

Ability Grouping and Teacher Expectations

Most highly industrialized societies claim to be meritocracies—societies that attempt to place and advance individuals based on their merits. Yet few achieve a perfect match between abilities and responsibilities. Testing, discussed in Chapter 2, is one method used to determine education and job placement, yet many hold strong sentiments against the use of standardized tests for placement and perceive poor, minority, disabled, and female students to be at a disadvantage. In the rush to make schools and teachers accountable, many states and districts instituted placement exams, one outcome of which is ability grouping.

INSTRUCTIONAL GROUPING.   The basic question is how best to educate large numbers of students whose backgrounds and abilities differ widely without limiting the instructional opportunities of lower-track students. This is a reasonable question. Efforts to deal with it, however, have often found low-income and minority students at the bottom of the ability grouping system (Burnett, 1995). Therein lies the problem. As recent research shows, even in very early childhood, cognitive differences are strongly associated with parental social status (Lee and Burkam, 2002).

Using measures of student achievement, even in kindergarten, thus divides students by their social origins.

All schools with more than just a few students must decide how to organize those students into groups for instruction. The most common dimension of this sorting is by age. We are used to the idea that generally children in the same grade are about the same age. In fact, "holding back" students because of their low achievement level is an emotionally powerful event for children because they are then placed with children younger than themselves. Getting off the regular age-grade progression is an early indicator of education risk; very high percentages of high school dropouts are "left back" in elementary school, often more than once (Hammack, 1989; Stearns et al., 2007).

In addition to age, gender is sometimes used to sort students, as in single-sex schools, an old practice in American education (Tyack and Hansot, 1990). Rising concerns for the academic achievement of girls and, during the last decade, of boys has produced new interest in this form of grouping. Federal policies forbid most of this form of segregation until recent changes were announced. It is too early to see whether this policy change will stimulate the creation of large numbers of single-sex schools, but in many urban areas, there is interest in how such schools might help improve academic achievement.

Academic achievement, itself, is a very common dimension of grouping. Sometimes called "ability grouping," using student achievement to create learning groups and classes has a long and controversial history in American education. The term reflects its history. The word "ability" is defined in the dictionary as the state of being able to perform; also, a natural talent or acquired proficiency (Webster's, 1974). Implied in this usage is that ability may be part of the genetic heritage of a person, a "natural talent," not something over which we have personal control. Early mental testing sought to uncover the "natural" intellectual abilities of individuals, and though our thinking has moved away to a more plastic and flexible conception of intelligence, the legacy of this usage remains. The usage of "acquired proficiency" or achievement is consistent with our understanding today (Lemann, 1999). Students may be grouped into the "robins" or "blue birds" reading groups based on their reading performance.

Achievement grouping is a common practice in schools because most teachers believe that it is easier to teach a group of students with similar levels of prior learning. Different grouping patterns emerge under different organizational structures, depending on the structural constraints and the school's atmosphere, or "culture." An example of a structural constraint would be students demanding to be placed in a particular track (Kilgore, 1991, pp. 201–202). Groupings are usually based on reading and math levels of students. In high schools, this grouping is often associated with divergent curricular pathways, called "tracks." Traditionally, American high schools developed as comprehensive schools, providing college preparation courses, as well as vocational and general education courses (Hammack, 2004). The sequencing of courses, especially in math and science, meant that if one wanted to go to college, the student needed to start the college prep classes as a freshman and continue to take them through the senior year. Mobility into, through, and out of this track was necessarily limited by the sequencing of courses. This meant that educational decisions that prepared students for college needed to be made late in elementary school, cutting off those who developed an aspiration to college later. Today, such rigid tracking systems are rare (Lucas, 1999). More common is a diverse curriculum with many student choices (Powell, Farrar, and Cohen, 1985), though sequencing is still very important, especially as high schools expand their Advanced Placement and other college-level course opportunities.

Most U.S. schools studied using national data sets have similar tracking systems and sequencing of courses in math (Hoffer and Kamens, 1992); there is more variation in science sequencing, though placement in math and science often go together. Studies show that as early as eighth grade, students' science grouping affects their future science curriculum and their chances to excel in the sciences (Schiller and Stevenson, 1992).

Unfortunately, not all students are placed on the basis of careful evaluation of their interests and abilities. Testing has been a primary method of placing students in tracks, but this method can increase social stratification (Darling-Hammond, 1994). A study of inner-city urban schools found that many factors operate in the placement of students—filling study halls or low-enrollment classes, filling remedial courses so that funding would continue at the school, and honoring staff preferences for course assignments (Riehl, Natriello, and Pallas, 1992). Movement from one track to another is usually downward, based primarily on achievement. A student's socioeconomic level, however, does affect assignments, with higher-socioeconomic-level students disproportionately in college tracks (Lucas, 1992). The effects of the differences in children as they enter school do not disappear easily (Lee and Burkam, 2002).

Schools in the United States rely more heavily on tracking than schools in any other nation (Oakes, 1990). However, national sequencing of courses, that is a common sequencing across a country, is less common in the United States than in many other countries because of local control of schools and no national governing bodies or tests. Standards set by teachers' organizations and college entrance requirements have some influence on national sequencing of courses and tracking of students in the United States (Schiller and Stevenson, 1992). Many states now require students to take and pass high school exit tests in order to obtain a diploma. This forces schools to offer a curriculum of at least minimal rigor for all students, and, reformers hope, will better prepare graduates for college opportunities and for work (Dougherty, 1996).

Japan, which values group conformity, is an example of a society with heterogeneous grouping in schools, treating all students alike by age cohorts. Though tracking within schools is rare, it occurs across middle and high schools in Japan, with some schools considered elite. Japanese parents and teachers believe in the philosophy that each child is expected to achieve in school, and they believe that all can, although some may need to work harder than others. An underlying assumption in American education, despite the efforts toward equality, is that some will fail because of our different abilities.

Conflict theorists argue that elites in the United States are unlikely to change basic structures that work for their class interests (Oakes, 1995). Thus, reforms in education have benefited some but have not changed their relative educational and economic position. Achievement grouping often begins in elementary school and continues through high school as students are "tracked" into distinctive curricular paths. The problem is to determine who gets placed where; too often, according to conflict theorists, placement correlates directly with the child's background, language skills, appearance, and other socioeconomic variables.

The Supreme Court's 1967 ruling in *Hobson v. Hansen* in Washington, DC, stated that separation of students into fast and slow tracks resulted in unconstitutional segregation of minority and nonminority students. Yet, many public secondary schools still offer core courses tailored to differences in student ability (Lucas, 1999). Many teachers argue that finding the best "fit" between students and teachers increases classroom effectiveness and that ability grouping of students makes it possible to teach them more effectively at their own levels (Hallinan, 1994).

Students in different groups have quite different school experiences. For instance, in average- to low-achievement classrooms there is a more disruptive learning environment (Mekosh-Rosenbaum, 1996), whereas students in honors classes participate more (Gamoran et al., 1995). These learning environments affect student life chances, self-concepts, motivations,

IQ and achievement levels, and other aspects of school and work experiences. Of the three major ways in which reproduction theorists argue that classes are reproduced (public versus private schooling, socioeconomic class composition of school communities, and achievement grouping of students), research shows tracking to be the most important mechanism in the reproduction process. Colclough and Beck (1986, p. 469) show that students from "manual class" (working class) backgrounds are more than twice as likely to be placed in a vocational track as are other students. Table 3.2 illustrates the importance of each of these factors in the reproduction of class.

Thus, we know that achievement is not a perfect predictor of placement in learning groups. Characteristics of schools such as "electivity" (how students are assigned to tracks), inclusiveness, and other school policies, plus student characteristics (socioeconomic status [SES] of students and community, race, percentage of minority students in the school, the proportion of students in the school in an academic track, and the methods for assigning tracks—self-selection versus assignment) are influential in a student's placement. The higher the SES, the more likely students will be in academic tracks (Jones, Vanfossen, and Ensminger, 1995). Placements tend to be fairly stable over the year. We know that students placed in high-achievement groups are taught more and at a

Table 3.2 Social Class and Schooling Structures

Schooling Structure	Mental Class	Manual Class	Overall
I. School Type			
Public schools			
Percent students recruited from	33.37	66.63	—
Percent class membership reproduced	52.92	70.85	64.87
Private schools			
Percent students recruited from	43.93	56.07	—
Percent class membership reproduced	62.02	53.94	57.49
II. School Community			
High-minority communities			
Percent students recruited from	26.59	73.41	—
Percent class membership reproduced	45.27	71.13	64.25
Low-minority communities			
Percent students recruited from	36.29	63.71	—
Percent class membership reproduced	55.33	70.72	65.14
III. Curriculum Track			
General track			
Percent students recruited from	26.96	73.04	—
Percent class membership reproduced	33.41	81.91	68.83
Vocational track			
Percent students recruited from	19.70	80.30	—
Percent class membership reproduced	16.67	90.27	75.77
College-bound track			
Percent students recruited from	45.63	54.37	—
Percent class membership reproduced	69.32	44.95	56.07

Source: Colclough, Glenna, and E. M. Beck, "The American Educational Structure and the Reproduction of Social Class: Table 3, Social Class and School Structures," *Sociological Inquiry* Vol. 56, No. 4, p. 469. Copyright © 1986 by John Wiley & Sons. Reproduced with permission of John Wiley & Sons.

faster pace than are those in low-achievement groups, making it more difficult for students in lower tracks to move up.

Studying the socioeconomic composition of students in different schools is also revealing. Anyon (1980) compared the socioeconomic composition of schools with the work tasks of students, studying five elementary schools with very different compositions based on parents' occupations: two working-class, one mixed (middle-class), one "affluent professional," and one executive elite. The school patterns train students for their respective social classes. In working-class schools, children follow procedures—usually mechanical, rote behavior. In the middle-class school, getting the right answer and following directions is important, but some choice is possible. In the "affluent professional" school, the emphasis is on independent creative activity in which students express and apply ideas and concepts. In the executive elite school, developing analytical intellectual ability, learning to reason, and producing quality academic products are important. Conceptualizing rules by which elements fit together is a key goal.

Tracking has other consequences for students who develop "student cultures" within each track. These cultures add to the perpetuation of attitudes and behaviors that reproduce social class. In Israel, a multiethnic society, students from the same ethnic groups have tended to group together. Vocational education has come under question because it reproduces the same class of students in the same occupations (Yogev and Avalon, 1987). This track-based student culture may limit or expand student engagement in school and academic achievement. The degree to which students enforce among themselves norms that support or undermine school and achievement has received much attention in the last decade or so. We will review that literature in more detail in the next chapter, but many scholars see such "peer effects" as powerful and strongly associated with the existence of achievement-based learning groups in schools (Ogbu and Simons, 1998).

Many writers have commented on the effects of grouping. A summary of findings follows.

1. Lower-ability groupings tend to include a disproportionate number of lower-class and minority children; this stratification influences educational attainment and is likely to affect students' later job attainments and earnings.

2. Children from low-socioeconomic backgrounds are more likely to be placed in low-ability groups because of low test scores, which some argue do not measure ability accurately. In addition, they are often stigmatized, and scores keep falling in relation to other groups.

3. Each school has its own stratification system, depending on students coming into the system, but children in any given grouping tend to be more homogeneous in terms of socioeconomic status and race than are children in the school as a whole. In other words, groupings within the school are highly related to the background of the students. Once students are labeled and grouped, there is less chance of their moving from one category to another. Schools in different neighborhoods have different outcomes. For instance, in higher social class districts with excellent schools, students have more college preparatory courses from which to choose (Jones, 1996, p. 21; Spade, 1994; Spade, Columbia, and Vanfossen, 1997).

4. Students in upper-ability groupings are disproportionately of higher socioeconomic status; are more motivated; and have higher achievement, class rank, and test scores, all of which give them a better start after high school. Teachers give more feedback and praise to high-ability groups and plan more creative activities for them. For the lower-ability groupings, the opposite is true. This same distinction by class status holds at junior and community colleges in the vocational versus academic tracks.

5. Summaries of research on the effects of ability grouping indicate that the practice benefits gifted students and those placed in high tracks. Lower-ability groups receive less

teacher attention and poorer instruction, setting them further behind in the quest for equal opportunity. Ability groups often reinforce race and class segregation and stereotypes, and they lower the aspirations and self-esteem of lower-group students.

6. Most problematic is the conflicting evidence on the effects of grouping. In a review of 29 studies on the effects of ability grouping, Slavin (1990) finds little evidence of beneficial effects. He does not address institutional and curricular differences in students' experiences, but mainly uses test scores.

Not only do some studies show no justification for the use of tracking but they also question programs such as Chapter I that "pull out" students from regular classes (Oakes, 1990). Most damning was a study showing minority students' disproportionate placement in low-achievement math and science classes with the least-qualified teachers and insufficient access to computers, science equipment, and quality textbooks. Students in low-achievement groups lose ground and perform poorly on reading and math achievement tests (Hallinan, 1990). Grouping can start as early as first grade and can have an impact for several years thereafter (Pallas et al., 1994).

Those in favor of heterogeneous grouping of students believe that tracking on the basis of presumed ability level harms students who are placed in the lower tracks and fails to help those placed in higher tracks. Proponents of untracking students also assert that tracking results in a lack of equity, is a violation of democratic values, produces low self-conceptions of learning ability, and causes a devaluing of self by those placed in lower tracks. Many argue that tracking programs based on presumed ability result in two unfortunate consequences: "more academic failure, and heightened racial and social class animosity" (Brookover, Erickson, and McEvoy, 1996, p. 116) that are more important than the gains it provides for those in the higher tracks.

In a series of studies of efforts to "detrack" middle and high schools, Oakes, Wells, and their colleagues have shown the resistance that can be generated to this change. Teachers in some subjects, particularly math and science, may believe that the curriculum should be graded by prior student achievement, and these subjects are often organized in a strictly hierarchical way. This tendency has been increased with the addition of college-level courses to the high school curriculum (AP courses, International Baccalaureate programs, dual-enrollment programs). Eligibility for these course opportunities is often determined by prior achievement. Parents of students in the high achieving groups or tracks strongly defend the benefit their children obtain from a hierarchically structured curriculum (Oakes and Wells, 2004; Wells and Serna, 1996). How students understand tracking and detracking is addressed by Yonezawa and Jones (2006).

Rosenbaum (1999–2000, pp. 1–7), a scholar who has studied tracking extensively, is not positive about the effects of detracking. A school he studied undertook a major detracking program in its social studies classrooms. Teachers found it hard to construct curriculum and class activities for heterogeneous groups. They were less likely to cover high-level topics; high achieving minority students did not receive material they would have in differentiated classrooms. Moreover, neither homogeneous nor heterogeneous groupings seem to assure high quality instruction (Gamoran and Weinstein, 1998, pp. 385–415).

Are there solutions to the problem of homogeneous versus heterogeneous grouping? Most suggestions focus on restructuring classroom groupings: Students work together in many subjects but are grouped in reading, language arts, and math. Low achievers are not stigmatized or made to feel they are "dummies." Low achievers are few in the class, so that the teacher can give them needed help. Success, experts argue, depends on small student-to-teacher ratios, high expectations by teachers, extensive oral communication in class, and experienced, effective teachers (Levine and Stark, 1983).

Some elementary schools in Britain and the United States have attempted alternatives to grouping, making constructive use of the diverse abilities and backgrounds of the students. In these schools, children work at their own levels of ability in reading and math. The teacher gives the class lessons on particular topics suitable for the range of abilities and works with individual children or with small groups, sometimes with the help of an aide. Cooperative relationships between children are encouraged—for example, children who understand a math concept may be assigned to help teach other students. This fosters not only cooperation but also feelings of self-worth because each child's particular talents are recognized. It also prevents some of the problems associated with labeling. The late Elizabeth G. Cohen, a sociologist of education at Stanford University, has studied how heterogeneous grouping in schools can be better managed by teachers. She and her colleagues have developed ideas about "complex instruction." In this method, "students use each other as resources while completing challenging group tasks that require the use of multiple intellectual abilities. Teachers work to create equal-status interaction within the small groups" (Cohen and Lotan, 1997, p. vii; also see Cohen, 1986).

TEACHER EXPECTATIONS AND STUDENT ACHIEVEMENT. What difference do teacher expectations of students make in student performance? In a pioneering study, Robert Rosenthal and Lenore Jacobson (1968) tested the effects of teacher expectations on interactions, achievement levels, and intelligence of students. A follow-up study in a San Francisco elementary school with a high percentage of lower-class and Mexican American students gave support to their hypothesis that once a child is labeled by the teacher and others, a "self-fulfilling prophecy" operates: The teacher expects certain behaviors from the child and the child responds to the expectations. Once this pattern is established, it is hard to alter (Bonetari, 1994).

Criticisms of their study have focused on its methodological weaknesses and have pointed out that their findings apply mainly to lower grades. Multiple factors enter into teacher

interactions with students; nonetheless, they pioneered in an important area of research that continues to provide valuable insights on teacher–student dynamics. The body of literature that has developed since their study has shown that teacher expectations play a significant role in determining how much and how well students learn (Bamburg, 1994). The focus of more recent studies has been on teacher expectations of their class.and how these expectations affect their teaching methods and the atmosphere in the class. What difference do teacher expectations of students make in student learning?

Teacher expectations are influenced by various factors, including records of the student's previous work and test scores; the student's dress, name, physical appearance, attractiveness, race, sex, language, and accent; the parents' occupations; single-parent and motherhood status (Cooper, 1995); and the way the student responds to the teacher (see Box 3.1). A study of Mexican American student achievement was shown to be related to teacher attitudes and expectations; teachers viewed the Mexican American students as different from Anglo students. Underachieving Mexican American students valued their cultural traditions more than the high-achieving Mexican American and Anglo students and became resistant to learning when these traditions were marginalized. Achievement was also related to their compliance, appearance, styles of communication, and willingness to support Anglo norms (Pena, 1997).

Teacher expectations are manifested in the teachers' behavior toward and treatment of individual children and their grouping of the children in classroom situations. Children pick up the subtle cues; the "self-fulfilling prophecy" can cause them to believe that they have certain abilities and can influence future behaviors. Many teachers in schools with low-achieving students become discouraged about the children's ability to learn. Their expectations for student learning are reduced, creating that self-fulfilling prophecy in which teachers expect less and students give less. Students are influenced by their teachers' expectations, and they internalize those expectations.

Teachers manipulate the classroom situation so as to affect student performance through achievement grouping and creating other groups within the classroom. An example of this is revealed in an experiment conducted by a classroom teacher in Iowa. She was concerned that her students really understand the impact of discrimination, so she set up an experiment, the results of which surprised even her. She divided the children in her all-white class into two groups: blue-eyed and brown-eyed. For the first day, one group was given privileges and made to feel superior. The situation was reversed the next day. The children took their roles very seriously, with the superior ones taking delight in putting down the inferior ones and in excelling in their own work. The inferior for the day were outperformed. The importance of this example is that labels can affect the self-concept of students and their treatment by others, even in such a short-term experiment (Peters, 1971). The major policy recommendation coming from studies of teacher expectations is that positive teacher attitudes and approaches toward learning are necessary if students are to believe that they can achieve; some inner-city schools that have rigorous expectations have raised levels of achievement significantly.

Another facet of the teacher expectations literature is how these expectations operate at the school level. A number of researchers have explored what is called "collective responsibility" for student achievement and how this school-level characteristic varies and how it affects student performance (Lee and Loeb, 2000). The basic idea here is that expectations are reciprocal—that is students' behaviors and achievements affect teacher expectations for individual students, for classrooms, and for schools. In turn, those expectations of teachers affect student behavior and performance. Most of the discussion this far has been at the individual student and classroom

BOX 3.1

Sources of Teacher Expectations

We need to guard against using the following factors that can impose lower expectations on undeserving students:

Sex. Young boys and older girls are sometimes the recipients of prejudicial low academic expectations. This often is a function of mistaken beliefs about the relevance of boys' maturation and sex-role discrimination, which harms females.

Socioeconomic status level. Low expectations are typically held for children of families with low-level income and education. Status based on the jobs held and the place of residence of the parents often are used to prejudge students.

Race and ethnic identifiers. African American, Hispanic, and Native American students receive lower expectations than other students. Asian students receive high expectations.

Negative comments about students. Negative comments by other teachers or principals often result in lower expectations.

The status of the school. Rural and inner-city schools often are associated with lower expectations than suburban schools. The racial, ethnic, and income level of the school is often a factor in such prejudice.

Appearance. Lower expectations are associated with clothes and grooming that are out of style, made of cheaper material, not brand name, or purchased at thrift or discount stores.

Oral language patterns. Nonstandard English often is the basis for holding lower expectations for students.

Neatness. Lower expectations are associated with general disorganization, poor handwriting, or other indicators.

Halo effect. There is a tendency to label a student's current achievement based upon their past performance evaluations.

Readiness. There are negative effects when teachers assume that maturation rates or prior lack of knowledge or experience are unchanging phenomena, thus precluding improvement.

Seating position. Lower expectations are typically transmitted to students who sit on the sides and in the back of a classroom.

Socialization by experienced teachers. Experienced teachers have a tendency to stress the limitations of certain students for new teachers rather than the need to work on improving the performances of students.

Student behavior. Students with poor, nonacademic behavior also tend to receive lower academic expectations from teachers.

Teacher training institutions. Some faculty within colleges of education perpetuate myths and ideologies of individual limitations of students. This results in prejudicially low expectations for large numbers of students.

Teacher education textbooks. Some textbooks also perpetuate myths and ideologies that individual students have limitations, which reinforce prejudicially low expectations for students.

Tracking or grouping. Students in a lower academic track are mistakenly presumed to have been placed there for good reason (i.e., they have limited capacities and can never be expected to learn critical knowledge and skills).

Source: Brookover, Wilbur, et al., *Creating Effective Schools: An In-Service Program* (Holmes Beach, FL: Learning Publications, Inc., 1996), pp. 75–76.

level. Increasingly researchers are recognizing that schools also operate as a single organization, and that the way teachers and administrators in a school think and act can have a significant effect on students. Thus, the notion of collective responsibility is the degree to which teachers and administrators believe that what they do can affect student behavior and performance. If teachers attribute student behavior and performance primarily to factors external to the school—to the family, the neighborhood—then they are unlikely to exert high levels of effort to educate students. These collective expectations are, of course, made up of those expectations of individual teachers, but together, they may in turn affect the attitudes of individual teachers, creating a school climate encouraging of student effort *and* teacher effort. Of course, the opposite effect is also possible; a situation referred to as a failing school. In the Lee and Loeb research referred to above, teachers in Chicago's smaller school were more likely to have a positive sense of collective responsibility for student learning than were large schools. Smaller school size seems to encourage a sense that the learning needs of students are achievable and not overwhelming as large schools may communicate.

Applying Sociology to Education: *How can teachers affect classroom interactions and student self-perceptions?*

Financing Schools in the United States

Wealthy school districts attract the best-educated and more experienced teachers. They can offer higher salaries, superior facilities and materials, support staff to handle problems, and a potentially achievement-oriented group of students. Poorer and minority schools get new, inexperienced teachers. There is also a tendency for minority teachers to be placed in schools with heavy concentrations of minority students, depriving all districts of an integrated teaching staff. These are some of the factors that indirectly affect student achievement (Elliott, 1998).

When schools were initially founded in the United States, they were largely funded by local communities. Individual communities decided to tax themselves to support education for their children. Few funds were available from the state, although the authority for schools resides with the state government. The tradition of local funding remains strong, as communities see their ability to control their children's schools in part assured by their raising the funds to pay for schools. The property tax became the chief means by which local funds to support schools were generated. This meant, of course, that the greater the value of property in a community, the more money it could raise at any level of taxation. Communities of wealth and of poverty, taxing themselves at the same rate, generate very different amounts of money. This inequality led to greater participation of states in funding schools so as to reduce the worst disparities, driven by lawsuits based on the equal protection clause of the federal constitution. These "foundation" state grants were based on an estimate of sufficient funding to provide an adequate education. But such disparities in the amount communities spend on schools are still large. A recent report about spending in New Jersey school districts found districts at the top spending over $29,000 per student a year and at the bottom, $7,426, while the statewide average was $12,098 (Hu and Fessenden, 2007).

This imbalance has stimulated several court cases concerning equal financing of education. In the 1974 landmark *Serrano v. Priest* case, the California supreme court ruled that forcing school districts to rely heavily on local property taxes created sharp inequalities between school districts in the state. In 1976, California was ordered to substantially reduce the gap between districts by 1980. Many other state courts considered cases on finances, one of which was heard by the Supreme Court. In *San Antonio Independent School District v. Rodriguez*, the supreme court left decisions regarding property tax funding of schools up to each state. Property tax is still a part of local school funding, but often it is not the most equitable way of collecting funds for education. School spending per student can be up to four times greater in wealthy districts than in poor ones. Property taxes are highest in cities, causing middle classes to leave and businesses to locate elsewhere, resulting in a smaller tax base. Urban students often require different types of programs—bilingual, vocational, compensatory, or special education—all of which cost additional money. On average, local districts with high percentages of students in poverty receive a higher percentage of school revenues from the state and federal government, though most federal support is for special programs, such as compensatory education (Brown, 2007).

States help support education through income tax, sales tax, and lotteries. Local districts use primarily property taxes to fund close to 50 percent of local school budgets. And this is where the conflict arises; some districts bring in significantly more tax dollars than others and can afford better education for their children. The federal government holds a big stick over local and state education by threatening to withdraw funding for special programs if districts do not comply with federal laws. The federal "No Child Left Behind" law requires annual testing of students and assessments of school progress in an effort to close achievement gaps, among other things. Assessment must be implemented by the states if they want to continue to receive federal education funding.

In recent years, however, the litigation over education funding has taken a new turn. Because education is not mentioned in our federal constitution, it is a state function, and all state constitutions spell out the state's responsibility for providing citizens with an education. The specific language varies from state to state, but often includes language such as a guarantee of a "thorough and efficient education." How one defines such an education has become the subject of litigation. But without operational state standards or definitions of what an education would look like, litigation based on the equal protection clause of the federal constitution was limited. In its place, an argument about "adequacy" has emerged. One common mechanism used to resolve this is known as a "costing out method." This method has several forms, but often involves examining how successful school districts achieve their results and finding out what those educational efforts cost. It identifies the resources and conditions necessary to provide all a reasonable education, an "adequate" one—which can increasingly be defined according to the standards that states have adopted for their credentials. For example, if a state has a high school exit examination, model school districts would be the ones that have the highest success rate for their graduates on that test. In adopting state standards, states have essentially defined what a "thorough and efficient" education means in practice. Thus, an unanticipated consequence of the movement to impose specific educational standards has offered litigants a new means of seeking greater equality of school funding (Rebell, 2006). As we will discuss in more detail in Chapter 4, with the 2007 Supreme Court ruling against using race to assign students to schools, this litigation is one of the few remaining means to salvage the effort to equalize the educational opportunities of children from different backgrounds.

Educators will continue to struggle over ways to involve all children fully in the educational process. For some, this means finding ways to alter the disadvantages of "cultural capital" brought to school by lower-class children. For others, it means restructuring the system so that all children have a place, regardless of family background and financing factors. In the next chapter, we discuss the effect of educational policies and attempts at equality of educational opportunity on specific groups of students.

Summary

Schools are the target for the frustrations of many groups; they represent at the same time a means to get ahead and an institution that is holding some students back.

I. THE CRISIS IN SCHOOLING

According to many experts, there is a crisis in schooling. Both the public and the educators are concerned about evidence indicating the failure of schools to meet expectations. It is also true, however, that we expect schools to solve some problems that have their roots in the structure of societal institutions. This chapter addressed the stratification system and its role in education and society, and equality of educational opportunity.

II. THE PROCESS OF STRATIFICATION: IS INEQUALITY INEVITABLE?

Stratification, a process that is interlaced through the whole societal structure, refers to our position in society's hierarchy. Our social class, the structure of American stratification, is determined by several variables, including wealth, power, and prestige. Educational attainment is closely associated with these variables. In addition, education is used to sort people into future societal roles. Thus, people look to education to improve their status in society.

There are two major theoretical explanations of stratification systems. Functionalist theorists see inequality as inevitable, and education as playing a role in selecting and training people for unequal positions in society. The question is this: How much inequality should be tolerated?

Among the criticisms of functionalist theory is the charge that, by assuming inequality, it assumes perpetuation of the status quo.

Conflict theorists disagree with the assumption that inequality is inevitable. They argue that it is perpetuated by those in power, the "haves." We are distinguished by status groups, with the dominant group controlling. Conflict theorists hold that education alone cannot solve the problems of inequality in society, but that it will take a restructuring of the whole society to bring about change.

III. STRATIFICATION AND EQUALITY OF EDUCATIONAL OPPORTUNITY

Equality of opportunity refers to all people having an equal chance of achieving a high-socioeconomic status in society, regardless of sex, race, or class. Related to schools, it refers to equal facilities, financing, and availability. Problems arise over different treatment and outcomes—the fact that certain groups come out consistently on the bottom.

Social classes are "reproduced" through several mechanisms, such as elite and private schools, tracking and ability grouping, and teacher expectations. For instance, certain school policies can influence groups negatively. Testing tends to favor middle-class, white students; ability grouping falls along race and class lines. Teacher behaviors and expectations can also affect student achievement. All of these factors can influence the child's achievement and attainment in school.

Many ideas have been proposed to bring about change, including legislation, changing the financing of schools, and compensatory education.

Putting Sociology to Work

1. What evidence, if any, do you see in your community for "the crisis in schooling"?
2. Do you have evidence that your social class, race, subculture, or sex has affected your educational experience? Document. Talk with others about their experiences.
3. Describe examples of differences in educational achievement by race, sex, or class from data available for your community or for other communities. How would a structural-functionalist explain these differences? How would a conflict theorist do it?
4. Talk to teachers or school officials about school policies that influence stratification: testing, ability grouping, and teacher expectations.

Gender, Race, and Class
Attempts to Achieve Equality of Educational Opportunity

Tanisha's mother had always stressed that she should apply herself to schoolwork; she had purchased books, engaged herself in computer learning programs, and often spent evenings reading with Tanisha. When Tanisha entered kindergarten, her mother made sure to make herself known to her daughter's teacher, and volunteered as often as she could for trips and activities requiring adult participation. As Tanisha entered grade school, her mother made certain that she found out about who were the best teachers and what programs might be available for gifted students. She sought out community activities that encouraged academic achievement and enrolled Tanisha in cultural programs that were offered during the summer months and after school. As a result, Tanisha was one of the top achievers in her school district. When it was time to enter high school, her mother applied to the selective, college preparatory track at the best high school in her town.

During the last few years, however, a number of teachers and some parents had been exploring the benefits and costs of curriculum tracking in high school. They reviewed research and sought out other models of organizing students in classes. The research that they had consulted noted that tracked classes usually benefit the high achievers, but not the middle or lower achievers. The higher track classes had fewer disruptions and covered more material. In schools with diverse student populations, poor and minority students and recent immigrants were often placed in the lower tracks, thus reinforcing the already low levels of achievement these students experienced. In particular, these teachers and their supporters became convinced that heterogeneous grouping (mixing students of all achievement levels in the same classrooms) was a more equitable way of distributing educational services to students. With the school board's approval, the district decided to detrack all its high schools and implement a new, heterogeneous class system that required all students to take the basic academic curriculum.

Tanisha's mother was outraged; all her efforts for the previous eight years were being undermined by this new system. She had anticipated her daughter being able to enroll in advanced placement and other classes with other high achieving students. Her daughter had earned these opportunities by her devotion to school and years of hard work. Now the chance to be one of the top performers in the school, to be identified as prepared for the most selective colleges in the country, and to be eligible for the scholarships necessary to attend those institutions seemed to be disappearing in an attempt to level the quality of education all students received. How unfair!

Scenarios such as this are playing out in school districts across the country as they try to more equitably organize education but are faced with reactions such as these. As we address issues of gender, race, and class in this chapter, think about how they influence the work of schools.

African American and white, female and male, Hindu and Muslim, rich and poor—such dichotomies in our ascribed statuses also imply different points on the continuum of educational experiences and outcomes. The positions that individuals hold in the societal and educational systems are influenced by their race, sex, cultural background, and social class. These background factors affect the stratification within educational systems and society as a whole; the dynamics of systems cannot be understood without regard for such factors. In this chapter, we focus first on the experiences of females and males in the educational system and on how this influences the status and roles of men and women in society. (A distinction is made in most discussions between "sex," which generally refers to biological aspects of an individual, and "gender," which refers to sociocultural aspects that determine appropriate behavior patterns (Rothenberg, 1995, p. 8). Here we use the terms *sex* and *sex roles* to refer to both biological and sociocultural aspects.) In the second section, we look at some attempts to rectify the unequal treatment of racial, ethnic, and other minorities in the educational system and examine the results of these attempts.

GENDER AND EQUALITY OF EDUCATIONAL OPPORTUNITY

Boys and girls attending the same schools and classrooms come out with different experiences, interests, achievement levels, and expectations (Curran and Renzetti, 1999). Theoretical explanations and scientific research on the different educational experiences focus on socialization, the role of education in societies, and "biological destiny."

Sex-Role Socialization

The socialization process begins the day we are born and ends the day we die. Informal education is a continuous process throughout life; formal education—schooling—is restricted to certain periods (Vogel et al., 2003). Girls and boys have different socialization experiences from birth, and by the time they enter nursery school, most children already have a good idea of their gender identity from parents, siblings, TV, and other "socialization agents."

The socialization function continues to take place in schools, where students spend more than six hours a day in classes and school-related activities. Teachers and schools become important sources of information on sex-appropriate behavior; children learn by observing and imitating adult roles, including the roles of teachers and administrators. They observe the ratio of males to females and the authority structure in the educational hierarchy. They learn their own sex-appropriate behavior through positive and negative sanctions, as well as through textbook examples and pictures.

Children's toys play a major role in sex socialization as well. "Boys' toys"—toy trucks, chemistry sets, doctor kits, telescopes, microscopes, building blocks, and Legos—encourage manipulation of the environment and are generally more career-oriented and more expensive than "girls' toys" (Richmond-Abbott, 1992, p. 87). Parents are generally very conscious of buying sex-appropriate toys for their children. Toy choices carry over to children's play, and by the time young children reach nursery school, they have already learned to play with sex-appropriate toys. Popular video games also portray traditional gender role stereotypes, women as sex objects, and violence against women; in a study of 33 popular video games, no female characters were included in 41 percent, and women were seen as sex objects in 28 percent (Dietz, 1998). The characterization of women in popular culture has also been widely decried (see, for example, http://www.amplifyyourvoice.org/mysistahs).

Books are a major source of messages about sex roles, and sexism in textbooks has received a great deal of attention. Among the best known of the many studies done on readers and storybooks are those by a group based in Princeton, New Jersey, called *Women on Words and Images* (1988). They evaluated gender portrayal in children's readers and have updated their findings as new editions from 18 major textbook companies were released. Content analysis of texts examines the sex of the main character, illustrations, positive and negative images of men and women, stereotypes, and many other factors related to the portrayal of sex roles in the societal system. Recent analyses show improvements, but imbalances still favor males in rate of portrayal and types of roles assigned (Goodman, 1993; Heilman, 2001; Purcell and Steward, 1990). Children's picture books also show greater male representation in titles, pictures, and central roles (Tepper and Cassidy, 1999). Studies reveal that science, social studies, and even math books depict girls and women in stereotypical sex roles. For instance, math problems involving girls often show them jumping rope, buying clothes, sewing, cooking, or calculating the grocery bill (Goodman, 1993; Keifer and Sekaquaptewa, 2007). These socialization experiences influence what boys and girls learn about their gender roles. Though textbook publishers are improving accuracy in examples and coverage, many school districts cannot afford to buy the updated books (Cohen, 1992, p. A1).

Differences in behaviors begin early, when children as young as three-and-a-half start to influence their peers. Girls tend to be ignored by boys and even teachers and may stop trying to get attention. Girls form intimate "chumships," whereas boys relate through groups organized around activities, such as sports, similar to future job structures. Even speech patterns differ, with boys using speech for egoistic purposes and girls for social bonding (Hibbard and Buhrmester, 1998; Tavris, 1990, p. B5). Both Paley (1984) and Barrie Thorne (1993) have closely observed children's play in school and other settings and have both emphasized that gender organizes many of the activities of both girls and boys. For example, Paley asserts that "kindergarten is a triumph of sexual self-stereotyping" as children act to restrict their playgroups to members of the same sex. She also notices, however, girls have some advantages. The range of their acceptable behavior was wider than for boys—girls could engage in "boy behavior" without punishment, but boys could not do girl activities. Thorne found that this segregation had its limits. Her older children (middle-school aged) also segregated their playgroups, but she notes that some of the opposite sex were usually included. She argues that educators and parents can act to limit the hegemonic view of gender as an oppositional dualism that neglects cross-gender similarities. Martin's research (1998) provides good evidence that much of gendered nature of girl and boy play is socially constructed. She notes, for example, how girls' clothing is generally less comfortable and restricts movement more than boys' clothing and that pre-school teachers were likely to "manage girls and their clothing" "tucking in their shirts, fixing a ponytail gone astray" (pp. 489–499).

Girls and boys learn "hidden" sexist lessons (Sadker and Sadker, 1994, p. 2). For instance, boys are called on more, asked to solve problems, disciplined more, and have more interaction with teachers. The accumulated messages may lead girls to experience other problems and disorders including eating problems, harassment, pregnancy and dropping out, and low self-esteem. On the other hand, boys may come to view schools as a place where girls excel and thus associate academic achievement with female traits, reducing their likelihood of sustaining motivation for achievement (Willis, 1977). The "crisis" in boys' education represented by lower levels of male achievement, high school graduation, college enrollment and graduation has stimulated school reform efforts (Hu, 2007). This is not a new concern, as Sexton (1969) identified many of its elements almost 40 years ago.

The "boy problem" has received much attention in the last few years, with many writers addressing the issue of underachievement. While the increasing success of girls and women has also received attention, the apparent lack of success of boys is generating much concern. Some authors emphasize the biological differences between boys and girls, especially the different structures and chemistry of their brains (Gurian and Stevens, 2005). Arguing that current pedagogies and school structures are ill suited to the ways boys learn, these authors promote more "boy friendly" practices. Others come down more strongly on the nurture side of the debate, asserting that while there are important biological differences and propensities between girls, little solid evidence exists that can explain their differential academic achievements (Peg Tyre, 2008). Others argue that nature (biology) and nurture are not unrelated and that the debate diverts attention to the search for educational practices that benefit all learners, whatever their gender. Moreover, the debate has ignored the reality that there is much overlap in how girls and boys learn; there is at least as much variation among each gender as there is between them (Corbett, 2009).

Societies' stereotypes of male and female behavior are learned early in a child's life. Evidence of these stereotypes is apparent around the world. Statistics on enrollments and literacy rates for men and women exemplify the different societal expectations for the sexes (see Table 4.1). Of 50 countries with significantly fewer girls than boys enrolled in school, most are located in the poorest regions of South Asia, Africa, and the Middle East, according to a study by Population Reference Bureau (Crossette 2011); however, this discrepancy is declining. Girls' enrollment in primary school improved in the 1990s from 93 percent in 1990 to 96 percent in 1999. Eighty-six countries have already achieved gender parity and another 35 are close to doing so. The gender parity index (GPI) improved for all countries over the decade. But overall the GPI remained below 0.9 and in favor of boys in South and West Asia, the Arab States, and sub-Saharan Africa. Women's participation in secondary education, however, remains a fraction of men's in most poor countries (UNESCO, 2002). Without education, women cannot participate fully in the economic and political aspects of society, yet access to literacy and education remains a major problem for much of the world's population.

Table 4.1 Regional Literacy Rates for Adult Men and Women (15+)

	Males (%)		Females (%)	
	1985–1994	1995–2005	1985–1994	1995–2005
World	82.6	87.4	70.1	77.4
Africa	63.3	71.0	43.5	51.7
North America	95.9	96.2	94.6	95.2
South America	89.4	91.3	88.1	90.3
Asia	79.1	86.2	61.1	73.1
Europe	99.1	99.3	97.7	98.7
Oceania	94.3	94.3	92.9	92.8

Source: UNESCO. Available: http://stats.uis.unesco.org/unesco/TableViewer/tableView.aspx?Reportid=201 (Retrieved January 25, 2008). Regions based on UNESCO categories.

Sex Differences in the Educational System

The sex-role differences in education in the United States are not new. The Puritans in the United States discouraged literacy for women, except to ensure salvation by reading the Bible. After the American Revolution, it became the responsibility of women to teach young children and pass on moral standards; thus, a limited amount of education became acceptable, perhaps even encouraged, in a male-dominated society. This attitude is illustrated in the following quotation from a school observer in the 1880s:

> We noticed the boys all writing, but none of the girls; turning to our friend Tullis for an explanation, he said it was not safe for girls to learn to write, as it would culminate in love-letter writing, clandestine engagements and elopements. He said women were allowed to study arithmetic, though, for Miss Polly Caldwell studied as far as long division, and Mrs. Kyle, while a widow, got as far as reduction. He says Polly Caldwell was a weaver, and required the aid of figures to make her calculations for warping. (*History*, 1973)

Societal systems are dependent on schools to pass along crucial beliefs and values—among them, sex-role behaviors and expectations. In part, this occurs formally through courses and texts used in the curriculum or through the structure that assigns privileges and tasks by sex. But many of society's expectations are passed on through the informal or "hidden" curriculum (discussed in Chapter 8), including materials, activities, differential treatment, and counseling. Sex roles in schools mirror those in society. Our behavior and our expectations for each sex, from child-rearing activities to school expectations, are greatly affected by stereotypes (Rothenberg, 1995, p. 8). Stereotypes about male and female characteristics are fairly consistently held by members of our society: Girls are docile, gentle, cooperative, affectionate, and nurturing; boys are aggressive, curious, competitive, and ambitious.

Higher education presents a mixed picture for women. Although the numbers of women enrolling are increasing, this is not the case in all fields. In 1833, Oberlin was the first U.S. college to open its doors officially to women, but their education was restricted to domestic subjects. With the development of women's colleges in the mid-nineteenth century came women reformers and women professionals. Since that time, the picture has been one of steady advancement for women in education, with both all-female and coeducational schools and with their entry into a wide range of professions, but not all. Recently all-women's Smith College established an engineering school to provide opportunities for women in this field. In recent years, many of even the staunchest male institutions have become coeducational. One area that continues to be controversial is women's athletics. Ongoing lawsuits in higher education point out the discrepancies—universities give less support to women's athletics than to men's, and Title IX requires equal treatment (Suggs, 2005).

Over the past 20 years, the gap between the number of women and men going to college has disappeared for the 25- to 29-year-old age group (see Figure 4.1). In 2006, over 59 percent of those enrolled for a bachelor's degree were women. Women are enrolling in graduate education in increasing numbers and are strongly represented in education, health professions, and the social and behavioral sciences. Between 2003–2004 and 2015–2016, women are projected to increase their proportion of Master's degrees by 41 percent while men's proportion is projected to increase by 28 percent. Women earned more first professional degrees than men in 2004–2005 (see Table 4.2) (NCES, 2006, p. 78).

Despite their increasing numbers, women do not always receive respect for intellectual achievements. For instance, African-American intellectuals, especially women, are caught in a bind, living in a basically "anti-intellectual society." They often believe that their intellectual work is

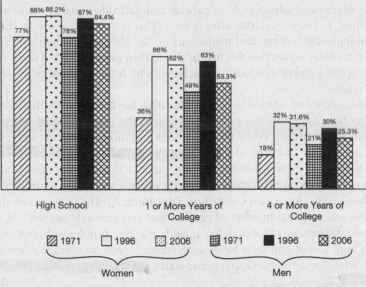

FIGURE 4.1 Percentage of 25- to 29-year-olds who have completed selected levels of education, by sex, March 1971, 1996, and 2006.
Source: U.S. Department of Commerce, Bureau of the Census, March Current Populations Surveys.

perceived as less valuable than that of activists (Hooks and West, 1991), though their contributions lay the groundwork for activism. "Be smart, but not too smart—and always expect confrontation with harsh realities" is the advice of one woman.

There is good evidence that girls and women are excelling in school, and that it is the boys who are dropping out in greater numbers and failing to equal women in higher education achievements.

Table 4.2 Percentage of Bachelor's Degrees Earned by Women and Men, by Field				
	1984–1985		**2000–2001**	
Major Field	**Female**	**Male**	**Female**	**Male**
Total	50.7	49.3	57.3	42.7
Biological/life sciences	47.8	52.2	59.3	40.7
Business	44.9	55.1	49.4	50.6
Computer science	36.8	63.3	27.7	72.3
Education	75.9	24.1	76.7	23.3
Engineering	13.1	86.9	19.9	80.1
Health professions and related sciences	84.9	15.1	83.8	16.2
Mathematics	46.2	53.8	47.7	52.3
Physical sciences and science technologies	28	72	41.2	58.8
Psychology	68.2	31.8	77.5	22.5
Social sciences and history	44.1	55.9	51.8	48.2

Source: National Center for Education Statistics, "Trends in Educational Equity of Girls and Women: 2004," 2005c, Table 29. NCES 2005–016.

Many statistics on educational participation and achievement now favor girls (Sommers, 2000). However, these educational advances do not always translate into equal access to all fields, better job opportunities, and equal salaries after school. This is especially true in the STEM areas (science, technology, engineering, and mathematics). Yet, girls and women continue to excel in school; Mickelson (2003) argues that this may be due to their perception that there are few alternatives, and there is still a payoff to educational achievement. It just may not be as large as the ones boys and men receive.

The predominance of women in higher education has become a matter of concern. More generally, many have lamented the relative decline in the proportion of our populace with higher educational credentials. While there has been a significant increase in higher education enrollments (detailed in Chapter 10), the rate of graduation has remained steady, and the United States has fallen below a number of other nations in graduates after leading for many years. Women now are about 57 percent of undergraduate enrollment, a number that has been steady since about 2000 (American Council on Education, 2010). Women earn the majority of Master's degrees and an equal number of professional and graduate degrees (ACE, 2010). The reasons for these differences are varied, but include pipeline problems: Males are less likely to graduate from high school and have lower achievement levels on average when they do; these differences are related to family socioeconomic status. The differences disappear for students at higher statuses (ACE, 2010).

Behavioral characteristics are clearly important as well. As Golden, Katz, and Kuzieko, (2006, pp.153–154) note: "Boys have a much higher incidence than do girls of school disciplinary and behavioral problems and spend far fewer hours doing homework. Controlling for these non-cognitive behavioral factors can explain virtually the entire female advantage in college attendance."

SEX-ROLE COMPOSITION OF SCHOOLS.   Major sex composition differences remain in the structure of educational systems. For instance, in the United States in 2003–2004, 68 percent of public school teachers were women; more elementary than high school teachers were women (NCES, *SASS*, Table 19).

The pattern of "the higher, the fewer" continues at the university level where 38.1 percent of the teaching faculty are women, primarily in lower ranks. Why do these inequalities exist? Socialization affects attitudes; structural barriers limit access. And the educational system is slow to change. For instance, socialization and the hierarchical and power structures of organizations have influenced women not to seek administrative responsibilities; interpersonal barriers confront aspiring women when they face the dominant power structure; organizational and institutional barriers occur during recruitment, selection, placement, evaluation, and other processes. Thus, at several levels women face obstacles to achieving higher positions in the structure.

Single-sex high schools and colleges have been dwindling since the 1960s, but research shows that they can provide support by separating academic from social concerns of adolescents. Some school districts are now considering single-sex classes in math and some sciences (Estrich, 1994, p. A11). Differences in learning styles and problems with teacher reactions to girls and boys could be eliminated with single-sex classes according to advocates. In academic achievement, achievement gains, educational aspirations, reduced sex-role stereotyping, and positive attitudes related to academics, single-sex schools have advantages. Recent federal rules are more tolerant of this form of segregation, and, especially in urban areas, a number of school districts are experimenting with all-male and all-female schools on the theory that the distraction of gender differences interferes with academic achievement (Riordan, 2002; Schemo, 2006).

As part of their efforts to address the "boy problem," already discussed, a number of urban districts are opening separate schools, often middle schools, for boys and girls. There is contradictory evidence about the effectiveness of these schools (Hubbard and Datnow, 2005). Like many educational innovations, it is very hard to isolate the factors that are responsible for the outcomes produced by the innovations. In this case, how much the fact of single-sex enrollment contributes to school effects must be carefully separated from other differences that may be introduced, such as curriculum, pedagogy, and school climate. There is evidence that when the right combination of school and teacher characteristics are present—e.g., a sense of brotherhood among the students, feelings of safety, culturally relevant and academically rigorous instruction, and ongoing professional development—at-risk boys can do very well in school (Martin, Fergus, and Noguera, 2010).

In higher education, research indicates that women at single-sex colleges have higher self-esteem and self-control than women from coeducational colleges (National Survey of Student Engagement 2007), though debate about the value of single-sex college education continues; evidence indicates that faculty members at coed institutions take male contributions to classroom discussions more seriously than those of females, and they permit males to dominate (Fiske, 1992, pp. 52–53). Studies at a formerly women's college that became coed indicated that there are now fewer overall interactions in all classes, which they attribute to a gender political environment (Canada and Pringle, 1995).

When all-women's Mills College in California decided to admit men, storms of protest arose. In this instance, the wishes of the students prevailed and the college remained all women. Without the social distractions of a coeducational institution and with norms of academic focus, encouragement to excel is stronger at single-sex institutions. Although no challenges have been through the courts, single-sex colleges may face "separate but equal" challenges in the future. Their chief problem, however, is that a limited number of women are willing to attend an all-women's college and thus their number is declining. According to a study carried out for what used to be Randolph-Macon Women's College, only 3 percent of female high school graduates would consider a single-sex institution (Salomone, 2007; also see her 2003 book).

EXPERIENCES AND ACTIVITIES IN SCHOOLS. Activities of persons in contact with children—parents, classroom teachers, administrators, and other school decision makers—also must be taken into account in understanding girls' experiences in schools. In elementary school, a child is most likely to have a female teacher. Although most classrooms are coeducational, many activities within the classroom are sex-linked. Evidence indicates that girls do not receive the same attention boys do; for instance, boys are encouraged to solve problems, whereas girls are given the answers. Thus, teacher actions reinforce sex stereotypes. Girls often are asked to water the plants and boys are asked to clean the blackboards. Children line up for activities by sex; even in discipline and in the amount of time teachers spend with children, there are sex differences. Studies find that boys receive more and harsher discipline, but also more teacher time and praise. Teacher expectations enter into differential treatment of students by sex as well as by class and race (National Association for Women in Education, 1996).

Activities reflect stereotypical attitudes, as exemplified by studies of classroom and playground play behavior. As early as preschool, girls' play is more cooperative, whereas boys' play is more functional or "purposeful" (Neppl and Murray, 1997). In fact, boys in elementary school come to believe masculinity is avoiding whatever is done by girls (Jordon, 1995). As one observer of playground activity writes:

Differences between the sexes are easily perceptible in the playground, always allowing for the presence of a few girls who are keen footballers and marbles players, and who are known (and accepted) as "tomboys," and a few timid little boys who stay under the protection of the older girls. Boys, in general, are more egotistical, enterprising, competitive, aggressive, and daring than the girls. They are comedians, exhibitionists. They do not mind making fools of themselves and provide most of the clowning that is such an important part of playground fun. They concentrate all their attention upon a game. (Opie, 1993, p. 7)

Many young women experience sexual harassment, usually from peers in school (see Box 4.1). In a recent study of students in grades 8–11, 83 percent of girls and 79 percent of boys experienced some form of sexual harassment, with sexual jokes, gestures, and comments most common, followed by touching or grabbing in a sexual way. The harassment takes a greater toll on girls who report feeling less confident and more afraid in school (American Association of University Women, 2001).

ACHIEVEMENT AND MOTIVATION: THE CASE OF MATH AND SCIENCE.   "Girls face pervasive barriers to achievement throughout their precollegiate schooling and are 'systematically discouraged' from pursuing studies that would enhance their prospects for well-paying jobs" (American Association of University Women, 1992). This finding came from a study in 1992, "How Schools Shortchange Girls." Since the report made the headlines, some change has taken place in math and science courses. Girls are taking more math and science courses, though not at the highest levels where there are still gender gaps, especially in physics and computer science. The computer science gap is particularly problematic as it is a "boys' club" in some schools (American Association of University Women, 1998; NCES, 1997).

BOX 4.1

Hostile Hallways

During your whole school life, how often, if at all, has anyone (this includes students, teachers, other school employees, or anyone else) done the following things to you when you did not want them to?

- Made sexual comments, jokes, gestures, or looks in your presence
- Showed, gave, or left you sexual pictures, photographs, illustrations, messages, or notes
- Wrote sexual messages/graffiti about you on bathroom walls, in locker rooms, and so on
- Spread sexual rumors about you
- Said you were gay or lesbian
- Spied on you as you dressed or showered at school
- Flashed or "mooned" you
- Touched, grabbed, or pinched you in a sexual way
- Pulled at your clothing in a sexual way
- Intentionally brushed against you in a sexual way
- Pulled your clothing off or down
- Blocked your way or cornered you in a sexual way
- Forced you to kiss him/her
- Forced you to do something sexual, other than kissing

Source: American Association of University Women, *Hostile Hallways: The AAUW Survey of Sexual Harassment in America's Schools,* 1993, p. 5.

An invisible "glass ceiling" begins in elementary and high school. The Gender Equity in Education Package introduced to Congress sought to redress these gender differences (Hegger, 1993, p. A5). In some science fields such as biology and biomedical sciences, females have surpassed males (see Table 4.3). Of the 2003–2004 bachelor's degree graduates in these subjects, over 62 percent were female. Recent reports of women's enrollment in science, engineering, and technology courses of study are encouraging. Massachusetts Institute of Technology (MIT), for example, reports that 38 percent of engineering students are female, up from 35.6 percent a year before. Renseelaer Polytechnic Institute has recorded a 54 percent increase in female enrollment over the last five years (Guess, 2007). This increase in enrollments around the country may well be attributed to a number of programs that have aimed to increase young women's interest in science, engineering, and other technical fields. A good example is the work of the Girl Scouts (see the website: http://www. girlsgotech.org). A review of these programs has been published by the American Association of University Women (2004).

On standardized test measures of achievement, the male and female scores depend on the content of the tests; girls do better in reading, writing, and literature, boys in math and science. Composite SAT and ACT scores are higher for males, though the gap is not great. In 2009, girls averaged 20.9 on the ACT test and boys, 21.3; on the SAT, the girls averaged 498 on the critical reading, and 499 on the math and writing sections, while boys averaged 503, 534, and 486 respectively (http://www.fairtest.org/university/ACT-SAT). High school females received somewhat higher science grades than males, but males tended to take more optional math and science courses than females (NCES, "High School Coursetaking," 2007c).

Most researchers theorize that the differences in mathematical achievement result from socialization and experiences of boys and girls. These experiences start as early as primary school. White males have been encouraged to be independent thinkers and can develop creative ways of dealing with mathematics rather than following rigid norms of math formulas. Many teachers expect boys to be better problem solvers and often ask them more high-level questions than girls, and high-achieving girls receive less attention than boys. A simple summary states that "males tend to attribute successes to internal causes and failure to external or unstable causes. Females tend to attribute success to external or unstable causes and failure to internal causes".

Table 4.3 Percentage of High School Graduates Taking Selected Mathematics and Science Courses

	1994		2005	
Mathematics and Science Courses	**Female**	**Male**	**Female**	**Male**
Mathematics				
Geometry	72	68	85	81
Algebra II	62	55	73	67
Trigonometry	18	17	8.6	8
Calculus	9	9	13	14
Science				
Biology	95	92	94	91
Chemistry	59	53	70	62
Physics	22	27	31	35
Biology, Chemistry, and Physics	20	23	26	28

Source: National Center for Education Statistics, *Digest of Education Statistics,* 2006, Table 139.

Women believe the stereotypes, just as do many minority students, that they are not as smart in math or science as their male counterparts though their scores are improving (Vedantam 2011). In an examination of the "gendering of math," Mendick (2005) describes how mathematics is considered a masculine endeavor and often those who are good at it are not very socially adept. Females who are strong at math are shown to often downplay their mathematics achievements so as not to be too closely associated with these stereotypes. The association of gender with subject matter undoubtedly affects student motivation to excel. Altering stereotypes, however, is not an easy process, especially when the adult role structure conforms to them.

Recent research on the "stereotype threat" provides a new angle on this issue. This research proposes that members of groups for whom strong stereotypes are present will feel stress when they are asked to perform a task that could confirm the stereotype. This stress interferes with their ability to perform the task and reduces their performance, thus confirming the stereotype (Spencer, Steele, and Quinn, 1999). This research has also included African-American group members, among others.

Parental support and involvement also influence attitudes toward math and science and other curricular choices in the United States and other countries. Parents with higher-socioeconomic status are more likely to be "active managers" of their children's school course selections (Lareau, 2003; Muller, 1998; Useem, 1991). These girls tend to have more advanced course work, which in turn contributes to social class reproduction (Useem, 1990). Cross-cultural studies of differences in parental support, teacher expectations, study habits, and values and beliefs that affect achievement indicate that girls in some countries excel in math. This is attributed to the country's gender stratification in education and occupational opportunities (Baker and Jones, 1993). For example, girls in Singapore, Japan, and Taiwan do much better in advanced math than American girls their age, and sometimes better than American boys. And over the past 30 years, American females have made tremendous gains in all scientific fields, including the most male-dominated ones (Ceci and Williams, 2006). Teaching styles also affect learning; math lessons in a Japanese school encourage children to think through the problem rather than give the answer. Comparative data show that female and minority students in the United States are not taught to think through a problem in other than a set formula or procedure.

This issue remains alive, as signaled by the American Association of University Women's report, "Why So Few?" Noting that there has been progress by women in science, technology, engineering, and math professions, the proportion of women major in these subjects in college is much lower than men. The report documents that women's achievements in math are considerable, yet they still lag behind men in selecting and completing college majors in these fields. The report also points to a number of cultural and organizational changes college and university departments and faculty could implement (Hill, Corett, and Rose, 2010). Attempts to narrow the gap between the mathematical performance of boys and girls have resulted in a plethora of innovative programs for teaching math and for attacking the problem from both attitudinal and organizational perspectives ("What We Know," 1993). For instance, according to a University of Michigan study, giving girls more "hands-on" lab work and reducing gender bias in texts can reduce the gender gap ("Science Study," 1995, p. E2). Positive female role models are another helpful way to increase young women's confidence in their abilities. As the socialization experience of students and school structural elements regarding math are altered in positive ways, we will continue to see positive changes and a narrowing of the gender gap in math and in the sciences (Committee on Maximizing the Potential of Women in Academic Science and Engineering, 2006).

Is there evidence that inborn characteristics are at the root of differences in educational experiences of girls and boys, that biological factors predestine some to success and some to failure by gender? Studies by sociobiologists look to possible biological factors to explain gender differences in girls' math and science ability, biological learning styles of each sex, and general intelligence of each sex. The problem with biological explanations is that they seldom give enough weight to the strong influence of cultural expectations and environmental constraints on students and, therefore, provide incomplete explanations when examined alone; evidence is still inadequate to draw conclusions about what role biology plays in sex differences in learning and achievement. Though researchers have looked for biological explanations for differences in math achievement, that does not explain Asian American women's relatively higher representation in science and engineering positions than the general workforce in the United States, let alone the significant achievement gains by all women in math and science courses in the last 30 years (Ceci and Williams, 2006). Explanations are found in culture and home environment.

Combating Gender Differences

Evidence indicates that subtle and blatant differences in treatment of girls and boys occur at all levels of the educational system. There is no one solution for dealing with these differences, but steps are being taken to lessen negative effects where boys or girls are disadvantaged by the system.

1. In teacher education, awareness of self-identity, stereotypes, and practices that commonly operate in the classroom can make teachers more sensitive to the formal and informal curriculum that perpetuates such practices. Simple changes in classroom practices are the easiest to tackle.
2. Dealing with concerns of women outside the classroom helps women learn in the classroom. Questions about relationships, career choices, violence, and futures are all concerns that impinge on the learning process (Gilligan, Lyons, and Hanmer, 1990, p. 26).
3. The Title IX program mandated that school districts provide a nondiscriminatory educational environment for students; the law covers admissions quotas by sex, different course offerings by sex, and athletic programs. Regulations for schools include analysis of existing programs and equal treatment of all students in courses, financial aid, counseling, services, and employment. In fact, many changes in school programs have been attributed to Title IX.

Probably the biggest impact of Title IX has been on men's and women's sports. Facilities, physical education equipment, and course offerings must be equivalent for men and women. In the 35 years since it was enacted, controversy over the implementation of this law has been steady. Recently, there have been debates over the specific details of how colleges can demonstrate that they are in compliance and the basis for claims that they are not (Powers, 2007). The consequences of these debates are not trivial. Since 1992, more than 350 men's sports teams have been eliminated at colleges around the United States and opportunities for men have dropped 12 percent, whereas opportunities for women have increased by 16 percent (Gavora and Schuld, 1999; for a thorough treatment of this topic, see Suggs, 2005).

Every institution in society has been affected by the changing roles of men and women. The changes are occurring rapidly, and we have not yet seen their end effect on education, other institutions, or equality of opportunity for women.

Opportunities in women's team sports have increased as a result of the Title IX program.

CLASS, RACE, AND ATTEMPTS TO RECTIFY INEQUALITIES IN EDUCATIONAL OPPORTUNITY

The question of how to achieve equality of educational opportunity is an issue considered by society's decision makers. The problems include disadvantage, poverty, and discrimination. Is it society's job to do something to correct the injustices suffered by racial minorities? One of the premises behind affirmative action is that it is.

Educational disadvantage stems from schooling, family, and community sources, which cannot be controlled by any individual student. There are demands for equal school facilities, experienced and trained teachers; equitable per pupil expenditures; an integrated racial composition; and preferential treatment, such as affirmative action, to make up for past inequities (Coleman, 1990). These demands will increase as minority populations grow.

Trends in Public School Enrollments

Dramatic shifts in public school enrollments are under way. In most states the number of white students will shrink, whereas the number of African-American and other minority students will increase (see Table 4.4). In 1972, minority children made up 22.2 percent of public school enrollment, with the largest minority, African Americans, at 14.8 percent, and Hispanics, at 6 percent. Today the picture looks quite different. In 2005, minority children made up 44 percent of public school enrollments, with African Americans comprising 17 percent of that group, Hispanics 21 percent, Asians 4.8 percent, and other groups small fractions of the total (NCES, *Digest*, 2009, Table 41).

Ninety-eight percent of the high school graduates in the District of Columbia are members of minority groups; and in California, Hawaii, Mississippi, and New Mexico, minority students became the majority in about 1995. In 2007, dropouts, students who were 16–24 who had not graduated and were not enrolled in school, varied by race/ethnicity, with 6.5 percent of whites, 11.2 percent of

Table 4.4 Percentage of Public School Enrollment by Ethnicity, 1966–2005					
	1966	**1976**	**1986**	**1996**	**2005**
Total Number	43,039[a]	43,714[b]	41,156[c]	43,775	50,000
Percentage					
White	80.2	76.0	70.4	62.5[c]	57.6
Total Minority	19.8	24.0	29.6	37.5[c]	42.4
Black	14.3	15.5	16.1	16.7	15.6
Hispanic	4.6	6.4	9.9	11.9	19.7
Asian	0.4	1.2	2.8	4.4[c]	3.7
American Indian	0.5	0.8	0.9	1.0[c]	0.7

[a]Number in thousands.

[b]Based on U.S. government projections that extended to 1997.

[c]Based on extrapolation of U.S. data and population reference data by author (Bouvier & Davis, 1982; Ornstein, 1984).

Source: From *The Condition of Education 1989*, Vol. 1 (Washington, DC: U.S. Government Printing Office, 1989), pp. 110–111; *Digest of Education Statistics 1976* (Washington, DC: U.S. Government Printing Office, 1977), p. 40; and *Projections of Educational Statistics to 2000* (Washington, DC: U.S. Government Printing Office, 1989), p. 5; *Conditions of Education Digest, 1999*, p. 152, Table 138; and *Condition of Education*, 2007, Indicator 3 and Table 5.1.

Blacks, 6.9 percent of Asian/Pacific Islanders, and 27.3 percent of Hispanics falling into this category NCES, Dropout and Completion Rates in the United States, 2007, NCES 2009-064.

The Underclass and At-Risk Students

The term *underclass* was coined by Gunnar Myrdal, a Swedish observer of American society, and was brought into current usage by William Julius Wilson. The ghetto underclass is characterized by "low aspirations, poor education, family instability, illegitimacy, unemployment, crimes, drug addiction, alcoholism, frequent illness, and early death" (Wilson, 1987, p. 4; also see Steinberg, 1995). It has also come to refer primarily to minorities.

However, some scientists disagree with the concept and its implications of "blaming the victim" for the problem; thus, underclass has become a political policy issue. Herbert Gans describes it this way: "On the right and the left, the former arguing that underclass behavior is the product of the unwillingness of the black poor to adhere to the American work ethic, among other cultural deficiencies, and the latter claiming that the underclass is the consequence of changes in the industrial economy" (Winkler, 1990, p. A5). One study of Hispanic populations points out that, despite poverty and deprivation, Hispanics do not have many of the traits associated with underclass, such as poor health indicators and family breakdown (Moore and Pinderhughes, 1993).

Research on Equality of Educational Opportunity

Although literature related to equality abounds, two studies stand out because of the impact they have made on the ensuing debate, and their comprehensive data collection, analysis, and contribution to understanding inequality: the Coleman Report (Coleman et al., 1966) and Jencks's study of inequality (Jencks et al., 1972).

THE COLEMAN REPORT.   The best-known study of desegregation is the Coleman Report. The Department of Health, Education, and Welfare hired Coleman and his associates to do a study 10 years after the *Brown* decision was handed down to determine the state of affairs in education.

Coleman's findings turned up both some expected results and some quite unexpected ones. Indeed, the report proved highly controversial, partly because it challenged some strongly held but untested assumptions about schools and education.

The purpose of the study was to evaluate opportunities and performance of minority students compared with white students. Coleman's survey extended to about 5 percent of the schools in the United States and covered 645,000 students at five grade levels. The children were given tests of several types; information about the children's backgrounds and attitudes was collected; and school administrators filled out questionnaires about their schools. Coleman's findings revealed a number of interesting points.

1. Minority students (except for Asian Americans) scored lower on tests at each level of schooling than did white students, and this disparity increased from the first to twelfth grades. Coleman attributed the disadvantage of minority students to a combination of out-of-school factors, many of which center on the family: poverty, parents' education, and other community and environmental factors.
2. The majority of children at the time of the report attended segregated schools. Teachers also tended to teach children of their own race.
3. The socioeconomic makeup of the school, the home background, and the background of other students in the school were factors that made the biggest difference in students' school achievement levels. This was a surprising finding and led to the recommendation that schools be integrated in order to have a racial-class mix of students.
4. Curriculum and facilities made little difference in student achievement levels—another surprising finding. In fact, school facilities turned out to differ very little across predominantly African-American or white schools.
5. White children had somewhat greater access to physics, chemistry, language labs, textbooks, college curricula, and better-qualified and higher-paid teachers, but the differences were not very great.

The findings have been tested and retested by researchers, and although there are variations in the results, Coleman's general conclusions have been upheld. It was these findings that led to Coleman's recommendation that one way to improve the academic achievement of poor and minority children would be to integrate the schools, putting minority children with white children to produce an environment for achievement and to provide educational role models. The study provided the impetus for increased efforts to desegregate, especially through the use of busing. Coleman's results regarding the importance of teachers and teacher characteristics have been challenged by some recent research. We will address this issue in Chapter 13.

JENCKS'S STUDY OF INEQUALITY.   Another famous and often-quoted study questions the use of schools to attain equal opportunity in society. In their report, Christopher Jencks and his colleagues reanalyzed the Coleman data plus many other data sets and argued that no evidence suggests that school reform can bring about significant social change outside of schools. A summary of Jencks's findings follows:

> [T]he evidence suggests that equalizing educational opportunity would do very little to make adults more equal. If all elementary schools were equally effective, cognitive inequality among sixth-graders would decline less than 3 percent . . . cognitive inequality among twelfth-graders would hardly decline at all and disparities in their eventual attainment would decline less than 1 percent. Eliminating all economic and

academic obstacles to college attendance might somewhat reduce disparities in educational attainment, but the change would not be large. (Aronson, 1978, p. 409).

Jencks points out that experience over the past 25 years suggests that even though the educational attainment gap between minorities and whites narrowed, economic inequality among adults continues to exist.

Jencks concluded that schools can do little to change people's status in society after graduation. Even school reform and compensatory education programs are not seen as effective in substantially changing the differences among adults. These conclusions both startled and angered educators and others; it is not pleasant to hear that schools make little difference. In the study, Jencks did not deny that schools are important for everyone—he did say that they cannot solve society's problems. He also concluded, as did Coleman, that the school achievement of children is dependent on one major factor—their families. Family background and attitudes toward education are primary determinants of school experience. Jencks argued that because school cannot achieve an egalitarian society and economic equality, we must redistribute income by changing the economic institution into a more socialistic system.

In further analysis of data, Jencks reports that family background accounts for about 48 percent of one's occupational status and 15–35 percent of income differences among individuals. The amount of education and family status are closely associated (Jencks and Phillips, 1998; Jencks et al., 1979).

Although the tests and retests of Coleman's and Jencks's conclusions come up with varied results, most uphold the importance of students' families and the backgrounds of peers. An important recent research report adds a new element to this conclusion, however. Douglas Downey, Paul von Hippel, and Beckett Broh (2004) clearly demonstrate that schools do, in fact, promote greater equality. While children are in school, they learn at about the same rate, even though they start and end the year at often very different levels of achievement: Everyone benefits from attending school. However, because of differences in learning over the summer months, inequalities are produced. Most students "fall back" in their academic achievement over the summer months, but more affluent children, who experience richer activities that their parents' resources can provide, fall back less, producing a gap in the September achievement levels that stay largely unchanged over the following academic year. Thus, if children were not in school, the gaps in their achievement levels would increase over the entire year. The gaps are held in check by attending school. In this sense schools are "equalizers," preventing the inequalities their family and community backgrounds produce from becoming as large as they otherwise might. The importance of desegregation in equal opportunity is discussed next, and the significance of school "climate" is discussed in Chapter 8.

The Battle over Desegregation

Poverty and racism have been ugly realities in the history of the United States. Kidnappings, lynchings, mob violence, and abuse could not stop protests against unfair treatment of large segments of the population. These problems were reflected in the school system as in every other part of society, and the schools developed as segregated institutions in much of the country.

When discussing desegregation, people often use two terms interchangeably; however, their meanings are technically different. "*Desegregation* of schools refers to enrollment patterns wherein students of different racial groups attend the same schools, and students are not separated in racially isolated schools or classrooms. *Integration* refers to situations in which students of different racial groups not only attend schools together, but effective steps have been taken to . . . overcome the disadvantages of minority students and develop positive interracial relationships" (Ornstein and Levine, 1985, p. 398).

Court Cases on Desegregation

In 1954, the Supreme Court pronounced its landmark "separate is not equal" decision in the *Brown v. Board of Education* case, a ruling that has been seen as a blessing by some and a curse by others. Has it made any difference in the education or social status of minority groups in our society? Ten years after the *Brown* decision, the courts still had made no rulings on what desegregation meant. Therefore, in 1964, the Civil Rights Act ruled that delays in desegregation were no longer tolerable. In order to achieve equality of opportunity, desegregation was ordered, meaning that schools had to have 20–30 percent enrollment from each group. Some major desegregation efforts, especially in the South, produced change, but large cities remained and became even more segregated. A 1973 court case in Denver ruled there was intentional segregation, and the city must change this pattern. This ruling led to change in other large cities as well, with most using busing of children to attain the goals. Patterns of enforcement have varied; however, and the rulings in test cases—from the Supreme Court down to district courts—have been inconsistent. Since the 1954 "separate is not equal" Supreme Court ruling, and the order to change with all deliberate speed, courts at every level have been busy interpreting the ruling for their districts. The picture remains muddled.

More than half a century has passed since the *Brown v. Board of Education* ruling. The U.S. Supreme Court rejected voluntary desegregation and required cities to initiate desegregation plans, but the national debate about desegregation continues. The pattern of segregation is like a patchwork quilt: Some areas have successfully desegregated, whereas others remain almost exclusively African American or white.

Early efforts to desegregate can be divided into five periods: first, the 1954 Supreme Court decision; second, the 1968 ruling requiring southern rural schools to adopt desegregation plans; third, in 1973, when desegregation moved from the South to the North and West when Denver was required to rectify segregation; fourth, the current court cases that are rescinding mandatory busing in some cities; and fifth, the emphasis on improving quality of education in minority schools. Minority schools are those that have 90 percent or more minority students, and in 1980 one-third of African-American students attended such schools (Orfield, 1983). Since then segregation has increased in our schools: In 2000–2001, 50.6 percent of black students attended schools whose enrollments were over 75 percent minority; 56 percent of Hispanic students were enrolled in such schools, while only 2.8 percent of whites were. By 2006–2007, the figures were 51.5 percent of black students, 57.3 percent of Hispanic students, and 3.3 percent of white students who attended schools with 75 percent or more minority students (NCES, *Condition of Education*, 2009, Table A-26-3).

The Coleman Report documented the extent of segregation in the nation's public schools and the benefits to children where integration had occurred. With these data, pro-integration forces stepped up efforts to force integration, bringing numerous cases before the courts. But by the mid-1980s, there seemed to be a slow but steady reversal of years of desegregation efforts.

A key trend in the 1990s was court cases that released school districts from court supervision of their desegregation efforts; several Supreme Court cases have approved dismantling of school desegregation plans, referred to as "unitary standards" (DeLacy, 1997). Examples include the following cases: *Board of Education of Oklahoma v. Dowell* (1991), *Freeman v. Pitts* (1992), *Missouri v. Jenkins* (1995), the Connecticut state case of *Sheff v. O'Neill* (1996), and *Wessmann v. Gittens* (1998). The results of the dismantling are that many students return to their segregated neighborhood schools. School segregation increased steadily in the 1990s, especially in non-Southern states (Weiler, 1998). This is because of a combination of dismantling plans, demographic changes caused by immigration (especially in urban areas), and the growth of suburbs. Hispanic students are more educationally isolated than African-American students (Orfield et al., 1997). More focus is being centered on access to education and within-school tracking as these affect academic performance of minorities.

The most recent Supreme Court rulings continue this trend. Voluntary desegregation plans used by the education authorities in Seattle, Washington (*Parents Involved in Community Schools v. Seattle School District No. 1*, 2007), and Louisville, Kentucky (*Meredith v. Jefferson County Board of Education*, 2007), were struck down by a 5–4 vote. The majority held that the use of race, even as a secondary factor in student assignment to schools, was illegal. The plans were of a type often called "controlled choice plans," which assign students to schools primarily by their choice and residence, but also limit the overrepresentation of students from one race to a faction close to the proportion of that group in the larger student population. This use of race, however, was seen by the majority as violating constitutional guarantees of equal protection. Asserting that the ruling was "faithful to the heritage of Brown," the majority all but ruled out any use of race in student assignment. While the dust is still settling on this ruling it seems clear that school authorities making efforts to avoid further racial segregation of the student populations will have to find other means to achieve that goal. The most widely discussed method at the moment is to employ a measure of student socioeconomic status in the assignment process (Kahlenberg, 2001). However, while income and race are correlated, family economic resources are a poor proxy for race, and in many cities, most of the students are poor whatever their race or ethnicity, so economic integration is not much easier to achieve than racial integration (Reardon, Yun, and Kurlaender, 2006).

Most recently, one of highly regarded voluntary plans in Wake County, North Carolina, which uses socioeconomic measures for creating more integrated schools, has been abandoned due to stiff community resistance. While there was wide support for the plan to equalize the distribution of children in schools by their socioeconomic status, other parents were very unhappy about their children being assigned to schools away from their neighborhoods. Since most neighborhoods are economically segregated, busing was necessary to equally distribute children among the schools. "We are giving the school system back to the families and taxpayers in this county," said a member of the school board voting for the new attendance plan (Aarons, 2010; Grant, 2009).

EXTENT OF THE DESEGREGATION–INTEGRATION PROBLEM. Social scientists have conducted more than 100 studies of busing and desegregation, with research focused on several primary questions:

1. Are desegregation plans accomplishing the goals of integrating schools, improving the quality of education for minority children, and improving relations between the races?
2. Are efforts to desegregate causing neighborhoods and schools to become more segregated because of "white flight" from the affected school districts?
3. What are the effects of integration on children's achievement and self-concept?
4. Can busing help accomplish the ultimate goal—equality of opportunity in society? Or are we piling our societal racial problems on a yellow school bus and shutting the door?

In some inner-cities, education officials, resigned to the growing segregation of schools, have tried to ameliorate the problem by instigating new, innovative programs for their minority constituents. This has led some to dispute whether "better but segregated" is just a return to "separate but equal." Concerned over the controversy about the importance and value of desegregation, a number of scholars, including Gary A. Orfield, presented a summary statement of social science research over the past 30 years. The findings fall into four areas and show the following:

1. The desegregation of a school district can positively influence residential integration in the community.
2. Desegregation is associated with moderate academic gains for minority-group students and does no harm to white students.
3. Desegregation plans work best when they cover as many grades as possible, when they encompass as large a geographic area as possible, and when they stick to clearly defined goals over the long haul.
4. Effective desegregation is linked to other types of educational reform. (Orfield et al, 1992)

A more recent study by Orfield from The Harvard Project on School Desegregation found that there was a significant decline in segregation in the South from the mid-1960s to the 1970s, followed by a stable period until about 1988, and an increase in segregation from 1988 to the present (Orfield, 2009; Frankenberg and Lee, 2002). This trend has also been documented in northern cities, such as Denver (Horn and Kurlaender, 2006).

Effects of Efforts to Desegregate Schools

What happens when minorities and whites go to school together? Are students helped or hurt? Studies have considered the interpersonal relations, the self-esteem of students, the academic achievement and social roles of both African-American and white students, and the effect of "white flight" on the communities involved. Volumes of information have been collected on each of these topics, and a Brief submitted to the Supreme Court for its most recent school desegregation rulings provides excellent summaries of this material from the American Educational Research Association (http://www.aera.net/uploadedFiles/News_Media/AERA_Amicus_Brief.pdf) and the material from the Civil Rights Project, now located at University of California at Los Angeles (http://civilrightsproject.ucla.edu/legal-developments/court-decisions).

SELF-ESTEEM, SELF-CONCEPT, AND ACHIEVEMENT.   Self-esteem is important to achievement in school. African-American children have been of concern to psychologists for many years because measurements of racial preference have shown that they lack a positive sense of racial identity and self-esteem. In a replication of studies conducted since the 1940s, questions about African American or white doll preference were asked. "Pick the nice, bad, pretty doll, and the one you'd most like to play with." Sixty-five percent of the African-American children and 75 percent of the white children preferred the white doll (Talan, 1987, p. E11). This finding is especially significant for African-American children in desegregated schools. The question raised is whether normally self-confident African-American students are less confident in integrated school settings. Study findings show that African-American students in integrated settings have lower self-confidence, self-esteem, and levels of aspiration than African Americans in less integrated schools, even though they do better, go to college more often, and are more successful in finding jobs and receiving higher incomes (Trent, 1997; also see Braddock and Eitle (2004) for a thorough review of the effects on minority student achievement of diverse school settings). And although schools may be desegregated, there is also concern about within-school segregation from tracking policies.

Student Goals, Aspirations, and Future Prospects

African-American students have high aspirations. Positive high expectations from teachers as well as parents can help aspirations become reality (Voelki, 1993). In fact, the high aspiration of African Americans may be responsible for the narrowing educational gap between them and whites, and those aspirations will continue to be useful to African Americans in making advancements (Cheng and Starks, 2002).

The effect of desegregation on aspirations and achievement has been an area of concern for researchers, especially because there has been a decline in African-American college entry compared with whites. Plans to complete four-year college programs increased for both African-American and white students, but the actualization of plans for African Americans and Hispanics rose and fell during the 1980s. Since the early 1990s, however, the percentage of 18- to 24-year-old youth enrolled in a degree-granting institution has generally grown: In 2003, 41.6 percent of white youth were enrolled, 32.3 percent of African Americans, and 23.5 percent of Hispanic youth (NCES, 2005, Youth Indicators, Indicator 22).

The norms that dominate in a high school influence what students believe is possible. Thus, African-American students in desegregated schools, especially males, have a higher likelihood of attending college and completing more years of schooling than do those from segregated schools. This is probably related to the aspiration and achievement levels at the schools and to available opportunities. African Americans who attend desegregated high schools also get better jobs than those from segregated high schools, and they have better chances for promotion (Trent, 1997; McPartland et al., 1985). Desegregation has been found to have a small positive effect on achievement in reading for African-American students but no effect on their achievement in mathematics (Schofield, 1995; McPartland et al., 1985). In summary, desegregation seldom lowers the achievement of minorities and most often raises it. Also, there is virtually no evidence that desegregation lowers the achievement levels of whites.

The results of numerous studies indicate that achieving the goals of integration and positive race relations will not be easy, but lessons from successful programs provide models for reaching goals. Key in these programs are good human relations within classrooms, use of cooperative learning to involve all students and reduce tracking, efforts to involve students in extracurricular activities, fair enforcement of clear rules, and positive involvement of parents and other community members.

"WHITE FLIGHT."   While citizens and policy makers were arguing over the effects of busing, social scientists began debating "white flight." Was busing or the threat of busing to achieve desegregation causing cities to become more segregated than before because whites were moving out of the cities to avoid school integration?

In 1975, James Coleman released some results of a new study. In it, he concluded that school desegregation contributed to "white flight" from big cities and was fostering resegregation of urban districts. Whites were leaving large- and middle-sized cities with high proportions of African Americans. Coleman and his supporters now seemed to be suggesting less integration and more segregation to remedy "white flight."

Table 4.5 (p. 132) illustrates the change in percentage of minority students in major city schools between 1968 and 2008. Other studies since Coleman's have revealed important variables related to "white flight" that account for much of the decline of the white population in large urban areas:

1. Higher birthrate of minority families, resulting in more school-age children
2. Economic and class differences in upward mobility with whites moving to suburbs
3. New minority families moving into urban areas
4. Discrimination against minorities in suburban housing
5. Differences in "white instability" related to percentage of African-American concentration. (McDonald, 1997)

Table 4.5 Minority Student Enrollment of the 25 Largest City School Systems, 1968–2008

City	1968		1978		1988		1998		2001	
	Student Enrollment	Percent Minority	Student Enrollment	Percent Minority	Student Enrollment	Percent Minority	Student Enrollment[a]	Percent Minority[b]	Student Enrollment	Percent Minority
New York City	1,063,787	54.2[c]	998,947	71.3	960,000	79.0	935,000	85	1,066,516	84.7
Los Angeles	653,549	42.6[a]	556,236	70.3	594,802	84.4	635,000	92	721,346	90.1
Chicago	582,274	61.5[a]	494,888	78.5	410,230	87.6	355,000	94	435,261	90.4
Philadelphia	282,617	61.0	244,723	69.0	191,141	76.5	160,000	81	201,190	83.3
Detroit	296,097	61.2	220,657	85.8	175,469	95.5	135,000	98	162,194	96.3
Houston	246,098	46.2	142,553	70.6	190,381	84.5	235,000	94	208,462	90.0
Dade County (Miami)	232,465	41.3	229,254	62.2	251,100	68.0	275,000	79	368,625	88.7
Baltimore	192,171	65.1	149,465	77.6	107,250	83.0	90,000	88	99,859	89.2
Dallas	159,924	38.4	133,289	66.2	131,582	81.8	145,000	91	161,548	92.2
Cleveland	156,054	57.9	103,627	67.6	73,350	76.0	60,000	85	75,684	80.7
Washington, DC	148,725	93.5	108,903	96.0	88,631	96.5	75,000	99	68,925	95.5
Milwaukee	130,445	23.9	95,502	49.4[c]	88,832	68.3	80,000	80	97,985	*
San Diego	128,914	21.7	115,007	38.3	117,057	58.6	125,000	70	141,804	*
Memphis	125,813	53.6	113,108	74.0	103,099	78.0	93,000	82		*
St. Louis	115,582	63.5	72,515	74.8	47,117[d]	80.7	40,000	88	58,230	*
Atlanta	111,227	61.7	76,625	90.5	61,718	93.4	55,000	96		*

District	1968 Enrollment	1968 % Minority	1980 Enrollment	1980 % Minority	1988–1989 Enrollment	1988–1989 % Minority	2000–2001 Enrollment	2000–2001 % Minority	Projected Enrollment	Projected % Minority
New Orleans	110,783	67.1	88,714	85.8	85,113	92.7	75,000	96	77,610	*
Columbus	110,699	26.0	82,691	36.8	65,160	50.4	55,000	60	64,511	*
Indianapolis	108,587	33.7	73,569	48.2[c]	50,143[d]	50.6	40,000	55	70,847	*
Denver	96,577	33.4	68,830	55.6	58,626	64.8	50,000	72	63,024	*
Boston	94,174	27.1	71,303	60.4	54,765[d]	75.5	45,000	85	63,024	*
Fort Worth	86,528	32.7	68,224	52.6	68,410	64.4	75,000	74	79,661	*
Albuquerque	79,669	37.7	81,913	46.7[c]	84,783	51.0	85,000	55	85,276	*
San Antonio	79,353	72.9	63,214	87.1	61,246	93.1	70,000	96	57,273	*
Newark	75,960	81.8	65,575	90.7	49,728[d]	92.3	40,000	95	*	*
Totals	5,468,072	51.9[e]	4,519,334	71.3[e]	3,863,027	85.8[e]	4,028,000[a]	87.2[e]		85.01

[a]Projections include a slight increase in student enrollments, most of it in California and Texas.

[b]Projections are conservative for minority enrollments, based on 50 percent or less of the growth rate between 1978 and 1988. The assumption is that most white flight has already occurred; however, immigration trends and family size of minorities will affect school enrollments.

[c]By 1980, these school systems (Milwaukee, Albuquerque, and Indianapolis) were more than 50 percent minority.

[d]From 1968 to 1978 the 25 city school districts were the largest city districts nationwide. By 1988–1989, Mobile (69,000), Fresno (65,500), Nashville (63,000), and Tucson (57,000) had replaced St. Louis, Newark, Indianapolis, and Boston in the top 25 list.

[e]Weighted percentage minority based on total population.

*Data not available.

Source: Ornstein, Allan C., "Urban Demographics for the 1980s," Education and Urban Society, August 1984, pp. 477–496; Ornstein, 1990, preliminary data from a nationwide survey, unpublished; reprinted in Ornstein, Allan C., "The Relationship of the School Organization to Minority Students," Peabody Journal of Education Vol. 66, No. 4, Summer 1984, published 1991; Date for 2001 from Young, B. A., 2002. Characteristics of the 100 Largest Public Elementary and Secondary School Districts in the U.S., 2000–2001 (Washington, DC: National Center for Educational Statistics, U.S. Department of Education, 2002), NCES 2002.

Court rulings have varied: In Denver, Boston, Memphis, and other cities courts ruled that "schools must be within 10 to 15 percent of the overall racial composition of the district," even if this requires busing. Other court rulings such as those in Dallas and Houston have allowed minority schools to remain segregated on the grounds that to integrate would be impractical. However, nonminority schools do have to desegregate (Levine and Levine, 1996, p. 266).

A national study evaluating the impact of school desegregation programs on white public school enrollment trends found that, comparing districts that desegregated with those that did not, desegregation enrollment trends are the same. Prior to desegregation, enrollments declined, and the largest decline occurred during the year of actual desegregation and increased racial contact. Districts with more than one-third African-American enrollment experienced twice as much enrollment loss (Wilson, 1985). Specific district-level characteristics associated with reduced white school enrollments include the proportion of African-American pupils in the district, implementation of minor desegregation programs, and substantial proportions of Hispanic pupils (Ornstein, 1991, p. 66). Otherwise, there is little evidence that desegregation promotes resegregation (Smock and Wilson, 1991). The most recent school desegregation ruling by the Supreme Court, however, takes away most tools that districts have used to encourage integration and the prospects for increasing segregation, which has already been rising in many urban areas, seem very strong (Frankenber and Lee, 2002).

The overall results of efforts to desegregate seem to be positive if measured in terms of benefit to most people. Because many schools remain predominantly minority, however, current efforts focus largely on instructional improvement in these schools and larger school reform efforts such as No Child Left Behind.

INTEGRATION ATTEMPTS

School districts have adopted numerous plans to work toward desegregation—redistricting, magnet schools, and busing and other student transfers, to name a few. In some cases, school districts have been desegregated, but separation exists within the schools. Segregated classes and tracks, minority groupings within classrooms, segregated athletics and extracurricular activities, differential discipline and suspension practices, and teacher assignments may all hamper efforts to integrate schools and classrooms (Metz, 1994).

Various steps have been taken to achieve educational equality within and between schools. The best known of these are the federally sponsored compensatory educational programs. The Elementary and Secondary Education Act was passed in 1965 with the expressed goal of improving the education of poor and minority children. Initially, $1 billion was appropriated, and the figure has continued to grow. Compensatory educational programs, funded primarily by federal government agencies, have included programs from preschool to higher education; the following describes several of these programs.

1. *Early childhood education.* Head Start and Follow-Through are the most common programs in this category. Whereas Head Start attempts to help disadvantaged children achieve "readiness" for the first grade, Follow-Through concentrates on sustaining readiness and supplementing in the early grades whatever gains are made by the children who have had a year's experience in Head Start. The children in those early childhood programs, which encourage child-initiated activities rather than teacher-directed activities, showed more short- and long-term academic and social development, and the children in these programs achieved benefits that the many unserved but eligible children did not (Schweinhart, 1997). These programs remain important tools in the effort to narrow the achievement gaps among American students.

2. *Bilingual education.* An estimated 3 million public school students cannot do regular work in English. The Supreme Court ruled that states must assist limited-English-proficient students, but it did not indicate how; states have developed a variety of programs, from bilingual education to English as a Second Language training. In 1997, 11 states mandated bilingual education programs, and 3 forbad bilingual education (Garcia and Morgan, 1997). Emphasis and content of these programs vary, but they commonly focus on children whose native language is not English.

Spanish-speaking children are the major target groups in these programs. Debate surrounding bilingual education centers in part on the best way to integrate non-English-speakers into American society (McGroarty, 1992, pp. 7–9). How people attain literacy in a second language is influenced by their culture and the social context in which the language training takes place. Effective programs will take this into consideration in developing methods of instruction. One concern among those teaching English as a second language is how long federal funds should support children in bilingual programs; the current limit is five years, but many argue that more time is needed to integrate students into regular classes (Schmidt, 1992, p. 21). There is great demand for teachers who can teach bilingual classes, and many schools are having difficulty filling these positions; in California alone, 8,000 additional bilingual teachers are needed (NCES, "High School Coursetaking," 2007; Office of Bilingual Education and Minority Languages Affairs, 1996).

3. *Guidance and counseling programs.* Various social, psychological, and vocational services have been provided for the disadvantaged. Social workers and community aides have been involved in helping to bridge the gap between the school and home.

4. *Higher education.* Special programs in higher education include the following: (a) identifying students with college potential early in the secondary schools and enriching their program; (b) accepting special provisions and lower academic requirements for college admission; (c) using admission criteria that allow open enrollment, whereby every high school graduate has the opportunity to attend a two-year or four-year college, thus favoring low academic achievers who might not otherwise be granted admission; (d) transition programs to increase the probability of success for disadvantaged youth once admitted into college; and (e) special scholarships, loans, and jobs based solely on financial need and minority status (Ornstein and Levine, 1985, pp. 546–548; also see the U.S. Department of Education site for the TRIO Programs, http://www.ed.gov/about/offices/list/ope/trio/index.html).

Special programs also help schools revise curricula, pay for instructional materials, hire auxiliary personnel for tutoring, and provide adult education programs.

There are other, less tangible results of compensatory education. Upward Bound is a federal program to help disadvantaged students prepare to enter and succeed in college (http://www2.ed.gov/programs/trioupbound/index.html). Students enter the program in their first or second year of high school and can remain through the summer after high school graduation. The program provides instruction, tutoring, and counseling. Statistics have revealed mixed results on achievement, indicating that many students stay in the program only a short time, and the program has little impact on high school graduation rates. However, it may impact students' postsecondary plans and experiences. Despite the inconclusive impact of the program, young minority and white students who have never before met children of other races live and study together, play together, and make new friendships. The overall atmosphere is cooperative. Gaining Early Awareness and Readiness for Undergraduate Programs (known as GEAR UP, http://www2.ed.gov/programs/gearup/index.html) is another federally funded program aimed at helping low-income high school students prepare for college. Many of these programs are held on college campuses where the students not only experience a campus atmosphere but also live in dormitories away from home. These students might not have seen college life as a possibility before this experience.

On the pessimistic side, some (e.g., Levine and Levine, 1996) believe that compensatory educational experiences do not provide significant results toward societal change and are insufficient to counteract the existing differences. Schools reflect and reinforce prejudices of the outside world, which cannot be equalized by special programs, improved teacher quality, or other patchwork remedies. A recent evaluation of comprehensive school reform models put in place at a number of Title 1 funded schools found essentially no difference in the achievement of their students from the achievements of students at a group of matched schools not adopting the new models, throwing into question whether current models of school reform can compensate for differences students bring to school from their homes and communities (Good, Burross, and McCaslin, 2005). We return to this question at the end of this chapter.

EDUCATIONAL EXPERIENCE OF SELECTED MINORITIES IN THE UNITED STATES

We have discussed minorities in general terms, lumping all groups together, but focusing mainly on African Americans. There are, however, unique differences in the problems facing specific groups. For instance, children of migrant farmworkers have little chance of receiving a consistent or continuous education, though mobile school programs have been set up to move from camp to camp with the migrants. Children whose native language is not English suffer from that limitation in the middle-class American school. Bilingual programs are provided in areas with a concentration of non-English-speaking groups—for instance, schools with heavy concentrations of Mexican American and Puerto Rican children. Influxes of Southeast Asian, Cuban, and Haitian refugees also have created a need for special language and culture programs.

Hispanic Students

Today close to half of America's population growth comes from immigration, primarily of Hispanics and Asians (Macionis, 2000). Hispanics are the fastest-growing ethnic group in the U.S. public schools, doubling over the past two decades from 6 percent in 1973 to 15 percent in 1997, and increased to 21.1 percent by 2007 (NCES, *Digest*, 2009, Table 41). Segregation of Hispanic students rose dramatically between 1970 and 2005, with 77.3 percent attending predominantly minority schools in 2005 (see Table 4.6). Almost 40 percent were in schools with minority populations of more than 90 percent that year. With the increase in numbers has come an increase in segregation in states with the highest Hispanic population. The average age of Hispanics is much younger than that of whites because of high birthrates and youth immigration. Hispanic preschool-age children are less likely than white or African-American preschoolers to be enrolled in school, but the difference evens out in kindergarten ("Hispanic Education Fact Sheet," 1999).

Although Spanish-speaking residents are often grouped under the label "Hispanic," there are differences among the groups, with Cubans and some other Latin Americans faring well in school compared with whites, Puerto Ricans, and Mexicans and some groups from the Caribbean, including Dominicans (Velez, 1994). Two factors stand out concerning Hispanics and schools.

| Table 4.6 | Percentage of Hispanic Students in Predominantly Minority and 90–100 Percent Minority Schools, 1968–2005 | |

Year	Predominantly Minority	90–100% Minority
1968	54.8	23.1
1970	55.8	23.0
1972	56.6	23.3
1974	57.9	23.9
1976	60.8	24.8
1978	63.1	25.9
1980	68.1	28.8
1986	70.0	33.0
1992		34.0
1998	75.6	36.7
2005	77.3	38.7

Source: Orfield, Gary, *Public School Desegregation in the United States, 1968–1980* (Washington, DC: Joint Center for Political Studies, 1983), p. 4. U.S. Department of Education data; *The Condition of Education,* 1995; and *Digest of Education Statistics,* 2005, Table 94.

First is the issue of increasingly segregated schools, and second is bilingual education (Moore and Pinderhughes, 1993; San Miguel, 2004).

The gradually increasing segregation leads to several results: As the number of Hispanics in an area grows, their percentage in school grows; many are concentrated in urban areas that are losing white population. Language and cultural barriers may limit interaction with others and encourage concentrations. High school dropout rates of Hispanic students are more than four times that of white students—27.3 percent of 16- to 24-year-olds who were not enrolled in school and had not completed high school versus 6.5 percent of non-Hispanics (NCES, Dropout and Completion Rates in the United States: 2007, NCES 2009-064); but, as many Hispanic youth are immigrants, these statistics can be misleading. The dropout group needs to be divided into those who have spent much or all of their schooling in the United States and those who immigrate after having left school in their native country. The native-born Hispanic dropout rate is about 14 percent (and has been declining), while the rate for immigrant Hispanic youth is over 30 percent. "Of the 529,000 16 to 19 year old Latino high school dropouts in 2000, one-in-three, or roughly 175,000, are immigrants who had little or no contact with U.S. schools. Nearly 40 percent of immigrant Mexican 16 to 19 year olds are dropouts, while the dropout rate for Mexican immigrants educated in U.S. schools is 20 percent" (Fry, 2003). It is important to note that Mexican Americans born and raised in the United States often fare as well as their classmates from other backgrounds.

BILINGUAL EDUCATION. A concentration of Hispanics means that many children are surrounded by Spanish-speaking people in their schools as well as their homes. The controversial issue of bilingual education has been debated for a number of years, not only for Hispanics but for other language minorities as well. Should state and federal governments provide special funds to teach minority children in their own languages? Will teaching in native languages help or disadvantage minority children? What will be the results for states and the nation?

Many argue that teaching children in their native languages hurts them in the competitive system and that English facility is crucial to get ahead (Levine and Levine, 1996, p. 324).

Others argue that children are disadvantaged by being taught in a language they do not know, that they wish to retain their cultural language, and that they resent being considered "unacceptable" the way they are. The debate continues even in minority communities. Nationally, almost 8 percent of all public school students received English Language Learner services, which include bilingual courses (NCES, 2003, Table 10). The current thinking seems to favor two-way bilingual education that gives English-speaking children and other native speakers the chance to learn in both languages; this policy is being implemented in California (Garcia, 1993). A study of Mexican American middle-school students found that those who were proficient in both English and Spanish had better grades and higher numbers of credits at the end of ninth grade than those from limited English or English-only backgrounds (Rumberger and Larson, 1998). Most students that were studied wanted to learn English, and only a minority remained fluent in their parents' language after a generation (Portes and Hao, 1998). The educational achievement of non-native English speakers, often referred to as English Language Learners (ELL students), are now caught up in debates over the provisions of the No Child Left Behind Act. This legislation requires schools to test groups of children and measure the degree to which they are making "adequate yearly progress" toward the standards set by each state. While most of the attention about this provision of the law has been devoted to racial and ethnic groups, non-English speakers are a group over which controversy has developed since including them as a separate group may make achieving the yearly goals more difficult (see the resources at the Center for Applied Linguistics, http://www.cal.org/topics/ell/).

Most recently, the method of identifying students in need of ELL services and means of providing it—in four-hour pull-out sessions—in Arizona has come under scrutiny from a federal court case, (*Miriam Flores v. State of Arizona*, 2007) and by the U. S. Office of Civil Rights (Zehr, 2010). Essentially the dispute is over whether Arizona is identifying all student in need of the services (by undercounting, they save money, the argument goes), and whether the pull-out program deprives the students of educational content they need, such as math and science (prolonging their ability to graduate on time). These are complicated and difficult issues that, given the level of immigration we now have, will continue to challenge educators for a long time to come.

Immigrants

Immigration is the "sincerest form of flattery"; people select a country because it is desirable (Rumbaut, 1995, p. 307). Much recent immigration stems from Africa, the former Soviet bloc countries, Kurds from Northern Iraq, the former Yugoslavia, from Central America, and from some Asian countries. Immigration often starts because of wars or military occupations, and economic problems and opportunities; once families are established in a new location, other members join them, expanding the immigrant community in the new location (Cammarota, 2005).

Most immigrant parents encourage their children to work hard and get good grades in the schools in their new homeland as means of getting ahead; children may believe adjusting socially is more important, and these two ideas can be contradictory (Ogbu, 1991). Children's ethnic identities influence their self-esteem and assimilation into the culture, and hence their attitude toward schooling (Rumbaut, 1994).

The United States is the world's leading immigration country, with about 35 million legal and illegal migrants, more than twice the number of any other country (Bean, Brown, and Rumbaut, 2006). Immigration accounts for one-fifth of the population growth in the past decade in the United States (Stewart, 1992), mostly from Latin America (especially Mexico and Cuba) and Asia (especially Southeast Asia). In recent years, the proportion of immigrants from Latin America and the Caribbean has been close to 48 percent; from Asia, 35 percent; and from Europe and Canada, 17 percent

Table 4.7 The Shifting Profile of Immigrants to the United States, 1951–2005							
Area of Origin	**1951–1960**	**1961–1970**	**1971–1980**	**1981–1990**	**1991–1993**	**1997**	**2005**
Europe and Canada	67.7%	46.3%	21.6%	12.5%	13.1%	18.4%	17.7%
Asia	6.1	12.9	35.5	37.5	30.0	26.5	35.7
Latin America and the Caribbean	24.6	39.2	40.3	47.1	49.9	61.5	48.2

Source: Rolph, Elizabeth, *Immigration Policies: Legacy from the 1980s and Issues for the 1990s* (Santa Monica, CA: The RAND Corporation, 1992); U.S. Department of Justice, 1991a; U.S. Bureau of the Census, 1995; U.S. Bureau of the Census, March 1997; Current Population Survey, Internet release date: October 5, 1999; and U.S. Bureau of the Census, The 2007 Statistical Abstract: The National Data Book, Table 8.

(Aguirre and Turner, 2001, p. 227) (see Table 4.7). The 1990 immigration law not only increased by 40 percent those permitted to enter but it also allowed more Europeans and Africans to enter. This means more and diverse students and faculty from abroad will be part of the U.S. educational systems. The law also requires that immigrants have contacts for employment or a skill to obtain employment, allowing them to become mobile in the society. Each group has a different history of why they immigrated and their experience in their new country (Sowell, 1994; also see Portes and Rumbaut, 2001).

A study of the educational aspirations and attainment of eighth- and ninth-grade immigrant children, both native- and foreign-born, resulted in the following findings: Three-fourths of the sample from a wide variety of immigrant groups preferred speaking English, the exception being Mexicans living near the border. Some groups—particularly Asians (Chinese, Japanese, Koreans, and Indians), followed by Vietnamese, Filipinos, Cubans, and Colombians—have high educational attainment and aspirations as shown by scores well above the norms on mathematics and other standardized tests. Below the national norms were Hmong, Mexican, and Cambodian immigrants, also reflecting socioeconomic status of the families. The Hmong, however, received very high grade point averages (GPA), compared to many other groups, and did more hours of homework. Immigrant groups as a whole outperform native-born American students in GPAs (Rumbaut, 1996, pp. 23–24).

Immigrant children have a number of impediments to their educational success. First is learning academic English, a task that often takes as many as seven or eight years (Suarez-Orozco, Suarez-Orozco, and Todorova, 2008). Learning the norms of the new country often leaves newcomers feeling alienated and disconnected with their new environment. Frequently, these factors lead to a decline in academic performance after several years of residence (Suarez-Orozco, Suarez-Orozco, Todorova, 2008). In the *Learning in a New Land* study, the Suarez-Orozco and their collaborator Todorova found that only 24 percent of their sample of immigrant youth could be said to thrive in school. Yet in their study of second-generation immigrants in New York City, Philip Kasinitz, John H. Mollenkopf, Mary C. Waters, and Jennifer Holdaway find largely positive results. For example, "*All* the second generation groups earn as much or more than the comparable native born group." (2008, p. 343). "We often attribute drive and creativity to the self-selection of immigrants, or to ethnicity itself, but the real second generation advantage comes from being located between two cultures" (*Inheriting the City: The Children of Immigrants come of Age.* Harvard U P, 2008). This position increases the options and choices available to those who occupy it.

Several issues become important in the new immigration wave. Each skilled immigrant who enters a new country is creating a "brain drain" in the country of origin. New immigrants have different needs, and schools are often forced to take into account different value systems and behavior patterns. Language barriers create challenges for school districts, and the issue of illegal immigrants raises questions about the educational rights of these groups.

Asian American Students

The list of Asian American cultures and languages is extensive—Chinese, Filipino, Hawaiian, Korean, Japanese, and many more—making categorization difficult. Asian Americans make up about 5 percent of the U.S. population, with 14.9 million in 2006 (Asian Nation, 2008). By 2050 the estimated population of Asian Americans will be about 33.4 million. More than 800,000 Southeast Asian refugees—Vietnamese, Cambodians, Laotians, and Hmong—have come to the United States since 1975. They now number more than 1 million. California has 40 percent of this population. Because their values differ from those of Americans in some key areas that affect education, it is important for educators to be aware of these differences and work with them. For instance, "filial piety," unquestioning loyalty and obedience to parents and other authority figures, means that some parents do not attempt to see teachers; yet it is important to have parental involvement to help children. Several factors are directly related to parental involvement: level of literacy, educational level, and perceptions of what the school expects (Marschall, 2006).

Asians often come from large, tightly knit kin groups; the largest groups are the Indochinese and Filipinos. There are significant differences among Asian groups, with Vietnamese children generally most successful (Blair and Qian, 1998; Rumbaut and Ima, 1987). Because close families and education are highly valued in many Asian cultures, especially those with a Confucian value system that emphasizes family closeness to achieve shared goals (Caplan, Choy, and Whitmore, 1993), students are cooperative and teachers are held in high esteem. The general attitude is that Asian students are good students, and schools with high percentages of Asian students are good. Yet this "model minority" stereotype is, like all stereotypes, only partly accurate (Lee, 1996, 2005).

Despite language barriers, Asian students as a group outscore other minorities, native-born white students, and international students on the International Assessment of Educational Progress and National Assessment of Educational Progress standardized examinations (Bracey, 1998; Levine and Levine, 1996, p. 312). Many Asian students take more courses in foreign languages, mathematics, and natural science than other students. Asian American students are also overrepresented in college-preparatory programs and in gifted-and-talented programs in high schools.

Explanations for the high educational achievement of Asian American students, and Chinese Americans in particular, are related to these groups' traditional family values and values placed on education, especially parents with advanced educations themselves; favorable socioeconomic characteristics; and small-business owners who believe education is a channel of intergenerational mobility (Goyette and Xie, 1999; House, 1997). Chinese Americans were among the most successful groups in the Kasinitz, Waters, and Holdaway study, *Inheriting the City*, referred to above.

Recent studies, however, are showing that with successive generations in American society, the Asian American achievement differential is coming more in line with white student achievement, rather than exceeding it (e.g., Goyette and Xie, 1999). This may be caused in part by successive strains on the close-knit family and community, and by integration into the dominant peer-group value system.

Native American Students

The case of Native Americans is unique. When colonists first settled in the United States, Native Americans spoke more than 2,000 different languages, 300 of which are still spoken today. At first, missionaries provided education, but by the 1890s education was under government control (Chavers, 1991, pp. 28–29). The government and churches believed it was their duty to "civilize the Indian population," to eliminate their linguistic and cultural differences. They were relegated to poor land, and today many live in poverty as a result of low incomes, poor education, and unemployment or underemployment.

In the early nineteenth century, Congress appropriated monies for a "civilization fund." Boarding schools were established to remove children from tribal and family influences and assimilate them into American culture (see Reyhner and Eder [2004] for an excellent history of American Indian education). In 1928, the "Meriam Report" (Report of the Board of Indian Commissions, 1928, pp. iii, 41) questioned the government's "respect for rights of the Indian . . . as a human being living in a free country," criticizing the government policy of boarding schools, where 40 percent of Native American children were enrolled.

Gradually policies changed; schools became day schools, and bilingual Native American teachers were employed. In 1968, the then president Johnson urged putting control of Native American schools into Native American hands, and in 1972 the Indian Education Act was passed, allowing tribes to control and operate their schools. For the most part, this shift has taken place, and it seems unlikely that control will revert again to the Bureau of Indian Affairs. In one plan, the Choctaw Indians have been given complete control of educational programs on a Mississippi reservation, and they have built a new, modern school. The result of this local autonomy from the Bureau of Indian Affairs is that educational programs are geared toward the needs of the community; more students are attending and staying in schools longer (Johnson, 1995).

In the early 1990s, more than 80 percent of the approximately 300,000 Native American students were in public schools, many in major cities. Others were in tribally contracted schools. Parental involvement is low in non-Native American-controlled schools, absenteeism is high, and the dropout rate for high school students is near 15 percent (NCES, *Condition*, 2010, Table A-19-1).

Of the American Indian/Alaska Native 1992 12th-graders who were likely postsecondary participants, 11 percent received a bachelor's degree as their highest degree by 2000 versus 31 percent for the total population of likely postsecondary participants. American Indians/Alaska Natives were less likely to have received a bachelor's degree by 2000 than white (34 percent), black (24 percent), and Asian/Pacific Islander (34 percent) students who were likely postsecondary participants (Indicator 7.4). The picture is not all bleak, however. Some groups have increased high school graduation rates and college attendance, and tribal colleges are meeting the needs of many students (Johnson, 1995). Academic success in college is greatest for students who have family support, student support services, and precollege preparation programs such as Upward Bound; the highest failure rates for college students are related to financial problems and cultural differences (Jenkins, 1999; Kastl, 1997).

In order to improve the educational and other opportunities for Native Americans, some tribal leaders have established businesses on reservations, including gambling casinos. Some, though not all, have been successful in bringing needed dollars to tribal coffers.

The clash of cultures experienced by Native American children in the traditional school setting is described in Box 4.2. In order to meet the needs of Native American children, educators need to understand the cultures and be sensitive to the needs of these children, as for all children by planning appropriate student-centered curricula, holding high expectations, and maintaining good home–school relations.

Special Education Students

Which children can attend regular classrooms, and which should be separated for part or all of their education? This question of school and classroom organization and where students with

BOX 4.2

An Indian Father's Plea by Robert Lake (Medicine Grizzlybear)

Dear Teacher,

I would like to introduce you to my son, Wind-Wolf. He is probably what you would consider a typical Indian kid. He was born and raised on the reservation. He has black hair, dark brown eyes, and an olive complexion. And, like so many Indian children his age, he is shy and quiet in the classroom. He is 5 years old, in kindergarten, and I can't understand why you have already labeled him a "slow learner."

He has already been through quite an education compared with his peers in Western society. He was bonded to his mother and to the Mother Earth in a traditional native childbirth ceremony. And he has been continuously cared for by his mother, father, sisters, cousins, aunts, uncles, grandparents, and extended tribal family since this ceremony.

The traditional Indian baby basket became his "turtle's shell" and served as the first seat for his classroom. It is the same kind of basket our people have used for thousands of years. It is specially designed to provide the child with the kind of knowledge and experience he will need to survive in his culture and environment.

Wind-Wolf was strapped in snugly with a deliberate restriction on his arms and legs. Although Western society may argue this hinders motor-skill development and abstract reasoning, we believe it forces the child to first develop his intuitive faculties, rational intellect, symbolic thinking, and five senses. Wind-Wolf was with his mother constantly, closely bonded physically, as she carried him on her back or held him while breast-feeding. She carried him everywhere she went, and every night he slept with both parents. Because of this, Wind-Wolf's educational setting was not only a "secure" environment, but it was also very colorful, complicated, sensitive, and diverse.

As he grew older, Wind-Wolf began to crawl out of the baby basket, develop his motor skills, and explore the world around him. When frightened or sleepy he could always return to the basket, as a turtle withdraws into its shell. Such an inward journey allows one to reflect in privacy on what he has learned and to carry the new knowledge deeply into the unconscious and the soul. Shapes, sizes, colors, texture, sound, smell, feeling, taste, and the learning process are therefore functionally integrated—the physical and spiritual, matter and energy, and conscious and unconscious, individual and social.

It takes a long time to absorb and reflect on these kinds of experiences, so maybe that is why you think my Indian child is a slow learner. His aunts and grandmothers taught him to count and know his numbers while they sorted materials for making abstract designs in native baskets. And he was taught to learn mathematics by counting the sticks we use in our traditional native hand game. So he may be slow in grasping the methods and tools you use in your classroom, ones quite familiar to his white peers, but I hope you will be patient with him. It takes time to adjust to a new cultural system and learn new things.

He is not culturally "disadvantaged," but he is culturally "different."

Source: Lake, Robert, "An Indian Father's Plea," *Teacher Magazine* Vol. 2, September 1990, pp. 48–53. Reprinted with permission from the author.

disabilities fit into this environment has stimulated both commentaries and research. In order to be classified as disabled, a child must have a health condition or impairment that limits the ability of the child to perform a major life activity for an extended period of time. Conditions include learning disabilities; speech, hearing, orthopedic, and visual disabilities; mental retardation; serious emotional disturbance; and other forms of disability.

The era of the special education student began with the 1975 passage by Congress of PL 94–142, the Education for All Handicapped Children Act. It stated that all children with disabilities must be educated in the "least restrictive environment" possible. More recently, PL 99–457 (the Individuals with Disabilities Education Act) has been added, requiring school districts to educate all disabled children between the ages of 3 and 21. The interpretation of these laws and how to carry out their intentions have varied greatly, but they brought to the attention of educators and the public the importance of considering each child's special needs and then designing programs suited to them.

Under the federal acts, about 13 percent of all children from birth to 21 years (most between ages 6 and 17) qualified for services under either Chapter 1 or Part B programs. This figure has steadily risen from 1976, when it was 8.3 percent of all students, until about 2005 and has since slowly declined. Students diagnosed as having specific learning disabilities are the largest group, comprising about 39 percent of the total. The next largest group had speech or language impairments (about 22 percent), mental retardation (about 7.6 percent), and serious emotional disturbances (about 6.7 percent) (see Figure 4.2; NCES, *Condition*, 2010, Table A-6-1). These increases are in part due to changing definitions of disability, especially learning disability, and techniques of diagnosis (Gallego, Duran, and Reyes, 2006; also see Aaron, 1997; Carrier, 1983).

Ninety-five percent of students with disabilities were served in regular school buildings and classrooms. About 54 percent are in regular classes most of the day, over 41 percent are in resource rooms for special help at least part of the day, and 3.3 percent are in separate classrooms or buildings. Services are provided for a variety of students. About twice as much money is spent to educate a disabled child as before PL 94–142, yet many are not receiving special education even now. Part of the problem is assessment: determining whether a child is learning disabled or has some other problem.

Research results show that integration of as many special education students as possible can have positive results; students have peer models from whom to learn social skills and competencies, and other students learn about disabilities. Integrating special education students into classrooms provides models and expectations that are powerful influences on children. However, there is a lack of evidence from methodologically strong studies that mainstreamed students learn more, and, where evidence does exist, the balance is only marginally positive. The research task now is to more thoroughly investigate the mediators and moderators that support the optimal education for children with special needs and disabilities (Lindsay, 2007). The effects of labeling students for special placement can influence peer-group relations, but the research has not clearly documented whether separate placement or mainstreaming has any detrimental effects. Of major concern is the number of minority students labeled retarded or learning disabled. The main criterion for eligibility for special education services in schools has been proof of intrinsic deficit. There are two problems with this. First, defining and identifying high-incidence disabilities are ambiguous and subjective processes. Second, the focus on disability has become so intertwined with the historical devaluing of minorities in the United States that these two deficit lens now deeply influence the special education placement process (Harry and Klinger, 2007). The end result is a disproportionate placement of some minority groups in special education (Klingner et al., 2005). Some encouraging directions are under way that may help schools focus on differences rather than on deficits. These include a change in the discrepancy model, the Response to Intervention model (RTI), which focuses on early intervention, and involving parents in the placement process (Fuchs and Fuchs, 2006). A new vision of special education is called for in which the notion of disability is reserved for students with clear-cut diagnoses of biological or psychological limitations and the categorization is used only for the purpose of delivering intensive, specialized services in the least restrictive education environment possible. Clearly, careful and fair assessment is in order.

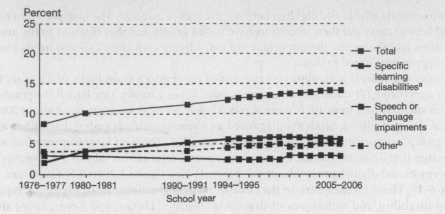

FIGURE 4.2 Number of children with disabilities in federal programs as a percentage of total public K-12 enrollment, by type of disability.

[a]A disorder in one or more of the basic psychological processes involved in understanding or in using language, spoken or written, that may manifest itself in an imperfect ability to listen, think, speak, read, write, spell, or to do mathematical calculations, including conditions such as perceptual disabilities, brain injury, minimal brain dysfunction, dyslexia, and developmental aphasia.

[b]Other disability types include mental retardation, emotional disturbance, hearing impairments, orthopedic impairments, other health impairments, visual impairments, multiple disabilities, deaf-blindness, autism, traumatic brain injury, and developmental delay. Note the nature of disabilities within this category are diverse; they are included together here to represent cases contributing to the total not otherwise presented in this graph due to relatively low prevalence in the population.

Note: Special education services through the Individuals with Disabilities Education Act (IDEA) are available for eligible youth identified by a team of qualified professionals as having a disability that adversely affects their academic performance and as in need of special education and related services. The total is the percentage of youth receiving special education services through IDEA in early education centers and public schools in the 50 states and the District of Columbia and in Bureau of Indian Affairs (BIA) schools through 1993–1994. Beginning in 1994–1995, enrollment numbers and percentages exclude BIA schools. See supplemental note 8 for more information about the student disabilities presented here.

Source: U.S. Department of Education, Office of Special Education and Rehabilitative Services (OSERS), Office of Special Education Programs (OSEP), *26th Annual (2004) Report to Congress on the Implementation of the Individuals with Disabilities Education Act,* vols. 1 and 2, 2006b; data from OSERS, OSEP, Data Analysis System (DANS), 1976–2005. Available: http://www.ed.gov/about/reports/annual/osep/2004/introduction.html and http://www.ideadata.org/index.html (Retrieved September 22, 2006 from 2006b).

Gifted Students

Few think of gifted students as disadvantaged, but if their talents are not being developed, we may argue that they are in a disadvantaged position. Societies need to develop and use the talents of their most gifted members, but this presents dilemmas and controversies in democracies: To single out some students for special treatment or training is to give advantage to some and create an elite intelligentsia; yet if ability is considered regardless of other factors, such as family position, we are developing and using needed resources. The problem here is that high levels of achievement are disproportionately found among privileged youth, and gifted and talented programs may be seen as equally and disproportionately benefiting them (Brantlinger, 2003).

Controversy continues when schools consider which students to place in gifted programs. Congressional Act PL 95–561 defined "gifted" as including general intellectual ability, specific academic aptitude, creative or productive thinking, leadership, and visual and performing arts talents. But who is gifted is actually defined by each program that singles out children for special treatment, and herein lies the controversy (see Box 4.3). Low test scores and institutional discrimination may hide the talents of some students, especially minority students. New York City's Department of Education has revised its rules for eligibility for its gifted programs several times in recent years to assure that these services are made available to all groups of students equitably (Winerip, 2010). We know that gifted students benefit from homogeneous ability grouping. But in the process, some students are labeled "better" than others, and a self-fulfilling prophecy can result in which there is added stress and pressure to succeed and play a "significant" role in society.

Although there is lack of agreement on one strategy, many feel that individualized instruction combined with some joint classroom activities with other students may best serve both groups. Separating students from their peers does occur when students are tracked, sent to special programs or classes, or "pulled out" of classrooms for any purpose. Most useful to gifted and other students are programs that support a variety of learning styles and use students in the teaching process (Van Tassel-Baska, 2006).

BOX 4.3

The Case of a "Dull" Genius

Perhaps a good place to begin is with the case of a boy who was a slow developer, particularly with respect to language. He did not begin to talk until after his second birthday, and language difficulties persisted for him into adulthood. He did poorly in school; his temper tantrums proved highly disruptive to the classroom. Both his parents and his teachers thought him dull, and neither envisioned much of a future for him.

Finally, however, when he was 14, his parents happened upon a different kind of school pursuing a more holistic approach to education, and a less exclusively linguistically oriented one. The boy blossomed and his world changed. His name was Albert Einstein. His later writings suggest what may well have been the key problem: Even as an adult, Einstein continued—unlike most of us—to think in visual images rather than in words. Thus, he might understandably have found classrooms dealing only in words very hard to handle. (It may be worth noting, however, that the apparent language deficiency that handicapped him as a pupil may have empowered him as a creative genius. It has been said that Einstein's ability to depart from traditional physics may well have been associated with his independence from its concepts, as he dealt instead with visual images.)

Source: Raywid, Mary Anne, "Separate Classes for the Gifted? A Skeptical Look," *Educational Perspectives* Vol. 26, No. 1, 1989, p. 44.

IMPROVING SCHOOLS FOR MINORITY STUDENTS

The U.S. educational system is built on the premise that all students should be educated regardless of race, ethnic group, sex, ability, or other characteristics. This responsibility has been entrusted to the state and federal government, to take an active role in ensuring rights for minorities, including African Americans, Hispanics, immigrants from other countries, women, and other disadvantaged groups. Although there is an impatience to reform education, any new programs need to consider all students; thus, reforms must come from old and new ideas, from the powerful and not so powerful in society, and from the various groups who will be affected (Coleman, 1990). Real change in the situation of minority students will not come about without individual and structural changes involving education, family, and other groups that act to empower minority students rather than disenfranchise them. This is a formidable task, considering the difficulty of changing power relations in society. Many programs only perpetuate the structure as it is and produce little change, in part because they deal with only part of the system. Some general conclusions and recommendations that stem from the research, especially that related to "at-risk" students, recommend that schools intervene early, make sure students spend time "on task," have high expectations of students and mainstream potential dropouts, provide support services such as day care for student parents, and reduce class sizes to fewer than 20 students (Lindjord, 1998). Many researchers and policy makers are experimenting with program ideas such as multicultural educational programs, school climates that reduce prejudice, and community service and career involvement programs to keep students in school.

EFFECTIVE SCHOOLS.   Effective schools create positive academic achievement environments, and they raise students' self-esteem, reduce student alienation and delinquency, encourage interracial friendships, and integrate teaching of racial equality into the school curriculum (Hammack, 1990). All students are highly involved in extracurricular activities, and teachers display behaviors that favor racial integration and prejudice reduction. In addition, many parents play an active role in these schools. Effective schools should benefit all students, including minority students, by attending to the following issues:

1. Clear-cut goals and objectives
2. Adequate funding and appropriate use of funds
3. Quality academic programs
4. Valid assessment programs and effective monitoring of progress
5. Parent, family, and community involvement
6. Teacher and staff development
7. High expectations for students
8. Comprehensive support services
9. Adequate school facilities
10. Productive school climate and culture
11. Multicultural instruction and sensitivity. ("Effective Schools," 1998; Levine, 1995)

What has been added to this mix in recent years has been an increase in measures of accountability and oversight. The increased testing required by No Child Left Behind has enlarged the transparency of school performance and provided for new measures of school effectiveness.

CHOICE PROGRAMS, VOUCHERS, AND CHARTER SCHOOLS.   Proposed plans for revitalizing education allow parents to choose the kind of school that meets their children's needs. In theory, this should provide competition and improve schools. The surge in the number of charter schools, in part a result of the Obama's administration's embrace of them in the Race to the Top competition, is among the latest trends in the efforts to improve the achievement of at-risk youth. However, there are many problems with the concept, as outlined in Chapters 5 and 13 of this text.

COOPERATIVE LEARNING.   Cooperative learning involves groups of four to six heterogeneous members who work together toward achieving a goal. This idea stems from the work of Slavin and others at the Center for Social Organization of Schools at The Johns Hopkins University (Slavin, 1983, 1995). Findings show that cooperative learning positively affects student relationships and achievement (Cohen and Lotan, 1997).

ATTITUDES OF SCHOOLS AND TEACHERS.   Among the many recent reports on how to improve schools are *What Works* and *Creating Effective Schools [Check DOE websites for these programs]*. They document a number of findings from research that result in effective schools. The general conclusions support our discussion here concerning the need for improving the achievement and attitudes toward minority students. Teachers must communicate high expectations to all of their students; schools need strong educational leadership that emphasizes academic achievement; and parents need to be involved in the education of their children (Brookover, Erickson, and McEvoy, 1996; Tenenbaum and Ruck, 2007).

COMMUNITY INVOLVEMENT.   Community involvement addresses the need to approach school reform from many angles as suggested by the systems model. Schools alone cannot change the situation for minority students; the involvement of parents and businesses help change the situation. For example, a New York City businessman promised 6th graders from his alma mater financial support to attend college if they finished high school. Instead of up to 75 percent dropping out, as was the norm, 83 percent finished high school and many have gone on to college. This one case started a national business–school liaison, the "I Have a Dream Foundation," to help 10,000 children pursue higher education (Sommerfeld, 1992, p. 1). There are many organizations that seek to facilitate the development of better relationships between communities and schools. Some examples are the Coalition for Community Schools (www.communityschools. org), Schools of the 21st Century (www.yale.edu/21C/index2.html), and Communities in Schools (www.cisnet.org).

The process of stratification pervades educational systems both as a reflection of the stratification patterns in the society and its institutions, and as a mechanism to reinforce and perpetuate those patterns within society. From children's homes, neighborhoods, and peer groups to the political and economic systems, children are socialized to play their roles in society and to occupy a place in the societal system. Issues of equal opportunity have been raised, especially by those who feel that they are receiving unfair treatment and unequal chances for the rewards society can offer. Education is a target for these criticisms because of its perceived importance in providing opportunities for a better life. The open systems perspective reminds us that problems of equality go far beyond the effect of schools alone. Schools may be the nursery of integration, but equal access to housing, health care, equal pay for equal work, employment opportunities, and many other areas must also be considered in the fight for equality of opportunity.

Educational reform today is greatly concerned with reducing the "educational achievement gap" between African Americans and Latinos and the rest of the country's youth. The impetus, for example, of the No Child Left Behind legislation was explicitly to reduce these differences in average achievement levels. The evidence of these differences is clear; they exist as children enter school and increase the more years of schooling students experience. This increase of the achievement gap has been a much researched topic. Some researchers have attributed its increase to actions of the schools that children attend and the teachers who teach them. Curriculum grouping, tracking, and negative teacher expectations are examples of the factors many feel are responsible for the gaps in student achievement (Blau, 2003).

OVERCOMING STUDENT RESISTENCE.   Others have also attributed the gap in achievement among minority students to oppositional behavior of the students themselves (Fordham and Ogbu, 1986). This is a complex argument that we need to address in some detail. The argument begins with the circumstances surrounding the immigration or inclusion of minority groups into society. Ogbu distinguishes between voluntary immigrants, those who, of their own volition, move to a new country, and those who are involuntarily brought to the new country. Examples of the former are immigrants who seek better life opportunities in a new country than they perceive are available to them in their home country. Involuntary immigrants are those who are forcibly brought to a new country as slaves, indentured servants, conquered peoples, and the like. Examples are African-American slaves, Native American peoples, and peoples of The Philippines, Puerto Rico, and other places who have become Americans involuntarily. For Ogbu (1994), these original conditions of relations between immigrants and their new society have powerful consequences. Voluntary immigrants are eager to take advantage of whatever opportunities may exist in their new home, seeking to learn the language and culture of their new home so that they can assimilate. Though they may face barriers to assimilation such as discrimination and prejudice, Ogbu notes that, because the move to the new society was voluntary, these immigrants are able to work to overcome these barriers. On the other hand, involuntary immigrants, also facing prejudice and discrimination, reject the dominant society as an oppressor and struggle to maintain their integrity in the face of the more powerful dominant society. Assimilation is tantamount to collaboration with the enemy, and differences between the minority and dominant society mark off their separation. While initial, or primary, differences between voluntary and involuntary minorities (such as language, religion, food, and so forth) are important, over generations these differences become smaller and less significant. For involuntary groups, however, the reduction in cultural differences does not pay off in a reduction of prejudice or discrimination. Moreover, not seeking assimilation, these groups work to create new differences between themselves and the dominant groups. Ogbu calls these differences "secondary cultural characteristics" and understands them (language, dress, and taste differences, for example) as means by which the involuntary groups maintain their cohesiveness and strength in the context of their disadvantaged status in the society. Such adaptations, in turn, maintain the distinctiveness of the group and may prevent its integration into the larger society when prejudice and discrimination are reduced.

Since the primary social institutions of society necessarily reflect the values, norms, and culture of the dominant group, involuntary immigrants and their offspring approach these institutions with suspicion. Anticipating that these institutions, including education, will not be welcoming and receptive to them, members of groups whose origins in the society were involuntary, are likely, according to Ogbu, to reject definitions of success promoted by those institutions. This rejection does not happen among the youngest members, but appears strongly during late childhood and adolescence (Harris, 2006; Tyson, 2002). Ogbu and Fordham described members of these groups as enforcing norms that rejected conformity to dominant institutions and culture. They labeled this rejection as "acting white." Members of these groups, they asserted, police themselves to limit the degree to which members adopt dominant patterns of behavior, and especially behaviors that might lead to success in the dominant society. Poor school achievement is thus seen as a badge of conformity to the subgroup's ways of behavior. Ogbu and his coauthors understand the achievement gap to be, in part, the result of these larger social dynamics, not simply the result of individual ability or effort, or of the lower resources these communities may have to support their children's education. This is especially so for males. For example, Carter quotes one of her female informants as follows:

> It's easier for a girl to be smart because if a boy is smart, he gets stuff from his crew or whatever like, 'Ah man you're soft, you're soft! I can't believe you know that poetry stuff.' So [boys] try to hide that they're smart, that they know stuff like that, [and] I think that it's easier for a girl. (2005, p. 87)

Carter goes on to say that her informant made it clear that the boys had come to define the classroom and certain aspects of their education as feminine, as soft. For many of the boys, then, not only is education seen as "white," but also feminine, a powerful combination that motivates them not to succeed. As Carter concludes, "Without sufficient social and economic resources, the consequences are that poor African American and Latino males, in their quest to assert manhood in a patriarchal and male-dominated society, are likely to collaborate in their academic and socioeconomic marginalization" (2005, p. 85).

From research such as that of Fordham and Ogbu and of Carter, it is clear that the negative connotation of "acting white" exists within the African-American and Latino communities. The question is how widespread it is and to what degree is it responsible for the achievement gap. Research by economists (Fryer and Torelli, 2005) as well as a number of sociologists (e.g., Ainsworth-Darnell and Downey, 1998; Carter, 2005; Cook and Ludwig, 1997 Harris, 2006; O'Connor, 1997, 2001; Tyson, 2002; Tyson, Darity, and Castellino, 2005) supports a conclusion of skepticism about how dominant the acting white admonition is among African-American and Latino youth. This research finds that regardless of race or ethnicity, high achieving students are likely to be called "nerds" and receive other negative reactions from less well-performing students. At the same time, these researchers also find that there is no significant difference between the attitudes toward education among students from different racial and ethnic backgrounds. Some students do have negative attitudes toward school, but these negative attitudes are not more prevalent among one group in contrast to others.

The ability of the "acting white" hypothesis to explain lower academic achievement of African Americans and other involuntary immigrant minorities is thus in doubt. Several researchers have proposed a rather different explanation. Harris, for example, drawing on the ethnographic work of Tyson (2002) and Carter (2005), as well as his own quantitative analysis, argues that African-American and other minority children enter school significantly behind in academic achievement, and that gap grows each year, to the degree that negative attitudes form, they are the result of educational failure, not the other way around. As Harris puts it " . . . poor performance early in the schooling process might be partially to blame for the counterproductive schooling behavior observed among some blacks during adolescence, a reverse order of causation than the resistance model suggests" (2006, p. 825). Alexander, Entwisle, and Olsen, using longitudinal data from Baltimore, track the educational achievement levels of students through their elementary school careers and on into high school and beyond. They find, as did Heyns (1978) over 30 years ago, that "prior to high school, the achievement gap by family SES traces substantially to unequal learning opportunities in children's home and community environments" (2007, p. 168). When children are attending school, these family and community influences are compensated for by the educational process of schooling (as we noted earlier when discussing the

Coleman Report). However, during the summer, the gap grows, and is never closed by schooling, because each fall, as students return to school, the previous summer's learning advantages of middle- and upper-class students put them further ahead of their less advantaged classmates. The learning gap at any point in time is substantially the result of the accumulation of these yearly summer differences in learning. Alexander and his colleagues conclude, "Our results show how out-of-school learning during the elementary grades is linked to the year 9 achievement gap by family SES: a gap that, in turn, separates college track youth from non-college track youth, and that distinguishes those who fall off the path to high school completion from those who attend four year colleges" (2007, p. 173). Alexander, Entwisle, and Olsen (2007) argue for early preschool interventions along with year-round opportunities for learning. Thus, schools do help equalize student achievement, but don't close the gap. Without schooling, the gap would be far wider. Our thinking about schools and their role in the process of educational stratification is benefiting from these new findings about the "seasons of learning."

In summary, education is still a route to social mobility for many students, but for those locked into minority schools and neighborhoods and those who suffer from other disadvantages, achievement is more of a challenge.

Applying Sociology of Education: *Do students encourage both antischool and achievement norms?*

Some scholars report that African-American and Hispanic students may encourage their friends not to work hard and be successful in school because to do so would be to "act white." Have students you know expressed such antiachievement sentiments?

Summary

In this chapter we continued our discussion of the process of stratification in education and society. We focused on the problem of sex inequality in schools and attempts to rectify sexism, followed by problems facing minority groups in American education, including discussions of African Americans, Native Americans, Hispanics, and Asian Americans.

I. GENDER AND EQUALITY OF EDUCATIONAL OPPORTUNITY

Girls and boys have different school experiences, partly because of differences in expectations, encouragement, and treatment. The sex-role socialization process begins at birth, influencing what children feel is appropriate to their sex. Male and female achievement is affected by parental expectations; books, texts, and other materials; TV and media; toys; achievement motivation; sex-role

models; teacher stereotypes and expectations; and peer-group pressures. The reasons for differences in math achievement are discussed, concluding that there is little evidence for biological explanations of differences. Efforts that combat the negative effects of sexism, such as Title IX programs, also are discussed.

II. CLASS, RACE, AND ATTEMPTS TO RECTIFY INEQUALITIES IN EDUCATIONAL OPPORTUNITY

Do schools make a difference? Findings related to this question indicate a complex interaction between family and schools that affects equal opportunity. Because of inequalities in educational opportunities for minorities, the political and legal systems have intervened. Numerous court cases have ordered school districts to desegregate through busing children. Attempts to bus, the effects of busing and "white flight," self-concept, and achievement are discussed. But there is no doubt that schooling prevents even greater inequalities from developing.

III. INTEGRATION ATTEMPTS

The attempt to rectify inequality through compensatory educational programs is described and evaluated.

IV. EDUCATIONAL EXPERIENCE OF SELECTED MINORITIES IN THE UNITED STATES

Hispanic students are the fastest-growing and most segregated group in schools, and they also come from many different backgrounds. Whether to teach these students in English or their native language is a controversial subject. Which will give them greater opportunity in the future?

Asian American students do best of the minority groups, whereas Native Americans have perhaps the most difficult time. Other groups, such as special education students, are discussed briefly.

V. IMPROVING SCHOOLS FOR MINORITY STUDENTS

Several programs that attempt to change the situation for minority students are discussed: changing patterns of interaction in schools, multicultural education programs, school climate, and community involvement are examples. It increasingly seems clear that schools have limited abilities to overcome the disparities in students' lives outside of schools. However, without schooling, the differences among youth from different backgrounds would be much larger than they already are.

Putting Sociology to Work

1. At your local library, randomly select a sample of children's books. Tabulate the following:

	Male	Female
Number of stories where main character is	___	___
Number of illustrations of	___	___
Number of times children are shown	___	___
in active play	___	___
using initiative	___	___
displaying independence	___	___
solving problems	___	___
earning money	___	___
receiving recognition	___	___
being inventive	___	___
involved in sports	___	___
being fearful or helpless	___	___
receiving help	___	___

2. Interview a group of 8th-grade girls, then boys, about their aspirations, future career plans, and high school curriculum plans. Compare these aspirations.
3. Talk with students who are being bused in order to desegregate schools. What are their experiences and

feelings both about busing and about its effects on the school, academic work, their own attitudes, and friendships or peer-group relations?
4. What are the admissions policies with regard to race and sex for professional schools (medical, law, nursing, dental) in your area?

CHAPTER

5

The School as an Organization

A visit to New Trier High School in a wealthy area of Chicago reveals the world of academic possibilities open to children. The physical setting is like a beautiful college campus with well-equipped labs for science, an Olympic-size pool, and facilities having the latest technology. Students have choices of many advanced high school courses, and teachers' class sizes average 15–20 students. Most students are white and from wealthy neighborhoods. Ninety-three percent of students go to four-year colleges, many to the best Ivy League schools.

Contrast this with P.S. 79, an elementary school in New York City. In this badly overcrowded school, classrooms hold over 30 students per class. The need for more space is apparent, as even the library and gymnasiums are used as classrooms. There is no room for a computer lab or science room. The building is in desperate need of repair (Kozol, 1991). Contrast the basics of these two schools—even the organizational structures differ because of the size and funding available in different school districts.

While some of the differences between these schools have to do with funding, organizational structures such as school size and decision-making processes also determine the effectiveness of each school. Most urban schools like P.S. 79 do not have the luxury of treating each child as an individual. They are like conveyer belts—put students in at one end, and hope they get spit out at the other. Warehousing students is another way to describe student experiences; adults control their behavior but have little connection to their many students. High school teachers in poor, large, crowded schools see 150 students a day, and in some overcrowded city schools 200. This allows no time to get to know students and their needs, and some get lost in the crowd. Teachers work in isolation, carrying out routines required by the administration.

We know from research what is needed to provide positive learning environments. For example, research shows that smaller schools and classrooms produce higher achievement; lower dropout, violence, and vandalism rates; more positive feelings toward school; and greater participation in school-related activities. Creating smaller schools or schools-within-schools, providing advising structures to deal with students' needs, and keeping students with the same teacher for more than one year are ways to structure the organization of schools so that students feel more connected to their school. Collaborative learning structures result in higher achievement (Darling-Hammond, 2010, p. 239).

Let's eavesdrop on a high school where students are beginning the day and note some of the organizational structures typical of many schools:

It is Monday morning, 8:45 A.M. We are entering a high school. Sounds of loud voices, banging lockers, and running feet greet us as the big, heavy doors slam behind us. A loud bell clangs through the chaos, and students begin disappearing behind closing doors along the corridor. And so another day begins. Each student knows his or her proper place in the system. If a late student enters, disrupting the organizational routine, the school personnel will use discipline to socialize this disruptive student into proper behavior and instill the value of punctuality.

There are many ways of looking at the school as an organization. In Chapters 6 and 7 we focus on the role structure of the school, and in Chapter 8 on its informal organization—classroom interactions, teaching and learning processes, and school climate. Here we look at the important structural components of the system and analyze aspects of the school as a bureaucracy.

Although each school has its own culture and subcultures, complete with legends, heroes, stories, rituals, and ceremonies, certain organizational facts are relevant to any discussion of schools. As seen in the example above, the size of a school is correlated with the type of organizational structure and degree of bureaucratization—the larger the school, the higher the degree of bureaucracy. The region of the country and a school's setting affect the degree of centralization—many rural schools tend to become more centralized because the area covered is more sparsely populated. Community residents in urban school districts often push toward decentralization because of the diverse needs of different urban populations and neighborhoods. The community's class and racial composition influence the school structure and climate, and private or religious schools are affected by other unique variables.

In considering the social structure of the school as an organization, our open system boundaries fall around the school and classroom (see Figure 5.1). Although the internal structure of the school organization is our focus, keep in mind that the system is shaped and changed through interaction with the environment. Schools serve purposes for other organizations and institutions in society, and they cannot exist independently of other organizations. For instance, when we discuss school goals we are really discussing what is expected of schools by their environments and how that is reflected in school goals. We separate out the school as an organization for analytical purposes only, as one part of understanding the whole educational system.

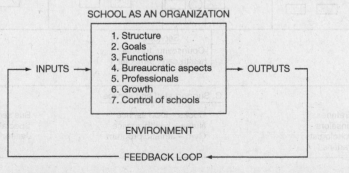

FIGURE 5.1 Open system model of educational organizations.

THE SOCIAL SYSTEM OF THE SCHOOL

Behind the hustle and bustle of the school hallway lies a system in which everyone knows their place—where to go and what roles they are to play in that system. According to the functionalist approach, the school system is composed of many distinct subsystems or parts, each with goals; together these parts make up a functioning whole (see Figure 5.2). If one of these parts experiences problems or breakdown or does not carry out its functions, other interdependent parts are affected. Each part is dependent on the others for smooth operation, for the materials or resources it needs to function, and even for its existence. As you read the following, picture a school with which you are familiar.

1. As we enter the school we are directed to the office. Here a member of the school staff, usually the secretary, greets us and ascertains our business. The office and its staff act as buffers to protect the rest of the school from interruptions in routine.
2. Classrooms take up most of the physical structure of the school; within the classroom, teacher and students are the main occupants. However, the order of the classroom—including seating arrangement, work groups, location, style of leadership, class size, and the types of students—affects the relationships between position-holders and the consequent roles they play. These in turn affect the activities taking place within the classroom. Each classroom has a distinct social climate and structure.

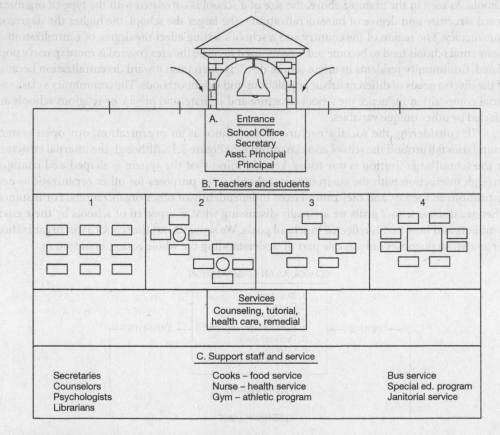

FIGURE 5.2 School system structure and roles.

3. Support services are necessary for classrooms to function; standard services include food, janitorial, and emergency health services. In addition, most schools have personnel and facilities for counseling, technology, special services such as psychological testing or tutoring, bus service, and library service. This total school system exists in a larger societal context, including the local community with its social classes, minority-group compositions, and interest groups; the regional setting; the state government with its board of education, legislative bodies, rules, and regulations; and the federal government with its federal regulations and funding. A school system—people, buildings, classrooms, textbooks, and equipment—becomes what it is through interaction with the environment.

GOALS OF THE SCHOOL SYSTEM

Formal goals serve several purposes for social systems. They provide guidelines for activities of the system and focus the activities of members; they imply social acceptance of the stated purposes and of means to achieve them; and they legitimize the activities of the system. There is not always consensus, however, on what goals should receive highest priority or how the goals should be achieved. Witness the controversies over school curricula: Some adults are concerned that schools are not putting enough emphasis on basic skills and that too many "frills" (art, music, and physical education, for example) are included in the program. Others argue that children need exposure to a broad curriculum for the development of "the whole child." Also, schools are under pressure from many community members to take on ever greater roles, especially in social service areas such as after school child-care programs and intervention in personal and family problems.

Thus, goals are constantly being "negotiated" and reconsidered. For functional theorists, addressing issues and problems helps keep the system in balance. For conflict theorists, problems often reflect inequalities and goal differences between the interests of powerful members of society and those wanting change. We now consider briefly some goal expectations of various societal sectors that influence official school goals.

Societal, Community, and Educators' Goals

Each society has certain goals for its educational system that, ideally, are put into practice in its schools and classrooms. Important school functions are to socialize the young to perform needed adult roles; keep the young occupied and delay entry into the job market; help perpetuate society by socializing the young into particular societal values, traditions, and beliefs; develop skills needed to live in society, such as reading, writing, and responsibility; and select and allocate the young people to needed roles, from professionals to laborers.

In homogeneous societies there is often consensus on key goals, and national educational programs result in uniform curriculum and materials; but heterogeneous societies have constituencies with competing goals. Functional theorists hold that goals give direction to the school, helping it to function smoothly and to support the societal system. Conflict theorists argue that school goals reflect the dominant power groups in society, that they represent only one segment of society, and that they serve to perpetuate an unequal stratification system. School systems are often at the center of political struggles for control of resources and ideas.

Over time, goals change. For instance, the early sociologist Émile Durkheim spoke of the social organization of the school classroom that fosters the moral habits that keep societies together (Durkheim, 1961). While keeping societies together may still be a goal, other goals have superseded

One goal for schools is that they function smoothly. Schools have difficulty dealing with disruptions to routine.

it in importance. Educators debate goals for school curriculum, structure, outcomes, and even what values and morals should be taught, if any (Jackson, Boostrom, and Hansen, 1993).

Each new *national administration* presents its goals for education. During the first George Bush administration, the plan was called *America 2000: An Education Strategy* (*America 2000*, 1991). The Clinton administration's plan was *Goals 2000: Educate America Act* (*Goals 2000*, 1994). It called for systematic national reform. The George W. Bush administration policy, *No Child Left Behind*, called for strict accountability and penalties for schools that do not measure up to the goals. The Obama administration seeks to modify the goals of *No Child Left Behind* and added a plan called *Race to the Top* to implement some of its goals. During each presidential campaign in the United States, the major candidates put forth platforms on education indicating their respective philosophies of the government's role in education.

The diversity of goals and expectations in the United States is exemplified by the fact that there are *competing interest groups* in communities and little consensus among those who have vested interests in schools—students, social scientists, educators, parents, and politicians, to name a few. This diversity of goals presents a dilemma for school districts beholden to their constituencies.

Noted educators also propose goals for reform that receive national attention. In K-12 education, Theodore Sizer has influenced educational reformers with his proposals to address problems in the school systems, not the teachers. For example, he recommends that to be successful, teachers should teach fewer subjects in greater depth and teach no more than 80 students in a day. Students should be active learners and receive diplomas only after mastery of certain subjects (Dykema, 2002; Sizer, 1985; Sizer and Sizer, 1999).

Another noted educational reformer, John I. Goodlad, who established the *Center for Educational Renewal*, focused on reform of K-12 education and teacher education. In the plan for reform, Goodlad and colleagues recommend smaller schools and more autonomy for individual schools. His writings have stimulated reform at teachers' colleges as well as propositions for improving education (Bernhardt and Ballantine,1995; Goodlad, Mantle-Bromley, and Goodlad, 2004). Many other reforms have been proposed: reduction in class size, especially for at-risk students; standardization of curricula so that there is some consistency across districts and states; and involvement of parents in their children's schooling (Darling-Hammond, 2010; Small school Reform Plans, 2005).

For the *community and family*, goals for schools include formalizing socialization experiences, facilitating peer interaction; structuring socialization experiences; helping meet family goals for successful children; giving children more options in the competitive marketplace; and producing young people who will fit into the community. Individual groups or families in a community may differ on goals because of their social class, religious affiliation, or minority status.

The expectations that *individual communities* have of their schools are likely to be far more specific than the general goals of society. For instance, schools in traditional small towns in rural areas, such as that described in the classic work *Elmtown's Youth* (Hollingshead, 1975), are likely to stress hard work, moral orientation, and other major American values (Williams, 1970). The dominant community members (business leaders and politicians) control school board elections and screen out teachers who might try to change things. Urban schools, because of the heterogeneous population served, have less consensus on academic goals and spend more energy on the "goals" of discipline and control. Suburban schools are likely to focus on success and achievement goals, reflecting their communities and constituencies. Emblems, mottoes, and student handbooks stating very general goals are redefined and operationalized constantly to meet community needs and expectations. Local school goals, influenced by political pressures from the community, put decision making in the hands of the local school.

It is precisely because of the constant pressures for change that educational goal statements are broad and widely acceptable: "Our goal is to prepare students for the global world of the future." This avoids clashes between schools and government, community, family, and other groups. Vague general goal statements, however, also mean that the schools receive little direction from these statements and schools are vulnerable to influence and pressure from many conflicting interest groups.

School Goals

A broad and generally accepted model for most schools' formal goal statements was developed in 1918 by the National Education Association's Commission on the Reorganization of Secondary Education. It recommended that secondary education should "develop in each individual the knowledge, interests, ideals, habits and powers whereby he will find his place and use that place to shape both himself and society toward ever nobler ends." Although it is dated, this statement reflects some basic American values that are reflected in many local schools: good citizenship, or fitting into society; and individuality, or making one's own way by using acceptable means. In reality, these goals are not working for some groups in American society. Equal opportunity is far from reality, as we discussed in Chapters 3 and 4.

The stated goals are often different from the operational procedures, which outline what is to happen and what programs are to be carried out in each school. These procedures focus on curricular content, classroom style, and organizational structure to accomplish the stated goals. It is in the school that stated goals must be translated into action; in this process, conflicts over purpose and interpretation can arise.

Subgroups within the community and school may have informal unstated goals that differ from, and perhaps even contradict, the stated formal school goals. For instance, teachers may seek to buffer themselves from the community to protect their professional autonomy, whereas the school may profess an open-door policy toward parents and community members. Teachers and schools put up protective barriers to maintain the school's operational goals and control over the academic programs.

Two models dominate the organizational control of schools: highly decentralized schools in which teachers have workplace autonomy, and top–down centralized bureaucracies in which teachers have little autonomy. The degree of control over goals, stated or unstated, and the autonomy of teachers and individual schools depends on what activities are considered and on differences in the degree of control exerted by boards of education, principals, and teachers in different types of schools (Ingersoll and Merrill, 2011b).

Individual Goals

Those who hold roles in schools are also likely to have different goals. Consider the different reasons for school involvement of teachers and other educational professionals and for students. For individual students school is obligatory; students are required to attend. However, school provides an opportunity for students to get together with peers and engage in sports and other activities. Students' educational goals will vary depending on individual motivations, ranging from dropping out at 16 to attending college. Many students can be encouraged to take challenging academic courses when they see rewards in doing so.

Goals of parents include providing opportunities for their children to get ahead or occupying their children during part of the day. Administrators and teachers desire high-quality education, but they also have personal goals such as the need for money, prestige, and satisfying work.

The goals just discussed reflect many of the functions or purposes (discussed in Chapter 2) that education serves in society and that help prepare children for society, but also illustrate the conflicts that can arise over goals.

> **Applying Sociology to Education:** *What conflicts over goals have dominated school board meetings in your local schools? What interest groups are involved?*

THE SCHOOL AS AN ORGANIZATION

Sally Joseph is a 5th grade teacher, popular among students and parents because of the results she achieves in reading and math and her ability to relate to children in her classes. Ms. Joseph has relative autonomy in leading her classroom. How she organizes and presents her materials is primarily her decision, within the parameters of her physical space and the broad goals outlined by the school district. Yet she functions within a larger organizational system that presents her with both opportunities and constraints. Traditionally, sociologists have viewed schools as bureaucracies, but they point out the limitations of this bureaucratic model for educational organizations; what works in formal bureaucracies such as business organizations may be dysfunctional in schools. We shall look at schools as bureaucracies, problems related to this model, and alternative models.

The School as a Bureaucracy

Bureaucracy! How often do we throw up our hands in disgust at the red tape, forms, impersonal attitudes, and coldness of bureaucracies? How infuriating is it to be treated as a number? Behind the stereotypical face of bureaucracy are millions of individuals with histories and feelings and experiences like ours. What is it that makes us bristle at the idea of bureaucracy? Bureaucracy is a rational, efficient way of completing tasks and rewarding individuals based on their contributions to the work that needs to be done. However, it can also represent an impersonal, inefficient, cumbersome organization unresponsive to human needs, as perhaps you have experienced when you waited in line to accomplish some task such as paying for purchases, registering for classes, or renewing a driver's license.

Although we may complain, bureaucracy serves a vital function in our society. A system based on nepotism and favoritism rather than selection and promotion based on merit, for example, would be certain to raise cries of unfairness and discrimination, and it would be dysfunctional for most societies. By dividing organizations into formal and informal parts (discussed in Chapter 8), we can better understand the working bureaucracy and the way it relates to schools.

A note of caution is necessary in discussing schools as bureaucracies, because schools are unique organizations. Schools are distinctive because they are expected to transmit values, ideals, and shared knowledge; foster cognitive and emotional growth; and sort and select students into different categories—college material, promising, bright, and so forth—with consequences for future adult status. Organizationally, schools are divided into classrooms, the day into periods, and students into groups by grades or performance on examinations (Hurn, 1993). Other bureaucracies have different purposes and structures.

Characteristics of Bureaucracy

The bureaucratic form of organization became prominent in Western Europe and the United States during the Industrial Revolution, primarily because it was believed to be the most efficient and rational form for organization with goals of high productivity and efficiency.

Max Weber, whose ideas were discussed briefly in Chapter 1, described the elements that make up a bureaucratic organization (Weber, 1947) in his typology of characteristics called an "ideal type." No real organization is going to match these ideal type characteristics completely, but it gives a set of characteristics against which to compare real organizations. The italicized points in the following six statements are Weber's characteristics, followed by an explanation of their relation to schools, as outlined by David Goslin (1965, p. 133).

1. An increasingly fine *division of labor*, at both the administrative and teaching levels, together with a concern for allocating personnel to those positions for which they are best suited and a formalization of recruitment, promotion, and firing policies.
2. The development of an *administrative hierarchy* incorporating a specified chain of command and designated channels of communications.
3. The gradual accumulation of *specific regulations and rules of procedure* that cover everything from counseling and guidance to schoolwide or systemwide testing programs and requirements concerning topics to be covered in many subjects such as history, civics, and social studies.
4. A deemphasis of personal relationship between students and teachers and between teachers and administrators, and a consequent reorientation toward more *formalized and affectively neutral role relationships*.
5. An emphasis on the *rationality* of the total organization and the processes going on within the organization. In general, the movement, particularly at the secondary school level, has been in the direction of the rational bureaucratic organization that is typified by most government agencies and many business and industrial firms.

6. In addition to these characteristics discussed by Goslin is Weber's point that the *positions individuals hold in the organization belong to the organization*. Thus, when an administrator, a teacher, or a student leaves the system, new individuals will move in to hold those positions.

Let us look at each of Weber's characteristics of bureaucracy and relationship to schools more closely.

DIVISION OF LABOR, HIRING AND FIRING, AND PROMOTION POLICIES

Division of labor. Each of us has specific tasks in our work, at home, and in school. We become specialists. With busy schedules, efficiency is high if we each know the tasks for which we are responsible and become adept at performing them. One problem that can result from a high degree of specialization is boredom; consider the assembly-line worker who faces eight hours daily at a single monotonous task. For a teacher, however, each student and class is different and challenging. There is constant updating of material and techniques, and learning of new knowledge. This relieves boredom, but the intensity of the work can also cause burnout, a problem discussed in Chapter 6.

Hiring and firing based on competence and skill. The following is taken from a teacher job description of a large school district:

Duties of teachers. Teachers shall take charge of the division of classes assigned to them by the principal. They shall be held responsible for the instruction, progress and discipline of their classes and shall devote themselves exclusively to their duties during school hours. Teachers shall render such assistance in the educational program in and about the buildings as the principal may direct, including parent-interviews, pupil-counseling, corridor, lunchroom, and playground supervision, and attendance at professional staff meetings. (Teacher job description)

With extensive certification regulations and testing, personnel policies, hiring committees and procedures, and equal opportunity regulations, school personnel must be clearly qualified for the positions to be filled. Training institutions become important for preparing individuals with the skills and attitudes necessary for the job. Colleges of education are usually accredited by state and regional organizations. They are required to teach the needed job skills and must be run in accordance with federal and state regulations governing education. The colleges also serve as screening points; those students studying education who can fit into the system and abide by rules are likely to be passed on to school systems with high recommendations.

Promotion and salary based on merit. Salary schedules and criteria for promotion are usually formulated by the superintendent's office and approved by the school board. These two are closely linked to the individual's level of education and number of years of service.

HIERARCHICAL SYSTEM OF AUTHORITY.
It takes only a little time in the halls of learning to know who is the boss and who is being bossed. The hierarchy of authority in any bureaucracy can be diagrammed, and most schools fit into the model shown in Figure 5.3. The hierarchy has implications for communication channels in schools. Depending on the position in the hierarchy, a person will receive and give out varying numbers and types of messages. Consider your college classrooms: There is a variety of teaching styles, class size, and information flow. One typical pattern is a downward flow of communication from instructor to student. Many educators believe

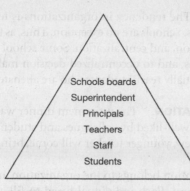

FIGURE 5.3 Hierarchical system of authority in schools.

that modifying the one-way flow and encouraging more interaction would lessen the alienation created in many large bureaucracies. More teachers would become "facilitators" in the learning process instead of "directors" or one-way communicators.

Part of the individual's responsibilities in the hierarchy involve reciprocal relationships, that is, relating to others in the organization. This is illustrated in the use of names: Teachers call students by first names, but the reverse is less common. The hierarchical differences are acknowledged in the teacher or administrator's formal title. The formal organization hierarchy chart alone cannot provide an accurate picture of where authority and power lie and how they are used, but it can give a picture of structure and formal relations.

RULES, REGULATIONS, AND PROCEDURES.   School begins at 8:40 A.M. Students who are late must report to the office for a tardy slip. At 8:50 A.M. students move to class period 1.... This is the routine set up by rules, but in addition there are rules covering most forms of behavior in the school, including dress, restroom behavior, cafeteria time, recess, after-school activities, bus behavior, and on and on.

Each individual is socialized into the system's rules and regulations. Often these rules are formalized in an orientation program for new students or written in a student or teacher handbook. Most of the expectations, however, are passed on informally through observation, discussion, and ridicule, or by more severe sanctions if rules are violated. Part of our anxiety about entering new situations is the fear of violating the rules, making faux pas, and being singled out for ridicule. Most of us wish to avoid such embarrassment, so we do our utmost to conform.

Formalized and affectively neutral role relationships.   Those individuals holding the same position in the bureaucratic organization are treated alike. At least that is the way it is supposed to be to avoid favoritism. The following familiar example illustrates this point. The school is giving standardized examinations. All the children will sit in rows in the auditorium, where they are handed a test book and told to "Begin," "Now turn the page," "Stop," "Close your test booklet," and "Pass it to the right."

Exceptions to rules such as those for giving standardized tests may cause problems for bureaucracies. Efficiency is based on an assumption of sameness, and each exception takes time and energy from the organizational routine. If an individual is treated "differently," there may be charges of preferential treatment, prejudice, or discrimination. Formalized, impersonal treatment pervades many aspects of our school systems, but where human relations are involved, formal relations are constantly being challenged. Human beings do not always fit into simple efficient boxes.

RATIONALITY IN ORGANIZATIONS.   The tendency in organizations is to seek more efficient means of carrying out goals and functions. Schools are no exception. Thus, as the size of schools has grown, so have formalization, specialization, and centralization. Some school districts are trying to move back to smaller schools, classrooms, and to decentralized decision making to bring human elements back into the schools and potentially reach students who are alienated.

POSITIONS BELONG TO THE ORGANIZATION.   The retirement dinner was crowded with well-wishers; she has been a popular teacher, well-liked by colleagues and students. She will leave, but the position will be refilled. Next fall a new, younger teacher will come, bringing a new personality and different talents to the job.

One thing is clear: The job description belongs to the organization and carries with it the rights and responsibilities of the position. Each individual hired to fill a role will do so in a unique way, interjecting his or her own personality and experience into the job. We know that Mrs. McCleary has a reputation for being a strong disciplinarian, Mr. Rahim for being good at teaching math concepts, and so forth. Yet each holds a position with the same job description.

The holder of the position has authority or legitimacy over others only in areas related to the job. Authority is one type of power that gives the role-holder the right to make decisions and exert influence and control in specified areas. In school systems, legitimacy is granted on the basis of expertise and position in the hierarchy. Should a teacher overstep the power vested in the position, the teacher's legitimacy could be challenged. For instance, your teacher or professor cannot require you to get a good night's rest, eat a good breakfast, or even spend a certain number of hours outside school working on school-related activities.

When a teacher retires, resigns, or is fired, the replacement assumes the same responsibilities, and allegiance is given to the new position-holder. Personal reasons for allegiance may vary—respect for authority or for the person's expertise, or knowledge that the person holds power in the form of job security, money, or responsibility for giving grades. But the position remains the same.

Professionals are generally highly trained and have more autonomy and freedom in the way they execute their roles than do those lower in the hierarchy. How much freedom they have depends on their reciprocal roles and the setting in which they are working, as discussed in Chapter 6.

Part of learning our roles in an organization involves understanding the reciprocal roles: students and teachers, teachers and principals, and students and peers. Symbolic interaction theory explains the process that is constantly taking place in our adjustment to situations as "taking the role of the other." This helps us learn our own roles and their limitations, and anticipate the mind-set of the reciprocal role-holders so that we can understand and meet their expectations.

Development of Schools as Bureaucracies

In the nineteenth century, schools were scattered throughout the country; their size depended on location, but most were small, often one room with multiple class levels, compared with today's large inner-city and consolidated rural schools.

> By 1865 systems of common schooling had been established throughout the northern, midwestern and western states. . . . The common schools of the period varied in terms of size, organization and curricula depending on their location. In rural areas, where the majority of Americans lived, one would most likely find the one- or two-room schoolhouse in which a pupil's progress was marked not by annual movement from one grade to the next but by his completion of one text and beginning of the next in the series. Only in larger towns and cities had grading been introduced. (Binder, 1974, pp. 94–95)

The movement to mass secondary schooling forced a change in early high schools to more modern models. The main changes included the bureaucratization of public education and the move from the innovative structures of individual schools to strong, centralized structures and administrations in which teachers had little power.

Since the turn of the twentieth century, schools have become larger and increasingly more bureaucratic, exhibiting many characteristics similar to those presented in Weber's "ideal type" bureaucracy. A result of the changing size of school populations and movement to urban centers was the centralization and bureaucratization of schools. These moves toward consolidation of school districts resulted in part from modernizing state bureaucracies that pushed for this change, and from increasing numbers of students. The enrollments in public and private elementary and secondary schools from 1970 to 2008 are presented in Figure 5.4 (NCES, "Elementary and Secondary School Enrollment," 2007). The growth of "corporate schooling," according to Meyer and Rowan (1978), relates to the worldwide trend of national development; educational bureaucracies serve the societies, not individuals or families, and as such they help those in control "sort, select, and allocate" individuals from the many groups in society into positions. Standardization of the system facilitates this process and has led to larger and larger bureaucracies with increasing numbers of administrators. Today there is more than one administrator for every 10 teachers, and in some districts less than half of the employees are teachers. The main role of many administrators has become to respond to requests for information and reports from higher administrative levels in the state or federal governments.

Problems in Educational Bureaucracies

Any time we attempt to put people into neat categories to maximize efficiency in an organization, there will be some who do not fit into the categories. In fact, its very structure as a bureaucracy may cause a school to experience difficulties. Consider the following types of problems:

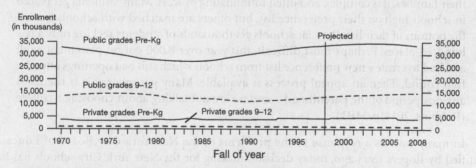

FIGURE 5.4 Elementary and secondary school enrollment, by control and grade level of school, with projections: Fall 1970–2008. *Source:* U.S. Department of Education, National Center for Education Statistics: (1999) *Digest of Education Statistics: 1998* (NCES 1999-036) (based on Common Core of Data); and (2007) Projections of Educational Statistics to 2016 (NCES 2007). Available: http://nces.ed.gov/programs/projections/projections2016/ (Retrieved: March 15, 2008).

Note: Enrollment includes students in kindergarten through grade 12 and some nursery school students. Beginning in fall 1980, data include estimates for the expanded universe of private schools. Projections indicate that enrollments will increase 9 percent between 2004 and 2016.

1. Huge enrollments make test scores, rather than in-depth knowledge of a student's family, background, problems, motivations, abilities, and other personal characteristics, the major criteria for screening and placement of students, and thus the determinants of his or her future.
2. Because relationships are expected to be impersonal, students, particularly the disadvantaged, cannot receive the counseling and support, or the exposure to "acceptable" role models from whom they need to develop a positive self-image.
3. Official rules tend to overcontrol the behavior of school personnel and are difficult to circumvent when problems arise.
4. Teachers and students often feel powerless to change school conditions and so become apathetic about solving problems.
5. Teachers, and particularly administrators, can develop bureaucratic personalities, becoming insecure, overly protective of their jobs, narrowly specialized, less and less concerned with teaching, and inflexible in their daily behavior.

For many students, the school bureaucracy presents a bewildering and alienating maze through which they must struggle. Our negative feelings toward bureaucracy come into play as the system gets larger and we are caught up in the rules and regulations; we are treated as numbers that are being processed.

> In an extreme example, eighth graders in New York City must apply to up to 12 high schools in order of preference, chosen from a total of almost 400 schools and more than 600 separate programs with individual applications. About 80,000 students go through the process every year, and their applications are processed by a computer program that takes into account whether or not the school has admissions requirements (is a "screened" school, which may include test scores, GPA, and attendance information, among others) or is limited to students in a particular geographic area of the City. While the process seeks to afford choice and options fairly to students and their families, it is complex and often intimidating process. Many students get placed in schools high on their preference list, but others are matched with schools toward the bottom of their list. Popular schools get thousands of students seeking only a few hundred places. Perhaps most difficult, this year over 8,000 got no placement at all and had to create a new preference list from schools which still had openings after the first round. Then an appeal process is available. Many parents say it is the most anxious period of the parenthood—and we are not talking about choosing a college (Robbins, 2011, p. MB1).

In many ways as a response to the problems of the New York City Board of Education identified by Rogers years ago, today decision making for the New York City schools has been removed by the state legislature from the central board and the 32 local boards. Instead, the city's mayor appoints a chancellor, who serves at the mayor's pleasure, and an appointed advisory board, the majority of members appointed by the mayor, control decision making. Thus the board in this case has no independent voice. Some argue that local residents no longer have democratic control of their public school system (Ravitch, 2010). School boards in other districts have seen their decision-making power dwindle as professional educators handle complex policy issues and government mandates (Maeroff, 2010). Yet because many communities demand a say in running of the schools, elected school boards are likely to remain powerful in many districts around the United States.

The larger the system and the more entrenched the bureaucracy, the more there is resistance to change. A teacher facing 30 or more students each period, six periods a day, is unlikely to recognize an individual student's problem and take time and energy to deal with it. Therefore, that individual student may retreat further and further into the faceless mass at the high school, where 5,000 bodies are processed through the system. As we shall see in our discussions, various solutions to the impersonal bureaucracy have been proposed, some of which include decentralization of decision making; dividing large schools into smaller units; reducing class sizes; curricular changes; personalizing instruction; and having students more involved in the school and community settings.

Understanding Schools as Modern Organizations: Structures and Models

What should be done with early adolescents? This is the question underlying debate about the virtues of middle school or junior high structures versus other organizational structures. Recent trends indicate a shift from junior high schools (grades 7–9) and middle schools (grades 5–8 and 6–8) to programs structured from K-8 or K-12. These two structural models are shown in Figure 5.5, along with the general structure of education in the United States.

Are schools "loosely coupled" or tightly controlled? That question introduces two approaches to schools as organizations. Let us consider both ideas.

Organizations in which activities and decisions made at one level are not necessarily reflected at other levels have been called *loosely coupled* organizations. This description characterizes many school districts. Part of this structure comes from the autonomy and physical separation of levels of hierarchy in educational systems. Teachers, such as Sally Joseph in the earlier example, are spatially isolated and professionally autonomous in classrooms (Gamoran and Dreeban, 1989); many teachers who desire autonomy support and prefer this situation. Actions of administrators also may facilitate teacher autonomy by granting them control over the organization of the classroom. Viewing schools as "loosely coupled" may be closer to the reality faced by teachers than trying to understand their behavior and feelings of control over decision making through more traditional theories that focus on bureaucracy, control mechanisms of schools, or environmental pressures. However, the "No Child Left Behind" policy called for increased accountability, testing, and changes in curriculum, all of which have tightened the coupling and resulted in more centralized decision making. Although the Obama administration's education policy provides funds for local schools, those schools are held accountable for the expenditures and results.

Attempts to impact classroom teaching are often failures. Decisions made at administrative levels often have little impact on classrooms, and what goes on in classrooms is removed from the school's formal hierarchy, according to the loosely coupled model. Many administrators end up spending very little time on instructional matters. The dilemma for schools and their administrators is central coordination of educational activities in a situation where teachers are largely autonomous (Weick, 1976).

One example of a loosely coupled educational system can be seen in large metropolitan districts with multiple layers of administration. In contrast, private schools in the United States, such as preparatory and Catholic schools, are more tightly coupled but with administrations that are less complex; the result of the latter in most cases is more curricular coherence (Scott and Meyer, 1984). Teachers have more sense of control over classroom practice within the curriculum guidelines in Catholic schools, which some studies indicate leads to higher levels of satisfaction (Lee, Dedrick, and Smith, 1991). Where administrations control the availability and use of resources, such as funds for materials and distribution of resources, allocation of time, and student

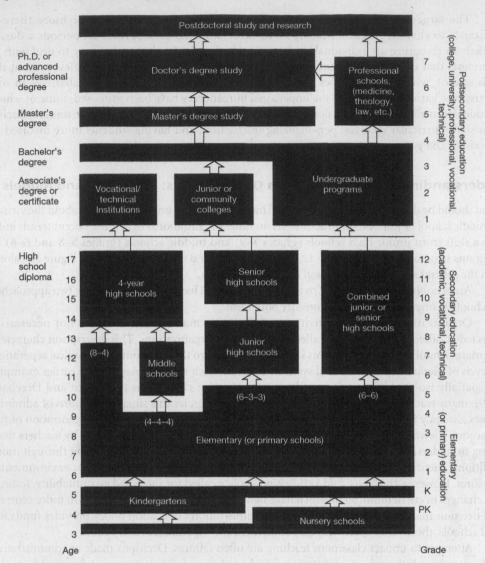

FIGURE 5.5 The structure of education in the United States.   *Source:* U.S. Department of Education, National Center for Education Statistics. Annual Reports Program, 2005. Available: http://nces.ed.gov/programs/digest/d05/figures/fig_01.asp

Note: Adult education programs, while not separately delineated above, may provide instruction at the elementary, secondary, or postsecondary education level. Chart reflects typical patterns of progression rather than all possible variations.

placements, units of the educational system may be more dependent on each other and more *tightly controlled.* How tightly or loosely coupled the system is also varies by grade and subject matter (Gamoran and Dreeban, 1989), and by pressure from communities, states, and the federal government for testing and for accountability of school systems and teachers. It is clear that the No Child Left Behind and Race to the Top programs have tried to tighten up the links between assessment and instruction, and between centralized educational goals and classroom teachers. We will see more of this in Chapter 6 when we discuss teacher evaluation and compensation.

Institutional theory and analysis are concerned with influence from the environment and broader cultural norms on educational systems. Researchers using this approach have several questions that guide their studies: Why do educational organizations located in different communities and even countries have similar practices and structures? How do these organizations adapt to changing conditions in their environments, both local and international? Do broader forces in cultures result in change across organizations? (Burch, 2007, p. 84).

Institutional theorists generally argue that broader cultural patterns guide organizations, and organizations adopt similar patterns to fit into the larger national and global systems. Schools are also influenced by the role-holders—administrators, teachers, and students—and their behaviors. For example, how teachers implement policies affects change; collectively teachers in classrooms can influence the larger system. Consider the introduction of technology into schools and classrooms. How teachers adopt and carry out technology programs influences the overall implementation systemwide (Spillane and Burch, 2006).

Educational organizations are shaped by external environments, from new technology to financial pressures (Meyer and Rowan, 1978). Their administrative structures become increasingly complex as educational organizations deal with new demands from their environments.

New programs in schools often come from external sources—profit and not-for-profit vendors such as private educational firms pushing test preparation courses, reading programs, or technology learning systems. The ways new programs are implemented may differ greatly across schools depending on the student needs and teachers who must carry out the new program. This is where institutional theorists and "loosely coupled" practices come together (Coburn, 2004). " . . . Studies that draw on institutional theory have brought needed nuance to our understanding of how educational policies and practices interact with institutional environments to shape policy outcomes" (Burch, 2007, p. 85). Figure 5.6 illustrates that institutional theory recognizes the broader educational and cultural forces that impact student achievement and good teaching (Burch, 2007).

Applying Sociology to Education: *In what ways is a bureaucratic organizational model useful to schools? In what ways can it be dysfunctional?*

CENTRALIZED VERSUS DECENTRALIZED DECISION MAKING: THE FIGHT OVER CONTROL OF SCHOOLS

In every system there are centers of power where decision making takes place. In the social system of the school, the locus of power has been in contention over the years. Key questions concern whether power should be concentrated in one central place or be distributed among parts of a system, who should make decisions for whom, and at what level. This section is concerned with how power and control are distributed in educational systems, with the politics of education, not primarily its organizational nature, as the last section emphasized. Some decision making takes place at each level of the system, from the school board to the superintendent to the teacher in the classroom to individual participants in the school (Barr and Dreeben, 1983). Most models break down decision making into two types: centralized and decentralized (Ingersoll, 1994, p. 150).

Centralization of Decision Making

The degree to which decision making is centralized varies with the size of the system; the loosely or tightly coupled status of the system, the degree of homogeneity of the people involved in the system, and people's goals for the system, whether it be at the international, national, state, or local/organizational level.

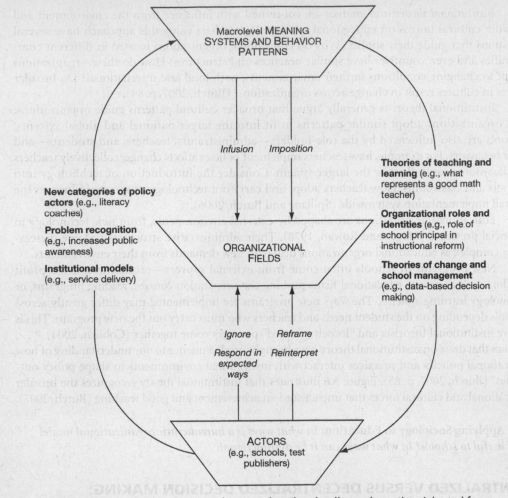

FIGURE 5.6 Institutional perspectives on educational policy and practice. Adapted from Scott and Meyer (1994). *Source:* Burch, Patricia, "Educational Policy and Practice from the Perspective of Institutional Theory: Crafting a Wider Lens," *Educational Researcher* Vol. 36, No. 2, pp. 84–95. March 2007. Reprinted by permission from SAGE Publications.

Powerful countries and international organizations influence policies and programs of less developed countries. For instance, the World Bank makes monetary policy, but it also "helps guide and create knowledge," which leads to the production of knowledge. Consider the impact foreign assistance has had on African educational systems. Education is essential for development, yet many African countries are unable to afford educational systems beyond elementary levels. Therefore, dependence on funds from foreign sources is necessary. The price is often centralization of curriculum, control, and decision making at the international level, and reduced local imagination and initiative in how to best educate a country's citizens.

The U.S. *federal government* has garnered increased control in education in recent years by determining areas of national concern, requiring schools to respond to initiatives, and allocating federal funds for education in those areas. When federal funds are provided for new programs, new administrators are hired to take on program responsibilities. This increases local educational bureaucracy and administrative expenditures, but without necessarily integrating the administrative unit into the educational system. This phenomenon of increased administrative size without integration has been called "fragmented centralization." For example, the federal government allocated funds for accelerated science and math programs in the "Sputnik Era" of the 1950s, when the U.S. government was concerned that the former Soviet Union was gaining a technological lead in the space program. In the 1990s, laws were passed requiring that all disabled children have access to education (Americans with Disabilities Act, 1990). More recently, accountability has been a theme. Centralized power and decision making in education, however, are not necessarily representative of the interests and concerns of the local community, resulting in potential fragmentation.

Another example of centralization is U.S. *state initiatives* in educational reform, spurred on by federal and private foundation commission reports lamenting the condition of education. State boards and commissions of education are recommending new policies at an unprecedented rate: preschool requirements for three- and four-year olds, schools in session 24/7 (Stevenson, 2007), new structures for schooling from K-8 or K-12, tougher graduation standards, proficiency exams, textbook and curricular revisions, longer school days, year-round school, and many other reforms. Consider the recent discussions over the teaching of evolution in Kansas when the Kansas school board voted to remove most references to evolution from state education standards ("Poll: Origin Theories," 2000). State representatives argued that until the local units and professional organizations take leadership, someone else must. (This decision by the Kansas school board has not gone into effect due to court challenges.)

Many of these new state initiatives are aimed at the very core of the instructional process—what is taught, how, and by whom—reducing the autonomy and decision making of local school boards (as in the case of New York City above), administrators, and teachers. Elected or appointed boards of education at the local and state levels have the ultimate decision-making power—on paper. In reality, as school districts have become larger and more centralized, and as the issues become more complex, requiring trained experts, school boards have tended to leave issues of educational policy to the school administrators, giving them rubber-stamp approval. They have retained for themselves the role of mediators between the schools and the community and the task of reviewing fiscal policies. In this way, professional educators in large educational systems have gained more autonomy over policy issues.

Another contender in the centralized "control of education" contest is *private organizations* such as foundations and industries, which have become increasingly involved in educational practice and policy. School boards are contracting with external organizations to perform services, negotiating with the company that can provide the most for the least. This occurs most often in noninstructional areas, such as food and janitorial services, but also in tutorial, reading, technology, and other instructional services. For example, private-company reading programs promise to raise reading levels of children. In some areas, businesses are providing financial support for teacher training and special programs for children.

Some *school districts* such as Tallahassee, Florida, Milwaukee, Wisconsin, Fairfax County, Virginia, and Houston, Texas, have "last-resort" or "second chance" programs in which they send high-risk or expelled students to charter schools or privately operated schools where the students find a more structured environment and sometimes more teacher attention (Hardy, 1999). Privatization of services could leave the school boards more time to deal with educational issues, but it also gives other organizations influence in school decision making and signifies another level of educational control.

Many suburban schools have a core of motivated *students and parents* who are involved in and influence the decisions of school boards and school officials. Involvement is possible when classes are small, expectations are high, and discipline is fair but firm, and where classrooms are structured for cooperative learning to meet more student needs than rigidly structured classes. In urban schools it is harder to get some parents involved, but schools face vocal concern from other parents and community members. Large school districts such as New York City have had major disputes over control of local schools, with concerned local citizens wanting to be involved in decision making concerning staff hiring and firing, building maintenance, construction plans, and curriculum.

Decentralization of Decision Making

Decentralized school management as opposed to central administrative decision making is a growing trend in the United States. Decentralization is often referred to as *site-based management*—"delegating authority to the school (site) instead of the central office, a shared decision-making model engaging various stakeholders and facilitative rather than directive leadership" (Cromwell, 2005, p. 1). Popular in discussions of educational reform, the idea involves shifting the initiative in public education from school boards, superintendents, and central administrative offices to individual schools. This gives local schools more responsibility for school operations (Cromwell, 2005). While many decision makers laud decentralization, others point out problems such as lack of clear parameters and standards for operation, lack of training for being autonomous, lack of control over accountability standards, and power issues that hamper decision making.

Some view decentralization simply as an administrative device—as a shift in administration from the national to the state or city governments, or from central city administrative offices to the local schools. Others insist that decentralization should embody a design for meaningful shifts in power from central administration to local community schools, and that plans should go beyond education to other crucial areas such as counseling and health for students and even families.

Advocates of local control maintain that only decentralization can temper the central bureaucratic monopoly on power and decision making. Studies of schools that have decentralized reveal that students improve in their academic achievement; this is especially true in smaller high schools. Local control can facilitate schools in meeting local needs, being flexible, being responsive to student talents and abilities, and providing mixed-ability classes and cooperative learning (Snell, 2006).

Philadelphia, with help from several agencies, funded a school initiative to give local school sites greater autonomy to coordinate curriculum and instruction across disciplines and grades. Teachers working together were the key to revamping schools' organizational structures and to ongoing success of decentralized decision making. The conclusions from this largely successful experiment indicate that restructuring initiatives should be teacher-driven at local sites with external change agents and funding of necessary components in the initial phases (Useem, 1994). Giving teachers decision-making power makes a difference in teachers' perceptions of their daily lives and quality of their teaching.

San Francisco developed a plan to decentralize through school choice, allowing parents to choose their children's public schools. The money follows students, but schools left with harder-to-educate students such as those with few English skills or special education needs get more funds per student. With site-based budgeting, each school decides where to put its funds. This plan has resulted in many niche schools in performing arts, language, and math and technology. Similar programs have been developed in Cincinnati, Houston, St. Paul, Seattle, and Oakland districts around the United States, and other cities are developing such programs (Snell, 2006). Research findings indicate that decentralized school plans reduce fraudulent or corrupt, nonresponsive bureaucracy; provide more money at the classroom level; and result in higher achievement (Ouchi, 2003).

Although the power struggles over control of decision making in public schools continue, some parents are expressing their concern about the direction of schools by withdrawing their children altogether and placing them in private schools or homeschooling them. Some proposals for alternative structures of education have been realized in the form of alternative and free schools. Parent and student input into decision making is built into these school structures. Charter schools have experienced rapid growth, but with their rapid growth have come many questions, court cases, and some failures. Educational critics such as Ivan Illich (1971, p. 154) have recommended total restructuring or "deschooling" of education as we know it today, in order to change the locus of power. (These alternatives are discussed in Chapter 13 on educational reforms, alternatives, and movements.)

One thing is clear: The issues that fuel locus-of-control fires are still hot. The issue of school control concerns more than just the control of education; for minority groups, it reflects issues of control over life chances.

Applying Sociology to Education: *Considering local needs, national needs, teacher and student morale, and other relevant factors, when and where is centralization versus decentralization the best organizational model for schools?*

REFORM OF SCHOOL ORGANIZATION

There is no shortage of suggestions for improving schools. One of those suggestions that is the subject of research and debate is small schools or schools-within-schools (Darling-Hammond, 2010; Honig, 2009).

Small Schools and Classrooms: Are They Better for Student Achievement?

In the 1940s, there were over 200,000 school districts in the United States; today there are fewer than 15,000 serving three times as many students (Meier, 2006). Many of these districts are huge and centralized. Research tells us that there is more involvement, more feeling of ownership, and more "membership communities" when schools are small. But is achievement greater? Do students become better citizens, learn more, and care more about learning in small schools? Are there disadvantages to small schools? Advocates of small schools characterize them as communities with engaged students and collaborative faculties (Lee and Ready, 2007; Raywid, 2006; Ready, Lee, and Welner, 2004). Those who question spending the funds and reorganizing schools argue that small schools have less diversity and fewer sports and other activities, and do not necessarily provide achievement advantages proportionate to the expenditures (Schneider, Wysse, and Keesler, 2006; Viadero, 2006).

While the evidence is mixed, the sentiment among educators is that small schools provide tangible and intangible results that large, more impersonal schools cannot. In recent years a number of researchers have pointed out both academic and personal values in small schools, both urban and rural; they tend to have higher academic achievement, are more personal, have higher student and teacher satisfaction and morale, lower dropout rates and behavior problems, and have more students involved in extracurricular activities. They have particular benefits for disadvantaged students. A small but consistent relationship exists between size and disorder as well. Small schools are safer, have greater communication and performance feedback, and have more individuals involved in decision making (Gottfredson, 1986). Because of the apparent advantages of small schools, some educators are creating mini-schools or schools-within-schools in larger school buildings, dividing students into small communities (McAndrews and Anderson, 2002). In fact, some researchers argue that small school size is essential if meaningful school reform is to take place.

The effectiveness of small classroom size (under 17 students) versus medium (17–25) and large (over 25) is also subjects of research—and policy disagreements (Biddle and Berliner, 2002). Some argue that the evidence clearly supports the benefits of small class size for learning and achievement; others using the same evidence argue that class size alone does not result in higher student achievement, but that other reforms in such areas as teacher education are needed to see benefits (Rees and Johnson, 2000).

Early studies of small classes and schools were experiments and field studies of individual or small groups of schools; large-scale surveys have also been used to gather data; and large field experiments in states including Tennessee, Indiana, Wisconsin, and California have provided extensive data. For example, California Partnership Academies with over 290 programs for 10th to 12th grades provide small learning communities and partnerships with businesses. For students, this integrates academic and career technical education (California Department of Education, 2009). Some conclusions using information from all of these studies are as follows:

1. Carefully planned and adequately funded small-class programs (generally fewer than 20 students) in early grades generate substantial gains;
2. The longer students are in small classes, the greater the gains;
3. Gains occur in both testing and other indicators of students' success;
4. Gains are retained through upper levels of schooling; and
5. Gains occur for all students, but are greatest for disadvantaged students who carry more gains to upper grades.

(Note: Limited evidence is available for the effectiveness of small class size at the high school levels.)

The explanations for these findings focus on the greater possible interaction of teachers with individual students; this allows students to better understand classroom rules and culture that carry over into future classrooms, a benefit especially relevant for students from disadvantaged homes. Learning the school culture is crucial in the early grades, hence the strong findings for positive effects of small classes for lower grades. Enthusiastic, well-trained teachers are also key to the small-class-size advantage. Classroom management and discipline take less time and energy, and students are more engaged in small classes and small instructional groups within classes.

In a comparison of the research on the effects of small classrooms on achievement, the authors conclude, "All students would reap sizable education benefits and long-lasting advantages . . . and students from educationally disadvantaged groups would benefit even more. . . . no other educational reform has yet been studied that would provide such striking benefits" (Biddle and Berliner, 2002, p. 22).

Despite ample evidence that small classrooms produce positive results for primary schools students, policy makers have been slow to move on these findings. Why? Perhaps it is because of ignorance about the issue; ineffective dissemination of results; prejudice against those students who might benefit the most (poor and minority); politicizing the issue by making funding a choice between high-stakes testing and more teachers; and practical problems such as finding space, hiring more teachers, and funding small-class initiatives (Biddle and Berliner, 2002, p. 22). We return to some of these themes in Chapter 8.

SUPPORTS FOR SCHOOL IMPROVEMENT

How schools are organized and operate can make the difference between successful and failed attempts at instruction in classrooms. The following are five aspects of schools that support life in classrooms and successful student achievement as gleaned from research (Bryk, 2010, pp. 24–25):

1. Coherent instructional guidance system: help for teachers in the form of instructional guidance in teaching; feedback mechanisms to help assess effectiveness of teaching; and materials, tools, and instructional routines shared by faculty to support their efforts.
2. Professional capacity: the quality of teachers, professional development to support them, and teachers working together improve instruction. This involves performance feedback and cooperation to solve problems.
3. Strong parent-community-school ties: student motivation and participation reflects the strength of parent and community ties with schools.
4. Student-centered learning climate: teachers, administrators, and staff in schools influence the learning climate in schools and set the tone for students to see themselves as learners. A safe environment is basic to learning as is belief in students' abilities and support for each student's needs.
5. Leadership drives change: principals in successful and improving schools serve as dynamic leaders. They involve the local community, and hire and develop effective staff.

The organizational structure of schools has a major impact on the success of schools. Other important influences on school success include the statuses and roles in schools and how they are carried out, which is the topic of our next chapter.

Summary

In this chapter we have discussed the school as an organization, focusing on formal aspects of the internal functioning of schools. In our systems model, the organization represents the actual school or system being considered. For analytical purposes, the focus here is on the internal organization more than on the interaction of the organization with its environment. However, when discussing goals and centralized versus decentralized decision making, the influence of the environment cannot be ignored. The following outline summarizes major topics covered.

I. SOCIAL SYSTEM OF THE SCHOOL

The relation of the organization to the systems model is discussed, summarizing structural components of educational systems such as classrooms and positions of participants within the school.

II. GOALS OF THE SCHOOL SYSTEM

School goals serve multiple purposes in helping define the system's activities. Goals are not the product of isolated educational systems but reflect the concerns of the larger society, the community, participants in the school, and individuals.

III. THE SCHOOL AS AN ORGANIZATION

Two models of school organization are discussed: bureaucracy and loosely coupled. Characteristics of bureaucracy as outlined by Max Weber are discussed:

1. Division of labor, recruitment, and promotion policies
2. Hierarchical system of authority
3. Rules, regulations, and procedures
4. Holders of similar positions being treated the same
5. Rationality of the organization.

Problems in using a bureaucratic model in education settings are outlined, and the relationship between growth and bureaucracy is discussed. Institutional model and loosely coupled organizations reflect activities and decisions that are made at one level, but not necessarily carried out at other levels. Because teachers often have a great deal of autonomy, this model may come close to fitting many schools.

IV. CENTRALIZED VERSUS DECENTRALIZED DECISION MAKING: THE FIGHT OVER CONTROL OF SCHOOLS

With the growth of schools has come more centralized decision making. However, challenges from local residents of huge bureaucratic systems have forced school officials to heed demands for greater local representation. One movement for decentralization is site-based management. Another is "choice."

Evidence is mixed on the value of smaller school size, but most educational researchers find evidence that small schools do provide significant benefits, especially for disadvantaged students. Small class size at the primary level, likewise, allows for socialization into school culture and benefits all students, especially disadvantaged students.

Putting Sociology to Work

1. Visit a high school—the one you attended, if possible. In your field notes, indicate examples of Weber's characteristics of bureaucracies and decision-making patterns in the school and classroom.
2. Imagine you are from another culture; describe the school you visit as if you had no familiarity with the education system. Note the norms (rules, behavior patterns, communication patterns, and so forth) and functioning of the organization.
3. What are your most memorable school experiences? How do they relate to the material in this chapter? (For example, what were your positions in the structure?)

4. Compare your goals for high school when you were a student with your goals for high schools now. What were your goals for college while in high school? Have they changed?
5. Visit a large high school and primary school and a small one. What differences do you note between them in school climate? Can you learn anything about teacher–student interactions in each and about student achievement?
6. What are the advantages and disadvantages of local, site-based management of schools?

6

Formal School Statuses and Roles

"The Way It Spozed to Be"

It was an exciting meeting! Half the town turned out to express their views and hear the discussion on the issue of a sex education course in the local middle school. The 7th graders were being shown anatomy videos and contraceptives, and a large group of parents disapproved, arguing that these matters should be dealt with at home. Other parents took the position that teenagers need all the information they can get, especially with the high rate of teenage pregnancy and disease. Because the topic is not dealt with in many homes, they felt schools should cover it. Of the various pressures confronting school personnel from both inside and outside of the school building, the question of sex education in schools is very much typical of the conflicting pressures facing schools around the United States. Involved in this real scenario are community members representing interest groups, parents, students, school administrators, teachers, and probably many others. In this chapter, we look at the roles of these stakeholders in schools and their influence in the educational process.

For each of us there is a degree of discontinuity in the statuses we hold. We have a high status in one social setting—parent, oldest sibling, supervisor over other workers, and president of a club—and low status in other social settings—patient, student, and low-guy-on-the-totem-pole at the neighborhood gym. This chapter on statuses (positions) and roles (responsibilities in those positions) in the organization and how they relate to each other is a continuation of our discussion of the organizational structure in educational systems.

THE MEANING OF ROLES

Recall your experience as a student in elementary and high school. Not only did your statuses (positions) and roles (responsibilities in your positions) change as you progressed through the system, but in some classroom situations your status was higher than in others. Perhaps you won the English composition competition but were unskilled in math; you may have been the fastest runner on the playground but could not spell "whether."

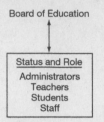

FIGURE 6.1   Hierarchy of positions.

Statuses and Roles in the System

Every organization is made up of an interrelated set of statuses or positions that members of the system occupy (see Figure 6.1).

These positions are needed to perform tasks and meet the goals of the system. Implicit in each position is a set of responsibilities or parts to be played by the individual holding the position; these activities make up the roles. Sometimes the specific requirements of the position are written out; these represent the ideal for that position. Sometimes positions are only roughly defined, allowing considerable room to determine one's own role behavior. Often, there is a great deal of flexibility in role performance, especially as one moves up in the hierarchy and gains seniority. All individuals bring their own experiences and personalities into the position. Principal A is not identical to principal B, although the job descriptions may be the same.

Role expectations held by decision makers affect the selection of persons for particular positions. Choices may reflect prevailing stereotypes or norms, such as those that encourage selecting women for elementary-level teaching positions or males for administrative positions.

The School Organization and Roles

The organizational settings in which we carry out our roles define and limit the ways we behave. For example, a classic description of centralization in the New York City system states, "to guarantee uniform standards across the city, to preserve professional autonomy from outside political interference at the local level, to prevent ethnic separation, and to maintain headquarters control over field officials" (Rogers, 1969, p. 272). "Most decisions on such matters as curriculum, staffing, budgeting, supplies, construction, and maintenance are made by professionals at central headquarters, several layers removed from the schools themselves" (Rogers, 1969, pp. 271–272). The result of organizational centralization means that decision making is removed from the classroom, and teachers' autonomy may be limited. Centralization is but one organizational factor that affects role performance of members of the system. Teachers in their own autonomous classrooms, however, have a great deal of flexibility in how to implement programs and the curriculum.

Role Expectations and Conflict

What we expect of principals, teachers, school counselors, and others varies depending on our position in the organization. Schools function smoothly when people agree on role expectations and roles are carried out in accordance with those understandings; however, when there is disagreement, conflicts arise. A key problem here is that the goals of education are often ambiguous, even contradictory, and not universally shared; this can cause confusion in role expectations.

From the functionalist perspective, role expectations as defined by the organization and agreed to by participants should benefit all by helping to maintain a smooth running system, assuming individuals carry out their role expectations as planned. From the conflict perspective, some roles put the role-holders in advantageous positions for obtaining the scarce resources of society; for students this includes good grades and test scores, admission to prestigious colleges, good jobs, and high salaries. The more authority there is in a role, the greater the possibility of conflict between that role and roles of those with less authority. For instance, persons in the teacher role have the authority to dominate those in the student role. This domination can be achieved in subtle ways through the socialization process, which forces students into a subordinate role.

Role conflict occurs for individuals when their own role expectations are in conflict with expectations of others or cannot be met. When students must study for exams and carry out family responsibilities, or teachers differ with parents over course content or discipline techniques, expectations between members of the system and the environment are in conflict. This conflict may happen when definitions of the position and the function the position plays toward meeting system goals differ among members of the organization.

Applying Sociology to Education: *Describe some statuses and roles you hold in the educational system. What can cause role conflict?*

PROFESSIONALS IN THE EDUCATIONAL SYSTEM

Sociologists characterize professionals by several factors (Ingersoll and Merrill, 2011a):

1. credential and licensing requirements for entry (into the profession)
2. induction and mentoring programs for entrants
3. professional development support, opportunities, and participation
4. specialization
5. authority over decision making
6. compensation levels
7. prestige and occupational social standing.

Certain occupations such as law and medicine fall clearly into the category of professions. Because of professionals' commitment to fellow professionals in their area of expertise, and to their professional organizations, conflict can arise between the principles governing the bureaucracies for which they work and those governing their profession. This role conflict can make it difficult for professionals to adjust to bureaucratic structures.

The school system presents a unique situation when considering occupations that are professional. Teachers—who make up the majority of staff members—are "marginal professionals," or what has been referred to as "semiprofessionals." They share this not-quite-professional status with nurses, social workers, librarians, and others (Ingersoll and Perda, 2008). These semi-professions have some common characteristics: They involve nurturing, helping, and supporting responsibilities. They also include a preponderance of females. For example, 82 percent of public elementary and secondary school teachers in the United States are female (National Center for Education Information, 2005); although more males have entered teaching in recent years, many are skimmed off for administrative positions at higher levels. Even at secondary school levels, teaching has been characterized as a "feminine role," although there are more male teachers at the high school level. Strong arguments have been made that only predominantly male occupations receive professional status and that predominantly female occupations have failed to reach this level because of a male political and economic elite that keeps job status and pay of teachers and other semiprofessionals down and leaves them little autonomy within the bureaucratic system.

Teachers have made claims to hold professional status in order to gain higher prestige and pay, but they have not yet developed the "teacher subculture" (unity as a group) to claim full professional status (Ingersoll and Perda, 2008). Professions have clear qualifications and boundaries for membership, whereas membership in the teaching occupation is much less clearly defined. This difficulty stems from several factors related to the nature of teaching. First, teaching was not considered to be "regular" employment in this country until the mid-nineteenth century when it acquired serious occupational status with the advent of free, public education, and the founding, in 1857, of the professional organization, the National Teachers Association (now the National Education Association). Teachers are still employed by bureaucracies, however, under the direction of principals, superintendents, and boards of education. Direction, then, comes from the bureaucracy rather than the professional organizations.

Professions have high prestige in occupational rankings. "Teacher" was not near the top of prestige rankings in an early ranking, however. In data comparing 60 countries with the United States on occupational prestige rankings, high school teachers ranked 64 out of 90 occupations (Tremain, 1977). Secondary school teachers in the United States had an occupational prestige score of 66, the same as registered nurses, the second of the two highest-ranked "female" occupations; and elementary school teachers have a score of 64 (*General Social Survey*, 1998). However, a recent occupational ranking shows teachers receiving higher rankings in the list of professionals and semiprofessionals (Taylor, 2002), and teaching is still one of the higher-prestige occupations readily available to women.

Whereas many professions operate on a "fee-for-service" basis, that is pay for providing a service, teachers receive a salary from the organization in exchange for teaching students; they are expected to prepare students for life after school. A further distinction is that professionals have expert training and a command of knowledge not generally possessed by lay persons, and they are scrutinized by colleagues, whereas teachers do not possess unique knowledge (though their skills are specialized), and are scrutinized and regulated by the bureaucracy and lay public. Thus, the knowledge and skills of professionals are seen as specialized and vital, whereas teachers' skills are more general.

In bureaucratic settings, many teachers must contend with close supervision, emphasis on rules, and centralization of decision making. These factors of standardization and centralization are alienating to those who want to be considered and treated as professionals. The desire for professional status and the frustration of trying to gain recognition, prestige, autonomy, and higher salaries in the bureaucratic setting have led to reform movements, militancy, and unionization of teachers.

ROLES IN SCHOOLS

No roles exist in a vacuum. Roles locate us in relation to others who hold reciprocal positions. Following the role hierarchy in Figure 6.1, we can now look at the role responsibilities of each of these position-holders and evaluate their relationship to one another.

School Boards: Liaison between School and Community

Community members with concerns about a school often express those concerns to school board members, their community liaison with the school. Hence, we first take a look at school boards and the role they play in bridging the boundary between school and community.

ROLE OF THE LOCAL SCHOOL BOARD. Lay school boards are a uniquely U.S. phenomena, stemming from the idea of public control of schools. Theoretically, local school boards (also called board of regents, board of education, board of trustees, or board of directors) have a tremendous amount of power awarded to them by most states. This power stems from the tradition in our country of democratic lay control over schools. Nearly every school at every level, public or private, has its board.

The National School Boards Association compiled the following list of formal duties to meet organization goals representing the legal role of school boards:

1. Hiring superintendent, principals, and teachers
2. Determining teachers' salaries and contracts
3. Providing transportation for students
4. Determining the size of the school budgets
5. Deciding the length of the school term
6. Building new schools and facilities
7. Changing school attendance boundaries
8. Selecting textbooks and subjects to be taught
9. Maintaining school discipline.

In reality, once the board has selected the superintendent, most boards exert little control over the administration, teaching, or curriculum, but concern themselves with school policy matters (Maeroff, 2010). Boards in large districts tend to be more diverse and political, with funding and student achievement being key topics, and decisions about special education, teacher quality, educational technology, and safety being important issues (Hess, 2002).

Recent policies in some school districts have removed the decision-making power from school boards and placed it in the hands of mayors or other officials. This move is seen by some as efficient, but by others as removing what little influence local communities have had on the direction of their schools through their locally elected school boards (Ravitch, 2010).

State boards of education, often appointed by state governors and subject to the approval of legislators, oversee state standards and district policies, especially where state monies are concerned. In recent cases of bankruptcy of large school districts, state boards of education have played major roles devising new financing plans. Although decisions over curriculum are primarily a local matter, states may wield considerable influence in decisions on curriculum issues (science teaching, civics, and sex education), expenditures, and methods for financing schools.

COMPOSITION AND EXPECTATIONS OF SCHOOL BOARDS. In the United States, each state's laws determine how board members are selected and what powers are delegated to local school boards. Almost all, 96.2 percent, of school boards are elected, although some states allow either elected or appointed school boards depending on local preference (Hess, 2002). Boards are composed predominantly of white, professional males (61.1 percent) with higher than average incomes and education (Hess, 2002). They are generally between 41 and 50 years of age and have children in school. Females make up 38.9 percent of board members nationally, African Americans, 7.8 percent, and Hispanics, 3.8 percent. In urban districts, African Americans make up 13 percent and Hispanics 7.5 percent of board members. The typical board has between five and eight members who serve four-year terms. The average member serves for 6.7 years, meaning many are re-elected for second terms. Two-thirds of board members receive no salary for their board work (Leal et al., 2004).

Many conflict theorists argue that minority views are not proportionally represented or influential in school decision making. Neo-Marxists Samuel Bowles and Herbert Gintis argue that schools serve the interests of those who dominate the economy in a capitalist system (Bowles and Gintis, 1976). Thus, in the few districts that appointed school board members, they are more likely than elected members to represent bourgeois interests of those in power; the potential for conflict with other community interest groups is great. Not all agree. Members of the community likely to serve on the volunteer school boards generally have a genuine interest in the educational system and represent a cross-section of community interests, yet they usually have little orientation or training for their job.

Community members have certain expectations of school board members. Although these may differ depending on whether the individual is a parent, taxpayer, professional, or other, six role expectations stand out: promote public interest in education; defend community values; hear complaints and grievances; supervise school personnel; conserve resources; and promote individual rights and interests within the school.

School board member priorities tend to focus largely on funding decisions and student achievement, but also on special education, teacher quality, and educational technology (Hess, 2002). When the priorities of school board members and the public are compared, the discrepancies represent the boards' concerns with managerial problems that sometimes differ from community and parent concerns. In fact, the gap between views of the public and board members is wide on a number of issues. Asked whether the schools are doing a good job, 71 percent of urban board members said yes, and only 37 percent of urban adults agreed. Although 82 percent of urban board members said their districts were effective at keeping violence and drugs out of schools, only 33 percent of urban adults agreed (National School Board Foundation, 1999).

FACTORS AFFECTING BOARD DECISIONS.   The most troublesome issues facing board members are state and federal mandates and money issues; for example, funds may be needed to renovate facilities and support after-school programs, but no funding is available for these initiatives. In addition, boards may become mired in controversial issues requiring funding that prevent them from dealing with long-term planning and policy issues.

Boards are limited in their effectiveness and influence in part because they are caught in the middle between the demands of electors and the needs of the school. As revealed in the example concerning sex education at the beginning of the section, some issues faced by school boards are specific, perhaps isolated, concerns, causing brief episodes of conflict. Most of the board's decision making, however, is more routine, and interactions are primarily with parent–teacher associations, administration, teachers, and concerned community members. School boards cannot be expected to command the knowledge of the professional educators—superintendents, principals, and teachers—and this fact alone limits their decision-making capabilities and control. In fact, boards often rely on the knowledge and expertise of professional educators such as superintendents and principals when making decisions.

Some educational analysts feel boards have too much power considering their limited expertise, and propose a more limited role for local school boards; some reports suggest that state boards of education should take on more responsibility for local decisions. In the case of New York City, the city with the country's largest school system with 1.1 million students, distrust of the 32 locally elected boards of education responsible for elementary schools, and an appointed board running the rest of the system, resulted in the state legislature giving the mayor sole authority to govern the schools. Although there is a citizen advisory board, its powers are very limited. (Ravitch, 2010).

School boards have reciprocal relationships with other role-holders in the system. The most direct link is through the superintendent they hire. This relationship has been compared to a marriage, and for the most part the partnership is a happy one, with board members supportive of superintendents. However, breaks do occur, primarily because of loss of confidence and faith, or evidence of mismanagement of finances.

This interdependence between roles also affects decision making. Boards receive carefully selected information on issues from teachers and administrators; some issues may be filtered out and never reach the board. Effective superintendents have developed good communication and trust, and they possess knowledge that no board member can fully master; by controlling information, superintendents have great influence over board decisions.

Applying Sociology to Education: *How is the school board selected in your community, what segments of the community are represented, and what issues do they deal with?*

Superintendent: Manager of the School System

The office was large. A long table covered with computer printouts and charts took up one side of the room, and a rather large desk faced by two easy chairs stood on the other side. Books on administration matters, teaching, and curriculum were shelved around the walls. As I entered, the superintendent jumped up, looking relieved to take his eyes off the figures for a few minutes. We discussed his role. The responsibilities of a superintendent of a small school district include a large number of routine roles: issuing budget reports; engaging in staff negotiations; answering mail and phone calls; meeting with principals, staff, and others; carrying out routine "blessings" on projects; giving symbolic gestures of support and approval; preparing reports for the board, the state, and the federal government; keeping up with new regulations; responding to questions; and making staff recommendations. These tasks take up the bulk of time. If time remains, matters such as long-term planning and curriculum and teacher evaluation can be considered.

Crises interrupt the normal flow of work, making it difficult for the superintendent to plan a firm schedule. An unexpected shortage of heating fuel, for example, can make it suddenly necessary to arrange for double sessions. Successful superintendents juggle their various constituencies—community groups, parents, the school board, principals, teachers, and staff—with skill. In large districts the responsibilities of the role may be divided between several assistant superintendents, each of whom specializes in an aspect of the role such as curriculum, public relations, or staffing.

The profile of typical superintendents was, until recently, predominantly white males. In 1982, only 1.2 percent were females. A 2010 survey by the American Association of School Administrators found that 24.1 percent were female. Most are still white while only 2 percent are black and another 2 percent were Hispanic/Latino, but that is twice the proportion of minority superintendents in 1982 (http:// www.aasa.org/NCE/NCEcontent.aspx?id=18176. accessed, May 16, 2011).

Large urban school districts are finding it increasingly difficult to attract superintendent candidates. Problems with hostile boards, shabby treatment, negative publicity, graft and corruption, conflicting expectations, and rigid requirements for the job make it unappealing to qualified candidates.

THE ADVENT OF ADMINISTRATION. Until the late nineteenth century, local boards were responsible for running the community schools. With smaller districts and fewer compulsory years of schooling, this was possible. As school systems became increasingly large, complex, and urban, a force of trained, full-time professionals took over the day-to-day running of the schools; school boards relied on these hired agents, delegating significant power to them. Tyack describes this transformation from village school to urban system as an organizational revolution that made educational systems move from a relatively informal relationship between school and community to a more systematic and rational system. This transformation paralleled changes in society to a more corporate, bureaucratic system run by professionals; values of industrialization, free enterprise, and capitalism resulted in large industrial organizations becoming the model for schools (Kantor, 2001; Tyack, 1974).

The move toward bureaucratic school systems resulted in what Callahan calls the "cult of efficiency," sacrificing educational goals to the demands of business procedures. The dilemmas about how to best run the schools are still prevalent today (Callahan, 1962). The number and specialization of administrators depend largely on the size and complexity of the system. Small districts may have one superintendent who is a generalist, as in the preceding example; large districts need specialized managerial expertise in such areas as business, legal matters, personnel, public relations, and data-processing operations.

POWER OF THE SUPERINTENDENT.   The actual power of the superintendent to make decisions for the system is related to a number of social and environmental factors: the type of community in which the position is held; the composition and role of the school board; baby booms which cause expanding student populations; teacher strikes; demands by teachers, students, and community for more power and autonomy in decision making; federal guidelines and requirements for accountability; and court orders. In attempts to exercise power, the superintendent may be faced with conflicting demands from these constituencies. For example, pressures may be brought to bear on superintendents to cut costs radically at the same time that the teachers are demanding higher salaries.

Often the outcome of power conflicts depends on the superintendent's style. Being politically suave in dealing with the board and the public and using expertise to its greatest advantage can put the superintendent in a powerful position. As Willard Waller, an early sociologist of education in the United States, suggested,

> [W]e must conclude that it is a difference in [superintendents'] personal techniques which accounts for this [ability to deal with the school board] . . . that ability to dominate a school board pleasantly is a greater factor in determining personal advancement in this walk of life than the ability to administer a school system of students and teachers. (Waller, [1932] 1965, p. 94)

Regardless of the distribution and degree of power, the role of superintendent has become a firmly established and essential part of most school districts.

The Principal: School Boss-in-the-Middle

Principals are managers and coordinators. Their roles include supporting teachers, disciplining students, counseling students and teachers, managing the budget, scheduling classes, dealing with concerns from the school's environment, and handling the myriad of other problems that arise each day in the school.

ROLE OF THE PRINCIPAL.   A careful look at the roles of the principal shows that most, by definition, involve interaction with other individuals—teachers, superintendents, parents, students, staff, and service providers. Principals have more direct contact with the public than do superintendents. They hold positions in the middle, often between conflicting interests. They are the bosses of their schools, and as such they must make recommendations on the hiring and firing of teachers, and at the same time give moral support to their teachers. Handling such potentially conflicting responsibilities is not easy. Many variables affect the role and expectations of a principal— size of the school and district, a rural or big-city location, and the social-class background of the children attending the school. When principals were asked about their main problems, they mentioned funding, micromanaging by superiors, politics entering into decision making, accountability movements, federal government mandates, and teacher quality and tenure issues. These problems differed in order of importance by large versus small schools and urban versus suburban and rural schools (Farkas et al., 2003). Principals face new challenges in the twenty-first century such as earlier onset of student puberty and growing diversity in schools (Tirozzi, 2001).

Principals interact with a variety of others in their school's environment, from professional and technical experts in education to parents and community members. Within the school, research stresses the importance of the principal (or designated leader) as instructional leader in creating an effective school culture to support strong academics and achievement (Brookover et al., 1996). If the principal works with the teaching staff and receives support from them, planned change from federal, state, and local mandates is more likely to occur (Deal and Peterson, 1993).

When we hear little from the principals' offices, things are probably going smoothly. They are busy managing their schools; facilitating the teaching and learning processes taking place; dealing with daily, routine, teacher needs and student concerns; and maintaining good relationships with groups outside the school. Principals report that their priorities are shaped by measures of school effectiveness such as enacting accountability standards, ensuring school safety, developing good teachers, maintaining effective community relations, and creating a sense of shared purpose within the school (Genzen, 2000; Lyons, 1999; Smith, 1999).

School administrators spend part of each day dealing with the unexpected; this includes building problems; student discipline and illness or accidents; occasionally disasters such as bus accidents, suicides or murders, bomb threats or weapons in the school; and natural disasters such as tornadoes. Here is a description of a typical day from a small-town elementary school principal:

> My day starts before the school opens. I check to make sure the building is in order and teachers in place. When possible, I like to be in the halls to greet students as they come in; seeing them gives me a lift.
>
> Many of my interactions with teachers take place in the halls where we exchange a few words about an issue or problems. Most problems for teachers can be solved in this way. Of course, we have team leaders' meetings too.
>
> Only severe discipline problems come to me. Most are handled in the classroom. But if students are damaging property or endangering other children or fighting, then I see them.
>
> There are always the routine things to do—reports, curriculum matters, budgeting, and so forth. But when a parent comes in, I drop everything, if possible, to see that parent.
>
> I think some people feel we sit behind a desk and shuffle papers, but that's only the tip of the iceberg. I have a daily plan, but more often than not things come up which need immediate intervention. (Interview with elementary school principal by the author)

What do principals "do" all day? Teachers are in their classrooms teaching the students, so does that not leave free time for the principal? The answer is a resounding "no." Principals in elementary schools have days fractured into numerous activities (Lortie, 2009). Meeting with various constituents including parents, writing reports and filling in paperwork, evaluating staff members, maintaining an open door for teachers, watching over hundreds of children's safety, working with contractors for lunch and cleaning services—these are but a few of the many tasks that fall to the principal.

The principals of middle schools or junior high schools face a different type of situation than elementary school principals. Students in the junior high age group have been described as a "jumble of hormones." They are trying to "get it all together," and each child copes in a different way. Children may be less manageable within the classroom and discipline becomes more of an issue at this level, thus involving the principal or assistant principal.

High school principals have the additional role of preparing students for the transition to college and the work world. High school principals and school districts are being held accountable for the students they pass from grade to grade and graduate. State and federal mandates control the degrees of freedom principals have to make decisions for their districts. Several legal suits have been brought against school systems on the grounds that they graduate students who cannot read or write at a 12th-grade or even 10th-grade level. Competency testing of students and testing of new teachers are often the responsibility of the principal. (These issues are discussed further in later chapters.) Being both effective managers and instructional leaders is difficult, and some suggest that these tasks should not fall to the same person.

In some districts the role of the principal has been enhanced. In New York City, for example, some principals have been given significantly more power over their school than is typical. They have greater control of the school's budget and make decisions about how to allocate much of it. They also have greater autonomy in selecting staff, deciding about special programs, and the like. The idea behind this is that principals should be managers of the schools with the prerogatives that managers have in other settings, and thus can be held accountable for the performance of the school. This idea is consistent with the move in many districts to increase the school options available to parents. The increase in school choice plans has fueled the development of a market for schools, where individual schools compete with each other for enrollments. For this to flourish, proponents argue, schools need to be free to innovate and to develop their own strengths.

In many systems today, a high priority for principals is the marketing of their school—a new role expectation. These pressures are increased as "school report cards" of various kinds are becoming widely available and used as the basis for administrator and teacher evaluation (Hemphill, and Nauer, 2010). Many persons in the school system play roles complementary to that of the principal. Principals cannot perform their own roles without giving some consideration to how their performance might affect or infringe on the roles of others. In essence, then, these others play an important part in the definition and delineation of the principal's roles.

PROBLEMS FACED BY PRINCIPALS.   A friend of Jeanne, an elementary school principal, recently retired. She was ill from the constant job stress: continually failing levies resulting in reduced teaching staff, shortage of classroom staff and supplies, low staff morale due to overwork, a student body that "came and went" due to parent(s) in marginal economic situations, students with many problems at home, continued government demands for higher academic achievement from children whose lives were falling apart and who needed stability and belonging, increasing time spent on paperwork rather than educating, demands to campaign for school levies—the list goes on. Her days were long, and rewards increasingly reduced. Ultimately, she felt powerless to help her school's children and bring about the needed change.

The role of the principal today is both demanding and increasingly stressful as illustrated by the case example above. "Many principals are unable to cope with the growing demands and the resulting stress. Exhausted, they are retiring silently" (Brown, 2006). Particularly difficult are the continually changing requirements from federal legislation. Some educational policy makers report that training programs are not preparing principals for today's demands. They call for more and different training for principals including changes in coursework to reflect the changing requirements and demands of the job, and more practical experience. Others argue that more fundamental change in the educational system is needed to alter the demands of the job.

Each school constituency has expectations of the school principal, and school safety is often at the top of the list. Reports of public concerns about schools place the responsibility for safety and feelings of being safe in schools on the principal. Eighty-five percent of public schools report at least one violent crime or theft per year. Although between 1992 and 2007 there was a decline in school violence, the rate remained the same between 2004 and 2007. However, of the 55.7 million students enrolled in pre-K to 12th grade in the 2007–2008 school year, (Snyder, Dillow, and Hoffman, 2010) 1.5 million were victims of nonfatal crimes and 43 were victims of school-associated violent deaths. More male students (10 percent) than female students (5 percent) have been threatened or injured with a weapon, and 10 percent of urban teachers have been threatened. Twenty-three percent of students from 12 to 18 years old report gang activity in their schools (NCES, "Indicators of School Crime and Safety," 2009).

Students who do not feel safe at school indicate that it is usually because of threats from bullies and weapons. Others, including large percentages of African-American and Hispanic students, report fear of being attacked at school or when going to and from school, usually by street gangs. High-profile incidents such as the shootings at Columbine High School or Virginia Tech University result in heightened concern among students. The guide *When Disaster Strikes* recommends that principals have a plan in place to deal with safety issues and tragedies. Using knowledge from the social sciences to deal with problems, knowing what to expect in the way of reactions and grief, and having the mechanisms in place are important steps a principal can take to prevent personal damage to children (McEvoy, 1992).

THE PRINCIPAL'S POWER.   Principals and other administrators have power to influence school effectiveness through their leadership and interactions. In the most effective schools, principals meet with teachers regularly, ask for suggestions regarding curriculum, and give teachers information concerning effectiveness (Lortie, 2009). Those concerned with effective schools argue that principals should spend the majority of their time improving instruction, but this seldom happens because of the many conflicting responsibilities facing principals.

Principals have power to exert control over the teaching staff by rewarding cooperative teachers and causing less desirable situations for less cooperative teachers through classroom placements, assignments of unruly students, and undesirable scheduling. The principal's expectations of teachers strongly influence teacher morale, performance, and self-concept; teachers indicate that they are more satisfied with principals who make clear what is expected and reward good work, yet allow for their involvement in decision making. Teachers also claim professional status and the need for autonomy. They expect the principal to stand up for them in situations where their authority is challenged, and they sometimes use their collective power to make this clear to the principal as in cases where grievances are filed or strikes occur.

We have learned that women dominate the field of education, and even in educational administration as principals, 50.3 percent are female. This is a big change from 1993 to 1994 when only one-third of principals were female (NCES, "Public School Principal Questionnaire," 2009). Female leaders have different styles of leadership than their male counterparts, with stress on the servant role, providing emotional support and materials to teachers (Fridell, Belcher, and Messner, 2009), "interacting with teachers as a resource provider" (NCES, *Digest*, 1999), and favoring a decentralized power model and parental involvement (Sobehart, 2009). "Women bring different leadership, communication, and decision-making styles, and instructional resource, communicator, and visible presence" (Mertz and McNeely, 1998).

Although the principal has the power to run the school, he or she is also constrained by the environment—the superintendent and board, teachers' unions, student demands, and state and local regulations. Principals are involved in decision making in many areas but share the responsibility with those holding reciprocal roles. According to some educators, to increase the effectiveness of principals to carry out their roles in today's climate, universities training principals should reconsider the curriculum to address demands on principals today (Brown, 2006).

Applying Sociology to Education: *What are some conflicting roles held by principals? Why is being a principal in today's climate difficult? Seek out the School Report Card for a local school, and examine the categories and data included in it. How might a principal influence the data it contains?*

Teachers: The Front Line

Looking back at our school days, the people we remember most fondly or with the greatest dislike are teachers. Occasionally a principal makes an imprint in our memory, or a counselor influences our decisions. But the teacher is the one with whom we have the most contact, and his or her classroom is where we lay ourselves open for scrutiny, praise, and criticism. Often not even our parents spend as much time with us and understand our capabilities as well as our teachers do.

WHY TEACHERS TEACH.   Why do teachers choose to become teachers? Most teachers indicated one or more of the following reasons: the desire to work with young people and impart knowledge; love of children; desire to do something valuable for society and make a difference; the challenges and responsibilities of teaching; interest and excitement about teaching and subject-matter field; security and financial rewards; and to fulfill a dream (Phillips and Hatch, 1999). Seeing students develop new skills and gain an appreciation for knowledge can be very rewarding (U.S. Bureau of Labor Statistics, 2007).

CHARACTERISTICS OF TEACHERS AND THE TEACHING FIELD.   Approximately 3.7 million U.S. citizens were employed as professional educators, with .5 million in private schools and 3.2 million in U.S. public primary and secondary schools (NCES, 2010). This constitutes about 4 percent of the U.S. workforce, and is 12 percent higher than in 1999. Of the 3.2 million public school teachers, 1.25 million were secondary school teachers, 1.57 million were elementary school teachers, and 231,833 were unclassified (Ingersoll and Smith, 2003; NCES Fast Facts, 2010; U.S. Department of Labor, 2007).Some characteristics of teachers are outlined in Table 6.1 (NCES, 2009).

Formal rules and regulations guide the behavior of students and teachers.

Of elementary and secondary teachers, 87 percent are white and 13 percent minority; more than 40 percent of schools have no teachers of color. Male teachers are "an endangered species" as well, comprising only 21 percent of teachers. "The typical public school teacher is white, female, 46 years old and married with school-age children . . ." (Taylor, 2004). Median years of teaching have increased from an average of 12 years in 1981 to 15 years in 2003.

An individual writing "teacher" in the occupation blank on a form would generally fall into the category "middle class." Some believe teaching is an easy route to upward mobility from lower classes, although teachers represent a broad range of class backgrounds. Not only is the cost of training for this profession lower than for many others, but the occupation is a familiar one.

Table 6.1 Selected Characteristics of Public School Teachers: Selected Years, Spring 1966 through Spring 2001

Selected Characteristic	1966	1976	1986	1996	2001	2006
Number of teachers (in thousands)	1,710	2,196	2,206	2,164	2,979	3,588
Sex (%)						
Male	31.1	32.9	31.2	25.6	21.0	29.9
Female	68.9	67.1	68.8	74.4	79.0	70.1
Median age (years)						
All teachers	36	33	41	44	46	46
Males	33	33	42	46	47	44
Females	40	33	41	44	45	47
Marital status (%)						
Single	22.0	20.1	12.9	12.4	15.2	13.2
Married	69.1	71.3	75.7	75.9	73.1	73.1
Widowed, divorced, or separated	9.0	8.6	11.4	11.8	11.7	13.8

(Continued)

Table 6.1 Continued

Selected Characteristic	1966	1976	1986	1996	2001	2006
Highest degree held (%)						
Less than bachelor's	7.0	0.9	0.3	0.3	0.2	0.1
Bachelor's	69.6	61.6	48.3	43.6	43.1	37.2
Master's or specialist degree[a]	23.2	37.1	50.7	54.5	56.0	60.4
Doctor's	0.1	0.4	0.7	1.7	0.8	1.4
College credits earned in last 3 years						
Percent who earned credits	—	63.2	53.1	50.2	46.3	55.7
Mean number of credits earned[b]	—	—	4	—	—	—
Median years of teaching experience	8	8	15	15	14	15
Teaching for first year (%)	9.1	5.5	3.1	2.1	3.1	1.8
Average number of pupils per class elementary teachers, not departmentalized	28	25	24	24	21	22
Secondary and departmentalized elementary teachers	27	25	26	31	28	29
Mean number of students taught per day by secondary and departmentalized elementary teachers	132	127	97	97	86	87
Average number of hours in required school day	7.3	7.3	7.3	7.3	7.4	7.4
Average number of hours per week spent on all teaching duties						
All teachers	47	46	49	49	50	52
Elementary teachers	47	44	47	47	49	52
Secondary teachers	48	48	51	52	52	53
Average number of days of classroom teaching in school year	181	180	180	180	181	181
Average number of nonteaching days in school year	5	5	5	6	7	7
Average annual salary as classroom teacher (current dollars)[c]	$6,253	$12,005	$24,504	$35,549	$43,262	$49,482
Total income, including spouse's (if married) (current dollars)	—	$19,957	$43,413	$63,171	$77,739	$87,630
Willingness to teach again (%)						
Certainly would	52.6	37.5	22.7	32.1	31.7	38.2
Probably would	25.4	26.1	26.3	30.5	28.7	27.2
Chances about even	12.9	17.5	19.8	17.3	18.4	16.1
Probably would not	7.1	13.4	22.0	15.8	15.7	12.7
Certainly would not	2.0	5.6	9.3	4.3	5.6	5.8

—Not available.

[a]Figures for curriculum specialist or professional diploma based on six years of college study are not included.

[b]Measured in semester hours.

[c]Includes extra pay for extra duties.

Note: Data are based upon sample surveys of public school teachers. Data differ from figures appearing in other tables because of varying survey processing procedures and time period coverages. Detail may not sum to totals because of rounding.

Source: U.S. Department of Education, Digest of Education Statistics, 2009, Table 69. (NCES, 2009). For 2006, U.S. Department of Education, Digest of Education Statistics, 2010, Table 73 (NCES, 2010).

We all "understand" teachers. Considering teacher hiring, attrition, and retirements, the percentage of growth in the teacher ranks between 2008 and 2018 is predicted to be 13 percent (Bureau of Labor Statistics, 2008).

In the 1960s there was a shortage of teachers brought about by the rapid increase in the number of school-age children from the baby boom. As the 1970s came to an end, however, more than 600,000 teachers were labeled "surplus" and most could not find jobs. The predicted job market low passed in 1983, and the situation for teachers has improved. The average number of students in public school classrooms in 2007 was only 15.2. In private school classrooms, the average size was 13.3 students (U.S. Census Bureau, 2010). These lower classroom figures reflect in part the impact of teachers who teach smaller classes of special education, compensatory education, and bilingual education.

In the late 1990s, there were again fewer jobs for teachers and a reservoir of unemployed teachers. The increase in applicants to teachers' colleges and the rising salaries of starting teacher which attracted some professionals from other fields to teaching made the situation difficult for new teachers. However, supply and demand forces balance the equation, and today the scales are tipping to favor those in search of teaching jobs, due in part to the large number of baby boom teachers retiring and to teacher attrition. When there are teacher shortages, more alternative routes to teaching emerge. Some recent paths for urban schools include Teach for America, a program for college graduates beginning careers; programs for retirees or individuals wishing to change careers that allow them to teach in their fields while completing required education courses; and programs for college graduates to take an additional year to be a certified teacher with a master's degree.

One of the most difficult tasks for school administrators is to predict the population fluctuations in their districts and prepare for them by having an appropriate number of teachers and classrooms.

WOMEN AND MINORITY TEACHERS.   At one time, teaching was one of the few career paths accessible to highly qualified women and minorities. In 1972, 37 percent of women college graduates were headed for teaching; by 1995, that number was only 14 percent (NCES, 1995). Most recent figures show about 9 percent of all college graduates majored in education; yet the percentage of women in that 9 percent is still high, 75.8 percent. Today 18 percent of women college graduates major in business, 9 percent in health professions, and just below that in third place is education (Tulshyan, 2010). On average, pay for starting education majors in the United States is $36,200, with mid-career averages of $54,100. Elementary education teachers receive somewhat less (O'Shaughnessy, 2009).

Asked if they would select teaching as a profession again, 66 percent said they would and 19 percent said they would not (NEA, 2010). After five years, 40–50 percent of new teachers have left the profession. The reasons are many, often involving personal reasons such as family or health. Reasons cited by new teachers who are dissatisfied with teaching are poor salaries (78.5 percent), student discipline problems (34.9 percent), poor administrative support (26.1 percent), poor student motivation, lack of faculty influence, large classes, and little opportunity for advancement (Ingersoll and Smith, 2003). The fact that there is a heavy preponderance of women in teaching's lower levels has not been overlooked by researchers or feminists. Over three times as many females as males teach in public schools, with 2,220,000 females to 723,000 males in the 2008–2009 school year. Between 75 and 90 percent of primary school teachers have been female for most years since the early 1900s. The figure for secondary school female teachers has fluctuated from 47 to 65 percent in the same period. Overall, about three-quarters of all public school teachers were female. Males predominate as school administrators and superintendents (NCES, 2010, Table 246).

Women who move into educational administration do so slowly, spending many more years in the classroom than men before becoming administrators. There appear to be two overlapping reasons for this: convenience and discrimination. For women, teaching has been more available and acceptable than other professions, and the accessibility of education is greater than in many other fields; time and cost of getting a degree are less in education than in some other fields; the hours, vacations, and schedule are compatible with home and children; the job can be pursued in many locations; and for many, the "nurturing" experience coincides with life experiences. Discrimination is a factor in the imbalance because many other career paths have been closed to women at the training or entrance level, and men have had a greater variety of career opportunities available. However, as more jobs become available, fewer highly qualified women and minorities choose education.

RETENTION IN THE TEACHING RANKS.   Of the 3,380,300 public school teachers in 2007–2008, 84.5 percent remained in the same school, 7.6 percent moved to a different school, and 8 percent left teaching (5.3 percent of leavers because their contract was not renewed) (NCES, "Teacher Follow-up Survey," 2010). Of those who left teaching, the most common reason was retirement, followed by pursuit of another career, pregnancy and child-rearing, and other family or personal issues. Those who leave because of dissatisfaction often do so because of low salaries.

Teachers' career cycles typically follow three stages: survival in the new setting and discovery of new challenges, stabilization through the middle years, and *disengagement* from their strong investment in teaching as their careers come to an end. Teachers' commitment differs depending on the career stage, with mid-career teachers having lower commitment to their jobs.

Today, 42 percent of teachers are over age 50, 27 percent are 40–49, 21 percent from 31 to 39, and 10 percent under 30 (NEA, 2010). There are certainly advantages to having a high concentration of older teachers. They have much teaching experience and consider themselves professionals. Collectively, they belong to more professional organizations and have more ties in the community than younger teachers. But there are disadvantages, too: Some tenured teachers are not competent, but they must be kept on; older teachers are more expensive to the system; and their presence prevents younger teachers from filling a percentage of the teacher slots. Young teachers bring new teaching ideas and new developments in the discipline to their first jobs, helping to keep older colleagues in touch with their fields. Thus, a two-way socialization takes place between older and younger teachers.

ROLE EXPECTATIONS FOR TEACHERS.   Are we asking too much of our teachers? Consider the following hypothetical advertisement characterizing the role expectations for teachers:

WANTED

College graduate with academic major (master's degree preferred). Excellent communication/leadership skills required. Challenging opportunity to serve 150 clients daily on a tight schedule, developing up to five different products each day to meet individual needs, while adhering to multiple product specifications. Adaptability helpful, as suppliers cannot always deliver goods on time, incumbent must arrange for own support services, and customers rarely know what they want. Ideal candidate will enjoy working in isolation from colleagues. This diversified position allows employees to exercise typing, clerical, law enforcement, and social work skills between assignments and after hours. Typical workweek: 50 hours. Special nature of the work precludes amenities such as telephones or computers, but work has many intrinsic awards. Starting salary . . . ("What Matters Most," 1996, p. 54)

Teachers are primary socializers of children; that is, they play an important role in teaching the child how to be a member of society. In elementary grades many teachers see their roles as "caring" and nurturing activities, but in recent years in both the United States and United Kingdom, more competitive and performance-driven expectations are altering that role. Increased testing, preparing students for enhanced performance at the next levels of schooling, and more school inspections in the United Kingdom all result in a changing role for teachers, especially women teachers in the elementary grades (Forrester, 2005). Yet strong intergenerational bonding between teachers and students also result in higher academic achievement and fewer disciplinary problems (Crosnoe, Johnson, and Elder, 2004).

The primary reciprocal role for the teacher is with students. It is an involuntary relationship for both. The teacher holds power and has several means of exerting it: adult authority, grades, punishments such as detention or humiliation—and also affective behavior, praise, reinforcement, and personal contact. The question of how to socialize young people most effectively in the schools is, according to some, the most pressing issue schools face. Although parents and principals may be in the background making curricular and instructional decisions (Apple, 1988), "the final responsibility for delivery of an effective school learning climate rests with teachers" (Brookover et al., 1996, p. 101).

Teachers are expected to teach children the three Rs—reading, 'riting, 'rithmetic, manage and facilitate classrooms, provide an atmosphere conducive to maximum learning, and in general be gatekeepers who control the flow of activity and students. As socialization agents, teachers are in very visible roles and are expected to set good moral examples for students. Yet what is defined as "good" is often controversial. For example, some court cases challenge teachers' negative influence on their students because of their dress, appearance, alcohol or drug charges outside of school, sexual orientation, or unseemly behavior with students.

Whether or not they have tenure, teachers can be fired only with good and just cause. Such causes, though difficult to prove, generally include incompetence (knowledge of subject matter, teaching methods); immorality (lying, falsification of records, misappropriation of funds, inappropriate behavior with students, and cheating); drug abuse; critical and derogatory statements about the employer; and profane language.

TEACHER PREPARATION.   The reality of facing that first class full of children challenges every beginning teacher—that is, one-third of the teaching force each year. More than 50 percent of public school teachers have returned to college for master's, specialist, or doctoral degrees. Fifty-six percent have master's degrees, a recommendation by The National Commission on Excellence in Teacher Education, which advocates that teacher-preparation programs be improved and extended to five years, in particular that teachers be required to obtain a degree in a particular content area and then take teacher training. Although these recommendations appeal to many, there is fear that a five-year program would discourage potential teachers.

Most teachers are certified in their main field of teaching. The majority of public school teachers (71 percent) believed they were well prepared to maintain order and discipline in their classrooms, but fewer (41 percent) believed they were prepared to implement new teaching methods or mandates from the state or district (36 percent). Only 21 percent of teachers believe they are prepared to integrate educational technology into their classrooms. With the new initiatives,

Table 6.2 Four Lenses for Examining Teacher Quality

Category	Definition and Example Indicators
Teacher qualifications	*Credentials, knowledge, and experiences that teachers bring with them when they enter the classroom, such as:*
	Coursework, grades, subject-matter education, degrees, text scores, experience, certification(s), and evidence of participation in continued learning (e.g., internships, induction, supplemental training, and professional development)
Teacher characteristics	*Attitudes and attributes that teachers bring with them when they enter the classroom, such as:*
	Expectations for students, collegiality or a collaborative nature, race, and gender
Teacher practices	*Classroom practices teachers employ—that is, the ways in which teachers interact with students and the teaching strategies they use to accomplish specific teaching tasks, such as:*
	Aligning instruction with assessment, communicating clear learning objectives and expectations for student performance, providing intellectual challenge, allowing students to explain what they are learning, using formative assessment to understand what and the degree to which students are actually learning, offering active learning experiences, and subscribing to cohesive sets of best teaching practices
Teacher effectiveness	*A "value-added" assessment of the degree to which teachers who are already in the classroom contribute to their students' learning, as indicated by higher-than-predicted increases in student achievement scores*

Source: National Comprehensive Center for Teacher Quality, report on "Teacher Quality and Student Achievement: Making the Most of Recent Research," March 2008, p. 2. Available: www.tqsource.org/publications/March2008Brief.pdf

technologies, and changing student populations, the demand on teachers to go beyond their preparation is great (NCES, 2001).

Education reformers are revamping many teacher education programs. While all states require teachers to be licensed, the expectations differ (U.S. Bureau of Labor Statistics, 2006–2007). Criteria for "What Makes a Good Teacher" are indicated in Table 6.2.

The Education Commission of the States looked at the research on teacher preparation and laid out key questions to guide research and discussions about improving teacher quality and reviewed the sometimes limited research literature in these areas. For example, "Do good teachers have adequate knowledge of their subject matter? Should teachers have more training in pedagogy or their subject matter? What is the value of field experience (student teaching) for teacher training? Are their viable alternative routes to teaching that are effective? Is special preparation needed for teaching in low-performing schools? Is it possible to select students who will be the best teachers? Do high accreditation standards help the quality of teaching?" While there is data on some of these questions, others are still being debated (Allen, 2003). We discuss some of these below.

Educational reformers focus on different aspects of quality teacher preparation, including some of those previously mentioned. For example, John Goodlad's (1984, 1998) recommendations in national reports provide models for changing teacher education. Some recommendations include having teachers major in their subject area with additional courses in pedagogy, giving teachers more say over what happens in schools, establishing a national board of standards, and increasing the number of minority teachers. In fact, a National Board for Professional Teaching Standards has been established and is working to implement recommendations.

Evaluating teacher education curricula and redesigning content to address current concerns include classroom management practices, multicultural and global education, special training for teaching in the middle grades, improved quality of math and science education, and work with differences in male and female learning styles (Banks, 1999).

When school districts are growing, they need to add new teachers, and school districts are resorting to several techniques suggested by experts to prepare and hire more teachers. One technique is to retool current teachers who are in fields with less demand by training them in other areas. Another is "alternative credentialing" to attract qualified individuals working in other areas into teaching. In addition, usually pedagogical training is provided when a person begins teaching. A year of graduate education for those with degrees in other areas can also qualify new teachers to be certified. Perhaps the best-known program of this sort is Teach for America, which is a national effort to recruit the highest achieving graduates of the nation's best colleges to teach for two years in understaffed urban and rural schools (http://www.teachforamerica.org/). Several cities have established their own programs, such as the New York City Teaching Fellows Program. These programs seek to serve several purposes, including raising the prestige of teaching (Teach for America receives many more applications than it accepts), and putting teachers who really know their subject into classrooms sometimes staffed by less accomplished teachers. Critics of these programs are concerned about the short preparation these teachers receive before being assigned a class and the fact that only a two-year commitment is required. One of the important problems hard-to-staff schools face is high turnover of staff, preventing the teachers and other staff members to develop strong collegial relationships. The Teach for America program does not help this problem, as few of its members stay at the same school much beyond their original commitment.

To improve teachers' effectiveness, especially in content areas, some educators propose a universal master's degree. Some states do require teachers to have a master's degree and technological training within a certain number of years of being hired (U.S. Bureau of Labor Statistics, 2006–2007). However, critics point out that this additional time and cost might discourage many potential teachers, including minority students, from studying for teaching degrees. Other efforts focus on providing settings in which prospective teachers can receive classroom training in professional development schools, schools that work in conjunction with colleges of education to provide training for new teachers (U.S. Bureau of Labor Statistics, 2006–2007).

TESTING, LICENSING, AND PROFESSIONAL DEVELOPMENT.   Teachers are required to have a bachelor's degree, a teacher training program, supervised practice teaching, and a test of basic skills. In an effort to raise standards, all states now require national or state tests to license teacher candidates for specific grades. The question is whether these tests help raise the quality of classroom teachers (Chaika, 2005). The tests have created a problem: Many prospective teachers are failing the tests—59 percent in Massachusetts alone. With some areas experiencing teacher shortages, how is this challenge between having competent teachers as measured by tests and filling vacant positions to be resolved? In addition, the number of minority students taking the Praxis I and Praxis II exams for teachers is disproportionately small, resulting in fewer minority students in the teacher pipeline. Some question the use of one test to determine a potential teacher's ability to be a successful teacher and argue that multiple criteria should be used (Chaika, 2005).

The National Teacher Examination and other tests are widely used by school districts. Some states have developed their own tests. The two national teachers' unions, the National Education Association and the American Federation of Teachers, support teacher testing, although their views of what is tested and the basic purpose for the tests vary.

"No Child Left Behind" legislation and "Race to the Top" competitions for government funds have put increasing pressure on schools to hold teachers accountable for their students' achievement. Yet, many noted educational scholars oppose government initiatives that dictate and limit teacher roles and autonomy (Apple, 2007). The concept of teachers retaining some autonomy illustrates that teachers maintain some degree of autonomy by working in their micro-networks of relations, often removed from the policy makers far from the classroom (Hupe and Hill, 2007).

Controversy over testing and licensing of teachers continues, with some arguing that skills tests may not be valid, are not the only measure of competent teachers, and may discriminate against minority teachers. Others support the testing, arguing that it is harmful to children to have teachers in the classroom who lack basic skills. Court cases challenging the fairness of state testing are pending in several states.

Whether teachers are teaching in their fields of expertise is also a question raised about teacher quality. Recent research suggests that many high school teachers, especially those in high-minority and high-poverty public schools, are teaching out-of-field in English, science, and math (Ingersoll, 1997; NCES, 2004; Nelson, 2006). At the other end of the educational continuum is preschool education, crucial to the brain development and preparation of young children for later school success. However, preschool teachers often lack training to work with young children. Concerned educators are asking that early childhood educators have at least a bachelor's degree, preferably in early childhood education (Early et al., 2007).

Professional development is offered to most teachers during the school year: 95 percent of teachers participated in a workshop, conference, or other training; 59 percent of teachers participated in subject-matter topic training during the years; and 73 percent in professional development on methods of teaching (Scotchmer, McGrath, and Coder, 2005).

RECOMMENDATIONS TO IMPROVE TEACHING AND TEACHERS.   The concern with high dropout rates of students, poor performance of U.S. students on international exams, and other educational problems has set off the alarm bells in the U.S. Department of Education and in private foundations and organizations devoted to improving the quality of children's education. Many reports have been produced, dealing with the "crisis in education" and making some radical suggestions for change. Some argued that before the United States could upgrade educational programs and curricula, it would have to make teaching a more attractive profession. As older, experienced teachers retire and gifted young ones leave for other professions, the qualifications of the teaching force dwindle. During teacher shortages, the United States will have to "scrape the bottom of the barrel" unless it raises salaries, provides benefits, and improves working conditions.

The catch-22 is that as more government administrations dictate policy to control the quality of education, fewer professional teachers will be attracted to education. Good teachers want autonomy and need competitive pay and working conditions. Some teachers also feel the demands on teachers for nonteaching duties that take 10–50 percent of teachers' time is not productive for their students; these duties include keeping records; monitoring playgrounds, lunchrooms, and hallways; making copies—many of which take away from important instructional duties.

Merit-, incentive-, or performance-based pay has been proposed as a way to reward teacher excellence, and some administrators such as in Washington, D.C., are implementing such plans. A majority of the public favors merit-based reward systems, and many states in the United States have projects on merit pay, especially those with Race to the Top funding. However, some argue that these plans lower teacher morale, create dissension, make the situation competitive, and are impossible to administer.

The latest research, however, does not offer much support for the ability of merit pay schemes to improve student achievement (Sawchuk, 2010). An evaluation of a voluntary program in which almost 300 Nashville, Tennessee, math teachers participated assessed whether the bonuses of between $5,000 and $15,000, based on whether the achievement of the students of those teachers rose, actually produced gains. The gains were calculated using a value-added technique that eliminated other sources of change in the students' achievements. The program did not "yield consistent and lasting gains in test scores" (Sawchuk, 2010). For gains to have been common, participating teachers would have had to be "holding out" in their work as teachers: "A lot of the discussion about performance pay is based on a faulty assumption that the reason we don't have higher test scores is that teachers are shirking their responsibilities," one commentator is quoted as saying. This research does not end the need for additional research, as there are other questions to be asked, such as whether the existence of such programs might influence who is attracted to teaching.

The call for performance pay is, in part, based on the newer research about the effects of teachers on student achievement that we have referred to before. More test data have allowed researchers to associate students' performance with the teachers they had, which has elevated the importance of teachers in the view of many. Yet this research raises questions about how much improvement over current test score levels these pay schemes are likely to produce.

Bad conditions in schools need to be rectified before real change can occur. Some private and parochial schools, which have less money for salaries, structure their schools so that teachers have more freedom and fewer bureaucratic rules, allowing professionals to flourish and share a mission in a team atmosphere. Public schools, because of the hierarchy and bureaucracy, must be routinized, standardized, and regulated. Currently the "No Child Left Behind" legislation and other government programs are adding to the requirements with initiatives that are transforming the role of the federal government in the U.S. education system (Apple, 2007)—for better or worse!

TEACHER STRESS AND BURNOUT.   "Burnout is used to describe a syndrome that goes beyond physical fatigue from overwork. Stress and emotional exhaustion are part of it, but the hallmark of burnout is the distancing that goes on in response to the overload" (Maslach, Schaufeli, and Leiter, 2001, p. 397). Burnout results from multiple stressors facing human service professionals that become emotionally exhausting and cause loss of sense of purpose (Dworkin, 2001). Burnout has psychological dimensions—an inability to cope with an array of life stressors, placing the blame for burnout on the victim. "Sociological dimensions consider structural constructs of alienation—powerlessness, meaninglessness, normlessness, isolation, and estrangement," all with organizational and structural roots (Dworkin, 2007).

Burnout results in schools losing teachers in three ways: teachers leave teaching altogether, they transfer to another school, or they are fired. Federal reforms in U.S. schools are meant to address threats to U.S. economic dominance and place in the global system, yet the result is that teachers feel more pressure and less appreciation for the job they do (Dworkin, 2001), factors that result in burnout. A review of the history of burnout shows that it has increased with each new reform. The 1977 pre-reform cohort of teachers had the lowest burnout rate. Burnout increased with the "A Nation at Risk" report, again with "Site-Based Decision Making," still further with "High-Stakes Testing," and now with "No Child Left Behind" and "Race to the Top" (Dworkin, 2007).

Problems in schools also affect teacher stress and burnout, especially in urban areas. Teachers often feel that their work is meaningless and that they are powerless to effect changes in their situations. They feel unappreciated by uncaring administrators and students. A number of factors contribute to the problem: Some are characteristics of teachers; others are found in societal pressures on schools. For instance, burnout often begins between 7 and 10 years of teaching; the level of burnout rises with age and years of experience in teaching, peaks at age 41 through 45, and then declines. Teachers with higher levels of education, and, therefore, higher career expectations, experienced more frustration. The following lists characteristics of typical burned out teachers:

1. Were under 30 years of age
2. Were white and from middle-class backgrounds
3. Were inexperienced, having taught for fewer than five years
4. Were racially isolated, teaching in schools where most of the student body is of a race other than their own
5. Felt that members of their own race have been targets of discrimination at their school
6. Preferred not to be assigned to the school at which they teach
7. Believed that fate or luck controls their destinies and, hence, their future is out of their hands
8. Disagreed with their principals on the appropriate role for a campus administrator.

> The research revealed that the best single predictor of the likelihood that a teacher would plan to quit teaching was a sense of burnout. Teachers who wanted to quit also fit the characteristics of the teachers who were burned out. (Dworkin, 1985, p. 9)

Are there solutions? These seemingly individual problems have environmental factors that, if dealt with, can help reduce stress and provide job supports. Inducting new teachers into the school culture; opening classroom doors and creating supportive teams; providing in-service training to meet individual staff needs; and restructuring school governance to allow for shared decision making are all suggested as ways to address and reduce burnout (School Mental Health Project, 2002). First, teachers need to feel a sense of control over their domain, so that they can be creative and spontaneous; second, supportive principals are a key factor in reducing stress and burnout. Those principals who use democratic personnel policies, are supportive and collegial, and involve teachers in decision making have fewer burned out teachers (Dworkin, Saha, and Hill, 2003).

In sum, when a group is faced with threats from its environment—low prestige and low salaries; poor working conditions; lack of autonomy and professionalism; physical threats; hurt pride; difficulty dealing with some students; and criticisms from angry minorities, parents, and administrators—there are bound to be reactions: stress, burnout, dropping out, and joining teachers' unions to fight for better conditions and more autonomy.

RECOMMENDATIONS TO IMPROVE THE ROLE OF THE TEACHER. All is not bleak! A 2009 Gallup-Healthways poll of teachers indicates that they hold the top position on several measures of well-being: the way they evaluate their lives overall, their capacity to access resources needed to lead a healthy life, their overall emotional health, their intention to engage in healthy behaviors, and their willingness to express optimism about the future (Lopez and Agrawal, 2009). Nonetheless, the picture is mixed. As one teacher put it: "My life is pretty good. I like the kids; I like the job; I like the satisfaction I get from the work. But I feel I'm not doing something which is really valued by society. Look at our pay scale and the lack of autonomy we as professionals have. So I don't know what the future holds for me or for the profession" (Dworkin and Haney, 1988).

Task forces and commission reports have made suggestions for sweeping changes, some of which we have discussed. Teacher satisfaction hinges on a number of factors. Important are the public's attitudes toward the teaching profession and changes teacher's want in work conditions that would make a difference: smaller class size, small learning communities, school safety, community and family involvement, professional development opportunities, resource allocation, and effective leadership ("Key Issues," 2008). This may be due in part to increasing recognition and appreciation among the public of the essential role teachers play in society.

The main message is that teachers need more pay, more respect, more professional treatment, and more opportunity for advancement if we are to attract and keep high-quality individuals in the field. Progress is being made on some of these ecommendations as shown by the recent positive attitudes of teachers and higher salaries in many districts, but faculty still report having little influence over school policies and only moderate control over classroom decisions.

Applying Sociology to Education: *Describe an effective teacher you know. What makes this teacher effective?*

Behind the Scenes: Support Roles in the School

SCHOOL STAFF: GUARDIANS OF THE GATEWAY.   On entering the school, students first contact may be with a school guard or part of the city police force, checking for weapons or other contraband. Adults' first contact is usually with an office worker behind a counter who serves the important functions of "buffering" and "filtering" the principals and teachers from dealing with the community. The irate parent comes in demanding to see the principal immediately; the text salesperson would like to speak to someone "in charge." To deal with the many tasks and demands on schools, they have support staff that includes both professional specialists and service workers. The office worker, serving as a buffer for principals and teachers, must determine the appropriate place for the request or complaint to go, screen out unnecessary interruptions of school personnel, and match the visitor with the appropriate person.

Office workers also control such key information as the contents of files. For example, if the vice principal needs information on the arrangement made with the food distributor for deliveries, he or she relies on the office worker to locate the material. Teachers and students also depend on office workers for many services and information, including record keeping. In this respect the person holding the role often wields a great deal of influence.

Other important support roles include librarians, special education teachers, counselors, paraprofessionals or teachers' aides, food service workers, bus drivers, and nurses. One important role is often overlooked: janitors. They are in a unique position. Although they hold little formal power in the hierarchy, they may be extremely influential members of the community in which a school is located. They have an insider's view about the running of the school, a vantage point almost no others, not even the principals, have. Although many janitors are neutral entities, some have used the position in a political way, as exemplified in the following excerpt from Waller:

> [T]he janitor is always a member of the local community, whereas teachers belong rather
> to the outside world . . . . The janitor is important, too, as a talebearer. Often he regards
> himself as an official lookout for the community; it is his role to see what he can and
> to report what he observes to his friends and connections by way of gossip. (1965, p. 80)

Another crucial role in schools is carried out by paraprofessionals—individuals with less than a four-year college degree. Although they do not have total control of a classroom, they do carry out numerous tasks in classrooms and schools. The largest number work with special education programs, including remedial and bilingual classes.

The role of school nurses has changed dramatically, from giving bandages and immunizations to handling medications for chronically ill and hyperactive students, to dealing with abuse, and to working with other social problems that affect health services. Sometimes this involves coordinating social services to get children the help they need. One controversial aspect of this role in some schools is sex education, pregnancy testing, and dispensing condoms.

COUNSELORS: THE SELECTION AND ALLOCATION FUNCTION.   As high schools have become larger and more diverse in programs and course offerings, their personnel have become more specialized. Counselors are hired by many school systems, mostly to deal with students at the high school level. They usually have degrees in school counseling and often have teaching experience. From the American School Counselor Association (ASCA, 2007) website comes a policy statement that includes a definition of the formal role of the counselor:

> . . . educators trained in school counseling with unique qualifications and skills to address all students' academic, personal/social and career development needs. Professional school counselors implement a comprehensive school counseling program that promotes and enhances student achievement. Professional school counselors are employed in many school settings . . . (American School Counselor Association, 2007)

In the past counselors had a great deal of power in determining what happened to each student—a "gatekeeping" role resulting in the road students follow when they leave secondary school (Brookover et al., 1996, p. 100). With all the student records at hand, they guided students into courses and programs to meet students' and society's needs. The counselor made lifetime decisions for young people. Counselors used not only the objective criteria of grades and test scores but also their impressions of the students, often formed during brief encounters taking place over several years. Labels attached to students from teachers and peers also influenced the counselor's impressions, factors such as the student's class background, dress, and manner of speaking.

However, this power to determine the future prospects and lives of students began to be challenged in the late 1960s and 1970s with several changes in society: the advent of community colleges with open-door policies, making college more accessible; parents taking active roles in their children's futures and challenging the schools' decisions if they did not meet their goals for their children; and the growing importance of college education and skills for the needs of the labor market. Therefore, in recent years U.S. high schools and counselors have adopted a "college-for-all" policy, avoiding criticisms of the selection and sorting function they formally played (Rosenbaum, 2001; Rosenbaum and Person, 2003). A dilemma is present for the counselor who is expected to keep "societal" goals in mind, get to know students well enough to plan their futures, and work with students and parents to achieve what are sometimes unrealistic goals.

SPECIAL SUPPORT ROLES.   Because of continuing concern in the United States over the apparent decline of basic skills, Title I (Elementary and Secondary Education Act) was passed to provide supplementary monies to districts for additional personnel and special programs. Schools can hire specialists in reading, mathematics, and sometimes preschool education to work with children who score below a designated level on standardized tests. In addition, needy children in Title I programs are offered some auxiliary services such as food, medicine, dental services, and clothing. Special education staff can make a significant difference for marginal students if they have high expectations and provide support rather than give up on these students (Brookover et al., 1996, p. 105). This is especially true for those students who have attention deficit disorder, are learning disabled, are emotionally impaired, or are mentally impaired. Schools also hire teachers' aides to provide teachers with instructional and clerical support, including recording grades and duplicating materials; to do tutoring; to give students individual attention by working one-on-one; to supervise lunch and playground activities; and to deal with special education students. Aides may be part-time or full-time. They held 1.3 million jobs in 2004, most in public schools (U.S. Bureau of Labor Statistics, 2006–2007).

With shortages of funds and personnel, volunteer programs abound. Extra hands to do special tasks can be invaluable. Retired teachers and other professionals, community citizens with skills, parents, business members, substitute teachers, even upper-level students, or college students volunteer in schools. They tutor; aid teachers or substitute in classes; give lessons on specific topics; help in the office, library, or other areas; chaperone; and run after-school programs in sports or other special-interest activities. Some programs use community resources to place students for internships, and in some communities businesses provide personnel and resources to the schools for special programs.

Alumni are the biggest school boosters and the strongest school critics. They provide financial support, especially at the college level, and are often community members in their high school hometowns, attending sporting events and volunteering help in various capacities. However, alumni can be a hindrance in efforts to change. For example, a prestigious preparatory school set quotas for accepting a percentage of minority students each year; it then considered becoming coeducational. Protests and loss of alumni support—including financial help—followed these moves.

None of the roles we have discussed would be possible without students, the topic of our next chapter.

> **Applying Sociology to Education:** *Draw a diagram of a school and describe different roles within the school. Consider roles in the school's environment (i.e., taxpayers) as well. Place yourself and other family members in this diagram.*

Summary

No system can work without individuals who fill the necessary roles, which in turn bring the system alive. Although the major obligations for most positions are usually clearly defined, individuals bring unique sets of characteristics, training, abilities, and background experiences with them when playing their roles. Hence, no one description can capture the richness and variety that enter into the system of roles.

I. THE MEANING OF ROLES

Roles refer to the parts individuals play in the social system. In school organizations, roles include administrators, teachers, students, and support staff. Conflicts may arise from incompatible demands on those holding particular roles. Reciprocal roles in the educational system illustrate the interdependence of parts; for instance,

without students other roles in the educational system would be nonexistent. Those taking on a role are usually socialized rather rapidly into that role; few can tolerate the uncertainty of an ill-defined role, and few want to face the ridicule or punishment likely to follow defiance of role expectations. Hence, the school system has a built-in guarantee into which most neophytes will fit nicely and without disruption. This is one reason that change in the system is often slow.

II. ROLES IN SCHOOLS

School boards consist of elected lay community members, or in some cases appointed members, who have varying degrees of control over school personnel, budget, and policy; these may be points of tension between community members and professional educators.

Superintendents are the overall managers of schools. They provide the liaison between the schools, the board, and the community.

Principals are bosses of individual schools, but their authority lies between that of the superintendent and the teachers. This often requires them to play a balancing act to keep both satisfied.

Teachers are on the front line, running the classrooms. The conflict between their desire for autonomy and pressures from the environment can lead to tensions. Recently, there have been controversies over teacher accountability, testing of teachers, and teacher training. Several national U.S. commission reports have addressed the problem of how to improve teaching.

A number of other support roles exist in schools, each playing an important role in the overall functioning of the school.

Putting Sociology to Work

1. Imagine yourself in the various roles of a specific school system. Compare your role behavior in each role.
2. Try to recall your education at different levels in your role as a student. What were the positions in the school hierarchy with which you came in contact?
3. Observe the people in a school. Note the differing roles and the reciprocal relationships.
4. View the documentary film *High School* and try to identify some of the formal school roles you see individuals performing. Describe the reciprocal role relationships.
5. Examine several of the "Problems in Teaching Series" (Science Research Associates) films of teaching anecdotes and identify the roles the teacher, students, and administrators are taking in performing their formal roles.

CHAPTER 7

Students
The Core of the School

Jeanne, one of your authors, chatted with a group of 4th-grade boys about their school experiences. There was no question about their knowing what was expected of them by the adult world and why they go to school. They all chimed in that they must learn to read and write to survive in today's world and that they wouldn't get a job if their skills weren't developed. What does it mean to be a good or bad kid in school? Again, they did not need to stop and think. A good kid is one who turns in assignments on time, listens and pays attention in class, and doesn't mess around. Bad kids are disruptive, sometimes mean and aggressive, and don't really care about learning. Is it hard to be a good kid in school? When the teachers are picky or in a bad mood, it is; but most of the time it's not, if you want to be good. Jeanne had a feeling of déjà vu; things hadn't changed much since she was in school. The continuity over time in expectations is remarkable.

STUDENT CHARACTERISTICS

Students come in many sizes, shapes, intellectual capacities, and motivation levels. They can be active learners, passive attendees, or disruptive troublemakers. Estimates indicate that most children in the world between the ages of six and nine attend school all or part of the time, but after about 3rd grade the picture is spotty. Attendance is near 100 percent in industrialized nations, but it is much lower in less developed countries, as we shall see in Chapter 11 (see Box 7.1).

In 1983, the report *A Nation at Risk* recommended that all students seeking a diploma be required to complete the "new basics." This included four units of English; three units each of science, social studies, and mathematics; and one-half unit of computer science. From 1982 to 1994, the percentage of public school students completing this curriculum jumped from 13 to 32 percent. By 2005, 51 percent of students completed this more demanding curriculum (Manzo, 2007). High school students are taking more courses (seven per year) than they did in 1982–1983, but they are spending less time on work for these classes. The largest increase in courses taken was in math and science, but there was also an increase in social studies and English. This trend toward more academic courses being

BOX 7.1

School Enrollments, 2007–2008

Total enrollment in the U. S. public and private elementary and secondary schools, K-12, in 2010–2011 was estimated at 55.4 million, according to the U.S. Education Department's National Center for Education Statistics (2007). Of that total, 49.4 million students were attending public schools. Private school enrollment was estimated at 5.8 million. Students attended one of the 99,000 public schools, including 4,700 charter schools in the nation. Minority students comprised 44.6 percent of total school enrollment in 2008. Current expenditures for public elementary and secondary education will be about $540 billion for the 2010–2011 school year. The national average current expenditure per student is projected to be $10,792, up from $10,297 in 2007–2008.

About 19.1 million students are expected to attend two-year and four-year colleges in the fall of 2010, an increase of about 3.8 million since the fall of 2000. Although most will attend full-time, around 7.2 million will attend part-time. The increase in enrollments is due to larger numbers of youth and a higher rate of postsecondary enrollment: 41.3 percent of 18- to 24-year olds were enrolled in 2009 compared with 35.5 percent in 2000. For the 2008–2009 academic year, annual prices for tuition, room, and board were estimated at $12,283 for public schools and $31,233 at private ones. (Information retrieved from http://nces.ed.gov/fastfacts/ on September 18, 2010).

offered and taken may reflect the recommendations of early commission reports arguing that we needed to upgrade our programs. These changes are affecting students of all types and abilities at all levels of the educational system. However, the scores on national assessment tests have not risen as one would expect from these changes in course-taking patterns. Some think while the names of courses have been changed, not enough of their content has been changed to reflect the new names. One observer states, "We've collected examples within the same school and the same course title of huge differences in the assignments and the expectations for students" (Manzo, 2007, p. 2). A related development concerns an effort by the College Board to better monitor the content of Advanced Placement courses, which have been proliferating as more and more high schools seek to offer courses that may carry college credit (Lewin, 2007). The following is a description of some of those students and their needs.

Minority students made up 44.6 percent of the nation's elementary and secondary students in 2008, and were a majority of all students in Arizona, California, District of Columbia, Hawaii, Louisiana, Maryland, Mississippi, New Mexico, and Texas (NCES, *Digest*, 2006, Table 40; NCES, *Condition*, 2010, Table A4-1). These students need minority role models and bridges between the middle-class culture of the school and minority subcultures. The number of minority teachers, however, declined from 12.5 percent in 1980 to 9 percent in 1996 (NCES, *Digest*, 1999b, p. 80). This number has since increased with 17 percent of all teachers in 2007–2008 from minority backgrounds; however, they are still only a small percentage of the teaching force compared to the percentage of minority students (NCES, *Condition*, 2010, Table A-27-1). The number of available minority teachers is especially important for minority students because the evidence is strong that black teachers have more positive evaluations of black student classroom behavior than do white teachers, a factor that may influence student success (Downey and Pribesh, 2004).

The low percentage of minority teachers is understandable considering the teaching conditions in unappealing classrooms and schools; relatively low salaries; and, what some claim are, culturally biased teacher exams (Stephens, 1999). Techniques for increasing the number of minority teachers must approach the problem at many levels, from individual incentives to teacher-college programs, to state and national policies. Equitable placement procedures, incentives, competitive salaries, mentoring programs, subject-area recruitment, and multicultural training are all recommendations (Stephens, 1999). In Georgia, the state has instituted a plan to train noncertified school district employees, mostly paraprofessionals, by giving them tuition and support so that they can become certified teachers (Dandy, 1998). In 2006, the city of Philadelphia, with 85 percent minority enrollment in its schools, but only 38 percent of its teaching staff minority group members, announced a new program: The Teacher Diversity Campaign, to recruit more teachers of color into its classrooms (Keller, 2006). Increasing the number of minority teachers would provide more role models for the many students coming through the academic pipeline.

Expectations for the Student Role

In most public school systems, formal role expectations for students are standardized by grade. Elaborate plans outline where a student's academic position should be. Formal student roles—club officer or athletic team member; or (at the lower grades) trash emptier, board eraser, or traffic guard—are found in most schools, but these roles do not capture the flavor and variety of the classroom and student roles. Many schools now have elaborate student handbooks, with considerable details about the expectations for behavior and the system of sanctions that may be imposed upon those who violate them. "Zero tolerance" policies toward drugs and weapons, for example, are controversial but common in schools today.

Student culture, which is a complex of "strange customs," constitutes a "participation mystique, complex rituals of personal relationships, a set of folkways mores, and irrational sanctions, a moral code based upon them" (Waller, [1932] 1961, p. 103). This description is part of the informal student role and reflects the uniqueness of student culture.

In describing the expectations for student roles in schools, we must consider both the formal and informal aspects of student culture. We were all a part of it once, but memories fade and times change, keeping the student culture apart from the world of adults. Students are at the bottom of the role hierarchy with a power structure looming over their heads. Although they are a numerical majority in the system, they are a distinct minority in decision making. Often students are spoken of as an almost alien group—the group to be "subdued," disciplined, or conquered by the school staff.

The student subculture determines for many young people the acceptable behaviors for peer survival, behaviors that are often at odds with adult expectations. Peer groups come in different types: Some support the importance of school learning and achievement, some are more interested in social activities, and a proportion of peer groups engage in delinquent activities. Those students whose friends care about learning have better educational outcomes than those whose friends have little interest in learning (Chen, 1997).

If a student's *friendship patterns* are "high-quality," meaning with students who value their education, students are more likely to adjust and even take on leadership roles. However, those students whose friends have been defined as having behavioral problems have a more difficult time adjusting, especially in junior high school (Berndt, Hawkins, and Jiao, 1999). Who children select as friends is not only a personal choice but also a cultural process, and may reflect their self-concept and feeling about their place in the society or in school practices such as tracking. In other words, friendship patterns can be seen as part of the process of class reproduction (Corsaro, 1994; also see the discussion of student culture in Chapter 13).

The following two studies of "jocks" and "burnouts" and of athletes and nonathletes provide examples of student subcultures. Class reproduction can occur through adolescent peer groups. "Jocks," college-bound, middle-class students, have an investment in the school system, whereas "burnouts," working-class students who often feel hostile or alienated in the school environment, are stigmatized in schools. Working-class students may engage in behaviors that will prevent them from succeeding in high school (Eckert, 1989; Willis, 1981). Scholar-athletes and pure scholars have higher self-esteem, extracurricular involvement, and leadership ability than do pure athletes or students who are neither scholars nor athletes; one example is that women who participate in sports (excluding cheerleading) have higher achievement in science (Hanson and Kraus, 1998; Snyder and Spreitzer, 1992; and, as regards cheerleading, see Bettis and Adams, 2003).

Another variable that affects the student role is gender. Even such subtleties as language usage can have an impact on the student experience. If teachers are aware of the different uses of language, they may be able to use this knowledge effectively in teaching girls and boys. According to a study of student language usage, girls tell secrets to their best friends, whereas boys participate in activities in larger groups and develop hierarchies of status. Boys are more comfortable putting themselves forward and are more willing to argue, whereas girls resist "hostile" discussions. Because of such differences, some argue that single-sex education may lead to more positive social and academic outcomes for female students (Riordan, 1990). Gender and achievement are discussed in Chapter 4.

Learning the Student Role

Each year a new crop of students must be socialized into their roles and the expectations of kindergarten and the elementary school classroom. Students preparing to enter a new classroom or school are concerned about making mistakes in front of their peers or getting in trouble because they have not yet learned their role expectations. Most children want to be accepted. Much of the student's role learning ties in with the social control function of education—learning how to adjust, take orders, and obey. To become a "good" student means to follow the school's routine and rules. These early experiences have an impact on the later adjustment of students and their attitudes toward schooling.

School deals with the intellectual abilities of the child; in contrast, the family deals with the whole child. Preschool programs and kindergarten introduce the child to the institution of education and have been described as "academic boot camp." In a classic article describing the kindergarten routine, Gracey (1967) recounts a day in the life of both the children and the teacher, pointing out the socialization of children into the formal world. Students are the most transient members of the educational system in that they move through and eventually leave the system; the school system is geared toward facilitating the successful movement of students through the system. Movement requires progress, which in turn requires control and cooperation. Because students are not in school by choice, most schools find it necessary to keep them in line by using incentives such as positive reinforcement and interesting subjects, or punishment such as extra work, detentions, and suspensions, and by giving grades as incentives for students to accomplish the school's goals. One of the chief concerns of the early grades of school is to ensure that students learn and accept these rewards (Dreeben, 1968).

> **Applying Sociology to Education:** *Collect your and your classmate's elementary school report cards or obtain a copy of a report card from a local school. Now analyze the categories of behavior and work that are explicitly graded by the teacher. See how these categories change by grade level. What are the grading systems used by the school? How might these documents differ from those used in adult work settings? Did the parent have to sign the card? Must the report card have been returned to the teacher? Think about the report card as a communication device used by the school to tell students and parents what is important in school.*

Learning the rules, roles, and routines is part of becoming a "good" student.

Each year's crop of students becomes a "class" and is processed through the system as a group, or cohort. Picture a giant sieve with layers. Students are put in the top and pass through the layers, which have succeedingly smaller holes. Those who fail to pass through a level are retained or drop out of the sorting and selecting process. At the bottom of the sieve comes graduation.

If students with common experiences and values are placed according to their ability levels, their labels—brains, jocks, and losers—may affect their role patterns. The fact that students are placed in different tracks also points to a major cause of variation in students' educational experiences. The courses students pursue are generally influenced by and selected on the basis of their future plans for either further schooling or work. In several European countries—Germany and England, for example—tracking or "streaming" becomes increasingly rigid as students move through the system. Exams at several school levels in Germany, at age 16 in England, and for university entrance in Japan and many other countries have a major impact on determining a student's future educational opportunities. SATs or other exams are required by many U.S. colleges and universities.

Conflicting Expectations for the Student Role

The school is expected to socialize children to be successful members of society; this implies academic and social skill development for students in the school. The school expects "successful" students to carry out two components of achievement at the elementary level, according to Talcott Parsons. The first is "cognitive" learning of information—skills, frames of reference, and factual information about the world. The second is a "moral" component, including responsible citizenship, respect, consideration, cooperation, work habits, leadership, and initiative (Parsons, 1959). To the extent that student peer groups rebel against these goals, division and conflict are created. High school students may have another agenda, centered on peer-group involvement and acceptance. Willard Waller points out this conflict between adult and student values very aptly. His analysis describes a basic function of schools, cultural transmission:

> Certain cultural conflicts are at the center of the life of the school. . . . A conflict arises between teachers and students because teachers represent the culture of the wider group and students are impregnated with the culture of the local community. . . . A second and more universal conflict between students and teachers arises from the fact that teachers are adults and students are not, so that teachers are the bearers of the culture of the society of adults, and try to impose that culture upon students, whereas students represent the indigenous culture of the group of children. (Waller, 1965, p. 104)

Student Coping Mechanisms

Students use different coping mechanisms to get through the levels of the system. Varying roles are adopted—the leader, the clown, and the bully. Playing these roles requires adapting to the demands of differing situations.

> Thus the leader may remain a leader, but he must adapt his leadership to the (usually) superior force of the teacher, which he may do through alliance, opposition, rivalry, or other means. The clown is still a clown, but his buffoonery must be disguised, it may become covert, or it may adopt a mien of innocence and pose as blundering stupidity. (Waller, 1965, pp. 332–333)

Waller points out that a clever teacher recognizes student roles, manipulates them, and uses them effectively. Teachers speak differently to students for whom they have high expectations and low expectations. Students can pick up cues about how teachers feel about them (Babad, Bernieri, and Rosenthal, 1991; Charles, 1999; Waller, 1965). Daniel McFarland has also contributed to our understanding of classroom life. Closely observing many classrooms over time, he has argued that the structure of classrooms and the instructional activities that take place within them have powerful effects on the behavior of students, which are also influenced by the status of students in the classrooms. Popular students, for example, can sway other students' behavior, either positively or negatively (McFarland, 2001, 2004).

> Some classes are more vocal than others because they have students with friendly interpersonal relations who are given the opportunity to interact with one another through group work and discussion. Moreover, some students are more vocal than others because they have various status resources [such as good looks or popularity] that make them legitimate participants in various classroom endeavors. (Daniel A. McFarland, 2005)

Powerful students may need to be coopted or circumvented by teachers, depending on the situation, for the work of the classroom to proceed.

Teachers may also have different stereotypes of male and female students, resulting in different experiences for boys and girls in school. For instance, many teachers believe that males have higher math capacity and, therefore, have higher expectations for males in math performance (Li, 1999). Students who are alienated from the system may also attempt to sabotage the teaching effort by maintaining an emotional detachment from what is happening in the classroom, devaluing what is taking place, cheating, daydreaming, or acting bored (Jackson, 1968).

Another student coping mechanism is apathy—protecting themselves against total failure in a competition they feel they cannot win. If their sense of self-worth is threatened, it may reduce their desire to try to achieve. Until these students see the possibility of success from effort rather than feeling a sense of futility, they are unlikely to put forth that effort. A Washington D.C. teacher put it this way: "What I see every day is bad. So many of our teenagers here struggle to read, and instead of asking for help, they feel a need to front—to show their toughness by refusing to participate" (Garfield, 2010). Failure at school can create a self-fulfilling prophesy— students may avoid investing effort in learning activities that they believe offer little reward, and it does not take many years of not doing well in school for students to decline to put in the kind of effort learning requires (Alexander, Entwisle, and Horsey, 1997). We discussed some of these processes at the end of Chapter 4 when we reviewed the literature on "acting white." Those students with positive attitudes are likely to be high achievers. Those who are defensive or have low self-esteem or other problems often need help to succeed. Although schools cannot solve society's problems, they can attempt to recognize students in trouble and collaborate with other human service agencies to meet student needs.

Why should we care about alienated, bored, apathetic students? The loss in human potential is tremendous. "Our society is aging and the number of children and youth in relation to other age groups in the population is declining. If current trends continue, a disproportionate number of our young will grow up poor, undereducated, and untrained at the very time that our society will need all of our young to be healthy, educated, and productive" (Children's Defense Fund, 1996). For many who drop out, illegal activity can be attractive, given the few opportunities available for them in the legitimate labor market. Evidence of this is that over 30 percent of federal prisoners and 40 percent of state prisoners are high school dropouts compared with about 18 percent in the general population. One-half of those on death row share this history of educational failure (Laird et al., 2007).

SCHOOL FAILURES AND DROPOUTS

Alienation is a sense of powerlessness, normlessness, meaninglessness, isolation, or self-estrangement. In schools, its roots are found in the formal, impersonal, bureaucratic, educational system. Complete overhaul of the school structure would be necessary to prevent the feelings that drive some students to drop out of the system. Dropouts (called "status" dropouts) are persons who are 16- to 24-years-old who are not enrolled in school and who have not completed a high school program, regardless of when they left school. People who have received General Education Development (GED) credentials are counted as high school completers (Sable and Gaviola, 2008). As we will see, efforts at school reform and restructuring are often motivated by a desire to make school less alienating to those students who drop out.

Who Drops Out?

Sheri is a high school dropout and an unwed mother, a double stigma. Her intentions were to finish high school while her baby attended day care; then she could get a good job to support the baby. But when winter came and the baby got sick, she could not get to school regularly and dropped out. Juan's family moved to a large city from his native Puerto Rico when he was in elementary school. He worked part-time while attending high school because his family needed the money. With the language barrier, need for immediate cash, and little support from home, he dropped out to work longer hours at his menial job. Sheri and Juan are just two examples of the many youths who leave high school.

Eight percent of all students between the ages of 16 and 24 dropped out of high school (NCES, *Condition*, 2010, Table A-19-1). Where ethnic diversity is greatest, retention rates are lowest. African Americans and Latino students feel more alienated, with a higher sense of powerlessness and isolation than white students; these feelings are especially influential in dropout decisions for males. Note the dropout rates for different groups in Table 7.1.

About one-third of all Hispanic students dropped out before completing high school from the 1970s through 1990s, many to help their families, but most ended up in deeper poverty. The percentage of Hispanics aged 16–24 years who had not completed high school by 2008 was 18.3 percent, reflecting a declining trend since about 1995 (NCES, *Condition,* Table 1A-19-1; Orfield, 2004).

Students from Mexican American non-English-speaking homes in the United States have additional possibilities of being alienated; bilingual students tend to cope better than non-English-speakers because they are able to acquire the institutional support for school success and social mobility (Stanton-Salazar and Dornbusch, 1995, p. 116). Moreover, research shows English language learners are overrepresented in special educational programs, a diagnosis that can prevent them from attaining regular educational achievement (MacSwan and Rolstad, 2006).

Dropouts are disproportionately male, older than average (often two or more years behind grade level), burdened with low grades and behavior problems, minorities, from low-income

Table 7.1   Event Dropout Rates[a] for Those in Grades 10–12, Ages 15–24, by Sex, Race–Ethnicity, and Family Income, October 1972–2007

		Sex		Race–Ethnicity[b]			Family Income[c]		
October	Total	Male	Female	White	Black	Hispanic	Low	Middle	High
1972	6.1	5.9	6.3	5.3	9.5	11.2	14.1	6.7	2.5
1980	6.1	6.7	5.5	5.2	8.2	11.7	15.8	6.4	2.5
1990	4.0	4.0	3.9	3.3	5.0	7.9	9.5	4.3	1.1
2000	4.8	5.5	4.1	4.1	6.1	7.4	10.0	5.0	1.6
2005	3.8	4.2	3.4	2.8	7.3	5.0	8.9	3.8	1.5
2007	3.5	3.7	3.3	2.2	4.5	6.0	8.8	3.5	0.9

[a]The event dropout rate is the percentage of those in grades 10–12, ages 15–24, who were enrolled the previous October, but who were not enrolled and had not graduated in October of the current year.

[b]Beginning in 2003, respondents were able to identify themselves as being "more than one race." The 2003 through 2005 White, non-Hispanic and Black, non-Hispanic categories consist of individuals who considered themselves to be one race and who did not identify themselves as Hispanic. The Hispanic category includes Hispanics of all races and racial combinations. Because of the small sample size for some or all of the years shown in the table, American Indian/Alaska Natives and Asian/Pacific Islanders are included in the total but not shown separately. The "more than one race" category is also included in the total in 2003 through 2005 but is not shown separately because of small sample size.

[c]Low income is the bottom 20 percent of all family incomes; high income is the top 20 percent of all family incomes; and middle income is the 60 percent in between.

Note: Beginning in 1992, the Current Population Survey (CPS) changed the questions used to obtain the educational attainment of respondents.

Source: U.S. Department of Education, National Center for Education Statistics, *Dropout Rates in the United States, 1997, 1999,* (based on the October Current Population Surveys); NCES. Dropout Rates in the U.S. 2005 (Washington, D.C.: U.S. Department, 2007, NCES 2007-059). NCES, Dropout and Completion Rates in the United States, 2007. NCES 2009-064.

families with low educational attainment, and with little educational encouragement. It is these individuals who make up the reserve labor force in capitalistic systems. Unemployment is directly related to educational attainment. The unemployment rate for those 25–64 years old without a high school diploma or equivalent was 9.7 percent during the three-year period between 2006 and 2008 compared to 6.2, 4.7, and 2.6 rates for those with a diploma, some college, and a bachelors' degree or better, respectively (U.S. Census, American Community Survey, S2301). For the same period, the median income of males with less than a high school diploma who were older than 25 was $23,638; for women, it was $14,682. By way of reference, the average income for all those aged above 25 during this period was $34,483 (U.S. Census, American Community Survey, S1501).

The dropout problem is growing worse in many major U.S. cities, where the average rate is more than 40 percent; in New York City, about 50 percent fail to graduate in four years (Bosman, 2007). In the nation as a whole, however, the rate has leveled off and is declining slightly (see Table 7.1).

Why Students Drop Out

Dropping out is perhaps best described as a process, not an event—a process of progressive academic disengagement that often traces back to children's earliest experiences at school. It is the result of an accumulation of often small events that become compounded (Alexander, Entwisle, and Kabbani, 2001). Evidence suggests that these events begin at the earliest enrollment of students. For example, in the Baltimore sample studied by Alexander and his colleagues, future dropouts were significantly more often absent as 1st graders than future graduates, a difference that grew larger in middle school and larger still in the early high school years (Alexander, Entwisle, and Kabbani, 2001). Students from low socioeconomic status (SES) backgrounds, with teenage mothers, and from families experiencing stressful change (such as frequent moves) were much more likely to be among the future dropout group. These background factors often produce lower levels of achievement, which leads to frustration and disengagement and lower academic achievement.

> The experiences at home and at school that shape children's development influence not just how they think but also what they do. Habits of conduct, once established, tend to persist, as do reputations grounded in those habits. Teachers, we know, rate children on the basis of their classroom deportment. We also know that children's work habits, classroom engagement, and compliance with school routines carry considerable weight in determining achievement levels and are implicated in achievement differences across social lines. In the present results, engagement behaviors at school rival test scores and report card marks in forecasting eventual dropout—and this holds all along the way, including 1st grade. (Alexander, Entwisle, and Kabbani, 2001, p. 802)

Some schools are so poor and crowded that they cannot begin to offer in-school support, much less coordinate with other agencies to meet student needs. Kozol describes differences in two Chicago-area schools—one wealthy, one poor. The wealthy school has an average class size of 24 children, and there are 15 students in classes for slow learners. The poor school has remedial classes with 39 students and classes for the "gifted" of 36 students. Each student at the wealthy school has an adviser assigned; at the poor school, one guidance counselor advises 420 children (Kozol, 1991, p. 66). It is difficult to cope with the requirements of the compulsory, rigid, formal, educational system, which has no room for misfits who frequently drop out when they reach legal age (National Dropout Prevention Network website, http://www.dropoutprevention.org/).

Problems such as teenage pregnancy and peer-group pressure from gangs are two examples of factors affecting dropout rates. Teenage pregnancy often prevents young mothers from finishing school. This problem is most prevalent in the inner city. Early intervention to provide sex education, parenting training, child care, and easy access to education is necessary. Many programs are being targeted to inner-city schools (Scott-Jones, 1991, p. 461; "Teen Pregnancy," 1998). Recent data show that these programs seem to be having a positive effect. The teen birth rate in 2005 was 21 per 1,000 young women aged 15–17, an all-time low. The rate in 1991 was almost twice as large, 39 per 1,000 young women (Federal Interagency Forum on Child and Family Statistics, 2007).

Gang violence is a threat to neighborhoods and schools. Armed, angry, and impulsive, these hostile youths have little regard for others. Social ills are directly related to youths joining gangs.

Gangs and Schools

Youth gangs are found in every area of the United States and many other countries. Why do youths join gangs? Joining a gang, some argue, is a class and ethnic group issue. Most gangs are made up of disaffected youth living in poor neighborhoods, having difficulty in school, and sometimes coming from ethnic groups that are not integrated into the mainstream society. Youths join gangs for protection and to show strong loyalty to their neighborhood and "to protect their turf." In localities where gangs are common, avoiding them can be hard. Their dominance of the street life leads parents in many communities to keep their children indoors as much as possible and to try to enroll them in schools outside of their neighborhood (Anderson, 1990, 1999). Gang involvement is also related to risk-taking behaviors, and the rate of delinquent acts is high for gang members (Crowley et al., 1997; Thornberry and Burch, 1997; Valdez, 2007). Add ethnic differences, difficulties assimilating, and limited opportunities, and one has a recipe for gang membership (Rodriguez, 1993; Umemoto, 2006). Immigrants join gangs to defend and maintain their ethnic identity and create a sense of belonging.

The National Youth Gang Survey (NYGS), sponsored by the U.S. Department of Justice (National Youth Gang Center, 2007, http://www.nationalgangcenter.gov/Survey-Analysis), has been conducted since 1995 and provides a representation of gang members and their activities. The survey is given to police and sheriff departments of all sizes. From these surveys, NYGS estimates that there were 27,000 active gangs and 788,000 gang members in the United States in 2007, an increase from the recent low of about 20,000 gangs in 2003 and about 693,500 members in 2001. Most members (92 percent) are male; female-dominated gangs exist, but are rare. The majority of gang members are aged above 18 (63 percent), while about 37 percent are under 18 years of age. Hispanic youth make up 48 percent of all gang members; African Americans, 36 percent; Caucasians, 10 percent; and others, 6 percent of gang members. About one-third of the gangs have a mix of ethnic groups. Though gangs are most prevalent in urban areas, they also are found in suburbs, small cities, and rural counties.

What do gang members do? Many gangs are involved in serious and violent crimes. Twenty-eight percent of the gangs were organized specifically for trafficking in drugs; other gangs committed assaults and robberies, sometimes along with drug activities. Fighting, stealing, alcohol drinking, and drug dealing lead to power and respect from other gang members. An estimated 50 percent of assaults involved carrying a gun.

How do gangs affect schools? In fact, the number of gang members in schools is usually fairly small, but the gang presence can be quite disruptive, bringing into schools fear, violence, drugs, and recruitment for gangs (Burnett and Walz, 1994). Recent research has also shown that youth who are arrested are less likely to graduate; the earlier their contact with the criminal justice system, the greater the likelihood they will drop out (Hirschfield, 2009). Some ethnic groups are labeled by teachers and peers in school and are expected to fail and to be gang members; Latino youth often experience this stereotype (Katz, 1997). By stereotyping certain students, they may be labeled unfairly. The school atmosphere can contribute to a sense of failure, restrictions on language, lack of respect for different cultures, and lack of a sense of belonging (Burnett and Walz, 1994).

What can schools do about gang influence? First, they can legally protect the learning environment for students from intimidation, fear, or threat of violence. Dress codes that forbid student gang apparel, however, are not legal unless it can be shown that the apparel interferes with learning and with freedom of expression (Gluckman, 1996). School atmosphere plays a significant role. Court rulings concerning student due process protections have been cited by some researchers as limiting what school authorities can do to curb gang activity. Arum (2003) notes that it is not so much the extension of these rights as:

> the wide-spread perception—shared by teachers, administrators and parents—that school discipline even for minor sanctions has been subjected to judicial, not simply administrative, oversight. The perception that a student can potentially invoke constitutional due process rights virtually anywhere and at any time has led not necessarily to greater protection for individuals, but to the legalization of school practices, the intimidation of school personnel faced with an ambiguous legal terrain, and an undermining of the school's moral authority. (p. 208)

In seeking to protect students from unfair disciplinary decisions, advocates for student rights have, according to this view, undermined a crucial educational resource. To counter this decline in the moral authority of schools to create appropriate socialization environments for youth, Arum and his colleagues argue that we need to limit the extension of court rulings into these matters and to be clear about the unintended consequences of extensions of student rights.

Communities can help youth by providing alternatives to gangs. For instance, youth clubs, sports activities, midnight basketball, boxing, rap sessions, and other activities draw youth away from gangs. The best remedy is to integrate all young people into the school so that they feel a vested interest in participating and know their efforts will lead to success in the job market.

School Crime and Violence

School-based crime and violence are among the most pressing concerns in public polls of attitudes toward schools. In its most recent annual crime survey, the Gallup poll found that having their school-aged children physically harmed at school was an important parental concern. The proportion of parents frequently worried about their children being harmed at school, however, has declined from a high of 20 percent in the 2006 survey to 14 percent in 2009 (Gallup Poll, 2010, http://www.gallup.com/poll/1603/Crime.aspx). Shootings in schools make the headlines, but many students face daily bullying, sexual harassment, and beatings. In fact, some children are afraid to go to school or they carry weapons to school for protection, issues discussed in Chapter 2 and elsewhere in the text. Parents, educators, and community members are concerned for the safety of students and the integrity of the learning process. According to the 2009 Indicators of School Crime and Safety report, rates of crime in schools have moved up and down, without any discernable overall trend for the last nine years: Rates have generally declined, though victimization at school has increased slightly (NCES 2010-012, http://nces.ed .gov/programs/crimeindicators/crimeindicators2009/index.asp)

Studies show, however, that most schools are safe and that 80–90 percent of school employees rate their schools as safe (Verdugo and Schneider, 1999). Why, then, is there a perception of unsafe schools? Newspaper headlines report dramatic happenings on school grounds, incidents that seem random yet are real. Educators in most schools affected are shocked by these incidents; it is the very randomness of the acts and lack of ability to predict them that frightens people. Though violent acts are unlikely in 90 percent of schools, the other 10 percent are problematic. The public seldom hears about problems in some inner-city schools where crime and violence are daily events and the schools are armed fortresses with metal detectors and police guards.

Consider the case of a group of Chicana adolescents. Conditions in their school are poor with overcrowded classrooms, underfunded programs, high dropout rates, many students in poverty, teacher burnout and discouragement, social promotions, sexism and racism, and no programs to remediate these students, resulting in few graduates prepared for college. Young women in the school make choices based on the reality of their situations, and those choices often involve early pregnancy, gang affiliation, and dropping out of school (Dietrich, 1998; Valdez, 2007).

Students like these girls who are engaged in antisocial behavior are likely headed for academic failure. Yet, programs that do exist to deal with the problems focus on either the antisocial behavior or academic success and do not link the two; programs also focus narrowly on changing attitudes or behaviors, but not the context or climate within which such behaviors occur. By identifying climates that allow for academic failure and antisocial behavior, schools may be able to attack the problems more effectively (McEvoy and Welker, 2000).

The Safe Schools Movement was formed to combat school violence. Movements arise when there is collective action around a common purpose. Violence reduction is a goal of all schools in the United States and of the Safe Schools Movement. However, developing effective school-based programs that are integrated into the school systems and can change the climate of the schools is challenging. Problems include "conflicts over violence reduction programs and services, lack of appropriate program evaluation, limited programs that attempt to change attributes of the individual rather than the environment in which violence emerges, and lack of a theoretical rationale to guide the development of school-based violence prevention and intervention efforts" (McEvoy, 1999).

Retention and Suspension: School Reactions to Problem Students

Schools need to rethink how they deal with "at-risk" and troublesome students based on sociological study results. Grade retention is one factor that contributes to the decision to drop out of school. Retention does not appear to improve school performance of poor students, but it does tell students that they are not considered capable, which increases the chances of their leaving because of frustration and disengagement (Roderick, 1994, 1995; Stearns et al., 2007; also see Alexander, Entwisle, and Dauber, 2003).

Students who are retained have low self-esteem and seldom make up the academic deficiencies that held them back in the first place (McCollum et al., 1999). Retained students lose achievement and have higher dropout rates. For example, a University of Chicago study found that 78 percent of those held back in the 8th grade had dropped out of school by their nineteenth birthday (Trotter, 2004). Estimates are that 2.6 million students are retained at a cost of $10 billion. These students are often young males with low SES, poor self-esteem, and low motivation, a description that matches that of the typical dropout (Nason, 1991; Stearns et al., 2007).

Schools seeking funding for special programs as alternatives to retention have had difficulty finding funds, leaving few alternatives to retention (Natriello, 1998). Thus, budgetary constraints are leading to retention, which is leading to a higher rate of dropping out, ultimately costing schools and society in both loss of human power and social services.

Unfortunately, too many schools use strategies such as suspensions that reduce expectations and stigmatize students. The students who are suspended are often at-risk students to begin with. Suspending students may eliminate the immediate problem but cause many long-term problems, including increased dropout rates because suspended students get behind in class work. "Tragically, although removing troubled and troubling students may provide systematic relief for schools, such strategies ignore the root causes of aggressive behavior and banish those children who are most in need of the benefit of a strong academic foundation, a caring school environment, and positive peer relations" (Hudley et al., 1998).

To prevent students from dropping out, programs that focus on the most vulnerable populations try to reduce causes of apathy and alienation, raise self-esteem and success of students, and begin early in students' careers. Most experts advise identifying at-risk students early and intervening quickly. Many intervention programs have been proposed and some have been tested at the elementary and middle school grades. Accelerated academics, alternative schools, and Saturday and after-school programs are some of the academic approaches used. Stearnes and her colleagues (2007) recommend that schools work hard to retain students with summer school opportunities and academics, especially when they keep children with their same-age peers, at the same time helping students to gain the skills they lack. Laws to deny drivers' licenses to students in academic difficulty or to those who drop out of school before age 18 are being passed in a number of states. Getting parents involved in programs to keep students in school and holding parents accountable for students who do not attend school are other strategies. Finally, for those students who do drop out, an increasing number of programs for completing high school are available.

Over 60 percent of the dropouts studied in the National Educational Longitudinal Study begun in 1988 eventually completed high school; some return to high school, whereas others complete the General Educational Development (GED) exam. Their completion of high school is associated with several variables: Those students who demonstrated academic ability even if they did not perform well were most likely to complete high school. Seventy-five percent of those students from higher SES families completed high school (Hurst, Kelly, and Princiotta, 2005). About one-quarter of dropouts enroll in postsecondary education, and of those with postsecondary experience, 27 percent report earning a license or certificate, and 9 percent report they earned an Associate degree or higher.

Adolescent Employment and Dropping Out of School

Adolescent employment creates conflicting expectations for students; adolescents supply labor as workers in fast-food restaurants, as newspaper carriers, and in many other positions in evenings and on weekends (Post and Pong, 2000). Work experience is a valuable training for adult roles, especially in responsibility, punctuality, working for a boss, following orders, handling money, and practicing whatever skills may be acquired. However, work takes time from studies, extracurricular activities, peer associations, and "growing up."

Two major questions have been asked about the effect of high school students' employment: What is the effect on school achievement of the number of hours worked, and are working students more likely to drop out of high school? More than half of 10th graders and almost all 11th and 12th graders work sometime during the school year (Schoenhals, Tienda, and Schneider, 1998). The number of hours worked and the type of employment significantly impact students' decisions to drop out of school. Students working in traditional student occupations such as babysitting, lawn work, odd jobs, and farming chores experience a different work environment than students working in retail or the private sector economy. Traditional work settings are less mundane and may entail meaningful interactions with adults, another source of socialization. However, long hours working in service sector occupations can be detrimental for both male and female students.

Unfortunately, this means that the majority of high school student jobs can have a detrimental effect on staying in high school. "Policy makers have long contended that one way to socialize teenagers to become young adults is to encourage them to work. However, these findings indicate that there is a negative unintended consequence of adolescent employment: a higher likelihood of dropping out" (McNeal, 1997, p. 217).

If adolescents work limited hours at times that do not interfere substantially with other activities, there are benefits from the experience. Many cite the ability to buy clothes, cars, electronic goods, MP3 players, and other desired goods as a motivation for working.

Dropping out of high school is related to the number of hours a student works during high school and to the motivation for work; some students work more hours than allowed by law. Other students work because they have school-related problems, need money, or have family problems. Though some students must work to help their families, fewer than one in ten donate part or all of their earnings to help support their families.

The answer to the question of whether employment during school hinders academic achievement and progress is elusive (see Table 7.2). Warren, LePore, and Mare (2000) show, as is generally the case, that the amount a student works is crucial to its impact: Students who work more intensively (more hours and in nontraditional jobs for youth) do less well in school and are somewhat more likely to dropout. However, whether this is due to their work or not requires more analysis. These researchers find that preexisting characteristics (lower grades, lower SES, lower achievement

Table 7.2 Reasons for Dropping Out

Reasons for Dropping Out	Total	Sex		Race–Ethnicity		
		Male	Female	Hispanic	Black, Non-Hispanic	White, Non-Hispanic
School related						
Did not like school	51.2	57.8	44.2	42.3	44.9	57.5
Could not get along with teachers	35.0	51.6	17.2	26.8	30.2	39.2
Could not get along with students	20.1	18.3	21.9	18.2	31.9	17.4
Was suspended too often	16.1	19.2	12.7	14.5	26.3	13.1
Did not feel safe at school	12.1	11.5	12.8	12.8	19.7	9.5
Was expelled	13.4	17.6	8.9	12.5	24.4	8.7
Felt I didn't belong	23.2	31.5	14.4	19.3	7.5	31.3
Could not keep up with schoolwork	31.3	37.6	24.7	19.5	30.1	35.8
Was failing school	39.9	46.2	33.1	39.3	30.1	44.8
Changed school and did not like new school	13.2	10.8	15.8	10.3	21.3	9.8

| **Table 7.2** Continued | | | | | |

Reasons for Dropping Out	Total	**Sex**		**Race–Ethnicity**	
		Male	Female	Hispanic	Black, Non-Hispanic	White, Non-Hispanic
Job related						
Could not work and go to school at same time	14.1	20.0	7.8	14.3	9.0	15.9
Had to get a job	15.3	14.7	16.0	17.5	11.8	14.3
Found a job	15.3	18.6	11.8	20.8	6.3	17.6
Family related						
Had to support family	9.2	4.8	14.0	13.1	8.1	9.0
Wanted to have family	6.2	4.2	8.4	8.9	6.7	5.4
Was pregnant[a]	31.0	NA	31.0	20.7	40.6	32.1
Became parent	13.6	5.1	22.6	10.3	18.9	12.9
Got married	13.1	3.4	23.6	21.6	1.4	15.3
Had to care for family member	8.3	4.6	12.2	7.0	19.2	4.5
Other						
Wanted to travel	2.1	2.5	1.7	(b)	2.9	1.9
Friends dropped out	14.1	16.8	11.3	10.0	25.4	10.9

NA, not applicable.

[a]Females only.

[b]Too few cases for a reliable estimate.

Source: U.S. Department of Education, National Center for Education Statistics, National Education Longitudinal Study of 1988 First Follow-up Survey, 1990.

test scores, and less optimism about going to college, for example) fully account for the negative association between employment intensity and academic course grades. In other words, it appears that students transfer their effort to work after finding little success in school. Identical findings for the link between work and delinquency have been published by Paternoster and colleagues (2003).

The Future for Dropouts

Many dropouts face a grim future. Only about 55 percent of recent high school dropouts were employed between 2006 and 2008 (U.S. Census, American Community Survey, S2301, and see Table 7.3). They are more likely to be on welfare and to have dependent children. A disproportionate number of dropouts end up in the nation's jails and prisons, and are four times as likely to engage in unlawful behavior. Dropouts have difficulty competing in the labor market, as they lack skills for today's jobs, have less knowledge for daily living, and have low self-esteem. But most important is the human cost to society of individuals who cannot compete in the world. Unfortunately, some proposals to raise standards in schools and require graduation examinations could also increase the dropout rates of marginal students, although a proportion of dropouts end up completing their high school degrees through GED exams.

A program for older students is the federal government's "ability to benefit" program that allows students without a high school degree or equivalent to pass a test administered by a college and qualify for federal aid to attend that college. Though these students are considered high-risk

Table 7.3 Employment Status of Young Adults Not Enrolled in School During the October When Age 21 in 2001–2006 by High School Graduation Status, Sex, Race, and Hispanic or Latino Ethnicity

Percent Distribution

High School Graduation Status During the October When Age 21	Employment Status During the October When Age 21				
	Total	Employed Civilian	Serving in Armed Forces	Unemployed	Not in the Labor Force
High school dropouts	100.0	60.6	0.3	8.6	30.5
Men	100.0	68.4	0.4	8.6	26.6
Women	100.0	49.8	0.1	8.7	41.4
White, non-Hispanic	100.0	68.7	0.2	7.1	25.9
Black, non-Hispanic	100.0	45.9	0.5	10.3	43.4
Hispanic or Latino	100.0	59.2	0.4	11.2	29.3
High school graduates, never enrolled in college[a]	100.0	71.5	5.4	6.0	16.0
Men	100.0	72.0	10.0	6.2	11.8
Women	100.0	70.8	1.4	5.7	22.0
White, non-Hispanic	100.0	76.6	5.6	4.7	13.0
Black, non-Hispanic	100.0	57.7	7.4	11.3	23.6
Hispanic or Latino	100.0	68.4	7.7	4.9	18.9
Some college, no longer enrolled	100.0	77.9	3.8	4.7	13.6
Men	100.0	78.7	5.9	5.0	10.4
Women	100.0	77.1	1.8	4.4	16.7
White, non-Hispanic	100.0	80.1	4.3	3.1	12.5
Black, non-Hispanic	100.0	72.9	2.8	9.5	14.7
Hispanic or Latino	100.0	74.4	3.9	4.7	17.1

[a]Respondents who have received a General Educational Development (GED) credential are counted as high school graduates.

Note: The National Longitudinal Survey of Youth 1997 consists of young men and women who were ages 12–16 on December 31, 1996. Race and Hispanic or Latino ethnicity groups are mutually exclusive but not exhaustive. Other race groups, which are included in the overall totals, are not shown separately because their representation in the survey sample is not sufficiently large to provide statistically reliable estimates.

Source: U.S. Department of Labor, Bureau of Labor Statistics, America's Youth at 21: School Enrollment, Training, and Employment Transitions Between Ages 20 and 21. Washington, D.C. 2009. USDL09–0079.

for dropping out, many find this opportunity to restart just what they need (Burd, 1996). Increased resources, more flexible time requirements, altered suspension policies, and special counseling services are but a few aspects of this program. This program has recently been debated as the federal government seeks to protect students from fraudulent student loan schemes, especially those associated with for-profit postsecondary institutions (http://www.ed.gov/news/student-aid-rules-protect-borrowers-and-taxpayers).

In the New York City borough of Queens, a new program at John Adams High School illustrates another approach. One of 20 Young Adult Borough Centers, the program, offered in conjunction with community-based organizations, is open to students with at least 17 credits of the 44 needed to graduate but who have dropped out of school or are many credits behind where they should be. In addition to courses and tutoring, the program offers career and college planning, job-skills development, and access to social workers and other community resources. Students can build their own schedules. Those with fewer than 17 credits, who are often younger and with weaker academic skills, have access to transfer schools that operate full-time and offer an intensive program aimed at bringing the youth up to high school-level attainment (Gwertz, 2007).

Schools can contribute to the dropout process—or, as some have referred to it, the "pushout" process—by giving signals that the schools cannot deal with certain students. Detentions, suspensions, expulsions, and no school support system are recipes for creating dropouts.

Criticisms of the Student Role

Students are generally well aware of where they stand academically. They have been labeled by teachers and other students from their earliest days in school. In one 2nd-grade classroom, the teacher divided the children into reading groups—the Rocket ships, Jet airplanes, and Piper cubs. There was no doubt in those children's minds as to where they stood! Even the types of subjects taken by older students encourage role definitions; there are "dumbbell" courses and "elite" ones. These placements and labels can have a permanent, sometimes detrimental, effect on a student's self-perception (McFarland, 2006).

Attitudes toward student learning differ across cultures. The Japanese have few student "failures," in part because they do not define students as failures. If students are not succeeding, parents and teachers expect them to work harder to accomplish what is expected. Instead of assuming that some students cannot do the work, the assumption is that all (except those with a disability) can pass if they put in enough time and effort. This corresponds with the findings on effective schools in the United States, which hold that high academic expectations for students and teachers result in high achievement.

According to anthropologist Jules Henry and other critics of schools, students are put in a position that compromises their integrity; they must "give the teacher what she wants." Henry elaborates the reason for this in his book *Culture against Man*:

> American classrooms, like educational institutions anywhere, express the values, preoccupations, and fears found in the culture as a whole. School has no choice; it must train the children to fit the culture as it is. School can give training in skills; it cannot teach creativity. . . . Schools deal with masses of children, and can manage therefore only by reducing them all to a common definition. (Henry, 1963, pp. 287, 320–321).

Thus, students are not encouraged to be creative, but only to toe the line, according to Henry.

Many educators have raised criticisms about the student role that concern the core of society itself. Bowles and Gintis (1976) argued that the roles of students in schools prepare them for the unequal stratification system in society at large. Students divided into tracks conform to different behavioral norms. "Vocational and general tracks emphasize rule-following and close supervision, while the college track tends toward a more open atmosphere emphasizing the internalization of norms." These differences in social relationships reflect students' social backgrounds and likely future economic positions.

> Thus blacks and other minorities are concentrated in schools whose repressive arbitrary, generally chaotic internal order, coercive authority structures, and minimal possibilities for advancement mirror the characteristics of inferior situations. Similarly, predominantly working-class schools tend to emphasize behavioral control

and rule-following, while schools in well-to-do suburbs employ relatively open systems that favor greater student participation, less direct supervision, more student electives, and, in general, a value system stressing internalizing standards of control. (Bowles and Gintis, 1976).

According to this perspective, docility, lack of creativity, and conformity are the goals being met by schools in preparing students for the work world. In our time of accountability and high stakes testing, this conformity to narrow criteria of academic achievement can seem even more oppressive.

The student role has not changed significantly in most school settings, even with educational movements advocating more rights, power, equal opportunity, and freedom for students. Students are the clients of education, yet they have almost no control over the service rendered. Do students have the right to determine what they learn and how they should learn it? Radical educators such as Illich (1971) and Kozol (1991) argue that this is a basic right that is being denied to students for reasons other than sound pedagogy.

> **Applying Sociology to Education:** *Describe your role as student at various levels of the educational system. How has it changed?*

STUDENTS AND THE INFORMAL SYSTEM

To carry out a role, individuals must believe that they can be successful. Therefore, students must believe that they can be high achievers in order to try. Our evaluation of our ability can be altered depending on what we believe to be the costs, rewards, and motivations involved. The following sections reveal the subtle influences on students' academic achievement and school experiences.

Student's Self-Concept

Wilbur Brookover and colleagues (1996) show that self-concept of academic ability is significantly correlated with academic performance. Labeling and conditioning influence the way we see our abilities in any area. If many students in a school have low achievement expectations, this influences the school's achievement level. Manipulating school variables may improve students' chances of academic success. School value climate, background experiences, peer-group relationships, and other factors in students' careers influence academic self-concept, and vice versa. Thus, the recommendation in the effective schools literature is to raise students' self-concept and academic expectations through helping them actually master the requirements of the curriculum.

School Value Climate and Student Achievement

Schools reward incompetence. So argues Jackson (1968), pointing out that the average student spends 20 hours a week on courses, does little to no homework, and plays dumb. The reward for success in school is more hard work, so why try? Here we examine how school affects student achievement.

Brookover and his colleagues (1973) set about to test Coleman's and Jencks's findings that the home environment supersedes school influence in students' school achievement. In ongoing research on school climate and performance, they administered questionnaires to students and teachers. Results showed that academic value climate of school for elementary students is affected by four types of perceptions:

1. Student perceptions of the present "evaluations/expectations" of "others" (parents, teachers, and friends) in their school and social system
2. Student perceptions of the future "evaluations/expectations" of "others" in their school and social system
3. Student perceptions about the level of feelings of futility permeating the social system of the school
4. Student perceptions of those academic norms stressing academic achievement that exist in their school and social system. (Brookover and Erickson, 1975).

The most important variable by far was the students' reported sense of futility—their feelings of hopelessness and their sense that teachers do not care about their academic achievement. The role of teachers' and classmates' attitudes in establishing these feelings is obviously an important part of the school climate. This finding is also reflected in the efforts to create smaller schools, so that students and teachers can develop more personal relationships, and students are less likely than in big schools to "fall between the cracks." The use of "advisories," for example, class periods with a teacher and a small group of students devoted to the students and their lives, often with the same teacher and students meeting over several years to provide continuity, is a common practice to thwart student disengagement (National Research Council and the Institute of Medicine, 2004).

Brookover and colleagues (1996) considered the effects of school social structure and social climate on student achievement. *Student achievement* was measured by reading and writing competencies, academic self-concept, and self-reliance. The *school social structure* was measured by teacher satisfaction with the school structure, parental involvement, differentiation in student programs, principals' reports of time devoted to instruction, and student mobility in school. The *school climate* was measured by student perceptions, teacher perceptions, and principal perceptions. More than 85 percent of the variance in student attainment was explained by the combination of these variables. In a summary of findings, which compared improving and declining schools, Brookover and colleagues found the following: The staff members of improving schools place more emphasis on accomplishing basic reading and mathematics objectives; they believe all students can master basic objectives and they hold high expectations; and they assume responsibility for learning and accept being held accountable. Principals in improving schools are instructional leaders and disciplinarians. In short, Brookover argues that schools can and do make a difference.

To illustrate this point and to put the concept of "school climate" into practice, Brookover and colleagues designed a pragmatic program in the Chicago public school system using the variables mentioned to alter school climate. As a result, school achievement levels increased significantly.

The findings of an English study confirm those of other studies on the following question: "What difference do schools make?" The researchers studied 12 inner-city London secondary schools, which varied greatly on factors such as student behavior and academic ability. School variations remained fairly constant over time, even when controlling for students' family background and personal characteristics. Examination results, behavior, and degree of delinquency were closely related in successful schools, but not related to school size, physical aspects of the building, or administrative structure.

Outcomes were related to school characteristics as social institutions—"academic emphasis, teacher action in lessons, the availability of incentives and rewards, good conditions for pupils, and the extent to which children were able to take responsibility." These factors could all be influenced by staff. The abilities of the children also affected outcomes. The combined factors created "a particular ethos, or set of values, attitudes, and behaviors which [will] become characteristic of the school as a whole. This is the school value climate. Behaviors and attitudes are shaped by school experience, and these in turn shape outcomes of schools" (Rutter et al., 1979, pp. 177–179).

Many recent commission reports encourage teachers to set high academic standards, assign well-constructed homework, and provide grades and meaningful comments. In fact, there is a relationship between the high standards and homework; research indicates that achievement and test scores improve with increased study time spent outside the classroom. High achievement performance standards set by teachers, parents, and peers also generate greater effort on homework. Higher standards are set by teachers and peers for high-ability students who can handle a challenge. Parents are more likely to set higher standards for lower-ability students less able to deal with the challenge. This difference may result from teachers' expectations of high-ability students and parents' response to their student's poor performance (Coon et al., 1993; Natriello and McDill, 1986; Pashal et al., 1984).

The bottom line is that student self-concept, home environment, teacher expectations, school climate, and many other factors all interact to affect a student's achievement. Whatever the academic norms of a school, students tend to conform. Where academic achievement is rewarded by faculty and peers, students tend to achieve better (McDill et al., 1967). School climate explains much of the difference in levels of school achievement, differences sometimes attributed solely to race, SES, and home effects (Brookover and Erickson, 1975). As we noted in Chapter 4, research is now clear that schools have positive effects on student learning—some may be more effective than others. But schools make a difference (Downey, von Hippel, and Broh, 2004).

Teacher and Student Expectations

Within schools, groups of student peers can be identified by their cohesiveness; along with that cohesiveness goes a set of expectations, values, and aspirations. Willis (1977) describes how boys in an all-male comprehensive secondary school in England were divided: A small group of boys was called the "lads," who "worked the system" to gain control over their time, and the large majority was called "ear 'oles" (ear holes, that is, passive learners who cannot shut their ears to resist what schools offer), who complied with authority and the expectations of the school. Lads learned to belong to the working class by rejecting the mental work expected by the school as offering upward mobility; they reinforced and reproduced their parents' status. The culture the lads reproduced for themselves was actually based on their realistic assessment of chances within the school and social class context, according to Willis. He starts his book with the following:

> The difficult thing to explain about how middle class kids get middle class jobs is why others let them. The difficult thing to explain about how working class kids get working class jobs is why they let themselves. (1977, p. 1)

School reformers argue that a sense of futility among students can be altered by setting high expectations: "No students are expected to fall below the level of learning needed to be successful at the next level of education" (*Effective School Practices*, 1990). But student motivation and effort is not something that is easy to create when it is not already present, especially when, as among Willis's lads, the students actively resist the goals of teachers.

> **Applying Sociology to Education:** *Are there groups of students who reject your community schools' value climate? How would you change the value climate of your community's schools to improve students' learning and achievement?*

Peer Groups and Student Culture

When we enter a school or observe playground activity, we see the school's unique culture manifest itself. The norms that control behavior of peer-group members are strong. One need only observe the conformity in dress, gestures, language, and slang to discover what is acceptable in a particular school. Fads and crazes are key aspects of student culture, holding the group together.

Playground activities and games help set the students' world apart from the adult culture. Even in playground games, children are learning to relate to their peers by following rules, taking turns, and verbally and nonverbally expressing themselves. These behaviors will carry over into their formal encounters with the adult world and are an important socializing agent in the child's life (Thorne 1999).

The student subculture has a strong influence in determining what happens in school. Because students are grouped together by age and subjected to a series of age-related requirements, they develop a separate subculture with norms, expectations, and methods or "strategies" for coping with these demands. This subculture of peers evolves as a result of the long period of school training, necessary for modern societies, that delays the entry of young people into the adult world. Peer groups serve a number of purposes for their members: Young people of similar age and status in the social and educational system can express themselves freely; experiment with social interactions and friendships while learning to get along with others; learn sex roles; and serve as reinforcers for norms, rules, and morality. Age-mates are important in this process because they are thrown together into school activities (Wilkinson, 2003).

In *The Adolescent Society*, Coleman (1961) writes that the strength of this subculture lies in its power over its members. He found that for an adolescent, the disapproval of one's peers is almost as hard to accept as that of one's parents, and that one pays a price for nonconformity. For most adolescents, their peers are a reference group that influences their dress, mannerisms, speech patterns, and preferences—their whole way of life. Smoking, involvement in early sexual activities, drinking alcohol, and using drugs, for instance, are closely correlated with best friends' and close peers' behavior (Bauman and Ennett, 1994; Ryan, 2001; Wang et al., 1995; Webb et al., 1993).

High school subcultures often place high value on athletics for males and on leadership activities for females, but little value—for either sex—on being very bright or academically oriented. For girls, good grades are often believed to detract from popularity. Some students even try not to appear smart for fear of losing peer-group approval. The students with the highest status in high schools tend to be from the dominant SES group in the school, oriented toward school activities, and not primarily concerned with gaining adult approval. Students who are academically outstanding gain little peer acceptance or reward and are sometimes ridiculed. Coleman (1961) suggests that schools could shift the focus so that the norms of the teen communities reinforce educational goals rather than inhibit them. However, in those high schools where students have high educational and occupational expectations, competition for grades can be intense. High achievement in these schools is rewarded, and some students may even resort to cheating rather than risk doing poorly (Attewell, 2001; McCabe, 1999). Student peer groups often form around neighborhood friendships, which may have existed since grade school. Their activities may have little to do with the academic aspects of school, though they can influence academic achievement and other organizational aspects, such as extracurricular activities (Garner and Raudenbush, 1991, p. 251).

Student peer-group actions are constructed within the framework or environment of the school. Philip Cusick outlines key parts of this *sociocultural environment*, which had the *intended effects* of denying freedom of activity and lumping students in an undifferentiated mass and the

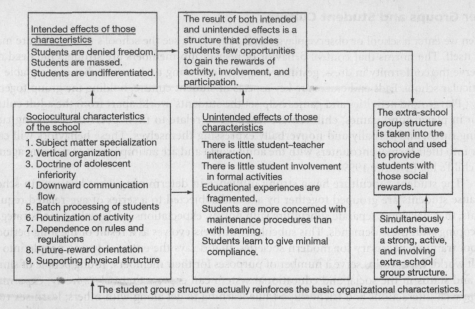

The student group structure actually reinforces the basic organizational characteristics.

FIGURE 7.1 Relationship between student behavior and the school organization.
Source: From Cusick, P. INSIDE HIGH SCHOOL, 1E. © 1973 Wadsworth, a part of Cengage Learning, Inc. Reproduced by permission. www.cengage.com/permissions.

unintended effects shown in Figure 7.1 (1973, pp. 216–217). As Cusick discovered in the high school he studied, "The tendency of the students . . . to maintain tight, in-school groups was a natural, but unrecognized, consequence of the school's basic organizational structure. As long as the supporting structure exists, the students will probably continue to form groups" (pp. 208–209). The more recent research of McFarland (2001) came to the same conclusion, again pointing to the intimate interconnections of behavior and its context.

Within this potentially alienating culture of high school, it is important to have friends with whom to walk, sit at lunch, and attend activities. There is usually a core of elite "jocks" and good-looking female students, and some schools may have high-status music and drama groups. There are, unfortunately, social isolates who have no friends and, therefore, no "protection" in the system (Cusick, 1973, p. 173). Generally, their number is small. In his study of high schools, Hargreaves (1967) describes two main student groups or subcultures: those with positive orientations and those with negative orientations. Students with positive orientations toward the values of schools end up in the higher groups, which reinforce their orientations; negative students end up in the lower groups. For members of the negative subcultures, peer culture becomes the primary identification, whereas positive students are influenced by school values as well as by peers. Much of the focus of recent research concerned with student subcultures and peer effects has been devoted to studies of the effects of race, especially on whether norms against "acting white" exist and influence student academic achievement. We have addressed this question in Chapter 4. Studies of "whiteness" and its relations with other ethnic identities and how they play out in schools are also increasingly common (e.g., see Perry, 2002).

School organization sometimes contributes to the polarization of students through ability grouping, or "streaming," as do social class differences in students. Willis gives evidence that those from working-class or lower-class backgrounds may see little hope for an improved future and concentrate in negative-orientation groups:

> [A]nti-school culture provides powerful informal criteria and binding experiential processes which lead working-class lads to make the "voluntary" choice to enter the factory, and to help reproduce both the existing class structure of employment, and the "culture of the shop floor" as a segment of the overarching working-class culture. (Willis, 1977, pp. 53–54)

There is evidence that the influence of peer groups is growing in many countries as the influence of family on adolescents decreases. Studies indicate that parenting practices do influence the child's peer associations (Brown et al., 1993). The amount of time parents spend with adolescents does affect their tendency toward delinquency, with more parental time inhibiting formation of delinquent friendships (Warr, 1993).

Although the family in the United States used to have the dominant influence on adolescent values and behavior, the home as a socializing agent is now in competition with peer groups for the child's attention (Goodlad, 1984, 1998). There has been particular interest in the consequences for peer socialization effects in inner-city areas. As Wilson (1996) postulates, the concentration of urban poverty increasingly common in U.S. cities has produced circumstances that help produce a number of social problems, including low educational aspirations and achievement. The specific mechanisms that produce these effects, however, have not been well documented. Ainsworth (2002) provides us with a look at how these larger social circumstances enter into and affect individual lives. He finds strong support for collective socialization theory (educational expectations and the amount of homework completed) as the vehicle that best mediate the relationship between neighborhood effects and educational outcomes.

Attention to school and parent and community communication obviously follows from these observations. Programs such as the National Network of Partnership School, sponsored by the Center for Social Organization of Schools at Johns Hopkins University, are a good example of the efforts being undertaken to strengthen the connections between schools and families (http://www.csos.jhu.edu/P2000/).

Student Coping Strategies

Student "coping" strategies, or ways of adapting to the power structure of school culture, are major aspects of the informal system. Students develop strategies related to their own needs, based on their own experiences with schooling, self-concept, peer-group relations, ability grouping, and other factors. School requires strategies very different from those learned at home in early socialization, although early learning is crucial to the student's success in school. The child is gradually eased into the competitive, judgmental, disciplined world of school. The social distance between students and teachers is established early because teachers have authority as a result of their position in the educational system. Thus, students begin to learn strategies to cope with the world of the school and classroom from an early age.

Much of the research in this area is an offshoot of the interactionist theoretical approach, which contends in part that we construct our realities within an environmental context and behave in accordance with those constructions. From this perspective, the development of strategies can be seen as a kind of negotiation requiring students to understand the teachers' roles and needs while attempting to maximize their own interests. Students' attitudes vary from almost complete compliance with the teachers' goals to total lack of commitment. Teachers have power, but getting students to do what is desired takes strategies other than the direct use of power (Woods, 1980). "Negotiations" between individual students, students and teachers, and the class as a group are constantly changing, although some interactions are fairly routine (Cusick, 1983).

Different strategies are appropriate at different times in the maturational development of students. Learning how to work and solve problems may be key at one time, whereas mastering skills in taking examinations is the focus at another stage in the student's career (Woods, 1980). Turning points in children's careers can change them from "drifters" to "experts," or from excited students to bored ones. Peers play a major role in students' self-concepts as the peers define the role of each student in the class and school. Unpopular teens may be labeled "nerds," a label that is overcome by some teens through activities and friendship groups leading to greater self-confidence (Kinney, 1993).

Martyn Hammersley and Glenn Turner (1980) have developed an interactional model that takes into account student and teacher strategies. It begins with an analysis of the intentions, motives, and perspectives for student actions. The student considers possible actions, their costs and payoffs, and makes a decision based on the perceived and actual consequences of various behaviors. The teacher sets guidelines, expectations, or "frames" that operate in the classroom situation or that relate to specific segments, lessons, or problems. Students may conform to teacher "frames" or set up alternative options or "frames" that deviate from the teacher's. Whether students conform or deviate depends in part on student peer-group behaviors and on their involvement in the lesson content (McFarland, 2004).

The sociocultural structure of the school is also important in determining student experiences and strategies. Recognizing this, Robert Merton developed a typology of students' reactions to school goals and means (the school's methods of attaining goals). Individual student reactions to school goals and means range from acceptance to rejection, as indicated by Merton's (1957) four types:

1. *Conformity:* acceptance of goals and means
2. *Retreatism:* rejection of goals and means
3. *Ambivalence:* indifference
4. *Rejection with replacement:* something else in mind.

Peter Woods (1980) tested the goals–means typology on English public boarding school boys and revised the model to make it represent more of the variations in individual pupils' responses. He adds to the goals–means typology several categories:

1. *Colonization.* Colonization combines indifference to goals with ambivalence about means. The students accept school as a place where they must spend their time and try to maximize available gratifications, permitted and not, official and unofficial. Parts of the school system are acceptable to them, but illegal means may be used to cope, such as copying work or cheating on tests.
2. *Indulgence.* There is a strongly positive response to goals and means.
3. *Conformity.* This is broken down into several categories.
   a. *Compliance.* Students "feel some affinity for and identification with the goals and means."
   b. *Ingratiation.* Students "aim to maximize their benefits by earning the favor of those with power, and are usually undisturbed by unpopularity among their peers."
   c. *Opportunism.* Students show "less consistent application to work and frequent but momentary leanings toward other modes," trying them out before settling on one. This can result in fluctuations of behavior.
4. *Intransigence.* Students adopting this strategy are indifferent to the school's goals and reject its means to achieve goals through rules, rituals, and regulations. They may disrupt lessons and

even physically assault staff or destroy property. Appearance may distinguish this type of student—hair, dress, shoes, or boots. These students are generally difficult for the school to handle.

5. *Rebellion.* Students reject the school's goals and means, but they substitute others. This is common later in school careers. The replacement of goals makes this group less of a threat than the intransigents.

In this model, developed by Merton and modified by Woods, student strategies in relation to school goals and means of achieving goals are laid out for students in elementary and high school. At the college level, strategies differ because of the different demands and nature of the situation. College students' coping mechanisms are oriented to the work they must complete in each class. Snyder (1971) documents many of the gaps between the hidden and formal curricula in higher education, that is, the implicit demands versus the visible ones, which can be recognized more easily (see Margolis, 2001, for a more recent treatment of this topic).

Some college students quickly discover that those who master the hidden curriculum, who learn to "play the system," have learned important coping strategies. For example, Miller and Parlett (1976) write about "cue-consciousness," the degree to which students pick up cues from professors on such things as exam topics and favored subject areas. They describe three types of students:

1. *Cue-conscious.* Students who rely on hard work and luck to do well. They are less well prepared for exams because they try to learn more topics. They pick up a limited number of cues.
2. *Cue-seekers.* Students who learn selectively. They often actively seek information from faculty and try to make a good impression while seeking cues as to which topics are important.
3. *Cue-deaf.* Students who pick up virtually no cues about what is important and try to study all of the material rather than being selective.

The researchers found a correlation between the most cue-conscious students and high exam scores. Some research on differences in achievement in higher education settings is investigating cue-consciousness as an example of inequality in cultural capital (Ibarra, 2001; Margolis, 2001).

In recent years, some researchers have studied students' learning styles. Each person has dominant modes of learning; if teachers are aware of the range of individual variations and class profiles in learning styles, they can plan lessons to match dominant modes or the variety of learning styles. Students who know their style can adapt study patterns. We learn from auditory, visual, and tactile stimuli; in cooperative groups; in competitive situations; or in isolation. Several scales to evaluate learning styles have been developed (see Box 7.2).

Student strategies result in a variety of individual roles and a variety of labels: conformists, drifters, planners, retreatists, intransigents, rebels, teacher's pet, nobodies, troublemakers, jocks, dumb kids, brains, eggheads, popular, sleepers, or hand-wavers (Jackson, 1968). Any label can change. Once labeled, however, a child may come to behave more and more in the manner associated with the label, carrying out the self-fulfilling prophecy (Rist, 2007).

When evaluating student strategies, it is important to consider the entire system within which the student is operating, including the power dynamics, strategies of other students and teachers, and the sociocultural structure or goals and means of the school. In their work on male-only schools, Martin and colleagues (2010) stressed the importance of the school and its staff to help boys learn how to "do" school.

the more students feel intellectually engaged with what they are learning and the better the quality of school-based adult relationships students have at these single-sex schools, the more likely they are to exhibit academically supportive behavior, which in turn bolsters their academic performance. (2010, p. 14)

BOX 7.2

Learning Styles Inventory

The following are sample statements from the Grasha–Reichman learning styles inventory (Grasha, 1975). (Students respond on a scale from "agree" to "disagree.")

1. Most of what I know, I learned on my own.
2. I find the ideas of other students relatively useful for helping me to understand the course material.
3. I try to participate as much as I can in all aspects of a course.
4. I study what is important to me and not necessarily what the instructor says is important.
5. I think an important part of classes is to learn to get along with other people.
6. I accept the structure a teacher sets for a course.
7. I do not have trouble paying attention in classes.
8. I think students can learn more by sharing their ideas than by keeping their ideas to themselves.
9. I like to study for tests with other students.
10. I feel that I must compete with the other students to get a grade.

The researchers analyze the responses of each student and of the class; with this information, both students and teacher have a better understanding of which style of learning is most effective in particular classes.

This is another example of the increasingly widespread recognition that the personal relationships between students and teachers, sometimes called the degree of "personalism" exhibited in a school, is important. This may be especially true for students from low socioeconomic status families, where fewer resources are available to help the children to address the challenges they face. As we have noted before, this is one of the rationales supporting the small schools movement (discussed in Chapter 5); researchers have concluded that smaller learning communities are less likely to allow students to "slip through the cracks." Using such practices as advisories, and periods set aside for teachers and students to talk about their lives and topics beyond the official curriculum, where personal knowledge can be shared, the schools hope to promote the social and academic learning of students (Hammack, 2008). These expanded roles for teachers, however, require support and professional training, not always available in school systems (Phillippo, 2010).

The environment in which students learn, whether single-sex or charter school, is crucial to the students' experience. We now consider the environments in which students learn.

> **Applying Sociology to Education:** *What strategies do you as a student use to cope with your course(s)?*

STUDENTS AND THEIR ENVIRONMENTS

Effects of Home Environment on Educational Achievement

A school social worker who had in her district an elementary school that served a poverty-stricken area told of children whose parents could not care for them because of their working hours, illness, or other social problems, and of young children who took care of younger siblings. She told of children who had cola and potato chips for breakfast; of children who came to school in winter with holes in their shoes and wet feet; and of children who had unexplained bruises and even rat bites. As a result of the current recession, the U.S. national poverty rate has jumped to the highest level in 15 years, with 14.3 percent of the population or 44 million people living below the poverty line (Eckholm, 2010). One in five children are currently living in poverty, as are over 25 percent of black and Hispanic citizens. Children facing such environmental hardships do not have the support system necessary to do well in school.

Studies from Kenya, Africa, and from India also find that students from poor home environments had lower achievement than those from higher-status home environments. This was especially true for boys in India. (In India, this was measured by Misra's Home Environment Inventory Scale, and in Africa by a home environment questionnaire.) The role of parents in children's motivation to do well was stressed as an important variable (Muola 2010; Siwach, 2008).

Government departments of education have also stressed the guidelines for parents and schools, by as shown in the following concerning "Parent Expectations and Student Achievement":

> The most consistent predictors of children's academic achievement and social adjustment are parent expectations of the child's academic attainment and satisfaction with their child's education at school. Parents of high-achieving students set higher standards for their children's educational activities than parents of low achieving students. (Michigan Department of Education, 2001)

Children's positions in school and society are determined in large part by their family background. Studies by Coleman et al. (1966) and Jencks et al. (1972), discussed in Chapter 4 and below, found that one-half to two-thirds of student achievement variance is directly related to home variables such as socioeconomic level (Greenwood and Hickman, 1991, p. 287). Family "processes" are a better predictor of positive achievement and grades than all other variables (Dornbusch and Ritter, 1992).

An underlying question here is how schools can meet every child's needs. We know that schools use social constructs, with organization and language that are more familiar to middle- and upper-class children. These children are more likely to have home experiences supporting the values, attitudes, and training in cognitive skills that will help them adapt to school demands. During the early formative years, children learn languages, values, and an orientation toward the world. The early home learning environment of children is crucial; Bloom estimates that 80 percent of our potential intelligence is developed by age eight. Stimulating environments can help recover lost potential, but the process becomes more difficult (Bloom, 1981).

Let us follow two five-year-old children of equal intellectual ability into school. Joey comes from a working-class family, Billy from a middle-class family. Why is it likely from the outset that Joey will achieve at a lower level than Billy? We must be ever cautious of generalizing from two cases, and we must be aware that there are many variations in patterns of child-rearing; yet research in the United States and Britain has identified some common class-related child-rearing patterns, and these give Joey and Billy different tools with which to approach the school experience.

Joey and Billy's differences fall into several categories: cultural capital they bring to school, learning right and wrong, attitudes and values, language ability and cognitive skills, family structure, and parent–child interaction. When Joey misbehaves, his parents are quick to discipline him. The most common punishments are threats about consequences of his actions or withdrawal of privileges or belting him with a strap. Billy is also disciplined, but the method is very different. His parents use reasoning, guilt, and shame to instill values. Joey's socialization may be useful training for living in a sometimes dangerous environment, but it does not help him meet certain demands of the classroom situation, such as creative or independent thinking.

Joey and Billy are likely to develop different language patterns. Both speak English, but middle-class children learn formal or elaborated language in addition to "public" language used in everyday conversing by both children. The more restricted "public" language limits the child's ability to conceptualize new ideas and concepts. Formal language allows Billy to deal with more complex ideas and feelings (Bernstein, 1981).

Although most parents place a high value on the education and achievement of their children, their methods of encouraging education are different. Working-class parents expect their children to "behave" in school, stressing conformity and obedience to authority, behaviors necessary for working-class jobs. Socialization of middle-class children stresses independence and self-direction, important in decision making and carrying out white-collar jobs.

Family Background and Parental Involvement

Children succeed in large part because of their family background and what parents do to support their children in their education. Parenting styles and parental expectations play crucial roles in setting the child's educational agenda. Guidelines about after-school and weekend activities, television watching, homework, and other school-related decisions give the child structure and help the child set goals (Covay and Carbonaro, 2010; Dornbusch and Ritter, 1992; Lareau 2000; 2003). Even the summer experiences children have can move them ahead academically. These experiences such as camps and classes may not be available to all children (Alexander, Entwisle, and Olson 2007).

One of the most important ingredients in a child's success in school is the degree of parental involvement in the educational process of the child. Questions concern what parental activities help or harm a child's school achievement. Involvement of parents is shaped by their social and financial resources, their opportunities to be involved, and their own orientation toward education (Darling-Hammond, 2010).

Some home environment factors that influence student achievement include social class of family, early home environment, parenting style, "type" of mother–child interaction, effect of the mother working, parent involvement in school decisions and activities, family and student aspirations, and number of children in the family. The more children in the family, the less time parents interact with each child. Let us consider several of these factors.

Social Class Background

Parents' involvement in the educational process differs by social class. A great deal of research has focused on the "cultural capital" that children bring to school from their family life (Kalmijn and Kraaykamp, 1996). Some types of cultural capital facilitate school learning, but some do not (Bourdieu, 1977). In fact, social class position can become a form of "cultural capital" leading to different schooling experiences. The cultural capital of middle- and upper-class children—for instance, those with educated mothers (Rosenweig, 1994)—provides useful resources for educational experiences, whereas that of the lower classes provides resources not valued by dominant social institutions such as education (Lareau, 2000).

Higher-class parents are active in managing their children's education at home and at school, whereas lower-class parents do what the schools ask but little more. Both sets of parents hold similar educational values, and parents are treated the same by the school. Higher-class parents, however, have more "cultural capital," and if they use it, their children benefit (Oakes and Wells, 2004). Parents of working-class children are often less comfortable dealing with schools and teachers than those of higher-class students, who feel more comfortable communicating with teachers and are more involved in school activities (Lareau, 2000).

Middle-class families tend to have more educational materials at home—books, newspapers, and magazines. These students read a lot at home and score higher than lower-class students on reading achievement tests. Their parents read, visit the library, and participate in school activities. They also visit more museums and attend concerts, and provide extra educational opportunities during school breaks (Entwisle and Alexander, 1995); all of these are activities that reinforce values of education and supplement learning.

Though children from different social class backgrounds attend colleges, their cultural capital is closely related to the type of college they attend. Students' choice of college is related to their family background, friends, and outlook on their life chances (McDonough, 1997). In addition, the long-term differences indicate that low-SES students' income levels, educational attainment, educational aspirations, and graduate school attendance were lower than those of high-SES students (Walpole, 2003).

Parenting Styles

Parenting styles also affect student achievement. Authoritarian, overprotective, and permissive parenting styles (very rigid or very lax) in the U.S. society are negatively associated with student achievement, and higher percentages of students from these backgrounds drop out of school (Ianneli, 2004; Taris and Bok, 1996). An authoritative style (guidance with reasoning) balances clear, high parental demands with emotional responsiveness and recognition of the child's autonomy. This latter approach is positively related to achievement (Darling, 1999). It involves a high degree of monitoring on the part of the parents, high support and involvement, and a high degree of psychological autonomy for the child (Lam, 1997). In some societies, rigidly structured and cohesive families are associated with high achievement.

Based on her close observations of a variety of families over many years, Annette Lareau has described two class-related approaches to child-rearing: "concerted cultivation" and "accomplishment of natural growth" (2002, 2003). Middle-class parents, either black or white, are likely to employ the concerted cultivation approach with their children. This involved making extensive use of organized leisure activities to cultivate the child's development and talents. The parents' interactions with the child are usually based on reasoning, and negotiating with the child about his or her activities and behavior. Working-class parents, again of any race, are more likely to use the accomplishment of natural growth approach to child-rearing. This entails providing all that the children need to become whomever they were destined to become, but with little parental direction. Children are largely left to their own choices for leisure activities, and parents use directive language far more often than they engage in negotiation as they seek to shape behavior. Of course, resources are involved here, as participating in many organized activities requires fees and parental time and involvement. We saw this difference previously when we reviewed the literature on summer learning and its effects in Chapter 4.

Family Aspirations

Family and student aspirations for the future are another aspect of the influence of class, race, or ethnic background. Parents who set high standards and have high aspirations for their children are more likely to have high-achieving children. James Coleman and colleagues found that

African-American and white seniors had comparable aspirations; the difference was in taking the necessary steps to carry out their goals. African-American students believed that they had less control over their environment and left their fate to luck and chance (Coleman et al., 1966), though many lower-class African-American mothers find multiple strategies to encourage their children's school achievement (Rosier, 1993). From Coleman's research in Equality of Educational Opportunity (the Coleman Report) comes evidence that the effects of the home environment far outweigh the effects of the school program on achievement. Educational and social class background is the most important factor in determining differences among students. The next most important factor is the school composition—the backgrounds of other children in the same school.

Another extensive study, by Christopher Jencks and others (1972), reached the same general conclusion: Family characteristics are the main variable in a student's school environment. In fact, Jencks's findings indicate that family background accounts for more than one-half of the variation in educational attainment. Regardless of the measure used—occupation, income, and parent education—family SES is a powerful predictor of school performance.

Today we have far better measures of the effects of teachers on students than did Coleman, as we have described in Chapter 6; as a result of the No Child Left Behind legislation, students' learning is assessed virtually every year by state tests, and it is now possible to associate individual children's achievement with their teachers. The evidence is strong that teachers differ significantly in their impact on students' learning. Having the best teachers in a school for several years in a row can lead to very high levels of achievement, no matter the family background of the student. Some interpret these data to mean that Coleman was wrong—that teachers are the most important variable affecting student learning. A consequence of this interpretation is that many are now calling for the evaluation of teachers to include a "value added" component: Part of teachers' annual evaluation would be a measure of the gains their students make on learning assessments tests. Teachers who are above average would be rewarded and those below the average would be identified as in need of improvement. Washington, D.C., schools just put in place a new teachers' union contract that calls for this kind of evaluation, with above average teachers receiving considerably higher salary increases than their average or below average colleagues. These policies are controversial and there are many questions about the measurement of student learning and how those data are factored into teacher evaluation (Dillon, 2010). As we noted in Chapter 6, the most recent research does not support the conclusion that teacher merit pay schemes can improve student achievement (Sawchuk, 2010). Moreover, there is no consensus that teachers are more important than student background in predicting achievement.

Single-Parent Homes

Twenty-five percent of households with children under 18 are headed by a single parent and 42 percent of 12–17-year-old black children lived with a sole adult parent (Kreider and Elliott, 2009). Children from one-parent households have lower grades, lower test scores, and higher dropout rates on average than those from two-parent households; these results also are influenced by the race or ethnicity of the family, the educational level of the parent(s), and low level of involvement by the absence of a parent. Warning signs that children are likely to have problems in school appear as early as ages three to five in many welfare children who receive little cognitive stimulation and emotional support. Unless there is significant parental support and supervision, these factors are correlated with children being tardy or absent from school, not doing homework, not having contact with their parents, and engaging in frequent dating and early sex (Cavanagh and Huston, 2006; Mulkey, Crain, and Harrington, 1992; Pallas, 1989).

Children who live with single parents may receive less parental encouragement and monitoring of schoolwork than children in two parent families. However, recent findings show no significant effect on educational achievement when compared to similar socioeconomic level students (Wie and Qi, 2006).

The Role of Mothers

Poor mothers are less likely to be involved in their children's schooling because of discomfort with teachers and lack of social support (Thurston and Navarrett, 1996). Children who are left to make their own educational plans and decisions, where parents have little involvement, are more likely to be dropouts (Rumberger, 1990). Single parents, however, who do become involved in their children's education can compensate for these problems (Pallas, 1989). Recent findings indicate that mothers who work part-time tend to be very involved in their children's education, and their children perform at a higher rate. Full-time work affects after-school supervised time for the child; it is here that differences exist (Duncan and Chase-Lansdale, 2000; Muller, 1991). A comparative study of 11 countries shows that national family policies that help to equalize family resources result in little difference between single- and two-parent families (Pong, Dronkers, and Hampden-Thompson, 2003).

Other evidence shows the impact of involvement of mothers in the schooling process. For instance, mothers with an 8th-grade education discuss similar strategies to other parents for encouraging their children's school achievement, but their use and implementation of these strategies differed by their socioeconomic level. College-educated mothers "managed" their children's high school schedule by selecting college preparatory courses. High-socioeconomic-background children do better in the school system partly because their parents have better management skills (Baker and Stevenson, 1986). In fact, some middle-class parents may try to "control" schools and take action if a child is having problems, whereas lower-class parents are likely to feel helpless and alienated in their interactions with schools (Lareau, 2000). When mothers from higher income families marry, there are slight academic advantages to the children (Wagmiller et al., 2010).

A question of concern to many families is the effect of working mothers on the achievement of children. Study results are mixed, and many variables are involved such as the number of hours worked and intensity of the work, care of children, and the socioeconomic level of the family (Williams, 1993). Summarizing the major findings, we can say that working women provide positive role models and their children often score higher on achievement tests (Radin, 1990). More specifically, African-American, single, working mothers have a positive effect on the achievement of African-American elementary school children. Working mothers from African-American two-parent families have little effect on children's achievement. Findings show little relationship between a mother's occupation and her daughter's occupational aspirations, perhaps because many mothers' occupations were routine jobs. When the mother was in a female-gendered occupation, however, the daughter was more likely to aspire to a female-gendered occupation (Mickelson and Velasco, 1998).

The Number of Siblings

The number of children in the family is another variable that affects school experience, especially the years of schooling that a child completes. Parents with smaller families offer children greater intellectual and educational advantages. We know that boys who come from families with a small number of siblings have more mobility; that is, they more often complete more years of schooling than did their fathers. The more siblings in a family, the more diluted the parents' attention and material resources (Blake, 1991), and the lower the achievement (Hanushek, 1992).

Children from families with a small number of siblings "gain many advantages of a personal nature, including markedly higher verbal ability, motivation to perform in school, a preference for 'intellectual' extracurricular activities, a family setting that is typically conducive to study and academic pursuits, and encouragement to go to college." Those from families with a large number of siblings, "on average, have lower verbal IQs, perform less well in school, engage less in intellectual extracurricular activities and more in sports and community activities, are less likely to be encouraged to go to college, and, as a consequence, are more dependent on being shored up by familial status if they are to graduate from high school" (Blake, 1986, p. 416; also see, Conley and Albright, 2004).

Schools play a role in making it possible to involve parents (Spencer, 1994, p. 5f). Not all schools are welcoming; teachers are overworked and parents add one more layer to the workload (Dornbusch and Ritter, 1992). Some parents expect too much from teachers or are downright abusive (Ostrander and Ostrom, 1991, p. 37). However, there are constructive ways to involve parents both in the education of their own children and in the school program (Epstein and Dauber, 1991, p. 289).

> **Applying Sociology to Education:** *What can families do to enhance the academic achievement of their children?*

Students make up the largest group of school participants and, therefore, have the major role in influencing the achievement level and climate of the school. The importance of understanding their roles is to know what they bring to the school in terms of environmental influences and what they take out of the school in terms of preparation for participation in society.

Summary

The largest group making up the school system are students. Schools exist to socialize students into productive roles in the larger society. This chapter deals with a variety of aspects of the student role.

I. CHARACTERISTICS OF STUDENTS

Minority student enrollments are increasing in primary and secondary education in the United States. Students are caught between school, peer, and the family expectations, affecting student achievement. Student subcultures and friendship patterns can influence a student's self-concept and achievement in school, as can social class and gender. Students learn their roles early in school—in nursery school or kindergarten—and carry out these roles throughout their school careers. Each new group is processed as a cohort or class. Some students face conflicting expectations between teachers and administrators representing adult authority, and peers. Students cope with expectations by adopting different roles in classrooms; they may be apathetic, alienated, or go along with the school program. For those who have problems with the system, failure is possible.

II. SCHOOL FAILURES AND DROPOUTS

Some students fail. These are the students who are most at-risk to drop out of school. Home problems, pregnancy, second-language issues, gang affiliation, immigrant status, poverty, and feeling alienated from the school system can all lead to dropping out. Youths join gangs for protection and belonging; many gangs are involved in illegal activities, and their influence can spill over into schools. Though their numbers may be small, their impact on schools can be great, creating fear, violence, intimidation, drug use, and gang recruitment. In order to control the influence of gangs, schools try to influence the learning environment so that it is more accepting of at-risk students, but at the same time protect schools for the other students. The Safe Schools Movement develops programs to reduce violence and the threat of violence in schools. Some students are retained or suspended from schools; often those students are more at risk for dropping out. Several suggestions for reducing these problems are given. Employment can be helpful or harmful to student achievement, depending on the type of work and the number of hours worked. Dropouts face a difficult future; therefore, trying to keep students in school is an important goal. Conflict theorists argue that school prepares students for their social class status in society.

III. STUDENTS AND THE INFORMAL SYSTEM

Self-concept impacts a student's achievement. Low expectations in a school or classroom result in low achievement. The value climate of the school influences expectations; schools do make a difference in student achievement, and characteristics of effective schools are discussed, such as teachers setting high standards. Teacher expectations of students and peer-group influences compete to affect student achievement. High school athletic groups are one example. Ability grouping can influence student peer grouping, not always with positive results. Coping strategies, discussed by interaction theorists, refer to ways students interpret and respond to school expectations. One model for looking at student strategies considers students' goals and means as related to their achievement.

IV. STUDENTS AND THEIR ENVIRONMENTS

Environments refer to influences outside the school that affect the student's role in the school. For instance, home environment has a major impact. Whether the student receives support from home, role models, and other requirements to do well in school will have an impact on his or her achievement. When parents are involved in their children's schooling, children's achievement is higher. Involvement of parents differs by social class and parenting styles. Family aspirations for the future also influence student achievement. More highly educated mothers, for instance, take a more active role in managing their children's education. Whether a mother's working affects the child's achievement varies. Number of siblings also can affect achievement, with smaller families giving more attention to each child.

Many factors, then, affect the student's achievement in school.

Putting Sociology to Work

1. Discuss how teacher expectations have affected your education or your children's education.
2. What peer groups or cliques were evident in your high school? How did these affect the attitudes toward school and achievement levels of the students involved?
3. How can a child's self-concept affect his or her learning? Give a specific case example.
4. Interview parents from several different backgrounds—class, minority status, and gender. Ask about their involvement in their children's schooling and what their philosophy of being involved is.
5. What are the most important influences in the lives of students you know—your children, siblings, and others you know—their families, peers, or other influences?
6. Investigate the evaluation of teachers in your community. Are value-added provisions being talked about or proposed?

The Informal System and the "Hidden Curriculum"

What Really Happens in School?

I was visiting an urban high school to evaluate a federally funded bilingual education program for recent immigrant students attending the school. As I walked along the main hall of the large, still beautiful old high school, located in a once thriving middle-class neighborhood now struggling with high rates of poverty among its largely immigrant population, my eyes caught a big plaque on the wall listing valedictorians and salutatorians over the school's 85 years. I scanned the names and dates on the list, and was surprised to notice that the last entry had been for students graduating 16 years before I visited the school. None of the last years' top students had their names engraved on the plaque. Perhaps as important, none of the current students at the school had names like the names on the plaque—the surrounding community had so changed in the last generation that entire groups of residents had moved away as new ones came into the neighborhood. While the school was still well maintained, and it still had a kind of "cathedral of learning" aura, the lack of attention to the regular updating of this plaque sent a loud message to the current student body. Every year there is a student with the highest and second highest GPA in the graduating class and these students are, in most schools, publicly celebrated and rewarded for their effort and achievement. They exemplify the values of the school and as such are held up as models for other students. But this school signaled its disdain for its highest achieving students by neglecting to keep the plaque up-to-date. No member of the staff saw it as their responsibility to keep the symbolic rewards of the students' hard work current. The program I was visiting to evaluate was terrific, but students who were not connected to it faced a very different school. Activities that could have reinforced the values of achievement, which could have aligned them with status in the school, were not being attended to. The rituals that celebrate the highest values of the school were neglected and the neglect was evidence of the climate in the school. The staff and the students were going through the motions of school, but there was no real life, no vitality in their actions.

During our time as students, we spend more than 1,000 hours each year in school (Jackson, 1968). Probably our clearest memories of school are the high and low points, not the daily routine. Ask your friends what they remember about early school experiences and you will hear about winning the spelling bee, standing in front of the class to recite a poem, getting detention for nothing, searching for the hamster that got loose in the school and missing math period, falling on the playground and getting stitches, and starring in the school play and forgetting the lines. These highs and lows help make up our attitude toward schools and how we shape our school experience. They are part of the *informal system*. In this chapter we look at several aspects of the informal system of schools, those unplanned experiences that happen apart from or as a result of the formal, planned curriculum of schools.

We tend to define ourselves in relation to those around us in school—our peers and teachers. We are tested, rewarded, accused, cajoled, punished, favored, ridiculed, praised, or mocked. And possibly, we fail. John Holt (1968) discusses this topic and in doing so points out some of the variables that shape children's school experiences:

> They are afraid, above all else, of failing, of disappointing or displeasing the many anxious adults around them, whose limitless hopes and expectations for them hang over their heads like a cloud. They are bored because the things they are told to do in school are so trivial, so dull, and make such limited and narrow demands on the wide spectrum of their intelligence, capabilities, and talents. They are confused because most of the torrent of words that pours over them in school makes little or no sense. It often flatly contradicts other things they have been told, and hardly ever has any relation to what they really know—to the rough model of reality that they carry around in their minds. (pp. xiii–xiv)

Our beliefs about school are affected by the teacher, by the atmosphere of the classroom, by events taking place outside the school, and by our own perceptions and interpretations. Yet most of us have not given much thought to our beliefs about school. Social scientists and educators have not paid much attention to this topic until recently. Judging by the scarcity of studies, students' beliefs about school would seem to be of little concern; after all, kids must go to school, so why question how they feel about it? What good would it do anyway? Schools have functions to perform and they cannot always be to the liking of students, who probably do not know anyway what is important to learn.

The informal system covers topics ranging from coping strategies of individual students and teachers at the microlevel of analysis to the structure and culture of schools at the macrolevel. Because the informal system permeates every aspect of education, we can only give examples of what this system is and how it works.

THE OPEN SYSTEMS APPROACH AND THE INFORMAL SYSTEM

The internal system of the school has both a formal part, consisting of roles and structure, and an informal aspect. Consider the model shown in Figure 8.1, and note the interaction between the internal system and the environment, which is discussed further in Chapter 9. Our topics in this chapter cover several aspects of the informal system: the hidden curriculum and reproduction theories, pedagogical "codes," educational climate and effective schools, peer cultures and peer-group influences, the school as an informal agent of socialization, power dynamics in the school, and student and teacher coping mechanisms.

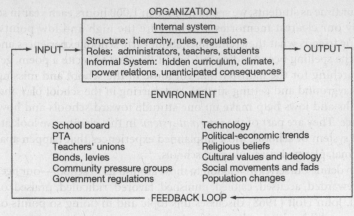

FIGURE 8.1 The open system of schools.

The Hidden Curriculum

Under the organized, structured curriculum lies another, the three Rs: rules, routines, and regulations of the "hidden curriculum," as demonstrated in the syllabus outlined in Table 8.1. Most of us have had similar questions as we entered each new class and evaluated each new teacher. The name *hidden curriculum* was coined by Philip Jackson (1968), and the concept has been used for many years by educators, sociologists, and psychologists in describing the informal system of schools. Snyder (1971) refers to the "implicit demands (as opposed to the explicit obligations of the 'visible curriculum') that are found in every learning institution and which students have to find out and respond to in order to survive within it" (p. 6).

From the systems perspective, the hidden curriculum is one part of the total system, and we can understand it only by understanding the context or school setting. We now review some of the elements that make up the informal system. Important elements of the hidden curriculum have been identified in higher education settings as well (Margolis, 2001).

Reproduction Theory and the Informal System

To conflict theorists, the social control function of the hidden curriculum reproduces the social class of students (Bowles and Gintis, 1976); for instance, working-class students learn to cope

Table 8.1 Syllabus for Course 101

Actual or Visible Curriculum	Hidden Curriculum
Instructor: Name	*Instructor:* What should I call the instructor?
Texts: Names	*Texts:* Do we really have to have them and read them?
Course topics: Listed	*Course topics:* What is the instructor really going to teach? What is he or she really interested in?
Requirements:	*Requirements:*
Readings	What do I really have to do to get by?
Projects	Will it help if I speak up in class?
Exams	Will it help if I go see the instructor?
Bibliography	*Bibliography:* Am I really supposed to use this?

with boredom in schools, which enables them to endure a life of boredom on the job. They learn through the hidden curriculum that they are "written off" in the educational system, like most of the students at the high school described at the beginning of this chapter.

The hidden curriculum, from this perspective, contains a social and economic agenda that is responsible for separating social classes, giving elites more freedom and opportunity, and training nonelites to accept their lot as obedient, punctual workers. Most students learn to accept their political-economic system as best, whatever their position within it.

Anyon (1980) documents the differences in school experiences and expectations by describing several types of elementary schools in contrasting communities, from working-class to professional and executive elite schools. Although many outward similarities exist, the hidden curriculum in each school addresses the "needs" of the social class represented by the majority of students in the school.

1. The working-class school stressed following the steps of a procedure, mechanically, by rote, with little decision making, choice, or explanation why it was done a particular way. Grading is based on following procedures.
2. The middle-class school stressed getting the right answer. There is some figuring, choice, and decision making; for instance, asking the children how they got an answer.
3. The affluent professional school stressed creative activity carried out independently, with students asked to express and apply ideas and concepts, and think about the ideas.
4. The executive elite school stressed developing analytical intellectual powers, reasoning through problems, conceptualizing rules by which elements may fit together in systems, and applying these to solving problems. Included here is successful presentation of self.

Anyon points out that these aspects of the hidden curriculum are preparing the students for their future productive roles in society. The working class is being prepared for future wage labor that is mechanical and routine, the middle class for bureaucratic relations to capital, the professionals for instrumental and expressive roles that involve substantial negotiation, and the elite for analyzing and manipulating the system. In conclusion, the hidden curriculum prepares students for their future roles in society, even as the formal curriculum may be virtually identical.

MacLeod (2009) describes the life of two groups of young men in a poor housing project in Boston. In his ethnographic study, he observes, "hangs out with," and interviews members of the groups; his focus is on their relationship to their schooling, the barriers to success in school and life, and the way they reproduce their life chances by their actions. In another ethnographic study, Lubeck (1984, p. 230) reports on early childhood education, documenting the importance of the use of time and space to transmit adult values. The differences between the Head Start and other child-care settings she studied illustrate the importance of values for reproducing class. In Head Start settings serving low-income children, time and space tended to be more rigidly structured for the children than in other centers where children had some control. The meaning for the students is in the long-term results of reproducing their class status.

But the hidden curriculum is always not so hidden. In report cards sent home, for example, schools make explicit judgments of the behaviors and attitudes of pupils along with the academic evaluations we normally associate with report cards. Typical of report cards in the early grades are assessments of the child's "work habits and behavior," and include individual grades for categories such as: works well independently, is organized, puts forth good effort, talks at appropriate times, completes work on time, completes homework, expresses ideas clearly, participates in class discussions, shows respect for others, works and plays well with others, follows classroom and school rules, and listens attentively. Students are expected to learn how to behave as students—learning no less important than the academic learning for which schools test.

Teachers need cooperative students; with 20 or more children in a room with one adult, cooperative students are a must. This necessity does not vary by the social standing of the parents, but is an organizational requirement of all schools. As Anyon and others have pointed out, however, not all schools are alike in the real academic and behavioral expectations they have of students. Schools serving more affluent students create environments for those children that can be vastly different from the environments of schools serving poor students.

Students at all levels of education develop coping mechanisms or strategies for survival within the structure of contradictions—delays while much of the day is spent waiting to hurry up, or denials when students are told the many things they cannot do. Students try to find the approved responses among the mixed messages; successful students become adept at beating the system (Holt, 1968).

Applying Sociology to Education: *How were your high schools' values supported, or contradicted, by its extracurriculum? How hidden were these aspects of life in the school?*

THE EDUCATIONAL "CLIMATE" AND SCHOOL EFFECTIVENESS

Let us enter the school again as we did when we discussed the formal school system. However, this time we are looking for the informal aspects of the system. We can observe only a handful of situations, but these few will provide examples of the informal system within schools.

"Climate refers to a general social condition that characterizes a group, organization, or community, such as the general opinion in a community" (Brookover, Erickson, and McEvoy, 1996, p. 26), as it affects what happens in schools and classrooms and as it contributes to

Much student learning takes place outside the classroom in interaction with peers.

effective schools. Put less formally, climate and culture are the unofficial happenings and the atmosphere that pervade each educational setting—warm and accepting, strict and intolerant, and large and impersonal. The concept of organizational climate has interested researchers since the 1960s; early research indicated that attention to the school climate could influence student academic achievement. Therefore, understanding conditions or environment needed to maximize student learning became a focus of researchers in both the United States and other countries (Johnson et al., 1999). Some elements of the informal system are fairly easily observed: the school's architecture, open versus closed classrooms, ability grouping, age grading, and team teaching. Many of these are discussed elsewhere in the text. Others are not so easily observed. Here we are particularly interested in the educational "climate" or "culture" as it affects the experience of school participants. Factors both inside and outside the school influence the value climate, our first topic.

The Value Climate

What affects students' motivations, aspirations, and achievement? Why are some schools more productive than others? Do peers have more influence over students than teachers and parents? It is difficult to unravel this interlocking group of questions, for the variables are closely interrelated and no single one can provide an answer. Each major research project concerned with the value climate has included slightly different research questions, variables, methods, and settings, resulting in conclusions that are often diverse and even contradictory. Although this is a field in the process of development and change, the studies cited here show the relationship of value climate to home environment, self-concept, achievement, and teacher expectations, and illustrate some of the major interests and findings in the field.

Schools teach more than reading, writing, and arithmetic. Both the formal and informal organizations include lessons in values and morals. Philip Jackson and colleagues (1993) studied practices in schools that pass on moral values to students. For instance, teaching of morals as a part of the formal curriculum of public schools was almost absent. Though lessons in morals came up within the curriculum content of other subjects, seldom was the purpose of a lesson to instill moral content. Moral education came in other forms, such as the rituals and ceremonies in schools—speakers on drug abuse, pep rallies, graduations, the Pledge of Allegiance, or holiday celebrations such as Martin Luther King Day. Visual displays of signs, pictures, and posters contained moral messages such as "Take pride in what you do" and "Peace on Earth," promoting a kind of "bumper sticker morality." At times teachers would interject moral lessons into the day: commenting on a theft, act of cruelty, or poor sportsmanship are examples. For instance, efforts today to reduce bullying usually contain explicit moral lessons about respect and tolerance (Aarons, 2010).

Some moral messages were not taught, but absorbed as part of the educational environment. For instance, each classroom and school has its dos and don'ts—rules, regulations, customs, and traditions. Teachers work hard to establish their expectations of student behavior early in the school year. Verbal and nonverbal cues let students know when their behavior is unacceptable. It is through these messages that students learn the informal lessons of school.

The School Climate and Effective Schools

Many aspects of schools are familiar: corridors, classrooms behind closed doors, a big clock, and signs directing us to the school office. But there is something unique about each school's environment or atmosphere, something intangible. This forms the school *climate*.

SCHOOL CULTURE.   Each school has a culture of its own, like a miniature society. This is part of school climate. It consists of the values, attitudes, beliefs, norms, and customs of those making up the system. Each school's culture includes its rituals and ceremonies (Waller, [1932] 1965). A key purpose or function of this culture is to bring about a group feeling of loyalty. Pep rallies, cheering at athletic events, assemblies, singing, devotions, fire drills, honors and awards ceremonies, opening exercises, and commencement constitute ceremonies common to most schools, but these are unique in each school. Many ceremonies take place around athletics; athletes are often leading figures among the students and may even be given special privileges and status in the school. Similar ceremonies are found at the college level in fraternities and sororities; they distinguish participants from the more "serious" world of academics and professors, and provide a buffer between the two.

In many places students are assigned to a public school by place of residence. The school culture reflects the immediate community in which the school is located and its students' characteristics. The racial and socioeconomic segregation of residential communities means that schools often differ widely in the kinds of students they serve and the environments that are created (Kahlenberg, 2001; Saporito and Sohoni, 2006). Increasingly, parents and students are being offered a choice of schools to attend. Schools usually differ according to a theme or an emphasis reflected in their curriculum. Some research on new small schools demonstrates that when larger schools are broken up into smaller units in the same building, the schools attract quite different groups of students, as friends want to continue to associate with friends, who often share common levels of achievement and attitudes about the school (Lee and ready, 2007). While these choices may be offered more frequently at the secondary level, they are common in cities at the middle and even elementary school level (Fuller, Elmore, and Orfield, 1996). As students and their families make school choices, they influence the culture of the school they attend.

Norms in both the school setting and the larger culture encourage distance between teachers and students. A new teacher who tries to be too friendly to students may receive sanctions from teachers, ranging from teasing to ostracism. In most school situations, teachers maintain distance as a sign of authority, and perhaps also to discourage close relations, which might lead to indiscretions between students and teachers. In many new small middle and high schools, however, teachers are encouraged to develop and maintain more personal relationships with students, on the theory that such relationships are likely to encourage and motivate students to remain engaged in school and to perform better (Committee on Increasing High School Students' Engagement and Motivation to Learn, 2003). As we have previously noted, "personalism" seems to help create a more positive environment for students and produces better attendance and feelings about school, but whether academic performance is boosted remains uncertain. Such personal relationships with students, however, may also be associated with questions about appropriate boundaries between students and teachers and may be associated with early teacher burnout as was addressed in Chapter 6 (also see Freedman, 1990).

A number of new small schools are dedicated to providing their students with an education that affords the possibility of educational and social mobility. Serving poor urban communities, these schools are relentless in their emphasis on college going and high educational achievement. They are explicit about offering their students a way out of the circumstances in which they find themselves. Restricting their curriculum to college preparatory subjects and often requiring a longer school day and a longer school year. These schools often have long waiting lists (Whitman, 2008).

Teachers represent the culture of the adult society and the dominant group; students have a more limited cultural boundary centered on age-peer group, school, and local community. The world-view held by the two groups is a separating influence. Teachers are considered "different" by students;

mystique surrounds them. Recall your impressions of various teachers, the rumors that circulated about them, and the nicknames they were given. Students make their own culture, which is passed on to each new generation entering the school; it involves language, dress, humor, music, games, and hazing (Corsaro, 2005). A reduction in the gap here is what some of the new schools seek to produce.

SCHOOL LEARNING CLIMATE.   We can all document problems found in schools, but how do we define effective schools? Learning climate refers to "the normative attitudinal and behavioral patterns in a school which impact on the level of academic achievement of the student body as a whole"—teacher expectations, academic norms, students' sense of futility, role definitions, grouping patterns, and instructional practices (Brookover et al., 1996, p. 28). The concept of effective schools addresses both formal structural variables and informal climate variables, recognizing the interrelationship between the two.

Pervading all of these characteristics is the idea that a positive school climate emphasizes and rewards academic achievement, the importance of scholastic success, and the maintenance of order and fair discipline. Complementing these should be positive home–school relations: a supportive home environment for students, involvement of parents with the school, and support of students doing homework (Epstein, 1995). Some researchers refer to the degree which a school surrounds its students with "academic press." Successful schools put academic achievement on top of their priorities and seek to infuse all their activities with opportunities to learn the curriculum that, increasingly, is assessed via tests which can determine whether the individual student will be promoted to the next grade. Phillips (1997) points to the personalism, described earlier, and to academic press as potentially in conflict with each other. She asserts that the findings from her research support the positive outcomes (higher attendance and achievement) and are associated with schools with higher levels of academic press. These relationships within the school and classroom context make up the system of education that must be manipulated at the local, state, and national levels to improve schools and make them more effective (Levine and Ornstein, 1993). Lee and Ready also find that creating a climate with high levels of academic press and personalism is not easy. As already discussed, some of the successful small and charter schools are quite explicit in trying to maintain both characteristics in their schools (Whitman, 2008).We will return to this issue in greater detail in Chapter 13.

> **Applying Sociology to Education:** *Based on what you have learned about effective schools, what needs to be changed to make your community schools more effective?*

Classroom Learning Climate

The class has often been described and viewed as a self-contained system, sealed off from society. Psychologists and sociologists have concentrated on the "one teacher–many students" model, rather than viewing the classroom in a broader context advocated by the open system model. The classroom also has been equated with a crowd situation (Jackson, 1968, p. 10): many people in close proximity and a central figure trying to maintain control, often through the use of discipline. Whatever the model, the dynamics of classroom behavior cannot be understood unless the importance of the environment is recognized. Did Johnny have breakfast this morning; did Linda have an argument with her best friend; are Stephen's parents separating; does the teacher have personal or professional problems?

The learning climate is made up of routines imposed on students in classrooms in order to maintain control and discipline. In fact, the instructional patterns are remarkably similar.

Students often play passive learning roles and are not actively involved in thinking or in hands-on activity. Teachers can take into account different types of intelligences and learning styles, however, in teaching to student needs (Lazear, 1992). Teachers call the shots and determine the activities. If they believe they can make a difference, they usually do (Weber and Omotani, 1994).

Classrooms, because of their structure and organization, assume certain behaviors and attitudes on the part of students—delayed gratification, for example, and support of group cohesion and purpose over individual desires. These attitudes are not taught easily in school but are necessary components of the teaching situation. Children must begin to acquire the behaviors and attitudes necessary for classroom learning before coming to school. The school experience can be meaningless for "unprepared" children. Problems in families, lack of discipline in some homes, and the influence of television have not aided the adjustment to traditional classrooms. Preparation for school can no longer be assumed by teachers. What can be done to prepare students? Suggestions range from solving societal-economic problems in order to increase family stability to promoting charter schools and merit pay schemes for teachers as described in Chapter 13.

Today, many children have school-like experiences in day-care centers and pre-school programs. (Can you remember your first day in school?) Well over a million children are expected to be enrolled in public prekindergarten in the fall of 2010, and approximately 3,693,000, a record, will be enrolled in kindergarten.(NCES, *Projections of Educational Statistics*, 2009-062). According to Hernandez, from 1940 to 1987, the "proportion of preschoolers who did not have a parent at home full-time nearly quadrupled from about 13 to 50 percent, and by 1987 about 40 percent of preschoolers were regularly cared for by someone other than their parents" (1993, p. 11). In 2005, about 57 percent of children ages three to five and those who had not yet been admitted to kindergarten were enrolled in a center-based program. Only 26.3 percent were in parental-care-only situations (NCES, *Digest of Educational Statistics*, 2009, Table 45; NCES 2010-013). Thus, nonfamily settings are familiar to many children, but that does not mean they are well prepared for school when they enter kindergarten or the first grade.

Students understand their classroom experiences in many different ways, most of which are influenced by relations among students. Especially for early adolescents, social and personal development needs suggest that cooperative learning activities are important and effective (Gilmore and Murphy, 1991). These activities, usually based on group learning designs, are especially appropriate for heterogeneous classrooms, composed of children with a wide range of levels of prior learning or in which disabled children are mainstreamed (Cohen, 1994; Cohen and Lotan, 1997).

Classroom climate can produce antischool feelings, especially in competitive, restrictive classrooms, or it can produce students who are motivated toward self-improvement, academic success, and enjoyment of learning. Where student motivation is low, increasing teacher concern and involvement may reduce classroom problems. An unfortunate downward trend in positive, encouraging teacher behavior occurs, however, as students progress through levels of school. By the high school years, "the frequency of teacher praise, encouragement, connection with guidance, and positive interaction with students had dropped by nearly 50 percent from the number of observed occurrences at the early elementary level" (Benham, Giesen, and Oakes, 1980, p. 339).

In extended observations of a number of high school classrooms in two schools, Daniel McFarland closely studied when the teacher's control of the classroom was challenged. His findings support the conclusion that resistance is likely to arise when instructional formats give students access to public speech and when students have powerful social networks of friends in the class. He found that the social opportunities of some kinds of learning tasks, coupled with political opportunities of networks, enable students to consistently undermine and redirect classroom affairs. "The results suggest that resistance behavior is more the result of classroom organizational features of social networks and instruction than student 'alienation' factors and is therefore rectifiable through classroom management" (McFarland, 2001, p. 612; also see McFarland, 2003).

CLASSROOM CODES: INTERACTION IN THE CLASSROOM.   A major process in the school system is interaction. Messages concerning expectations, power relations, and attitudes toward others and the learning process are passed on through verbal and nonverbal cues. The type and extent of classroom interaction is related to teacher styles, which can be grouped into three types:

- *Authoritarian:* Formal power is vested and used by the teacher.
- *Democratic:* Students are involved in the decision making that affects classroom activities.
- *Laissez-faire:* There is general freedom in the classroom.

The daily student–teacher interactions and interpersonal relations determine the atmosphere of the classroom. In the average classroom a routine develops, though a day in a classroom is seldom really routine. Consider the fact that between 300 and 600 interactions take place in one hour of class time. Consider also that for every spoken message there are several unspoken messages given through tone, gesture, and facial expressions. The silent language can tell us more about the atmosphere of the classroom than any spoken words.

Basil Bernstein, an English sociologist who has written extensively on processes in schools, was concerned with the formal and informal processes that take place in classrooms, the rules that govern interaction, power relationships between teachers and students, and how these relate to the social class of students. He argued that these classroom dynamics lead to the social reproduction of class (Bernstein, 1996). Classrooms, he contended, have interaction "codes"—rules, practices, and agencies regulating communication that determine the distribution of power. *Code* refers to a "regulative principle which underlies various message systems, especially curriculum and pedagogy." *Pedagogy* refers to the means of transmission of knowledge, the activities in which students and teachers engage to master the content of the lessons, usually through structured curricula. Among the codes are hierarchy—the interaction between the transmitter (teacher) and acquirer (student); the sequencing and pacing, or progression and rate, at which information is transmitted; and the criteria, or whether the student accepts as legitimate or illegitimate what is being transmitted in the educational process. All of these factors affect the student's learning. Control, then, relates to the power structures and social division of labor. Those who control *what* knowledge is transmitted in the curriculum also have control over *how* knowledge is transmitted—the materials, organization, pacing, and timing of knowledge transmitted and received (Bernstein, 1990). "That schools require an elaborated code for success means that working class children are disadvantaged by the dominant code of schooling, . . . difference becomes deficit in the context of macro-power relations."

In a test of Bernstein's concept of "pedagogical codes," Kalekin-Fishman (1991) studied the way messages are transmitted between teachers and students in kindergartens in Germany and Israel. The "noise" patterns in classrooms reflected the goals and structure of classrooms. For instance, a teacher's authoritarian directives resulted in more controlled noise patterns, with children speaking when permitted. This pattern was more effective in some settings, such as working-class areas, in bringing about desired results. Teachers as "facilitators" produced more "white noise" or undifferentiated sound in the classroom, because students were freer to talk with fewer direct teacher commands. The different pedagogical codes do affect the learning environment and the reproduction of social class. While more work needs to be done on these processes, it is clear from McFarland's and Kalekin-Fishman's research that classrooms cannot be taken for granted—they are complex and highly interactive settings in which student learning and behavior are often problematic, especially as students get older.

Student Friendship and Interaction Patterns in the Classroom

Who students "hang out" with is an important part of the informal experience in schools. These friendship patterns affect each student's peer-group affiliation and in turn aspirations for educational attainment. Student friendship patterns and interactions vary depending on whether the classroom is structured in an open or a traditional manner. Open, flexible, and democratic classrooms stress the affective or emotional growth of students (Grubaugh and Houston, 1990), whereas traditional classrooms are teacher-centered and often stress learning the basics. According to a study of friendship patterns (Hallinan, 1976), affective classrooms include increased interaction and shared activities, more uniform distribution of popularity among students, and an increased opportunity for students to be good at some task. Open classrooms encourage more and longer-lasting friendships. Hallinan considered the context in which students meet friends in traditional and open classes. Students in open classes had fewer best friends (Hallinan, 1979), but more general friendships. In traditional classrooms, children have potential friends who are seated near them because of imposed seating assignments.

Friendship patterns begin in preschool; children develop friendships in the course of their play, and these patterns continue through childhood (Corsaro, 1994; Evaldsson and Corsaro, 1998; also see Boocock and Scott, 2005). Having friends is related to popularity of young children and facilitates socioemotional growth and behavior (Walden, Lemerise, and Smith, 1999). For adolescents, having a best friend is important as a source of mutual intimacy and provides acceptance, understanding, a place for self-disclosure, and mutual advice. Loyalty and commitment become increasingly important aspects of friendships as adolescents become older.

Peer social status and friendships do not necessarily go hand in hand. Some rejected, neglected children have friends, and some popular children do not. The point is that all children need social peers and close friends to feel that they belong; to the extent that teachers can facilitate these relationships, children's achievement may improve (Vandell and Hembree, 1994).

There are clear differences between female and male popularity and friendship patterns: Females are closely knit and egalitarian, sharing intimacies and problems; males are loosely knit, with clear status hierarchies based on shared activities such as sports (Corsaro and Eder, 1990). Popularity of boys and girls in elementary school relates to gender socialization. Boys achieve high status because of athletic ability, coolness, toughness, social skills, and success in cross-gender relations. Girls are popular because of their parents' socioeconomic status, their appearance, social skills, and academic success (Adler, Kless, and Adler, 1992; also see Thorne, 1993).

Eder (1985, Eder et al., 1995) describes a hierarchy of cliques that are evident among girls in junior high school. Popular girls avoid interactions with lower-status girls, but this engenders dislike toward the popular girls, hence a cycle of popularity. Many girls want to appear friendly and interact with people they dislike to avoid a "snobbish" or "stuck-up" label. Adolescent boys are often insensitive and aggressive—patterns they adopt as part of the stress on competitiveness for success (Eder et al., 1995; Thorne, 1993). For the most part, different experiences of girls and boys in elementary school classrooms result from gender-role expectations; there are subtle differences in teaching boys more self-reliance and independence, and girls more conformity and responsibility (Brophy, 1985).

The organizational structure of the school can also affect interactions. For instance, tracking or ability grouping constricts the number and variety of students with whom one comes in to contact, influencing student contacts such as racial interactions in schools where groupings break down along racial lines. Interracial friendships are important as a training ground for future work environments and as an influence on college aspirations and attendance. The closer the peers, the greater the influence, especially in the same track and gender (Hallinan and Williams, 1990). Teachers often manipulate the classroom situation in order to have better control over interaction patterns of individuals or groups of students. Moving seats, rearranging desks, and regrouping students all influence interaction patterns and climate. The educative value of inter-racial and cross-class contacts has increasingly been identified as an important objective of schools and colleges. In fact, it formed one of the most important arguments in the Supreme Court's ruling in favor of affirmative action at the University of Michigan (Moreno et al., 2006).

Special events or organizational changes can alter the classroom routine and also affect classroom participation: when a substitute teacher comes, when a child moves from one reading group to the next level group, when the principal visits the classroom, when testing days are held, and when the school has a special assembly or holiday program.

SEATING ARRANGEMENTS AND PHYSICAL CONDITIONS IN CLASSROOMS AND SCHOOLS.

A persistent question in the field of school facilities planning is the relationship between the building environment and the performance and behavior of users, particularly students (Earthman and Lemasters, 1996). Evidence points to the influence of classroom structure and school conditions in the achievement of students.

Most classrooms are set up so that the teacher is the center of activity; students face the teacher and are placed so that maximum attention can be focused toward the central point. In this way, students' attention can be better controlled by teachers. If a student is inattentive, or a group of students is disruptive, seat reassignment may solve the problem.

The location of a student's seat affects both that student's behavior and the teacher's attitude toward the student. Students focus better on individual tasks when they are in rows; one study showed that time on task went from 75 percent in rows to 56 percent in groups, back to 79 percent when reorganized into rows. For some tasks, sofas and effective room decor, such as popular posters, create an optimal learning environment. The message is that the seating arrangement is most effective when it matches the task; group seating is most appropriate for cooperative learning tasks (Arnold, 1993; Hastings, 1995; Marx, Fuhrer, and Hartig, 1999).

Studies from elementary schools to college classrooms show that students sitting in the front or center of the classroom participate more and achieve better. These students are also regarded more highly by teachers and peers. Teachers tend to be more permissive in their verbal interactions and use fewer formal directives with pupils who are near the front. In college class-rooms, students in these positions tend to be brighter and more interested, to get better grades, and like the instructor better, perhaps because they can see and hear better, are more involved, and can watch and participate more. Yet for some students, seating choice is related to the need for privacy (Pedersen, 1994; Stires, 1980); they may select seats out of the focus area.

Attention has also been paid to the physical conditions that produce the best working condi-tions, including open-space programs, school building age, thermal factors, visual factors, color and interior painting, hearing factors, windowless facilities, underground facilities, site size, and building maintenance (Earthman and Lemasters, 1996). Estimates indicate that 25 percent of learning is dependent on the physical environment (Hayward, 1994). Researchers found that the most important factors affecting student performance and achievement were the thermal environ-ment, lighting, adequate space, and equipment and furnishings, especially in science education. The ideal temperature for optimum learning in the classroom is about 20°C (68° F), with variabil-ity depending on such factors as activity, clothing, and amount of stress. Little research has been done on lighting, though windowless schools are not considered advisable. Even the "electrical atmosphere," or ionization of the climate, has been suggested as a factor that affects learning and performance, with negative ionization thought to be beneficial (Kevan and Howes, 1980). Other factors, such as types of seats, wall color, shape of room, music and noise level in and outside the classroom, all have some effect on learning, though evidence in this field is scanty.

A look at one of the largest school systems in the United States, New York City public schools, illustrates the problems of aging facilities. The system is trying to provide for a large increase in student enrollment while improving conditions of old buildings. Unfortunately, the results are not positive. In the 1990s, already crowded school buildings grew more crowded; class sizes increased; the conditions of buildings deteriorated; and academic achievement remained poor, with average reading and math scores at least one grade level below average. The average class sizes in 1996 were 32 or more in high schools, 26 in grades 4 through 9, and 29 for kindergarten through grade 3 (Rein, 1997). By 2006, progress on reducing these class sizes had been made. According to official statistics, high school classes averaged between 26 and 27 students, while kindergarten through grade 3 averaged 21.1, grades 4 and 5 averaged 24.6, and 6 through 8 averaged 28.5. These figures are somewhat higher than in immediate previous years due to the recession (2009–2010 Updated Class Size Report; NYC Department of Education, p. 3).

SIZE OF SCHOOL AND CLASSROOM.   One assumes that "smaller is better" in the classroom; that smaller classes mean fewer control problems, less work for teachers, and more interaction and communication between teachers and students. There is evidence at the elementary level (K–3) that reduced class size does enhance achievement. In fact, the federal government spent $1.2 billion in 1999–2000 on the administration's "Class Size Reduction Initiative," and several states including California and Tennessee have introduced programs to lower class size at the elementary level (Sullivan, 1998). Tennessee's Project STAR (Student/Teacher Achievement Ratio) began in the 1991–1992 school year, and reduced class sizes in grades 1–3 to a ratio of 1 teacher for 15 students. The Lasting Benefits Study (Nye et al., 1994), an evaluation of the project, revealed that reduced class size increased achievement and improved instruction (Achilles, Harman, and Egelson, 1995), and those effects lasted at least through 5th grade. Minority and inner-city students gained the most (Black, 1999).

Another question to ask is this: "What happens in small classes and small groups within classes?" Schools with smaller class sizes and fewer students per teacher have more positive classroom climates, a factor associated with higher achievement. Classrooms in which children teach each other specific material in small groups also have high achievement levels. However, teachers do not always take advantage of the smaller class size to create climates more conducive to learning (Galton, 1998). Teacher training is important to maximize learning potential in small classes.

As early as 1974, smaller school size was recommended by the Panel on Youth (Coleman et al., 1974, pp. 154–156), chaired by James Coleman, because of the impact on social interactions. Since that time, other studies have pointed to the benefits of small schools, including greater interest in school activities, higher achievement levels, and more social equality (Griffith, 1995; Lee, 1995). Students can play a more active role in school life, and interact more informally with teachers and administrators in smaller schools. In contrast, the climate in large schools leads students to be more passive with adults, to be followers, to depend on others to manage their affairs, and to have fewer leadership opportunities. Percentage of participation decreases with increased size of the school. Certain types of activities, such as hobby clubs, can increase in size to include any number, but other activities—athletic teams, music, and drama—are inelastic; students attending larger schools are at a disadvantage because a smaller percentage of the school population can participate. At the same time, small schools have to limit the number of extracurricular activities they sponsor. At one new small school visited by an acquaintance of one author, the prospective student said after a tour, "I might not make the basketball team, but I would like for the school to have one."

In the last decade or so, several major foundations, such as Gates and Carnegie, have given out hundreds of millions of dollars to help establish new small schools and to break up large ones into smaller schools-within-schools. New York City, for example, has founded over 150 of these schools, most enrolling no more than 500 or 600 students. Some schools are free-standing and have newly renovated space and others are located on floors or wings of large buildings where they have to share the library, science classrooms, the cafeteria, and other necessary facilities. As noted earlier, the logic for this reform has centered on the research that has shown that existing small schools have a more positive social environment and some research also found higher levels of achievement among students attending the smaller schools. The older model of a comprehensive high school providing a variety of curricular tracks to a large group of students has been criticized for trying to do too many things at once, without doing any of them well. College preparation, vocational education, and general education curriculum have little in common. With a more narrow curricular focus, critics say, schools can be more personal and more academic.

According to recent research, however, the formula for creating these more effective small schools, especially schools-within-schools, has eluded the managers of urban school systems. It is still fairly early in the reform period, but several studies are now urging caution in the widespread adoption of this reform (Lee and Ready, 2007). The enthusiasm of several of the foundations supporting the reform is waning (Thompson, 2005). A major problem of comprehensive high schools was that their curricular tracks were stratified, with college-prep tracks having the highest status. Often, the theme-based schools-within-schools re-create this stratification across the small schools, with a science and math emphasis school, for example, being selected by the higher achieving students, and others sorting themselves among the rest of the schools. Lee and Ready stress the need to have options for students that are of equal educational value, each with a primary academic core. Finally, they found no necessary connection between small schools and new and more effective teaching methods

Chicago has also been very active in creating small high schools, and a recent study of them produced similar findings. These schools are likely to have more highly committed and collegial teachers than average who create supportive academic and personal contexts for students. Dropout rates decline and graduation rates are somewhat higher for some groups of students, but not all. The authors of a recent study, however, do not find better instruction, nor has the overall student achievement improved (Kahne et al., 2008). A recent newspaper article makes the point another way in its title, "4100 Students Prove 'Small Is Better' Rule Wrong" (Dillon, 2010). The article describes the achievement gains attained at Brockton High School in Massachusetts, an urban school with a majority of students from poor families and with many immigrants. Small size does not automatically produce improved teaching or learning, though it does seem to produce school environments that students and teachers prefer (Xiaofend and Mayer, 2005).

ARCHITECTURE OF SCHOOLS.   Architectural designs reflect the purpose that a building is to serve; in turn, the design influences activities within a building, and how these will interact with surrounding activities and buildings. School architectural style and sites make schools stand out among buildings, indicating their distinct function. Whether school buildings are squeezed between other buildings or located on sprawling campuses, their fenced-in area or other physical separation distinguishes them from the community at large. Some educators object to this physical isolation from the surrounding community. Separation isolates schools from valuable interactions with the wider community. Yet it serves the function of concentrating students in one place for one specific activity ("An Architectural Revolution," 1990, p. 9).

The school is composed of many dynamic parts that fit together, from buildings that make possible certain interaction patterns to the atmospheres or climates that influence the learning process. All these are part of the complex informal system of education. We now turn to another major aspect of the informal system: power relationships.

> **Applying Sociology to Education:** *Describe what you would call an ideal school in terms of architecture, size, and physical conditions.*

POWER DYNAMICS AND ROLES IN THE INFORMAL SYSTEM

In the classroom, there is a delicate balance between formal expectations and informal processes. Many rules prescribing formal behavior in schools are informally transmitted. Some argue that this informality serves the school and classroom well; the classroom is less bureaucratic than many formal organizations (Dreeben, 1973), providing a smoother transition from home to workplace than might otherwise occur. When students are not hampered by formal rules, they are more likely to unconsciously assimilate rules. Through this informal process, students learn to deal with the formal and informal expectations of organizations. Broadly defined, *power* refers to the ability to get others to do what they would not do on their own. Teacher power in actual practice promotes teacher and adult interests, based on the assumption that the adults know best what is best for the children.

Theoretical Explanations of Power Dynamics in the Classroom

The theoretical approaches that have been discussed in other chapters are also important in discussions of power dynamics. Functional theorists emphasize the consensus resulting from the socialization function of the classroom as it prepares students for societal roles (Parsons, 1959). Another primary function is that of selection and allocation, which begins in elementary classrooms and continues throughout schooling. Not only achievement but also obedience and cooperation are important aspects of schooling. Children learn quickly what is expected of them, and their cooperation makes the school system work. Those most successful in meeting achievement and behavioral expectations do best in the school system. Students are "selected" according to how successfully they have been socialized into the system and how well they cooperate with those in power. Their reward for preparing themselves in school for adult roles is to find an appropriate adult occupation. Not all adult roles are equal in their rewards, and inequality results, but it is inequality that supports the needs of the larger society, this view argues.

Conflict theorists have other interpretations of classroom dynamics. They see a power struggle between school staff, representing the dominant group and values of the adult world, and students, who must be controlled, coerced, and coopted using a variety of strategies. The theme of conflict in the classroom is dominant in Waller's book, *The Sociology of Teaching*, written in 1932 (1965). He describes the difference between adult and student cultures, mechanisms to maintain the social distance between the two, and the "battles" in classrooms over requirements.

Capitalism, which, according to conflict theorists, demands that schools prepare a loyal, docile, and disciplined workforce for society, is seen as a societal force behind the "coercion" in classrooms:

> Schools foster types of personal development compatible with the relationships of dominance and subordinancy in the economic sphere . . . through a close correspondence between the social relationships which govern personal interaction in the workplace and the social relationships of the educational system. (Bowles and Gintis, 1976, pp. 11–12)

From this perspective, conflict is seen as built into the dynamic system. Power influences which (or whose) "cultural capital" is transmitted and reproduced. Teachers control the use of space and time, initiate interactions, and define the rules. Thus, the routines and rituals of schools represent the dominant value system that the schools are passing on to young people. Those who are successfully selected, classified, and evaluated in school are likely to be successful in society as adults (Bernstein, 1990; Bourdieu, 1977). Parents who aspire for higher social standing for their children may work hard to get their children admitted to "excellent" schools in the belief that these schools will better prepare their children for a life the parents could not themselves attain nor for which they could prepare their children, lacking the cultural and social capital necessary for social mobility. A number of such "schools for social mobility" have been created to serve the urban poor and explicitly hold out the promise to provide the social and cultural capital that parents do not themselves possess. (Hammack, 2010; Kalmijn and Kraaykamp, 1996). Parents of minority students "play their hands" in a variety of ways, depending on the interplay between the individual parents and the particular school that is dealing with their child (Fordham, 1996; Lareau and Horvat, 1999; Yonezawa, Wells, and Serna, 2002).

Schools alone do not determine their own internal power structure or their unequal outcomes. Rather, we must view schools within the larger societal context of social class, ideological, and material forces (Apple, 1980). Some of the recent "reforms" of education coming from government sources and justified by conservative ideologies and policies are exacerbating inequalities (Apple, 1996, 2006), yet educational theorists have spent little time analyzing the impact of power systems outside schools.

From the interactionist perspective, each member of the class has a distinctive perception of the world of the classroom. Each individual's plan of action is dependent on how she or he views the world and responds to it (Hatcher, 1998). Many factors affect perceptions. Consider Howard Becker's classic study of Chicago teachers (Becker, 1952). Their perceptions of students were related to cultural differences and class origins among pupils, which in turn related to the degree of trouble teachers had with students.

Students are often labeled early in their school careers and put into rigid, inflexible tracks. For instance, one teacher grouped students into "tigers, cardinals, and clowns"; labels given were internalized by pupils and acted as a self-fulfilling prophecy. Tigers received the most positive interaction, whereas those in lower groups were given less attention. The groups were correlated by researchers with students' social class—for example, tigers being from higher classes than the other groups (Gouldner, 1978). These different expectations based on class influenced the selection and allocation process, with students from lower-class backgrounds at a disadvantage. Another indication of the effect of labeling on student behavior is seen in a study of individual students' perceptions of their teachers' disapproval; perceptions of teacher disapproval are related to more delinquency (Adams and Evans, 1996; also see Rist, 2007).

Student perceptions of their own chances for success influenced their decisions about what role to play in school. For example, some studies show that the "climate" in all-women's classes is more conducive to women's participation if separation does not lead to different opportunities and values (Stromquist, 1995, p. 423). Issues surrounding women's education continue to generate controversy and research, as discussed in Chapter 4. In another example, Hatcher (1998) discusses how students from different class positions perceive education opportunities through very different lenses, and make their choices, such as to apply or not to demanding courses or programs, rationally according to their judgment of the likelihood of a positive payoff in relation to the effort required.

Teacher Strategies and the Informal System

" 'Classroom management' refers to the entire range of teacher-directed planning, managing, and monitoring of student learning activities and behavior. The school climate incorporates not only collective classroom management by the staff, but also schoolwide rules and norms for defining and enforcing proper student behavior" (Brookover et al., 1996, p. 184). Different teacher strategies are necessary in each new circumstance. The philosophy of the teacher and school, the organization of school and classroom, available resources, number of students, and their interest level—all affect the goals and strategies of teachers.

Martyn Hammersley and Peter Woods outline several alternative techniques or strategies that may be used by teachers to deal with classes:

1. Formal organization implies that the teacher is the center of activity; typical strategies are to have students recite material, or do question-and-answer and written work. Informal organization implies groups of students working together and more interaction between class members.
2. The teacher may supervise student action and intervene when deviation occurs. Alternatively, the teacher may act more as participant.
3. The teacher may make use of orders and demands backed by coercion and the authority of the position. Alternatively, the teacher may make personal appeals to the rights and obligations of any person, backed by legitimate resources.
4. Class or school tests may be used for comparison of student performance. Alternatively, there may be no formal assessment. Many commonly used informal strategies of grouping are based on age, ability, or "troublemakers" versus random grouping based on student choice, friendship groups, or no formal grouping (Hammersley and Woods, 1977, p. 37).

Techniques employed by teachers influence the climate of the classroom and type of learning taking place, though on many dimensions there is no clear evidence which technique is more effective (See Box 8.1).

Students often challenge teacher authority, and teachers often end up going further in adjusting to students than students to teachers. Students in lower tracks, according to Mary Haywood Metz, most often use physical and verbal disorder strategies in challenging, whereas those in higher tracks test the teacher's mastery of the subject. Students challenge teachers on the ground where they feel most competent (Metz, 1978, pp. 91–92). Students and teachers may enter into bargains in which students agree not to be too disruptive and teachers agree not to be too demanding (Sedlak et al., 1986). New teachers, even when armed with the best training and

BOX 8.1

Differentiated Instruction

How the curriculum gets taught, not what gets taught, characterizes differentiated instruction. Even in fairly homogeneous classrooms, students vary not only in what they know but in how they learn. These differences are expanded in heterogeneous classrooms. A recently evolving approach to teaching in these classrooms tries to accommodate student differences through varying the means and types of instruction teachers deliver. The variations include the pace at which topics are introduced, the depth of knowledge and understanding of the material introduced, and the degree to which students' interests are taken into account. Initially, teachers need to assess each student's strengths and weaknesses at the beginning of the year. With this information, teachers can begin to differentiate the content—the knowledge and skills—students need to learn. The processes by which this content is introduced can also be varied. The product students produce, the assessments they master, and the projects they develop can be varied depending on the initial characteristics they provide. Differentiation is about understanding the needs and abilities of a class and providing alternatives within multiple, but limited constraints. This puts additional demands on teachers and professional development experts, but offers the potential to improve the instruction teachers are able to provide.

Source: Carol Ann Tomlinson, "Mapping a Route toward Differentiated Instruction," *Educational Leadership* Vol. 57, No. 1, September 1999, pp.12–16.

teaching techniques, must experience the realities of the classroom to develop their own strategies to meet goals for their classes.

Consider the task of getting and keeping student attention. Teachers have plans in their minds for the activities and lessons of the day, but they must convince students of the importance of the lessons and motivate them to comply—and even to participate. Time on and off task is related to classroom management; "teachers in typical classrooms lose approximately 50 percent of their teaching time because students are off task or otherwise disrupting learning" (Charles, 1999, p. 107). Studies of effective schools find that teachers can save wasted time by having well-planned and paced lessons, making quick transitions between topics, using students to do some simple tasks and paperwork, establishing daily routines, and using other time-saving techniques (Brookover et al., 1996, pp. 185–198).

The teacher must defend the lesson from disintegration and internal defection. The student is being asked to pay attention to the "official environment"—that is, what is going on in the class directed by the teacher—rather than to a friend, comic book, or other distraction. In the typical situation, teachers are at the front of the classroom with students facing them. They watch for inattention and may use strategies such as questioning to get attention. Students may attempt to disguise illicit activities. Today, many schools ban cell phones because students may use them to surreptitiously send text messages to their friends about assignments or test questions. Teachers can exert power in the form of control over valued things—recess, physical education, and games.

Most people perceive deviant students as detrimental to the classroom situation. Some teachers, however, find that using disruptive students as a "resource" may turn them into an asset. Deviants are products of the social organization of the classroom; by considering three factors in their place in the total social context, teachers may discover how to manipulate the classroom structure to their benefit: (1) how ranks of deviants are established; (2) how deviant status is maintained; and (3) how deviants contribute to maintaining order or gain from their disruptions (Rist, 2007; Stevenson, 1991).

Students today have a need to be entertained; they expect instant gratification. Attention spans are shorter. They need more attention, are harder to please, have higher expectations of teachers, are less willing to put forth effort to learn, and are motivated by external rather than internal rewards.

Applying Sociology to Education: *What coping strategies do(es) your professor(s) use in class?*

DECISION MAKING IN THE CLASSROOM.   We have discussed teachers' roles in the educational system in Chapter 6 and the effect of teacher decisions and actions on students' achievement in Chapter 4. Implicit in these discussions is the teacher's role as the primary decision maker in the classroom. What really happens in the classroom and what influences the decision-making process is complex. Much of the research on this topic comes from "interaction" theorists and the "new sociology of education," and focuses on the dynamics of classroom interaction and how individuals perceive the situation. It is not easy to observe these dynamics, but, despite methodological difficulties, the "how and why" of decision making is now a topic of concern.

Most of a teacher's decision-making behavior is almost instinctive, based on experience. But teachers do have decision-making strategies, conscious or unconscious. They may be "situationally specific decisions, or negotiative strategies," used to deal with special circumstances that arise. Teachers' strategies, especially those of the new teacher, are often based on a textbook ideal world. Students deviate from ideals, however, forcing teachers to deviate from their ideal models to more realistic strategies for the situation.

Using a role conflict model, which focuses on incongruities in the teacher's role, we can see how decision making is influenced not only by the views and expectations of students, parents, other teachers, and administration but also by teachers' own definitions of the task to be performed. Teachers must consider what they can and cannot, will and will not do. They may exploit rules, use their expertise, and bargain to gain power. Decision making is a complex process influenced by many interacting elements. In many ways, teaching is a performance art, much like a stand-up comic; while there is a text (a script or a set of jokes on which the performer has worked long hours), the delivery of the material in front of the audience can be a daunting experience. Of course, the audience changes nightly for the stand-up performer while the teacher has the opportunity to get to know the students in class well. On the other hand, the comic does not get evaluated on how well the audience remembers the jokes. Teacher dissatisfaction and burnout are increased when teachers are given little control in determining the classroom environment (Lee, Dedrick, and Smith, 1991) or get less support from the principal and other administrators (Liu and Mayer, 2005).

The importance of recognizing the informal system of schools—the hidden curriculum, the educational climate, power dynamics, and other topics—is in understanding aspects of the educational system that lie beneath the surface. This chapter has provided a few examples of this large part of education. Also crucial to dynamics of schools is the environment, our next topic.

Summary

To understand the processes taking place within the school and classroom, one must be aware of the informal system, an important area of social research. In this brief discussion, we have attempted to acknowledge its importance for a complete understanding of the system and its integral part in a systems approach.

I. THE OPEN SYSTEMS APPROACH AND THE INFORMAL SYSTEM

The hidden curriculum of the informal system includes the curriculum students learn that is not part of the formal curriculum—implicit demands, values, and latent functions. Some conflict theorists argue that schools reproduce students' social class, largely through the hidden curriculum, though many of these demands and values are explicit on school report cards. Students experience schools differently depending on their class backgrounds.

II. THE EDUCATIONAL "CLIMATE" AND SCHOOL EFFECTIVENESS

The climate or atmosphere of schools and classrooms includes the school's architecture, type of classroom, ability and age grouping, and other aspects of the school. Value climate influences motivations, aspirations, and achievement of students. Factors such as home environment, self-concept, and school values influence the effectiveness of schools. The school culture is distinctive in each school. Interaction patterns in classrooms are also part of the climate. Factors, such as gender, that affect interaction are discussed.

III. POWER DYNAMICS AND ROLES IN THE INFORMAL SYSTEM

Power dynamics are present in any hierarchical system. In schools, a look at the teacher–student relationship acquaints us with some of the issues. Both students and teachers develop coping strategies to deal with the dynamics. Power in schools can be actively used or can be seen as latent potential to keep students in line. Functional theorists argue that students learn societal roles by cooperation with adult-enforced rules, whereas conflict theorists feel that there is constant potential for conflict because of power dynamics.

Teachers attempt to maintain a delicate balance between overt use of power and gaining student cooperation. Teachers must make decisions about strategies to use in the classroom; numerous factors affecting these decisions are discussed. The strategies used range from power to subtle cues to changing the physical or social arrangement of the class.

In order to understand how educational systems work, an understanding of the informal system is essential.

Putting Sociology to Work

1. Interview a sample of students concerning their outstanding memories of school experiences.
2. Describe the student peer subculture in your high school and college. Were there social isolates, and can you recall their characteristics? Compare your high school with a high school today through observation or interviews.

3. What were some roles students played in your high school? Talk to some students about the roles they play today.
4. What are some strategies used by teachers you observe in high schools to get students to cooperate?

CHAPTER

9

The Educational System and the Environment

A Symbiotic Relationship

It did not take long for John Heegard to put the clues together. Valencia McMurray was one of the most promising students in his Advanced Placement U.S. History class at North High School in Minneapolis. But the junior was missing three, four, five days in a row, often just showing up to pass an exam—no small feat, considering the legendary toughness of Heegard's tests.

Heegard tried but was unable to reach Valencia or her family to check if she was okay. When she did show, he noted her usual wit and intellect were often muted by depression. "It was evident something was up," Heergard says. "When a kid's that bright, it doesn't take long to figure out they're having some kind of trouble."

This teacher had developed trust with his students and eventually Valencia shared the problem—she was homeless, and had been bouncing from living space to living space for over a year. At that point the two started to connect her to resources she needed to be successful.

According to government definitions, homeless children and youth lack a fixed, regular, and adequate nighttime residence. They sleep in shelters, transitional housing, cars, campgrounds, motels, and share shelters with others (NAEHCY, 2009).

"North Minneapolis is a community stressed by unemployment and poverty, where youth are forced to grow up fast and wary . . ." This was the situation for Valencia and for thousands of children and youth like her. In the 2008–2009 school year, 954,914 homeless children were enrolled in public schools, a 20 percent increase from 2007 to 2008, and a 41 percent increase from 2006 to 2007, and these figures are an underestimation because of the difficulty accounting for all the homeless (NAEHCY, 2009; Teaching Tolerance, 2010).

The question is this: How can education systems deal with children who have many problems outside of school and expect them to be successful in school? The children's environments make learning a severe challenge for schools. This chapter focuses on the school environment including what the participants in school bring with them and other environmental influences on schools.

230

Our environment surrounds us. It engulfs us. No one and nothing exists in a vacuum, for we cannot exist outside our environment. It includes all of those individuals and organizations that shape us—family, religion, politics and the legal system, economics, health care, communities, trends in society, and many other influences that affect our lives—and those of our schools. Each person's environment differs because of our different experiences, just as the environment differs for each educational system. What makes our environment unique depends on our background experiences, the family into which we were born, and the individuals and institutions with which we come into contact. Similarly, each school environment is unique.

As college students, our environment sets out certain role expectations: pay tuition, take classes, study, receive grades, and eventually graduate. Events related to one part of the environment and set of behaviors or roles will affect the other roles we play because they are all interrelated. Let us suppose that we have an important exam coming up. We may experience role conflict because of time pressure. Perhaps our family or friends will be neglected; perhaps we will decide not to spend much time studying for the exam in favor of attending a party with friends. Every element of our environment is affected by demands from other elements.

In this chapter we consider the meaning of environments and examples of institutional environments of schools. As part of the larger societal system, school systems are surrounded by pressures from ideological groups, political systems, economic conditions, and trends in society. Each sphere of society is interrelated; schools cannot ignore the political, economic, and cultural-ideological spheres that make up their environments (Apple and Weis, 1986).

THE ENVIRONMENT AND THE EDUCATIONAL SYSTEM

Think of children as sponges, waiting to absorb the knowledge presented to them, and many parts of the environment—government, community pressure groups, and religious and other special-interest groups—demand input into what children are taught and how they are taught. Therefore, educational systems have many pressures from these environments. Schools are particularly vulnerable to environmental influences where issues relate to their function of socializing the young.

Population changes, technological advances, fads, and social movements are examples of environmental factors that influence the educational system. In the 1960s, there was much experimentation with avant-garde educational programs in the United States, producing ideas that influenced the public schools. In the 1970s, there was great concern with establishing more discipline in schools; "back-to-basics" became the theme. The 1980s and 1990s brought accountability and proficiency testing of teachers and students. In the beginning of the twenty-first century, many of the same issues persist—accountability, testing, and efforts to achieve opportunity for all students to succeed are major influences on schools.

In our discussion of the internal workings of the system, we considered the connection between the many individual positions people hold in educational systems and the structural units of the school organization. The point is that no organization, unit, or individual can exist without being dependent on and influenced by the environment. Figure 9.1 emphasizes the relationship between the organization and its environment.

All individuals and organizations depend on their environments in order to survive and to provide organizational needs; in turn, they affect the environment in which they live by leaving personal or institutional imprints on individuals and institutions.

The interdependence of organization and environment can be seen clearly in many systems. Consider the complexity of a system such as New York City and the problems that occurs when

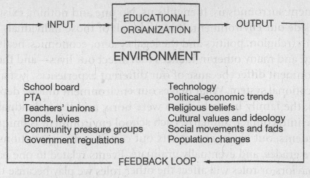

FIGURE 9.1 Environment of school systems.

one part of that system malfunctions (Darling-Hammond, 2010). If the power goes out, or the sanitation engineers, subway workers, telephone operators, or schoolteachers go on strike, the city's interdependent structure breaks down and all parts of the system are strained to the breaking point. New York City's school system is complex and changing. Until recently, the schools were controlled by an appointed board and 32 local elected community boards, with their own superintendents and staff. Those were all eliminated and the mayor was given total control of the system by the New York Legislature in 2003. The system employed 92,287 teachers in 2007, with an additional 17,368 instructional aides, and several thousand administrators and support staff (librarians, counselors, and technicians); it served about 1.1 million students (New York City Board of Education, 2007). The school budget is paid by 50 percent local revenues, 43 percent state revenues, and 7.3 percent federal moneys (NCES, 2005). Interdependence of parts of this tremendous school system forces it into a delicate balancing act between competing community interests.

Types of Environments

Some parts of our environment are more important to our survival than others; these are our immediate environments. Less important to survival are secondary environments. Our families are key to our emotional, physical, and financial well-being, whereas a Friday night party is not a matter of survival for most of us. For school organizations, the relevant parts of the environment fall into a number of categories: government, including local, state, and national legislatures and agencies; the judicial system; financial support units; the "physical" community surrounding each school, including the demographic composition (age, sex, religion, race, and social class); interest groups in the community; the technological environment, including teaching innovations and new scientific research; consumers of educational system products, such as those who hire graduates or incorporate new knowledge from educational systems; and religious institutions.

The distinction between immediate or primary environments and less crucial secondary environments is not always clear. Importance can change over time, but the fact remains that there are differing degrees of importance in environmental factors. Recognizing this allows us to single out those environmental factors that most affect decision making in a school system at any one time. The school is affected less as environmental units become farther removed, just as ripples in a pond become weaker as they move out from the center.

Organizations are not closed systems but depend on the environment for resources, materials, people power, and, ultimately, existence. The importance, or salience, of environmental

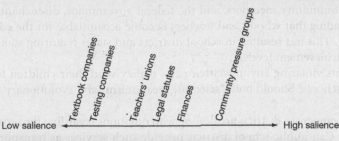

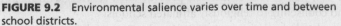

FIGURE 9.2 Environmental salience varies over time and between school districts.

units for educational systems can be illustrated as a continuum (see Figure 9.2). The salience of environmental units will vary depending on the individual school situation being considered.

Another point needs to be explained. We generally consider the individuals who fill positions in the schools—the administrators, teachers, students, and support staff—to be parts of the internal organization. These groups fill the positions in the internal structure of the school and carry out the processes of the school. They also provide the bases for the informal relationships in the school. However, there is no question that each of the position-holders in the school brings a unique background and personality into the school, which could be considered an "environmental influence." (Some sociologists consider students as clients of the school system, and, as such, they became a part of its environment.) Further, some school personnel, such as principals, school counselors, and social workers, carry out roles to provide a bridge between the school and the home or community environment. These "boundary-spanning" roles facilitate the movement of ideas and products in and out of the school system and are essential in maintaining relations and contact with the environment.

To summarize, the importance of environmental units must be viewed as varying in degree; some are crucial to the well-being, even survival, of the organization at a particular time. Effects of problems in one sector of the system's environment or in relations with the environment will have ramifications for other sectors, depending on that part's salience to the survival of the system.

In this chapter we focus on the institutional environment of the school: family, religion, the economic system, political and legal systems, and community influences. There are many elements in any school's environment, from the individuals who make it up to the ancillary organizations that surround it, put pressures on it, and provide services to it.

Applying Sociology to Education: *List some influences from various types of environments on your local schools. Categorize these on a continuum into primary and secondary environments.*

SCHOOL SYSTEMS' ENVIRONMENTS: INTERDEPENDENCE BETWEEN INSTITUTIONS

School officials deal daily with issues from their external environments. Consider the interactions between families, religion, the judicial system, the political and economic systems, and special-interest groups:

- Parents, community members, and the federal government, disenchanted with schools, are demanding that schools and teachers become accountable for the education they are providing. This has resulted in school districts and states requiring standardized tests to measure achievement levels.
- Are parents violating any unwritten rules if they send their children to nonaccredited religious schools? Should both "scientific creationism" and evolutionary theory be taught in schools?
- Courts in numerous districts are dealing with questions regarding the separation of church and state: Can public school districts provide such services as transportation, remedial classes, and counseling to religiously affiliated schools?
- Financing schools leads to controversies when some districts have more property tax money for education than others.
- Hot debate rages in communities between special-interest groups representing differing points of view on minority studies, selection of textbooks, role of the schools in sex education, and numerous other issues.

In this section, we look into some examples of environmental pressures and resulting issues affecting schools: home and family influences, the institution of religion (church and state), the economics of education (financing schools), politics and legal institutions, and communities and their schools.

Home and Family Influences on Schools

When children walk into the school building they bring with them ambition; motivation; pressures; expectations; physical and mental strengths or weaknesses; and sometimes abuse, insecurities, stress, and other problems. Therefore, knowledge of the social and family context that students bring into school is essential for teachers in dealing with students and a key part of the school, classroom, and students' environment. In Chapter 7 we discussed the influence of the family on achievement of students. Here we reemphasize the link between the family institution and education.

Many families balance work and parenting. They must find reliable child care for preschool children. In 2005, 11.6 million (63 percent) of the 18.5 million children under five years were in some type of regular child care arrangement; 40.2 percent were with relatives and 26.5 percent outside of the home in organized care facilities (Johnson, 2005). Because of the variety of types and quality of early childhood care settings, the U.S. Congress passed the National Child Protection Act of 1993 to help safeguard young children in child care from abuse when they are outside the home.

The "curriculum of the home" refers to the development of attitudes and habits that support learning and the value placed on personal development. This informal curriculum is influenced by family size, reading materials and reading at home, vocabulary development, time spent watching TV, parental involvement in school decisions, and family resources. A much-sited research study found that "in four years . . . an average child in a professional family would have accumulated experience with almost 45 million words, an average child in a working-class family would have accumulated 26 million words, and an average child in a welfare family would have accumulated 13 million words" (Hart and Risley, 2003). In addition, the authors found that affluent parents speak to their children in more encouraging language, while poor parents often use punitive, authoritarian language. As illustrated by this study and others, the preparation children receive in the "home curriculum" has a major impact on their success in school.

About 1.5 million children in 2007 actually went to school at home in the United States, and the numbers of homeschooled children are growing rapidly, up 74 percent since 1999 and 36 percent since 2003 (Lloyd, 2009). In total, almost 3 percent of school-aged children in the United States are homeschooled. This educational movement is the largest change to types of education in recent years, surpassing voucher and charter school programs in numbers and creating new educational forms. Reasons cited by parents for homeschooling include "concern about the school environment—safety, drugs, and peer pressure, 88 percent; parents wanting to teach religious and moral instruction, 83 percent; dissatisfaction with instruction at public schools, 73 percent; and wanting a nontraditional approach to instruction, 65 percent (Lloyd, 2009).

Public schools in a growing number of states are allowing homeschooled children to participate in individual courses, sports, music, and other extracurricular activities and support services. Both states and private organizations are developing curricular materials for homeschooled children, and courses on the Internet are mushrooming.

Two types of homeschooling dominate; one stems from the liberal alternative school movement, the other from the Christian day school movement; both originated in the 1960s and 1970s. Although very different in their philosophies, both are concerned with control over children's education and the importance of family in society today. This social movement with supporting curricular materials has developed organizational strategies for pursuing their goals, and most parents of homeschoolers receive support from local and national groups. On state and national tests most homeschooled children are quite competitive, and they go on to succeed in colleges (Stevens, 2003).

For students who attend public or private schools, the key finding is that the higher the parents' involvement in their children's schooling, the higher the overall academic performance of the children. Parents affect children's educational achievement and aspirations in several major ways. For example, the socioeconomic background of the family makes a difference: Some parents are isolated from what is required for school success, and their patterns of interacting with children do not fit well with the school culture (McDermott, 2003/2004; Souto-Manning and Swick, 2006). Boys and girls are strongly influenced by the "defining" behavior of parents through which expectations for appropriate behavior are established (Cohen, 1987). Also important, especially for girls, is "modeling," or emulation, of parents. Family influence is strong across social class, but mothers with higher educational status are more involved in school activities, have more contact with teachers, and choose college-preparatory courses for their children. Again, the major finding of studies is that children of parents who are involved in schools have higher school performance levels (Baker and Stevenson, 1986; Cotton and Wikelund, 2001; Stevenson and Baker, 1987). Children from homes in poor neighborhoods however, experience negative effects on their educational attainment (Cooper, Lloyd-Reason, and Well, 2003; Epstein, 1987a, 1987b, 1988b).

Parental involvement in schooling is also correlated with children staying in school longer and doing better in school. Research findings indicate that what parents do with their children during the 70 percent of waking hours children are not in school can make a major difference in children's achievement: higher grades, test scores and graduation rates; better attendance at school; higher motivation; and lower suspension, drug and alcohol use, and violent behavior (Michigan Department of Education, 2007). Home environments that encourage learning are more important than income or education level of parents. Reading experiences at home, such as parents reading aloud to children, increases the chance of reading success; parents who talk to their children about school encourage school success; parental involvement in monitoring and organizing the child's time, helping with homework, and discussing school problems helps children; and in addition to higher achievement, parental involvement results in improved behavior (Michigan Department of Education, 2007; National Education Association, 2007). Thus, developing school and family partnerships enhances learning and helps children succeed in school and later life. Children's summer activities also influence their achievement in school.

Researchers at The Center on Schools, Family, and Community Partnerships at Johns Hopkins University suggest the types of parental involvement, discussed in Box 9.1. Parents' investment in their children and support for higher education are related to parents' views of status attainment. Some parents perceive children as an investment, following the "human capital theory." Others view payment for education as "resource-dilution," often related to how many children are in the family compared with available resources. Parents tend to be more willing to pay for higher education for their children if their parents paid for their education and they believe this to be a responsibility; they are also more willing to pay if the number of children in the family does not drain their resources (Steelman and Powell, 1991).

BOX 9.1

Epstein's Framework of Six Types of Involvement

1. **PARENTING:** Help all families establish home environments to support children as students.
   - Parent education and other courses or training for parents (e.g., GED, college credit, and family literacy).
   - Family support programs to assist families with health, nutrition, and other services.
   - Home visits at transition points to pre-school, elementary, middle, and high school.
2. **COMMUNICATING:** Design effective forms of school-to-home and home-to-school communications about school programs and children's progress.
   - Conferences with every parent at least once a year.
   - Language translators to assist families as needed.
   - Regular schedule of useful notices, memos, phone calls, newsletters, and other communications.
3. **VOLUNTEERING:** Recruit and organize parent help and support.
   - School and classroom volunteer program to help teachers, administrators, students, and other parents.
   - Parent room or family center for volunteer work, meetings, and resources for families.
   - Annual postcard survey to identify all available talents, times, and locations of volunteers.
4. **LEARNING AT HOME:** Provide information and ideas to families about how to help students at home with homework and other curriculum-related activities, decisions, and planning.
   - Information for families on skills required for students in all subjects at each grade.
   - Information on homework policies and how to monitor and discuss schoolwork at home.
   - Family participation in setting student goals each year and in planning for college or work.
5. **DECISION MAKING:** Include parents in school decisions, developing parent leaders and representatives.
   - Active PTA/PTO or other parent organizations, advisory councils, or committees for parent leadership and participation.
   - Independent advocacy groups to lobby and work for school reform and improvements.
   - Networks to link all families with parent representatives.
6. **COLLABORATING WITH COMMUNITY:** Identify and integrate resources and services from the community to strengthen school programs, family practices, and student learning and development.
   - Information for students and families on community health, cultural, recreational, social support, and other programs/services.
   - Information on community activities that link to learning skills and talents, including summer programs for students.

National Standards for Parent/Family Involvement

Building upon the six types of parent involvement identified by Joyce L. Epstein, Ph.D., of the Center on School, Family, and Community Partnerships at Johns Hopkins University, National PTA created program standards of excellence.

National Standards for Parent/Family Involvement Programs

Standard 1:	Communicating—Communication between home and school is regular, two-way, and meaningful.
Standard II:	Parenting—Parenting skills are promoted and supported.
Standard III:	Student Learning—Parents play an integral role in assisting student learning.
Standard IV:	Volunteering—Parents are welcome in the school, and their support and assistance are sought.
Standard V:	School Decision Making and Advocacy—Parents are full partners in the decisions that affect children and families.
Standard VI:	Collaborating with Community—Community resources are used to strengthen schools, families, and student learning.

Source: Joyce L. Epstein et al. "Epstein's Framework of Six types of Involvement." Baltimore, MD: Partnership Center for the Social Organisation of Schools, 2000.

Applying Sociology to Education: *What aspects of a positive or negative home environment affect a child's achievement in school?*

The Institution of Religion: Church and State

In many societies, religion and state are synonymous, and the educational system reflects the beliefs and values of both. Religious groups may have their own schools, and they may tolerate the dominant religious themes. For instance, holidays of non-Christian students living in England, a multicultural but predominantly Christian society, are often discussed to promote intercultural understanding.

HISTORY OF RELIGION AND EDUCATION IN THE UNITED STATES   In the United States, a unique experiment was attempted. Since the time of the U.S. nation's founding, the principle of separation of church and state has been espoused. Expressed in the First Amendment, it states: "Congress shall make no law respecting an establishment of religion, or prohibiting the free exercise thereof." The framers of the U.S. Constitution built in guarantees to avoid the religious conflicts that had arisen in many other countries. The government's responsibility was to protect the rights and freedoms of all and favor none. Yet, keeping church and state distinct has not always been easy. The roots of the problem lie in the pluralistic society, where freedom of worship is an integral part of the value system and political ideology (see Box 9.2).

We have seen in our open systems model the interdependence of institutions, meaning that religion is interdependent with other institutions. When individuals segment religion from the rest of daily life, in institutions of family, economics, politics, health, and education, conflict is not likely to arise. But where religion is integrated into all aspects of a person's life, including education, there is pressure on the schools from the religious environment.

RELIGIOUS COURT CASES.   In the United States, religious pressures on schools have led to court cases, initiated by both religious groups and those favoring secular education. Three types

BOX 9.2

Church and State in American Education

Should prayer be allowed in schools? Under what circumstances? Should students be allowed to lead prayers at events such as graduation? Should religious schools receive federal funds for special education? Should state schools pay for student religious publications?

In 1971 the U.S. Supreme Court established guidelines for what constitutes a violation of separation of church and state (Cook, 1995, p. 17). The Lemon test (from a court case *Lemon v. Kurtzman*, 1971) "established a prohibitive test of constitutionality. The challenged government action must (1) have a secular purpose; (2) have a principal or primary effect that neither advances nor inhibits religion; and (3) not foster an excessive government entanglement with religion" (Cord, 1992). Despite the guidelines, in recent years the Supreme Court has given little clear guidance to school districts as an increasing number of cases reach the courts. They have sought to avoid the appearance of persecuting religious groups and also to avoid advancing or endorsing religion. In the 1992 case, *Lee v. Weisman*, the court ruled that giving a nonsectarian invocation of God at a public school graduation ceremony violated the constitution.

Consider the case of a community, Kiryas Joel, of Hasidic Jews outside New York City. Yiddish is the main language, and dress and other cultural patterns are distinctive to the group. Children go to Jewish parochial schools funded by the Hasidic community.

Children with disabilities from the community went to school in an adjacent school district to receive special services, but parents withdrew them because of the "panic, fear, and trauma which (the children) suffered in leaving their own community . . . " (Drinan, 1994, p. 9). A new school district was set up in Kiryas Joel for the 220 children, attended only by children with special needs, taught in English, and with no religious symbols. A legal battle concerning students with special needs raised the question: Are the schools intended to help religion? The school was challenged and New York's highest court found the district violated the First Amendment of the Constitution, and in 1994 the U.S. Supreme Court upheld this decision (Rabkin, 1994).

Recently, the U.S. Supreme Court ruled on the funding of religious-oriented student publications in a case from the University of Virginia, declaring that the university must pay the printing cost for a religious-oriented student publication from the Student Activities fund. The court's argument was that by denying the group funding, the university violated free speech rights (Hernandez, 1995).

The separation of church and state is a controversial political issue and is unlikely to be resolved in a clear and straightforward manner any time soon.

of cases have dominated the courts. First are those that claim that a school or its policies infringe on individual beliefs. For example, saying prayers in class or at ceremonies may be seen as a school promoting a particular religion while rejecting others. Another example is the teaching of the theory of evolution which contradicts some religious beliefs.

The second type of cases occurs when school officials or policies prevent individuals from participating in religious activities during school hours or on school premises, such as religious use of public school facilities and resources. Still another set of cases have dealt with how much and what kind of public assistance religiously affiliated private schools should receive. The following paragraphs review important Supreme Court cases related to religion and schools.

As early as 1948, religious released-time classes in public school buildings were ruled unconstitutional. In 1962, an extremely controversial ruling was passed by the Supreme Court against required recitation of prayers in public schools, drafted by the state Board of Regents in New York (*Engle v. Vitale*, 370 US 421). The idea was to forbid schools from instructing, guiding, or encouraging people toward any particular form of religious worship. Several states then passed laws allowing for voluntary prayers; by 2008, 32 states had laws permitting or requiring silent prayer, reflection, or meditation for between one and five minutes at a time (LRU, 2008). These laws allow for a "period of silence," often "in silent contemplation of the anticipated activities of the day." This has been ruled constitutional because it does not "advance religion"; however, reciting the Lord's Prayer and forcing students to recite the Pledge of Allegiance have been ruled unconstitutional.

The 1992 case of *Weisman v. Lee* again addressed school prayer, this time related to the constitutionality of including prayer at graduation or promotion ceremonies. One side argues that invoking God's name should be upheld as constitutional; others argue that this violates the rights of separation by favoring some religions over others, and by making nonadherents feel that they are outsiders and that the public school system does not belong to them. The Supreme Court banned student-led prayers at football games, arguing that this amounted to offering prayers in public places; in this Texas case, the issues of separation of church and state versus students' free-speech rights were at issue (*Santa Fe Independent School District v. Doe*, 2000) (Leveritt, 2000; Mauro, 2000). According to a national poll, two-thirds of Americans think students should be permitted to lead such prayers (Carelli, 2000).

Other court cases return to the complex issue of extracurricular religious clubs. In a 1981 ruling (*Widmar v. Vincent*), the Supreme Court granted public university students the right to form religious clubs on campus; in a June 1990 ruling (*Westside Community Schools v. Mergens*), it extended the ruling to apply to secondary schools under some circumstances (Sendor, 1990, p. 15). The Equal Access Act states that if a school allows any noncurriculum-related clubs to meet—recreational, political, and philosophical—it must also allow religious groups to meet. The U.S. Congress has also entered into the issue of church and state, considering whether the Ten Commandments can be displayed in schools.

In 1963, the decision in *Abington Township, Pennsylvania v. Schempp*, the "school prayer" decision, prohibited school officials from organizing or leading prayers and devotional Bible readings in public schools. Religious freedom for students of all faiths and those with no faith required neutrality in schools. Bringing up the importance of religious education, the decision said: "One's education is not complete without a study of comparative religion and its relationship to the advancement of civilization . . . ." The argument was that we cannot ignore religions as a field of academic study because they encompass a large part of many people's lives and have had a large impact on the development of society. Therefore, schools can teach about religion, comparative religion, history of religion, or the Bible as literature, but not promote a religion.

The next Supreme Court decision on school prayer was in the 1985 case of *Wallace v. Jaffree*. This decision struck down Alabama's moment-of-silence law that was for the purpose of "meditation and voluntary prayer," arguing that neutral silence is appropriate, but could not include a religious motive.

The most recent Supreme Court case regarding school prayer was *Santa Fe v. Doe* in 2000. The ruling held that schools may not ask students to lead prayers over the public address system before football games; this was because students would be speaking for the school, not as private students (First Amendment Center, 2010).

The issue of separation of religion and state is not over; more cases are being sent to the Supreme Court, though the Court is not taking all of them. This will be an interesting issue to watch in the years to come.

SCIENTIFIC CREATION AND EVOLUTION.   One of the most controversial cases involving separation of church and state was heard before the Little Rock, Arkansas, state courts in 1981 and 1982.

Referred to popularly as Scopes II, *McLean v. Arkansas Board of Education* was similar to the 1925 trial of John Scopes for teaching evolutionary theory in the classroom. The 1981–1982 case dealt with requiring equal time in the classroom for "scientific creationist" and "evolutionist" theories. This and similar cases have centered on the battle between "absolute truth" believed by creationists and "relative truth" of those who have been labeled by fundamentalist Christians as "secular humanists." Those in favor of teaching several views argued that evolution is not a proven theory and that other theories should receive equal time; those opposed, maintained that the creationist view is taken from the Bible and would bring religion into the classroom.

After lengthy expert testimony, the court ruled that allowing the creationist view to be taught would be a violation of church and state separation. The case was particularly important because it set a precedent for cases being considered in 18 other states. One of these was brought before the Supreme Court in June 1987; the argument was that "creation science" had as much right to be taught in the classroom as evolution. Proponents argued that creation is a respectable scientific theory, that life forms did not evolve but appeared suddenly, and that this thesis should be given equal time. But by a 7 to 2 vote, the Court again held that this was a subterfuge to bring the Bible back to class and would violate First Amendment rights ("Louisiana Creationism Law," 1987, p. 23).

The issue arose again in Kansas where the State Board of Education passed the "Kansas Curricular Standards for Science Education"; it did not include the theory of evolution in the required science curriculum, leaving the choice of teaching evolution up to the local school boards (Larson, 2004). Polls on public opinion concerning the issue indicate that 83 percent of Americans want the theory of evolution taught in science classes, and 70 percent do not see a contradiction between evolution taught in science classes and creationism as a religious concept. Less than 30 percent want creationism taught in science classes (People for the American Way, 2000). Another case in Harrisburg, Pennsylvania, challenged the Dover Area School District for passing rules that encourage children to consider alternatives to evolution. It proposed inserting *intelligent design* (ID) into the biology curriculum (Biever, 2005). "*Intelligent Design* is the controversial assertion that an intelligent agent rather than an undirected process such as evolution is responsible for certain features of the universe and living things" (Biever, 2005, p. 44; italics added). The ruling barred the Dover school board from teaching the concept in public schools as it found that *intelligent design* was religiously motivated and promoted and advanced religion (Boyle, 2005).

Considering federal and Supreme Court rulings on separation of church and state, most findings have come down on the side of preserving separation, though some rulings leave remaining questions. However, the issue has not died.

VOUCHERS AND CHARTER SCHOOLS.   Voucher systems and charter schools continue to be controversial, especially when religion is involved. These schools are popular among parents who want more control over their children's education, but organizations such as "Save Our Schools" argue that public schools need the funds being diverted to other programs to maintain schools (Postlewaite, 2003). Evaluations of charter school programs show mixed results in terms of "achievement, access, integration and civic socialization" (The Rand Corporation, 2007). While scholars and policy makers debate their merits, the number of charter schools is growing. A recent controversy in Washington, D.C., arose when the Catholic diocese, short of funds for its schools, requested permission to open seven charter schools. A similar controversy has accompanied thee opening of Hebrew language charters schools (Medina, 2010; Jennifer Medina, 2010, June 25. "Success and Scrutiny at Hebrew Charter School." The New York Times, A1). This again raised the question of separation of religion and state because charter schools receive public funding (Martin and Sanchez, 2009). In Washington, D.C., 20 percent of the students are in various types of charter schools. However, students in traditional public schools do slightly better on 4th-grade National Assessment of Educational Progress tests than charter school students. This does not take into consideration how long the schools have been in existence or the background of students ("The News Hour," June 11, 2007, PBS).

Several state and federal court rulings on voucher systems and charter schools have created confusion over funding of private schools, especially religious schools. According to a ruling in the case of *Ridgecrest Charter School v. Sierra Sands Unified School District in California* (2005), public and charter school students must be treated equally. Charter students are district public school students. The general concern is that vouchers are providing subsidies to students who attend religious schools, violating the church–school separation principles of the Constitution. The courts seem to be encouraging states to focus on improving the public schools rather than looking for solutions in funding private schools.

Another issue in the church–state controversy is the clash between state standards and those of private schools. Many religious groups would prefer to have control over both the type and the amount of schooling children receive. One case in point occurred in Darke County, Ohio, in 1976, when the Tabernacle Christian School, serving the Dunkard religious group, was told that it had failed to comply with the state board of education requirements. Because the school had not met state standards, the parents would be charged with failure to send their children to school. This was seen by supporters and sympathizers of the school as an attempt to crush evangelical Christian schools. Other cases involve conflicts between religious groups such as the Amish and the states in which they live, centering on attendance laws. Despite the disparity between the state's and religious groups' conceptions of and expectations for education, accommodations between them have been reached in most areas.

A related controversy has to do with providing parochial schools with instructional materials and services from public monies. In a 1975 Supreme Court case (*Meek v. Pittenger*), the conflict between strict and loose constitutional constructionists came to a head. The court ruled that "a state government may lend secular textbooks to pupils attending parochial and other religiously oriented schools." Government may also provide nonpublic schools with buses; lunches; fire protection; water; police; sewers; tax exemptions; standardized tests and scoring; in-school diagnosis of speech, hearing, and psychological disorders; therapy, guidance, and remedial services off the school premises; payment for field trips; and loans to students of instructional materials and equipment. It was ruled unconstitutional, however, to make direct loans of instructional materials and provision of auxiliary services that might result in the direct and substantial advancement of religious activities.

FUNDING OF RELIGIOUS SCHOOLS. In 1985, the case of *Aguilar v. Felton* legally required public schools to administer federal aid to all children, but questions about how to do so remain. Some court decisions have supported withholding aid to private schools for certain equipment, such as computers and photocopiers, which could be used for religious purposes (Crawford, 1986, p. 15). Other cases have found that financial aid may be denied to certain academic disciplines; for example, the U.S. Supreme Court ruled that states giving aid to college students do not need to support students majoring in theology (Bloomberg.com, 2004). Clearly, there is a fine line between the acceptable and unacceptable, and more test cases are being brought to the courts.

Applying Sociology to Education: *Present arguments for and against religious presence, such as clubs and prayer, in public schools.*

The Economics of Education: Financing Schools

Most societies view education as an investment in the future. Training youths functions to socialize them into productive roles in society, prepares them to contribute to society, and "selects" them for future roles. In many countries, central governments provide local districts with funds to carry out equitable public education. These policies are based on goals of efficiency, equity, and liberty. However, wealthy members of society may buy their children elite private educations, thus ensuring them high positions that reproduce the stratification system.

Schools prepare students for the ever-growing expansion and technological sophistication of the economic sector. This is reflected in the rapid growth of schools to train populations for jobs. Consider the dramatic growth of schooling in the United States. From 1890s to the 1960s, secondary education expanded from an enrollment of 7 percent of the high school-age people to more than 90 percent. From 1985 to 1990 public secondary school enrollments dropped 8 percent, but rose 31 percent from 1990 to 2005 due to the baby boomlet, providing a net increase of 20 percent. In 2010 the enrollment in public high schools was 14.7 million students, compared to 13,270 in 1998 (NCES, 2000; NCES, *Projections of Educational Statistics to 2015*, 2006; NCES, 2010).

The growth of schools is seen by functionalists as meeting the economic needs for an educated labor force. The two go hand in hand to support the economy of nations. The growth and improvement of schools enhance worker skills and character traits, which in turn improve economic growth and social progress. More schooling for individuals opens more economic possibilities for individuals and nations.

A counterargument to the functionalists states that educational improvements alone do not cause social development. Schools serve as sifting and sorting institutions. Conflict theorists believe schools train individuals to meet the economic, occupational demands of society. Training stratifies by credentialing selected individuals for elite positions and others for the labor force, just as testing sorts individuals, but it does not necessarily imply social progress.

The financial environment of schools in the United States is uncertain. Actual dollars for education keep rising; but school costs are rising faster than inflation, and school levies to help meet rising costs often fail. The average cost of educating public school students who attend school regularly has risen from $453 per student in 1919–1920 to $8,313 in 2002–2003 to $10,297 in 2007–2008, and most recently to $10,792 (in constant dollars) (NCES, The Condition of Education, 2006; NCES, 2010). This figure per pupil varies greatly across the United States. For example, Phoenix, Arizona, pays a low of approximately $12,000 per year to educate a student, whereas New York City metro area pays a high of $27,000 for some children (Schaeffer, 2010).

School financing occurs at three levels: local, state, and federal (Reyes and Rodriquez, 2004). State funding has, on balance, provided the most funds for public education; however, this balance is shifting. The state share of funding grew steadily to about 50 percent in the 1980s. Then state funding began to decline as local funding rose from 43.9 percent in 1986–1987 to 46.9 percent in 2005. In 2009, state funding totaled $264.2 billion and made up 47.6 percent of total school budgets. The balance varies by state. For instance, in Nevada, 65.3 percent of the funding comes from state sources, whereas state funding provides 87 percent in Hawaii, 85 percent in Vermont, and 70 percent in Minnesota and New Mexico. The federal share was 8.5 percent in 2009 (Hill, 2006; NCES, "Statistics of State School Systems," 1999, p. 170, Table 158; NCES, 2006; NCES Digest, 2009).

Inner-city schools with higher expenditures are particularly hard hit in attempting to fund schools: Teachers' unions in cities are strong and often successfully demand more pay; school buildings need repairs; special programs, such as compensatory education, are greater in inner cities; and turnover of students is higher. Unfortunately, as the tax rates go up to support the schools, some residents move to the suburbs, further reducing the city's tax base. Therefore, federal and state funding is higher in poor areas such as inner-city districts that do not have a strong tax base. In school districts with a high percentage of children in poverty, the federal government pays almost 13 percent of schools' revenues, the state pays 60 percent, and local revenues amount to 27 percent. Even with government subsidies, comparing poor districts with wealthy districts, the funding picture looks quite different: Federal funding in wealthy districts is as low as 3 percent, state funding 41 percent, and local funding 56 percent.

LOCAL FUNDING.   Property taxes have been the main collection method for local funding, but the disparities between districts are great. Inner cities have lower tax bases from property taxes and continue to lose their tax base as wealthy individuals move to suburbs and industries relocate. Therefore, suburbs have greater tax bases to provide better schools. Should property taxes not provide adequate funds, bond levies can be put up for a vote, but the record of success does not bode well for schools depending on this source. Per pupil expenditures in central cities are generally less, though needs are usually greater to provide for students in poverty, to maintain and upgrade old school buildings, and to collect property taxes.

Across the United States, large districts and small towns alike face shortages of funds. By 1974, local taxes supplied 26 percent of the school budget, and in 1990, 47 percent; however, this figure declined to 43 percent in 2002 (NCES, "Statistics of State School Systems," 2006). Today, an average of 43.9 percent of total school revenue in the United States comes from local funding sources (NCES Digest, 2010, Table 172). A major problem, as mentioned earlier, is that the tax base is shrinking in many areas, and in many areas local property taxes to support schools are declining as taxpayers are rebelling against this heavier burden.

School finance reform has been a top priority in most states, and state support is providing an increasing proportion of school budgets, whereas local and federal taxes provide less. In addition, the local tax bases are affected by crises such as the closings of military bases and the bankruptcies of industries. To cope, some local districts are resorting to four-day workweeks, selling children's art, and holding lotteries to raise needed educational funds.

STATE FUNDING.   In recent years, state funding of education has increased to almost 60 percent of the total funding in poor districts; the money comes primarily from sales taxes, personal income taxes, and special funding like state lotteries. Sales taxes are as high as 7.75 percent (some counties in Nevada) and zero in five states. Forty-one states have income taxes, most based on federal tax return reports. Property taxes are the biggest source of local revenue. Personal income tax makes up the remainder, and these tax rates vary by state for an average state contribution to schools in the United States of $264.2 billion, or 47.6 percent of total school budgets. An increasing number of states are using lotteries and gambling to raise funds for education ("State Sales Tax Rates," 2007; Retirement Living Information Center, 2007; NCES Digest, 2010, Table 172).

Schools are often dependent on local funding sources such as tax levels.

The issue of school funding was first initiated almost 30 years ago and is still an issue in the courts, with many states involved in litigation. The concern in distribution of funds is how to be fair to all groups and areas of a state. State monies come to local districts through four main methods:

1. *Flat grants* provide the same amount to all districts for all students regardless of special needs; some states modify this to provide more for poor districts.
2. *Foundation plans*, the most common approach since the *Serrano* case [discussed later], provide for a minimum annual expenditure per student.
3. In *power-equalizing plans*, "the state pays a percentage of the local school expenditures in inverse ratio to the wealth of the district."
4. *Weighted-student plans* allow students to be rated according to their special needs: bilingual, disabled, and vocational education. (Ornstein and Levine, 1985, pp. 258–259; italics added)

Several of these plans attempt to take into consideration the differential in local ability to support schools and special needs of some districts, thus attempting to provide more equality among schools ("State Aid to Schools," 2005).

A continuing debate, which has reached the courts in a number of states, concerns the use of property taxes to help finance schools. The argument of groups opposed to property taxes is that wealthier districts have more money to pour into schools and can afford a better-quality education for their children. Thus, states are seeking ways to reduce the disparities in funding between local districts. Two well-known court cases addressed the issue of local school funding through property taxes. In 1971, in the case of *Serrano v. Priest*, the California supreme court ruled that "this funding scheme invidiously discriminates against the poor because it makes the quality of children's education a function of the wealth of their parents and neighbors." This landmark ruling affected school funding legislation in 46 states (Pennington, 2006). In a 1973

Texas case, *San Antonio v. Rodriguez*, the plaintiffs argued that education is a fundamental right and all schools should have the same financial base. This case reached the U.S. Supreme Court, which held that "education is not a fundamental interest or right." This meant that the use of property taxes to support schools was left undisturbed, although states were urged to devise new taxing and spending plans.

Other cases have resulted in a redistribution of monies for education among local, state, and federal funds. Since the *Serrano v. Priest* (1971) and *San Antonio v. Rodriguez* (1973) landmark cases, court rulings on funding plans have sent mixed messages about equality and funding (Fulton and Long, 1993; Pennington, 2006). With the advent of specific state standards for educational credentials, litigants have had a new angle from which to pursue their cases—educational adequacy instead of equity arguments (Rebell, 2006). The *Abbott* case in New Jersey and the *Campaign for Fiscal Equity* case in New York State, for example, have successfully used state standards for educational achievement to force an increase in the state contribution to school funding in order to assure that schools have adequate funds to support a successful educational system.

FEDERAL FUNDING. Federal funding for education is influenced by the economic state of the nation. When recession plagued the United States in the early 1980s, as it does in the late years of the first decade of the 21st century, available monies from government revenues dropped.

A nation's priorities and leaders' philosophies also influence how schools are funded and the role of government. During the Reagan and Bush administrations, the philosophy was to leave education and decision making to state and local governments. Thus, federal programs for disadvantaged students, except for Head Start, were reduced. Twenty-seven federal programs were put together into single grants to states, resulting in some programs being lost at the state level, especially if they were unpopular among more powerful groups in the state; this caused many to argue that the federal government should continue to support programs to enhance equal opportunity. Urban schools are likely to suffer most from loss of programs and money. The end result is that the United States spends less money per student on education than many other industrial nations, with a current average of $10,792 per pupil (Organization for Economic Cooperation and Development—OECD, 2003 NCES, The Condition, 2010) (see Table 9.1). Several ideas have been proposed to improve funding of education: Tuition tax credits, vouchers and charter schools, private-sector support and companies running schools, and lotteries are among the most common methods suggested. As mentioned, vouchers have generated controversy in various circles. The basic idea is that children and their families would receive a voucher to pay for a school of their choice, or for schools that would meet special needs of their students. Some critics of this idea argue that it could lead to segregated schools, challenge teachers' unions, allow special-interest groups such as religious groups to dominate education, and destroy the concept of mass public education.

Because of financial pressures, schools are put in the situation of having to market themselves to the environment, sell their program advantages, justify their staffing, and prove their success. The programs that are considered by the community to be "frills" are scrutinized most carefully. Thus, extracurricular activities—sports, music and art programs, counseling services, yearbooks, newspapers, debate teams, plays, and concerts—are often the first to be eliminated in a budget crunch. The financial environment of the school has a great impact on the type of school programming and planning that takes place.

Applying Sociology to Education: *What are some implications or results of the balance of funding sources—local, state, and federal—for public schools?*

Table 9.1 Relative Proportions of Public and Private Expenditure on Educational Institutions, for All Levels of Education (2007)

Distribution of public and private sources of funds for educational institutions after transfers from public sources, by year

	2007					2000		Index of change between 2000 and 2007 in expenditure on educational institutions	
	Public sources	Private sources				Public sources	All private sources[2]	Public sources	All private sources[3]
		Household expenditure	Expenditure of other private entities	All private sources[1]	Private: of which, subsidised				
Notes	(1)	(2)	(3)	(4)	(5)	(6)	(7)	(8)	(9)
OECD countries									
Australia	69.5	23.0	7.5	30.5	4.4	73.2	26.8	120	143
Austria	91.0	4.8	4.1	9.0	4.6	94.0	6.0	108	168
Belgium	94.4	4.4	1.2	5.6	1.7	94.3	5.7	115	112
Canada	74.7	10.7	14.6	25.3	0.5	79.9	20.1	111	149
Chile	57.7	40.0	2.3	42.3	1.2	55.2	44.8	139	125
Czech Republic	88.7	7.6	3.7	11.3	m	89.9	10.1	147	167
Denmark	92.5	3.9	3.6	7.5	m	96.0	4.0	115	225
Finland	97.5	x(4)	x(4)	2.5	n	98.0	2.0	124	152
France	91.0	7.1	1.9	9.0	1.7	91.2	8.8	106	108
Germany	85.4	x(4)	x(4)	14.6	m	85.6	14.4	105	106
Greece	m	m	m	m	m	93.8	6.2	m	m
Hungary	m	m	m	m	m	m	m	146	m
Iceland	90.1	8.6	1.3	9.9	m	90.0	10.0	149	149
Ireland	m	m	m	m	m	m	m	160	m
Italy	91.1	7.3	1.6	8.9	1.4	94.3	5.7	101	164
Japan	66.7	21.7	11.6	33.3	m	71.0	29.0	101	124
Korea	57.6	30.8	11.5	42.4	2.1	59.2	40.8	154	164

Notes: 2 | 3

Luxembourg	**m**	m	m	**m**	m	m	m	m	m
Mexico	**80.3**	19.5	0.2	**19.7**	1.2	85.3	14.7	127	182
Netherlands	**83.8**	7.3	8.9	**16.2**	1.5	84.1	15.9	123	126
New Zealand	**80.6**	19.1	0.2	**19.4**	m	m	m	109	m
Norway	**m**	m	m	**m**	m	95.0	5.0	126	m
Poland	**90.6**	9.4	m	**9.4**	m	89.0	11.0	127	107
Portugal	**91.7**	6.9	1.3	**8.3**	m	98.6	1.4	m	m
Slovak Republic	**86.2**	7.9	5.9	**13.8**	1.7	96.4	3.6	130	555
Spain	**87.3**	11.7	1.1	**12.7**	0.4	87.4	12.6	128	130
Sweden	**97.4**	n	2.6	**2.6**	n	97.0	3.0	120	102
Switzerland	**m**	m	m	**m**	m	92.1	7.9	109	141
Turkey	**m**	m	m	**m**	m	98.6	1.4	m	m
United Kingdom	**69.5**	20.1	10.4	**30.5**	19.7	85.2	14.8	109	274
United States	**66.1**	19.9	14.0	**33.9**	m	67.3	32.7	125	131
OECD average	**82.6**	~	~	**17.4**	**2.8**	~	~	**123**	**165**
EU19 average	**89.2**	~	~	**10.8**	**3.3**	~	~	**123**	**178**
Partner countries									
Brazil	**m**	m	m	**m**	m	m	m	166	m
Estonia	**93.5**	6.0	0.5	**6.5**	1.4	m	m	148	m
Israel	**76.7**	16.7	6.5	**23.3**	2.3	80.0	20.0	112	136
Russian Federation	**82.5**	12.1	5.4	**17.5**	m	m	m	326	m
Slovenia	**86.7**	11.6	1.7	**13.3**	n	m	m	m	m

1. Including subsidies attributable to payments to educational institutions received from public sources.
2. Year of reference 2006
3. Year of reference 2008.

Source: Education at a Glance 2010: OECD Indicators, OECD 2010 (September 6) Indicator B3, How much public and private investment is there in education; OECD.
See Annex 3 for notes (*www.oecd.org/edu/eag2010*).

The political climate and philosophy of education directly affect funding for education. Our next environmental institutions are the political and legal sectors.

The Political and Legal Institutions

Governments have direct involvement in education, whether through influencing content and values taught, funding for special programs, or setting policy. Educational systems in many countries are controlled by the central government, usually through a ministry of education. Other governments often have legal and financial control and influence over schools. Some of the political issues facing schools are worldwide; others are unique to particular systems. Consider the following issues that face local to national educational systems.

1. Should children be provided with broad, comprehensive education or tracked, with some taking vocational education and others academic courses?
2. Should schools be administered from a central "ministry of education" or a local authority?
3. Should parents be allowed to educate their children in schools of their choice (even if unaccredited, such as some church schools) or at home, or should children be required to go to accredited schools?
4. Should vouchers be given to parents to choose their children's school?
5. Should groups of parents with particular ideological concerns be allowed to ban textbooks from schools because they are offensive to the group?
6. Should controversial community or societal issues such as AIDS and sex education be taught in the classroom?

In many ways, education and politics cannot be separated:

• School programs are influenced by economic needs; some countries with planned economies designate how many people can be trained for each type of position.
• Parents and communities put pressure on schools to prepare children for success.
• Different interest groups conflict over what knowledge should be passed on to children through curriculum content and textbooks (Apple and Weis, 1986, p. 8).

State governments set standards for child care centers, especially in low-income communities (Fuller et al., 2004).

In the United States, the states set standards and test for adequate achievement in math, reading, and other subjects. These standards differ dramatically between states as shown by the National Assessment of Educational Progress (NAEP) test; some state standards are above these norms, others well below. Many educators argue that this is a flaw in the "No Child Left Behind" legislation; states may set their own standards low so as not to be penalized for failing to meet goals (Lewin, 2007). Yet others argue that state populations differ by poverty levels, immigrant populations, and other factors; to judge all by the same standards would be unrealistic. Recent research findings suggest that many of these state exit exams, that is, exams given to those aspiring to graduate from high school, are harming the students who fail them and not benefiting the students who pass them (Warren and Grodsky, 2009). A closer look at this government accountability role is in order.

Schools have always been the testing ground for societal changes. In the United States, this means responsibility for public education and "promoting the general welfare." Early in U.S. history, the federal government was involved in setting aside land for education and raising funds as ordained in the Northwest Ordinance of 1785 and the Morrill Act of 1862 and in passing laws to ensure education for specific groups of students such as Native Americans. In recent years, laws have been passed to guarantee education for all groups of students. One example is Affirmative Action legislation that has had a major impact on college acceptances of minorities around the United States (Brown and Hirschman, 2006).

Courts at each level of the judicial system hear cases on education ranging from religion in schools, as previously discussed, to desegregation and education for the disabled, to voucher systems and charter schools. School districts, community residents, or interest groups initiate cases that are brought before the courts, several of which we have considered throughout this text: prayer in schools, creationism, textbooks, school funding, busing and integration, special education, and many others.

Examples of the enormous impact legislation can have on schools are seen in the 1954 *Brown v. Board of Education* case; the 1964 Civil Rights Act; Public Law 94–142; and the Education for All Handicapped Children Act, enacted in 1975, requiring schools to "mainstream" disabled children from ages 3 to 21. More recently the Individuals with Disabilities Education Act (IDEA) changed the lives of many children. Before the passage of PL 94–142, 1 million disabled children could be excluded from the public school system, and hundreds of thousands more were denied appropriate services. Now many disabled students are graduating from high school, going to college, and entering the workforce. Arguments for integrating these students into the public schools include the following (IDEA, 1997).

1. The disabled can achieve higher levels academically and socially if not isolated.
2. Regular school settings help them cope with the world in which they must live as adults.
3. Exposure to the disabled helps other children understand the differences between children.

Each year the Department of Justice Enforcement issues a status report on the effectiveness of the Americans with Disabilities Act (ADA), a comprehensive civil rights law for people with disabilities. Over the years, their conclusion has been that from mainstreaming students and ensuring participation in activities to offering fair testing opportunities, the situation for disabled students has improved greatly since the law went into effect (Department of Justice, 2010; "Enforcing the ADA," 1995). There are still concerns about definitions of who qualifies for protection and opportunities under the law, especially the 12.4 million cognitively disabled Americans whose status is unclear ("The Disabled ADA," 2006).

Opponents of the ADA law argue that many disabled children suffer from the taunting of classmates and from untrained teachers trying to make the program work. They recommend caution in placements, special training for teachers, and a limited number of disabled children in any one classroom.

Governmental bodies and agencies at various levels in the school's environment have responsibility for passing and enforcing legislation related to the functioning of schools, and, therefore, they have an impact on the school's internal operation. Whole educational systems are affected and the structures must be altered to include appropriate materials, physical facilities, and support personnel; roles must be redefined to address the new expectations; and school goals must be restated to avoid conflicting statements. Laws requiring change in schools, classrooms, curricula, and individual role responsibilities mean a restructuring of the system and repercussions for structure and positions at each level.

Applying Sociology to Education: *What role does the political system play in your community's schools? Think of specific examples.*

Communities and Their Schools

Groups of parents complain that the school should not be teaching about sex. Businesses put pressure on the school to train students in industry-oriented computers and technology. Some immigrant groups want the school to teach students in their native languages. Peer groups compete with schools for the attention and loyalty of students. All of these examples show the vulnerability of the school system to environmental pressures from a variety of community sources. The composition of the community in which schools are located determines the "raw material" entering the local school.

At some time, most of us will take sides on an issue that is confronting the school system. It may involve the proper role of schools, the educational content of curricula, or the hiring or firing of personnel. Because of the school's vulnerability to environmental demands, the school administration is in a double bind. It is under pressure to consider all opinions on an issue, yet not all views can be accepted.

SCHOOL PARTNERSHIPS.   Corporate America, realizing that its future workforce is at stake, is paying more attention to schools. This attention takes several forms, from outright cash donations to operating schools on corporate premises. Foundations are particularly active in awarding grants to school districts for projects; some are diverting funds that formerly went to universities in attempts to shore up elementary and secondary schools.

Businesses have become increasingly involved in schools, especially in some large cities where high school students are given internships, graduates are promised jobs, and those going to college are given tuition scholarships. Business leaders consider this support to be in their interests to provide a trained labor force and more livable cities. The link between corporations and students from inner-city schools who go on to attend college encourages some students to continue with their high school educations. Local small businesses give donations for special programs, libraries, and sports programs. Corporations also express frustration, however, not always knowing the outcomes of their cash and in-kind contributions to schools. Measuring effectiveness is difficult, and many corporate leaders are questioning whether their efforts are having any impact. Yet major corporate donors such as the Bill and Melinda Gates Foundation and Mark Zuckerberg of Facebook continue to fund schools. The Gates Foundation gave $335 million to study effective teaching and to help fund several school districts, and Mark Zuckerberg made a $100 million gift to the Newark, New Jersey, schools in September 2010 (Del Falco and Henry, 2010).

Some school personnel question the role of business in public education, fearing undue influence from the corporate sector that has money to influence curriculum and policies; others feel that corporate partnerships provide hope for infusing more funds into poor school districts and for trying creative ideas to improve achievement levels.

Another partnership is special-interest groups. Their influences can make a positive contribution to schools, or they can make constant demands on the school:

• More money should be funneled into athletic programs.
• Sex education is not the role of the schools, but should be taught at home.
• Teaching diverse cultural heritages should be a high priority for schools.
• Students should learn discipline and respect in the school in order to become solid citizens.
• Minority students should have special cultural programs.

Peer groups are one example of a special-interest group; they become increasingly important for children as they progress through the teen years. Each child is likely to be influenced by several different groups—some are formally organized by the school, as in team sports; some are community activities through religious groups or scouts; and some are informal, such as neighborhood and school friendship groups.

Minority programming is another example of an issue put forth by special-interest groups. Classrooms are becoming more diverse in students' social class ethnic composition. Over the years, minority groups have requested that a number of programs be added to the school curriculum; African American, Hispanic, Native American, Asian, women's studies, and others have been initiated. More recently, grant money from such philanthropic organizations as the Ford and Rockefeller Foundations have funded projects in ethnic studies. Many educators agree that the standard curriculum—originally designed to socialize children to be like the dominant group in society, and to assimilate groups to be "Americans"—needs revision. Trends today are in the direction of multicultural programs supporting the diversity of groups within the system. This could eventually put each group into historical perspective in the national picture and stress respect for cultural diversity and pluralism.

The stronger the power base of the interest group pushing an issue in a community, the more consideration the issue is likely to receive. Some small groups have had disproportionate influence because they were willing to speak out. Consider the examples of censorship of books in Chapter 2. The school's institutional environment shapes the internal processes of schools around the world, making each a unique organization within its educational setting.

The many influences from the educational system's environment bring about some similarities between schools, but they also make each school unique because of different contributions and pressures from that school's unique environment. In order to understand the policies and activities within the school, it is necessary to understand the environmental pressures on schools.

Summary

I. THE ENVIRONMENT AND THE EDUCATIONAL SYSTEM

In order to survive, schools respond to the many and varied demands of their environments. Because they depend on the environment for resources, demands from the environment cannot be ignored. In this chapter we have focused on the institutional environment of schools: family and home, religious groups, financing and the economy, political and legal systems, and the community.

Conflicts of interest are an inherent part of the schools' environment, with opposing groups demanding that their views dominate. In order to receive the resources necessary for survival, schools must expend more energy dealing with the demands of the more salient parts of the environment.

II. THE SCHOOL SYSTEMS' ENVIRONMENTS: INTERDEPENDENCE BETWEEN INSTITUTIONS

Key institutions that make up the environment include the home, religious organizations, financial environment, government and legal systems, and the community and special-interest groups.

1. Children bring their attitudes toward school, among other attributes, from home. Parents have varying degrees of involvement in schools; the more active the parents, the more positive the results for their children's school experience.
2. In some societies, religion and the state, including education, are one and the same. In the United States, the separation of church and state has caused conflict on several issues, most notably what constitutes teaching

religion in schools and what to teach in the classroom. The "creation story" issue is a prime example.

3. Funding of U.S. education comes from three primary sources: federal, state, and local levels. The percentage supplied by each of these has shifted over the years. Court cases have challenged some local plans for financing schools as being unfair to poor districts, and in recent years there has been an increase in state funding. Funding comes from several sources: personal income tax, sales tax, property tax, levies, and—in some states—lotteries. Methods of distribution of funds also vary by state. Federal funding supports special programs for minorities, the disabled, and other targeted projects. Proposals for change, including tax credits and vouchers, continue to be discussed.

4. The government role in education involves passing laws and setting policies. Although local control in the United States is paramount, the federal government has great leverage by restricting funding of education to those who fail to adhere to federal educational guidelines. Where there are questions related to laws and policies, the courts are asked to make judgments; for instance, laws setting policy for education for the disabled have dramatically affected this group, and cases brought before the courts continue to test the law.

5. Communities provide the "raw material" entering the schools, as well as influencing the type of education offered in a particular community. Composition of the community determines the need for special programs such as bilingual education. Special interests in the community also put pressure on schools to accommodate their interests.

6. The school environment has a dramatic effect on the internal functioning of schools. We cannot completely understand schools without considering this crucial element affecting the educational system.

Putting Sociology to Work

1. Describe the parts of your environment that affect your role as a student. Do any of these cause role conflict?

2. What are some social movements or population trends affecting your school district? Ask teachers and principals what they perceive to be pressures on the schools related to current trends.

3. Find out how your local schools are funded and if there are any special sources of funding.

4. What are your local schools' immediate and secondary environments? Diagram them.

5. Discuss several examples of school system change brought about by environmental feedback.

The System of Higher Education

"The path from school to college is poorly marked" (Boyer, 1987, pp. 13–14). Some of us have models—older siblings, parents, or a counselor—to point the way through college-preparatory curricula, college testing, the application and selection process, and admission. Others have little guidance, and often these are the very students who have less chance of going to college and succeeding in higher education. Elementary and secondary schooling are compulsory, but we choose whether to attend an institution of higher education. The atmosphere, the professional manner of the faculty, and the organization of the system are all unique features of higher education as compared with primary and secondary schooling.

In this chapter we deal with the system of higher education—its development and meaning; access to the system; the structure, process, and role relationships within the system; environmental pressures toward change; and outcomes and reforms in higher education. The open systems model helps us draw together the many aspects of higher education and see them in relation to the total educational system (see Figure 10.1). This model shows the parts of higher education systems today. However, it would look unfamiliar to many who have been involved in higher education throughout history.

HISTORY AND DEVELOPMENT OF HIGHER EDUCATION

Walking through the colleges at Oxford and Cambridge universities in England, one is reminded that many traditions in higher education were established in the twelfth and thirteenth centuries in those very settings, with their courtyards, spires, formal gardens, long halls with stained-glass windows, and statues of notable early scholars. In the ancient Bodlien library at Oxford University, medieval scholars sat and studied just as students in jeans with laptops in their backpacks do today. The tradition of transmitting knowledge began with the early universities: Paris in France, Bologna and Venice in Italy, Salamanca in Spain, and Oxford and Cambridge in England. Founded mostly as centers of religious thought, along with such universities as Al Azhar University, in Cairo,

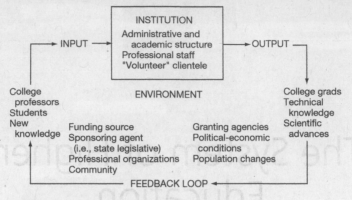

FIGURE 10.1   Systems model of higher education.

Egypt, an ancient center of Sunni Islamic learning, many of these universities established a delicate balance between independence and autonomy over their decision making and interaction with the church and state, a balance that set precedents for church–state–institution relations through the centuries and up to the present time.

Historical Functions of Higher Education

In the nineteenth century, a new mission or function was added to the traditional one of transmitting knowledge; research became an end in itself. This new mission created tension between teaching and research, causing strains on the teacher–student relationship and between faculty members with different orientations and interests. This tension is familiar to us today as professors divide their time between students and research. In many countries, research wins out because more monetary and prestige rewards are attached to these activities than to teaching Ballantine and Hammack 2009; Cuban, 1999).

Over time, changes have occurred in the governance, the administrative structures, the curriculum, and the composition of the student body in higher education. New disciplines developed rapidly, requiring adaptation of existing structures. Pressure for more representative multicultural curriculum and higher educational opportunities for more segments of populations around the world became key issues over the years.

Trends in the Development of Higher Education

Higher education developed differently in the United States compared with European countries such as England and Spain. In the colonial period, several small colleges were established in the United States, most sponsored by religious groups but run by laypersons, a pattern that was also typical in Scandinavian countries. The primary aim of these colleges was the education of clergy to lead the communities of faith that supported them. In the period that followed, many other colleges sprang up—and many failed. The colleges were meant to serve men from "respectable families" and a few lucky young men selected from poor families. Generally, they were established by upper-middle-class men and perpetuated the existing distinctions between social classes in the United States. In 1776, only about one man in 200 had a college education, but many other young men learned from tutors or were self-taught (Jencks and Riesman, 1968, pp. 90–91). Women were excluded from higher education at this period; however, a few women met in small private groups to receive training from broad-minded male professors at nearby universities.

It was not until the Civil War, with the passage of the Morrill Act in 1862, that many states established public land-grant colleges and universities with the purpose of providing liberal and practical education for a wide range of students. The legislation had come before Congress earlier, but Southern states had objected to the Federal intervention into education matters, considering it a states rights issue. By 1862, the South was at war with the Union and Northern states supported the transfer of federal public land to the states to support the foundation of public universities. By the late 1800s, public teacher-training colleges, or "normal schools," also sprang up to meet the growing need for teachers. At about the same time, the undergraduate college began to join with free-standing graduate and professional schools to form what we now know as universities. The first American colleges to provide graduate education and become universities were Harvard University, chartered in 1869 (Harvard College was established in 1636), and Johns Hopkins, in 1876.

By 1900, there were several hundred small, private, undergraduate colleges, most with a "classical" curriculum of Greek, Latin, mathematics, morals, and religion. Most of these colleges had a fixed, required curriculum, offering no choice to their students. Departments did not exist, and most colleges employed faculty who were generalists, not scholars with advanced degrees in their specialization. In the next few years, faculty began to specialize, often traveling to Germany to study in their advanced higher education institutions, and returned to colleges in this country to advocate for the establishment of academic departments with autonomy based on their collective expertise in their specialties. In addition, more specialized colleges, forerunners of today's professional schools, were emerging—for example, the Massachusetts Institute of Technology (MIT) and the California Institute of Technology, both specializing in engineering.

England today has increased the number of higher education institutions and college graduates who now comprise about 39 out of 100 individuals between ages 20 and 24 (the typical age of graduation). In contrast, the United States, with nearly 5,000 higher-education institutions, including two-year colleges (*The Chronicle of Higher Education Almanac*, 2010), has about 36 graduates out of every 100 individuals aged between 22 and 24 (our typical graduation age). Once the nation with the highest rate of young adults age 18–24 enrolled in college, the United States now ranks behind 16 nations in the Organization for Economic Cooperation and Development including Iceland (62.8 per 100), Australia (59.6 per 100), New Zealand (53.5 per 100), as well as Poland (44.8 per 100) and Korea (41 per 100) (NCES, *Digest*, 2010, Table 413).

Various historical factors led to the more restrictive model in some countries, but the mass education model developed in the United States has become the international standard. Without a federal university or a central educational authority (the U.S. Constitution does not mention education), the states created their own education law, and often encouraged private institutions to develop. These new private colleges, however, had to support themselves since states were unwilling to tax themselves to support education during the nineteenth century. This is why the Morrill Act's public colleges, the "Land Grant Colleges," have been so important in our education history.

The advent of two-year colleges, today called "community" colleges (the former name was "junior" college), is a twentieth-century phenomenon. They provide terminal degrees or act as feeders for four-year colleges and universities, or both. "In comparison with four-year colleges and universities, community colleges are more likely to enroll academically less well prepared students, minority students, part-time students, economically less well-off students, commuter students, older students, and first generation college students" (Oromaner, 1995, p. 1; Pascarella et al., 1998). This original American institution serves multiple purposes: a focus on students, remedial education where needed, vocational courses, community service, and nontraditional and minority student accessibility as well as the option to transfer to a four college (Grubb, 1991; Vaughan, 1991). About 43 percent of new first-year students began their college careers at two-year colleges in 2008 and 57 percent started at four-year colleges (NCES, *Digest,* 2010, Table 198). More than 45 percent of minority students are enrolled in community colleges (NCES, *Digest,* 2010, Table 198). Of those in higher education who attend community colleges, about one-fifth graduate from four-year colleges, a figure that has been constant over the past decade (Cohen, 1997; Dougherty, 2002). The likelihood of graduating in six years from a four-year college was the same (69 percent) for transfer students as for those who started at four-year institutions, though transfer itself is strongly affected by students' parental socioeconomic status, their academic preparation, and their age (the higher the age at entering the community college, the lower the probability of transfer). Graduation is influenced by the ease of admission to the four-year college, the financial aid made available to transfers, and whether community college credits are accepted (Dougherty and Kienzl, 2006).

Four decades ago, Burton Clark observed that junior colleges in California in the 1950s served two functions: to provide terminal two-year degrees and to give a small group of students the preparation to transfer to four-year institutions. Clark pointed out that when it became clear that many students wished to transfer, the low achieving were dissuaded by the junior college and told of the virtues of the career-oriented, two-year terminal programs. Clark called this the "cooling-out function" (Clark, 1960), that is the school tried to lower (or cool off) the high (or hot) ambitions of many students who struggled academically by redirecting their academic ambitions to vocational and occupation programs that did not prepare their students for transfer to a four-year college. Rather than failure in the transfer program, the college's logic was that the students could succeed in the terminal programs, although they would have to give up their dream of a four-year degree and the occupations requiring it.

This idea of the "cooling-out function" has been the stimulus for much debate about the role of two-year colleges. Elitists argue community colleges are inferior and do not measure up to academic standards of four-year institutions; mainstream critics are supportive in principle of community colleges, but believe they could do a better job of serving less advantaged students and promoting transfers to four-year colleges; and structural critics see a stratified system of higher education producing inequalities, and two-year colleges playing a role in that system (Pincus, 1994). The structural critics argue that community colleges serve as a sieve to eliminate poor and minority students or prevent them from moving up the educational ladder; marginal students, who are often minority students, are filtered out from the higher education system. For example, six years after starting college at a four-year public college, 34 percent of low-income, first-generation students earn bachelor's degrees. However, only 5 percent who begin at community college finish a four-year degree, though both groups have the same goal (Russell, 2008). Thus, entering a community college seems to provide less chance of getting a four-year degree than entering a four-year college (Dougherty, 2011); this is changing with more articulation agreements between community colleges and state universities. Many minority students have inadequate college preparation programs at inner-city high schools, and nearly 90 percent of these students spend time in developmental educational programs at community colleges, taking courses that do not carry college-level credit.

For instance, Hispanic students disproportionately attend two-year colleges (Velez and Javalgi, 1994). The interpretation of this disproportionate enrollment pattern, however, is not self-evident. Rouse (1998), for example, studied the degree to which two-year colleges increase educational attainment, and found that the availability of two-year colleges increased overall access to higher education, but may have lowered the attainment of four-year degrees. Among students with similar characteristics, those who begin at two-year colleges are less likely to ever receive a four-year college degree than those who initially begin at four-year schools. As Dougherty put it, " . . . the community college's contribution to baccalaureate production is small because its 'diversion' effect largely, though not completely, cancels its 'democratizing' effect" (Dougherty, 2002, p. 316). Since there are a higher proportion of Hispanic students in states with many community colleges (such as Florida, California, and Texas), it is hard to disentangle the causes of their enrollment patterns. Yet, completing the associate of arts degree may actually hinder a student's chances of getting additional years of education (Monk-Turner, 1992a; O'Connor, Hammack, and Scott, 2010). Community college, then, can perpetuate stratification in higher education.

While the debate over the consequences of community colleges for student adult attainment is over 30 years old, it has recently flared brightly. In articles and a book, James Rosenbaum has argued that the expansion of access to community colleges has had the opposite of its intended effect (Rosenbaum, 1998; Rosenbaum, 2001). Encouraging poorly prepared high school graduates to go to college ("college for all") has produced many frustrated students, who are unable to attain their goal. He argues that they should be offered clear information about their real chances in college and also be told of noncollegiate occupational and vocational education programs from which they might better benefit. This argument has been seen as a new variant of the criticism that higher education expansion has diluted its value and created a form of class and race segregation, an academic apartheid (Attewell and Lavin, 2007, p. 160). Attewell and Lavin, on the other hand, argue that the more open doors that allow many low-achieving high school graduates to attend college have produced positive results for them. Their data show that remediation courses help both colleges to maintain academic standards and those who pass the courses to succeed in their regular college courses (Attewell and Lavin, 2007, p. 171). These students go on to attain better jobs and higher incomes than they might have otherwise. Rosenbaum replied with a review of the Attewell and Lavin book, *Teachers College Record*, 2010, noting that most poorly prepared students seeking higher education degrees do not graduate, even though some do. It is clear that scholars in this area care deeply about the problems they study.

Another debate surrounding community colleges focuses on the shift in their purpose toward service to the corporate culture, with custom-contracted training programs to meet business needs. Because this is more of a community and vocational purpose, the traditional liberal arts and transfer functions of community colleges are weakened, some argue (Pincus, 1989). In October 2010, President Obama convened a major initiative to link community colleges with job opportunities in communities, stressing the need to prepare large numbers of students for business and government jobs (Gonzalez, 2010). Until 1970, a majority of community college students were enrolled in programs intended to prepare students to transfer to four-year schools; by 1980, 70 percent of community college students were in two-year vocational programs. In a recent review of the situation, several reasons for this dramatic shift were suggested, from the high responsiveness to economic, social, and political environments of the community college, to students' choices of programs (Dougherty, 2000; Dougherty and Bakia, 2000).

Research shows that the community colleges themselves may have pursued the more vocational and semiprofessional courses because it was an available niche in the higher-education marketplace, with four-year colleges taking control of the preparation of occupations with higher status (Brint and Karabel, 1989). However, contracting with businesses to provide training, courses, and workshops for business employees points to the fear that community colleges may find the financial benefits more appealing than their educational autonomy and serving the educational needs of their unique student constituencies.

Educators are concerned also about the drop in the numbers of transfers, although articulation programs with four-year colleges can make transferring easy. Some argue for the importance of the transfer function because it confirms the academic purposes of community colleges;

many students do aspire to a four-year degree but are discouraged in the process; and claims to be egalitarian depend on the transfer function, which purports to give all students an opportunity for a four-year higher education (Grubb, 1991, p. 194). The decline in the transfer rate may also be due to the increasing vocationalization of the community college. Their vocational programs may attract initially transfer-oriented students into terminal programs (Dougherty, 2002).

What effect do community college degrees have on occupational placement and success? The type of college we enter shapes our occupational status. Community college male entrants achieve lower occupational status than those who begin at four-year colleges. For women, occupational return for each additional year of education is lower for community college entrants than for four-year entrants. On average, community college entrants achieve a lower occupational status than four-year college entrants. As we noted earlier, however, on average, community college students are less well qualified than four-year college students, thus these groups of students are different from each other before college as well as after. The important question is whether attending either kind of college benefits the student personally and in the job market. According to Dougherty's recent review of the evidence, "students who graduate from community college vocational programs receive substantially better wages than to high school graduates, although lower payoffs than college graduates" (2002, p. 302). Their wages are 20–30 percent higher than comparable high school graduates (also see Kane and Rouse, 1999).

Monk-Turner, however, considers this economic payoff modest (Monk-Turner, 1992b). Vocational education offered at community colleges leads to certain types and levels of jobs, such as building trades or electronic or business skills; it benefits employers who need skilled workers and may give workers an opportunity to rise above low-paid, dead-end jobs (Pincus, 1985), but it may also lock workers into lower-level positions, as feared by conflict theorists.

It is clear that two-year colleges, in some places termed "short-cycle" colleges, serve a distinct role and, despite the controversy, are expanding their presence and variety around the world. For example, Britain has added "sixth-form" colleges to many comprehensive schools; these are similar in structure and function to two-year colleges. Japan also offers selected courses of study at two-year colleges, with the majority of their students being women. Canadian two-year college courses cannot be transferred to the university sector.

> **Applying Sociology to Education:** *What role do you think community colleges can or should play for students and communities?*

THEORETICAL APPROACHES TO HIGHER EDUCATION

Higher education has expanded rapidly around the world in the past half-century. Major theoretical questions are why and what are the results of this rapid expansion? Another major theoretical debate has centered on access to higher education—whether some groups have greater opportunity than others. Let us look briefly at these two debates through the eyes of functional and conflict theorists.

The Expansion of Higher Education

Functionalist or consensus theorists think that universities can go a long way toward solving societal problems through development and use of new knowledge; conflict theorists argue that universities often perpetuate the status quo and that more basic societal change is needed if we are to alter the current state of inequality.

FUNCTIONAL APPROACH.   According to the functionalist perspective, higher education has developed rapidly in the United States and other countries for several reasons. First, higher education is desirable to help improve individual opportunities. Second, higher education increases the possibility of equal opportunities by teaching the skills required in a complex technological world, and thereby improving an individual's ability to compete and fit into the system in a productive way. Third, society needs higher education to help prepare individuals to fill essential roles; this argument has been put forward to expand higher education in developing regions.

CONFLICT APPROACH.   Conflict theorists view the growth in higher education as directly related to changes in the needs of the capitalistic system. They believe that higher education, like primary and secondary education, is structured to serve the needs and perpetuate the advantaged position of the elite. Just as the secondary schools channel students into vocational or academic tracks, so too the higher education system can be viewed as a series of tracks. The illusion of upward mobility is present, but its reality has been questioned. There is a major difference in the occupational status of the student graduating from a two-year college or technical school compared with that of the elite university-trained student. Samuel Bowles and Herbert Gintis interpret most of the system of higher education as channeling students to lower-level, white-collar occupations that permit little autonomy or discretion. Students have more choice and long-range work without supervision in institutions preparing students for elite status (Bowles and Gintis, 1976, Chapter 8, 2002). These authors are doubtful that even an elite education encourages students to raise questions about the system and its legitimacy. Research funding, they argue, is also guided by the interests of the elite and perpetuates the status quo.

Another conflict approach has been developed by Randall Collins (1978), who argues that education is a tool in the competition among status groups in society. Rather than seeing increasing education requirements for jobs as a result of the higher cognitive demands of the work, as functionalists posit, he asserts that the establishment of educational credentials for jobs is evidence of efforts to close off access to those "unqualified" by their lack of credentials, not their lack of skill or ability to do the job. Groups, sometimes defined by their education levels or by their racial or ethnic group membership, seek to expand their advantages against other groups through creating specific educational credentials, much to the pleasure of educators, who then get more students. The credentialism that is created becomes a self-perpetuating machine, inflating educational requirements of occupations. The collegiate curriculum has become increasingly "vocationalized" as students now major in business subjects, not economics, and in communications, not English.

To understand the politics of this "gatekeeping" (Karen, 1990), or who has access to elite colleges and programs, one must study all parts of the educational system, including those who make decisions about access, which includes both college admissions officers and high school counselors (Rosenbaum et al., 1996), the criteria they use, and what type of university they are trying to create. The admissions process reflects the university's position in the larger society and how selective it can be. Therefore, the struggles for access in the society are reflected in the admissions process (Soares, 2007; Stevens, 2007).

Access to Higher Education

The issue around the globe is who gets into what university, and why. True or not, the belief in most countries is that education is the road to advancement and success. In many societies, the elite do dominate the halls of ivy, and as the opportunity structures change with modernization, others in society are demanding a share of the profits.

Old universities around the world are pressured to reconsider their restrictive entrance requirements, and new universities are opening their doors to new groups of students. For example, in Malaysia, the National University now serves primarily Malays, the indigenous group that until recent years was underrepresented in higher education compared with Indian and Chinese groups in the population.

In the United States, the situation is different. Admission to elite universities is similar to that in England and Japan, but it is not based primarily on a university exam. Most of the public institutions in the United States have "open-door policies," meaning that any high school graduate with required prerequisites will be admitted. Private schools are divided between open-door and selective admissions. Since 1980, public four-year institutions have become more selective, meaning that expectations for high school coursework and achievement test scores have increased. At one prestigious institution, Harvard College, admission decisions are tied to both the elite status of some students and affirmative action considerations for others (Karen, 1991). With this gradual closing of the doors has come protest over access to systems and elitism in higher education.

The competition for access to elite colleges highlights the status hierarchy in colleges and universities in the United States. Unlike most other countries, there are old and prestigious private colleges as well as powerful public ones. The "pecking order" among them has been illuminated by the rise of college rankings, such as those published by *U.S. News and World Report*. In addition, the proportion of high school graduates continuing their education into college has steadily risen to a figure now over 70 percent. With a much bigger enrollment in high schools than even a few years ago (a result of a mini-baby boom during the late 1980s and early 1990s), and little or no expansion of the number of seats available in the top sectors of the hierarchy, the college admissions scramble is tighter than ever. Top colleges now admit 10 percent or fewer of their applicants. This has had the effect of making colleges a little lower on the hierarchy more attractive and so, too, more competitive (Athaveley, 2007). A final factor that has fueled these developments is the emergence of a broad national market for colleges. While previously most high-performing students attended college in their home state or region, it is common now for them to apply to and attend colleges across the country (Davies and Hammack, 2005). All of these factors have led students to apply to 10 or even more colleges, again boosting the competitiveness of the admissions process. Demographic trends show that these intense college admissions pressures will ease somewhat in the next few years as the number of high school graduates declines.

Stratification and Equal Opportunity in Higher Education

In the United States, several factors are considered by college admissions officers—high school grades, activities, recommendations, and test scores (Stevens, 2007). Controversy centers on test scores in particular. Those in favor of using standardized test scores in the admissions process argue that scores help screen out students who "can't make it." Critics of the achievement tests argue that the tests do not give an accurate representation of what students have learned, that students who can afford it can be coached to raise their scores, that the tests do not measure what they say they do, and that they are unfair to minority students. The scores of minority students have improved somewhat; on the SAT, scores of most groups rose slightly, as shown in Table 10.1.

In many countries in Europe, Latin America, Africa, Asia, and other parts of the world, one exam for university entrance determines one's future. Pass or fail—simple as that! This has created a category of young people in Japan called "ronin" (Samurai warriors without a lord)—students who failed the exam for the university of their choice and spend an extra year or more studying to

▌Table 10.1	Average Scores on the SAT by Sex and Racial and Ethnic Group 2010			
	Critical Reading	**Mathematical Section**	**Writing**	**Total**
	Score	**Score**	**Score**	
Men	503	534	486	1,523
Women	498	500	498	1,498
American Indian	485	492	467	1,444
Asian, Asian American or Pacific Islander	519	591	526	1,623
African American	429	428	420	1,277
Mexican American	454	467	448	1,369
Puerto Rican	454	452	443	1,349
Other Hispanic or Latino	454	462	447	1,363
White	528	536	516	1,580
All	501	516	492	1,509

Note: Each section of the SAT is scored on a scale from 200 to 800.

Source: Fairtest http://www.fairtest.org/2010-collegebound-seniors-average-sat-scores.

retake the entrance exam. Some students in Japan, however, simply give up the competitive battle for top university placement and go to less prestigious institutions or to work; more often these are children of blue-collar workers, thus perpetuating the existing class system.

Gaining admission to Oxford University in England typifies the process of entrance to elite universities of the world: The university's entrance exam is most important. Next come the British A-level exams, which each high school graduate contemplating college takes. Socioeconomic variables (especially the type of school from which the student graduated) are highly significant in determining university admission. Pressure to open university admission to more students, stimulated by rapid social, economic, and political change in many countries, is forcing governments to consider new models such as the multiversity, to open more positions, and to consider allowing more private universities (Hayhoe, 1995). Partly as a result of the controversy over access, more institutions are adopting open admissions policies, our next topic.

Elite versus Public Colleges

Students from lower socioeconomic backgrounds are most likely to go to colleges with lower selectivity, such as two-year and open-enrollment institutions, regardless of their ability, achievement, and expectations. Although high school students in the United States know that some schools will accept them, fewer middle-class students are enrolling in selective schools. For example, a recent report on the enrollment of students at state flagship universities notes that they are becoming "disproportionately whiter and richer" (Gerald and Haycock, 2006; Haycock, Lynch and Engle, 2010). In general, American higher education is becoming increasingly segregated by students' family income (Mortenson, 2005a).

Elite boarding school students have the highest probability of attending highly selective colleges and universities (61 percent from elite schools versus 39 percent for a general sample of college-bound students) (Karen, 1990, p. 238). Admissions officers at private colleges are working toward diversifying the student populations at their campuses, usually voluntarily, though they have complete autonomy in whom they choose because of their independence from regulations (Farnum, 1997). However, these efforts have caused controversy and raised affirmative action questions.

Admissions and the Courts

Admission of minority students has not always been a voluntary decision by the institution. The government has put pressure on institutions by offering funding for special programs, passing affirmative action legislation, and denying research funds to universities that do not comply with government-set standards in minority admissions and staff hiring.

Increasingly the courts have become involved in major decisions affecting the direction of education at all levels; this sector of the educational systems' environment has taken on increased importance. In higher education, court decisions and their implications have ranged from admissions and affirmative action to financing school sports and questions of students' rights. Two early cases related to equal opportunity demonstrate the role of the courts in the environment of higher education.

What is considered preferential treatment of minorities by some has not gone unchallenged. In 1970–1971, a case was brought by Marco DeFunis, Jr., who was denied admission to the University of Washington law school; he claimed that minority students with lower scores were given preference. The case reached the Supreme Court, which ruled in his favor but left unclear the issue of minority admissions and quota systems.

Admissions officers hoped that the 1978 *Bakke* case would resolve the unanswered questions about minority preferential treatment in minority quotas resulting from the *DeFunis* case. In this case, the medical school at the University of California at Davis set up quotas. Allan Bakke came close to admission, but special applicants with lower scores were admitted. Bakke filed suit, arguing reverse discrimination. The Court supported the idea that institutions may attempt to achieve racial balance through admissions and affirmative action programs. But the

Systems of higher education range from open admissions to highly selective.

idea of protecting individual rights was not to be ignored in admissions; thus, types of race-conscious plans other than quota systems should be adopted. This eagerly awaited decision left almost as many questions unanswered as answered. Postmortems ranged from disappointment that the Court was stepping backward in the push for minority progress, to realization that more cases must be heard to test the ramifications.

Then in March 1996, the U.S. Fifth Circuit Court of Appeals struck down the admissions policy of University of Texas School of Law. In *Hopwood v. State of Texas* the court barred their policy favoring Mexican American and African-American applicants. The result has been a dramatic decline in the number of minority admissions to the school (Diaz, 1997). The ruling has left some states such as Louisiana and Mississippi with conflicting affirmative action directives (Healy, 1998).

Another recent issue facing higher-education admissions that has come under attack is race-based scholarships. A number of institutions have set aside scholarships for minority students to help with recruitment and retention, though these scholarships represent only 5 percent of all scholarships. Because of recent rulings against the practice, many colleges are dropping minority-only scholarships. A case in point is the University of Maryland. The Supreme Court has ruled that their scholarship program for African Americans only is unconstitutional ("Supreme Court," 1995, p. 22). Now some colleges are attempting to comply with the rulings by offering "first-generation student scholarships" that would include some disadvantaged white students as well as minority students (Gose, 1995). Critics argue and evidence indicates that minority enrollments will drop with rulings against race-based scholarships.

Most recently, the Supreme Court ruled in two cases from the University of Michigan. The undergraduate admission process at Michigan added points to the admissions scores of minority students increasing their likelihood of acceptance. Two white applicants who had been denied admissions filed suit against this process (*Jennifer Gratz and Patrick Hamacher v. Lee Bollinger*). At the Law School (*Barbara Grutter v. Lee Bollinger*), race was one of several admissions factors taken into account, but unlike the undergraduate process, there was not a fixed benefit accorded to minority applicants. In its rulings, the Law School's admissions procedures were approved because race was only one factor in a process that considered the whole application. In addition, the Court accepted the argument that diversity in education was an important goal for state systems of higher education and could justify using race as a factor in the admissions process. The Court rejected the undergraduate admissions process, asserting that adding points to improve chances of acceptance was discriminatory because the points were awarded to all minorities, not distributed individually. This was important because our history of racial discrimination that had been used to justify affirmative action policies has been criticized for not applying to all current minority students who have not faced racial segregation. Guaranteeing that this issue will remain with us, the Court asserted that in 25 years there should no longer be a reason to take race into account at all in college admissions (http://www.law.cornell.edu/supct/html/02–241.ZO.html).

Given the difficulty of using affirmative action today, many colleges are exploring ways to make possible higher enrollment rates for students from low-income families. Recently there has been a move to accept more students from lower-income families if qualified. Several universities, including Harvard, the University of Pennsylvania, and Stanford and Davidson College, have adopted policies to award low or free tuition to students whose family income is below $60,000. As many minority students are from low- and lower-income families, this approach would improve both minority and low-income enrollments in higher education. But few colleges and universities are wealthy enough to adopt this policy so its impact will be limited.

> **Applying Sociology to Education:** *How can institutions of higher education provide equal opportunity and be fair to all groups of students?*

CHARACTERISTICS OF HIGHER EDUCATION IN THE UNITED STATES

Higher education is a catchall term for programs offering some academic degree after high school. In general, however, we will not be referring to vocational or occupational training programs in this section.

In selecting our college, we can pick from two-year, four-year, or university systems, public or private. Once we have made our selection, we move into the system where we will remain until either (1) we are graduated after two or four years, (2) we drop out, or (3) we transfer.

There are more than 5,000 institutions of higher education in the United States offering associate and bachelors degrees (NCES, *Digest of Educational Statistics*, 2009, NCES 2010–013). First, sponsorship is an important division, with two main categories—public and private. Within the public category, institutions of higher education exist at the local, state, and even federal level. Most often public institutions are state-sponsored. Locally sponsored institutions tend to be two-year colleges and technical training institutions. More than half of the private institutions are religiously affiliated, usually with Protestant and Roman Catholic parent organizations.

Second, student composition tells us something about the institutions: percentage of males, females, minorities, foreign-speaking students; and age and background of students (see Table 10.2).

Third, types of programs distinguish one institution from another: two-year, four-year, master's or graduate level, Ph.D.-granting, and professional schools such as law or medicine. Many of the institutions develop certain specialty areas or professional schools for which they become well known. Some institutions, especially public, state-sponsored systems, have moved toward multicampus facilities. The public higher education system of California is a case in point, with its 10 university campuses, 23 four-year state universities, and 112 two-year campuses, which can either be terminal or feed into the other parts of the system.

Table 10.2 Racial and Ethnic Background of College Freshmen and Women 1998, 2006, and 2009

Racial and Ethnic Background	1998 (in percent)	2006 (in percent)	2009 (in percent)
American Indian	2.1	2.2	2.5
Asian American	4.0	8.6	8.9
African American	9.4	10.5	11.0
White	82.5	76.5	73.1
Latina(o)	4.5	7.3	11.2
Other	2.3	3.6	3.4

Source: Higher Education Research Institute at UCLA, "The American Freshman: National Norms for Fall 2009."

Within each classification, there may be further variations. For instance, there are many types of professional schools, including

Architecture	Journalism	Optometry
Business	Law	Pharmacy
Dentistry	Library science	Public health
Education	Medicine	Social work
Engineering	Music	Theology
Forestry	Nursing	Veterinary medicine

These schools vary as to size, financial resources, graduate or undergraduate training, relevant affirmative action legislation and sex distribution, and according to specific attributes of the universities with which they are affiliated. Although the variations between systems of higher education are great, what they have in common is their service to students who have completed 12 years of schooling and who are voluntarily furthering their education.

Higher education experienced a period of phenomenal growth and has now leveled off. We look at these trends and their implications next.

Growth of Higher Education

The growth of American higher education since the late nineteenth century (and especially in the 1960s) has been phenomenal when compared with any previous time. Despite the rapid increase in the size of institutions of higher education, the dropout rate has remained about the same throughout the period. Recent data show enrollments of 19,102,814 students (full-time and part-time) in fall of 2008. This number has risen from 13,818,637 in 1990 and 15,312,289 in 2000 (NCES, *Digest of Educational Statistics*, 2009, Table 189). The minority population in these figures is also rising, whereas the white population is dropping slightly.

The School-to-Work Transition and the Credential Crisis

Does everyone have the right to go to college? Do those who do not go to college have a right to work? Who should decide who has the right? And, ultimately, must some people trying to enter college and the job market fail?

The United States does less to help its high school and college graduates prepare for and find jobs than other industrial countries. A number of countries provide stepping stones into jobs—from high school to college or trade school to apprenticeships to jobs. These can be planned economies with a certain number of jobs available, planned transitions from school to work, or planned vocational and technical training, often with apprenticeships included (Buehler and Konietzka, 2010; Kohlrausch and Baas, 2010; Van Houtte and Van Maele, 2010). Those graduating from high school have seen little connection between school and work, yet they must adjust to the demands of the job market. College graduates fare better because they have trained in specific fields, though many of them major in areas in which there is no direct connection to work. Employers need workers with specific skills that new employees often lack. This means employers must go to the effort and expense of training new workers, using supervisors' time to explain and oversee tasks. In addition, employers make extra efforts to keep their skilled employees (Alexander, 2001; Rosenbaum and Binder, 1997).

An issue that affects college graduates is the "credential crisis," which has arisen because graduates can no longer be guaranteed a job after college. Large numbers of college graduates remain unemployed or are returning to graduate school to improve their chances of employment (Bivens et al., 2010). Various new types of credentials are being proposed and requirements for jobs are being raised, not as a result of new educational knowledge, but because of the increased number of people seeking higher-level jobs in the system. Thus, many people are overeducated for the jobs they receive, a phenomenon referred to as the "job gap." Jobs once held by poorly educated people are now held by more highly educated individuals until they can find appropriate jobs for their training. This is in part because the job pool for 2010 graduates is already crowded with 2009 graduates (Talk of the Nation, 2010). Recent research finds that there are even more people overqualified for their jobs than earlier research found, and that they have lower levels of job satisfaction as a result (Vaisey, 2006). But it is no longer rare for a college graduate to be employed as a retail clerk (in a book store, for example, or a Starbucks), something that was uncommon when the college degree itself was uncommon. We have adapted to this change, and, while we lament the apparent lack of appropriate opportunities for all college graduates, this dissatisfaction has not generated much of a movement for change. We will return to this topic at the end of Chapter 13.

The inflation of credentials is closely related to the economic and stratification system; students want higher credentials to get better jobs to have higher status, and in fact college graduates in the United States earn nearly $22,000 more than those with just a high school diploma ($55,700 versus $33,800), and their earnings increase more rapidly (College Board, 2010). However, the image of college and university as "a sure route to the better life" has lost ground (Karen and Dougherty, 2005). The value of a college degree remains because of the large decline in the job market value of the high school diploma, though not all college graduates benefit equally (Brand and Xie, 2010). In fact, many college graduates accept positions unrelated to their college majors. The current economic picture challenges the functionalist interpretation of expanding educational opportunities to meet societal needs. Tensions produced by the presence of large numbers of dissatisfied graduates could, according to conflict theorists such as Collins, mentioned earlier, force a restructuring of the economic system, and in turn, of the educational system.

Applying Sociology to Education: *Should everyone have access to higher education, or are we overeducating the population? Who should make these decisions?*

FUNCTIONS OF THE HIGHER EDUCATION SYSTEM

Higher education serves certain functions or purposes in society. What these purposes are or should be is a matter of debate and may cause conflict between parents, educators, students, government officials, and other groups in society. In the following discussion we consider the university as a community, the functions of the university, and conflicts over functions.

The University as a Community

One way to consider the functions of the university is through the concept of community: what members have in common, the division of labor, and the interdependence among members (Sanders, 1973, p. 57). Universities are communities with an overall academic program, centralized physical settings, a form of governance, and a range of services. One can eat, sleep, and work there. Perhaps the best way to describe the modern university is as one institution fulfilling numerous functions.

The full university, with its expanse of programs, research facilities, graduate and professional schools, and support services, has set the standards for all academic systems of higher education. Yet it is caught between contradictory goals, especially in the area of organizational structure and autonomy. Bonds such as shared beliefs, attitudes, and values, which traditionally held the university together, have been disintegrating as more formal structures, rules, and procedures have replaced them. Questions have been raised about some basic values of the university community—the nature of the academic programs; what kinds of factual knowledge, values and beliefs, and practical skills should be taught; the meaning of freedom of inquiry for students and scholars; and what should be included in the activities of a university. As the curriculum has been expanded to include more and more subjects, the kind of consensus around fundamental academic questions that once may have existed has become more and more difficult to create and maintain.

The Function of Research

The expansion of knowledge is a generally accepted purpose of higher education, especially in universities with strong research components. In the sciences and engineering, the direction and extent of research programs have been determined largely by the financial support provided by business, industry, and government. This influence on the direction of research efforts has led some researchers to ask, "knowledge for whom?" Some research, especially in pure rather than applied science, is being eliminated because it is not a priority in this time of financial cutbacks. This could lead to future gaps in our knowledge, some argue. The cutting back of state and government funding from the university's environment will significantly affect research institutions dependent on such funding to support research scholars, students, and other departments ("The American Research University," 1993), making them even more dependent on private and philanthropic funding. Certainly since the mid-twentieth century, research has grown as a function of higher education, no longer concentrated primarily in big research universities, but is important everywhere with the exception of the community college. Many states have attempted to use their higher education system to stimulate economic development (Brint, 2002).

The Function of Teaching

Concerns regarding the balance of teaching and research roles of professors dominate institutions of higher education, especially those with graduate programs. Stanford University, followed by Cornell and others, took the lead in the early 1990s when they announced that evaluation of teaching would be a significant part of the promotion process. A number of disciplines are producing teaching materials and promoting professional development in teaching. Professional schools are also putting more emphasis on the art of teaching.

Increasingly faculty at all types of colleges and universities are expected to publish their work. Academic publishing involves peer review, in which other specialists in the subject matter of the research are directly involved in the editorial selection process (usually anonymously), assuring that the quality of the research has been positively reviewed by other experts (peers). Thus, a record of successful publishing means a faculty member's work has been reviewed and approved by other experts in the field, a judgment that cannot always be reliably done at the home institution. One's teaching, however, can best be evaluated locally. Untenured faculty, with usually no more than six years of employment before an up or out tenure decision is made, put their effort into research and publication, teaching and possibly service on committees. Publications are now required at most types of four-year colleges, and teaching is sometimes in second place (Fairweather, 1993).

Beginning in the early 1990s, however, another voice has been heard calling for a return to an emphasis on teaching and on the priority of educating students (Boyer, 1990). Included in criticisms of faculty work is an overemphasis on the knowledge production (research and publishing) function over the educational (teaching) function of colleges and universities. Recently, a commission appointed by the Secretary of Education issued a report that laments the rising cost of higher education and the lack of "accountability mechanisms to ensure that colleges succeed in educating students" (U.S. Department of Education, 2006, p. x). The commission calls for reforms that lead to "high quality instruction while improving efficiency in order to be more affordable to students" (U.S. Department of Education, 2006, p. xi), and seeks common measures of what students learn while in college.

One response to these calls for new ways to assess student learning is the Collegiate Learning Assessment (CLA), a test created by the Council for Aid to Education. The 90-minute test asks students to draw on a set of documents concerning a topic, including quantitative and other forms of information, and write a two-page memorandum that describes and analyzes the arguments relevant to the topic. Unlike multiple-choice questions, the CLA aims to measure a student's ability to assess different kinds of evidence and to make an argument (Glenn, 2010). Given over several semesters, the test can be seen as a measure of the improvement in students due to the experiences they have had in college. Some of the research on the test questions how much students are really learning (Arum and Roksa, 2011). These researchers find that students' scores improve more if they take courses that require more than the usual amounts of reading and writing, a program of studies uncommon on many campuses.

The Function of Service

Another function or purpose of the university is that of public service in the wider community. The faculty are expected to disseminate knowledge developed in research programs through such channels as publications, the media, and teaching and lecturing. This diffusion of ideas has wide repercussions, even to the point of stimulating social change in countries around the world. The degree to which faculty scholars should become involved in attempts to sway opinions through social awareness or act to bring about changes is a matter of debate. However, students in many colleges are involved in community service work, sometimes as a required part of their education. The rise of "service learning" on many college campuses has widely increased the number of students involved in off-campus service as well as the amount of time they devote to these activities.

The Function of the "National Security State"

Higher education, sometimes assumed to operate autonomously, is, in fact, central to the training of individuals for high-level technical human resource requirements; this is seen by some as necessary to national security and for a developing economy. The university power structure is headed by boards of trustees who, some argue, serve corporate interests; these interests impact on the organization of universities (Rhoades and Slaughter, 1991). Liaisons between universities and the corporate world, created by graduates employed in these organizations and research funded by private interests, provide evidence for the links. The debate continues about whether this liaison is constructive for educational institutions, businesses, and society.

University professors create ideas in laboratories; some of these ideas become commercial products. Structures for transferring the technology from labs to commercial use are most often controlled by university administrations, who use the idea of "the public good" to control the transfer; university faculty, however, hold that scientific norms should guide the transfer of technology.

How the information is transferred affects who receives credit, patents, and financial benefits (Rhoades and Slaughter, 1991, p. 75). The control over the intellectual property created by faculty research funded by private sources as well as with public money has become an important issue as some inventions such as new drugs have become extremely valuable (Blumenstyk, 2007, April 6; also see Kirp, 2003).

Conflicts over the University's Function

It is a crisp autumn Saturday afternoon. The stands are packed for the big game, the traditional rivalry that will determine who goes to an important college bowl game. College athletics is big business worth millions of dollars, and the issues surrounding athletics have become major targets in the conflicts over the functions of a university. For universities with successful athletic programs, sports can be a big moneymaker and attracts new students. Critics argue that athletics is not part of the major function of universities—the acquisition and transmission of knowledge, service, or other traditional functions. This case illustrates the conflict over the academic function of universities versus a big-business orientation (Dowling, 2007).

The Academic Function of Universities versus Business Functions

Issues that have been raised in recent years illustrate the conflicts. The "athlete as a hunk of meat" is one of these issues. Scouts and recruiters see star high school players and sign contracts. It is illegal to offer rewards or bribes such as cars or fancy living, but it has been known to happen. What is more common is that pressure to succeed in athletics is so great that there is temptation to skirt the rules. Reports of grade fixing at several institutions have caused scandals and led to sanctions against individuals and institutions. Young men and women with weak academic backgrounds may be recruited to compete, but they sometimes fail to make progress toward a degree. Minority students are particularly affected. In recent years, however, beginning college student athletes have been entering as first-year students with higher credentials than in the past, and their graduation rate after six years is 63 percent compared to 61 percent of all students at Division I institutions.

Statistics collected by the National Collegiate Athletic Association (NCAA) (http://web1. ncaa.org/app_data/instAggr2008/1_0.pdf) show that African-American athletes attending Division I colleges are less likely to graduate (53 percent) when compared to all scholarship athletes (67 percent). However, a higher percentage of African-American scholarship athletes graduate in six years than all other African-American students (53 per cent versus 45 percent). Over 90 percent of Division 1A football teams in the Football Bowl Subdivision for 2009–2010 season graduated more than 50 percent of their players. However, the gap between the rates for whites and African Americans remains large: While 22 teams graduated less than one-half of their African-American football athletes, only two teams had such a low rate for their white players (The Institute for Diversity and Ethics in Sport, 2006; http://www.tidesport.org/Grad%20Rates/ 2009-10_Bowl_APR_GSR_Study%20UPDATED.pdf).

Using participant observation, two sociologists spent several years studying athletes at a Division I college, observing the conflicting roles of players. Most players come to college expecting to play ball, have a social life, earn a degree, and perhaps to go on to the National Basketball Association (NBA) or other professional leagues. Many quickly become disillusioned, however, and some feel exploited by the fans and even the coaches, who are interested in them only as long as they can perform well. The problem is that many athletes come poorly prepared for academics, and training is all-consuming. They are often housed separately, isolated from campus, and made to feel like outcasts. Some of the middle-class athletes graduate, but few recruited from the lower classes do so (Adler and Adler, 1991).

Another problem is the lack of support athletes get once they enter college. In some institutions they are used as long as they can play for the team; then they are dropped, leaving them little future. Several proposals have been made to curb the "meat market" phenomenon. In order to be considered a "qualifier," that is to play during their first year, starting in 2008, athletes had to have graduated from high school, completed a core curriculum (primarily English, science, and math) of 16 academic courses, and have a combination of grade point and SAT or ACT score specified in the NCAA academic eligibility standards. The NCAA uses a sliding scale to judge GPA/test score qualifications. For example, if a student has a 3.5 GPA, the SAT score needs to be 410 or above and the ACT 38 or above. Since they only count the verbal and math sections of the SAT, and the minimum score is 200, a high GPA is seen to compensate for a low test score. As the GPA falls, the SAT/ACT score requirement increases, so that a student with a 2.2 GPA needs a SAT score of 940 or above or a 79 or higher in the ACT (http://web1.ncaa.org/ECWR2/NCAA_EMS/pdf/Quick_Reference_Sheet_for_IE_Standards-6-18-09.pdf). Many coaches and athletics boosters see these rising academic requirements as disadvantaging minority athletes. Others see them as a means to combat the exploitation of these students (Dowling, 2007).

One proposal is to let athletes play five years, giving them more time to complete their college work. Programs for special tutorials, restrictions on "the season" and practice time, and counseling services are being put in place in many schools and could help poorly achieving students. Tutoring and mentoring programs at many universities are meant to supplement the athletes' programs; some help, some don't. Some of those athletes who flunk out or drop out end up sweeping floors or doing other menial labor. The academic "teaching" function is brought into question when emphasis is on business or income-producing activities, such as big-time athletics.

What Type of Curriculum?

Conflicts persist over curricular issues. On the one hand are those who would have the university retain its traditional focus on a liberal education in the arts and sciences, which transmits to students knowledge for its own sake and produces a well-rounded person. On the other hand are those who advocate a practical, career-focused training that stresses the social utility of the knowledge transmitted. These conflicts are particularly relevant today, when universities and colleges face periods of sometimes flat enrollment growth, and when economic conditions put pressures on students to get a degree they can "use"—one that will be functional and lead directly to employment. Most colleges still require "general education" courses of first- and second-year students, whatever their major will be. Many schools use a distribution model for these courses, requiring students to have several courses from different categories, including sciences, mathematics, social sciences, and humanities. Some schools have developed a set of these courses that are required of everyone; there may be no choices for some of the general education courses. These schools hark back to the nineteenth century when there were few if any choices in a college's entire curriculum. Only a few elite schools may be able to resist the pressures to diversify the curriculum and introduce more applied or practical programs as opposed to "pure" arts and sciences. For most institutions, ability to adapt to changing or conflicting environmental demands may determine survival (Kraatz and Zajac, 1996). Occupationally-oriented majors account for about 60 percent of all degrees and over 80 percent at many colleges and universities (Brint et al., 2005).

Societal conflicts are reflected in debates over curriculum content and pressure to be "politically correct." Racism, discrimination, prejudice, intolerance, differential treatment, sexual harassment, and homophobia are all hot topics on university campuses. Extremes range from those who would throw out the "old" curriculum and replace it with entirely new materials sensitive to abuses of the past, to "hate speech," and to racial or sexual incidents on campuses. The debate is between competing responsibilities to protect freedom of speech and to protect students, faculty, and staff who are victims of hate crimes (Munitz, 1991, p. 4). The Supreme Court has ruled in one decision that "hate speech" is free speech, but other court rulings challenge use of such words as the "N" word by teachers and students except in literature (Zirkel, 1999). Recent campaigns against "killer coke" and for a green campus and sustainability are other topics that have engaged students.

Most colleges are "internationalizing" their curricula to include Third World and environmental concerns; the numbers of students majoring in these fields are also increasing (Dodge, 1990, p. A31). Requirements to engage in community service show a curricular trend toward service learning and citizenship development. Increasingly, too, study abroad is becoming common and sometimes required. Some colleges are even developing branch campuses in other countries (Altbach and Knight, 2006). New York University just opened up a free-standing branch campus in Abu Dhabi (http://www.insidehighered.com/layout/set/print/news/2010/06/21/nyu), during the same year that Michigan State University closed its outpost in the United Arab Emirates. George Mason University also opened and closed a campus in this region. It is not automatic that these projects succeed.

Conflicts over purposes can also be seen in the changing roles of various members of the university community. For instance, in the 1950s administrators were expected to watch over their students like parents; hence the term *in loco parentis.* Dormitory hours were rigid, lights-out regulations were enforced, separation of the sexes in living quarters was expected, and the atmosphere was one that not only perpetuated an adolescent dependence but also carried the home structure to the school. Following student discontent and attacks on the university administration in the 1960s, most administrators gradually reduced or eliminated this role. With new technology, faculty roles are changing as well, as described in Box 10.1.

BOX 10.1

The Future of Higher Education: Case of the Virtual University

Imagine a university that comes to all citizens who have a desire to learn and wish to take courses, from high school age to senior citizens. The setting can be the home, a library, or any place with Internet access.

No need to imagine! In Kentucky and several other states, this scenario is reality. Faced with the changing state, national, and global economy that made former occupations in coal mining and tobacco growing obsolete, Kentucky's virtual university is being used as one solution to the problem of unemployment and poverty.

How does the process work? The virtual university staff of 20, sitting in an office with cubicles and computers, arranges for services to be delivered online to students around the state and beyond. Public and private universities in Kentucky offer up to three-quarters of required degree credits online. Other services include contracts with professional designers of courses, online library resources, student counseling services, and bookstore services.

The role of faculty changes from lecturing to mentoring—from discussing issues and problems with students to utilizing services such as online writing assistance, and, of course, grading student work.

(Continued)

(Continued)

Concerns about lack of face-to-face interaction are being addressed by seeing the professor or class members on the computer screen.

In the virtual university, students as consumers have control over the process of learning, are able to register and carry out all tasks online, move at an individually comfortable pace, watch and interact with professional online courses that include projects and assignments, read the text from online bookstores, and interact with the professor online. According to Susman, president of Kentucky Commonwealth Virtual University, virtual universities involve an "orbital shift." No longer do students need to be on-site, running around between offices to register or to obtain professor permissions and parking passes. No longer are they concerned with getting to class on time—the Internet has 24-hour access.

Looking for recreation as a part of the college experience? Join the virtual football team. Michigan Virtual University has challenged Kentucky's team to a match. Other opportunities for games such as chess, book clubs, and chatrooms in courses are being created as you read this; the possibilities are endless.

The bottom line is that the university experience for some students is likely to be a very different one in the future with technology leading the way. The KY Virtual College has grown considerably since its founding (http://www.kyvu.org/).

Source: Taken in part from a lecture by Mary Beth Susman, President, Kentucky Commonwealth University, August 11, 2000, Bethesda, MD, at the meeting of the Society for Applied Sociology. See their website at: http://www.kyvc.org/

Applying Sociology to Education: *Should universities meet the needs of the community, remain independent of community needs, or find another option?*

HIGHER EDUCATION AS AN ORGANIZATION

Higher Education Structure and the Bureaucratic Model: Does It Work?

Universities face particular contradictions when trying to run on a bureaucratic or business model, yet that is what most are doing. The hierarchical charts of universities may resemble business organizations, but most of the similarities stop there.

1. There are two distinct structures in the university: the flat academic structure and the hierarchical administrative structure.
2. Many of the employees are knowledge specialists, professionals who by tradition expect autonomy and academic freedom; they may have only temporary loyalty to the institution but permanent allegiance to their disciplines.
3. Colleges are to a large extent detached from the community and larger society in pursuing their primary activities—transmitting knowledge and conducting research.
4. Teaching and research require individual faculty autonomy over the end product.
5. Policy decision making is spread throughout the organization, and students sometimes have a substantial voice in issues.

Let us consider the problems of hierarchy and decision making in greater detail.

THE DUAL HIERARCHY. Academic institutions have two hierarchies. The *academic structure* of the university, with its many departments and programs, has one form of hierarchy, usually based on rank and tenure. Although faculty members hold differing ranks, their formal status within the university is the same. However, informal influence, power, responsibilities, and salary may differ across institutions. The *administrative structure* approximates more closely the business model and Weber's bureaucratic division of labor. At the top of the hierarchy are the board of trustees, the president, and other top administrators, including deans. Other administrative personnel carry out diverse functions, providing health services, bookstores, food services, building and grounds maintenance, financial services, and counseling.

The structural looseness of the university, with its focus on academic freedom, may generate conflict with centralized decision making. The professional faculty expect to make decisions in their areas of expertise and resent others usurping this power or making rules that infringe on this "right"; this is especially true in the area of hiring, promotion, retention of faculty, and curriculum matters. Once faculty members are granted tenure, a process that begins with their peers but includes the president and board of trustees, their independence from administrative decisions is increased. Finally, there is inherent conflict between providing a good education and running an administratively economical and efficient operation—as is called for in business or a bureaucratic model. Nevertheless, the for-profit sector of higher education has been expanding— The University of Phoenix, for example, with classrooms in office buildings and strip malls across the country, is now the largest institutions of higher education in the United States. Distance learning, too, is on the rise (see, for example, Jaschik, 2007).

The difficult times that the economy of the world is facing in the last several years has had its effects on higher education. Many universities have seen their endowments fall and state appropriations decline, sometimes very steeply. Not only have colleges and universities suffered, but corporate giving is down and many foundations have found their own endowments in decline, leading to fewer and smaller gifts to higher education (Miller and Fabrikant, 2008).

These problems and inconsistencies have been accentuated by the rapid increase in size and corresponding administrative complexity of the "multiversity." With added departments, programs, and research components, the administrative structures increase in complexity along with the academic structure.

THE UNIVERSITY HIERARCHICAL STRUCTURE AND DECISION MAKING.   Despite the incongruities, it is useful to use characteristics of the bureaucratic model to describe the university, because this model is closer than any other to the realities of the situation. There are seven levels within the higher-education hierarchical structure.

1. *Department.* The department is an administrative unit with a head or chair who may be appointed or elected, or the position may rotate among department members. The chair is accountable to both department members and higher-level administrators. The position has inherent role conflict, because a chair must both support faculty and sit in judgment of them for salary increases and, sometimes, promotions. Departments are hierarchically structured, the usual ranks being instructor, assistant professor, associate professor, and professor. Power and decision making for the unit are usually distributed among members, who use democratic procedures to make major unit decisions. An increasing number of faculty are employed in non-tenure bearing positions—that is they are not eligible for tenure and are on term contracts. Some are full-time, others are part-time, or adjunct faculty. Their role in department, school, and university decision making varies widely and is an increasingly important issue as their numbers increase, as we noted above.

2. *College.* Several related disciplines are grouped as a college with a dean as administrative head. Professional schools in universities have similar status. At this level of the administrative hierarchy, decisions are made about finances, salaries, scheduling, new programs, and so forth, which affect all unit parts.

3. *Administration.* The president or chancellor, vice-president, deans, and assistants may or may not be active faculty members. They have responsibility for various aspects of the university, including academic matters, student services, and financial matters. Usually those overseeing academic issues and faculty have had experience as faculty members and often as department chairs. But many of the important aspects of higher education, such as the registrar's office, financial aid office, and bursar's office, have little connection to academic work and are run much like a nonacademic business.

4. *Faculty representative bodies.* Faculty councils or senates composed of representatives from the various colleges and schools have decision-making or advisory power over academic issues.

5. *Board of trustees.* These laypersons from the community have ultimate legal responsibility. Members are usually selected through election, by other board members, or through appointment by state governors or other bodies for public institutions. Most boards will give their formal approval to recommendations of the institution's president and faculty senate. Central committees have been formed as coordinating structures for some multicampus universities. These "superboards" have ultimate control just as boards of trustees, but they remove decision making even further from the faculty and individual campus (Clark, 1976).

6. *Regional accrediting associations.* There are six voluntary associations around the country that evaluate institutions' achievements in comparison with their goals, using professionals from within the regions: North Central, North West, New England, Middle States, South, and West. The attempt is not to equalize or standardize institutions, but to help institutions achieve the standards they set for themselves. Recent concerns about quality and accountability, however, have led to efforts to strengthen the hand of regional and national accreditors (U.S. Department of Education, *A Test of Leadership,* 2006). In addition there are many professional accrediting agencies for specific fields, such as accounting, medicine, and the law.

7. *National organizations.* Many countries have national coordination of public institutions. Although there is no formal national control of decision making in the United States, the federal government does wield its influence in many ways. To some extent a national educational policy has been developed in response to international pressures and competition, and national needs in areas of economics, politics, and the military. Federal funding has had a major influence on what research an institution pursues, and it may constitute the financial support of entire programs in the university. Student financial aid is another important source of revenue for most campuses; changing eligibility requirements is another way the federal government can influence higher education practices across the country. Many institutions would suffer severe crises if they lost federal support.

CONTROL AND DECISION MAKING.   Major decisions are made or approved by the institution's president and board of trustees. The multiplicity of diverse programs is coordinated through the administrative hierarchy. Although the number of coordinating structures has been increasing, demands also are increasing for decentralized decision making, with power held by individual units.

Lower-level participants in the university wield power that is not always recognized officially but that is influential in decision making. For instance, office workers have access to and control over people, information, and technology. Many office workers are irreplaceable because of the knowledge they hold. However, their compensation is seldom commensurate with their subtle power (Reyes and McCarty, 1990).

Students have varying degrees of power in the decision-making structure. They are with the organization for a short time; they bring new perspectives; they pass through and leave their mark. Because of their short stay in the institution, students are not usually primary decision makers, but they may provide much-needed impetus for evaluation and change of the status quo. Of course, students may make their voices heard in many ways, including through organizing and protest. Though not as common as during the antiwar movements in the 1960s, student movements remain a potentially powerful means of influencing the direction of individual campuses and higher education more generally.

Applying Sociology to Education: *Can you identify areas of conflict between the university hierarchical structure and the business model?*

ROLES IN HIGHER EDUCATION

Each of us has a role in the system of higher education. This is only one of our many roles, and herein lies one of the problems for higher education, as for any organization—it must compete for the loyalty of members who have multiple role obligations. A student may have family, work, and other role obligations. Faculty members have multiple loyalties, which lead to problems for the organization. Keep in mind the dilemma of conflicting role obligations as we discuss major roles in the system of higher education.

Roles in Higher Education: The Clients

Without students there would be no institutions of higher education, and most professors would be out of work. Students are clients of the system, buying a service, and members of the system, playing an integral part in its functioning. At different times students have held different degrees of power in the system, from an ineffectual group that comes and goes and has little real power to a group that, by their choices, determines which faculty members, programs, and even universities will survive.

The students of the 1950s were a cautious "silent generation." By the 1960s, students began to demand a major role in the governance of universities and other institutions and to create pressures for change. This politically active student population flexed its muscles with the Free Speech Movement at Berkeley; it went on, in greater strength, to the Vietnam War protests in the late 1960s and 1970s. What was remarkable about the revolt of the 1960s was that the youth culture profoundly impacted other members of the higher-education community with ideas and practices then adopted by adults. Changes initiated by students affected all members of higher education because of their reciprocal role involvements.

Through the baby-boom years, college enrollments expanded dramatically; then came the bust and retrenchments. Between 1979 and 1985, the number of 18-year-old high school graduates decreased by a half-million. Colleges feared that there would not be enough students to sustain them, but increasing recruitment among nontraditional students, a recession that kept students nearer their home institutions, and increases in the number of high school graduates attending colleges forestalled disaster for many small institutions. College marketing budgets have increased dramatically, using direct mail, videos, telephone contacts, invitations to visit, and scholarships to academically talented students for recruitment. Ironically, at a time when it seems that underrepresented groups might have an advantage, many colleges did not lower but increased their admissions requirements and expectations, recruiting students with high SATs and those from wealthier areas rather than poor, disenfranchised minority students.

More than 19.1 million students enrolled in higher education for the fall 2008 semester, up from 15.3 million for the fall 2000 semester. Private college enrollments were also up, from 3.6 million to 5.1 million for the same periods (NCES, *Digest of Educational Statistics*, 2009, Table 189). Fluctuations in enrollments are caused by many factors, including the numbers of college-age students in the population. For students of college age, 1996 was a record low year in the 1990s, but future enrollments are expected to grow (NCES, *Digest*, 2006, Table 3). The number of high school graduates is about to decline, however, lowering some of the admissions pressures so prominent in recent years. The major change in higher education enrollments, however, is in the for-profit, or proprietary, sector. Encouraged by large increases in federal support over the last decade for college students, these schools, including many occupational and trade schools, but also large multicampus academic enterprises such as Phoenix University and Kaplan University, tripled in size from an enrollment of 450,000 in the fall of 2000 to 1,469,142 in the fall of 2008 (NCES, *Digest of Educational Statistics*, 2009, Table 189). This is an important development which has taken place quite quickly and needs thorough study (Wilson, 2010).

The profile of the typical college student is becoming more diversified, with older nontraditional students, minority students, and married students attending college in greater numbers. In 1965, only 4.8 percent of all U.S. college students were African American. One percent of law students were African American. These numbers have changed dramatically over the past 30 years (Bowen and Bok, 1998). In the fall of 2008, African-American enrollees made up close to 13.5 percent of college enrollments, whereas just over 11.5 percent were Hispanic (NCES, *Digest of Educational Statistics*, 2009, Table 227). Native American enrollments also rose, and today there are 23 tribally controlled colleges in the United States.

At 28 selective colleges, 75 percent of African-American students graduated within six years, and 4 percent more graduated from schools to which they had transferred (Bowen and Bok, 1998). These percentages are higher than for many other groups. Ninety percent of African Americans in professional schools complete their training and earn twice what African-American men with bachelor's degrees earn. Despite the success of some students who would not have been admitted without affirmative action, the courts have changed some laws to deny special consideration.

Gender and Race in Higher Education

The number of women attending college in the United States has doubled since the 1970s. In fact, in 2010 college women outnumbered men by 10.9 million (57.4 percent) to 8.18 million (42.6 percent). Part of the increase results from nontraditional-age women returning to college. But the gap in enrollments is receiving wide attention. A hope for some institutions of higher education with weak enrollments lies in attracting women from nontraditional-age categories. In recent years, this group has been a target for admissions officers. These women are already entering, or returning to, college in large numbers. There are more than 1 million "reentry women" in higher education. Many reentry women are attempting to fulfill two sets of expectations: family roles and educational roles. Changes in family status often require that they go back to school. Survey data indicate that most reentry women are committed to their studies and have confidence and energy. Several colleges, including elite women's colleges, admit reentry women as a percentage of their college classes and provide special programs for them.

The social and economic consequences of this shift in levels of attained education are only beginning to be perceived. Many colleges are concerned that the number of males enrolled has reached a critical point. Several colleges that did not have football as an athletic option have introduced it in an effort to make their school more attractive to male applicants (Pennington, 2006).

There is evidence, however, that women's participation in higher education in noncore developing nations is being hindered by multinational corporations, which hire men in high-status occupations, thus creating less demand for educated women (Clark, 1992).

Women earn more graduate degrees in the humanities, social and behavioral sciences, education, and health professions, and men earn more degrees in natural sciences, computer sciences and engineering, and business management. Although there has been significant converging of the majors of men and women (Jacobs, 1996), the differences are particularly striking in engineering and computer science (Olsen, 1999). Since math achievement is the gateway to many high-paying careers in the sciences and engineering, women's achievement in math and science courses at all levels of education continues to interest researchers. In college, women's and men's grades are similar in math courses through calculus, though fewer women enroll in these classes (Bridgeman and Wendler, 1991, p. 283).

The median annual income of year-round, full-time male workers 25 years and over in 2008 with a bachelor's degree was $65,800; those with associate college degrees averaged $50,150. Women in the same categories averaged $47,030 with bachelor's degrees and $36,760 with associate's degrees (NCES, *Digest of Educational Statistics*, 2009, Table 384). Though factors such as time out for childrearing can be taken into consideration, women continue to receive lower income for similar levels of education.

Most women students seem reasonably satisfied with their college experience, including professors, other students, and classroom and study conditions. Students at all-women's colleges tend to be very satisfied with their experiences. They perceive their ability to acquire skills high, and their educational aspirations, including the likelihood of attending graduate school, are also high (Smith, 1990, p. 181). Yet the number of these schools continues to decline, as few female high school seniors express an interest in all-women's colleges (Salomone, 2007).

Many colleges are offering more non-degree courses for adult men and women through continuing education or lifelong learning programs. Not only do these programs enable interested adults to learn for pleasure, but they also help offset budget deficits in programs being run at a financial loss. Courses are taken by a wide range of adults—"do-it-yourselfers"; senior citizens; those who have a specific motivation, such as learning a language for a holiday trip abroad; and those who wish to prepare for college reentry, to have contact with others, to increase mental stimulation, or just to have fun (survey by author of students in continuing education classes).

Although women are gaining ground in academic settings, the story for other minorities is mixed. In 2010, almost one-third of the nation was African American or Hispanic. By 2050, the non-Hispanic white population is projected to be 52.8 percent of the total U.S. population (U.S. Census Bureau, 2000). Yet the numbers of minority groups in higher education do not reflect this diversity (see Table 10.2).

FACTORS RELATED TO MINORITY STUDENT SUCCESS OR FAILURE.   Student success in higher education is based not only on individual goals, motivations, and abilities but also on social class, race, sex, and early labeling. "Success" or "failure" begins early in life with the different advantages and disadvantages their backgrounds provide and labeling of children. By the high school years, teachers, counselors, students, and parents have a fair idea of the student's academic achievements. Tracking into college-preparatory or vocational courses is often an easy decision. Conflicts arise for those who have high aspirations but little support in the form of teacher recommendations, test results, counselor evaluations, and parental encouragement. Once in institutions of higher education, students report barriers to learning and success from their own backgrounds (financial problems and child care issues), and from the institution (Ballantine and Feltey, 2007) (see Box 10.2).

BOX 10.2

"Barriers to Student Learning"

Why is learning sometimes tough if not impossible? This is exactly what researchers Feltey and Ballantine wanted to know. From a sample of over 1,000 randomly selected students, the researchers learned about the major barriers to student learning. These barriers fall into several categories: personal student issues, role conflicts, issues with teachers, environmental issues, and course and classroom issues. The following is a summary of major factors; factors under each heading are listed in order of importance:

Personal Student Issues: Time, money, tuition, interest in subjects, learning disabilities, being tired, being ill-prepared, not doing homework, getting behind in courses, poor reading skills or not liking to read, laziness/procrastination, poor time management, difficulty focusing/not paying attention, not enough sleep, and long driving time.

Role Conflicts: Sick relatives/children, work conflicts, personal life/romance, family responsibilities, socializing, recreation, sports, and distractions (TV, video games, and cards).

Issues with Teachers: Poor/boring teachers, impersonal professors, inaccessible professors, foreign professors, teaching styles, teachers unwilling to be wrong or who will not answer questions, students who ask too many questions or are disruptive, and long lectures.

Environmental Issues: Uncomfortable chairs, noise level in class, temperature in classrooms, and parking.

Course and Classroom Issues: Tests/exams poorly constructed, only one method of evaluation or one assignment/test, too many students in class, classes scheduled at inconvenient times, stressful tests, Internet distraction, multiple assignments due at the same time, workload of classes, fast pace of classes, boring books, group projects, and uneven ability of students in class.

Class attendance also sheds light on barriers. About 15 percent of the students indicated they never skip class. Close to 60 percent miss 1–5 classes in a semester, 13 percent miss 5–10 classes, and 8 percent miss 10–15 times. The most frequent reasons for missing classes were illness, followed by studying for other classes, attendance not required, and "teacher is boring."

By understanding barriers to learning, students, faculty, and administrators can work to eliminate the causes of problems for students in higher education.

Source: Study by Jeanne Ballantine and Kathy Feltey, 2007.

Applying Sociology to Education: *Think about barriers to your own education. Do they parallel the above factors?*

Students who are not prepared for the college experience face extra challenges. Basic skills in reading, writing, and math, plus lack of college-preparatory curricula, can put students "at risk" in college. Early diagnosis and remedial action to build basic skills of students while they are still in high school can help students achieve, and many colleges are offering special services in remedial and developmental education.

Students with limited economic means are eight times less likely to graduate from college than other students (Levine, 1995), and options for funding are becoming more limited with government and campus cutbacks ("The Widening Gap . . . ," 1996). Almost 75 percent of students from the top income quartile completed a bachelor's degree in 2003, while almost 28 percent from the third quartile, about 13 percent of the second quartile, and 8.6 percent of the lowest income quartile were able to achieve this degree (Mortenson, 2005b). Many of those in the lowest income quartile are also minority students who make up 33.3 percent of higher-education enrollments (NCES, *Digest of Educational Statistics*, 2009, Table 227).Of those students receiving a bachelors degree in 2006–2007, 72.1 percent were white, 9.6 percent were black, 7.5 percent were Hispanic, and 6.9 percent were Asian/Pacific Islanders. American Indians comprised .007 percent of the total (NCES, *Digest of Educational Statistics*, 2009, Table 287). The difference often begins in earlier years of schooling, and many universities find themselves offering remedial courses for low-achieving students with weak skills. Urban universities in particular are being hit by underfunding and cutbacks in services, making them unable to respond effectively to many minority students' needs. Combined with increases in tuition, and increases in the level of student debt in the shift from grants to loans, many students are facing significant financial pressures.

Many minority students who enter college fail to complete their degree work, not because of ability level, but because of poor academic preparation, financial issues, and campus climates. As an example, Latino college students who had memberships in religious or social organizations and who had contact with other students outside of class in their first two years of college were more likely to continue in college, compared to those who faced a hostile racial climate (Hurado and Carter, 1997). Those who do graduate have lower grades and less chance of going on to graduate school (Steele, 1992). States such as California with large Latino populations (almost 50 percent of schoolchildren) are concerned about raising the education and achievement levels for the benefit of the state's economy (Lempert, 2010). The number of Doctor's degrees granted to African Americans rose slightly between 1997 and 1998 from 4.5 percent of all doctorates to 6.1 percent in 2007–2008 (NCES, *Digest of Educational Statistics*, 2009, Table 291). The percentage of doctorates earned by other minority groups is shown in Table 10.3.

Even with adequate preparation, many minority students feel undervalued, stigmatized, and vulnerable. It is as though others look for reasons to "confirm" racial inferiority (Steele, 1992). College is an impersonal, unfamiliar, even hostile world for many. It challenges self-respect and self-esteem, especially if one is insecure about one's ability to cope with college work and believes that others are questioning that ability too (Kraft, 1991). Racial incidents on campuses such as hate speech hinder efforts to integrate African Americans and other minorities and to improve their self-esteem. One explanation is that these incidents are sparked by the competition for scarce resources—grades, acceptance to competitive programs, graduation, and ultimately jobs and income. Recent research suggests that policies and practices that teach

Table 10.3 Characteristics of U.S. Citizen Recipients of Doctorates, 2008 (all fields)

	(in percent)
American Indian	0.4
Asian	8.3
African American	6.6
Hispanic	5.7
White	75.4
Other	3.7

Source: The Chronicle of Higher Education Almanac, 2010,
http://chronicle.com/article/Characteristics-of-Recipients/124009/

first-year students as early as possible how to use campus resources, that make the classroom into a community, that develop early warning systems to support students when they need help, and that connect each student with an activity or positive role model can promote higher levels of student success (Kuh et al., 2007).

STUDENT SUBCULTURES OR PEER GROUPS.   Students belong to peer groups, which have great influence on their activities, interests, and academic success. Some years ago, a typology of student subcultures or peer groups was developed by Burton Clark and Martin Trow (1966). Students were categorized into one of four types:

1. *Collegiate*—sports, dates, fun, fraternities and sororities, "Joe College," some money
2. *Vocational*—job preparation, no-nonsense attitude, financially less well-off, often working, married
3. *Academic*—intellectual, identification with faculty, time spent in library and lab, planning graduate and professional training
4. *Nonconformist*—several types: the aggressive intellectual, the student seeking personal identity, and the rebellious student.

With the radical student movements of the 1960s, new student types emerged that did not fit clearly into these categories. Although these types may have altered, the concept of a "reference group" that provides both a sense of belonging and a model for behavior has not changed.

Fraternities and sororities function to provide group identity for some students in higher education. These "formalized" peer-group relationships generally fall into the collegiate subculture. They provide an alternative to the academic side of college life. Although Greek organizations declined in number during the 1960s, since the mid-1970s they have increased in strength and number on many campuses. This growth has led to some serious charges, from hazing of pledges in sororities and fraternities (Nuwer, 1990) to date rape and even gang rape (Sanday, 1990), sometimes linked with alcohol usage. Though many college officials have strict policies and states have criminal laws that cover Greek activities, critics argue that these laws are ineffective and problems continue (Gose, 1997). The good news is that drug and alcohol use is down somewhat on campuses, and some fraternities are eliminating drinking parties. On many campuses, however, Greek life is strong and many students find it attractive (O'Donnell, 2009).

The vocational subculture dominates on some campuses because of economic pressures, competition for jobs, and many first-generation college students trying to improve their chances for upward mobility.

The Graying of College Graduates

During the 1980s, the traditional college-age population of 18- to 22-year-olds dropped by 2.7 million students. However, the overall number of college students rose by 1.8 million. Why? The increase in the number of students over age 25 rose significantly; since that time, however, the proportion of older students has stabilized. The Census Bureau reports that college enrollments were made up of 37.1 percent of students age 25 and older in the United States in 2008. The older, nontraditional students are upgrading their job skills, changing careers, and seeking personal improvement by taking classes for credit or audit, especially in a period of economic recession. Education becomes important in retooling for the paid labor force that many older people enter. Financial aid, including federal and state assistance, is available to help older citizens pay for schooling, and senior citizens often attend for free. The patterns of enrollment show that older students are more likely in community and other two-year colleges and many attend part-time, attesting to their other responsibilities. Yet, as the Attewell and Lavin (2007) research so strongly demonstrates, these students often persist and they and their children benefit from their education, even if it takes them longer to attain it.

This demographic shift is having an impact on curricula and on campus life. Evening and weekend classes have increased; more convenient off-campus sites have been established, especially in metropolitan areas; distance learning classes are increasing; much of the course work can be done at home; and some universities provide transitional programs for older students.

Many older students accept the stereotypes imposed on them, however, fearing to go back to school after so many years. They fear that they might prove to themselves or others that they are unable to cope with the college crowd, the work, the new and demanding environment, or the stress. Although there may be some performance decline with age, many older people remain highly productive and enjoy college life. Older people make good students, and they are highly motivated and dependable (Cox, 1996).

The postwar baby boom increased the number of births from 2.75 million in the 1940s to 4.35 million in the 1960s. The population of people age 65 and over is projected to increase from 39 million in 2010 to 69 million in 2030, using middle series projections. About 20 percent of the total population would be over 65 by 2030, compared to 13 percent in the late 1990s (U. S. Department of Commerce, Current Population Reports, 1996). This group also will be living longer because of continuing medical advances. As this group ages, it will be more active than its predecessors. Although ageism has historically plagued older cohorts, the baby-boom generation will probably defy most of the age-related stereotypes because of its proportion of the population. Federal and state legislation addressing the needs of older people has also been passed in some countries, including the United States, ensuring educational opportunity for all citizens "without regard to restrictions of previous education or training, sex, age, handicapping condition, social or ethnic background, or economic circumstances." For example, all state-funded colleges and universities in Ohio must provide free enrollment, on a space-available basis, to those 60 years and older (Ohio Revised Code). Countries that educate and make use of their older citizens can enhance their economic and social systems.

The profile of clients of higher education is changing, and their needs must be taken into consideration. Institutions will see a more diverse student body with a variety of goals and interests. It will take a flexible faculty to meet the changing needs.

Applying Sociology to Education: *What role(s) do you play in the higher education system, and how do(es) your role(s) compare with those of others around you in higher education?*

Roles in Higher Education: The Faculty

Universities expect professors to teach well, be knowledgeable and current in their disciplines, and produce work that will be influential and prestigious. The institution thus gains prestige, which in turn produces resources. Students, parents, and others in the institution's environment also hold certain expectations of faculty. The following section deals with some specific aspects of this role.

CHARACTERISTICS OF FACULTY.   Sociologists identify groups of people in part by the characteristics they have in common. Faculty are no exception. They can be characterized by their race, sex, type of institution, and academic discipline (see Table 10.4). In 1940, 15,000 people were employed on the faculties of U.S. colleges and universities. The 1960s brought a tremendous

Table 10.4 Percentage of Faculty Members by Sex, Rank, and Racial and Ethnic Group, Fall 2007

	Total[a]	White (%)	Asian (%)	Black (%)	Hispanic (%)	American Indian (%)	Nonresident Foreign (%)	Race unknown
Rank, full-time faculty members								
All	691,588	78.1	7.8	5.5	3.6	0.5	4.5	11,875
Men	402,455	78.1	8.5	4.4	3.3	0.4	5.2	6,660
Women	289,133	78.2	6.7	7.0	4.0	0.6	3.6	5,215
Professor								
All	172,086	85.9	7.1	3.4	2.4	0.3	0.9	1,309
Men	126,515	85.7	7.9	2.9	2.3	0.3	1.0	973
Women	45,571	86.6	4.9	4.8	2.8	0.4	0.6	336
Associate professor								
All	142,064	81.1	7.8	5.5	3.3	0.4	1.8	1,628
Men	85,622	80.6	8.8	4.8	3.2	0.4	2.2	1,038
Women	56,442	82.0	6.2	6.6	3.4	0.5	1.2	590
Assistant professor								
All	164,915	71.3	10.5	6.5	3.8	0.4	7.5	3,593
Men	86,796	69.6	11.6	5.3	3.8	0.3	9.4	1,945
Women	78,119	73.2	9.3	7.7	3.9	0.5	5.3	1,648
Instructor								
All	99,079	78.3	5.3	7.5	5.9	1.0	2.0	2,350
Men	45,533	78.6	5.4	6.4	6.1	1.1	2.4	1,066
Women	53,546	78.1	5.2	8.5	5.6	0.9	1.7	1,284
Lecturer								
All	30,603	76.7	6.8	5.2	4.9	0.5	5.9	661
Men	14,437	76.5	6.6	5.0	4.2	0.5	7.1	347
Women	16,166	76.9	7.0	5.4	5.4	0.5	4.8	314
Other								
All	82,841	70.8	6.9	5.4	3.0	0.5	13.3	2,334
Men	43,552	68.3	7.2	4.1	2.7	0.5	17.3	1,291
Women	39,289	73.5	6.6	7.0	3.4	0.6	8.9	1,043
Part-time instructional staff members								
All	612,882	81.4	4.1	8.0	4.4	0.6	1.6	55,323
Men	306,541	82.4	4.2	6.6	4.5	0.6	1.7	28,208
Women	306,341	80.3	4.0	9.5	4.2	0.6	1.4	27,115

[a]Excludes: Race Unknown

Note: The Chronicle subtracted from the total of all faculty members (not shown) the number whose race was unknown, then divided by the number of faculty members in each race/ethnicity category and by the number of nonresident foreigners. The number of faculty members whose race was unknown is shown at far right for reference. The category "other" includes faculty members with no academic rank and instructional employees without faculty status. Figures for part-timers include some lacking faculty status. Total numbers may differ from those reported elsewhere because of varying survey methodologies. Percentages are rounded.

Source: The Chronicle of Higher Education analysis of Fall Staff Survey, U.S. Department of Education.
http://chronicle.com/article/Percentage-of-Faculty-Members/123927/

increase in numbers of faculty along with increases in the student body, and by the 1970s full-time faculty numbered more than 600,000. By 1992, the number of faculty had dropped to 526,222, and in 2007 had risen to 691,588 (*The Chronicle of Higher Education Almanac*, 2010a).

A problem of increasing complexity is the rise in the numbers of part-time, adjunct faculty as well as the sharp increase in the proportion of full-time, non-tenure-track faculty. Today, many courses are taught by faculty who have only part-time appointments, sometimes teaching one or two courses at several different college campuses. Many of these faculty members would like to have full-time jobs, but cannot find them. Stitching a life together from several part-time posts usually makes the time for research and publication, increasingly a necessity for a full-time appointment, very difficult.

The situation of "contract faculty," full-timers but not on tenure tracks, may be better in that they often receive full benefits and may have multiyear contracts, but they still lack the ability to fully engage the faculty role in many colleges and universities. Their positions usually do not require the trilogy of faculty obligations: teaching, research, and service. Most often, these faculty members teach and provide student and administrative services, but are not expected to do the research and publication required of tenure-track faculty. Some are concerned that the decline in the proportion of tenured and tenure-track faculty threatens the quality and autonomy of higher education (http://www.aaup.org/AAUP/pubsres/research/conind2006.htm), while others see this as a necessary adjustment to the changing economic realities facing higher education. One thing is certain: Higher education is changing.

Another important trend that has taken place among collegiate faculty has been the rise in proportion of faculty working part-time. Their share of the total faculty has increased by 85 percent over the period from 1993 to 2007. During this same period, the number in tenured full-time faculty positions rose by only 8 percent, and full-time tenure-track faculty by 20 percent (*The Chronicle of Higher Education Almanac*, 2010b). Many think the need for flexibility in staffing, as the curriculum has shifted to more vocational subjects, has fueled this shift away from full-time, tenure-track faculty. Others see it as an example of the commercialization of the academy—evidence of the ascendancy of the business needs of the academy over its academic integrity. Of course, the economic downturn of the last three years has had a very negative effect on college and university budgets and has led to canceling searches for new faculty members, furloughs for some, and reductions in employees in others. These, among other trends, have spawned anxiety among some concerning the future of the profession (Finkelstein, 2003).

The proportion of females and males on the faculty varies depending on the program. In nursing, women make up nearly 100 percent of the faculty, but in engineering and agriculture they constitute less than 1 percent of faculty ranks. Women were found more frequently in teaching faculties rather than research institutions and in departments with low prestige. Their total numbers in 2007 were 289,133 out of 691,588 total faculty.

There has been little change in the number of full-time African-American faculty in institutions of higher learning in the United States in the past four decades, with 5.5 percent of all faculty in 2007. Recent figures indicate that the proportions of female and minority professors are growing, but slowly. However, those faculty are less likely to be tenured or in tenure-track positions, and more likely to be foreign-born (Finkelstein, Schuster, and Seal, 1995) (see Table 10.4).

To have increases in the number of faculty, more students must be coming through the system. We have already seen that there has been little increase in the number of African Americans going to graduate school and receiving Ph.Ds. The same is true for students coming from manual or blue-collar backgrounds, but they receive no special consideration because they are not considered an "official" category. Faculty representation from Catholic and Jewish backgrounds about doubled in the first half of the twentieth century, but has leveled off or dropped in recent years.

Faculty Issues in Higher Education

Three issues related to the role of faculty in higher education have been particularly important: professionalism, collective bargaining, and status of women faculty and staff in higher-educational institutions.

PROFESSIONALISM AND ORIENTATION: THE FACULTY ROLE.   Faculty members go through several years of intense training in order to become professionals. The primary mark of acceptance into professional status is the highest degree in the field; for example, the Ph.D. (Doctor of Philosophy), L.L.D. (Doctor of Laws), and M.D. (Doctor of Medicine). During the education period, intensive training and professional socialization take place as the graduate students learn not only their subject areas but also the appropriate attitudes, behaviors, and ethics of their discipline. Typically, graduate school training for a Ph.D. involves two or three years of course work, followed by comprehensive examinations and a major work of original research—the dissertation. Having been through an intense common experience, graduates become part of a "fraternity" protecting the entrance gates of the discipline by maintaining the traditions. These traditions are most highly protected in the most prestigious professions, such as medicine.

Yet this socialization process has had its critics. Some graduate students complain that their training lacks relevance to the professional tasks they will be performing. Some have limited practical experience. Others claim that they receive little or no training in teaching techniques, and that their research focus is usually very narrow. In addition, preparation for being faculty members may be minimal. In general, regular tenure-track faculty are expected to teach classes, develop and carry out their own research agenda, and provide service to their academic unit and to the university through working on committees (such as developing curriculum) and working with students out of class. Increasingly, faculty work can be done from home or away as well as in an office. While some relish their ability to access entire libraries from their home, others see telecommuting as nothing but "work, work, work" (Fogg, 2008).

The Association of American Colleges and Universities and the Council of Graduate Schools started a project in 1993 called "Preparing Future Faculty" (DeNeef, 2002). A number of institutions do provide training for future university teachers, and many provide ongoing professional development for faculty (Cage, 1996, p. A19). Seminars for teaching assistants (TAs) and faculty are offered at a number of universities. More institutions are emphasizing the importance of quality teaching. As noted earlier, there has been a concern that faculty spend too much of their time and energy on research and too little on teaching and working with students. This criticism varies, of course, by type of higher education institution; research universities expect their faculty to be deeply involved in research while liberal arts colleges expect a more equal balance between teaching and involvement with students and research. As higher education in state institutions has become a bigger factor in state budgets, scrutiny over how faculty spend their time has increased. This is certainly reflected in the attention given to teaching in the recent report on higher education (*A Test of Leadership*, 2006).

Once on the job, faculty members face differing role expectations. Teaching is the primary task at two-year institutions and at four-year liberal arts colleges, whereas research takes a large percentage of faculty time at most universities. The orientation of faculty is also related to the type of institution. "Cosmopolitan" faculty—those who have attachments and professional interests outside their institution—develop their research and writing in relation to a wider audience; they attract more grant money and prestige. "Local" faculty focus their attention within the institution, are active and concerned about institutional matters, and tend to be more loyal to the institution. Although both types are found at all institutions, higher percentages of "local" faculty are likely to be found at two- and four-year colleges (Gouldner, 1957).

The most prestigious institutions, which attract the most prominent faculty members, also have problems retaining them. These faculty teach less, and spend a great deal of time consulting, lecturing, attending conferences, or working at other institutions as visiting scholars or lecturers. Committee assignments and teaching often fall to younger faculty members. Universities tolerate this because having respected, well-known faculty enhances the prestige of the university and may attract other top scholars and students as well as more funds.

A difficult problem for many faculty is the incongruity between the demands of teaching and research. This dilemma often hits young scholars hardest; they must "prove themselves" in order to be retained and given tenure. This means performing well not only in teaching and university service but also in research and publishing, which may not receive the attention they actually need in the early years of a career. Young faculty members with family responsibilities may be forced to make hard decisions between family and career. Some argue that faculty have been pushed to "get it written rather than get it right." Thus, college faculty are hired to teach students, but are often expected to publish—or perish. Despite the pressures, professors are generally pleased with their careers, with 65 percent of males and 59 percent of females indicating they would pursue an academic career again if given the choice (Leatherman, 2000).

PROFESSIONALS, UNIONS, AND COLLECTIVE BARGAINING.   Academic professionals are characterized by belief in academic freedom, autonomy over decisions related to their discipline and educational process, and service to the community. The American Association of University Professors (AAUP) has traditionally represented faculty interests, setting down guidelines for salaries, promotions, and policies. AAUP's "clout" with institutions has been the backing of the membership and the threat to blacklist an institution so that faculty would resist taking employment there.

Support for union representation among faculty varies considerably. Many faculty members are reluctant to address their grievances to the administration through a mediating union, preferring instead to retain individual control over problem solving. At two-year institutions, faculty are more likely to consider themselves "employees," to follow more closely the secondary school model, and to expect to gain by union representation. Faculty at prestigious universities are less likely to use union bargaining agents because they have less to gain by being represented. Many already have high salaries relative to others, and they have the flexibility to relocate if they are dissatisfied. Yet, many faculty members do belong to representative organizations—professional associations and the AAUP—and the idea of organizational membership is an established one. In fact, on unionized campuses today AAUP represents faculty interests in such areas as due process and faculty salaries. The American Federation of Teachers (AFT) and the National Education Association (NEA) are unions of elementary and secondary teachers that have been competing to represent college faculty.

Higher education has expanded rapidly, especially at the two-year college level, which has fewer faculty members with terminal Ph.D. degrees. Economic problems have caused an uncertain job market in academia. Administrative decision making has become further removed from faculty, and young faculty members come from more varied backgrounds, providing a large core of faculty open to collective bargaining as a tactic (Morgan, 1992, pp. 2719–2720; also see, Saltzman, 2001). Thus, in recent years, faculty unions and collective bargaining have begun to look more attractive to large segments of the academic community. Collective bargaining in public colleges is determined by state law, and many states now have laws that permit unionization.

Private colleges are governed, like private businesses, by the National Labor Relations Board and federal law, which is more restrictive of collective bargaining.

Since the Yeshiva decision, most private colleges and universities have been off-limits to unionization. This Supreme Court ruling determined that faculty at most private four-year colleges and universities had duties that included participating in managerial decision making and were thus members of management, and not regular employees, who are eligible to unionize. This decision is still controversial among many faculty members who would like to be eligible to unionize, especially in the current economy (Wilson, 2009).

GENDER ISSUES IN HIGHER EDUCATION.   Women are more heavily concentrated in the two-year institutions than in universities, and in all institutions the percentage of women with tenure is lower than their percentage of the total faculty, meaning that women are concentrated in the lower ranks. One reason for this pattern, according to women's studies scholars, is the long tradition of male-dominated academic institutions. Traditional approaches to research are based on the male life cycle, following an established series of steps to success (Gilligan, 1979). Women, however, may pursue research with different career assumptions, such as entry into professions after childbearing years or shared academic positions. Acceptance of alternative models has been limited, a fact that has penalized women who are competent and effective—with consequent loss to the academic community.

"Women working on campuses face hostile environments," concluded a study of conditions facing women in academia. Not only is sexual harassment a continuing problem, but discrimination in the form of less pay for the same job, lower positions, and fewer promotions is common (Blum, 1991, p. A1; Ceci and Williams, 2006; Lomperis, 1990, p. 643). African-American women sometimes feel they must "outshine, outthink, and outperform their minority counterparts [white women in academia] to achieve legitimacy within the academy," and they often feel a sense of intense isolation (Fontaine, 1993, p. 121).

The proportion of female faculty has grown slowly in recent years, with women making up 41.8 percent of full-time faculty members in 2007: 26.5 percent of full professors and 47.4 percent of assistant professors (*The Chronicle of Higher Education Almanac*, 2010a). Women are dismissed in disproportionate numbers when faculty and staff are laid off. Women and minorities are less frequently hired in positions from which they have been excluded in the past, such as administrative positions. Also, women faculty are found disproportionately in female-dominated fields and lower-paying, lower-prestige institutions.

Roles in Higher Education: Administrators

Administrators must be jugglers, maintaining a delicate balance of goodwill between the environmental players crucial to the institution and the academic interests of faculty and the student body.

In public institutions, primary authority over fiscal matters and programs falls to a state (or local) board of trustees or regents, and may depend on the attitudes and prejudices of state legislators and governors, who in theory reflect the mood of the public.

At private institutions, administrators depend in part on support from private funds, often from alumni, foundations, and corporations. Such private sources of support are becoming increasingly important to public institutions, too, as levels of state funding have declined. But again, this funding is tenuous and depends on retaining the goodwill and continuing interests of donors. In the case of one prestigious institution, pressure from alumni influenced decision making. The alumni newsletter reported various impending changes in the traditional structure of the university: admitting women to the formerly all-male school, opening the doors to more minority students, and reconsidering the practice of giving preference in admission to relatives of alumni. Cries of outrage were heard from alumni who threatened to or actually did cease to contribute. The issues became policy, but in modified forms more acceptable to alumni. The trustees of Mills College, in Oakland, California, a women's college, voted to admit men to the fall 1991 class for the first time in the schools 138-year history. Students struck the campus refusing to attend classes and occupied buildings. The alumnae protested and threatened to withdraw support. The trustees reconsidered their decision and voted to remain a women's college. The president and many of the members of the board of trustees had left the campus within a year.

As faculty members have concentrated more on their disciplines and their academic pursuits, their role in college and university life has narrowed. For example, their participation in student life is less today than it was historically. Student affairs administrators, including those in residence halls, in student centers, and other student services, have increased in numbers as faculty have focused more on their teaching and research.

Critics of the increased role of administrators argue that the university has become "top heavy" with highly paid administrators who are moving the university into the business model of a competitive and profit-making institution. They also point out the high salary increases received by administrators in many institutions. For instance, their median salary was 4 percent higher in the 2006–2007 academic year, and salaries have outpaced inflation for the past 10 years (June, 2007). Most recently, of course, the economic recession has resulted in salary freezes, furloughs, and firings of faculty and administrators.

The system of higher education cannot be understood without referring to the environment such as alumni. The next section in our chapter considers some examples of the higher-education environment.

ENVIRONMENTAL PRESSURES ON HIGHER EDUCATION

Environmental pressures affecting the higher education system come from government, the courts, teacher organizations, publishing companies, churches, community, parents, and other interest groups (see Figure 10.2). Institutions of higher education are playing a game of survival;

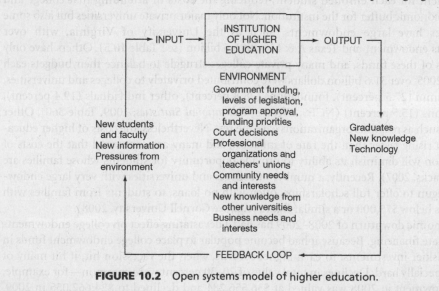

FIGURE 10.2 Open systems model of higher education.

whatever parts of the environment are most crucial to that survival will have the greatest impact on decision making and changes that take place. Let us consider several key sources of environmental influence on higher education.

Funding of Higher Education

Government has a degree of power over institutions of higher education through the control of money. The combined federal, state, and local government funding for higher education made up 44.79 percent of public institutions' budgets in the 2006–2007 academic year (see NCES, *Digest of Educational Statistics*, 2010, Table 352). This is down from 57.7 percent in 2000–2001. Although declining, government influence over public institutions is great, though private institutions often depend on governmental support for research and special programs as well. Tuition and fees play the largest role in most private institutions. Religiously affiliated institutions are generally least dependent on and influenced by government, although government regulations sometimes are seen as interfering with their ability to express their faith. For example, Bob Jones University decided to forgo its eligibility to receive federal funds so as to protect its campus rules against interracial dating (Connell, 1983).

If priorities for funding programs and research are established by the government in AIDS and cancer research or mental retardation, for example, then researchers are drawn to these areas to seek support funding. Some fields have higher funding priorities than others and, in fact, may be sustained by funding. Change in the funding priorities can bring about change in the number of faculty and staff in an academic department. Those staff on "soft money," or funded projects, may be cut back or not renewed. Laboratory or other facilities, faculty teaching loads, number of students attracted to a department as majors, and even a department's or institution's chances for survival can rest on levels of government support.

Colleges also receive funding from alumni, corporations, foundations, and religious organizations. Monies are often earmarked for special projects. Funds received by colleges are used for a variety of purposes. Some of these funds are placed in the institution's endowment, money that is invested and whose interest or return is available for spending, but the principal is left intact for generations. Some colleges (such as Princeton and Yale) have more than a million dollars in their endowment for each enrolled student, reducing the costs of attending that college and providing an economic buffer for the institution. Not only major private universities but also some public colleges have large endowments, such as the University of Virginia, with over 3.6 billion in its endowment and Texas A & M with 5.6 billion (see Table 10.5). Others have only small amounts of these funds, and many private colleges struggle to balance their budgets each year. In 2004–2005, over 31.6 billion dollars were contributed privately to colleges and universities, most from alumni (27.5 percent), foundations (28.8 percent), other individuals (19.4 percent), and corporations (15.5 percent) (NCES, *Digest of Educational Statistics*, 2009, Table 360). Other organizations such as religious organizations gave the rest. Nevertheless, the costs of higher education have been rising faster than the rate of inflation, and many are concerned that the costs of higher education will diminish its ability to provide opportunity for students whose families are not wealthy (Sacks, 2007). Recently, a number of colleges and universities with very large endowments have begun to offer full scholarships, often with no loans, to students from families with family incomes below $75,000 or a similar figure (e.g., see Cornell University, 2008).

The economic downturn of 2008–2009 has had a devastating effect on college endowments as well as on state financing. Because it had become popular to place college endowment funds in increasingly riskier investments, to earn higher returns, when the recession hit, it hit many of these funds especially hard. Declines in total value of 20–30 percent were common—for example, Harvard's endowment in 2008 was valued at $36,556,284 and declined to $24,662,055 in 2009.

Table 10.5 30 Largest College and University Endowments, Fiscal Year 2010

Institutions	$(000)	(%) Increase from 2009*
1. Harvard University	27,557,404	5.4
2. Yale University	16,652,000	2.0
3. Stanford University	14,391,450	14.1
4. Princeton University	14,052,220	15.5
5. University of Texas System	13,851,115	9.8
6. Massachusetts Institute of Technology	8,317,321	5.5
7. University of Michigan	6,564,144	9.4
8. Columbia University	6,516,512	10.6
9. Northwestern University	5,945,277	9.2
10. University of Pennsylvania	5,738,289	12.9
11. University of Chicago	5,668,937	9.6
12. The Texas A&M university System and Foundation	5,638,040	10.7
13. University of California	5,441,225	10.2
14. University of Notre Dame	5,234,841	9.2
15. Duke University	4,823,572	8.6
16. Emory University	4,694,260	8.5
17. Washington University in St. Louis	4,473,180	9.6
18. Cornell University	4,378,587	10.4
19. Rice University	3,906,823	9.2
20. University of Virginia	3,786,548	4.8
21. Vanderbilt University	3,044,000	6.2
22. Dartmouth College	2,998,302	6.1
23. University of Southern California	2,947,978	10.4
24. New York University	2,370,000	13.2
25. University of Minnesota and Affiliated Foundations	2,219,925	12.3
26. Brown University	2,195,740	5.3
27. Johns Hopkins University	2,155,330	6.8
28. University of North Carolina at Chapel Hill & Foundations	2,032,798	10.6
29. University of Pittsburgh	1,979,222	3.9
30. The Ohio State University	1,869,312	13.2

Note: % change in market value from FY 09 to FY 10 reflects net impact of: withdrawals to fund operations and capital expenses; payment of endowment management and investment fees; donor gifts and other contributions; investment gains or losses.

Source: http://nacubo.org/Documents/research/2010NCSE_Public_Tables_Endowment_Market_Values_Final.pdf

The real problem was that colleges with high endowments used the returns from those investments to fund large proportions of their budgets. When the returns dropped sharply, these schools had very large deficits in their operating budgets that had to be filled or their expenses trimmed dramatically (Foderaro, 2010). They could have sold endowment to cover the deficits, but because the markets were down so much, most were reluctant to do that realizing that they would get much less for the securities than they were worth in better times. The alternative was to borrow the money, and many very endowment-rich schools had to do just that: Harvard borrowed $1.5 billion to cover its needs. (McDonald, 2010). Ironically, the recession hurt the endowment-rich colleges and universities worse than less affluent schools.

The federal government provides grants and loans for students with financial need to help them meet the costs of college. Controversy erupted in late 1990 when the U.S. education secretary announced a ban on scholarships based exclusively on race; race could be used as only one factor in awarding scholarships to increase diversity on campuses, or used to remedy proven discrimination. By 1995 the Supreme Court upheld a similar case, striking down race-based scholarships (Myers, 1995, p. A13). The main source of federal scholarship support is the Pell Grant, which for a number of years was not increased and inflation reduced its value. However, in 2010 the Obama administration increased the funding for Pell grants.

Higher education has socioeconomic implications beyond the individuals who attain an education. The private economy in capitalist states is stimulated by government spending on higher education—especially on research—more than spending in general. Spending on research activities has long-lasting effects on private enterprise. This is especially true because the university is a primary location for pure research, which allows industry in the United States to spend its money on applications of research findings.

With government and family working together to help finance higher education, we have another example of the impact of environment and the interdependence of institutions. Government has also worked with schools in developing and funding curricula to meet national priorities. Yet with college costs increasing at a rapid rate, affordability remains a very big issue for many families (see Table 10.6).

Table 10.6 Average College Costs, 2009–2010

	4-Year Public Colleges		**Private Colleges**	
	Resident ($)	Commuter ($)	Resident ($)	Commuter ($)
Four-Year Colleges				
Tuition and fees	7,020	7,020	26,273	26,273
Books and supplies	1,122	1,122	1,116	1,116
Room and board[a]	8,193	7,969	9,363	8,163
Transportation	1,079	1,483	849	1,332
Other	1,974	2,318	1,427	1,788
Total	19,388	19,912	39,028	38,672
Two-Year Colleges				
Tuition and fees	—	2,544	—	—
Books and supplies	—	1,098	—	—
Room and board[a]	—	7,202	—	—
Transportation	—	1,445	—	—
Other	—	1,996	—	—
Total	—	14,285	—	—

[a] Room not included for commuter students.

— Insufficient data.

Note: The figures are weighted by enrollment to reflect the charges incurred by the average undergraduate enrolled at each type of institution.

Source: The Chronicle of Higher Education Almanac, 2010. http://chronicle.com/article/Average-College-Costs-2009-10/ 123949/

The Courts and Affirmative Action

The law generally prohibits discrimination on the basis of race, sex, color, religion, ancestry, national origin, age, disability, veteran status, or sexual orientation by public institutions and those that receive federal funds. Federal law also requires universities to use "affirmative action" to eliminate or correct the effects of past discrimination, intentional or not. At the same time, the courts have issued some contradictory decisions as in the previously mentioned *Hopwood v. Texas* ruling.

Affirmative action includes a broad range of activities, such as publicly advertising vacant faculty positions instead of filling them through the "old-boy network" or by "word-of-mouth" connections, eliminating inappropriate barriers that tend to exclude certain groups disproportionately, and ensuring that admission and employment decisions are actually based on the announced criteria.

The types of affirmative action that often cause controversy are (1) consideration of race or sex as a criterion in admission or employment decisions, and (2) establishment of numerical goals to measure progress in increasing the presence of minorities or women. One objection to the use of *goals*, which are defined as *targets* to be pursued by good-faith efforts, is that sometimes goals are interpreted to mean *quotas* (i.e., numbers that must be achieved in order to avoid some penalty). The result of establishing quotas would be that failing to base decisions on race or sex could result in loss of all federal funding, including grants, research contracts, and even student loan receipts.

Affirmative action has existed for almost half of a century, since Executive Order 11246 was issued in 1965; it has also been resisted for that amount of time. Great progress has been made toward eliminating discrimination based on race, sex, and various other criteria in educational and employment opportunities, but achieving equal opportunity will require additional effort.

In 1995, the U.S. Supreme Court ruled that government affirmative action programs that provide benefits on the basis of race or ethnicity must be subjected to "strict scrutiny" by the courts. That means such programs must be "necessary" to achieve a "compelling state interest" (i.e., government purpose). In its University of Michigan rulings, referred to earlier, the Supreme Court accepted diversity among students as a "compelling state interest" and approved of affirmative action as an acceptable policy, as long as it was applied individually to applicants (*Grutter v. Bollinger*). Giving all members of under-enrolled minorities the same preference, as the undergraduate admissions process did at Michigan, was found unacceptable.

Environmental Feedback and Organizational Change

"On September 30, 1964, five students concerned with civil rights were cited by the dean of men at the University of California, Berkeley, for violating rules which prohibited political propagandizing on campus" ("Ten Years Later," 1974, p. 1149). According to Neil Smelzer's theory of collective behavior (Smelzer, 1962), this was the "precipitating factor" that stimulated the confrontations between students and university administrators that lasted for four months and set an example for student protests at other campuses around the world. Such events as the following occurred:

> On December 2, 1964, 1,000 students, their morale bolstered by folk singer Joan Baez, occupied the administration building [at Berkeley]. What ensued was the sensational spectacle of some 700 police and sheriff's deputies bodily removing the unrelenting demonstrators. Instantaneously and spontaneously the number of sympathizers and collaborators multiplied. ("Berkeley Student Revolt," 1965, p. 51)

A university is concerned with its public image because of the effect image has on the public and private monies it receives and on the students it attracts. The Berkeley Free Speech Movement changed both the environmental image and the decision-making structure of the University of California. Many attempted to analyze the events. Some argued that the movement was the result of students trying to seize power in the educational system; others argued that they were responding to such concrete deprivations as lack of freedom of speech ("Berkeley Student Revolt," 1965, p. 51). In the years following the uprisings, there were intense debates over the purpose of the university, and pressures for change were felt by most institutions of higher education. In some cases, the institutions incorporated more students into the decision-making structure or were more tolerant on the issue of free speech. Other institutions reacted in the opposite way, tightening control over decision making in response to community pressures

This example indicates that feedback from the primary environment—the students viewed as clients—and from the secondary environment—the community—bring about alterations and change. The dramatic and intense reaction at Berkeley was a form of feedback demanding attention and action, which led to change and long-term searching for alterations and improvements in the system (Cohen and Zelnik, 2002).

The variables affecting change in each situation will differ, but the process of constant change can be traced and studied through the open systems model. Using this approach, the organization does not appear static—a criticism frequently made of functional analysis of organizations; nor will change necessarily be seen as resulting from continuous power struggles between factions or interest groups—as in conflict theory. Rather, change can be seen as a natural part of organizational process and function. The impact of the environment is seen in the tenuous budgets of many state universities, the election cycle, and who become governor and state representatives. Change is an ongoing, dynamic process in any system; organizations must rely on feedback from the environment and must constantly adapt and alter to meet changes in environmental demands if they are to survive.

> **Applying Sociology to Education:** *What are some environmental pressures on your institution of higher education? How is the institution dealing with these pressures?*

OUTCOMES OF HIGHER EDUCATION

Higher Education: Attitudes, Values, and Behaviors

What effect does college education have on the students who attend? This is the key question in studies of changes in students' political, religious, and moral attitudes and values over time. In the annual survey of first-year students conducted by the Higher Education Research Institute, changes over the past 29 years have been recorded: In 1966, for instance, 57.8 percent of students indicated that "keeping up with political affairs was very important or essential." This figure has declined over the years, reaching the lowest point in 1994, with only 31.9 percent saying this was important to them, and more recently increasing to 37.3 percent of students in 2005 (Hurtado et al., 2007). It rose to 39.5 in 2008 and fell back some to 36 percent in 2009, after President Obama's election (UCLA, Higher Education Research Institute, *Research Brief: The American Freshman, National Norms for 2009, http://www.heri.ucla.edu/cirpoverview.php*).

These are data concerning incoming freshmen; they do not tell us about how students change during the course of their higher education. This turns out to be a difficult research question.

First, traditional college-age young people are not only experiencing whatever college has to offer but are also maturing into adults, whether they attend college or not. They are having critical life experiences that affect their orientation, attitudes, and values whether they go to college, work, begin a family, or go into the military. Sorting out college effects from maturation effects is not easy. Moreover, even deciding how to measure "college effects" is complicated.

Colleges differ greatly from one another: Some are primarily residential and the residence hall experience is integral to the experience while other colleges are attended entirely by commuters. Some are highly selective in their admissions, while others are not. Some are isolated in rural areas, while others are located in the heart of major cities. Science majors are likely to experience a different set of norms than are arts majors. In short, we need to be very circumspect in generalizing about the effects of attending college on students.

Over the years, undergraduates revealed substantial changes in attitudes and beliefs. The largest positive changes relate to supporting feminism, making a commitment to clean up the environment and to promote racial understanding, developing a meaningful philosophy of life, and supporting legal abortion. Declines are seen in the emphasis on being well-off financially.

A notable finding in the fall 1999 survey is that almost one-third of first-year students feel high degrees of stress; many must work to make ends meet, and they express concern about competition. In 2005, the majority of first-year students have some degree of concern about financing their college education, although less than one-third of the respondents work for pay on- or off-campus. Less than half of the students "frequently" felt overwhelmed, lonely, or homesick, and worried about meeting new people in the first year (Hurtado et al., 2007). Women tend to feel more stressed about concern over money. Women also spend more time studying, doing volunteer work, participating in student activities, and doing housework or taking care of children than men. Men report spending more time on leisure activities.

Other trends indicate that drinking and smoking continue to decline; only half of incoming first-year college students say they drank beer frequently in the past year. The percentage of students who smoke was 14.2 percent, down from 15.8 percent in 1998 (Sax et al., 1999) and had dropped all the way to 4.1 percent by 2005 (Hurtado et al., 2007).

The Value of a College Education

Do higher-education credentials lead to higher occupational status and higher future earnings? College graduates earn up to 61 percent more than high school graduates. The median income for year-round full-time male workers 25 years old and over in 2008 with less than a high school diploma was $29,680; $39,010 with a diploma; $45,820 with some college, but no degree; $50,150 with a two-year college degree; $65,899 with a bachelor's degree; $80,960 with a master's degree; and $100,000 with a professional degree (NCES, *Digest of Educational Statistics*, 2009, Table 384). Other factors, such as the college attended and major, may become more important in predicting future status and earnings (see Figure 10.3 for those aged between 25 and 34). The website http://collegestats.org/articles/2010/02/whats-a-college-degree-actually-worth-20-good-answers/ has links to 20 recent articles on the value of college degrees.

Students who have gone to a prestigious school have greater chances for higher earnings than those who attend less selective colleges; however, this effect is strongest for students who came from lower-family-income backgrounds. For men, "selecting a profitable major and making prompt progress toward a degree had a larger effect on future earning than did the characteristics of the college they attended" (Fitzgerald, 2000). Female earnings, for reasons that are

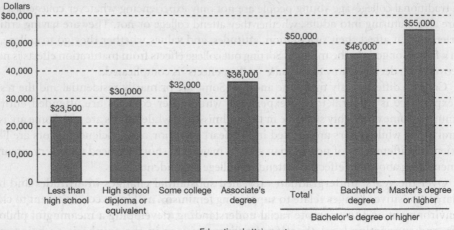

¹Total represents the median earnings of those with a bachelor's degree or higher.

FIGURE 10.3 Median annual earnings of full-time, full-year wage and salary workers ages 25–34, by educational attainment: 2008.

Note: Full-year worker refers to those who were employed 50 or more weeks during the previous year; full-time worker refers to those who were usually employed 35 or more hours per week. For more information on the Current Population Survey (CPS), see *supplemental note 2*.

Source: U.S. Department of Commerce, Census Bureau, Current Population Survey (CPS), March and Annual Social and Economic Supplement, 2009. *The Condition of Education*, 2010, Indicator 17.2.

not entirely clear, seem to benefit more from the characteristics of their colleges than is true for males. For both, however, the data are clear: Graduation from any college is better than attending but not graduating from the most selective college, and the variable economic rewards of occupations that are connected to majors are large (Davies and Hammack, 2005).

There is recent evidence that the benefits of attending college are not evenly distributed. In an innovative paper, Brand and Xie (2010) find that, other things being equal, those less likely to attend college derive the greatest benefit from attending. Thus, minorities and representatives of lower socioeconomic groups, who are less likely to attend and graduate from college, both men and women, and for every stage of the life course, derive a larger benefit from graduation than members of groups more likely to attend college. One may think of this finding as a result of these graduates being more scarce than their more common fellow graduates, and thus more valuable in the labor market.

Many students are accepting jobs in areas unrelated to their majors. This and the reduced economic advantages of college are causing young people to ask if college is worth the time and money. Consider Figure 10.3. The comparison shows that college graduates earn more than high school or elementary graduates but that these figures have declined in recent years, and the gap between groups is narrowing. Recent labor market changes, however, have continued to reduce the economic payoff of all less than college graduate categories.

The less tangible results of college have been summed up by Pascarella and Terenzini (2005). College helps students develop a positive self-image and better interpersonal and intellectual competence. They adopt more liberal political views and attitudes (which may or may not last) toward social issues, and their religious orientation decreases.

Applying Sociology to Education: *Is college worth the time and money? Why or why not?*

PROBLEMS AND REFORM IN HIGHER EDUCATION

With the increasing pressure on the educational system for accountability, higher education is in the critical eye of the public and policy makers. The ivory tower is facing more challenges, and many institutions are responding to problems: improve quality of teaching, attempt to control the costs of attending, evaluate the educational program, increase access for minority students, and prepare students with knowledge and skills for a good future.

Colleges are in the limelight for certain "unethical" practices: Sports scandals are one example. Another is grade inflation; between the 1960s and 1970s it was rapid, but has leveled off. Cheating by students is being firmly addressed in many institutions, with misconduct policies and procedures in place. Curriculum and credit given for courses is undergoing both internal and external review. Reports of misuse of funds are being investigated, and curriculum reform is a constant process.

All organizations have their critics; higher education is no exception. Some critics have an ideology to back their reformist critiques. In recent years, several authors have made sweeping criticisms of higher education, especially of humanities and social sciences. The conflict centers on views about the correct way to teach and the correct knowledge to learn. Issues of "political correctness" on campuses, stimulated in part by these critics, has brought about changes in curriculum and dominant issues on campuses. The conflicts represent an underlying tension between privilege and patriarchy on the one hand, and affirmative action and cultural diversity issues on the other (Wilkinson, 1991, pp. 550–551). While these issues are not new on campuses, there is continuing controversy about them. For example, a recent report asserted that over 90 percent of campus speech codes prohibit constitutionally protected speech (Foundation for Individual Rights in Education, 2006). The most recent attack on higher education is by one of its own, sociologist Andrew Hacker (with Claudia Dreifus, 2010). The book repeats many of the common criticism of colleges today, including their high costs, the proliferation of expensive amenities (such as elaborate recreation centers), the faculty members' emphasis on research as opposed to teaching, and the like.

Institutions of higher education are highly revered in most societies. They serve to expand equality of opportunity; provide a forum for discussion of national issues; and enable serious students to achieve their goals. Yet colleges are targets for criticism because their products (graduates) are visible and measurable. Consider colleges of education. Some commission reports push for increasing the status of education as a major, whereas others argue that students should major in a subject area and take education during a fifth year (Astin, 1993). As noted in Chapter 8, there is a new recognition of the importance of teacher quality in the United States, both as a result of the No Child Left Behind legislation, and because of research findings that show that teachers make a difference in student achievement. This has increased the scrutiny of the work of colleges of education (Olson, 2007).

The conventional wisdom is that universities are for the conservation, advancement, transmission, and interpretation of knowledge. The permanence of purpose implied by the almost universal acceptance of the definition throughout most of the twentieth century does not necessarily require permanence of method or curriculum content. Far from being detached from society, universities are very much a part of their environment, and their staff and students experience the societal tensions and strains caused by rapid economic and technological changes.

Summary

There is no one system of higher education. To the extent that generalizations can be made across systems, we have discussed some common characteristics and problems: the development and meaning of higher education; access to the system; the structure, process, and role relationships within the system; the environmental pressures toward change; and some outcomes and reforms in higher education.

I. HISTORY AND DEVELOPMENT OF HIGHER EDUCATION

Organized higher education dates back to the twelfth and thirteenth centuries. Over time, its structure and functions have changed dramatically. It now has a two-part structure—administration and faculty—and has taken on several additional functions such as research and service. The twentieth century brought the two-year college, and with it new structures and functions.

II. THEORETICAL APPROACHES TO HIGHER EDUCATION

We can gain a better understanding of how sociologists view higher education through functional and conflict theories. The systems model helps integrate aspects of higher education for a more comprehensive view. The issue of access to higher education, who gets in and why, is of major concern to educational theorists. They focus particularly on the admissions process and testing, and public versus private institutions. There have been legal challenges to admissions decisions to professional schools, with unclear outcomes.

III. CHARACTERISTICS OF HIGHER EDUCATION IN THE UNITED STATES

Institutions vary depending on sponsorship, student composition, types of programs, and degrees offered. The rapid growth of higher education threatened to weaken the value of college. Changing enrollments and economic patterns also forced cuts in programs and staff.

IV. FUNCTIONS OF THE HIGHER EDUCATION SYSTEM

The university can be viewed as a large community. With growth has come controversy over functions of the university: the form curriculum should adopt, the relationship between research and teaching, and the role service should play in the community. Controversy over the academic function of the university is illustrated by the role of "big business" sports on some campuses and the type of curriculum the university should have.

V. HIGHER EDUCATION AS AN ORGANIZATION

Higher education has been administered using a bureaucratic model, which many argue is not appropriate for the unique composition of the university. Decision making varies by constituency in the university, as do areas of decision-making responsibility. For instance, faculty generally retain control of curriculum matters.

VI. ROLES IN HIGHER EDUCATION

Students are becoming a more diversified group, with older students, minorities, and married students attending college in greater numbers. More women students are moving through the system and into graduate school today, assuming multiple roles, than in the past. Colleges wrestle with the problem of underprepared students who lack necessary skills to complete college.

Three issues facing faculty are discussed: professionalism, collective bargaining, and gender issues.

VII. ENVIRONMENTAL PRESSURES ON HIGHER EDUCATION

Several issues related to the environment of higher education were used to illustrate its importance: funding of higher education, court actions, and community pressure on programs.

VIII. OUTCOMES OF HIGHER EDUCATION

Outcomes of higher education include the value, attitude, and behavioral changes that take place and the financial outcomes of having a college education.

IX. PROBLEMS AND REFORM IN HIGHER EDUCATION

Finally, some problems and reforms in the areas of challenges to the higher education system and ethics are briefly discussed, including several critiques of faculty and curriculum. Proposals for reform are considered.

Putting Sociology to Work

1. List the institutions of higher education in your geographical area.
   a. What is the purpose served by each? (What courses and degrees are offered, and who is served?)
   b. What sorts of students go to each?
   c. What did your high school classmates do after graduation? college? work? other?
   d. Are there individuals who have not been accommodated by higher education in your area after high school?
   e. Do you see any gaps in the system of higher education in your area?
2. Think of a recent controversy in your institution. Put yourself in the place of other students who represent different viewpoints on the controversy, of a faculty member (or members), of an administrator involved with the controversy. How do they differ

in their perspectives on the controversy? It may be useful to interview those involved.

3. Consider several issues in higher education that were raised in the text or others that are of concern to you. Explain how a functionalist and conflict theorist would interpret these issues differently.
4. What problems do you see in the program or curriculum of your institution or in your major area? Designate alternatives to the present system at your institution that could help solve the problems.
5. Who holds formal power and decision-making rights in your institution in various areas? Who holds informal power? Give some examples. It may be useful to interview others on this question.
6. With what areas of the environment must your institution interact? Talking with an administrator about pressures on the university would be informative here.

CHAPTER

11

Educational Systems
Around the World

A Comparative View

I n a rural village in West Africa, a few children sit under a tree, some with slates and chalk. A book is shared, and there are no papers, pencils, or other supplies. The teacher who has only a 6th-grade education himself tries to help the children focus on learning to read. Several thousand miles to the north children sit at desks in a classroom well equipped with materials and technology for their education. Let us visit two individual children in these systems and observe how their educations and life chances differ.

Aminu is eight. He falls somewhere in the middle of nine brothers and sisters. He and his family live in a small, rural village in West Africa, in the northern part of his country. Farming is the primary occupation of the villagers, with each family tilling their own plot. Aminu's family uses a hand plow in the fields. It is not an easy life, but the family generally has enough to eat—mostly a starchy diet of millet, cassava roots, bananas, and some bits of meat. Aminu has other relatives living in the village too—cousins, aunts and uncles, and grandparents.

From an early age Aminu helped the family in the fields; his father taught him about farming and his grandfather about his family and religion. Although he was one of many children, there was always some relative to whom he could turn for help. His life was secure and happy.

At age six, he began attending the village school. All the children went there from ages six to nine, as mandated by the central government. Aminu didn't much mind; he saw his friends there and could play during free time. The teacher was a young local man who had been away to secondary school and came back to take charge of the one-room schoolhouse located in the village meeting hall. Molam Hassan seemed a nice man but was very strict and frequently resorted to striking pupils with a ruler or punishing them by making them stand in a corner. With older and younger children in one class, it was difficult to teach materials pertinent to all. Aminu learned basic mathematical functions, which he rather enjoyed doing,

Schooling around the world takes place in many settings.

though he saw no use for them. He could read simple books. They were about English boys and girls going on picnics with their dog. Aminu studied the Koran and learned to recite passages. He disliked being called on to stand in front of the class and recite, for if he forgot, he would be punished. He had no time, peace, or quiet to sit down at home and learn the recitations. But writing was worse. The children were required to write down dictations, and Aminu could never get it right.

When planting and harvest time came, Aminu and his brothers stayed away from school to help with the farming. When anyone was sick, the children took turns staying home and helping. One time Aminu missed a month of school to help his father and travel with him to the big town 20 miles away.

At the end of this school year, Aminu will leave school along with most of his friends. Only two boys are considering going on to the secondary school in the big town, the two top boys in the school. One has relatives in town with whom he can live. But the other is doubtful about going; his father needs his help and cannot afford the additional money his son would need to live away from home, though the education is free. Besides, many of the villagers are critical of boys who have left to study; they seldom return, and when they visit, they seem to have a superior air.

Joan is 10. She lives in an urban area in Britain. Her parents have a nice home in a residential section of town from which her father commutes to his business each day. Joan began school at age three in a private nursery, where she learned her letters, numbers, and nursery rhymes, and to follow rules, routines, and schedules. Then she went to infant school and primary school near her home, and she is to enter a girls' public school next fall. ("Public school" in Britain is equivalent to private school in the United States. Tuition must be paid. Attending public school is generally considered to be preparatory to getting into a good university.) Here she will study the regular academic subjects, including Latin and French, plus horseback riding and a musical instrument. She particularly likes drawing and will have private lessons. Joan's parents stress education; she studies or reads for at least one hour each evening and is rewarded when her reports are good. Her parents both read a great deal and have many books, magazines, and newspapers at home. Her mother was trained as a teacher; her father studied mathematics at Oxford University and is a successful businessman. She has one brother, who is at a public school for boys. Joan is a good student and applies herself. When she completes public school she will go on to the university.

These two scenarios provide a glance at two educational systems representing two worlds children are experiencing. The division is not only between two children, but between two educational systems, two countries, and two worlds: one rich and developed, the other poor and developing. This distinction must be kept in mind as we consider the world system of education. As different as they are, there are also commonalities in these two educational systems. In this chapter we explore some of these commonalities and differences.

We begin with a consideration of the global educational system; first we look at the field of comparative education, some examples of comparative educational studies, and approaches used to study education across cultures. Then we look at various theoretical views and typologies in comparative education. This is followed by a discussion of the interdependence of institutions within and among societies. Finally, we present examples of educational systems including higher education in different types of societies around the world.

COMPARATIVE EDUCATIONAL STUDIES

"Research on globalization and education involves the study of intertwined worldwide discourses, processes, and institutions affecting local educational practices and policies" (Spring, 2008). Sociology of education provides new insights, ideas, and perspectives on both one's own society and also global education trends. It provides information on what is unique in educational systems and what is universal. Although research on globalization and comparative education is interdisciplinary, sociologists have been major contributors to the field, developing useful methodologies, identifying key variables, constructing analytical models, and carrying out research projects. Most of the research findings can be used by policy makers for applied, practical purposes.

Comparative Education as a Field of Study

The field of comparative education has moved from primarily descriptive data and case studies of specific educational system in selected countries and problems in these systems to an inter-disciplinary field that looks at educational systems in comparative context using a variety of methodologies (Altbach, 1991; Spring, 2008). Research in the field ranges from studies using descriptive anthropological and ethnographic methods to large-scale data collection as found in comparative achievement studies (Baker, 2002; Rotberg, 2006).

Today many theories are employed, including world culture, world systems, postcolonial, cultural, feminist, poststructural, and postmodern theories (Spring, 2008). Some theoretical approaches used in comparative research are also used in other sociology of education studies: Marxist, neo-Marxist, correspondence, resistance and reproduction theories, dependency theory, and feminist theory.

Methods used to study educational systems range from historical comparisons of the development of educational systems and content analyses of curricula to large-scale studies based on international data sets and area, or regional studies using a variety of techniques from observation to interviews and questionnaires. Although a variety of social research techniques have been used by comparative researchers, many studies from individual countries still do not use comparative research techniques, but rather descriptive or case studies (Cummings, 1999; Rust et al., 1999).

William Cummings (1999) describes the field as having progressed through several historical phases of development:

1. Mid-nineteenth century: "Borrowers" and "predictors" used comparative inquiry to perfect and advance their own systems.
2. Mid-1950s: Classification of facts led to historical and area studies.
3. 1960s: Focus on education's role in transforming newly emerging developing nations.
4. Early 1970s: Relative neglect of comparative studies because of the idea that the United States was the leading society with little to learn from other countries.

More recently several themes have dominated comparative studies in education: globalization's effect on education, international development and partnerships (Crossley and Holmes, 2001), globalization of curricula (Boli, 2002; Brint, 2006), textbooks and teacher training (Benavot, 1992), quality and quantity of education, internal structure of systems and educational goals, educational finance, teaching techniques and effectiveness of education, control of decision making in education, education of specific demographic groups (Bray and Thomas, 1995, p. 1), scientific literacy (McEneaney, 2003), and new forms of learning (Broadfoot, 2000). Research topics of recently published comparative studies show great diversity: They include gender issues, in-school variables, dysfunctional aspects of schooling, the role of the state, curriculum and textbook issues, scientific literacy, comparative international achievement tests, legitimacy of knowledge, effects of globalization, and others (McEneaney, 2003). They are influenced by international organizations and worldwide trends and issues. Three of these themes are discussed in this chapter: comparative international achievement tests, legitimacy of knowledge, and effects of globalization.

As the field has developed, so have differences of opinion on the focus of comparative education. Consider the following opinions:

1. The process of developing an educational system is key for each country, and this should be done by "local cultural authorities," not external countries or organizations. Education should reflect the self-identified needs of each country.
2. Single solutions are the key to educational success in countries around the world: technology, vouchers, distance teaching and learning, and so forth.
3. Comparative models of education and universal standards of excellence developed by international organizations should guide development of educational systems.
4. How individuals and nations affect and are affected by globalization pressures and resulting change should be the focus of studies. However, this last focus on comparing the education

of individual countries has been eclipsed because countries are no longer autonomous states with individual national education systems, but exist in a global environment (Carnoy and Rhoten, 2002; Dale, 2005).

In actuality, none of these views is always the correct one, but these views and many others have been proposed for educational systems struggling to deal with their place in the world.

Comparative educational research is complicated by methodological problems such as differences in school starting ages, gender differences in schooling, different curricula models, different types of schools, testing and record-keeping techniques, all examples of why it is difficult to find standard comparative techniques and data. In addition, comparative studies must take into account differences in languages and methods of collecting data.

To help standardize data collection, the United Nations has established some common measurement techniques to be used by member countries, and as these techniques are adopted, comparative analysis is expanding with the help of more reliable data and governments' interest in international studies. This leads to a variety of new research questions, theoretical approaches, and methodologies.

Comparative Studies of Educational Achievement

Achievement tests are taken by children around the world, and many governments are curious about the findings to see where they stand and what they can do to improve. This is an important research area for most countries. The educational level of the workforce in industrialized countries gives an idea of the skills available in each country. Although secondary school completion levels are similar in top industrial countries, several countries stand out for their very high rates, preparing more students to go on to higher education. The percentage of the population between 25 and 64 completing higher education degrees has increased dramatically in a broad range of countries and is highest in Canada and the United States, with Japan close behind (see Figure 11.1).

International studies of academic achievement provide comparative data on reading proficiency, mathematics, and science achievement at different levels of education, and comparisons of access, completion, and learning within countries by income, social class, region, and ethnic group (Wagner, 2006). Use of international studies is increasing because of their value in providing new ideas and alternative perspectives on educational practices, school curricula, school policies, student backgrounds, and other sociocultural variables that affect teaching and learning.

The International Association for the Evaluation of Educational Achievement (IEA) carried out the most extensive comparative research endeavor ever. The original study is a classic in the field of comparative studies, not only because of its extent and its advanced comparative methodological techniques but because such a multimillion-dollar project may never again be possible (Passow et al., 1976, pp. 12–13). A number of volumes based on the data have resulted, with topics covering the significance of the study, methodology, and comparative findings. Follow-up studies have provided additional data for comparisons.

A primary purpose of the study was to identify key characteristics affecting national systems of education and relate them to outcomes of learning (Passow et al., 1976, p. 12). The

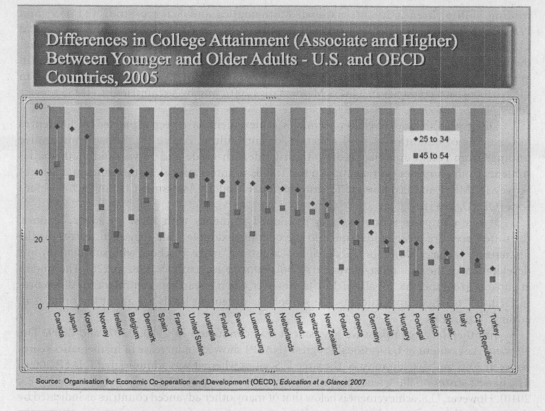

Source: Organisation for Economic Co-operation and Development (OECD), *Education at a Glance 2007*

FIGURE 11.1 Differences in College Attainment (Associate and Higher) Between Younger and Older Adults--U.S and OECD Countries, 2005.

study analyzed school subjects—math, science, reading comprehension, literature, civic education, and French and English as foreign languages. Test results were compared for 10-year-olds and 14-year-olds, and for the year before students left school. Key variables included age of school entry and leaving, size of school and classroom, proportion of total age cohort in school at graduation or leaving time, specialized versus comprehensive curricula, student socioeconomic status, and sex differences.

Such a vast amount of data was collected and processed, and so many hypotheses were tested that it is difficult to provide an accurate summary of the findings. However, this much can be concluded from the data analysis: After a country reaches a "critical threshold," educational efficiency and achievement between like nations is similar. Differences between developed countries are probably best explained by how many resources are put into what aspects of education. The IEA studies show only modest differences in achievement among advanced, primarily European, countries, although the range between subject areas such as math, science, reading comprehension, civics, and technology varies greatly (Suter, 2001).

Currently there are three comparative achievement tests from which most of the findings are taken. Progress in International Reading Literacy Study (PIRLS) measures reading ability; Trends in International Mathematics and Science Study (TIMSS) and Program for International Student Assessment (PISA) both measure mathematics; and TIMSS also measures science achievement. European and some Asian countries score highest on the tests, but the United States is above average on most. International comparisons of 4th graders reveal that the United States is outperformed by 10 of 45 participating countries in PIRLS 2006, by 8 countries in TIMSS Mathematics 2007, and by 4 countries in TIMSS science 2007 (NCES, 2009).

Differences that exist between countries' achievement have been explained by differences in financing of education, school structure, or curriculum. Figure 11.2 shows comparative findings from recent ongoing studies of 4th-grade, 8th-grade and 15 year old mathematics students from countries participating in the Trends in International Mathematics and Science Survey (TIMSS) and Programme for International Student Assessment (PISA) achievement tests (OECD, 2005).

If one compares schools in less developed countries with those in advanced ones, the differences are great as illustrated in the opening example. One suggested reason for the discrepancy is that children in less developed countries "arrive at school with substantially less development of the skills most relevant to school performance" (Inkeles, 1982, p. 228). The schools are unable to compensate for all the deficits. However, when researchers control for the differences in facilities, teachers, and students, the schools' achievement levels are about the same as in advanced countries.

Another large comparative assessment was conducted in 2003, 2007, and 2009. The National Assessment of Educational Progress (NAEP) showed an increase in mathematics scores between 2003 and 2009 in most of the large U.S. cities where it was administered (NAEP, 2009). The newest scores on the science portion were not yet released at the time of publication (NCES, 2010). However, U.S. achievement is below that of many other advanced countries as indicated by the combined international tests scores. Yet, interpretations of recent comparative test results show U.S. primary and secondary scores in math, science, and reading have increased (Salzman and Lowell, 2007). Fourth graders showed improvement, with higher literacy scores than students in 23 of the 34 participating countries in 2001 (Nohara, 2001). Internationally the United States held second place in science scores (Salzman and Lowell, 2007). Findings indicate that high expectations, rigor of the curriculum, and quality and content of instruction were key in high achieving schools.

Comparative achievement test can alert us to other trends in societies. For example, for each additional year of schooling attained by women in Global South (countries around the world that lie below the equator) countries, nearly 10 percent fewer children will die before age five. That is, 8.2 million fewer children dying in 2009 ("Better Education Attainment Saves Lives," 2010).

Applying Sociology to Education: What can educational policy makers in countries learn about their own countries from studying achievement scores in other countries, and what might they do with the findings?

Comparative Education and the Systems Approach

We cannot ignore the impact that countries have on each other and the interaction between education and other institutions in societal systems. The systems approach is again useful for piecing

Country	TIMSS 4th grade	TIMSS 8th grade	PISA 15-year-olds
Australia	▼	●	▲
Austria	†	†	▲
Belgium[1]	†	†	▲
Canada	†	†	▲
Czech Republic	†	†	▲
Denmark	†	†	▲
England	▲	*	*
Finland	†	†	▲
France	†	†	▲
Germany	†	†	▲
Iceland	†	†	▲
Ireland	†	†	▲
Japan	▲	▲	▲
Korea, Republic of	†	▲	▲
Luxembourg	†	†	▲
Netherlands	▲	▲	▲
New Zealand	▼	●	▲
Norway	▼	▼	▲
Poland	†	†	▲
Slovak Republic	†	●	▲
Switzerland	†	†	▲
Hungary	▲	▲	●
Scotland	▼	●	*
Spain	†	†	●
Sweden	†	●	●
Greece	†	†	▼
Italy	▼	▼	▼
Mexico	†	†	▼
Portugal	†	†	▼
Turkey	†	†	▼

† Not applicable. Did not participate in this assessment.

[1] Only Flemish Belgium participated in TIMSS 2003. Scores for Flemish Belgium were higher than the United States at grades 4 and 8 in TIMSS 2003.

* Scotland and England participated separately in TIMSS 2003 at both grade levels but jointly as the United Kingdom (including Northern Ireland) in PISA 2003. However, England did not meet response rate standards for grade 8 in TIMSS 2003 or for PISA 2003, so no comparisons are reported with the United States for England for grade 8 in TIMSS 2003 or for the United Kingdom for PISA 2003.

Note: Countries are ordered according to their performance relative to the United States in PISA and then alphabetized, except for England and Scotland, which did not participate in PISA separately.

Source: Organization for Economic Cooperation and Development (OECD) Program for International Student Assessment (PISA) 2003, and International Association for the Evaluation of Educational Achievement (IEA) Trends in International Mathematics and Science Survey (TIMSS) 2003. Scott Elais. National Center for Education Statistics (NCES). "Comparing NAEP, TIMSS, and PISA in Mathematic and Science" (Washington, DC: U.S. Department of Education).

Key:

▲ Average score is higher than U.S. average score

● Average score is not measurably different from U.S. average score

▼ Average score is lower than U.S. average score

FIGURE 11.2 Average mathematics performance of fourth-graders, eighth-graders, and 15-year-olds for all participating countries, relative to the U.S. average (2003).

together these dynamics. Using the open systems approach helps us conceptualize the world context within which each country exists (Figure 11.3). From this perspective, the world system is the environment for individual countries. How they interact economically and politically and their level of development within the world system influence the type of educational system they develop.

The systems approach is also useful in picturing the different *levels of analysis* at work in education. Educational systems can be viewed from the macro-, meso-, or micro-levels. *Macro-level analysis* considers the big picture: How is globalization affecting development of schools, power structures, and world trends in school structures and curricula. *Meso-level analysis* is the institutional level: how schools are organized; structures, categories, and rules (especially what is common in the organizational structure across educational systems); shared functions; and environmental pressures on institutions and organizations. *Micro-level analysis* focuses on a number of issues. The following are some examples: how people and small groups interact, including their speech and gestures; the way individuals present themselves to others; the setting for interaction; and individuals' interpretations of the situation (such as their place in the school system). Figure 11.3 shows some major concerns at different levels of analysis, from macro- to micro-level (Brint, 2006, p. 21).

Level of analysis	Major concerns
MACRO-HISTORICAL	
Development of school structures and purposes	Origins of school purposes and structures in comparative perspective
	Historical change in school purposes and structures in comparative perspective
	Consequences of school purposes and structures for society and particular groups in society
MESO-INSTITUTIONAL	
Operation of schools as social institutions in particular times and places	Organizational structures and practices for channeling energy and attention
	Environmental influences on schooling
	Interests and relationships of major categories of actors
	Consequences of institution for learning, socialization, and social selection
MICRO-INTERACTIONAL	
Staging and interaction processes involved in classroom activities	Structural influences on interaction within schools
	Methods used to develop learning communities
	Interaction-based successes and failures in instructional activities
	Consequences of school interactions for learning, socialization, and social selection

FIGURE 11.3 Levels of sociological analysis of schooling.

Source: SCHOOLS AND SOCIETIES, 2/e, by Stephen Brint. © 1998 Pine Forge Press; 2006 by the Board of Trustees of the Leland Stanford Jr. University. All rights reserved. Used with the permission of Stanford University Press, www.sup.org <http://www.sup.org/> .

The range of topics in comparative education analysis and levels of analysis at which these topics are studied is illustrated in Figure 11.4. Note in the cube the levels of analysis on the front, some topics of educational research on the right side, and some groups that are affected in unique ways by educational systems and policies on the top of the cube (Bray et al., 2007).

The questions that guide our research design include what we wish to compare, and how we should do it. These underlying questions lead to the following five research models and examples of each, which are by no means exhaustive of the approaches that exist:

1. Models comparing countries on specific aspects of education such as subject-area achievement (language, science, and math literacy);
2. Approaches identifying key elements in the internal structure of educational systems that can be compared cross-culturally (school-to-work transitions);
3. Societal system "strategies" or approaches to the development of educational systems to meet the needs of society (education in planned economies);
4. Models showing the link between mass education curricula, growth and expansion of nation-states, and similarities between curricula and structures (Schofer and Myer, 2005); and
5. Models showing the interrelationships between societal institutions and the environment (effects of globalization and international models).

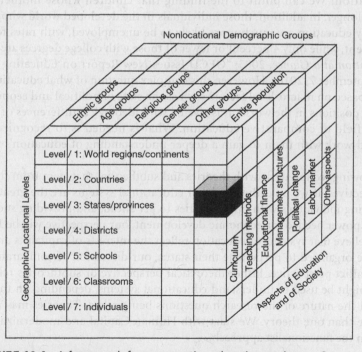

FIGURE 11.4 A framework for comparative education analyses. *Source:* Mark Bray and R. Murray Thomas, "Levels of Comparison in Educational Studies: Different Insights from Different Literatures and the Value of Multilevel Analyses," HARVARD EDUCATIONAL REVIEW, 65:3 (Fall 1995), pg. 475. Copyright © by the President and Fellows of Harvard College. All rights reserved. Used by permission. For more information, please visit www.harvardeducationalreview.org.

Comparative models or typologies such as the one in Figure 11.4 are like the frame of a house. They provide the foundation and support for each unique unit. We vary the rooms, the decor, and the outside covering. Yet each house has a foundation based on common principles of construction. Likewise, the models above provide frameworks for developing or studying the same types of systems, in this case, educational systems. A model is useful insofar as it reflects reality when matched against actual cases. Models commonly relate to either specific aspects of education or comparisons of systems. As methodologies become more sophisticated, so do models for comparative studies. The model presented in Figure 11.4 shows three dimensions for analysis that include most of the variables used in studies today: aspects of education and of society, geographical/locational levels (levels of analysis), and nonlocational demographic groups.

THEORETICAL PERSPECTIVES IN COMPARATIVE EDUCATION

Education is viewed by much of the world's population as a gateway to opportunity. Many bright, eager Global South children beg foreign visitors to help them get more education, whereas children in many developed countries think they would like nothing more than to be free of the compulsory burden of school. But what can education actually do for the people of a nation? We can point to the finding that children whose mothers have more education live longer. In addition, those individuals in the developed world who do not complete secondary education are much more likely to be unemployed, with rates for this group topping 9 percent, while only 4 percent or fewer of those with college degrees are unemployed (OECD, *Education at a Glance*, 2003; "OECD Issues New Report on Educating the U.S. and the World," September 7, 2010). However, this complex question of what education can do for individuals is based on macro-level factors such as the state of political and economic systems and countries' positions in the world. It is riveted with ideological differences of opinion that permeate the field of comparative education. What is needed is to recognize ideological differences and work with them to gain a deeper understanding of education's role in world development.

The following section deals with theories and subtheories that stem from functional and conflict perspectives. If we hold the view that educational systems are the great "levelers" of society, providing individuals with opportunities to get ahead, and providing society with the skilled human power needed for economic development, our perspective will be functional. If, however, we believe that systems of education reflect the interests of capitalists and the elite in society, and are organized to perpetuate their status, our discussion of comparative education will have a conflict perspective. Either theoretical perspective or subtheories related to these perspectives might be used to understand educational systems, depending on the view of the researcher and the nature of the research questions being asked. Theories may also combine elements more than one theory. We start with Human Capital and modernization theories stemming from the functionalist approach.

Human Capital Perspectives

Since World War II, there have been dramatic changes in the workplace. Between 2008 and 2018, the United States is expected to experience the biggest losses in manufacturing jobs, declining by about 9 percent, or 1,206,000 jobs. Construction jobs are seeing growth because of stimulus monies for building and roads, up 19 percent for 1,337,000 jobs. The largest growth is in the service sector, with 14.5 million new jobs projected by the year 2018 (Bureau of Labor Statistics, 2010–2011). These growth areas point to the rise of the knowledge-based economy and the importance of new technology. Many researchers look at this relationship between education and areas of economic growth and development.

Modernization and human capital perspectives, which dominated comparative education theory in the 1960s and early 1970s, pointed to the importance of education in transforming people's beliefs, values, and behaviors into those necessary for economic modernization—such as, diligence, rational calculation, orderliness, frugality, punctuality, and achievement orientation (Slomczynski and Krauze, 1986)—and new social values such as meritocracy—getting ahead because of one's own ability (Becker, 1993). Developing and cultivating human capital was seen as an investment; therefore, investing in education should be positive for economic growth (Hudson Institute, 1997). Global South or peripheral countries play a role in this view as they often supply the needed low-wage workers, causing manufacturing and low-skilled jobs to move to peripheral countries.

Although there is a clear relationship between the global economy and the role of education to prepare workers for needed tasks in that economy, some ask whether the workplace can absorb all the educated workers. Many countries are not able to use all of their trained workers, and this is causing a "brain drain" of workers, where workers who cannot find work in their own countries leave for other opportunities. For this and other reasons, human capital perspectives have been criticized as explained below:

1. Meritocracy is an ideal reached in few countries. Review of data from 20 countries representing different types of political–economic systems shows that former "Eastern European nonmarket economies" (Poland, Czechoslovakia, Hungary, and the former USSR) were closer to ideal meritocracy than the industrial market economies of Western Europe (France, Great Britain, Switzerland, Netherlands, Germany, Finland, and Sweden). Contrary to widespread beliefs, Japan and the United States are very far from ideal meritocracy—much farther than some less developed countries (Kerbo, 2000).

2. The Human Capital perspective has a built-in "ethnocentric" assumption that all nations will emulate the Western model of development. In fact, countries do not always lose their indigenous educational systems even if they adopt Western ones. Countries may tailor models from other countries to meet their own needs (Brown, 1999). For example, traditional Islamic schooling may be maintained along with the increase in Western influence on schooling (Morgan and Armer, 1987).

3. Making individuals "modern" through education may not result in a modern society (Benavot, 1987). Lack of jobs, gender inequality, and low wages for the educated may cause discontent and "brain drain." A new structure of international mobility is creating a "brain circulation" in which "highly skilled personnel" move from one country to another. For example, one-third of Silicon Valley, the high tech industry hub in California, is foreign born (Cao, 1996; Saxenian, 2005).

4. Most new jobs are in the service and sales sectors and require only some training. There is little evidence that new skilled jobs will be created as workers receive increased training (Redovich, 1991).

Two alternative views, world systems perspective and dependency theory, challenge the claim presented above that education is a positive force that enhances economic development.

> Dependency and world system scholars argue that: (1) the global capitalist economy is a holistic system characterized by structural inequalities both between and within nation-states; (2) the economies of Third World nations were systematically plundered and underdeveloped in earlier historical epochs and now constitute a peripheral component of the global system which continues to supply raw materials and cheap labor to the industrial centers; (3) the expropriation of profit and surplus value by core nations and multinational corporations depended upon the complicity and power of national elites who were usually educated in Western school systems; and (4) by seeking to maximize returns to foreign investments and by setting national priorities according to foreign standards, the actions of the national bourgeoisie have intensified internal inequalities, reinforced the dependency of Third World nations, and retarded long-term economic development. (Benavot, 1992, p. 8)

These theorists look instead to "a nation's structural position in the world economy, trade flow, dependence on primary product exports, state strength, degree of foreign investment, and the presence of multinational corporations" (Benavot, 1992, p. 8). They argue that education plays a limited role in determining or influencing economic development.

However, some reproduction theorists argue that education *does* affect development. For example, they point to Western-educated Global South leaders who have perpetuated former colonial patterns that keep their countries in dependent positions. Education systems in peripheral nations have reproduced and reinforced the class structure, strengthening the position of national elites (Carnoy, 1982). Although some economic growth has taken place, the profits go outside the country and the masses see little change. Other peripheral countries are using education to develop human capital and become competitive in today's work; India, China, and Korea are examples.

The United States is losing some of its formerly unchallenged competitive edge to these burgeoning economies. To continue to be competitive as many jobs are outsourced, some scholars recommend that the United States draw on its strengths—creativity of the workforce developed throughout schooling. Innovation, risk taking, and entrepreneurship are human capital strengths in the United States, and the educational system plays the key role in developing these strengths. The United States has 5 percent of the world's population, one-third of the scientists and engineering researchers, 40 percent of the research, and 35 percent of the research articles published in the world. Much of this strength comes from cross-disciplinary teams (Wince-Smith, 2006), resulting in the competitive edge that is being challenged.

"Legitimation of Knowledge" Perspective

The study of comparative educational knowledge has gone through two broad phases of development (Welch, 1991). The first was to study the process whereby educational knowledge becomes "legitimate" (i.e., accepted by the government and citizens), and how that knowledge base changes over time. The second was to consider the relationship between the legitimation of educational knowledge and power relations in the modern state. Conflict or "critical" theorists have taken the lead in these discussions. They use as a foundation writings by Max Weber, Karl Marx, Jurgen Habermas, and others.

In the 1970s, with the advent of the "new" sociology of education, Michael Young (1971) and others no longer assumed that education represented the social consensus or agreement of citizens of a country; in fact, "critical" sociologists questioned every assumption and structure. Some viewed education as a form of "ideological domination" by those in power to control the knowledge taught and to stay in power.

Three central questions are related to the issue of legitimate knowledge: How does certain knowledge become legitimate? Under what circumstances does it become changed? And what does a comparative comparison of such processes tell us (Welch, 1991, p. 515)? The hypothesis underlying these questions was that in the process of knowledge transfer (education of children), some groups in society may be left out of decision making about curricula.

The underlying theme in much of the recent writing is that curriculum and acceptable knowledge transmission are not neutral, but rather are driven by social elements such as who is in power and who has economic control (Archer, 1979; Habermas, 1978). Some argue that the form schooling takes, such as "comprehensive school structure" in Europe, is influenced by the needs of capitalist labor markets (Levin, 1978). Another influence is international organizations that "define and promote overall world-level principles and ideas that then are used to guide state policy behavior . . . national policy aims tend to be consistent with international organization decisions and policies" (McNeely, 1995, p. 504).

Even the day-to-day routines that take place in schools around the world have been studied for hidden messages children receive from external influences, including international organizations. This "hidden curriculum" is exemplified in the African thought process. Science education is more closely associated with a Western cause–effect view of the world than with a worldview from traditionally agricultural, religious countries. As science becomes an integral part of most countries' basic curriculum, these new Western worldviews are transmitted. Some argue that these "hidden messages" lead to a more rapid increase in a country's standard of living (Benavot et al., 1991; Holsinger and Lowell, 2000). But such a worldview may also perpetuate unequal stratification systems that give some elite members of society more access to elite education, making them competitive for global positions.

Despite the conflicting views over the role of education in societies, all nations have some form of formal education. In the next section we consider cross-national studies in comparative education: rich versus poor countries, studies of internal structure of educational systems, and societal strategies for education.

Rich versus Poor Educational Typology

Niger is the poorest country in the world, according to the United Nations Human Poverty Index. This index measures life expectancy, knowledge (including level of education), and standard of living. Indicators include sanitation, drinking water, electricity, children in school, and malnourished individuals. Educating the population in poor countries has major challenges, not least of which is the level of development as seen in the following demographic figures. In Niger, the vast majority of the 15.3 million citizens engage in subsistence-level agriculture. Infant mortality rate (deaths from birth to one year) is a high 116.7 per 1,000 births, and many infants are underweight. Deaths result from hepatitis, malaria, meningitis, and other infections and diseases. Life expectancy is 52.6 years. A majority of the population lives on less than one dollar a day. Population growth at 3.7 percent annually, with a birth rate of 7.7 children per woman (highest in the world), does not help the situation. Adult literacy, those 15 and above who can read, is 28.7 percent, but the sex disparity is great: 42.9 percent of males are literate, but only 15.1 percent of females. The average number of years of schooling is four overall and three for girls. Yet despite the bad news, there is some improvement with primary school enrollments rising from 24 percent in 1990 to 38 percent in 2002, and more girls are attending school. Other countries in the top ten poorest (from number 2 on) include Ethiopia, Mali, Burkina Faso, Burundi, Somalia, Central African Republic, Liberia, Guinea, and Sierra Leone—all in Africa, and most in sub-Saharan Africa (Hindman, 2010).

Despite implementation of various government programs to improve the basic health, welfare, and educational level, many barriers have to be overcome. Subsistence agriculture demands that all hands work, so children have little time for schooling and little opportunity to be educated however much they may value education. The population growth rate requires that the government spend money just to keep up with the additional children. Girls are involved in household chores and child care, and long distances from school make attendance difficult. Teacher quality also affects attendance rates. The government, by implementing a vast system of adult education that is reaching thousands, hopes to break the cycle of illiteracy. This is but one example of a country's efforts and challenges to improving formal education in developing countries.

Learning takes place in many ways and settings: For the rich of the world, much learning is formal. It takes place in classrooms and specially designed buildings. For the poor, there may or may not be a classroom. Often formal learning is a small part of the poor child's education; mostly he or she learns informally through imitating elders and learning the family trade. An anthropology professor once warned that before we scoff at informal learning we should consider its impact. He asked us to imagine ourselves transferred to the Kalahari Desert. How would we survive? Where would we find food and water? Without help we would likely perish. Yet the Bushmen survive and flourish there; they have been learning survival techniques, passed on from early childhood through the generations. The film *The Gods Must Be Crazy* shows the contrasts between the lives of Europeans and Bushmen.

There are about 653 million children of primary school age and 388 million of lower secondary age in the world. Half of these children live in South, West, and East Asia and the Pacific. That adds up to more than 1 billion primary and secondary school students in the world (UNESCO Institute for Statistics, 2010). Yet we must look at individual countries to get the whole picture. The proportion of children attending primary school in Niger is 22 percent, in Angola 27 percent, in Djibouti 30.6 percent, and in Ethiopia 31 percent (Maps of the World, 2006). However, in rich Western countries primary school enrollment is 100 percent (see Table 11.1). The number of children in school in any country is closely related to that country's wealth and level of economic development. Illiteracy and economic development are related; Global South countries that are struggling economically also have the highest illiteracy rates, with up to two-thirds of women and one-third of men illiterate. World adult literacy is 78.5 percent (UNDP, 2007–2008), 81 percent for men and 65 percent for women (UNICEF, 2002).

Unfortunately, the quality of schools in many of the poorest Global South countries is eroding, and public spending per pupil is dropping. Although middle-income countries show a rise in school quality, the overall differences in comparisons of Global South countries with industrial nations are great and the gap is widening. Why the differences? The reasons are many, but they center on the position of poor countries in the world system. Influencing the educational situation are the level of wealth in a country; the rapid growth in enrollments, which forces

Table 11.1 Children of Primary and Secondary School Age Out of School

Region	Primary		Lower secondary		Total	
	Percent	Million	Percent	Million	Percent	Million
Sub-Saharan Africa	25.8	32.2	36.8	21.3	29.3	53.5
Arab States	13.9	5.8	19.5	4.3	15.8	10.0
South and West Asia	10.2	18.0	27.3	29.1	16.6	47.2
Central Asia	4.8	0.3	4.9	0.4	4.8	0.7
East Asia and the Pacific	5.2	9.0	10.0	10.6	7.0	19.7
Central and Eastern Europe	7.0	1.6	9.6	1.9	8.3	3.5
North America and Western Europe	3.8	1.9	4.3	1.3	4.0	3.3
Latin America and the Caribbean	5.1	3.0	5.5	2.0	5.3	5.0
World	11.0	71.8	18.3	71.0	13.7	142.8

Sources: UNESCO Institute of Statistics. 2010. Table 1 "Out-of-school adolescents." www.uis.unesco.org/template/pdf/EducationGeneral/OOSA_EN.pdf (Retrieved March 28, 2011).

limited resources to be spread even thinner; and other factors related to dependent and debtor nations (Fuller, 1986; Gallagher, 1993). Unfortunately, rapid population growth in some of the poorest regions will only exacerbate the problems.

Within many countries, there are unofficially two educational systems: one in rural areas and the other in urban areas (Hannum, 1999). Some urban education is elite education. Village schools, as seen in the opening scenario in this chapter, have fewer resources, often less qualified teachers, and less parental support. They may be state-run or attached to a local temple, mosque, or mission; religious education may be the main emphasis. Urban schools in developing nations are usually organized and run on a Western or colonial model, often patterned after the English or French forms of education. Many serve the nation's elite population. Within the poor nations are families who cannot afford to take advantage of available preschool and elementary education because their children are needed to help with the farmwork, and survival has priority over schooling. In some countries (such as Latin American countries), however, early-childhood intervention programs are available and provide useful information, services, and support to the family and child. This provides one method for governments to increase the health and nutritional awareness of families.

Many of the comparative analyses of elementary school curricula show worldwide standardization in major subject areas, reflecting ideologies, rules, and customs that are transnational in character and that cut across regions and economic systems. Instead of individual countries or regions determining content, a world system based on scientific values guides the process of curriculum development (Benavot et al., 1988; Meyer, Kamens, and Benavot, 1992). As mentioned, standardization usually reflects Western models that are not always most relevant for developing countries. Some theorists disagree with the indicators used to show that there is a world system of education, but similarities in educational systems have been supported.

Secondary curricula, too, show homogeneity across cultures. In a study of 120 countries comparing curricula for students preparing for university, standard world models were apparent, although in secondary schools distinct curricular types, such as tracks in the arts and humanities or in math and science, were found in some systems (Kamens, Meyer, and Benavot, 1996). Secondary education is more elusive than primary education for rural children of developing nations, partly because they may be required to pay for transportation, boarding, books, or clothes that often make education impossible.

The educational system often serves to perpetuate inequality by being available only to elites, usually those from urban areas. Inequality is found in wealthy, developed, industrial societies as well as poor, emerging, developing, and modernizing ones. The inequalities between individuals are related to class, race, sex, and religion as well as to rural versus urban residence. Even the age at which children start school and the preprimary enrollment rates vary by country. For instance, 80 percent of students in industrialized (developed) societies attend preprimary education. However, in Africa and the Middle East the figures are 20 percent or lower. In Finland and Norway, two countries with high scores on international achievement tests, primary school starts at seven.

Globalization and Education

"Research on globalization and education involves the study of intertwined worldwide discourses, processes, and institutions affecting local educational practices and policies" (Spring, 2008, p. 330). Think of our systems model with its levels of analysis and its many environmental factors that affect what happens in school systems. These include worldwide discussions among educational experts about what children need to know to fit into the global system and models for achieving this education. Think of all this and you have a cursory view of the next theoretical approaches, all dealing with the concept of globalization and education.

Globalization is a complex and sometimes controversial concept. It was first coined by Theodore Levitt to describe changes in global economics affecting production, consumption, and investment (Spring, 2008, p. 331), and refers to shifts in patterns of transnational economic activities and movement of capital (money) and finance. It also refers to the shaping of new political and cultural patterns (Popkewitz and Rizvi, 2009).

Three contrasting views on globalization are put forth by the "globalists," the "skeptics," and the "changing rationalists." "Globalists" view globalization as a "significant historical development that alters all aspects of our lives." They see it influencing our social, cultural, economic, and political lives (Held and McGrew, 2007, p. 8). "Skeptics" view globalization as an ideological construction that has limited value in understanding schools or society; they point out that global change has been taking place since at least the 1880s—so what is new now? "Changing rationalists" see world trends such as immigration, poverty, development, security, and ethical governance as principles that need to be understood in terms of global change and to guide social reform, including school reform in a rational manner (Held and McGrew, 2007).

We have noted that although there are some common trends in educational policy and change, schools are not made from cookie-cutter models (Anderson-Levitt, 2003). In addition to the different theoretical views on globalization, there are those theorists who are critical of the global trends bringing change, arguing that many of these changes threaten local languages and cultures and perpetuate the status of the rich and encourage environmental degradation and violations of human rights. Cases in point are situations in African mines in the Congo that have enabled conflicts, rape, and poverty, and the human rights abuses in the Darfur region of Sudan.

One influential theory that falls into the globalization camp is World Systems Theory, discussed in the next section.

World System Analysis

This global conflict perspective views stratification between world countries just as conflict theory studies stratification within race, class, and gender within countries. "Core" (developed capitalist) states are often involved in the educational development of "periphery" (developing) states, a factor some argue serves the core states by training the workforce to capitalist specifications, resulting in a return of capital to the core nations (Clayton, 1998; Wallerstein, 2004).

World system theorists consider education within the transnational social structural system, and observe the effects of this global system on individual countries and regions (Wallerstein, 1974). Both ideological systems and organizations (political, economic, and religious) affect the direction of educational development. States or national governments are the means by which capitalists control the world market, including educational systems (Chase-Dunn, 1980). For instance, most countries are caught up in the "myth of progress" (Ramirez and Boli-Bennett, 1987, p. 18). Because all states respond to this common global ideology, educational developments have been similar, with the underlying assumption that growth is good for society and the individual.

An example of world system analysis is seen in the theoretical model developed by Robert Arnove (1980, p. 49), who uses "dependency theory" to explain the relationships between societies and education. A chain of exploitation exists at several levels: metropolitan (developed) countries and world organizations over peripheral (developing) countries; centers of power in Third World countries over peripheral rural areas; and so on down to the village level. In this system, the peripheral areas may gain by getting needed resources, but the price is domination (by the metropolitan or center areas) over local affairs—curricula, texts, and reforms, for example.

To illustrate the world system of education, scholars (Meyer, Kamens, and Benavot, 1992; Ramirez and Boli-Bennett, 1987) point to the many international organizations coordinating education worldwide: the Ford and Rockefeller foundations, the Organization for Economic Cooperation and Development, the United Nations including UNESCO and UNICEF, World Bank, World Trade Organization, international testing organizations, and so on (Spring, 2008). These organizations have the power and money to promote ideas and programs around the world, and models advocated by international agencies have spread around the world. Some of these programs are successful, others disappointing—as in the case of rural India, where emphasis on "nonformal education" gave the government an excuse not to provide classrooms for students. Faculty in higher-education institutions in Global South countries have been sponsored by organizations such as the Rockefeller Foundation. To some, this seems like philanthropy at its best, but to conflict theorists, this exemplifies international organizational philanthropy spreading capitalist ideologies and shaping Global South educational systems to meet the needs of international, multinational, and American corporate needs. They point out that the World Bank is financed by wealthy capitalist countries to give advice to developing nations.

Theorists moving away from the traditional world system theory contend that subordinates in periphery states are often aware of their status in relation to others and do act in relation to their knowledge, often by resisting dominance of core countries. In some countries, this is taking the form of controlling development of their own educational systems. Moving from macro-level analysis to postmodern interpretations, which include a consideration of periphery states as "conscious actors" in the process, parallels developments in conflict theory (Clayton, 1998).

Each societal system of education is influenced by the larger world system. Few societies in today's interdependent world can be studied without careful consideration of their place in the world community. Yet this is not an easy task, because comparing complex and different systems presents methodological difficulties.

Whatever theoretical perspective one holds, it can be agreed that education does not stand alone in society. Education must be considered in relation to other institutions in the society, and in relationship to each society's international environment. This is particularly important in the case of developing nations, many of which are in a postcolonial period and have inherited the educational system of former colonial powers. In the following section, examples of the interdependence of institutions are discussed.

> **Applying Sociology to Education:** *What is a comparative research topic or problem that interests you? Now apply two of the above explanations to this problem. Which seems more appropriate for providing a theoretical framework to study your question?*

GLOBAL INSTITUTIONAL INTERDEPENDENCE

Every society shares a set of common institutions: family, education, religion, politics, economics, and health systems. As the world shrinks with the aid of technology, communication networks, and transportation systems, different institutional models around the globe become more similar. However, political systems, economic systems, and religious beliefs are major variables separating countries. For instance, a rough separation in world countries divides the northern and southern hemispheres, with those countries in the southern hemisphere more often a part of the developing world, characterized by recent independence (since 1945), saddled with legacies of colonialism and debt to wealthier countries. Problems of poverty, disease, hunger, rapid population expansion, and illiteracy occupy governments and force educational issues onto the back burner in poor countries. News reports tell us of death and suffering in a constant string of wars, famines, epidemics, and refugee crises in a number of Global South countries.

Approaches to institutional interdependence can be *global*, as in the case of the "world system perspective" (Wallerstein, 1974); *cross-national*, as in the case of Williamson's economic-political typology of societies or studies of curricula, knowledge, or tests (discussed below) (Williamson, 1979); *institutional*, focusing on the institution of education in relation to other institutions (Benavot, 1997); or *national*, focusing on countries in relation to the global system. In the *global approach*, countries are conceptualized as a part of the world system with interdependent units. Internal and external changes in educational systems are linked to relationships between countries. Much research related to this theory has dealt with economic and political institutions, though cultural and ideological elements have been examined as well. More recently, this approach has been expanded to take an international view of forces that produce similar patterns of social change across societies, as mentioned earlier.

Several themes are common in the newer *institutional approach* to the study of education:

> First, it focuses on the origins and expansion of modern, secular mass systems of schooling in Europe and North America and their worldwide institutionalization during the twentieth century. Second, it analyzes the institutional underpinnings of education in society . . . .Third, this approach examines the ways in which mass and elite education alter important social constructions and institutional arrangements in society. (Benavot, 1997, p. 340)

From this perspective, institutionalists see education as creating a redistribution of political and economic power in national societies. Consider the interconnections between education and religion, family, and economic institutions, discussed in the following section.

Education and the Institution of Religion

Within one country—even within one village—the relationship between education and religion is complex and sometimes contradictory. A few examples may clarify:

- *Northern Nigeria.* A Koranic school for boys stresses traditional religious beliefs, attitudes, and behavior patterns, and is not supportive of change. It exists next to a state-run village school, formerly run by Christian missionaries, which stresses "modern" attitudes and the importance of education in "getting ahead."
- *Northern Ireland.* The Catholic parochial schools and the state schools attended primarily by Protestant children protect and perpetuate a distinction between segments of the society, and may enable the hostilities between the two religious groups.
- *Iran.* Fundamentalist Muslim schools (madrassas) support the status quo and reflect the leadership and views of Muslim imams, or religious leaders.
- *United States.* Fundamentalist Christian schools stress some values opposed to the constitutional separation of church and state; they express the group's alienation from the technological society. Examples of the latter are controversies about textbooks and the questioning of certain scientific teachings on evolution.
- *Israel.* Religion and education work hand in hand to accomplish the goals of the state. Hebrew language and religious training provide unifying themes in an otherwise heterogeneous society. Religion and political beliefs blend in many cases, however, as seen in the 2008 suicide bombing of a Jewish religious school by a Palestinian woman.

Religion is often closely linked to a group's ethnic, racial, or national origins; therefore, it may provide for the group a point of stability in a time of rapid and confusing change in which norms break down—a situation sociologists refer to as "anomie." Attitudes toward change are reflected in religious schools, or in state schools where the religion is represented. If a change is consistent with the principles of the religion, the church may in fact be a leader in that change. Religion may also serve to retard change, however, especially if the change threatens the principles of the belief system.

Family, Social Class, and Education

The family is the primary social bond and purveyor of values. In the family we develop an attitude toward ourselves and what we can become; we develop expectations concerning our education. It is in the environment created by the family that we receive informal education, and also encouragement, support, and proper behavior for success in formal educational pursuit. Deviation from this early influence probably means that some alternative model is available to us and is seen as realistic. The child may be influenced by a teacher, minister, or older child; or the community may require children to attend school and encourage the brightest to continue, perhaps even providing support.

Families in some poor communities may be too poor to take advantage of educational opportunities; formal education may not be a realistic part of their lives. Thus, the cycle of poverty for some and great opportunity for others—both in individual countries and in the world—is perpetuated. Paulo Freire, a former Brazilian minister of education for the state of Sao Paulo, worked to develop education for the poor, especially those in rural agricultural areas. He has written about what he sees as the hopelessness of the poor classes, caused in part by their inability to see beyond immediate problems and to look at the world critically. This inability allows a system of elite landowners to dominate rural, uneducated peasants (Freire, 1970, 1973, 1987; Torres, 1994). The peasants adopt a fatalistic attitude about life, supported by supernatural religious beliefs, which serve to hold them in their inferior places.

As a society becomes more literate, certain attendant changes occur: urbanization, mobility, and modernization. These have a direct bearing on the family. Extended families begin to break down as some members move to urban areas for more opportunities. As urbanization increases, the birthrate decreases because it is difficult to house and feed a large family in a cramped urban apartment. Women's status often changes with entry into urban life as many women enter the industrial workforce and have fewer children. Again, changes in one part of society inevitably affect other parts. The position of one's family in the social structure affects both one's chances for education and one's place in an educational system.

Parents in developed countries generally want to have a say in their children's education, to "manage" their school careers. For instance, in American schools, parents who manage the daily activities of their children raise the academic standing of their children. In Germany, parental management differs by the type of secondary school the child attends. It is greater in the college preparatory school (gymnasium) than in trade/vocational schools. In Japan, parents support schooling activities outside of the formal setting by tutoring their children and providing extra classes, which they feel enhance examination preparation and future opportunities (Baker and Stevenson, 1989, p. 348).

In a well-known typology, Turner (1960) suggested that the pattern of upward mobility shapes the school system. He compared English and American schools, concluding that the values in England support what he called the "sponsored" form of mobility, where elites select elites and perpetuate themselves. This compares with "contest" mobility in America, where an individual's abilities and competition are more important in placement. These values underlie the institution of education in each country.

Many parents want to choose the school their children will attend, including the religious affiliation, pedagogy, and curriculum. Minority and immigrant parents may make special efforts to influence their children's education (Baker and Stevenson, 1990; Glenn, 1989; Golan and Peterson, 2002). The importance of one's family background for educational achievement is discussed in other chapters throughout the book.

Education and Economic Institutions

Most countries believe that there is a relationship between education, economic development, and modernization. Governments act on this premise even though the facts do not always uphold it. They invest in education, and education generally reflects the political philosophy of a country and the goals of the group in power. Many governments have the power to adopt or reject educational programs, or even to totally revamp the educational system, as in China and Cuba during the communist revolutions. If the government establishes certain priorities for the society, the educational system is likely to reflect these in curriculum, texts, and other aspects of the program.

In order to meet a country's goals, trained personnel are needed. Human capital theorists argue that individuals are like pieces of machinery—a capital good—and can increase their value in the labor market by increasing their education and training in occupational skills (Becker, 1993; Bowles, 1976). This argument is challenged by Samuel Bowles and Herbert Gintis (1976), among others, who contend that individuals are labor, not capital.

However, the system of supply and demand of educated persons does not always work perfectly. Illiteracy and low levels of schooling are the major social problems confronting the Global South, problems that can inhibit economic growth and political stability. For instance, those from developing countries who receive a higher education will be among the elite, but the prestigious fields for which their training prepares them are not necessarily those where the country's need lies.

India, for instance, has many trained lawyers and engineers who cannot be absorbed into the system. This has caused a number of highly skilled individuals to leave India. China is experiencing a similar phenomenon as many students go abroad to study. China tries to lure the talent back with promises of higher wages and better social, political, and economic status.

Unfortunately, much of the supply–demand problem has arisen because of unsuitable models of education. Some have been adopted from or left by colonial powers; others are copies from Western science and technology. China has studied Western systems in attempts to modernize its educational system, but this creates the problem of trying to develop a system that is suited to China's needs by studying Western education. Today China is taking lessons from other countries but adapting them to the Chinese educational system.

Structures left from formerly colonized countries still influence power relationships in these countries, as seen in the case of the lower status of women in former colonial societies (referred to as "gender colonization"). Until these relationships are altered, countries cannot use their human resources, especially women, to their fullest (Acosta-Belen, 1990). When both the host countries and the multinational corporations see the value of economic development in education, women's progress may be enhanced.

Some multinational corporations hire large numbers of workers in Global South countries, especially women, but often for unskilled jobs that need little education. Many of these jobs are in manufacturing and are moving out of Global North countries to Global South where labor is cheaper and not unionized.

Educational reforms relate to religious, social, economic, and political ideologies. Countries as varied as Iran, Nicaragua, and Tanzania have moved away from Western models. Many comparative educationists advocate the development of educational programs based on the countries' needs. Tanzania received attention in this respect in the 1970s and 1980s for its program called "education for self-reliance," advocated by President Julius Nyerere from 1964 to 1980, to train people in needed skills; Kenya's Harambee school movement, started by leader Kenyatta after independence, encouraged local areas to form schools to meet local needs. However, today these schools have become less respected than government-run secondary schools.

The relationship between education and other institutions in society is constantly changing as illustrated in the next section.

Applying Sociology to Education: *Can changes in the institutions of one country affect others? Explain how this might happen, especially as it relates to education.*

STAGES OF ECONOMIC DEVELOPMENT AND EDUCATIONAL CHANGE.   The development of educational systems is most often related to three technological stages. In the first stage only a limited number of people, a privileged few, are involved in education—cloistered monks and political elite, for example. The second stage involves education that reaches further, training a core of the population for factory work and the civil service and to be leaders of business, industry, and government. Third is the training required for the technological age, for the "communication society," where education, work, and society are closely interrelated and available to all (Bell, 1973).

EDUCATION FOR MODERNIZATION—"MODERN MAN."   As a society moves through these stages, the values of the population and attitudes toward education and development also change (Inkeles and Smith, 1974). In his functional perspective of the modernization process, a society that places emphasis on economic development needs includes what they call "modern man." Modern man has "those personal qualities which are likely to be inculcated by participation in large-scale modern productive enterprises such as the factory . . . if the factory is to operate efficiently and effectively" (Inkeles and Smith, 1974). These personal qualities include

1. Openness to new experience
2. Readiness for social change
3. Growth of opinion, disposition to hold or form opinions, awareness of diversity of opinions, and the placing of positive value on variations in opinion
4. Interest in acquiring facts and information
5. Acceptance of fixed schedules, punctuality, present-time orientation
6. Belief that man can exert control over the environment and advance goals
7. Long-term planning in public affairs and private life
8. Calculability or trust in the world and others
9. Valuing technical skill
10. Educational and occupational aspirations
11. Awareness of and respect for the dignity of others
12. Understanding of production and the decision-making process.

These 12 personal qualities were closely related to other factors in the individual's background experience and society: kinship and family, women's rights, religion, the role of the aged, politics, communications, consumerism, social stratification, and work commitment. This "modern man" places a high value on formal education and schooling in skills such as reading, writing, and mathematics, and has the skills and attitudes needed for economic development.

THE CHALLENGE OF BECOMING MODERN.   The Industrial Revolution was a simple, gradual transition in its early stages. One development led naturally to another and to the increased investment of capital. Today, developing countries face pressures to make that transition rapidly. The technology is available, but economic development requires a change in the whole structure and value system of society. Subsistence agricultural societies must make enormous transitions to become "modern." Imagine for a moment a traditional, largely rural, agriculturally based country, with its internal structure reliant as much on extended family relationships as on any central or even regional government. In order to modernize, leaders must gain support for massive and rather rapid changes involving all institutions in the society. Some religious and political systems make the transition easily. Others resist change. Transportation and communication, health systems, economic planning, and capital to build an educational system for many levels, and types of knowledge and skills will all be needed. Developing the human capital necessary to carry out the economic development requires willingness to modernize and be mobile, motivation to pursue the education or training needed, and cooperation with the goals set by those in power. In other words, economic development depends on the attitudes and values of the population quite as much as on the technological machinery and necessary capital.

Dependency on rich nations may occur in the development process, for it takes massive input of capital and expertise for such a mobilization. Countries often bargain for aid from the developed world—socialist or capitalist—with the implicit understanding that they owe some degree of allegiance to the provider. International organizations, including the World Bank and the International Monetary Fund (IMF), have become involved in the global economy, playing a role in the development of Global South countries by providing expertise and funding; however, that involvement is criticized for perpetuating debt and dependency status of Global South countries.

Political–Economic Divisions between Societal Systems

Sociologists have laid out major political–economic divisions among societies and broad generalizations about the implications of those divisions for educational systems. For instance, socialism ranges from Marxism to social democracy, and capitalism from free-market economies to state-regulated capitalism and the welfare state. Socialist models put special emphasis on "egalitarian and relevant" education, as we shall see in the case study of China presented in Chapter 12. Capitalist models, predominant in Western Europe and the United States, tolerate inequality and stress "classical" as well as "practical" subjects in the curriculum, as we shall see in the case on Britain. Generally, educational systems reflect the position of the dominant group in society.

With many countries in Latin America, Asia, and Eastern Europe moving toward more representative democratic forms of government, scientists have raised questions about education's role in both the emergence and stability of these new political systems. Modernization theorists argue that mass education prepares the population for the responsibilities of living in a democracy where participation is expected. They see education as preparation for successful democracies. Conflict theorists see the potential for directing the mass population into desired positions as a way to perpetuate the existing power structure, even in democracies.

In a systems model that illustrates the interdependence of institutions, Williamson (1979) combines elements from the political and economic institutions. He contends that the educational system reflects the political structure and distribution of power in society. It is also important to understand the historical comparative context of a country in order to encompass its past, present, and future environments. This is especially important in cases of postcolonial educational systems. Williamson divides the world into four predominant types of societies (see Figure 11.5).

DEVELOPED SOCIALIST SOCIETIES.   The former USSR, now Russia, and some other Eastern European societies can be understood as socialist societies whose special features flow historically from the programs of industrial development followed by Lenin and Stalin. The Soviet system provided the model for the development of a number of Global South agricultural countries. However, today Russia has moved toward much more of a private enterprise economy."

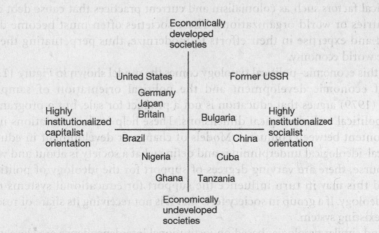

FIGURE 11.5   Models of development and type of economy.
Source: Williamson, Bill, *Education, Social Structure, and Development*
(London: Palgrave/Macmillan, 1979), page 36. Used with permission
from Palgrave/Macmillan.

UNDERDEVELOPED SOCIALIST SOCIETIES.   Peasant societies try to build socialist societies. Because most are predominantly agricultural, accumulating capital for industrialization is difficult. This has forced them into a dependency role in relation to other societies. Underdeveloped socialist societies face the structural problem of involving peasants and rural workers in revolutionary change; they must satisfy both immediate demands for a better life and longer-term demands for capital accumulation, which involves sacrifice and deferred consumption. Cuba is an example, but it, too, is experimenting with aspects of capitalism.

ADVANCED CAPITALISTIC SOCIETIES.   Capitalism has been described in many ways and has undergone many changes over the years. The main features of capitalism as described in classical theory include the following:

1. Private ownership of the means of production
2. A free market in labor
3. The concentration of production into factories and the incorporation of agriculture into the capitalist market
4. Production geared to a market and aimed at realizing profit
5. The rationalization of economic life to principles of clear capital accounting
6. Production geared to a world market.

In today's world, multinational conglomerates spread across the globe, competing for cheap raw products, labor, and world markets.

DEPENDENT SOCIETIES.   Dependent societies are characterized by an "interdependence of poverty, low income, low productivity, high mortality rates, urban squalor, economic dependence, political corruption and illiteracy" (Williamson, 1979, p. 39). They account for about two-thirds of the world's population. In Williamson's view, economic backwardness is the result of poor societies having had their economic and social systems distorted by the overseas expansion of capitalist enterprises. Thus, poverty is not intrinsic to these societies but results from historical factors such as colonialism and current practices that cause debt obligations to richer countries or world organizations. These societies often must become dependent on Western aid and expertise in their efforts to modernize, thus perpetuating their dependent status in the world economy.

From this economic–political typology comes the model shown in Figure 11.5, combining the level of economic development and the political orientation of sample countries. Williamson (1979) argues that education is not a product for sale, but a program of action in that it has political and ideological dimensions. These help explain variations in educational form and content between countries. Models of change or development in education reflect these political-ideological underpinnings and define what a society is about and what actions it takes. Of course, there are varying degrees of support for the ideology of political groups in control, and this may in turn influence the support for educational systems reflecting the dominant ideology. If a group in society feels that it is not receiving its share of resources, it may oppose the existing system.

This and similar typologies based on institutional interdependence are closely related to the open systems approach; they make paramount the relationship between the institution of education and other institutions in the national system and international environment. As societies change, these models will need to be adapted.

HIGHER EDUCATION AROUND THE WORLD

In 1989, students in China occupied Tiananmen Square in a fight for democracy in that communist stronghold. In 2008, Tibetan students, monks, and others demonstrated for independence, and in 2009–2010 other groups such as the Uyghurs in this vast and diverse country did the same, seeking a better, more independent life and preservation of their customs and language. The youthful uprising among a number of Arab and North African states in the winter and spring of 2011 are the most recent examples. The government has routed out the dissidents. Some leaders have been imprisoned; others have emigrated or gone underground. Students at the universities are closely watched, and in China new students go through intensive political indoctrination. Yet underneath the surface, the democratic movement still has adherents. Institutions around the world, from China to South Africa, experience student activism over issues of concern. They also share common trends: rapid growth in the demand for higher education, rising expectations, increased financial support for students, growing involvement of research and continuing education, diversification of the types of education offered, gender equity issues, and concern about dropouts. These and other issues can lead to student activism and disorder.

Some common themes encircle the world's higher-education institutions. As outlined by Altbach and Davis (1999), these themes include the following:

1. Access and equity
2. The link between education and work
3. The transition from school to work
4. Effects of technological developments
5. Transfer of talent across borders
6. Expansion of graduate education
7. Privatization of higher education
8. Crisis in academic professions
9. Accountability.

These common themes permeate the world system of higher education. Consider the first point, access to higher education. People around the globe see higher education as the key to future jobs, but countries vary greatly in their ability to meet the demand. In China and India, a growing percentage of recent high school graduates attend college, but in most of Africa only a fraction have access to higher education. Higher-education systems face dramatic change from serving the elite to providing mass universal access to a wide range of students.

With increased access comes the question of funding the additional students. Should countries invest in citizens' higher education, taking funds from other essential services including education at lower levels? Should citizens pay for their higher education, making it available to a limited number in the population and perpetuating an elite educational system? Or should financial support come from external sources, including international organizations, businesses, and private contracts, resulting in higher education being influenced by these sources? Each of these plans has advantages and disadvantages that impact global issues and themes.

In some regions, institutions of higher education are creating links between their universities. For instance, the European Union (EU) created the Bologna Process in 1999 with the express purpose of modernizing higher education throughout Europe. Forty-six countries with 5,600 institutions of higher education and 31 million students are a part of this unprecedented agreement. A main goal was to establish the European Higher Education Area (EHEA) in order to enhance worldwide employment and mobility of people. This plan is resulting in more

Table 11.2 Foreign Students' Countries of Origin, 2008–2009

Country or Territory	Students	1-Year Change (%)
India	103,260	+9
China	98,510	+21
South Korea	75,065	+9
Canada	29,697	+2
Japan	29, 264	−14
Taiwan	28,065	−3
Mexico	14,850	no change
Turkey	13,263	+10
Vietnam	12,823	+46
Saudi Arabia	12,661	+28
Nepal	11,581	+30
Germany	9,679	+9

Sources: Institute of International Education. "Record numbers of international students in U.S. higher education." www.iie.org/en/Who-We-Are/News-and_Events/Press-Center/Press-Releases/2009/2009-11-16-Open-Doors-2009-International-Students-in-the-US (Access Date: October 13, 2010).

collaboration and internationalizing of higher education in European countries, with student exchanges and research collaborations (Hunter, 2010).

Table 11.2 shows the number of foreign students studying in the United States. The numbers are the highest in recent times, with an 8 percent increase from 2007–2008 to 2008–2009. Enrollments of new students is up 16 percent. The most popular majors are business and management. International students' numbers are largest in California, New York, and Texas, with University of Southern California having the largest number of students at 7,482 (Institute of International Education, 2009a).

The United States also sends thousands of students abroad to study in countries around the world. The number of U.S. students studying abroad increased by 8.5 percent to 262,416 students in 2007–2008. About 40 percent of the students study in mid-length programs, and 56 percent study in short-term programs from 2 to 8 weeks. Of the 25 top destinations for U.S. students, 4 are in Western Europe—United Kingdom, Italy, Spain, and France. However, 15 of the top 25 countries are outside Western Europe and 19 are countries that speak languages other than English. For example, students studying in Africa increased by 18 percent, in Asia by 17 percent, and in Latin America by 11 percent. Europe still hosted 56 percent of U.S. students studying abroad, Latin America 15 percent, Asia 11 percent, and Africa 5 percent of the total group (Institute of International Education, 2009b) (see Table 11.3).

Study results of exchange students who go from the United States to other countries indicate that they return more interested in current events and international affairs, have an increased appreciation for foreign cultures, and seek international experiences and employment more frequently than students who have not had international study experiences (Carlson et al., 1990; Kraft, Ballantine, and Garvey, 1994).

There is a potential downside to studying abroad. Some countries are losing their best and brightest in the "brain drain" as record numbers of students go abroad for education and job opportunities. Again refer to Table 11.2, which shows the numbers of international students from various countries studying in the United States. The number of research doctorates awarded to

Table 11.3 Top 2007–2008 Destinations for U.S. Students.		
	Number of students	**1-Year Change(%)**
1. Britain	33,333	+2
2. Italy	30,670	+10
3. Spain	25,212	+5
4. France	17,336	+.6
5. China	13,165	+19
6. Australia	11,042	+3
7. Mexico	9,928	+5
8. Germany	8,253	+12
9. Ireland	6,881	+19
10. Costa Rica	6,096	+13
11. Japan	5,710	+14
12. Argentina	4,109	+14
13. Greece	3,847	+13
14. South Africa	3,700	+15
15. Czech Republic	2,739	+9

Source: Institute of International Education, 2009. "Americans study abroad in increasing numbers." www.iie.org/en/Who-We-Are/News-and-Events/Press-Center/Press-Releases/2009/ (Access Date: October 13, 2010).

non-U.S. citizens was 15,115 out of 44,515 total recipients, or 34 percent (Survey of Earned Doctorates, 2007). The numbers of non-U.S. Ph.Ds in science and engineering grew by 6 percent and nonscience majors by 7.1 percent between 2007 and 2008 (Inside Higher Education, 2008).

For many countries struggling to advance, some forms of higher education may be inappropriate. These societal needs and institutional demands could change the structure of higher education in these countries to models that are more suitable for jobs available. Many students, even in developed countries, are demanding a more vocationally oriented, practical education to help them get jobs. However, until developing countries can absorb their graduates, the brain drain will remove some of the young talent.

In order to provide examples of educational systems in the world, Chapter 12 presents countries falling into three quadrants of Williamson's typology: United Kingdom in the economically developed, capitalistic orientation; China in the socialistic orientation, developing societies quadrant; and West Africa, especially Ghana, in the developing societies that lean more toward capitalism. Only a few countries fall into the fourth quadrant, developed and socialist. We now move to an exploration of the educational systems of these countries.

> **Applying Sociology to Education:** *What are the advantages and disadvantages of studying abroad?*

Summary

This chapter is about education around the world. It discusses issues facing educational systems, covers theoretical approaches, and presents typologies to understand similarities and differences among systems.

I. COMPARATIVE EDUCATIONAL STUDIES

The field of comparative educational studies has been largely descriptive in the past, using case studies of selected countries. Theories and typologies are advancing our knowledge of the area. The systems approach helps us conceptualize the links between countries. One approach to comparative studies has been assessment of achievement in different subject areas across societies.

Institutional interdependence means that each institution is affected by each other institution. A change in one means that adaptations will be necessary in others. World system analysis stresses the interdependence of nations of the world, with "metropolitan" core centers and nations dominating over "peripheral" areas.

II. THEORETICAL PERSPECTIVES IN COMPARATIVE EDUCATION

Recent theoretical approaches contrast functional and conflict theoretical approaches; several of these focus on the relationship between educational and economic growth and development. Earlier theories focused on changing individuals to fit modern society. Human capital, legitimation of knowledge, rich versus poor countries, globalization and education, and world system analysis are reviewed.

World system analysis stresses the interdependence of nations of the world, with "metropolitan" centers and nations dominating over "peripheral" areas. Comparative studies all fit into several types: contrasting rich and poor nations, studying the internal structures of educational systems, and studies of institutional interdependence.

III. GLOBAL INSTITUTIONAL INTERDEPENDENCE

Institutional interdependence means that each institution is affected by each other institution. A change in one means that adaptations will be necessary in others.

In comparing nations, relationships of education to religion and family were discussed. Examples of "world environment" were given. Most emphasis has been put on political–economic systems as they influence educational systems. Williamson's typology illustrates this point.

Higher-education structures have ranged from Western forms to indigenous models. A problem faced by some countries is that elite students are educated in foreign countries and bring back Western political and legal models; these models are not necessarily best for countries struggling with development and literacy. Also, some of the educated elite may not find the need for their skills in their developing countries and may become alienated.

IV. HIGHER EDUCATION AROUND THE WORLD

The "brain drain" is claiming some young, educated, talent individuals who are leaving their countries of origin because their countries cannot absorb all the professionals that are being produced. The number of students studying abroad is increasing worldwide, and new forms of higher education are emerging to meet the needs of a globalized world.

Putting Sociology to Work

1. Talk to several international students about educational systems in their countries. Ask about the structure, access for various groups and classes of students, and how their systems differ from that in the United States.
2. Find out how you would be educated in your major field if you were studying in another country of your choice.
3. Select two developing countries, one capitalist, the other socialist. How do their educational systems

differ? Can this be attributed to their political ideologies?

4. Put yourself in the position of a minister of education in a developing country. What would be your primary concerns in planning the educational program?

5. Pose a question about comparative educational systems. Which of the theoretical approaches would be useful in dealing with your question?

Educational Systems Around the World

Britain, China, and Postcolonial Africa

Each country must ask itself this question: Education for what? Is the country trying to provide basic skills for survival; educate citizens for the needs in their daily lives such as subsistence farming; prepare the most competent students to leave the village for further education; provide different skills needed in the economy, one education for the laborers and another for the elites or leaders; give all citizens an equal chance for educational advancement? Country leaders struggle with these and many other questions about the purpose of education for their citizenry, and what proportion of their national budgets should be devoted to education to achieve national goals. In this chapter, we consider three different types of societies and their challenges in dealing with questions such as the purpose of education, the structure educational systems should take, and equality of education for groups in society.

Education provides a trained labor force and gives unity and identity to nation-states, qualities needed for individual and national progress (Benavot, 1992). Educational systems in newly developed nation-states often develop along Western models. But not always as we shall see! Ramirez and Boli argue that economic competition between states has caused the pressure for all nations to organize educational systems in similar ways, leading to the universality of state schooling and similarities between systems. Pressures from the economically integrated and dependent developed world have caused newer nations to commit themselves to state-funded mass educational models as part of nation building (Ramirez and Boli-Bennett, 1987). Commonalities in national curricula exemplify this trend.

The worldwide trends in education include increased enrollments; the establishment of educational ministries; compulsory education laws; increased state funds for education; educational opportunity for all, including women and minorities; and schools serving the purpose of both socializing agents for the nation and sorting systems for business and government.

Despite these world trends, social scientists must be cautious not to assume that all systems are similar because of cross-national pressures and dominant powers. Even though education

Countries' educational systems are influenced by demands from the global environment that determine their needs to fit into the world system.

may be influenced by colonial models and world trends (Archer, 1987), each system brings its own country's unique culture into education. As discussed in Chapter 11, some nations or groups within nations actively resist adopting Western models.

In the following case examples we see both the similarities and the differences in educational systems. These case studies represent systems that fall into different sectors of Williamson's (1979) political–economic typology (see Figure 11.5). Britain is located in the economically developed countries' sector, with a political system more clearly capitalistic than socialistic in orientation. China represents a system in the socialist tradition. Finally, Ghana, a former colony of Britain, is economically dependent and developing along capitalistic political lines.

Discussions of each country will include the historical background leading up to the present system; the national goals for the educational system; structural aspects of education, such as the number of years of schooling and type of curriculum; equality or inequality in the educational system; and higher education.

EDUCATION IN BRITAIN

Britain is the land of monarchies, peerages and nobility, and pomp and circumstance, a land that once ruled one-third of the world. The sun never sets on the British empire! It is also a land that was devastated by two world wars, that experienced extreme poverty for much of its population in the wake of industrial prosperity, and that has a legacy of immigrants from former colonies who have moved to Britain and must be educated and integrated into the society. The following section summarizes some key elements of the British education system, a system that has influenced its former colonies and much of the world.

Development of Education in Britain

Formal education started to take shape in Britain during the Middle Ages, with schools organized by religious organizations to teach students to read religious texts. In the late 1300s the first grammar schools, including Seinte Marie College of Winchestre and Eton College (both still in existence today), prepared students to enter Oxford University. By the second half of the nineteenth century, some leaders were advocating for widespread education; however, education was slow to spread as the majority of working-class people had few means and sometimes little interest in attending. Churches had handled most of the education to that time and some feared government intervention. In 1870, the first Education Act (also known as the "Forster Act") was passed, providing for voluntary denominational schools and nonde-nominational state schools.

Britain was one of the early industrialized and urbanized countries. The process of creating an educational system took place gradually, aided by a mobile peasantry able to provide the needed labor and by an international trade market anxious to buy goods. During this evolution, the rigid class structure in Britain was strengthened and was reflected in the educational system. Marxist interpreters have described the development of education in Britain as serving the needs of the elite. An educated mass was needed for the expansion of capitalism, with a trained labor force for various levels of industry. Morality, obedience, and frugality could be taught through the schools, and these goals were reflected in their curricula. The subordination of the lower orders had several aims—political control, the suppression of crime and drunkenness, the propagation of Christian morality, and the preparation of the lower orders for a life of industry and toil (Williamson, 1979, p. 55).

As the working classes grew and became more organized, they demanded greater access to education, among other rights. This was to the advantage of the elite, who needed an ever more sophisticated and skilled labor force. First, secondary education opened to the working class, and compulsory attendance, beginning at age 5, was eventually extended to age 11. Parents were and are required to see that their children receive an education for this period. After 5 years of secondary education, about age 16, students take the General Certificate of Secondary Education.

During the period after World War II, with the 1944 Education Act (known as the "Butler Act"), education became free for all—including university, if one qualified. But the school divisions still perpetuated class distinctions: grammar schools, secondary comprehensive schools with academic programs, and secondary technical schools representing trade-training programs. Increased access to higher education took place in the 1960s with the establishment of additional universities, polytechnics and "red-brick universities" (now part of the university system), colleges, and the Open University (distance and correspondence education for those who might not otherwise be able to attend an institution of higher education).

The official goals for British education, as stated in the Education Reform Act of 1988 and other education acts which have followed, are to raise standards at all ability levels; give parents a wider choice of schools and improve the partnership between schools and parents; make further and higher education more economically relevant and available to larger numbers; and obtain good value for money from the educational service as a whole. Assessment of this far-reaching act indicates that it served to increase parents' choice of schools and gave local schools more power. However, some question how much power schools actually held (*Education in Britain*, 1995; Powell and Edwards, 2005).

Education for the elite and upper-middle class is a different matter. English "public schools," similar to private preparatory schools in many countries and too expensive for the commoner, served those who wished to retain a social distinction—and they still do. "Public" schools—such as Eton, Harrow, Rugby, Winchester, and other elite secondary schools—serve a unique role. Eton, for instance, is set in a small town a short distance from Windsor Castle. The young students can be seen walking purposefully, surrounded by stately old buildings resonant with English tradition. "You are destined to be a statesman and gentleman," Eton seems to suggest to its inhabitants. Following rigid rituals and ceremonies and dressed in their uniform of black-and-white pin-striped trousers, white bow ties, black vests and waistcoats, and braided tailcoat, an Eton lad would never be mistaken for a state school student.

These "public" schools provide both excellent academic foundations and training in the art of being "ladies and gentlemen," fostering the mannerisms and speech patterns typical of the elite. They give the well-rounded education necessary to pass entrance exams for elite universities such as Oxford and Cambridge. A large number of senior civil servants and business and professional leaders were and are drawn from these schools, although highly qualified students from lower classes have some chance to attend elite schools as scholarship students.

Until recently, students attended grammar schools beginning at age 5, followed by secondary modern schools or secondary technical schools, compulsory to age 16. State-funded nursery and preschool programs are also available. Because of high unemployment, especially among the young who left school at age 16, The Education and Skills Act of 2008 raised the compulsory school age to 18, a law that will go into effect in 2013 for 17-year-olds, and in 2015 for 18-year-olds. The National Curriculum includes a number of required core subjects: English, mathematics, science, design and technology, information and communication technology, history, geography, modern foreign language, music, art and design, physical education, and citizenship. Several other courses are compulsory, including religious education (British Council, 2009). Government-sponsored training programs with work–study plans aid in the school-to-work transition, but only a small proportion of those in need can be accommodated. The result is that large numbers of youth are leaving school disillusioned and with little hope of employment.

Control and Decision Making in British Education

Historically, local control has been valued in Britain. The 1988 Education Reform Act, however, gave control to the national government to carry out national research and planning, recommend major revisions in the structure of education, and determine the basic national curriculum. Students were required to take a nationally mandated curriculum. The day-to-day decisions and running of the school was retained by local communities through the Local Education Authorities (LEAs); these bodies had wide-ranging power and duties. Each school had a governing body ideally consisting of equal numbers of local authority representatives, school staff including the head teacher, elected parents, students in older classes, and community representatives. LEAs held responsibility for the management of schools and the proper conduct of administrators. Both county (state-supported) and voluntary (usually church) schools have been under the jurisdiction of LEAs. Teachers have complained that they had less autonomy at the local level and more paperwork with this governance structure required by the government.

A recent change is transferring duties of the LEAs to Directors of Children's Services in each county or borough (The Children's Act of 2004 and amendments in 2006) (National Statistics, 2009). One of the concerns raised about the new structure is whether it will take some decision-making authority away from locally elected LEAs and move it to a government-controlled agency. The Minister of Education has been criticized by those who feel that increased privatization of education in Britain could destroy state schools. Privatization would mean self-governed schools under religious foundations, groups of parents, and even private individuals (Baker, 2010). With privatization some schools would receive not only government funding but also funding from private sources. In addition, these schools might be able to set their own curriculum and draw the best students, depriving state schools of quality students. According to critics, all of these factors will further stratify the school system between the wealthier and poorer students (Illingworth, 2010).

Structure and Composition of the British Educational System

State-supported British infant and primary schools have received a great deal of attention, and they have provided models for many elementary schools in the United States and around the world. The widely read Plowden Report, *Children and Their Primary Schools* (Central Advisory Council for Education, 1967), detailed a system of British primary education, in which schools are noted for their informal and open approaches to education. The visitor to a British primary school has the feeling of entering a child's world. From the ceiling hang mobiles; the walls are covered with artwork; books and educational toys line the walls. Classroom activities are minimally structured, with emphasis on individualized work. Older children help younger children in multiage classrooms. Curricula include plenty of active and creative time, music, art, time for special projects, and a range of opportunities for TV education, theater trips, and museum visits.

The structural levels of British education have been undergoing changes as described above at the upper-secondary and higher-education levels. Comprehensive schools were formed in the 1970s to counter the streaming of children into elite and working-class schools. They combine what were formerly grammar (more academic) and secondary-modern schools. At the turn of the century, 3.7 million children attend secondary schools. Approximately 10 percent of high school students go to "public" preparatory schools (British Council, 2009). Within secondary schools, there was some differentiation between students on the basis of academic versus vocational tracks, but the stated goal has been to identify talent and allow children to develop their capabilities.

Ninety percent of children in England and Wales, or 8.5 million, attended one of the 30,000 publicly funded state schools in 2009. Another 830,000 students attend 5,000 schools in Scotland, and 350,000 students in Northern Ireland attend 1,300 schools (British Council, 2009).

Effective schools in Britain share many characteristics with effective schools in other countries. A much-quoted study conducted in London singled out characteristics of effective primary schools: small school and class size, teacher planning periods and involvement in curriculum planning, lesson plans, progress reports on each child, low turnover of all school personnel and students, and an orderly work environment (Mortimore et al., 1988).

Exams and Credentials

Students' advancement in the British system is determined by national examinations. Today students take the General Certificate of Secondary Education (GCSE) after five years of secondary education, following which they may continue their education at vocational or technical college, or after an additional year of school they may take the AS-Level (advanced subsidiary-level) exams. After an additional years above AS-level study, students may take A-Level exams (advanced level), required to qualify for university (British Council, 2009).

The Education Reform Act of 1988 reflects international pressures for change. The primary impact is that all schools are to follow a common curriculum and examination plan, prescribed by law, in 10 subjects. Britain is a highly "credentialed" society, placing great emphasis on exams and certificates. It also claims a 99 percent literacy rate. Each student takes exams in several subject areas. At about age 16, students take the GCSE exam in major subjects such as mathematics and literature; following two more years of study, students take A-level exams. Between these two are the AS exams, equivalent to two GCSE exams or one A-level exam. Universities generally require three A-level exams for entrance. The national Department of Education, which determines the national curricula, publishes guidelines to provide the basis for the GCSE exam, which all students take before they leave school. This exam is written and marked by independent examination boards, and students take up to 10 exams in single subjects.

There is yet another very prestigious exam—the International Baccalaureate—taken by some sixth-form (16- to 18-year-old) students and requiring competence in six subject areas: one's native language, a foreign language, the study of man (history, geography, social science, or philosophy), experimental science, mathematics, and an art subject or advanced work in one area (International Baccalaureate, 2005–2007). The program has 546,000 students in 125 countries, including Britain as well as the U.S.

Critics of the exam system argue that those who can afford the "elite" education are best prepared for A-levels and elite university entrance exams, and that the exam system helps perpetuate the class system. Also, pressure on children from families to succeed on exams is often intense, and children who do not do well on the examinations are limited in their opportunities.

Inequality in Education and Occupational Mobility

Several British sociologists have written about the resistance to schooling found among some young British adolescents. This "counterculture of resistance" among working-class males in particular is seen in patterns of behavior—dress, truancy, smoking, vandalism, and rudeness—and represents their view that school is irrelevant to the lives they will enter (Corrigan, 1979; Lees, 1994, p. 86; Willis, 1981). Great strides have been made toward providing opportunity for students of all social backgrounds to move as far as possible in the educational system. However, there are at least two kinds of problems encountered in this endeavor. The Plowden Report and more recent studies point to the special problems of deprived neighborhoods such as inner-city areas, where health and housing standards are low and child mortality is high. Many young people from immigrant groups and those who fall into the poorest classes of society live in these areas. The Plowden Report recommended that schools in these blighted areas be given extra funds from the national educational budget, although the report also said that educational disadvantage cannot be solved in schools alone (Garner and Raudenbush, 1991, p. 251).

Another problem inhibiting mobility is the distinction between "public" schools and state-supported schools. With the tradition behind the elite schools and the excellent education they provide, plus the tendency for elite universities and government and industry to fill their top ranks with graduates of these schools, mobility at the top remains the prerogative of a limited, select group. Education reflects the history and traditions built up over long periods in Britain. Complete equality seems impossible without altering the basic structure of the educational system.

What does educational inequality mean for occupational attainment? Depending on the measures used, we can generally say that until recently one's class origins are more important in Britain than in the United States in occupational attainment (the thesis of 'American exceptionalism, Solon, 2002'). In the United States, educational attainment is more important, especially for one's first job placement (Kerckhoff, 2001; Kerckhoff et al., 1989). Although the process of career mobility in the two countries differs, the degree of openness or mobility is about the same when we look at occupational status 10–20 years after labor force entry.

Higher Education in Great Britain: Elite versus Mass Education

Oxford and Cambridge universities—prestigious institutions with spires, and courtyards, and divided into colleges with long traditions—have been the models for educational systems around the world. Classical, traditional education can be obtained from robed dons behind the cloistered walls; students are affiliated with a college in the university.

For centuries, these universities provided access to high positions and perpetuated the intellectual elite. With the worldwide trend toward more access to all levels of education by all groups in society, and the need for a more educated populace to fill the technical positions in an industrialized society, several changes have occurred: The great universities opened their doors a crack to let in larger numbers of qualified students from state-supported schools, and other institutes and colleges developed to meet growing needs for trained personnel. University access is still limited, and children of elites and professionals stand a much better chance of acceptance than do those from lower socioeconomic levels.

The government, however, is expanding access to many universities for the three-year degree courses, and masters degrees in four years. In addition, a number of polytechnics were developed, beginning in 1966, to meet the need for trained engineers, technical experts, and technicians. They are closely associated with business and industry. The goal was to have 31–33 percent of the 18- and 19-year-olds in one of the 88 institutions of higher education (Whitaker, 2000). In 2009, 1.8 million students were in institutions of higher education. About one-third entered at age 18 following secondary school (50 percent in Scotland), and many more mature students are returning to school or taking online courses (British Council, 2009). Institutions of higher education such as polytechnics give access to those who fail university entrance exams for the most prestigious universities or who wish to pursue specialized studies.

There are also differences between female and male faculty at universities. Male full-time professors outnumbered females by a ratio of 6 to 1, and less than one-third of lecturers were women. In 2003–2004, women were paid an average of 20 percent less than men in some major universities, with the overall gap of 14 percent, regardless of age and discipline (Baty and Czerski, 2005). Yet more women than men are students in institutions of higher education.

Another development in British higher education is distance learning through the Open University. Begun in 1971, it provided a model to many institutions around the world of successful distance education, and it gave opportunities to people who might not otherwise be able to attend university (e.g., teachers, those working, those at home, and those living at a distance from institutions of higher education). The idea caught on to the extent that, by 1976, the Open University received about 53,000 applications and was enrolling up to 20,000 students a year.

By 1980, enrollment had grown to 70,000 students, with 6,000 graduating each year. Today more than 180,000 students are taking classes (The Open University, 2007). More people study at the Open University than at any other United Kingdom universities: 150,000 undergraduates, 30,000 postgraduates, 11,000 higher degrees, 10,000 students with disabilities, and 25,000 students outside the United Kingdom. Most students are part-time (The Open University, 2007).

Open University students pay tuition and sign up for courses. They tune in to lectures on British Broadcasting Corporation (BBC) radio or TV. Texts are developed for the courses, and assignments are sent to tutors who correct and return them. At the end of the year students take examinations. A wide range of courses are offered through the Open University, with most degrees being given in general arts and science. The average student takes six years to complete a degree, compared with three or four years for students in residence on a campus, and the dropout rate is higher than at campuses.

The number of Open University students continues to grow as the program nears its fourth decade. The Open University has graduated well over 100,000 students, with 1,800 in 2003–2004 alone, mostly adult homemakers and full-time employees wishing to upgrade their credentials (BBC News, 2007).

Part of the recent growth in higher-education enrollments is because of reduced job opportunities in British society. Changes being initiated to help cope with the increased demand are familiar: larger classes, use of teaching assistants, and availability of intensive "24-month degrees" in some fields of study that normally take three years to complete. In the future, Britain will face pressures to open its educational system further and provide opportunities for the many unemployed working-class and immigrant members of society.

EDUCATION IN THE PEOPLE'S REPUBLIC OF CHINA*

China has the largest population in the world living on a huge landmass. In 2010 the country's population was 1.4 billion and it is estimated to reach more than 1.5 billion by 2025 (Infoplease, 2007; Rosenberg, 2010). The current fertility rate is 1.7 children per woman, a figure below population replacement level. Although the population is still growing, by 2030 the population growth will level off and begin to drop. Today China contributes 20 percent to the world's 6.7 billion people, one in every five (Rosenberg, 2010).

The territory covers almost a quarter of the world's land surface. Its Communist government officials send some officials and scholars to study in foreign countries, and admit both curious tourists and foreign scholars into its vast reaches. In fact, the second largest number of foreign students in the United States is from China, with 98,510 in 2009, second to India, with 103,260. Of the Chinese foreign students in the United States, 26,275 are undergraduates and 57,451 are graduate students, with the percentage of undergraduates growing (Lewin, 2009).

China has made significant strides in education and literacy for its vast population. In the early twentieth century, China's closed-door policy kept the West out. Since 1979, however, China has opened its doors again to the West with extensive trade and educational exchanges.

Recent Historical Events Affecting Education

Several key dates mark major transitions in China: In 1949, the Chinese Communist Party won national power and declared the founding of the People's Republic of China (PRC). At this time the borders closed to the outside world. China closed 2,200 private schools, about 4 percent of the nation's schools. In 1976, Chairman Mao (Mao Tse-tung) died; this event ushered in a new era of changing policies and programs and opened China's borders to the outside world in 1979. Since the adoption of market socialism in 1978, more than 90,000 private schools have reemerged (Ministry of Education of PRC, 2007). These are referred to as "society-run," "community-run," or "people-run" schools and are privately owned proprietary institutions with few government ties.

In 1989, pro-democracy protests led by university students were forcefully repressed, and contacts with Western countries were curtailed. The situation has eased since the late 1990s, and most exchanges have been carried out freely. Social science research, however, has only recently been expanded.

---

* With assistance from Dr. Zhiyong Zhu, Beijing Normal University.

No period can be ignored in reviewing Chinese education; each has been a reaction to the previous era, yet each reflects the changing political–economic scene of that time.

The Drive toward Modernization

China's Confucian educational legacy served the interests of China's power elite with its subtle underlying antiegalitarian political ideology, justifying elite privileged education. But in recent years, the growing realization of the need to expand education in order to modernize has gained popularity. In addition, there has been a realization that national development and modernization go hand in hand with basic education for all. Fundamentally, education in China is "intended to meet basic learning needs" with foundation-level education, early childhood and primary education, literacy, and general knowledge and life skills ("Meeting Basic Learning Needs," 1990, p. ix). Preparing a literate population to participate in the global economic rise of China is its current goal (Ministry of Education of PRC, 2010). China has made great strides in literacy of the population, with 93.9 percent of adults and 98.9 percent of youth reported as literate in 2009 (Human Development Report, 2009; UNESCO, 2007). The issue for Chinese education is how to provide educational opportunity to a vast and diverse population.

Deng Xiaoping became the leader of China in 1977, and with his leadership the Communist ideology was reinterpreted and economic changes put in motion. Some Western technology and management techniques were introduced to speed up modernization. With these changes came reform of the educational system.

Some degree of decentralized educational authority and reduction in strict central governmental policies is needed at all levels of the educational system for modernization reforms to take place (Du, 1992). The central government is giving more autonomy to communities and to private schools, seen as a necessity for reform. Chinese leaders also realize they cannot meet all needs and thus have allowed private schools to be established. These schools are not ethnic or religious, but are for-profit in the market socialism system.

Typically, the provincial education administrations have been given the power to compile textbooks for their own community schools since the mid-1990s. Of private schools started in the late 1980s, about half are trade schools and half academic; they are responding to the demand for education that cannot be met by the government, and they do meet part of that need. Educational systems reproduce, maintain, and perpetuate the existing social order, especially where they are government controlled. However, when the society is in transition, the education system will experience change as well.

The "quiet revolution" in education has transformed China from a largely illiterate country in 1949 to a country where almost all children attend school for 9 years of compulsory education and 15- to 24-year-olds are 99 percent literate (Ministry of Education of the PRC and UNESCO, 2010). Yet China still faces challenges in its attempt to educate all Chinese.

The Chinese government with the help of international organizations such as United Nations Educational, Scientific and Cultural Organization (UNESCO) has identified four primary challenges that are reflected in the goals for China in the next 10-year plan (2010–2020). First, the amount of the national budget that is spent on education needs to increase from the current 4 percent to 6 percent to reach the country's education goals. Second, the inequity in spending needs to be dealt with. Currently, large cities such as Beijing and Shanghai receive much higher amounts for education than most other areas. Third, there are still 71 million illiterate people aged 15 and over, and two-thirds of these are women. Fourth, education for girls and women needs to be improved to enhance women's status (Ministry of Education of the PRC and UNESCO Office in Beijing, 2010).

Equality of Educational Opportunity

Who receives the best educations in China has been shaped by political processes, and these processes have differed over time depending on who was in power and the policies of that group. Sometimes family status mattered and sometimes political priorities mattered. Immediately following the Cultural Revolution (1966–1976), having a father with high-rank status was a significant positive, though all schooling was limited during this time. At other times, family status was not significant or was of benefit only to those in political favor. The class status of a family has had a strong impact on individual educational attainment in China since the 1940s (Li, 2005b; Zhou, Moen, and Tuma, 1998).

In the period from 1978 to 2004, China experienced increased educational inequality between urban and rural areas, the eastern and western regions, and working and middle classes, with rapid economic growth and reform (Li, 2005a). With economic development, the central government has increased the investment in basic education in western and middle China's rural areas. From 2007, nine years of free compulsory education has been implemented in rural schools in these areas of China.

The rise of private schools, for instance, has given access to those with money. Those who are benefiting most from changes are urban residents from high-ranking cadres, professionals, and men (Zhou, Moen, and Tuma, 1998). The urban and rural differences in education stem from the "two track" funding models established before 1949: Rural schools were locally funded and urban schools were nationally funded. Even the purposes of primary education were seen as different. The new goals for 2010–2020 stress the need for financial understanding and cooperation between the different levels of government involved, and the integration of primary education with goals for economic growth and sustainable development (Fu, 2005). One of the ministry's goals for the next 10 years is to distribute more funding to education in rural, impoverished areas with ethnic and vulnerable groups (Ministry of Education of the PRC and UNESCO, 2010).

Status and Structure of Education in China

A typical day in a Chinese elementary school includes courses in Chinese, math, physical education, music, drawing, painting, and moral (political) education. Language study takes up to one-third of the day. The day starts with an exercise period, followed by four periods in the morning. There is a two-hour break for lunch and rest, followed by three more periods. After school, which ends about 4:00 P.M., some students stay for special help. After school on Saturday morning there are organized activities such as sports (Hauser, 1990, pp. 44–45). Foreign language study begins in 3rd grade; history, geography, and science begin in 4th through 6th grade. Classes range in size from 40 to 55 students.

According to Chinese statistics, 38 percent of pre-primary children and 99.27 percent of primary-age children (that is 107 million primary school students) attend 341,600 primary schools (Ministry of Education of PRC, 2010). Seventy-four percent of secondary-age children attend school, and 20–22 percent of college-aged students attend institutions of higher education (UNESCO, 2007). College students compete for scholarships to pay for their education.

CHAIRMAN MAO SAID:

Sweeping away illiteracy from 80 percent of the population is an important mission for New China. We must work energetically to realize this goal, so that workers and peasants can easily grasp scientific learning [and] become weapons for [class] struggle and [socialist] construction—complete and developed weapons for the people's democratic dictatorship. (Stites and Semali, 1991, p. 73)

His goal is close to being accomplished, with the 93 percent and above literacy rate among adults in China.

Authority structures in Chinese schools are based on personal ties and networks and on loyalty to authority and the political system. Because the party leadership perceived weaknesses in education that could prevent modernization, structural changes are taking place in the educational system. This did include local districts' obtaining their own financial resources for schools, but the resulting inequality between urban and rural schools has changed the goal to more equal distribution of funds between areas. Also, some changes in structure are taking place in private schools, in part because of the influences from abroad such as effective methods for teaching.

Recent changes in government policy concerning education muddle the picture. For instance, with the move toward individual rather than collective responsibility has come an emphasis on rural self-sufficiency, including local funding of rural schools. But many children have left school to participate in individual family moneymaking ventures.

Higher Education in the PRC

"Sustaining China's rapid economic growth in the future will come to depend in large part on the quantity and quality of the human resources it can mobilize" (Sun and Barrientos, 2009, p. 191). With the emphasis on rapid economic development, education is fundamental to developing the human resources needed for growth, and higher education is key in this process. Today about 22 percent of young people attend university; these are the best students who have attended 12 years of schooling and passed competitive examinations for entrance into the limited spaces in universities. In addition, the purposes and emphases of higher education have changed with the times.

Beginning in the late 1990s, the number of higher education institutions expanded rapidly. This has opened more university slots for the increasing number of secondary student graduates. The government made the decision that expansion would stimulate domestic consumption, ease the immediate pressure on the labor market from secondary school graduates, and address public demand (Wan, 2006). Thus, the time was right for the Chinese government to expand higher education. They saw the need to make the transition from elite to mass higher education (Zhao and Sixin, 2008). This expansion has benefitted one-child families, largely in urban areas, more than minorities—women and others from the central-western regions and rural areas (Li and Xing, 2010).

However, with this rapid expansion came problems with the old system and the pressure to reform that system to meet new demands. Financial and structural strains have caused some institutions to depend on bank loans rather than the government for their expansion. As graduates from these new higher education institutions reach the job market, there are not enough positions to absorb them; 1 million of the 5 million graduates are unemployed (Zhao and Sixin, 2008).

Chinese higher education dates back more than 3,000 years. Before modern times it was dominated by Confucian ideas and served primarily to prepare government officials for their positions. China has long held the belief that education and the economy are integrally linked. Hence, most changes have reflected this belief and current thinking along these lines. Higher education is undergoing radical change, with increased emphasis on science, applied research, foreign languages, the emergence of business schools, and restructuring of the management of education in the form of a Western model of scientific management. How long these measures will last is uncertain in the rapidly changing environment of Chinese education.

During the Cultural Revolution, the Ministry of Education in China was dismantled; it was reestablished in 1975. Major changes began in 1976, with the separation of politics and higher-education decision making—putting education in the hands of academics, the Ministry, and local committees. The Ministry controlled programs, curricula, and admissions. In May 1985, a State Council Education Commission (which was subsequently renamed "The Ministry of Education" [Ministry of Education, 2008] in the reform of state administration departments in 1998) replaced the Ministry to allow for closer regional control and to reflect the needs of regions.

Universities have been under strict controls and intense political indoctrination since the fall of the Maoist Gang of Four who led the Cultural Revolution in 1976 (Sautman, 1991). After the rebellious "counterrevolutionaries" protested at Tiananmen Square in 1989, students have been required to study ideology and be repoliticized (Robinson, 1991). First-year students at universities and colleges were required to take military training for ideological and political education. In the early 1990s, the State Education Commission has made reform more possible. Reform of higher education has focused on two areas of concern: management and structure, and curriculum and instruction (Du, 1992). This focus involves increasing the credentials of faculty and expanding access to higher education.

After "Decisions of Strengthening Educational Reform and Improving Quality Education Overall" and "Action Plan for Vitalizing Education for the 21st Century" were issued by the State Council and Ministry of Education in 1999, higher education in China has jumped into a period of expanding access and merging institutions. The access rate to higher education in 2005 increased to 22 percent from less than 10 percent in 1998 (Ministry of Education of PRC, 2010), which indicates that higher education in China has been moving from elitism to popular mass education. Concurrently, emphasis has been increasingly laid on access to and equity in higher education, addressing disparities between rural and urban areas, eastern and western regions, gender differences, and Han Chinese the dominant ethnic group in China, and ethnic minorities (Yang, 2006). Market reform, financial decentralization, and economic globalization in recent years have greatly accentuated China's social and regional inequalities (Postiglione, 2006). With the implementation of private education law in 2003, private institutions are increasing opportunities for higher education as well.

Since 2005, the central government and scholars have started to review and reflect the impact of the following: industrialization and privatization of higher education, globalization and localization of universities, the relationship between academic power and administrative authority, academic ethics and norms, and academic freedom and university autonomy (Fen, 2005; Luo, 2007). In "The 11th Five-Year Plan for China's Educational Development Outline" proposed by the Ministry of Education in 2007, improving the educational quality of higher education has been given the highest priority (Ministry of Education of PRC, 2007).

Emphasis on applied research in keeping with economic development has led to a professorate concerned with contract research more than pure research or teaching. Joint university projects with other countries, such as the United States, Canada, Japan, and Western Europe, are often initiated by the Chinese and generally involve mutual sharing; yet there is concern that the "foreigners" do not understand the culture with which they are interacting.

Some efforts to contain Western influence take the form of controlling exchanges, often available to scholars and students only after five years of work; repoliticalization programs; and limits on the type of research allowed. The government is trying to seek a balance between the need for scholars and Western knowledge, and the need for loyalty and indoctrination. One still sees patterns of patron–client relations, where political rulers offer prestige, privilege, and protection in return for support from scholars. It remains to be seen whether allowing intellectuals freedom to pursue their research is compatible with Chinese interests.

China has had a period of independence from the influence of other nations and is now interacting with others on its terms; however, much of Africa labors under a colonial legacy that has major implications for education.

FORMAL EDUCATION IN COLONIAL AFRICA

In the nineteenth and early twentieth centuries, Europeans conquered most of Africa and established boundaries around their colonies. Ostensibly the purposes were ending the slave trade, spreading Christianity and civilization, and opening the area for trade. Hardly mentioned were the expansion to new lands and the wealth of raw products that the colonial powers enjoyed as a result of their exploits.

Early in the colonial period, missionaries set up schools to teach Christianity and Bible studies. Colonial governments also organized schools according to the mother country's system of education, whether England, France, Germany, Portugal, or other colonists. Their purpose was to teach the language of the colonizing power and develop a cadre of Africans to help fill lower posts in colonial administrations, as well as to develop understanding and acceptance of European-style law and order. Many Europeans wanted to limit African education to technical, vocational, and agricultural skills, which would be helpful to Europeans in exploiting the resources of the countries. However, many Africans saw this type of training as an attempt to keep the country's population in their places, and they sought the academic education of the Western elite. Some went abroad to receive training, often with European encouragement and financial support.

Those few Africans who moved up the colonial education ladder often adopted European views and worked for the colonial administrations. They were often alienated from their own people and traditions, strangers in their own lands. With independence, some of these same European-educated Africans became postcolonial leaders. Their proposals were often greeted with skepticism by the people.

Whether the colonial power was French, British, or another European country makes a difference in the structure of education and access to schools today in the former colony. Colonial powers brought their political, legal, and educational systems with them, and the structures of those systems influence education in Africa today. The relationship of education to other institutions, what should happen in schools, the curriculum, who should teach, and who is responsible for educating the populous and making decisions have all been influenced by colonialism.

In sub-Saharan Africa, former French colonies tend to have centrally planned institutions, including education. Although French colonial schools started with lower enrollment levels overall, there has been more rapid expansion in recent years due to the trained professional leadership of schools and resources from economic development and growth that have gone into education. Former British colonies initially stimulated more local demand for schooling with a blend of European and African education, but the results have not always been successful at reaching more citizens with high-quality education. Most postcolonial countries today must make choices between rapid expansion of mass education with lower quality versus higher-quality education for fewer citizens (Garnier and Schafer, 2006; Wedgwood, 2007). In addition, for many citizens who see little advantage from education in their daily lives, the "promise of schooling" is waning (Coe, 2005).

In order to stimulate interest and create relevant systems of education, some countries are developing curricula that create and build on national culture and traditions through schooling. These programs involve teaching history, culture, African beliefs and practices, and skills needed in everyday life such as agriculture and health care (Coe, 2005). States are even contracting with private groups to develop such programs.

Although some sociologists of education argue that the world education system is developing similar patterns and curricula, there are many examples of former African colonies that are combining Western models with African traditions to meet local needs. Let us now turn to one example of an African education system—Ghana in West Africa.

Education in Ghana

"The Gold Coast," hub of the slave trade and dotted with slave castles, or fortresses, lies along the coast of Ghana. During the slave trade, Ghana profited slave traders, entrepreneurs, African middlemen, and colonial powers. The Portuguese, the Dutch, the Danes, and then the British (beginning in 1820 and lasting until independence in 1957) ruled the "Gold Coast," as Ghana was called. It was a prize colony, rich in mineral resources and later valued for its cocoa plantations.

History of Education in Ghana

When Ghana achieved independence in 1957, it was economically stable and its institutions were based on British models. Since independence, however, several different governments have ruled and been overthrown. In 1961–1966 there was a period of rapid expansion of education at all levels in Ghana. After 1966, however, enrollment in public primary schools in many parts of the country declined steadily (McWilliam and Kwamena-Poh, 1975, p. 116).

The early rapid growth was curtailed when a military government took over in 1966. The government ordered a study of the education system, which resulted in the following recommendations: "reorganizing and adopting new approaches to teacher training; creating new places at secondary Form I level and strengthening the secondary base in advance of university expansion; and considering the country's needs in the development of technical education" (McWilliam and Kwamena-Poh, 1975, p. 117). Despite the studies and recommendations, however, for many years following 1966 there was little change in the educational system. Political instability led to coups in 1979 and 1981, probably related to mistrust of the government by the people, the rich–poor division in the population, lack of opportunity for many in the country, or the government's lack of movement in the area of education. Enrollments dropped after a peak of 66.8 percent in 1965 for children from 6 to 11 years of age, followed by a drop of almost 14 percent for this age group in a 7-year period to 1972.

In 1974 the government designed an experimental structure for education for a few, but 90 percent of students still followed the old system. By 1983 the primary school enrollment during the first six years of school had risen again, this time to 79 percent (89 percent of boys, 70 percent of girls); middle schools enrolled 38 percent of the school-age children (48 percent of boys, 28 percent of girls). Elections in both 1992 and 1996 resulted in Jerry Rawlings being selected, providing for a period of stability in a country and the education system; this followed periods of political instability. In 2000, 75 percent of primary school students and 50 percent of secondary school students were enrolled in school (Bridges to the Future Initiative: Ghana, 2000), and the numbers have continued to increase slowly. Approximately equal numbers of boys and girls were enrolled in primary school in 2000, but boys continue further in school. Recent primary school completion rates show an overall rate of 72 percent, but only 47.4 percent for girls (Nationmaster.com, 2010). Girls report problems such as bullying, rape, and other violence, factors that play a role in their leaving school (Feldman-Jacobs, 2006). Ghana is somewhat ahead of other countries in sub-Saharan Africa where the average of 70 percent of students were in primary school in 2007.

The adult population literacy rate in Ghana was 66 percent in the latest estimates. For males between 15 and 24, however, the figure is close to 82 percent (Nationmaster.com, 2010; Center for Global Development, 2010); that compares with literacy rates lower than 50 percent in some least developed countries, many of which are in sub-Saharan Africa (UN Development Programme Report, 2005). With overwhelming problems of poverty and hunger in much of Africa, increasing the literacy rate has a low priority compared with feeding the population. At the same time, developing countries cannot compete with developed countries if their populations are illiterate. Most developing countries have had literacy as part of their educational goals with the hope that a literate population will translate into reduced poverty. However, this has not materialized in all countries. For example, in Tanzania the result is that mass access to education reduced quality of education and confidence of the citizens in the value of education, resulting in little reduction in poverty from education (Wedgwood, 2007).

Ghana and other countries have initiated a number of programs to increase literacy and school attendance. Some of these have been sponsored by nongovernmental organizations. For example, the Worldreader program is providing Kindle e-Readers to school children in several areas in Ghana to see if this technology will help boost literacy and increase the resources available to children (Heimbuch, 2010). Religious groups such as the Baha'i group have initiated literacy programs as well. "Enlightening the Hearts" is one such program to teach literacy in the native language, in the Ghanaian case, Twi. By teaching the native language first and supplementing it with English, they claim that overall literacy increases (Baha'I International Community, 2010).

Forms of Education

Education existed in Ghana and other African nations long before modern boundaries and European systems were introduced. It is important to distinguish, therefore, between traditional and formal education in many African countries.

> There were systems of education in Africa before the colonial period; for every community must have a way of passing on to the young its accumulated knowledge to enable them to play adult roles and so ensure the survival of their offspring, and the continuity of the community.
>
> In African communities, the older generation passed on to the young the knowledge, the skills, the mode of behaviour and the beliefs they should have for playing their social roles in adult life.
>
> The young were taught how to cope with their environments; how to farm, or hunt, or fish, or prepare food, or build a house, or run a home. They were taught the language and manners, and generally the culture of the community. The methods were informal, the young learnt by participating in activities alongside their elders. They learnt by listening, by watching, by doing. In many practical ways they learnt how to live as members of their community. (Busia, 1964, p. 5)

Many educators have asked how traditional systems can be used as a base for meeting the educational needs of modernizing countries. Options range from continuing French, English, or other colonial models to developing completely new indigenous types of education. Formal schooling is still primarily for the urban elite. The question becomes this: What kind of education should be offered in rural peasant communities?

One curriculum issue has to do with the language used for teaching. If the former colonial power's language is used, some feel that it imposes "linguistic imperialism on the country"; but if a native tongue is used, one group might gain dominance over another. Therefore, several countries are promoting learning for each group in its mother tongue to preserve cultural diversity and avoid conflicts, and a second world language. Rwanda, Africa, recently changed its official language from French to English, partly to become part of the East African Community, an economic which uses English. This community promises more economic integration into the world economy.

In many Third World countries, international funding agencies have attempted to direct the development of education. Consider the well-intentioned efforts in Ghana to increase literacy. However, these efforts may cause problems because the policies tend to emphasize the funding agency's goals and political agendas rather than country needs. One example is the World Bank. In the process of carrying out research on development and providing development funding, the development expertise and experience of the organization may end up setting standards for curriculum and knowledge in the countries receiving help. Those standards may not be working toward the country's goals.

Nonformal Education in Africa

In a remote village in Niger, Africa, with little access to schools, villagers (mostly the women) have organized to bring in experts from aid organizations to teach them skills and knowledge useful to their daily lives; many will never become literate, but they will gain by learning skills and information they need to improve their lives. Such projects fall into the category of "nonformal" education and "basic" education. "The shape of nonformal education programs varies according to the setting and the needs of the populations they serve" (Cavanagh, 2002, p. 10). Sometimes nonformal education projects involve a teacher or the most educated member of the community leading community members in learning reading or math, perhaps in someone's home. The education may involve training in agriculture, health care, or vocational training. Nonformal education has the advantages of reaching remote areas, costing little to provide, and providing flexibility to meet the needs of the community (Cavanagh, 2002). Around the world, researchers report on such educational projects, often funded by foundations or nongovernmental organizations. Nonformal education is distinguished from "formal school" because it is ongoing throughout people's lives. "Educational opportunities, formal and nonformal, must relate to each other both horizontally (e.g., school, home, mosque, media, work experience) and vertically throughout the different stages of a learner's life" (Hawes, 1979, p. 163). The methods, materials, and delivery systems must also vary to suit purposes and means available.

"Nonformal" and "basic" education seem to work together. Neither puts age or time strictures on education; both provide many varied paths to education, individual attainment of goals, and lifelong learning; and both involve various agencies—family, school, and community. Subjects range from functional literacy to knowledge of processes, such as health and sanitation; crops and animals; and household skills, including caring for the sick, making clothes, and civic knowledge. An attempt at nonformal, grassroots education is seen in the Community Development experiment, which has been tried in several communities. Informal courses or training in preventive medicine, health, nutrition, cooking, sewing, and other skills are made available to any person in the villages (Clemons and Vogt, 2004). Other programs have been developed to preserve African ways but teach Western skills. For many countries, the question is how to maximize development and still preserve national cultures and traditions.

> **Applying Sociology to Education:** *Will "basic" or "nonformal" education and mother-tongue teaching meet the needs of individuals and countries in the twenty-first century, or will their implementation perpetuate the rich–poor dichotomy without significantly raising the developing countries from the poverty level?*

Structure of the Ghanaian Educational System

Many societies develop education reform plans every few years to meet new challenges and demands from the local, national, and global environments. In 2007, Ghana approved a new reform act that increases the requirements for children; a few of the basics follow:

1. Universal Basic Education is now free for 11 years: 2 years of kindergarten, 6 years of primary school, and 3 years of junior high school.
2. Free and cost sharing arrangement is in place for senior high and higher education levels.
3. Courses are taught in a Ghanaian language and English.
4. At the basic level, literacy, mathematics, creative arts, and problem solving skills are the basics. Greater emphasis will also be put on information and communication technology.
5. After junior high, students may be streamed into senior high, or enter an apprenticeship.
6. Teacher training colleges will be improved and special incentives offered to rural teachers.
7. There will be local control over infrastructure, supervision, and monitoring, and a National Inspectorate Board will inspect schools to insure quality.
8. Appropriate curriculum for each level has been determined.
9. Teacher education is being upgraded, and distance education made available for current teachers.
10. Special educational needs are being addressed. (Education Reform 2007 at a Glance, 2007)

The 2007 reforms are a change from the previous plans which required children to enter school at age 6, with some going on to secondary school at age 12, which lasted 5 years. The stated goal was compulsory education for 10 years, but Ghana had a long way to go to achieve that level of schooling. Modeled after the British system, today Ghana "has 12,130 primary schools, 5,450 junior secondary schools, 503 senior secondary schools, 21 training colleges, 18 technical institutions, . . . and five universities . . . school enrollment totals almost two million" (GhanaHomePage: Education in Ghana, 2007).

Previously, the subjects taught in secondary schools generally follow the British model: language, mathematics, general science, social studies, religious education, and physical education. The exception was "cultural and practical activities," which focus on African heritage and necessary skills for daily life. Examinations also followed the British model. With the 2007 reforms, the senior high schools' core subjects include English, mathematics, integrated science, social studies, and information and communication technology (ICT). Every senior high student must also take one of these course programs: agriculture, business, technical, vocational, or general arts and sciences (Education Reform 2007 at a Glance, 2007).

Equality of Opportunity in Ghanaian Education

Sons and daughters of the urban elite have a disproportionate share of places in education as one progresses upward through the system. However, there is an economic motivation to provide free education for all children—to be competitive in the world and achieve social equality. Education has been free and even compulsory for 6 years since 1961, and now for 11 years, but many children still do not have access to schools or teachers.

Families in Ghana, as in other countries, make educational choices for their children based on a number of factors. These factors include cost to the family, school quality, travel time, and anticipated return on cost. Of those children who enroll in school at the appropriate age and stay in school, those with higher ability do have more opportunity to attend good schools, take competitive examinations for university places, and move ahead.

Differences in opportunity for education between the elite and the masses, however, persist in most African countries. In Ghana, these differences are to some extent regional. For instance, in northern Ghana many of the people have never been to school. One final point on the topic of equality: Ability to speak the English language has become a potent force of "academic colonialism," separating the educated elite from the rural illiterate.

Although each African system is unique, some general observations apply to many postcolonial countries. Education was seen as a high priority following independence from colonial control, for it was thought that through education countries could become truly independent of foreign domination and provide the indigenous leadership needed for technological development, industrialization, business, and movement toward becoming members of the economic global community. The educated elite could afford to send their children abroad where they often pursued prestigious fields such as engineering or law (but also Greek and Latin, less directly useful in modernizing a country). Returning students brought with them not only their expertise but also foreign ideologies and models for curricula. However, the development of technical and agricultural skills, emphasis on preventive medicine within the context of traditional tribal medicine, and integration of new knowledge with existing values and traditions may be more relevant to the needs of the nations than European models of education.

Applying Sociology to Education: *In order to modernize, is it preferable for a sub-Saharan African country to adopt a European educational model or to develop curricula that meet the needs of the local population?*

Higher Education in Postcolonial Africa

Africa has many fine universities, some of the oldest in the world. Today's universities offer a combination of "Western" models and subjects along with traditional and indigenous subjects. For instance, Ghana has two diploma-awarding institutions and five universities serving a population of 17 million, plus training colleges and technical institutions (GhanaHomePage, 2007). The University of Ghana at Accra offers excellent programs in traditional African arts, music, dance, and oral traditions in literature, as well as courses of study patterned after European models.

Another West African country, Nigeria, has 45 universities, of which 25 are federal, 16 state, and 4 private. Including other higher education institutions, nearly 1 million students are enrolled (Jibril, 2004). Nigeria's plan has been to improve the technological base of the country by providing an appropriate mix of students, with 60 percent in sciences and 40 percent in arts, but the reality is that they are still working to reach these figures.

The changing demands of the marketplace, the global political economy and globalization, corporate demands for highly educated workers, shift to information and knowledge production and service economies, increased mobility, and instant transmission of information—all these world trends affecting African education have resulted in demand for highly educated leaders and skilled labor. Several problems in African countries have also affected educational development: civil wars, autocratic rulers, corruption, lack of infrastructure and export of raw products, disease and pandemics such as HIV/AIDS, and colonial histories that have created conflicts between traditional cultural groups. Universities are attempting to keep up with new demands and repositioning themselves to provide education to make students competitive in the world.

A problem for many universities is that reduced national funding coincides with more student demand. In a report on higher education in sub-Saharan Africa, the experts reviewing the situation found rapidly growing enrollments and demand for higher education, poor revenue and expenditure patterns, declining quality, and insufficient relevance to the needs of the countries being served; the results were systems severely strained (Samoff and Carrol, 2003).

Meanwhile, a high percentage of university graduates in Africa are disillusioned because they cannot find jobs in African economies (Sawyer, 2003). Some members of the African elite rejected their own countries' traditional values, cultural uniqueness, and tribal ties in favor of Western models. Others became dissatisfied and alienated because they were overeducated for the available jobs. There is high prestige in being a lawyer or an engineer, but a developing country can absorb only a limited number of them. It might be better able to use schoolteachers and agricultural technicians.

In the future, African leaders searching for ways to improve standards of living will be looking at new models of education. Although political and economic factors may prevent rapid changes in educational systems, there is greater awareness of the problems, and alternative educational models are becoming more prevalent.

The three systems discussed in this chapter—Britain, China, and Ghana and other former colonial African countries—represent three types of political–economic structures in the world system. Whether we divide the countries of the world into these political–economic quadrants, or core and periphery countries, or Global North or South, or rich and poor, or postindustrial and agricultural, or developed and developing, the fact remains that children are receiving very different educations and are prepared for very different lives. Most children around the world receive some formal education, but the amount and circumstances vary greatly depending on the country's culture and place in the world political–economic system.

Summary

All countries provide some form of education to their citizens. These forms differ depending on the level of development, colonial history, and needs of the country's citizens.

I. EDUCATION IN BRITAIN

Education in Britain originated to prepare the elite to lead. With the need for skilled workers, education filtered to the masses, first as training for trades, and eventually as primary and secondary schooling for everyone. Though elite "public schools" still prepare a select group of students, opportunities for most young people have increased greatly at all levels of education.

II. EDUCATION IN THE PEOPLE'S REPUBLIC OF CHINA

Beginning with an educational philosophy influenced by Confucius, education has always been valued in the PRC. During the Cultural Revolution, the educational system was in shambles. By the late 1970s, education was again under firm government control and had spread throughout the country. One recent change has been in the number of private schools that have been created to fill a demand for education, especially in higher education. Today China claims 93.9 percent overall literacy in its vast territories and is increasingly establishing educational links with other countries.

III. FORMAL EDUCATION IN COLONIAL AFRICA

Formal education in colonial Africa was established and controlled by European colonists. With independence, African countries have had to struggle with what type of education is best for their varied cultures. In some cases the new hybrid educational systems are combinations of European and indigenous systems. Ghana is a case in point. The discussion traces issues and problems faced by Ghana in establishing a modern educational system that meets both internal needs and prepares Ghanaians for the future.

Putting Sociology to Work

1. Interview someone from another country about their educational experiences. Ask about their country's system: its history, access and equity, funding, curriculum, and preparation of the population for the twenty-first century.

2. In this chapter you have read about the experience of Ghana as a former colonial country. Read about another former colonial country and compare the differences.

3. Some countries have centralized control of education (China). Others allow more local control of schools (United States and Britain). What are the advantages and disadvantages of each?

4. Chapter 12 does not provide an example of a developed socialist country. Research the educational system in such a country. You might start by looking at some European countries.

13

Educational Movements and Reform

Among the most active areas of educational reform today are what some call "no excuses" schools. These mostly small middle and high schools have an explicit goal of moving poor and minority students, who seldom attend college, into demanding college preparatory curricula and into colleges (Whitman, 2008). They seek to generate in their students the ambition to get ahead through education and to provide them with the academic skills to be able to do so. In the process, the schools teach middle-class habits and attitudes and try to separate the students from the influences of the street culture dominating their neighborhoods. Many are charter schools, and many have extended school days and school years; a number of them require Saturday attendance and run mandatory summer sessions. At a number of these schools, competition for admission is great, and lotteries are frequently used. The recent documentary films, *Waiting for Superman* (http://www.youtube.com/watch?v=ZKTfaro96dg) and *The Lottery* (http://www.youtube.com/watch?v=Khlm4fa-_cE) describe the problems many feel exist with most of the schools these children attend and the promise of attending a "no excuses" school. These films are intended to generate more good schools and a movement to support the educational ambitions they embody.

This chapter considers these schools and the movements that they represent, and assesses the available literature on how well the schools are doing. Along the way, we will examine earlier movements toward education reform and change, and explore the roots of the reform impulse in American education.

Every generation struggles with how to provide the best education to meet the needs of children and society. In recent years, numerous commissions, task forces, and individuals have produced documents lamenting the condition of education in the United States and arguing the need for reform. States have followed suit with hundreds of reports and proposals for reform, many of which have been implemented. One notable area is accountability; in 2008, 41 states required prospective teachers to pass a test before entering the classroom, and others require students to pass achievement tests at various levels before they can move to the next level or be graduated (NCES, *Digest*, 2009, Table 171). As you read, consider how the major educational movements discussed have affected your own educational experience.

Educational movements are more common in countries that lack centralization of decision making in the educational system because influencing education at the local level is easier. Each school district has ultimate jurisdiction over its own educational decision making—a factor that encourages many points of view on education. Unlike most countries, our federal Constitution does not mention education, leaving it to state-level control.

At the time our Constitution was created, education was a minor matter handled primarily by religious groups. Illiteracy was common and not understood to be a matter of public concern. States were largely unwilling to raise taxes to support the creation of public schools until the mid- to late nineteenth century, when the common school movement gained momentum. Individual communities could decide to tax themselves for the support of schools, and those who did took pride in the local control of their schools. In most communities, local residents elect members of a board of education who decide educational policy and hire professional educational administrators to manage the schools on a day-to-day basis. These school superintendents, principals, and others serve at the pleasure of the boards and are thus cautious about introducing policies that don't have widespread community support. At the same time, this tradition of local control assures that the schools are open to the influence of community forces. Countries with more centralized educational decision making and more homogeneous populations have less diversity in educational programs and fewer popular movements for change.

In recent years, demands for accountability and court cases on desegregation, censorship, separation of church and state, and financing have led U.S. state legislatures and boards of education to play a greater role in educational decisions that affect the local level. Societal attitudes swing like a pendulum, from right to left and back again (see Figure 13.1). Education is but one of the institutions in society, and the educational pendulum reflects broad societal trends, movements, and attitudes as we shall find in our discussion of movements.

Theoretical approaches also enter into an understanding of movements. Some conflict theorists argue that attempts by conservatives and minority groups to stress basics will only widen the gap in the opportunity structure. The argument is this: The more the schools stress on basic subjects, rigidity, and discipline, the more compliant will be the future laborers. This in turn perpetuates or reproduces the unequal class structure by creating a well-trained compliant workforce—exactly what those in power need to perpetuate the class differences. These conflict theorists argue that only a restructuring of the obsolete educational and economic systems can lead to expansion of the opportunity ladder. If one accepts this theory, it seems ironic that many persons in those very groups that would be most hurt by stress on basics and discipline—minorities—are among those

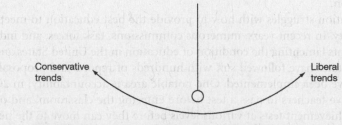

FIGURE 13.1 The pendulum of societal attitudes.

pushing for changes in these directions. But if the aim is to advance individual students' career opportunities, then preparing them to advance in the existing structures is what is appropriate.

The role of schools in preparing young people for the workplace has been in the forefront of educational reform movements, and there is a correspondence between schools and workplaces. However, conflict theorists are concerned that schools controlled by the state also produce the workers for the capitalistic system. Strong democratic social movements for equal opportunity in schools and society can help counter what conflict theorists see as reproduction of the social class system (Carnoy and Levin, 1986).

The view of functionalist theorists is very different. They believe that more stress on basics, discipline, and accountability will help people achieve a niche in the competitive economic system of society. Education in the basics provides individuals opportunity, even though it is unlikely to create a fundamental change in the stratification system of society.

THE NATURE OF EDUCATIONAL MOVEMENTS

Systems change because of constant internal and external pressures from many sources. Figure 13.2 notes some sources of change in educational systems. You can undoubtedly think of more.

When change is brought about in one system or subsystem of society, such as education or politics, it will affect other systems. Social movements are one major indication of the direction in which a society is moving and of the constant pressure for change on parts of the system.

The concept of social movement has been used to refer to numerous collective efforts for change or resistance to change—women's rights movement, civil rights movement, prohibition movement, antiwar movement, right-to-life movement, and the Tea Party movement. Movements arise because large groups of people are dissatisfied with existing conditions. Adherents focus on a general guiding ideology or philosophy, a strong idealism and dedication to this ideology, and some form of action. Movements often generate countermovements which seek to prevent reformers from achieving the changes they seek (e.g., the gay marriage movement versus the groups seeking to restrict marriage to a man and a woman).

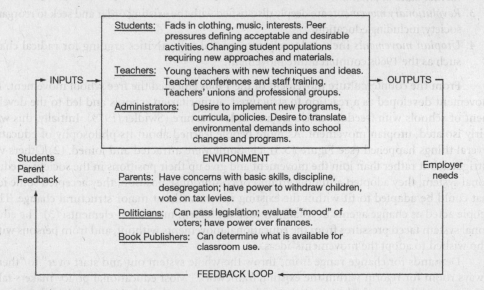

FIGURE 13.2 Sources of change in the school system.

There has never been a time when all members of a society were content with the society or its educational system. The supporters of a movement are generally attempting to bring about or resist some change in society; their motives for involvement in a movement vary from idealism to the personal satisfaction of belonging to a group of believers and having a "cause." Problems in society may first come to light because of a growing social movement. If a movement "catches on" and attracts large numbers of adherents, it is likely to have a direct impact on the existing system. It often starts out as a small fringe group bucking the general trends; with the development of leadership and a communication network such as a newsletter and website, and with the attention of the media, more people are attracted to the movement. Eventually, ideas from the movement may be adopted by schools or other institutions and become "institutionalized," that is, accepted as integral parts of society. Some social movements attract few followers and eventually die. These are often groups pushing for ideas that are not easily integrated into the existing system. Any large social movement is likely to include splinter groups or smaller groups of reformers or radicals supporting specific, related ideologies and causing internal dissent as movement supporters quarrel over means and ends.

Movements may be organized, or they may be unstructured and without clear leadership, as in the case of the counterculture movement from which free schools were spawned. However, individuals or books presenting common threads or ideologies, such as the desire for individuality and freedom, hold movements together. A current example is the conservative "Tea Party" movement that seeks to return to what they understand to be our country's founding principles. Leaders who have written influential books that generate and espouse the movements' philosophy and ideological bases provide common focal points.

Several typologies of movements have been constructed. The following is a summary of types of social movements most relevant to our discussion:

1. *Reform movements* believe that certain reforms are necessary, usually in specific areas of society such as education.
2. *Regressive movements* aim to "put the clock back," reverse current trends, and return to a former state of affairs.
3. *Revolutionary movements* are deeply dissatisfied with the existing order and seek to reorganize society, including education.
4. *Utopian movements* include loosely constructed collectivities arguing for radical change such as the 1960s counterculture movement.

From the counterculture movement of the 1960s emerged the free school movement. This movement developed as a reaction to structured, authoritarian schools and led to the development of schools with freedom of choice and little structure (Swidler, 1979). Initially, this was a fairly isolated, utopian movement. As more people learned about its philosophy of education, several things happened (see Figure 13.3): (1) Some were attracted and joined. (2) Others were intrigued, but rather than join the movement and give up their positions in the society or educational system, they adopted a middle ground or compromise position; they accepted some ideas that could be adapted to fit within the existing system without major structural change. These people acted as change agents in what now took on reform movement elements. (3) The educational system faced pressures from the educational movements without, and from persons within who wished to adopt the movements' ideas.

Demands for change range from "throw the whole system out and start over" to "there is always room for reform within the existing framework." Most educational policy makers take a cautious middle ground when it comes to changes because gradual change makes planning and

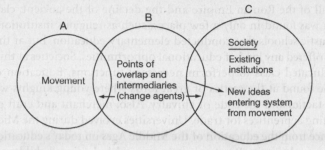

FIGURE 13.3 Educational movements can bring about change in systems.

adaptation possible without much disruption to the existing system. However, this approach appears unresponsive to some who want major structural and ideological change.

Caution must be exercised in using the label "movement" when referring to very specific or short-term changes. For example, many technological "fads" such as language laboratories and computers, and programmed texts brought about significant structural change, but they would probably not be considered movements. They might be subsumed under a larger "movement" such as "classroom technologies."

The purposes of the remainder of this chapter are twofold: to stress the impact of educational movements on school systems, and to discuss some major educational movements that have influenced education in the United States and other countries. Because the ideology behind education helps determine its structure, functioning, and change in the system, an understanding of these major movements is important.

> **Applying Sociology to Education:** *What are some specific examples of sources of change in the schools in your district?*

EARLY EDUCATIONAL MOVEMENTS

Influences on Western systems of education have come from around the world. Education has always been a part of a society's way of acculturating its young, of teaching a child to become a member of a society. Education is found in several forms: nonformal, informal, and formal. It is nonformal when a child learns the ways of his or her culture by being a member immersed and participating in that society, such as modeling parental behavior; it is informal in that a child may be taught through out-of-school activities such as the girl scouts or youth soccer teams; it is formal when a teacher provides instruction about certain aspects of his or her culture in a specific place, such as a school.

Early European Education: Purpose and Function for Society

In ancient Greece and Rome, privileged boys (seldom girls) were educated by wandering teachers called *Sophists,* who taught youngsters the skills needed to develop their reasoning power and rhetoric; that is, the art of persuasion. This "formal" education met the needs of the society and times. Philosophers and great teachers such as Socrates, his student Plato, and Aristotle are still studied for their concepts of the educated person, freedom of thought, and rational inquiry.

After the fall of the Roman Empire and the decline of the ancient, classical civilization, formal education was found in only a few places, such as religious institutions. Many towns in Europe had monastic schools that conducted elementary education, but at the secondary level, only monasteries offered any kind of educational opportunities. Societies at this time did not rely on a formally educated class to perform necessary functions. Education of a formal type, however, could be found at the castles of great lords where young knights were trained in the skills of military tactics and the code of chivalry. Also, merchant and craft guilds maintained means of instructing apprentices for trade. Universities evolved during the Middle Ages.

One influence from the education of the Middle Ages on today's educational movements is the concept of human depravity. Because lust was considered a sin, all children were conceived in sin and, thus, were born depraved. Early religious leaders, such as St. Augustine, and later John Calvin and Martin Luther, stressed that corruptive weakness could be corrected by a strong teacher who used authoritarian methods. Similarly, in the early colonies of New England "Old Deluder Satan Acts" were the first compulsory education laws requiring the reading of the Bible to save children from the temptation of straying from the faith. Many today still advocate the use of authoritarian methods and religious training in the classroom.

During the Renaissance in Europe the concept of the well-rounded and liberally educated person was developed. There was great interest in the humanistic aspects of Greek and Latin classics. In contrast to the sectarian education of the Reformation, with its God-centered worldview, the secular education of the Renaissance focused on the earthly experience of human beings. These views continue to influence curriculum movements, especially in higher education, which in the United States focuses on developing well-rounded students.

Another period of European history that had an effect on American education was the Enlightenment of the eighteenth century. It was believed that people could improve their lives by reason, by using their minds to solve problems; education would enable society to progress toward a new and better world, and schools were believed to be instruments for cultivating the reasoning powers of youth.

Educational Movements in the United States

THE PUBLIC SCHOOL MOVEMENT.   Until the early nineteenth century, many children in the United States attended only primary schools if they attended school at all. Schools at the secondary level were for the elite children, who were sent there to prepare for university, which would lead to occupations in the church or in commerce. This pattern perpetuated an elite and commercial class. However, demands for more access to education and other concerns led to movements for increased opportunity for schooling:

1. With the industrialization and urbanization of the northeastern United States, many people were concerned about the well-being of children; school provided one alternative to working long hours in the factories.
2. Industrialists sought ways to educate and urbanize those coming to towns from rural areas to make them reliable, compliant workers.
3. Many wanted to Americanize and assimilate immigrants.

The school appeared to be the institution that could solve these problems.

Horace Mann, a member of the Massachusetts legislature during the late 1820s and 1830s, was the most forceful advocate and leader of the public school movement. It was Mann who pushed for the establishment of schools for all children free of charge, without religious teaching, and financed through public taxation. He said, "Let the home and the church teach faith and values, and the school teach facts" (Blanchard, 1971, p. 88). He also advocated locally elected boards of education to remove control of the schools from conservative church ministers and schoolmasters. Local districts were supervised by and under the influence of a centralized bureaucracy—the state board of education. Mann himself was appointed head of this agency in Massachusetts.

Another innovation of Horace Mann was to seek the professionalization of teachers: Teacher training colleges, or "normal schools," were established; higher salaries were paid to attract better-qualified teachers; and scientific methods were used for the evaluation of teachers. This reform movement came at a time when societal needs favored development of mass education. Following Massachusetts's lead, people in other states pressed for laws establishing universal, free, primary education. This movement also extended to secondary education, but it was not until after the Civil War, with the need for a more highly educated labor force, that the cry of "more education for more people" really made an impact. As new schools were opened, new teachers were needed. Previously a predominantly male occupation, during the latter half of the nineteenth century, teaching, especially in elementary grades, became an increasingly feminized occupation (Rury, 1989). An important element of this shift was the lower cost of employing a woman. This change had implications for the pedagogy of the time. As Finkelstein (1989) shows, the emphasis changed from "spare the rod and spoil the child" to more benign techniques characterized the actions of teachers as instruction became more important than discipline and character development during the nineteenth century.

Yet it is hard to underestimate the importance of religion in the early development and expansion of schooling in the United States, especially in the North and West. According to Meyer and colleagues (1979), urbanization and industrialization during the nineteenth century were not prerequisites to the creation of schools. Rather a combination of evangelical Protestantism and the outlook of small entrepreneurs produced an ideology of nation-building through education that was also very important. The expansion of secondary education was rapid and widespread, with enrollments doubling every 10 years from about 1880 to 1940 (Hammack, 2004). This expansion produced a major debate over the purpose of high schools. Traditionalists asserted that the curriculum should mirror, as it historically had, the college curriculum—which was largely fixed on the liberal arts and science (electives and majors were uncommon until after 1890). Reformers believed that the high school curriculum should offer opportunities to students who were not intending to prepare for college and they promoted occupationally relevant subjects (Hammack, 2004). By the 1920s, reformers had won the day and the comprehensive high school became the dominant model—with several curricular routes (tracks) for all of a community's children: college preparatory, vocational preparation, and general education, all leading to high school diploma. Earning this diploma became the expectation for all youth by the late 1940s, when initial concern for "drop outs" developed (Dorn, 1996).

THE PROGRESSIVE EDUCATION MOVEMENT. The movement for public education during the first half of the nineteenth century paralleled the wider social trend to integrate newcomers into an increasingly urban and industrial society (Swift, 1971). Similarly, the progressive education movement extending into the 1920s and 1930s paralleled the political progressive movement of the 1890s. Led by the philosopher John Dewey and several of his students and associates, usually women, including Elizabeth Irwin, Lucy Sprague Mitchell, Caroline Pratt, Helen Parkhurst, and others, the movement was exemplified by New York private schools such as The Little Red School House, City and Country School, and the Dalton School. These famous schools influenced public and private educators across the country (Sadovnik and Semel, 2002). The title of Irwin's early book (coauthored with Lewis Marks), *Fitting the School to the Child* (1924), points to the child-centered orientation progressivism brought to schooling, a big contrast with the perspective described by Finkelstein in teacher narratives during the middle and late nineteenth century (also see Davies, 2002).

Recent controversies have surfaced over an offshoot of progressive education philosophy—"life skills." Courses in sex and drug education, marriage, parenting, death and dying, values clarification, money management, consumer knowledge, driver education, house buying, insurance, and other practical skills are seen by some as essential skills for students to have before leaving high school. Others believe that schools should concentrate on basic skills and that life skills should be taught at home, an offshoot of debates over what should be included in the high school curriculum and who should decide this.

THE ESSENTIALS.   Theodore Brameld (1977, pp. 118–120), who has written extensively on the various movements in American education, used the term *essentialist* to describe those involved in a 1950s movement opposing progressive education. Essentialists were particularly vexed about an offshoot of progressive education called the life adjustment movement, which they believed reduced education to teaching survival skills such as home economics, driver education, and hygiene—ignoring the intellectual mission of schooling to teach disciplines.

Conflicts over curriculum content continued. Essentialist critics, such as Arthur Bestor and Robert Maynard Hutchins, decried the "intellectual flabbiness and soft-headedness" of school curricula. Navy Admiral Hyman Rickover complained that he could not find enough scientists and technicians to build and run the Navy's nuclear submarines; and many church leaders and their followers deplored the teaching of cultural relativism and the ignoring of the eternal truths. Politically, the 1950s was a time of fear; Joseph McCarthy stressed the communist threat, with communists lurking in the teachers' lounges and superintendents' offices of the nation's schools. Some saw progressive education as a movement that would weaken educational institutions and were thus opposed to it as a threat to the nation. Echoes of these criticisms can be heard more recently in calls to improve educational attainment by concentrating on basic skills, a tendency strongly supported by the NCLB legislation. Its focus on tests is seen as strongly narrowing the curriculum in both elementary and high schools.

HUMANISTIC EDUCATION.   American education in the twentieth century follows the pendulum-swing theory, from rigor to relevance. Progressivism was in many ways a reaction to the crimping, stultifying schools of Victorian authoritarianism; essentialism was a reaction against progressivism; and the humanistic education movement of the 1960s and 1970s was a reaction to the authoritarianism that had never been given up by the schools. It was a rediscovery of the teachings of the child-centered progressives.

Leaders of the humanistic movement said that schools should eliminate coercive rules and regulations. More opportunities should be created for students to participate in shaping educational goals, especially at the secondary level. This movement was greatly influenced by the client-centered therapies of such psychologists as Carl Rogers and Abraham Maslow. In practice, educators such as Sidney Simon (*Values Clarification*) and Lawrence Kohlberg (*Stages of Moral Development*) presented teachers with a variety of techniques to clarify the values and develop the moral base of their students. Charles Silberman's *Crisis in the Classroom* (1970) was a keynote book on humanistic education. His analysis of American education described the schools as overly formal, devitalized, and often inhumane. He looked at the informal classroom of the English primary school as a model for reform. From the humanistic education movement came interest in an area of "preparation for life" called *moral education*, also known by such terms as *moral development, civic education, citizen/moral education, moral sensibility, moral reasoning,* and *values clarification.* Moral education does not "teach" morals; rather, through the use of classroom exercises, it helps children deal with ethical issues that affect them and the world in which they live, and that will be involved in their decision-making processes (Simon, 1972).

ALTERNATIVE EDUCATION AND RELATED MOVEMENTS

From the humanistic philosophical perspective came the origins of the alternative education movement, with its emphasis on the whole child. It is impossible to speak of one philosophy that all in the movement share, but terms used to describe the schools loosely adhere to philosophical tenets including *free, open, innovative, experimental, new,* and *radical.* Many of these philosophical underpinnings have been spelled out in books that have become the "Bibles" of alternative school advocates.

Free schools refer to schools that gave people freedom and choice; reflect qualities of openness, informality, flexibility, parental and community involvement, and integration in contrast to segregation; stress intellectual, social, and emotional development; encourage self-knowledge, independence, and interdependence; stimulate creativity in an environment of shared responsibility; and minimize failure, competitiveness, authoritarianism, top–down administration, and expensive facilities.

Summerhill was a small residential school set in a village in England; it advocated a totally free learning environment and unrestrained spontaneity. The late A. S. Neill (1960), who founded Summerhill in 1921, believed that to become fulfilled adults, children must be allowed to have a "free" experience, unfettered by rules. The few rules of the school were established by the whole community in a democratic way. Although regular classes from primary through secondary levels were offered, attendance was voluntary (Hart, 1970). Some free schools in the United States were patterned specifically on the Summerhill model; others adopted aspects of the model.

The free school movement was not, however, simply a reaction against repressive school structures, outdated curricula, or ineffective teaching methods, but one against the school as an instrument of the mainstream culture. Many, though not all, free school advocates were motivated by the philosophy that education should be regarded as a means to a political end, that the child should develop freely according to his or her own needs and abilities, not the curriculum of the establishment and dominating political beliefs. "No Child Left Behind" is at the opposite extreme of the philosophical beliefs and principles of the free school movement.

The largest group of students in free schools were children seeking escape from the anxiety and boredom of more traditional schools. They also included students who experienced academic failure and were potential dropouts. For both of these types of students, free schools met a need. Although the movement waned in the 1980s and 1990s, there are a few alternative schools, both public and private, today. They serve students who do not fit the rigid curriculum and test-oriented schools of today (Swidler, 1979). The small schools movement of today draws on the example of many of these earlier alternative school ideas and practices.

Third World Alternative Educational Movements

Changing the educational power structure was also the goal of some Third-World educators. In *Pedagogy of the Oppressed* (1970), Brazilian educator Paulo Freire asserted that literacy among oppressed peasants could be increased by leading these people to an awareness of their cultural reality (the powers that oppress them) and thus giving them the knowledge and its attendant power to fight back against the oppressor. Freire devised a new method of teaching reading that achieved considerable success among the people of poverty-stricken northeastern Brazil. The result was an increased politicalization of the peasantry, which was perceived as a threat by the government. Freire was jailed and eventually forced into exile. He returned in 1980 after a democratic government was reinstituted to continue his work, this time in Sao Paulo. Ivan Illich (1971), a former priest and reformer who worked in Mexico, viewed schools as among several institutions that are coercive, discriminatory, and destructive to the individual. He claimed that by disengaging education from "schooling," deinstitutionalization of the social order would occur, allowing for change. Illich also argued that one does not have to go to school to get an education and that schools can actually inhibit education.

English Primary Schools

The open primary school model of English Primary Schools features a commitment to individualized education and stresses the basics—reading, writing, and mathematics. In this system, children work at their own level in basic skills, which are taught in conjunction with other subjects such as history, science, music, and art. An evaluation of this system states the following:

> The back-to-basics movement in America and in Britain seems to assume that if children will spend longer periods of time working in a narrower way at basic skills they will achieve more. Our major national survey suggests that the opposite is true. If the basic skills are embedded in a web of direct experience on the part of the child that engages the many facets of his personality and being, then basic skills grow most strongly. ("A British Administrator," 1979, p. 61).

The impact of the alternative education movement can be seen in many school systems and classrooms where students are taught in less traditional ways, and in school districts where alternative types of schools or classrooms are available.

Many public school systems established "alternative public schools" for those students who were potential dropouts and could not function effectively within the traditional high school system (Foley and McConnaughy, 1981; Swidler, 1979). These "fringe" public high schools included many of the features of private alternative or free schools. They were informal and small, with personalized learning, student involvement in decision making, innovative learning techniques, and community involvement. Some major cities have retained alternative high schools for limited numbers of students and the contemporary movement to create smaller schools, especially small high schools, draws on this legacy (Jacobowitz et al., 2007; Semel and Sadovnik, 2008).

Open Classrooms

"Open classrooms" have their roots in the progressive education movement. Sometimes called *open education, open schools*, and *open space*, they began in the 1970s and are characterized by the following:

1. Concern over quality of teacher–child interaction; warmth, acceptance; children's thoughts taken seriously
2. Emphasis on cooperation, not competition; few behavioral problems

3. Freedom of movement and use of materials, within certain boundaries; communication among children

4. Other factors related to positive self-image and willingness to take risks and persist.

The teacher facilitates learning and helps students in their activities. The teacher's role is supportive, guiding, and child-centered. The physical environment presents an atmosphere of informality. Desks are grouped, and different activities are available in different areas of the room. Open classrooms are most commonly found in elementary schools.

Parents tend to be involved in open classrooms, volunteering help or bringing in projects for the children. Open education results in different interaction patterns in the classrooms; there is generally more interaction among students and less formal teacher–student interaction. Open education is particularly beneficial for some students, such as Native American children, who come from a culture that holds values similar to those of open education—cooperation, sharing, and individual responsibility for decision making.

In our current time of standards, accountability, and back-to-basics movements, perhaps best exemplified by yearly standardized testing requirements of the No Child Left Behind Act, open education classrooms have come under attack as "schools without failure," automatically promoting children without identifying lack of achievement. Some open education structures have been replaced by more traditional classrooms with desks and chairs in rows, but many teachers have retained some semblance of the open education atmosphere in their classrooms.

Back to Basics

From the alternative education movement, the swing of the pendulum moved to the conservative side. The movement, referred to as *back to basics*, features good, old-fashioned reading, writing, and arithmetic with a good dose of discipline thrown in and none of the "frills" such as humanistic education and the arts. Supporters of basic-skills education argued that schools should be guided by essentialist principles, including the following:

1. The elementary school curriculum should aim to cultivate basic tool skills that contribute to literacy and mastery of arithmetical computation.

2. The secondary curriculum should cultivate competencies in history, mathematics, science, literature, English, and foreign languages.

3. Schooling requires discipline and a respect for legitimate authority.

4. Learning requires hard work and disciplined attention (Routman, 1996).

Having completed such a school curriculum, the students should be able to apply their knowledge to solve many problems. Back to basics places more emphasis on basic skills; initially the pressure came from parents concerned about their children's skill levels. Additionally, pressure comes from commission reports, state legislators, international test score comparisons, and concerns of the public about the decline in achievement test scores. A good example of this is the *Nation at Risk* (National Commission on Excellence in Education, 1983) report by a commission appointed by a Reagan Administration secretary of education which asserted that we were "committing unilateral educational disarmament" for not paying enough attention to promoting excellence in our public schools.

Our historical summary shows that back-to-basics education is not new. In Puritan times most schools were set up to teach basic skills and religion so that children could develop an understanding of morals, religion, and law. Young boys from elite homes attended grammar schools where Greek and Latin literature were taught; always the emphasis was on basic skills. As

BOX 13.1

Excerpt from a McGuffey Reader: Things to Remember

1. When you rise in the morning, remember who kept you from danger during the night. Remember who watched over you while you slept, and whose sun shines around you, and gives you the sweet light of day.

2. Let God have the thanks of your heart, for His kindness and His care. And pray for His protection during the wakeful hours of day.

3. When you are at the table, do not eat in a greedy manner, like a pig. Eat quietly, and without noise. Do not reach forth your hand for the food, but ask someone to help you.

4. Avoid a pouting face, angry looks, and angry words. Do not slam doors. Go quietly up and down stairs; and never make a loud noise about the house.

5. Be kind and gentle in your manners; not like the howling winter storm, but like the bright summer's morning.

6. Do always as your parents bid you. Obey them with a ready mind, and with a pleasant face.

7. Never do anything that you would be afraid or ashamed that your parents should know. Remember, if no one else sees you, God does; from whom you cannot hide even your most secret thought.

8. We must do all the good we can to all men, for this is well pleasing in the sight of God. He delights to see his children walk in love, and do good, one to another.

Exercises—What should you remember in the morning? Whom should you thank, and for what should you pray? How should you behave at the table? What should you avoid? How should you behave to your parents? What should you do at night? Whom should you always trust?

Source: McGuffey, William H., *Third Eclectic Reader* (Cincinnati: Wilson, Hinkle, 1857; 2nd ed., 1965), pp. 55–57.

the colonies expanded, different types of schools were founded to meet the differing needs of students and society, but always stressing basic skills. McGuffey Readers reigned as the primary texts used in classrooms for almost a century, from 1836 to the 1930s. In addition to basic skills, the texts stressed morals and manners (see Box 13.1), which provides a clear example of cultural transmission of dominant values.

The Council for Basic Education, founded in 1956, acted as a liaison group for those interested in basic education, or basic skills. Proponents of basic education today have a variety of interests and motives. Some advocate use of the paddle and stress truth, virtue, justice, religious principles, and dress codes as the primary focus of schools. Others mainly want to be assured that the three Rs are being mastered.

The main uniting ideologies for back-to-basics proponents include reaction to the failures of promised miracles, to desegregation, and to the ban on Bible-reading and prayers in classrooms; a "break-down in the moral fiber of society"; and a need for "patriotism, morality, manners, adult authority, discipline, order, and quality education" (Egerton, 1976). This reaction has also stimulated the home schooling movement (Stevens, 2001).

What did this mean in terms of changes in the schools? Many open classrooms were eliminated. Courses other than basics were questioned or eliminated, including art and music appreciation, sex and drug education, physical education, and drivers' education, as were emphases on the well-being of the whole child and use of counselors and other social service programs. Discipline and basic skills took their place. In recent years we have seen a swing of the pendulum back with the slow return of some social programs and additional courses, although the emphasis remains on basic education and explicit standards of student achievement.

Private Schools

The private school business owes a great deal to back-to-basics proponents. Private schools thrive on the discontent of frustrated parents who want a reprieve from the conflicts over desegregation, the perceived lack of discipline, and apparent lowering of standards. Today, about 10.7 percent of all elementary and secondary students in the United States attend private schools (NCES, Fast Facts, http://nces.ed.gov/fastfacts/display.asp?id=65).

Categories of private schools include the following: elite preparatory schools such as Choate, Phillips-Andover, Groton, and Lawrenceville, which cater to the wealthy who plan to go to elite colleges (Cookson and Persell, 1985; Peshkin, 2001); special schools for the disabled or gifted; military academies; and religious, sectarian day schools sponsored by Catholic, Jewish, Baptist, Lutheran, Quaker, fundamentalist Christian, and other religious groups. Today, the largest number of private schools students attend are Catholic-affiliated schools, though that number is down from 54.5 percent to 42.5 percent of private schools during the period 1989–1990 to 2007–2008. (Council for American Private Education, http://www.capenet.org/facts.html, downloaded October 9, 2010). These private schools meet the preferences of many different people holding various beliefs about the role of education.

One type of private school that experienced tremendous growth in the 1970s was the fundamentalist Christian school. Some of these schools were established in reaction to a sense of negativity about the public schools, others in response to integration of schools. At the core of this movement is a distrust of the educational system, which seems to some to be imposing an alien value system on their own.

Fundamentalist Christians believe that education and Christian teachings cannot be separated. They object to public school teachings that include such ideas as humans having evolved from lower forms of life, denying the literal biblical interpretation of the Creation; the idea that humans are animals, implying that humans do not have a soul; and other specific teachings. Reaction to such teachings in public schools has led to an upsurge of interest in Christian schools. In this, as in other movements, one senses an in-group–out-group or we–they tone. "They" are destroying our children's faith in God, implanting alien ideas in their minds (see Peshkin, 1986).

Since 1991, private school education has received a boost from the government in the form of a push for "choice" systems. This allows parents to select from various schools, which in turn receive funds for each student enrolled (*America 2000*, 1991). Thus, more students are able to attend private schools. These "voucher" plans have been controversial as they can lead to public funds being used to support religious schools, what some see as a violation of our constitutional requirement of separation of church and state, though current court rulings (*Zelman v. Simmons-Harris*, 2002) allow such funding.

Applying Sociology to Education: *Should parents and students be able to select the school of their choice? What are the pros and cons?*

Accountability Movements

Accountability refers to a means of controlling educational standards of competency and measuring outcomes against expenditures. The accountability movement arose in reaction to the humanistic emphasis in education. Of paramount concern was the attempt to account for dollars spent and to hold someone responsible, usually teachers, for the output of schools, as measured by student achievement. Some educational writers arguing for reforms in the schools supported the idea of accountability. Nat Hentoff, for one, urged parents to speak up against the "great consumer fraud" and demand competent teachers, although he noted that teachers are almost never fired for incompetence (Hentoff, 1978, pp. 3–8). In order to try to ensure accountability, many proposals have been set forth for measuring teachers' performance, from student performance on standardized tests to the National Teacher Exams. For instance, competency-based education (CBE) in teacher training institutions requires students to master certain skills before graduation.

Low student test scores, violence in schools, and high dropout rates are cited as reasons for recent calls for accountability. Many states are requiring students to pass exams at one or more points in their school careers. These "high stakes" tests that can determine whether students get promoted to the next grade or graduate from school are put in place as a result of states adopting explicit standards for achievement. With such tests, not only can students be measured, but so too can teachers and schools as we described in Chapter 6.

Some states and local school districts have proposed that teacher pay be tied to student test results. This practice is likely to reduce creativity in classrooms, as teachers teach to the tests. Movements for accountability have increased the power and influence of testing agencies in the school environment. School districts desiring to evaluate their student populations compared with state or national norms rely on standardized tests. A decline in standardized test scores on the College Boards or SAT, put out by the Educational Testing Service (ETS), and on the ACT was cited as a major reason for the back-to-basics drive in the late 1970s and early 1980s. The desire to hold students, teachers, and schools accountable for meeting the state standards is at the heart of the most important educational movement of a number of years, the No Child Left Behind Act of 2001 (PL107–110), which we will discuss shortly.

Humanists point out that accountability may turn the schools from humane, spontaneous, creative places that encourage positive self-concepts and success to cold, formal places with measurement procedures and clearly delineated objectives, allowing for little spontaneity and creativity.

According to the systems approach, problems in education cannot be attributed to only one source. Teachers are not the only villains, nor are the students. Perhaps the schools are scapegoats, blamed because of expectations that they can solve all of society's problems. Government at all levels is involved, as are all those who serve the school. And families also play a role in school achievement.

Some critics of the accountability movement argue that there are numerous causes for educational problems besides the teacher or school administrators, including parents, community residents, school board members, taxpayers, and, most important, the students themselves. Recently, families and teacher education programs have faced their share of criticism for school failures. The point is that numerous people play a role in educating the child. Concentrating on only one aspect of the system and the environment will produce a "bandage effect," but it probably will not result in solutions to problems.

These issues are well illustrated by a debate that evolved during the Obama presidential campaign and into the early years of his administration. Citing the need to reduce the achievement gap between poor, urban populations and middle-class, suburban students, policy makers fell into two camps as they sought solutions: those who thought an unrelenting focus on schools and teachers was the best approach and those who argued that the causes of the gap were multiple and that school reform efforts should be joined with programs of community development and health promotion. While there is common ground between these two approaches, their emphases are different. Those adopting the former approach emphasize the importance of high quality teachers, small schools, and a singular focus on academic skill development. These proponents point to how teachers and schools can "trump" the social class origins of students: "When all factors are controlled, it is the quality of the teacher that makes the difference in student learning. Teacher quality is more important than any other variable" (Fallon, 2000, p. 5).

Advocates of the other approach, sometimes called the "Broader, Bolder Approach," emphasize the importance of school reform, but assert that it alone will not do the job (http://www.boldapproach.org/). Perhaps the best example of this latter approach is the Harlem Children's Zone developed by Geoffrey Canada. This is a nonprofit organization that funds and operates two charter schools and a network of neighborhood-based social service programs in a 100-block area of Harlem (Whitehurst and Croft, 2010). The network includes early childhood programs, after-school programs, support for the area's graduates who have entered college, fitness programs, nutrition and asthma management programs, tenant associations, community centers, and others. The Zone has received wide philanthropic support (over $100 million) and media attention (see the book by Paul Tough, *Whatever It Takes*). The Whitehurst and Croft report concludes that "There is no compelling evidence that investments in parenting classes, health services, nutritional programs, and community improvement in general have appreciable effects on student achievement in schools in the U.S." (p. 8). These programs are all justifiable on their own terms, but evidence so far does not support the conclusion that they produce higher levels of school achievement (Otterman, 2010).

Effective Schools and Educational Reform

A recent buzzword in the halls of education is *effective schools*. Exactly what is meant by this term varies, but common themes include schools in which students are achieving at a high level or in which achievement has risen significantly. Drawing from multiple studies of effective schools, we can summarize the characteristics that enable students to achieve at a high level:

1. Professional staff holds high expectations and believes all students can reach these.
2. Students understand high expectations, have high self-concepts, and have low sense of academic futility.
3. Role expectations of teachers and students include high achievement.
4. The school reward structure is centered on achievement.
5. Stratification of students and differentiation of instructional programs are minimal.
6. School goals and objectives are shared.
7. The school climate is conducive to learning (Brookover, Erickson, and McEvoy, 1996).

How to achieve effective schools is the subject of even more studies and reports. The highest rates of improvement in school achievement have been reported when there is clear articulation of grade-level expectations and standards in each area, clear homework policies throughout the school, and all students are taught the curriculum for their grade level. Other findings focus on instructional techniques, classroom expectations, and rules; how students are grouped for subjects; and other specific recommendations, some of which are discussed in earlier chapters (Talbert, 1995).

There is the danger in reform movements (such as effective schools) that schools, districts, or states will simply attempt to institute a "list" of reforms rather than consider carefully what is best for each school. Some influential reformers argue that the individual school must be the center for efforts to improve schools. In a large research project based on extensive descriptive data from 38 schools in 13 diverse communities, Goodlad (1984) investigated the following aspects of schools: school functions, the relevance of schools to students, how teachers teach, circumstances surrounding teaching, curriculum, distribution of resources for learning, equity, hidden curriculum, satisfaction with school quality, and the need for school data collection. He argues that school reform must take place at the individual school and classroom level, not at some distant central location. Uniformity imposed from a central office hinders real change, and decentralization of decision making is essential. The strong leadership of a principal who gives teachers power and works with them will have the greatest impact on achievement in the school (Bernhardt and Ballantine, 1995). As the saying goes, "the devil is in the details." Reform models must be implemented in real schools with real students, teachers, and administrators in real communities. The variety of ways a program is implemented can be enormous, each leading to different outcomes. We need to be wary of solutions to educational problems that don't concentrate on teachers and students, and on classrooms and the interactions that take place within them.

A major risk with back-to-basics, accountability, and effective schools is that some of the ever-growing number of disadvantaged students who fall in the bottom half will be left farther behind and eventually drop out.

STRUCTURAL AND CURRICULAR CHANGES IN THE SCHOOLS

Changes introduced in educational systems affect structure and role relationships. When movements produce new ideas, concerns, and programs, there are often efforts to incorporate them into the existing system. This requires adaptation of the physical and role structure of schools. Structural changes can take place at the system level (e.g., magnet schools, voucher systems, or charter schools); the school level (e.g., tracking students, integrating the disabled, programming for gifted children, or installing architectural alternatives); and the classroom level (e.g., alternative curriculum models, team teaching, or open classrooms).

The "School Choice" Movement

Several educational movements advocate options and choices for students and parents. They fall into four categories: charter schools, home schooling, open enrollment, and vouchers. School choice is a fast-growing innovation in public education with almost 27 percent of public school students in the United States participating in some form of choice (Grady and Bielick, 2010). Charter schools are increasing in popularity in many states, though the lack of state authorizing laws limit their expansion; they are allowed in 40 states as of 2010. Home schooling allows parents to arrange for their children's schooling. Open enrollment gives parents the option to choose where their children go to school, generally within a district. Vouchers also allow parents to send their children to any of a number of schools, depending on their preference (Education Commission of the States, 1999b).

Although the idea has been practiced in some cities for many years, only recently have districts formally adopted magnet school policies to desegregate and integrate, often leading to system-wide change. Magnet schools were established in some cities to distribute students and desegregate schools on the basis of special interests or talents: science, mathematics, art and music, and vocational education. The plan is in place in some cities, sometimes as part of a busing-desegregation plan. In 1992, there were 5,000 magnet schools nationwide, and the number was growing until districts began to explore other alternatives. Research indicates that magnet schools can improve the choices for students, help in desegregation efforts, and improve the quality of education (Blank and Archibald, 1992), but the rise of charter schools and other alternative schools has reversed their growth. According to recent data, there are fewer than 2,000 magnet schools now operating. These data, however, are not considered a good reflection of the actual number, because many states did not report the number of such schools operating in their boundaries (NCES, 2007c, "Overview").

Charter schools—publicly funded, free-standing schools with their own governing boards—are not always part of a regular public school district. They are a more recent innovation dating only from the early 1990s, and were begun by reformers who believed that rigid public educational bureaucracies were stifling innovation; they also allow for choice and are similar in some ways to magnet schools. A very fast growing phenomenon, their number increased from 1,500 in 1999–2000 to 4,400 in 2007–2008 (NCES, Condition of Education, 2010, Table A-32-1); these schools enrollments have increased from 340,000 in 1999–2000 to 1.3 million in 2007–2008. They are more likely than other public schools to be small and urban. Though most have been in operation only a short time, some are already closing, failing to meet the academic or financial performance levels required by their charters. New charter schools are established to serve at-risk or minority children or to meet concerns of parents. Any time choice is involved; however, some families are going to forego that choice, resulting in continued or greater inequality for some children (Rofes and Stulberg, 2004; Wells et al., 1999).

A new development is the rise of charter management organizations (CMO) that sponsor a set of schools, usually following a common model. Perhaps the best-known CMO is KIPP (Knowledge is Power Program schools [http://kipp.org/]), which currently runs 99 schools in 20 states, enrolling over 26,000 students. Other CMOs include Green Dot schools, Uncommon Schools, and Aspire Public Schools. These schools run on a franchise model, where each school is set up and follows a common philosophy and set of practices. KIPP schools are good examples of the "no excuses" schools mentioned at the beginning of this chapter. Most charters, however, are not members of these networks; rather, they are individually sponsored and governed, and vary widely in quality. Some CMOs are for-profit (Edison Schools is one example) and others are not-for-profit organizations. In either case, there is an entrepreneurial spirit in many of these schools as educators seek to improve the schooling many inner-city youth experience. The "no excuses" schools have shown some success with their inner-city students (Maxwell, 2010), but there are questions as to whether the demands they make on families and students can be met by most of those they seek to serve. The motivation of parents and their children to succeed must be very strong to endure the longer school days and years, the weekend and summer sessions, and the singular emphasis on college subjects and skills (Hammack, 2010). Some of these schools have high attrition rates, and few of them provide services to typical proportions of English language learners or students eligible for special education services. Their ability to transform the lives of typical inner-city students remains to be seen.

Another issue that has arisen as the charter school movement has grown is its effect of school segregation. The Civil Rights Project has documented that racial and ethnic segregation is greater in charter schools than in regular public schools (http://civilrightsproject.ucla.edu/research/k-12-education/integration-and-diversity/choice-without-equity-2009-report). In some locales, these schools seem to have become havens of white flight, while in others, they almost exclusively enroll children from a single racial or ethnic group. While desegregation was not the intent of the proponents of charter schools, this result is a negative consequence of their rapid expansion.

Community schools are similar to charter schools, but often integrate social welfare services dealing with health and emotional needs (Coltoff, 1998). Like charter schools, community schools focus on a particular method, theme, or curriculum; they are publicly funded but give parents and students autonomy in governance (deMarrais and LeCompte, 1995, p. 298). Voucher systems also produce system-wide changes. School districts establish schools with a variety of philosophies, educational programs, kinds of discipline, and services. Theoretically, communities and parents become involved in both the selection and the operation of schools.

Each family receives money vouchers for school-age children. The vouchers are good for a year of education at the school of their choice. However, the vouchers rarely cover the cost of independent private schools. Debate over using vouchers at religiously sponsored schools involves the separation of church and state in the use of public funds.

Each of these options falls into the category of school choice. Choice-movement leaders have advocated parental and student free choice of schools so that parents can select between educational philosophies and curricula. One argument for these programs is that competition between schools for student enrollment and voucher money could raise standards. If schools have to compete with each other, the logic goes, educational improvement will result—just as any market is thought to improve the products and the efficiency with which they are produced. Of course, consumer choice requires that information about choices be readily available. For example, New York City allows extensive choice of secondary schools, but the rules about who can apply where, and what their chances of getting their top choices actually are has stimulated a small industry publishing guides to the schools in addition to the official directory published by the school system itself (a Manhattan phonebook-sized document). Not all parents are able to take advantage of this information, however, and usually the more advantaged and savvy parents are the beneficiaries (Smrekar and Goldring, 1999). In a time when students' achievements are woven into accountability systems, school leaders may care very much about the characteristics of students who attend them. Much like students and their parents who try to "game" the admissions systems, school leaders may use their own methods to shape their student bodies in ways that make it more likely the school will meet its achievement benchmarks (Jennings, 2010).

The "market analogy" has become widespread in education, with its notion that education is like any other commodity consumers can obtain and that competition among providers is the best way to determine what forms are available and at what price (Gwirtz, Ball, and Bowe, 1995). Many support its application while others question the consequences for the society as well as individual students and families of an unregulated market of educational services. In each case, a major goal is to involve parents in the educational decisions regarding their children.

Opponents of choice have several key concerns: urban public schools might become the dumping ground for students not enrolled in other schools; and private schools supported in part by public funds might create further divisions in society by becoming more selective about their student bodies. Some have predicted the demise of public school education and heterogeneous grouping in schools. Voucher plans remain high on the agenda of some reformers who seek alternatives to regular public schools, but the legal battles are not over (Scott, 2005). The message is unclear about whether choice systems improve schooling for low-income youth. On the one hand, it could encourage more youth and family involvement and give the children alternative school options. On the other hand, it could perpetuate the gap between wealthy and poor youth because high-income youth would continue to receive better educations than poor youth because of their choices (Manski, 1992, p. 1; also see Smrekar and Goldring, 1999; Wells et al., 1999). One finding from research on the break up of large comprehensive high schools and the creation of several small themed high schools (to be discussed below) shows that students choose schools according to where their friends are going, often perpetuating the curriculum placements in the larger high school by choosing the smaller school that corresponds to their prior track placement (college prep track students are more likely to choose a science and math themed school than are general education track students (Ready and Lee, 2008).

It is also clear that the larger neighborhood context in which choice systems develop and operate is important (Lauen, 2007). The mix of school qualities, characteristics of local residents, availability of transportation, peer effects, and other forces determine who chooses and whether their choices are successfully realized. The importance of a school's attendance zone is long gone, and the increasing number of schools and their variety now complicates the distribution of students among schools.

> **Applying Sociology to Education:** *What are some effects of recent choice movements on your district's schools?*

Small Schools Movement

An important related development to the school choice movement has been the trend to create smaller schools. Fueled by the findings that students attending smaller school generally had better test scores and better attendance and graduation rates, a number of educational decision-makers began to support the closing of larger schools and replacing them with smaller ones, often within the same building, and to open new schools with fewer students. Often noting that private schools for the children of the wealthy seldom enroll more than a few hundred students, these proponents emphasized the importance of smaller classrooms, greater, more personal individual attention, and the unity of the curriculum (Kafka, 2008). During the first decade of the twenty-first century, smaller schools were promoted as a major vehicle of reform. Several large foundations (most notably The Gates Foundation) gave hundreds of millions of dollars to urban school systems to break up their large high schools and create many smaller ones. Toward the end of the decade, Gates Foundation decided to change its funding priorities since its smaller schools were able to raise graduation rates, but the academic achievement of students and their preparation for college did not improve (http://www.eschoolnews.com/2009/05/29/gates-foundation-teachers-trump-class-size/; Shear et al, 2008). The size of the school was not important in comparison with the quality of the teacher.

This finding has been repeated by others (e.g., Iatarola et al., 2008). Size alone does not improve achievement; it must be accompanied by improved instruction by competent teachers. When good instruction by competent teachers exists, students are likely to improve, no matter how large or small the school.

Technology and the Classroom

Concern over declining achievement scores brought a flood of cure-alls beginning in the late 1950s. Teaching machines, reading programs, talking typewriters, educational television, tape-cassette machines, and other technological innovations were introduced into classrooms across the nation. Computers in the classroom and computer-assisted instruction (CAI) began in the late 1960s. Proponents of the new technology argued that schools should take advantage of the technological revolution, just as business and other institutional sectors were doing. "Traditional" classrooms could be changed into individualized instructional centers to meet a wide variety of learning styles and interests. Today, computers are an integral and essential part of education at all levels of schooling in developed countries, and are taking root in developing countries as reduced-cost hardware and software make dissemination possible. Distance learning is also linking home and school learning. Though the specific types of technology in the classroom have changed, technology is here to stay. As new capabilities develop, new uses for technology are implemented. We are in the early stages of this far-reaching technological movement as we enter the twenty-first century.

Classrooms and the role of the teacher may be very different in the future. Information retrieval using electronic means will be key, and distance learning will bring unlimited learning potential around the world, having a lasting impact because of its importance to train students for future jobs in society.

One of the more interesting experiments now taking place is the "classroom of one" project in some New York City public schools (Coates, 2010) (http://schools.nyc.gov/community/innovation/SchoolofOne/default.htm). As the name implies, this model involves individualizing the educational experience of children, made possible with a computer for each participant. Currently being adopted at a few schools, this program first establishes a learner profile of each student, based on prior performance and the students' learning preferences and interests. An elaborate "learning algorithm" then tailors a specific instructional program for each student that incorporates the skills and knowledge the student needs to know with settings and tasks appropriate for the student based on the profile. Currently being used in 5th through 7th grade math, the 77 skill areas and knowledge areas are available in 1,100 lesson plans. Students may be placed in small or larger group for instruction; they may receive one-to-one tutoring or peer study; computer games and other e-learning options are available. From these smaller parts, progressively arranged, students develop mastery of the material and can progress at their own pace. Preliminary evaluations have been positive and the Department is moving ahead to expand the experiment. It remains to be seen whether the model is successful with wider groups of students, and whether it can as readily be applied to other school subjects. But it is clear that the continuing development of computer technology is allowing for further development of applications to schools. Optimists argue that experiments such as School-of-One will finally pay off. Arthur Levine, the current president of the Woodrow Wilson National Fellowship Foundation is an enthusiastic supporter: this " . . . may turn out to be the single most important experiment in education so far. It is the future." (http://schools.nyc.gov/NR/rdonlyres/9435AD08-90F3-42AA-838C-6372C3B5D2E6/0/SchoolofOneBrochure_FINAL.pdf).

Technology has its skeptics, however, in those who fear the loss of the human side of education and learning, which involves using the senses and learning through contact with others (Jones and Smart, 1998). There is little data suggesting that student achievement has improved as a result of the introduction of technologies into schools, but studies continue. In any case, students need computer skills to be literate and prepared for the job market. Whatever the future role of technology, learning remains a social activity. The importance of student motivation and effort is not magically eliminated by technological innovation (Giacquinta, Bauer, and Levin, 1993).

No Child Left Behind Act of 2001 and Race to the Top competition of 2009–2010

Counted by many as the most far-reaching educational reform effort of the federal government in U.S. history, No Child Left Behind legislation has come to dominate the educational reform and policy landscape today. Passed with bipartisan support, this legislation included the reauthorization of the Elementary and Secondary Education Act of 1965, itself a landmark of federal education legislation passed during the height of the "war on poverty." In 2008–2009 (this law allocated almost $15 billion in federal funds to support education at the local level [NCES, *Digest*, 2009, Table 379]). While this is a fraction of the total funds expended in support of public elementary and secondary education, most of which comes from state and local sources, it gives the federal government considerable leverage in directing educational policy.

This legislation, however, required states to test elementary aged children every year against state-developed standards for each grade (The Education Trust, n.d.). Thus, the law did

Computers are now common in classrooms.

not set national standards for what children were to "know and be able to do," but did require states to set explicit standards and to incorporate those standards into their achievement tests for each grade. While some states have used these tests to determine whether students get promoted to the next grade, the law requires states to gather these data for each school; the data are published to show the degree to which each school is preparing its students to achieve the standards set by the state. These data are to be published for each demographic group of students enrolled in the school (unless the number in a group is very small), and, if students are not performing at grade level, the schools are required to develop plans for improving their instruction. The law also required all teachers to be "highly qualified" by 2006; but, again, to avoid setting up national standards, the federal government leaves it up to the states to define what "highly qualified" actually means. While the details of the law's implementation have evolved over time, and may well change when the law next comes up for reauthorization, the law requires schools and districts to meet annual performance targets, based largely on test scores, for their student populations overall and for subgroups of students who are poor, speak limited English, have disabilities, or belong to racial or ethnic minorities. Schools and districts that fail to meet their targets for adequate yearly progress, or AYP, for two or more years face sanctions such as reduction in federal funds. Ultimately, the school may be forced to close. The legislation projects that by 2012 no gaps will exist between the different groups of students (http://ehistory.osu.edu/osu/origins/article.cfm?articleid=41). This legislation contains the largest and most important elements of federal education policy and the bill must be reauthorized periodically. As of 2010, it has not been reauthorized and many changes in it have been proposed. It will have to be reauthorized to continue the flow of federal funds to states and school districts, but for now it is impossible to say what its provisions will be.

The requirement that schools make progress on standard levels of achievement for all students is aimed directly at reducing the "achievement gap" that exists in the performance of students from advantaged and disadvantaged backgrounds. However, some states question provisions of the law, especially extensive and expensive testing requirements that have been seen as onerous; also, some states set standards at the lowest possible achievement levels to improve their state's performance scores.

The frequent testing forces teachers to teach to the test, and encourages schools to limit the variety of curriculum they offer in order to concentrate on the subjects deemed essential in the standards (Berliner, 2008; Hamilton et al., 2007; McGuire, 2007; Schemo, 2007; Warren and Grodsky, 2009). The use of these tests for assessing schools and evaluating teachers and their compensation has grown, even though there are good reasons to be skeptical about the validity and reliability of the tests (Medina, 2010). Critics also question the basic premise of the law—that schools have it within their power to overcome the achievement differences produced by inequalities among families and communities. Rothstein (2004) makes this case as follows:

> . . . eliminating the social class differences in student outcomes requires eliminating the impact of social class on children in American society. It requires abandoning the illusion that school reform alone can save us from having to make the difficult economic and political decisions that the goal of equality inevitably entails. School improvement does have an important role to play, but it cannot shoulder the entire burden, or even most of it, on its own. (p. 149)

This comment sounds like the broader, bolder approach described above, which, while seeking to develop many aspects of community life, especially in poverty areas, has not shown a significant impact on student academic achievement. This reflects back to long-standing issues in the sociology of education. Remember that Jencks, in confirming the Coleman findings of the importance of student background variables in explaining school achievement, argued against using educational policy to fight poverty. He asserted that reforming schools was an indirect and inefficient method to achieve a reduction in the rate or effects of poverty (Jencks et al., 1972). This argument remains very contemporary. The most recent federal efforts at education reform stem from the American Recovery and Reinvestment Act of 2009 (Public Law 111-5) and provides about $100 billion to state education systems and supplemental appropriations for several Department of Education programs. Most of this money was for a one-time supplement to state and local budgets hard-pressed by the economic recession of 2008–2009. One part of it, however, represents the Obama administration's school reform effort—the Race to the Top. This $4-billion program awards grants to states that adopt standards and assessments that prepare students to succeed in college and the workplace. It also helps build data systems that measure student growth and progress, and inform teachers and principals about how they can improve instruction; recruit and develop, reward and retain effective teachers and principals; and turn around the lowest-achieving schools (http://www2.ed.gov/programs/racetothetop/index.html).

While most of these provisions sound direct and logical, in actual practice, they have been surrounded with much controversy. We have already discussed the complexities of performance pay for teachers, but many think the development of state-level student data systems is a good idea. Yet, there are privacy issues and technical ones as well that will have to be addressed. The setting of common standards, pushed by many national educational and policy groups, goes against over two centuries of state autonomy in education matters (http://www.corestandards.org/).

Educational reform has been based on ideologies, philosophies, and social movements more than on solid research. In other fields, research informs practice in more direct ways. For example, experimental research is used to determine whether new drugs are introduced or not (Gewande, 2000). An experiment is a research methodology in which participants are unaware of whether they are receiving an actual drug or a placebo (a pill that looks like the real one, but contains no active agent). Findings from experiments yield valid and reliable findings about whether specific methods (or drugs) produce real achievement gains (or greater health). Only recently have experimental methods been strongly promoted in education; however, because they require the manipulation of students and pedagogy, there has been strong resistance to such studies. Learning is a complex, volitional activity that requires the willing and active participation of the learner, unlike the more passive pill swallowing of medical solutions. There are limits to the application of science-based or technologically based solutions to achievement differences (Lagemann and Shulman, 1999).

The problems that have stimulated efforts to change educational systems in the past continue—how to educate all children to prepare them for the twenty-first-century demands. The growing numbers of low-income and minority children, dropouts, and failures in societies around the world point out the contradictory values of equality and individual liberty. Though some would have us return to "the good old days" of education, no period in history has been free of educational critics and problems in schools, including high dropout rates, nonreaders, boredom, violence, and undisciplined students. We can predict that the pendulum of change will continue to swing.

This is especially so as there are different goals reformers seek to maximize, and sometimes these goals are incompatible if not contradictory. David F. Labaree (1997) identifies three goals that he argues Americans seek from our educational system: democratic equality, social efficiency, and social mobility. The first refers to the promise of equality of citizenship. All citizens are to be treated equally in their dealing with the state as they are prepared to assume the duties of citizenship (voting, serving on jury duty, and the like). Second, we expect schools to prepare people to do the work required by our economy. Finally, we expect schools to offer the opportunity for social mobility. Labaree argues that these three goals have become more or less important at different times in our history. The last one, however, has become paramount in our thinking. Schools are today mostly thought to be engines of individual social mobility—go to school and get ahead. The problem is that education for social mobility has become education for credentials and status attainment over the acquisition of knowledge. As we seek to maximize individual opportunity, we are less likely to emphasize the needs of the larger economy for educated workers, and of the larger society for well-educated citizens. These divergent goals keep our collective dissatisfaction with education at a high level, supporting continuing demands for reform. It is well to try to identify the goals reformers prioritize as they call for change.

A Look into the Future

Understanding that education is deeply connected with all other aspects of society leads to the insight that change in education is unlikely to take place without change also taking place in other sectors of society. One of the important changes of the twentieth century has been the expansion of education and the lengthening of the period between childhood and adulthood. We have seen the advent of adolescence and a delay in age of marriage. This period has now grown beyond what we have come to think of adolescence. A recent article argues that a new life stage has emerged, early adulthood (Furstenberg et al., 2004). Due in part to an increasingly demanding labor market, many young adults are busy building up their educational credentials and practical experience well into their 20s and even their early 30s. An increasing number of positions require a master's degree and internships and other forms of work experience that do not provide a full salary and benefits—essential ingredients for assuming adult status and responsibilities in society. In the 1950s, for example, most women were married and had a child before they were 23. Their husbands were full-time wage earners in the labor force.

> Our findings . . . confirm that it takes much longer to make the transition to adulthood today than decades ago, and arguably longer than it has at any time in America's history . . . In 2000, just 46 percent of women and 31 percent of men aged 30 had completed all five transitions [leaving home, finishing school, becoming financially independent, getting married, and having a child], compared with 77 percent of women and 65 percent of men at the same age in 1960. (Furstenberg et al., 2004, p. 35)

These authors argue that the primary reason for the prolonged early adulthood is that it takes much longer now to get a job that pays enough to support a family. College is now essential for most middle-class occupations, and for many students more than four years are required for graduation. Thus, schooling is not finished for many until well into their 20s, and often work experience cannot be accumulated until schooling is advanced. Of course, it takes resources to support these young adults in their quest for the requirements of good jobs. Dependency on one's family for financial, if not emotional, support assumes that families have the extra resources to spare, and many do not. "Youth from less well-off families must shuttle back and forth between work and school or combine both while they gradually gain their credentials. In the meantime, they feel unprepared for marriage or parenting" (Furstenberg et al., 2004, p. 38). Thus advantage is perpetuated over generations.

Attention to life's transitions is essential, and there is good evidence that these transitions are problematic for many youth and young adults. Education and other institutions (such as the military) that help youth bridge these stages need the attention of researchers, policy makers, and legislators, as the old timetables no longer apply.

Applying Sociology to Education: *What kinds of changes do you predict in schools as we move through the twenty-first century?*

Summary

Social and educational movements reflect the diversity of opinion present in a society. They reflect the range of perceived options. Systems experience pressure to change from movements in society; change may involve minor modifications in existing programs or major structural and curricular changes. Movements are only as effective in changing societal institutions as the attention they attract and the feasibility of the programs they propose and stimulate. Some movements seek separation from the existing structure. In this chapter we have reviewed theory of movements; the educational periods that have influenced today's education; movements in the United States, with specific examples; and trends in movements.

I. THE NATURE OF EDUCATIONAL MOVEMENTS

Educational movements come and go like the swing of a pendulum, reflecting the mood of the times. They influence educational systems acting as pressure groups in the environment. Some movements stimulate development of schools outside the traditional or public school system; others press for reform within the system.

II. EDUCATIONAL MOVEMENTS THROUGHOUT HISTORY

Three influences from early European education on educational movements and systems today include:

1. Influential methods of teaching such as "reasoning power, rhetoric, and the art of persuasion" and rational inquiry
2. Human depravity of children, which encouraged authoritarian methods
3. The Renaissance concept of well-rounded, liberally educated persons.

Several movements have dominated educational history in the United States: the public school movement, progressive education, essentialism, humanistic education, and the accountability movement.

III. ALTERNATIVE EDUCATION AND RELATED MOVEMENTS

The alternative education movement came at a time when all institutions in our country were being challenged. It focused on what adherents felt was the oppressive nature of schools. Influential in movement philosophy were Summerhill and the English primary schools. From the movement came free schools outside the existing system, and alternative schools and open classrooms within.

IV. STRUCTURAL AND CURRICULAR CHANGES IN THE SCHOOLS

The back-to-basics movement is a backlash against the "permissiveness of alternative education." It stresses basic skills and places less emphasis on "nonessentials." It gave rise to private schools, competency-based education, and other submovements, such as accountability.

Accountability has meant many things, but it usually includes the frequent testing of student learning against specific and explicit standards of achievement set by states. Schools not achieving set standards of pupil achievement are required to develop plans for achieving them.

Effective schools are concerned with how to help students achieve, and studies point out variables that schools should consider to raise levels of achievement. The idea here is that achievement is not just a classroom-level variable, but also a characteristic of schools, and that school-level attributes contribute independently to student achievement.

Some movements have a lasting effect; others, thought to be cure-alls, fizzle. Some early forms of educational technology, for example, did not live up to expectations, but technologies are having a major impact on schools and the educational process. Vocational education and some structural changes—magnet schools and voucher systems—have had mixed success. Open education has left a permanent, if limited, mark.

Societal movements are reflected in higher-education systems through curriculum and structural changes. Some institutions have produced alternative educational models.

Change related to educational movements has been reflected in proposed innovations, radical reforms, and other alternatives. Many concerns of individual groups are reflected in these changes. Predictions are that concerns for equal education will continue and that practical education will be a focus because of economic conditions.

Putting Sociology to Work

1. Find out what alternatives in primary and secondary education exist in your community.
2. Have any of the reforms mentioned in this chapter been tried in schools in your community? Are they still in use? What has been their success or failure record?
3. Design a hypothetical school at any level of the system of the type you would like to attend. Include features of systems discussed in this chapter and others you would like to add.
4. Conduct an informal survey of parents in your neighborhood about their attitudes toward education for their children and toward alternative versus basic education.
5. Spend some time observing in two local schools or classrooms that represent different philosophies.

REFERENCES

AARON, P. G. "The Impending Demise of the Discrepancy Formula," *Review of Educational Research*, Vol. 67, No. 4, 1997, pp. 461–502.

AARONS, DAKARAI I. "Busing Fight Highlights Struggles with Diversity," *Education Week*, April 7, 2010a, p. 16.

AARONS, DAKARAI I. "Efforts to End Bullying, A Challenge to Leaders, Gain Momentum," *Education Week*, May 12, 2010b.

"A British Administrator Looks at British Schools" (interview with John Coe by Vincent Rogers), *Phi Delta Kappan*, September 1979, p. 61.

ACHILLES, C. M., PATRICK HARMAN, and PAULA EGELSON "Using Research Results on Class Size to Improve Pupil Achievement Outcomes," *Research in the Schools*, Vol. 2, No. 2, Fall 1995, pp. 25–30.

ACOSTA-BELEN, EDNA "From Structural Subordination to Empowerment: Women and Development in Third World Contexts," *Gender and Society*, Vol. 4, No. 3, September 1990, pp. 199–320.

ADAMS, MIKE S., and T. DAVID EVANS "Teacher Disapproval, Delinquent Peers, and Self Reported Delinquency: A Longitudinal Test of Labeling Theory," *Urban Review*, Vol. 28, No. 3, September 1996, pp. 199–211.

ADDINGTON, LYNN A., SALLY A. RUDDY, AMANDA K. MILLER, JILL F. DEVOE, and KATHRYN A. CHANDLER *Are America's Schools Safe? Students Speak Out* (Washington, DC: U.S. Department of Education, National Center for Education Statistics, November, 2002), pp. 79–81.

ADLER, PATRICIA A., and PETER ADLER *Backboards and Blackboards: College Athletes and Role Engulfment* (New York: Columbia University Press, 1991).

ADLER, PATRICIA A., STEVEN J. KLESS, and PETER ADLER "Socialization to Gender Roles: Popularity Among Elementary School Boys and Girls," *Sociology of Education*, Vol. 65, No. 3, July 1992, pp. 169–187.

AGIRDAG, ORHAN, JANNICK DEMANET, MIEKE VAN HOUTTE, and PIET VAN AVERMAET "Ethnic School Composition and Peer Victimization: A Focus on the Interethnic School Climate," *International Journal of Intercultural Relations*, September 8, 2010. Doi:10.1016/j.intrel.2010.09.009.

AGUIRRE, ADALBERTO, JR., and JONATHAN H. TURNER *American Ethnicity: The Dynamics and Consequences of Discrimination*, 3rd ed. (Boston, MA: McGraw-Hill, 2001).

AINSWORTH, JAMES W. "Why Does it Take a Village? The Mediation of Neighborhood Effects on Educational Achievement," *Social Forces*, Vol. 81, No. 1, 2002, pp. 117–152.

ALEXANDER, KARL L. "Public Schools and the Public Good," *Social Forces*, Vol. 76, No. 1, September 1997, pp. 1–30.

ALEXANDER, KARL L. "The Clouded Crystal Ball: Trends in Educational Stratification," *Sociology of Education*, Extra Issue, 2001, pp. 169–177.

ALEXANDER, KARL L., and AARON M. PALLAS "Private Schools and Public Policy: New Evidence on Cognitive Achievement in Public and Private Schools," *Sociology of Education*, Vol. 56, 1983, pp. 170–182.

ALEXANDER, KARL L., and AARON M. PALLAS "In Defense of 'Private Schools and Public Policy': Reply to Kilgore," *Sociology of Education*, Vol. 57, January 1984, pp. 56–58.

ALEXANDER, KARL L., and AARON M. PALLAS "School Sector and Cognitive Performance: When Is a Little a Little?" *Sociology of Education*, Vol. 58, April 1985, pp. 115–128.

ALEXANDER, KARL L., DORIS R. ENTWISLE, and CARRIE. S. HORSEY "From First Grade Forward: Early Foundations of High School Dropout," *Sociology of Education*, Vol. 70, No. 2, 1997, pp. 87–107.

ALEXANDER, KARL L., DORIS R. ENTWISLE, and LINDA STEFFEL OLSEN "Lasting Consequences of the Summer Learning Gap," *American Sociological Review*, Vol. 72, No. 2, April 2007, pp. 167–177.

ALEXANDER, KARL L., DORIS R. ENTWISLE, and NADER KABBANI "The Dropout Process in Life Course Perspective: Early Risk Factors at Home and School," *Teachers College Record*, Vol. 103, No. 5, 2001, pp. 760–822.

ALEXANDER, KARL L., DORIS R. ENTWISLE, and SUSAN L. DAUBER *On the Success of Failure: A Reassessment of the Effects of Retention in the Primary Grades*, 2nd ed. (New York: Cambridge University Press, 2003).

ALLEN, MICHAEL "Eight Questions on Teacher Preparation: What Does the Research Say?" Education Commission of the States, 2003. Available: www.ecs. org/tpreport (Retrieved September 21, 2010).

ALTBACH, PHILIP G., and JANE KNIGHT "The Internationalization of Higher Education: Motivations and Realities," in H. S. Wechsler (ed.), *The NEA 2006 Almanac of Higher Education* (Washington, DC: National Education Association, 2006), pp. 27–36.

ALTBACH, PHILIP G., and TODD M. DAVIS "Global Challenge and National Response: Notes for an International Dialogue on Higher Education," *CIES Newsletter* (New York: Institute of International Education, January 1999), No. 120, p. 1+.

America 2000: An Education Strategy (Washington, DC: U.S. Department of Education, 1991).

American Association of University of Women, *How Schools Shortchange Girls: The AAUW Report* (Washington, DC: Author, 1992).

American Association of University Women, *Hostile Hallways: The AAUW Survey of Sexual Harassment in America's Schools* (Washington, DC: Author, 1993), p. 5.

American Association of University of Women, "Gender Gaps: Where Schools Still Fail Our Children," 1998. Available: www.aauw.org/learn/research/upload/GGES.pdf (Retrieved April 2, 2011).

American Association of University of Women. *Hostile Hallways: Bullying, Teasing, and Sexual Harassment in School* (Washington DC: Author, 2001).

American Association of University of Women, *Under the Microscope: A Decade of Gender Equity Projects in the Sciences* (Washington DC: Author, 2004).

American Council on Education, *Gender Equity in Education, 2010* (Washington, DC: American Council on Education, 2010).

American Library Association, *"The Chocolate War" Tops 2004 Most Challenged Books List* (Chicago, IL: American Library Association, 2006).

American Library Association, "The 10 Most Challenged Books of 2006," Copyright 2007. Available: www.ala.org/ala/oif/bannedbooksweek/challengedbanned/htm

American Library Association, "Top Ten most Frequently Challenged Books of 2009," October 2010. Available: http://www.ala.org/ala/issuesadvocacy/banned/frequentlychallenged/21stcenturychallenged/2009/index.cfm (Retrieved March 16, 2011).

American School Counselor Association, "Professional School Counselor," Copyright 2007. Available: www.schoolcounselor.org/content.asp?contentid=133 (Retrieved April 22, 2007).

Americans with Disabilities Act, 1990. Available: www.dol.gov/esa/regs/statutes/ofccp/ada/htm (Retrieved April 2, 2011).

"An Architectural Revolution Is Going on Inside Schools," *The American School Board Journal*, August 1990, p. 9.

ANDERSON, E. *Streetwise: Race, Class, and Change in an Urban Community* (Chicago, IL: University of Chicago Press, 1990).

ANDERSON, E. *Code of the Streets: Decency, Violence, and the Moral Life of the Inner City* (New York: W.W. Norton, 1999).

ANDERSON-LEVITT, K. "A World Culture of Schooling?" in K. Anderson-Levitt (ed.), *Local Meanings, Global Schooling: Anthropology and World Culture Theory* (New York: Palgrave Macmillan, 2003).

ANDREWS, RICHARD L., and MARGARET R. BASOM "Instructional Leadership: Are Women Principals Better?" *Principal*, Vol. 70, No. 2, November 1990, p. 38.

"A New Divide between Black and White," *Newsweek*, June 21, 1999. New York City Board of Education, *2000 Annual Report.*

ANYON, JEAN "Social Class and the Hidden Curriculum of Work," *Journal of Education*, Vol. 162, 1980, pp. 67–92.

ANYON, JEAN "Social Class and School Knowledge," *Curriculum Inquiry*, Vol. 11, 1981, pp. 3–42.

ANYON, JEAN *Radical Possibilities: Public Policy, Urban Education, and a New Social Movement* (New York: Routledge, 2005).

APPLE, MICHAEL W. "The New Sociology of Education: Origins, Current Status and New Directions," *Review of Educational Research*, Vol. 48, No. 1, 1978, pp. 495–503.

APPLE, MICHAEL W. "Analyzing Determinations: Understanding and Evaluating the Production of Social Outcomes in Schools," *Curriculum Inquiry*, Vol. 10, 1980, pp. 55–76.

APPLE, MICHAEL W. *Teachers and Texts* (New York: Routledge, 1988).

APPLE, MICHAEL W. *Official Knowledge* (New York: Routledge, 1993a), p. 215.

APPLE, MICHAEL W. "The Politics of Official Knowledge: Does a National Curriculum Make Sense?" *Teachers College Record*, Vol. 95, No. 2, Winter 1993b, pp. 222–241.

APPLE, MICHAEL W. "Power, Meaning and Identify: Critical Sociology of Education in the United States," *British Journal of Sociology of Education*, Vol. 17, No. 2, June 1996, pp. 125–144.

APPLE, MICHAEL W. *Educating the "Right" Way: Markets, Standards, God, and Inequality* (New York: Routledge, 2006).

APPLE, MICHAEL W. "Ideological Success, Educational Failure? On the Politics of No Child Left Behind," *Journal of Teacher Education*, Vol. 58, No. 2, March/April 2007, pp. 108–116.

APPLE, MICHAEL W., and LOIS WEIS "Seeing Education Relationally: The Stratification of Culture and People in the Sociology of School Knowledge," *Journal of Education*, Vol. 168, No. 1, 1986.

ARCHER, MARGARET *The Social Origins of Educational Systems* (London: Sage, 1979).

ARCHER, MARGARET "Cross-National Research and the Analysis of Educational Systems," paper presented at American Sociological Association meetings, Chicago, August 1987.

ARNOLD, ANITA C. "Designing Classrooms with Students in Mind," *English Journal*, Vol. 82, No. 2, February 1993, pp. 81–83.

ARNOVE, ROBERT F. "Comparative Education and World-Systems Analysis," *Comparative Education Review*, Vol. 24, 1980, p. 49.

ARONSON, RONALD "Is Busing the Real Issue?" *Dissent*, Vol. 25, 1978, p. 409.

ARUM, RICHARD A. "Do Private Schools Force Public Schools to Compete?" *American Sociological Review*, Vol. 61, February 1996, pp. 29–46.

ARUM, RICHARD A. *Judging School Discipline: The Crisis of Moral Authority* (Cambridge, MA: Harvard University Press, 2003).

ARUM, RICHARD A., and JOSIPA ROKSA *Academically Adrift: Limited Learning on College Campuses* (Chicago, IL: University of Chicago Press, 2011).

Asian Nation, "14 Important Statistics About Asian Americans," Copyright 2008. Available: http://www.asian-nation.org/14-statistics.shtml (Retrieved September 8, 2010).

ASKOV, EUNICE N., JEROME JOHNSTON, LESLIE I. PETTY, and SHANNON J. YOUNG *Expanding Access to Adult Literacy with Online Distance Education* (Cambridge, MA: National Center for the Study of Adult Learning and Literacy, Harvard Graduate School of Education, 2003).

ASTIN, ALEXANDER W. *What Matters in College?: Four Critical Years Revisited* (San Francisco, CA: Jossey-Bass, 1993).

ATHAVELEY, ANJALI "College Reject Record Numbers," *The Wall Street Journal*, April 3, 2007, p. B9.

ATTEWELL, PAUL "The Winner-Take-All High School: Organizational Adaptations to Educational Stratification," *Sociology of Education*, Vol. 74, No. 4, 2001, pp. 267–295.

ATTEWELL, PAUL, and DAVID E. LAVIN *Passing the Torch: Does Higher Education for the Disadvantaged Pay Off Across the Generations?* (New York: Russell Sage, 2007).

ATTEWELL, PAUL, and DAVID E. LAVIN *Teachers College Record*, Copyright December 05, 2008. Available: http://www.tcrecord.org ID Number 15457 (Retrieved October 6, 2010).

BABAD, ELISHA, FRANK BERNIERI, and ROBERT ROSENTHAL "Students as Judges of Teachers' Verbal and Nonverbal Behavior," *American Educational Research Journal*, Vol. 28, No. 1, Spring 1991, pp. 211–234.

Baha'i International Community, "In Ghana, Innovative Literacy Program Brings Dramatic Results," Copyright 2010. Available: http://news.bahai.org/story/591 (Retrieved October 2, 2010).

BAKER, DAVID P. "International Competition and Education Crises: Cross-National Studies of School Outcomes," in David L. Levinson, Peter W. Cookson, Jr., and Alan R. Sadovnik (eds.), *Education and Sociology* (New York: Routledge/Falmer Press, 2002), pp. 393–397.

BAKER, DAVID P., and DAVID L. STEVENSON "Mothers' Strategies for Children's School Achievement: Managing the Transition to High School," *Sociology of Education*, Vol. 59, July 1986, pp. 156–166.

BAKER, DAVID P., and DAVID L. STEVENSON "Parents' Management of Adolescents' Schooling: An International Comparison," Chapter 20 in Klaus Hurrelmann and Uwe Engel (eds.), *The Social World of Adolescents* (New York: Walter de Gruyter, 1989), p. 348.

BAKER, DAVID P., and DAVID L. STEVENSON "Institutional Context of an Adolescent Transition: Going from High School to College in the United States and Japan," *Journal of Adolescent Research*, Vol. 5, No. 2, April 1990, pp. 242–253.

BAKER, DAVID P., and DEBORAH PERKINS JONES "Creating Gender Equity: Cross-National Gender Stratification and Mathematical Performance," *Sociology of Education*, Vol. 66, No. 2, April 1993, pp. 91–103.

BAKER, MIKE "Gove Takes Control of the Curriculum," Copyright June 15, 2010. Available: http://www.guardian.co.uk/education/2010/jun/15/schools-curriculum-michael-gove (Retrieved September 29, 2010).

BAKER, RUSS "Stealth TV," *The American Prospect*, Copyright 2001. Available: http://www.prospect.org/print/V12/3/baker-r.html (Retrieved April 12, 2007).

BALLANTINE, JEANNE H. "The Role of Teaching Around the World," *Teaching Sociology*, Vol. 17, No. 3, July 1989, pp. 291–296.

BALLATINE, JEANNE H., and K. FELTEY "Factors Related to Minority Student Success or Failure," paper presented at the North Central Sociological Association Meetings, Chicago, IL, 2007.

BAMBURG, JERRY *Raising Expectations to Improve Student Learning* (Oak Brook, Illinois: North Central Regional Educational Laboratory Monograph, 1994).

BANKS, JAMES A. "Multicultural Education in the New Century," *School Administrator*, Vol. 56, No. 6, May 1999, pp. 8–10.

BARBU, S., G. CABANES, and G. LEMANER-IDRISSI "Boys and Girls on the Playground: Sex Differences in

Social Development Are Not Stable Across Early Childhood," No. 1, January 28, 2011, p. R16407. Available: www.ncbi.nlm.nih.gov/pubmed/21297987 (Retrieved May 7, 2011).

BARNETT, W. STEVEN, JASON T. HUSTEDT, K. B. ROBIN, and K. L. SCHULMAN *The State of Preschool: 2005 State Preschool Yearbook* (New Brunswick, NJ: The National Institute for Early Education Research, 2005). Available: http://nieer.org/yearbook/ (Retrieved June 21, 2006).

BARR, REBECCA, and ROBERT DREEBEN *How Schools Work* (Chicago, IL: University of Chicago Press, 1983).

BATY, PHIL, and HELEN CZERSKI "Deplorable Pay Inequity Persists," *The Times Higher*, September 30, 2005.

BAUDRILLARD, JEAN *For a Critique of the Political Economy of the Sign* (trans. Charles Levin) (St. Louis, MO: Telos Press, 1984).

BAUER, L., P. GUERINO, K. L. NOLLE, and S. TANG "Student Victimization in U.S. Schools," Copyright October, 2009. NCES 2009–306. Institute of Education Science, U.S. Department of Education, Washington, DC. Available: http://nces.ed.gov/pubs2009/2009306.pdf (Retrieved August 26, 2010).

BAUMAN, KARL E., and SUSAN T. ENNETT "Peer Influence on Adolescent Drug Use," *American Psychologist*, Vol. 49, No. 9, September 1994, pp. 820–822.

BBC News, "Male Professors Outnumber Women," Copyright May 14, 2007. Available: http://news.bbc.co.uk/2/hi/uk_news/education/6653705.stm (Retrieved July 10, 2007).

BEAN, FRANK D., SUSAN K. BROWN, and RUBEN G. RUMBAUT "Mexican Immigrant Political and Economic Incorporation," *Perspectives on Politics*, Vol. 4, 2006, pp. 309–313.

BECKER, GARY S. *Human Capital: A Theoretical and Empirical Analysis with Special Reference to Education*, 3rd ed. (Chicago, IL: University of Chicago Press, 1993).

BECKER, HOWARD S. "The Career of the Chicago Public Schoolteacher," *American Journal of Sociology*, Vol. 57, 1952, pp. 470–477.

BEGLEY, SHARON "Your Child's Brain," *Newsweek*, February 19, 1996, p. 55.

BELL, DANIEL *Coming of Post-Industrial Society: A Venture in Social Forecasting* (New York: Basic Books, 1973).

BELL, TERREL "A Nation at Risk," National Commission on Excellence in Education, April 1983 report, p. 5.

BELLISARI, ANNA "Cultural Influences on the Science Career Choices of Women," *Ohio Journal of Science*, Vol. 91, No. 3, 1991, pp. 129–133.

BENAVOT, AARON "Education and Economic Growth in the Modern World System, 1913–1985," paper presented at American Sociological Association meetings, Chicago, 1987.

BENAVOT, AARON "Curricular Content, Educational Expansion, and Economic Growth," *Comparative Education Review*, Vol. 36, No. 2, May 1992.

BENAVOT, AARON "Educational and Political Democratization: Cross-National and Longitudinal Findings," *Comparative Education Review*, Vol. 40, No. 4, November 1996, pp. 377–403.

BENAVOT, AARON "Institutional Approach to the Study of the Education," in Lawrence J. Saha (ed.), *International Encyclopedia of the Sociology of Education* (Oxford, England: Elsevier Science Ltd., 1997), pp. 340–345.

BENAVOT, AARON, and CECILIA BRASLAVSKY *School Knowledge in Comparative and Historical Perspective: Changing Curricula in Primary and Secondary Education* (Hong Kong: Comparative Education Research Center/Springer, 2006).

BENAVOT, AARON, DAVID KAMENS, SUK-YING WONG, YUN-KYUNG CHA, and JOHN MEYER "World Culture and the Curricular Content of National Educational Systems, 1920–1985," paper presented at American Sociological Association meetings, Atlanta, August 1988.

BENAVOT, AARON, ET AL. "Knowledge for the Masses: World Models and National Curricula: 1920–1986," *American Sociological Review*, Vol. 56, No. 1, February 1991, pp. 85–100.

BENHAM, BARBARA J., PHIL GIESEN, and JEANNIE OAKES "A Study of Schooling: Students' Experiences in Schools," *Phi Delta Kappan*, Vol. 61, January 1980, p. 339.

"Berkeley Student Revolt," in S. M. Lipset and S. S. Wolin (eds.), Review. *Newsweek*, Vol. 66, September 6, 1965, p. 51.

BERLINER, DAVID C. "Why Rising Test Scores May Not Equal Increased Student Learning," Dissent 2008. Available: http://dissentmagazine.org/online.php?id=156 (Retrieved October 15, 2010).

BERNDT, THOMAS J., JAQUELINE A. HAWKINS, and ZIYL JIAO "Influences of Friends and Friendships on Adjustment to Junior High School," *Merrill-Palmer Quarterly*, Vol. 45, No. 1, January 1999, pp. 13–41.

BERNHARDT, GREGORY, and JEANNE BALLANTINE "General Education and the Education of Educators," *Record in Educational Leadership*, Vol. 14, No. 2, Spring/Summer 1995.

BERNSTEIN, BASIL "Social Class and Linguistic Development: A Theory of Social Learning," in A. H. Halsey, J. Floud, and Arnold C. Anderson (eds.), *Education, Economy and Society* (New York: Free Press, 1961), pp. 288–314.

BERNSTEIN, BASIL "Sociology and the Sociology of Education: A Brief Account," in John Rex (ed.), *Approaches to Sociology* (London: Routledge, 1974), pp. 145–159.

BERNSTEIN, BASIL *Class, Codes and Control: Towards a Theory of Educational Transmissions*, Vol. 3 (London: Routledge, 1975).

BERNSTEIN, BASIL "Codes, Modalities and the Process of Cultural Reproduction: A Model," *Language and Society*, Vol. 10, No. 3, December 1981, pp. 327–363.

BERNSTEIN, BASIL *Class, Codes and Control: The Structuring of Pedagogic Discourse*, Vol. 4 (London: Routledge, 1990).

BERNSTEIN, BASIL *Pedagogy, Symbolic Control and Identity: Theory, Research, Critique* (London: Taylor and Francis, 1996).

BERNSTEIN, RICHARD J. *The New Constellation* (Cambridge, MA: MIT Press, 1993).

"Better Education Attainment Saves Lives," *Education Week Spotlight,* Copyright September 17, 2010. Available: http://blogs.edweek.org/edweek/inside-school-research/international-comparisons-of-a/ (Retrieved October 12, 2010).

BETTIS, P. J., and N. G. ADAMS "The Power of the Preps and a Cheerleading Equity Policy," *Sociology of Education*, Vol. 76, No. 2, 2003, pp. 128–142.

BIAGI, SHIRLEY *Media/Impact: An Introduction to Mass Media*, 3rd ed. (Belmont, CA: Wadsworth, 1998).

BIDDLE, BRUCE J., and DAVID C. BERLINER "Small Class Size and Its Effects," *Educational Leadership*, Vol. 59, No. 5, February 2002, pp. 12–23.

BIDWELL, CHARLES E. "The Sociology of the School and Classroom," paper presented at American Sociological Association meetings, Boston, August 1979.

BIEVER, CELESTE "Court Case may Determine How Evolution is Taught in U.S.," Copyright 2005. NewScientist.com. Available: http://www. newscientist. com/article.ns?id=dn8042 (Retrieved May 10, 2007).

BINDER, FREDERICK M. *The Age of the Common School, 1830–1865* (New York: Wiley, 1974), pp. 94–95.

BIVENS, JOSH, KATHRYN ANNE EDWARDS, ALEXANDER HERTEL-FERNANDEZ, and ANNA TURNER "The Class of 2010: Economic Prospects for Young Adults in the Recession," Economic Policy Institute: Briefing Paper #265 May 11, 2010. Available: www.epi.org/publications/entry/the_class_of_2010 (Retrieved October 10, 2010).

BLACK, SUSAN "Less Is More," *American School Board Journal*, Vol. 186, No. 2, February 1999, pp. 38–41.

BLAIR, SAMPSON LEE, and ZHENCHAO QIAN "Family and Asian Students' Educational Performance: A Consideration of Diversity," *Journal of Family Issues*, Vol. 19, No. 4, July 1998, pp. 355–374.

BLAKE, JUDITH "Sibship Size and Educational Stratification: Reply to Mare and Chen," *American Sociological Review*, Vol. 51, 1986, p. 416.

BLAKE, JUDITH "Number of Siblings and Personality," *Family Planning Perspectives*, Vol. 23, No. 6, November 1991, pp. 272–274.

BLANCHARD, JOHN F., JR. "Can We Live with Public Education," *Moody Monthly*, October 1971, p. 88.

BLANK, R. K., and D. A. ARCHIBALD "Magnet Schools and Issues of Educational Quality," *The Clearinghouse*, Vol. 82, No. 2, 1992, pp. 81–86.

BLAU, JUDITH R. *Race in the Schools: Perpetuating White Dominance?* (Boulder, CO: Lynne Rienner Press, 2003).

BLAU, PETER M., and OTIS DUDLEY DUNCAN *The American Occupational Structure* (New York: Wiley, 1967).

BLOKHUIS, JASON C. "Channel One: When Private Interests and the Public Interest Collide," *American Educational Research Journal.* Copyright June 1, 2008. Available: http://aer.sagepub.com/content/45/2/343.abstract (Retrieved August 24, 2010).

BLOOM, BENJAMIN S. *Human Characteristics and School Learning* (New York: McGraw-Hill, 1976).

BLOOM, BENJAMIN S. *All Our Children Learning* (New York: McGraw-Hill, 1981).

Bloomberg.com. "U.S. States Can Deny Scholarships for Ministry Study," February 25, 2004. Available: http://quote.bloomberg.com/apps/news (Retrieved May 10, 2007).

BLUM, DEBRA E. "Environment Still Hostile to Women in Academe, New Evidence Indicates," *The Chronicle of Higher Education*, October 9, 1991, p. A1.

BLUM, DEBRA E. "Athletes' Graduation Rates," *The Chronicle of Higher Education*, July 7, 1995, p. 34.

BLUMENSTYK, GOLDIE "Intellectual Property's Land Mines," *The Chronicle of Higher Education*, Vol. 53, No. 31, April 6, 2007, p. A17.

Board of Education of Oklahoma v. Dowell, 1991. Available: http://www.law.cornell.edu/supct/html/89-1080.ZD.html

BOLI, JOHN "Globalization," in David L. Levinson, Peter W. Cookson, Jr., and Alan R. Sadovnik (eds.), *Education and Sociology* (New York: Routledge/Falmer Press, 2002), pp. 307–313.

BONETARI, D. "The Effects of Teachers' Expectations on Mexican-American Students," paper presented at the annual meeting of the American Psychological Association, New Orleans, April 1994.

BOOCOCK, SARANE SPENCE, and KIMBERLY ANN SCOTT. *Kids in Context: The Sociological Study of Children and Childhoods* (Lanham, MD: Rowan and Littlefield, 2005).

BORMAN, KATHRYN M., and BRIDGET A. COTNER "No Child Left Behind—And Beyond: The Federal Government Gets Serious about Accountability," in Jeanne Ballantine and Joan Spade (eds.), *Schools and Society: A Sociological Approach to Education*, 4th ed. (Thousand Oaks, CA: Pine Forge Press).

BOSMAN, JULIE "Klein to Overhaul Alternative Schools Programs to Deter Potential Dropouts," *The New York Times*, May, 25, 2007, Section B, p. 5.

BOULDING, KENNETH E. "General Systems Theory: The Skeleton of Science," *Management Science*, Vol. 2, No. 3, April 1956, pp. 197–208.

BOURDIEU, PIERRE "Cultural Reproduction and Social Reproduction," in R. Brown (ed.), *Knowledge, Education, and Cultural Change* (London: Tavistock, 1973), pp. 71–112.

BOURDIEU, PIERRE "Cultural Reproduction and Social Reproduction," in J. Karabel and A. H. Halsey (eds.), *Power and Ideology in Education* (New York: Oxford University Press, 1977), pp. 487–511.

BOURDIEU, PIERRE, and JEAN CLAUDE PASSERON (eds.) *Reproduction in Education, Society and Culture* (London: Sage, 1977).

BOWEN, WILLIAM G., and DEREK BOK (eds.) *The Shape of the River: Long-term Consequences of Considering Race in College and University Admissions* (Princeton, NJ: Princeton University Press, 1998).

BOWEN, WILLIAM G., MATTHEW M. CHINGOS, and MICHAEL S. MCPHERSON *Crossing the Finish Line: Completing College at America's Public Universities* (Princeton, NJ: Princeton UP, 2009).

BOWLES, SAMUEL "Unequal Education and the Reproduction of the Social Division of Labor," in Jerome Karabel and A. H. Halsey (eds.), *Power and Ideology in Education* (New York: Oxford University Press, 1977), p. 137.

BOWLES, SAMUEL, and HERBERT GINTIS (eds.) *Schooling in Capitalist America: Education and the Contradictions of Economic Life* (New York: Basic Books, 1976).

BOWLES, SAMUEL, and HERBERT GINTIS "Schooling in Capitalist America Revisited," *Sociology of Education*, Vol. 75, No. 1, 2002, pp. 1–18.

BOYER, ERNEST L. *College: The Undergraduate Experience in America* (New York: Harper & Row, 1987).

BOYER, ERNEST L. *Scholarship Reconsidered: Priorities for the Professorate* (Princeton: Carnegie Foundation for the Advancement of Teaching, 1990).

BOYLE, ALAN "Judge Rules against 'intelligent design,'" 2005. Available: http://www.msnbc.msn.com/id/10545387/ns/technology_and_science-science/ (Retrieved April 2, 2011).

BRACEY, GERALD W. "Test Scores of Nations and States," *Phi Delta Kappan*, Vol. 80, No. 3, November 1998.

BRAMELD, THEODORE "Social Frontiers: Retrospective and Prospective," *Phi Delta Kappan*, October 1977, pp. 118–120.

BRAND, JENNIE E., and YU XIE "Who Benefits Most from College? Evidence for Negative Selection in Heterogeneous Economic returns to Higher education," *American Sociological Review*, Vol. 75, No. 2, 2010, pp. 273–302.

BRANTLINGER, ELLEN A. *Dividing Classes: How the Middle Class Negotiates and Rationalizes School Advantage* (New York: Routledge, 2003).

BRAY, MARK, BOB ADAMSON, and MARK MASON (eds.) *Comparative Education Research: Approaches and Methods.* "Introduction," p. 9. CERC Studies in Comparative Educaton 19. Comparative Education Research Centre, University of Hong Kong, Hong Kong, 2007.

BRAY, MARK, and R. MURRAY THOMAS "Levels of Comparison in Educational Studies: Different Insights from Different Literatures, and the Value of Multilevel Analyses," *Harvard Educational Review*, Vol. 65, No. 3, 1995, pp. 479–490.

BRIDGEMAN, BRENT, and CATHY WENDLER "Gender Differences in Predictors of College Mathematics Performance and in College Mathematics Course Grades," *Journal of Educational Psychology*, Vol. 83, No. 2, June 1991, p. 283.

"Bridges to the Future Initiative: Ghana 2000," Copyright 2004. Available: http://www.literacy.org/Projects/BFI/countries_ghana.html (Retrieved July 23, 2007).

BRIGHOUSE, HARRY "Channel One, the Anti-Commercial Principle, and the Discontinuous Ethos," *Educational Policy*, Vol. 19, No. 3, July 2005, pp. 528–549.

BRINKLEY, ELLEN HENSON *Caught Off Guard: Teachers Rethinking Censorship and Controversy* (Boston, MA: Allyn & Bacon, 1999).

BRINT, STEVEN (ed.) *The Future of the City of Intellect: The Changing American University* (Stanford, CA: Stanford University Press, 2002).

BRINT, STEVEN *Schools and Societies*, 2nd ed. (Stanford, CA: Stanford University Press, 2006).

BRINT, STEVEN, and JEROME KARABEL *The Diverted Dream: Community Colleges and the Promise of Educational Opportunity in America, 1900–1985* (New York: Oxford University Press, 1989).

BRINT, STEVEN, MARK RIDDLE, LORI TURK-BICAKCI, and C. B. LEVY "From the Liberal to the Practical Arts in American Colleges and Universities: Organizational Analysis and Curricular Change," *Journal of Higher Education*, Vol. 76, No. 2, 2005, pp. 151–180.

British Council, "UK Education Systems," Copyright 2000. Available: www.britishcouncil.org/

usa-educaton-uk-system-K-12-education.htm (Retrieved September 29, 2010).

BROADFOOT, PATRICIA "Comparative Education for the 21st Century: Retrospect and Prospect," *Comparative Education Review*, Vol. 36, No. 3, 2000, pp. 357–371.

BROOKOVER, WILBUR B., and EDSEL L. ERICKSON *Sociology of Education* (Homewood, IL: Dorsey Press, 1975).

BROOKOVER, WILBUR B., FRITZ J. ERICKSON, and ALAN W. MCEVOY. *Creating Effective Schools: An In-Service Program for Enhancing School Learning Climate and Achievement* (Holmes Beach, FL: Learning Publications, 1996).

BROOKOVER, WILBUR B., RICHARD GIGLIOTTI, RONALD D. HENDERSON, and JEFFREY M. SCHNEIDER. *Elementary School Social Environments and Achievement* (East Lansing, MI: College of Urban Development, Michigan State University, 1973).

BROPHY, JERE. "Interactions of Male and Female Students with Male and Female Teachers," in L. Wilkinson and C. Marrett (eds.), *Gender Influences, Classroom Interactions* (Madison, WI: University of Wisconsin, 1985).

BROWN, B. BRADFORD, ET AL. "Parenting Practices and Peer Group Affiliation in Adolescence," *Child Development*, Vol. 64, No. 2, April 1993, pp. 467–482.

BROWN, IVY "Advertising to Kids Limited," *Television Week*, Vol. 23, No. 8, 2004, p. 1.

BROWN, PAMELA F. "Preparing Principals for Today's Demands," *Phi Delta Kappan*, Vol. 87, No. 7, March 2006, pp. 525–526.

BROWN, SUSAN K., and CHARLES HIRSCHMAN "The End of Affirmative Action in Washington State and Its Impact on the Transition from High School to College," *Sociology of Education*, Vol. 79, No. 2, April 2006, pp. 106–130.

BROWN, TONY "Challenging Globalization as Disclosure and Phenomenon," *International Journal of Lifelong Education*, Vol. 18, No. 1, January–February 1999, pp. 3–17.

BRYK, ANTHONY S. "Organizing Schools for Improvement," *Phi Delta Kappan*, Vol. 91, No.7, April 2010, pp. 23–30.

BUEHLER, CHRISTOPH, and DIRK KONIETZKA "The Transition from School to Work in Russia During and After Socialism: Change or Continuity?" papers presented at the International Sociological Association World Congress of Sociology, Sweden, July 2010.

BURCH, PATRICIA "Educational Policy and Practice from the Perspective of Institutional Theory: Crafting a Wider Lens," *Educational Researcher*, Vol. 36, No. 2, March 2007, pp. 84–96.

BURD, STEPHEN "Who Has the 'Ability to Benefit'?" *The Chronicle of Higher Education*, January 12, 1996, p. A25.

Bureau of Labor Statistics, "College Enrollment and Work Activity of 2006 High School Graduates," Copyright 2007. United States Department of Labor. USDL 07-0604. Available: http://www.bls.gov/news.release/archives/hsgec_o4262007.pdf (Retrieved April 3, 2011).

Bureau of Labor Statistics, "Teacher Earnings," Copyright May, 2008. Available: http://www.bls.gov/oco/ocos318.htm#emply (Retrieved September 14, 2010).

Bureau of Labor Statistics, "Employment Situation Summary," Copyright 2010. Available: http://www.bls.gov/news.release/empsit.nr0.htm (Retrieved August 8, 2010).

Bureau of Labor Statistics, "Occupational Outlook Handbook," Copyright 2010–2011. Available: http://www.bls.gov/oco/ocos318.htm (Retrieved August 8, 2010).

Bureau of Labor Statistics, "Overview of the 2008–2018 Projections," *Occupational Outlook Handbook*. Copyright 2010–2011. Available: www.bls.gov/oco/oco2003.htm (Retrieved October 12, 2010).

BURNETT, GARY. *Alternatives to Ability Grouping: Still Unanswered Questions* (New York: ERIC Clearinghouse on Urban Education, December 1995), ED390947, Digest Number 111.

BURNETT, GARY, and GARRY WALZ *Gangs in the Schools* (Washington, DC: Office of Educational Research and Improvement, July 1994).

BUSHAW, WILLIAM J., and JOHN A. MCNEE "Phi Delta Kappan/Gallup Poll of the Public's Attitudes toward the Public Schools," September, 2009, p. 10. Available: http://www.pdkintl.org/kappan/docs/k0909pol.pdf (Retrieved August 8, 2010).

BUSHAW, WILLIAM J., and SHANE J. LOPEZ "A Time for Change: The 42nd Annual Phi Delta Kappan/Gallup Poll of the Public's Attitudes toward the Public Schools," *Phi Delta Kappan*, Vol. 92, No. 1, August 2010, pp. 9–26.

BUSIA, KOFI ABREFA *Purposeful Education for Africa* (London: Moutin, 1964).

CAGE, MARY CRYSTAL "Learning to Teach," *The Chronicle of Higher Education*, February 9, 1996, p. A19.

California Department of Education, "California Partnership Academies," Copyright 2009. Available: http://www.cde.ca.gov/ci/gs/hs/cpagen/asp (Retrieved August 31, 2010).

CALLAHAN, RAYMOND E. *Education and the Cult of Efficiency* (Chicago, IL: The University of Chicago Press, 1962).

CANADA, KATHERINE, and RICHARD PRINGLE "The Role of Gender in College Classroom Interactions: A Social

Context Approach," *Sociology of Education*, Vol. 68, No. 3, July 1995, pp. 161–186.

CAO, XIAONAN "Debating the 'Brain Drain' in the Context of Globalization," *Compare*, Vol. 26, No. 3, October 1996, pp. 269–285.

CAPLAN, NATHAN, MARCELLA H. CHOY, and JOHN K. WHITMORE "Indochinese Refugee Families and Academic Achievement," *Scientific American*, Vol. 266, No. 2, 1993, pp. 36–42.

CARELLI, RICHARD "Divided Supreme Court Hears Arguments on School Prayer," *Texas News*, March 30, 2000.

CARLSON, JERRY S., BARBARA B. BURN, JOHN USEEM, and DAVID YACHIMOWICZ *Study Abroad: The Experience of American Undergraduates* (New York: Greenwood Press, 1990).

CARNOY, MARTIN *Education as Cultural Imperialism* (London: Longman, 1974).

CARNOY, MARTIN "Education for Alternative Development," *Comparative Education Review*, Vol. 26, 1982, pp. 160–177.

CARNOY, MARTIN, and DIANA RHOTEN "What Does Globalization Mean for Education Change? A Comparative Approach," *Comparative Education Review*, Vol. 46, No. 1, 2002, pp. 1–9.

CARNOY, MARTIN, and HENRY M. LEVIN "Educational Reform and Class Conflict," *Journal of Education*, Vol. 168, No. 1, 1986, pp. 35–46.

CARRIER, JAMES G. "Masking the Social in Educational Knowledge: The Case of Learning Disability Theory," *American Journal of Sociology*, Vol. 88, No. 5, 1983, pp. 948–974.

CARTER, PRUDENCE L. *Keepin' It Real: School Success Beyond Black and White* (New York: Oxford University Press, 2005).

CAVANAGH, SEAN "Foreign-Aid Groups Use 'Nonformal' Strategies to Education Youngsters," *Education Week*, Vol. 22, No. 15, December 12, 2002, p. 10.

CAVANAGH, SHANNON E., and ALETHA C. HUSTON "Family Instability and Children's Early Problem Behavior," *Social Forces*, Vol. 85, No. 1, 2006, pp. 551–581.

CECI, STEPHEN J., and WENDY M. WILLIAMS (eds.) *Why Aren't More Women in Science? Top Researchers Debate the Evidence* (Washington, DC: American Psychological Association, 2006).

Center for Science and Technology Policy Research, *Prometheus: A Public Understanding of Science Paradox* (Boulder, CO: University of Colorado, 2004).

Central Advisory Council for Education, *Children and Their Primary Schools* (London: H.M. Stationery Office, 1967).

Center for Global Development, "Ghana-literacy," 2010. Available: www.cgdev.org/section/initiatives/_active/mcamonitor/mcacountries/_ghana (Retrieved March 28, 2011).

CHADDOCK, GAIL RUSSELL, ET AL. "A Challenge for Public Schools: Educating Minds and Hearts," *The Christian Science Monitor*, May 4, 1999.

CHAIKA, GLORI "Testing Teachers Makes Teachers Testy!" *Education World*. Copyright 2005. Available: http://www.educationworld.com/a_issues/issues/issues128.shtml (Retrieved April 23, 2007).

"Challenging Assumptions about Lead and IQ," *Environmental Health Perspectives*, Vol. 113, No. 5, May 2005, pp. A324–A325.

CHARLES, C. M. *Building Classroom Discipline* (New York: Longman, 1999).

CHASE-DUNN, CHRISTOPHER "Socialist States in the Capitalist World-Economy," *Social Problems*, Vol. 27, June 1980, p. 506.

CHAVERS, DEAN "Indian Education: Dealing with a Disaster," *Principal*, Vol. 70, No. 3, January 1991, pp. 28–29.

CHEN, BRIAN X. "How the iPhone Could Reboot Education," Copyright December 8, 2009. Available: http://www.wired.com/gadgetlab/2009/12/iphone-university-abilene/ (Retrieved August 24, 2010).

CHEN, XIANGLEI *Students' Peer Groups in High School: The Pattern and Relationship to Educational Outcomes* (Washington, DC: NCES, 1997), ERIC (ED410518).

CHENG, SIMON, and BRIAN STARKS "Racial Differences in the Effects of Significant Others on Students' Educational Expectations," *Sociology of Education*, Vol. 75, No. 4, 2002, pp. 306–327.

CHERNIAVSKY, JOHN C., and ELIZABETH VANDERPUTTEN "The Controversy of Technology in Education," Copyright 2003. Available: http://cenasy.com/AERA%20Paper%204.21.03.htm (Retrieved August 24, 2010).

CHERRYHOLMES, CLEO *Power and Criticism: Poststructural Investigations in Education* (New York: Teachers College Press, 1988).

Child Health USA, "Population Characteristics," Copyright 2003. Available: http://mchb.hrsa.gov/chusa03/pages/population.htm (Retrieved April 13, 2007).

Child Trends Data Bank, "Children in Head Start," Copyright 2005. Available: http://www.childtrendsdatabank.org/?q-node/352 (Retrieved August 24, 2010).

Child Trends Data Bank, "Early Childhood Program Enrollment 2007," Copyright 2007. Available: http://www.childtrendsdatabank.org/indicators/8EarlyChildhoodProgram (Retrieved March 11, 2008).

Children's Defense Fund, *A Children's Defense Fund Budget* (Washington, DC: Children's Defense Fund, 1996).

Children's Defense Fund, "Protect Children, Not Guns," Copyright September 16, 2010. Available: http://www.childrensdefense.org/child-research-data-publications/data/protect-children-not-guns-report-2009.html (Retrieved August 26, 2010).

Children's Law Center of Massachusetts, "School Suspension and Expulsion," 2002. Available: http://www.clcm.org/student_suspension.htm (Retrieved April 30, 2007).

ChildStats.government, "America's Children: Key National Indicators of Well-Being 2009," 2009. Available: http://www.childstats.gov/americaschildren/famsoc3.asp (Retrieved August 24, 2010).

CHUBB, JOHN E., and TERRY M. MOE *Politics, Markets and America's Schools* (Washington, DC: The Brookings Institution, 1990).

CLARK, BURTON R. "The Cooling-Out Function in Higher Education," *The American Journal of Sociology*, Vol. 65, 1960, pp. 569–576.

CLARK, BURTON R. "Structure of Academic Governance in the United States," Working paper, Institute for Social and Policy Studies, Yale University Press, New Haven, CT, 1976.

CLARK, BURTON, and MARTIN TROW "The Organization Context," in Theodore Newcomb and Everett Wilson (eds.), *College Peer Groups: Problems and Prospects for Research* (Chicago, IL: Aldine, 1966), pp. 17–70.

CLARK, ROGER "Multinational Corporate Investment, and Women's Participation in Higher Education in Noncore Nations," *Sociology of Education*, Vol. 65, No. 1, January 1992, pp. 37–47.

CLAYTON, THOMAS "Beyond Mystification: Reconnecting World-System Theory for Comparative Education," *Comparative Education Review*, Vol. 42, No. 4, November 1998, pp. 479–496.

CLEMONS, ANDREA, and CHRISTINA VOGT "Theorizing, Restructuring and Rethinking Nonformal Education in East and West African Communities," *Current Issues in Comparative Education*, Vol. 6, No. 2 (New York: Teachers College, Columbia University, 2004), pp. 88–99.

COATES, TA-NEHISI "The Littlest Schoolhouse," *The Atlantic*, July/August, 2010. Available: http://www.theatlantic.com/magazine/archive/2010/07/the-littlest-schoolhouse/8132 (Retrieved August 2, 2010).

COBURN, CYNTHIA E. "Beyond Decoupling: Rethinking the Relationship Between the Institutional Environment and the Classroom," *Sociology of Education*, Vol. 77, No. 3, 2004, pp. 211–244.

COE, CATI *Dilemmas of Culture in African Schools: Nationalism, Youth, and the Transformation of Knowledge* (Chicago, IL: University of Chicago Press, 2005).

COHEN, ARTHUR M. *The Transfer Rate: A Model of Consistency* (Los Angeles, CA: Center for the Study of Community Colleges, July 1997).

COHEN, ROBERT, and REGINALD E. ZELNICK (eds.) *The Free Speech Movement: Reflections on Berkeley in the 1960's* (Berkeley, CA: University of California Press, 2002).

COHEN, ELIZABETH G. *Designing Group Work: Strategies for Heterogeneous Classrooms* (New York: Teachers College Press, 1986).

COHEN, ELIZABETH G. *Designing Group Work: Strategies for Heterogeneous Classrooms* (New York: Teachers College Press, 1994).

COHEN, ELIZABETH G., and RACHEL A. LOTAN *Working for Equity in Heterogeneous Classrooms: Sociological Theory in Practice* (New York: Teachers College Press, 1997).

COHEN, JERE "Parents as Educational Models and Definers," *Journal of Marriage and the Family*, Vol. 49, May 1987, pp. 339–351.

COHEN, MURIEL "Gender Bias: A Textbook Case," *The Boston Globe*, March 1, 1992, p. A1.

COLCLOUGH, GLENNA, and E. M. BECK "The American Educational Structure and the Reproduction of Social Class," *Sociological Inquiry*, Vol. 56, No. 4, Fall 1986, pp. 456–473.

COLEMAN, JAMES S. *The Adolescent Society: The Social Life of the Teenager and its Impact on Education* (New York: Free Press of Glencoe, 1961).

COLEMAN, JAMES S. *Equality and Achievement in Education* (Boulder, CO: Westview Press, 1990).

COLEMAN, JAMES S., ET AL. *Equality of Educational Opportunity* (Washington, DC: U.S. Department of Education, 1966).

COLEMAN, JAMES S., ET AL. *Youth: Transition to Adulthood* (Chicago, IL: University of Chicago Press, 1974).

COLEMAN, JAMES S., THOMAS HOFFER, and SALLY KILGORE *Public and Private Schools, Report to the National Center for Education Statistics* (Chicago, IL: National Opinion Research Center, 1981).

COLEMAN, JAMES S., THOMAS HOFFER, and SALLY KILGORE *High School Achievement: Public and Private Schools Compared* (New York: Basic Books, 1982).

College Board, "Education Pays: 2010 Report Shows College Grads Weather Recession Better than Others," Copyright September 21, 2010. Available: http://www.collegeboard.com/press/release/213393.html (Retrieved October 10, 2010).

COLLINS, RANDALL *The Credential Society* (New York: Academic Press, 1978).

COLTOFF, PHILLIP *Community Schools: Education Reform and Partnership with Our Nation's Social Service Agencies* (Washington, DC: Child Welfare League of America, 1998).

Committee on Increasing High School Students' Engagement and Motivation to Learn, *Engaging High Schools: Fostering High School Students' Motivation to Learn* (Washington, DC: National Academies Press, 2003).

Committee on Maximizing the Potential of Women in Academic Science and Engineering, *Beyond Bias and Barriers: Fulfilling the Potential of Women in Academic Science and Engineering* (Washington, DC: The National Academies Press, 2006).

CONLEY, DALTON, and KAREN ALBRIGHT (eds.) *After the Bell: Family Background, Public Policy, and Educational Success* (New York: Routledge, 2004).

CONNELL, CHRISTOPHER "Bob Jones University: Doing Battle in the Name of Religion and Freedom," *Change*, May/June 1983, pp. 38–47.

COOK, RONALD J. "The Religious Schools Controversy," *America*, Vol. 172, No. 5, February 18, 1995, pp. 17–19.

COOKSON, PETER W., JR. *School Choice: The Struggle for the Soul of American Education* (New Haven, CT: Yale University Press, 1994).

COOKSON, PETER W., JR., and ALAN R. SADOVNIK "Functionalist Theories of Education," in David L. Levinson, Peter W. Cookson, Jr., and Alan R. Sadovnik (eds.), *Education and Society: An Encyclopedia* (New York: Routledge/Falmer Press, 2002), pp. 267–271.

COOKSON, PETER W., JR., and CAROLINE HODGES PERSELL "English and American Residential Secondary Schools: A Comparative Study of the Reproduction of Social Elites," *Comparative Education Review*, Vol. 29, No. 3, August 1985a, pp. 283–284.

COOKSON, PETER W., JR., and CAROLINE HODGES PERSELL *Preparing for Power: America's Elite Boarding Schools* (New York: Basic Books, 1985b).

COON, H., ET AL. "Influence of School Environment on the Academic Achievement," *Intelligence*, January/March 1993, pp. 79–104.

COOPER, HARRIS, and CONSWELLA J. MOORE "Teenage Motherhood, Mother-only Households, and Teacher Expectations," *Journal of Experimental Education*, Vol. 63, No. 3, Spring 1995, pp. 231–248.

COOPER, MARK, LESTER LLOYD-REASON, and STUART WELL "Social Deprivation and Educational Under-achievement: Lessons from LONDON," *Education and Training*, Vol. 45, No. 2, 2003, pp. 79–88.

CORBETT, KEN *Boyhoods: Rethinking Masculinities* (New Haven, CT: Yale University Press, 2009).

CORD, ROBERT L. "Church, State and the Rehnquist Court," *National Review*, Vol. 44, No. 16, August 17, 1992, pp. 35–37.

CORNEA, GIOVANNI ANDREA, RICHARD JOLLY, and FRANCES STEWART. *Adjustment with a Human Face* (Oxford: Clarendon Press, 1987), UNICEF.

Cornell University Chronicle On Line, "Cornell Drops Need-based Loans for Students from Families Earning under $75,000," Copyright 2008. Available: http://news.cornell.edu/stories/Jan08/finAid.html (Retrieved January 2, 2008).

CORRIGAN, PAUL *Schooling the Smash Street Kids* (London: Macmillan, 1979), p. 92.

CORSARO, WILLIAM A. "Discussion, Debate and Friendship Processes: Peer Disclosure in U.S. and Italian Nursery Schools," *Sociology of Education*, Vol. 67, No. 1, January 1994, pp. 1–26.

CORSARO, WILLIAM A. *The Sociology of Childhood*, 2nd ed. (Thousand Oaks, CA: Pine Forge Press, 2005).

CORSARO, WILLIAM A., and DONNA EDER "Children's Peer Cultures," *Annual Review of Sociology*, Vol. 16, 1990, pp. 197–220.

COTTON, KATHLEEN, and KAREN REED WIKELUND "Parent Involvement in Education," 2001. NWREL. Available: www.nwrel.org/scpd/sirs/3/cu6.html (Retrieved March 20, 2008).

COX, HAROLD G. *Later Life: The Realities of Aging*, 4th ed. (Englewood Cliffs, NJ: Prentice Hall, 1996).

CRAIG, THOMAS TOCH, and JERALD ERIN DILLON "Surprise—High School Reform is Working," *Phi Delta Kappan*, Vol. 88, No. 6, Fall 2007, pp. 433–437.

CRAWFORD, JAMES "Chapter 2 Limits Set in Suit Settlement," *Education Week*, September 17, 1986, p. 15.

CROMWELL, SHARON "Banning Books from the Classroom: How to Handle Cries for Censorship," *Education World*, Copyright 2005a. Available: http://www.educationworld.com/a_curr/curr031.shtml (Retrieved April 3, 2011).

CROMWELL, SHARON "Site-Based Management: Boon or Boondoggle," *Education World*, Copyright 2005b. Available: http://www.educationworld.com/a_admin/admin/admin176.shtml (Retrieved May 11, 2007).

CROSNOE, ROBERT, MONICA KIRKPATRICK JOHNSON, and GLEN H. ELDER, JR. "Intergenerational Bonding in School: The Behavioral and Contextual Correlates of Student-Teacher Relationships," *Sociology of Education*, Vol. 77, January 2004, pp. 60–81.

Crossette, Barbara "A Reality Check on the Status of Women," *The Interdependent*, March 29, 2011. Available: http://www.theinterdependent.com/11-329/a-reality-check-on-the-status-of-women (Retrieved May 7, 2011).

CROSSLEY, MICHAEL, and KEITH HOLMES "Challenges for Educational Research: International Development,

Partnerships and Capacity Building in Small States," *Oxford Review of Education*, Vol. 27, No. 3, 2001, pp. 395–409.

CROWLEY, CAROLYN L., BARBARA LAVERY, ALEXANDER W. SIEGEL, and JENNIFER H. COUSINS *Moving Beyond Labels: Approaching Gang Involvement Through Behavior* (Washington, DC: Society for Research in Child Development, 1997), ERIC 417240. Available: http://www.eric.ed.gov/ERICWebPortal/ search/ detailmini.jsp?_nfpb=true&_&ERICExtSearch_Search Value_0=ED417240&ERICExtSearch_SearchType_ 0=no&accno=ED417240 (Retrieved April 3, 2011).

CUBAN, LARRY *How Scholars Trumped Teachers: Change Without Reform in University Curriculum, Teaching, and Research, 1890–1990* (New York: Teachers College Press, 1999).

CUBAN, LARRY *Oversold and Underused: Computers in the Classroom* (Boston, MA: Harvard University Press, 2001).

CUMMINGS, WILLIAM K. "The Institutions of Education: Compare, Compare, Compare!" *Comparative Education Review*, Vol. 43, No. 4, 1999, pp. 413–437.

CURRAN, DANIEL, and CLAIRE RENZETTI *Social Problems: Society in Crisis,* 5th ed. (Boston, MA: Allyn and Bacon, 1999).

CUSICK, PHILIP A. *Inside High School: The Student's World* (New York: Holt, Rinehart and Winston, 1973).

CUSICK, PHILIP A. *The Egalitarian Ideal and the American High School: Studies of Three Schools* (New York: Longman, 1983).

D'ENTREMONT, C., and L. A. HUERTA "Irreconcilable Differences? Education Vouchers and Suburban Response," *Educational Policy*, Vol. 21, No. 1, 2007, pp. 40–72.

D'SOUZA, DINESH *Illiberal Education: The Politics of Race and Sex on Campus* (New York: Free Press, 1991).

DALE, R. "Globalization, Knowledge Economy and Comparative Education," *Comparative Education*, Vol. 41, No. 2, 2005, pp. 117–149.

DANDY, EVELYN B. "Increasing the Number of Minority Teachers: Tapping the Paraprofessional Pool," *Education and Urban Society*, Vol. 31, No. 1, November 1998, pp. 89–103.

DANIEL A. MCFARLAND "Why Work When You Can Play? Dynamics of Formal and Informal Organization in Classrooms," in Larry V. Hedges and Barbara Schneider (eds.), *The Social Organization of Schooling* (New York: Russell Sage Foundation, 2005), pp. 147–174.

DANIEL A. MCFARLAND "Curricular Flows: Trajectories, Turning Points, and Assignment Criteria in High School Math Careers," *Sociology of Education,* Vol. 79, No. 3, July, 2006, pp. 177–205.

DARLING, NANCY *Parenting Style and Its Correlates* (Champaign, IL: ERIC Clearinghouse on Elementary and Early Childhood Education, March 1999). ERIC #ED427896.

DARLING-HAMMOND, LINDA "Performance-based Assessment and Equation Equity," *Harvard Educational Review*, Vol. 64, Spring 1994, pp. 5–30.

DARLING-HAMMOND, LINDA *The Flat World and Education: How America's Commitment to Equity will Determine our Future* (New York: Teachers College Press, 2010).

DARLING-HAMMOND, LINDA, and MILBREY W. MCLAUGHLIN "Policies That Support Professional Development in an Era of Reform," *Phi Delta Kappan*, April 1995, pp. 597–604.

DAVIES, SCOTT "Leaps of Faith: Shifting Currents in Critical Sociology of Education," *American Journal of Sociology*, Vol. 100, No. 4, 1995, pp. 1448–1478.

DAVIES, SCOTT "The Paradox of Progressive Education: A Frame Analysis," *Sociology of Education*, Vol. 75, No. 4, 2002, pp. 269–286.

DAVIES, SCOTT, and FLOYD M. HAMMACK "The Channeling of Student Competition in Higher Education: Comparing Canada and the U.S.," *Journal of Higher Education*, Vol. 76, No. 1, 2005, pp. 89–106.

DAVIS, KINGSLEY, and WILBERT MOORE "Some Principles of Stratification," *American Sociological Review*, Vol. 10, 1945, pp. 242–249.

DEAL, TERRENCE E., and KENT D. PETERSON *The Principal's Role in Change: Technical and Symbolic Aspects of School Improvement* (Madison, WI: University of Wisconsin, Wisconsin Center for Educational Research, National Center for Effective Schools, 1993).

DELACY, DAN R. "Unitary Status," *American School Board Journal*, Vol. 184, No. 12, December 1997, pp. 22–24.

DELANY, BRIAN, and LYNN W. PAINE "Shifting Patterns of Authority in Chinese Schools," *Comparative Education Review*, Vol. 35, No. 1, 1991, pp. 23–44.

DEL FALCO, BETH, and SAMANTHA HENRY "Mark Zuckerberg Makes Massive Donation to Newark Schools," Copyright September 23, 2010. Available: http://www. csmonitor.com/USA/Latest-News-Wires/2010/0923/ Mark-Zuckerbert-makes-massive-donation-to-Newark- schools (Retrieved April 3, 2011).

DEMANET, JANNICK, and MIEKE VAN HOUTTE "Social- Ethnic School Composition and School Misconduct: Does Sense of Futility Clarify the Picture?" *Sociological Spectrum*, Vol. 31, 2011, pp. 224–256.

DEMARRAIS, BENNETT, KATHLEEN, and MARGARET D. LECOMPTE *The Way Schools Work: A Sociological*

Analysis of Education, 2nd ed. (White Plains, NY: Longman, 1995).

DENEEF, A. L. *The Preparing Future Faculty Program: What Difference Does It Make?* (Washington, DC: Association of American Colleges and Universities, 2002).

Department of Justice, "ADA Enforcement," 2010. Available: http://www.ada.gov/enforce.htm (Retrieved September 26, 2010).

DERRIDA, JACQUES *Of Grammatology* (Baltimore, MD: Johns Hopkins University Press, 1982).

DEVINE, JOHN (ed.) *Maximum Security: The Culture of Violence in Inner-City Schools* (Chicago, IL: The University of Chicago Press, 1996).

DEVOE, JILL F., ET AL. "Indicators of School Crime and Safety: 2002," *Education Statistics Quarterly*, Vol. 4, No. 4, 2003 (Washington, DC: National Center for Education Statistics).

DEWEY, JOHN *Democracy and Education* (New York: Free Press [1916], 1966).

DIAZ, IDRIS M. "What's at Stake: The Court Decisions Affecting Higher Education and Diversity," *Black Issues in Higher Education*, Vol. 14, No. 22, December 25, 1997, pp. 19–21.

DIETRICH, LISA C. "Chicana Adolescents: Bitches, 'Ho's,' and Schoolgirls,". ERIC #ED425036. Copyright 1998. Available: http://www.eric.ed.gov/ERICWebPortal/search/detailmini.jsp?_nfpb=true&_&ERICExtSearch_SearchValue_0=ED425036&ERICExtSearch_SearchType_0=no&accno=ED425036 (Retrieved April 3, 2011).

DIETZ, TRACY L. "An Examination of Violence and Gender Role Portrayals in Video Games: Implications for Gender, Socialization and Aggressive Behavior," *Sex Roles: A Journal of Research*, Vol. 38, Nos. 5–6, March 1998, pp. 425–442.

DILLABOUGH, JO-ANNE, and MADELEINE ARNOT "Sociology of Education: Feminist Perspectives: Continuity and Contestation in the Field," in David L. Levinson, Peter W. Cookson, Jr., and Alan R. Sadovnik (eds.), *Education and Sociology: An Encyclopedia* (New York: Routledge/Falmer Press, 2002), pp. 571–585.

DILLON, SAM "4100 Students Prove 'Small is Better' Rule Wrong," *The New York Times*, September 27, 2010a.

DILLON, SAM "Formula to Grade Teachers' Skill Gains Acceptance, and Critics," *The New York Times*, August 31, 2010b.

DODGE, SUSAN "More College Students Choose Academic Majors That Meet Social and Environmental Concerns," *The Chronicle of Higher Education*, December 5, 1990, p. A31.

DORN, SHERMAN *Creating the Dropout: An Institutional and Social History of School Failure* (Westport, CT: Praeger, 1996).

DORNBUSCH, SANFORD M., and PHILIP L. RITTER "Home-School Processes in Diverse Ethnic Groups, Social Classes and Family Structures," in Sandra Christenson and Jane C. Conoley (eds.), *Home-School Collaboration* (Silver Spring, MD: National Association of School Psychologists, 1992), pp. 111–125.

DOUGHERTY, KEVIN J. "Opportunity-to-Learn Standards: A Sociological Critique," *Sociology of Education*, Extra Issue, 1996, pp. 40–65.

DOUGHERTY, KEVIN J. "The Community College: The Impacts, Origins and Future of a Contradictory Institution," in Jeanne H. Ballantine and Joan Z. Spade (eds.), *Schools and Society* (Belmont, CA: Wadsworth, 2000).

DOUGHERTY, KEVIN J. "The Community College: The Impact, Origin, and Future of a Contradictory Institution," in Jeanne H. Ballantine and Joan Z. Spade (eds.), *Schools and Society: A Sociological Approach to Education* (Thousand Oaks, CA: Pine Forge Press, 2001).

DOUGHERTY, KEVIN J. "The Evolving Role of the Community College: Policy Issues and Research Questions," in J. S. Smart and W. G. Tierney (eds.), *Higher Education: Handbook of Theory and Research*, Vol. XVII (New York: Agathon Press, 2002), pp. 295–348.

DOUGHERTY, KEVIN J., and GREGORY S. KIENZL "It's Not Enough to Get Through the Open Door: Inequalities by Social Background in Transfer from Community Colleges to Four-Year Colleges," *Teachers College Record*, Vol. 108, No. 3, 2006, pp. 452–487.

DOUGHERTY, KEVIN J., and MARIANNE F. BAKIA "Community Colleges and Contract Training: Content, Origins, and Impacts," *Teachers College Record*, Vol. 102, February 2000, pp. 198–244.

DOWLING, W. *Confessions of a Spoilsport: My Life and Hard Times Fighting Sports Corruption at an Old Eastern University* (University Park, TX: Pennsylvania State University Press, 2007).

DOWNEY, DOUGLAS B., PAUL T. VON HIPPEL, and BECKETT A. BROH "Are Schools the Great Equalizer? Cognitive Inequality During the Summer and the School Year," *American Sociological Review*, Vol. 69, October, 2004, pp. 613–635.

DOWNEY, DOUGLAS B., and SHANA PRIBESH "When Race Matters: Teachers' Evaluations of Students' Classroom Behavior," *Sociology of Education*, Vol. 77, No. 4, 2004, pp. 267–282.

DREEBEN, ROBERT F. *On What Is Learned in School* (Reading, MA: Addison-Wesley, 1968).

DREEBEN, ROBERT F. "The School as a Workplace," in R. Travers (ed.), *Second Handbook of Research and*

Teaching (Skokie, IL: Rand McNally, 1973), pp. 450–473.

DRINAN, ROBERT F. "The Constitution and Handicapped Hasidim Children," *America*, Vol. 170, No. 7, February 26, 1994, pp. 8–11.

DRORI, GILI S. *Global E-litism: Digital Technology, Social Inequality, and Transnationality* (New York: Worth, 2006).

DU, RUIQUIG *Chinese Higher Education: A Decade of Reform and Development (1978–1988)* (New York: St. Martin's Press, 1992).

DUNCAN, G. J., and L. P. CHASE-LANSDALE *Welfare Reform and Child Well-Being* (Chicago, IL: Joint Center for Poverty Research, 2000), ERIC ED 452 289.

DUNN, SAMUEL "The Virtuality of Education," *The Futurist*, March/April, 1980, pp. 34–38.

DURKHEIM, EMILE *Education and Sociology* (trans. Sherwood D. Fox) (Glencoe, IL: Free Press, 1956), p. 28.

DURKHEIM, EMILE *Moral Education* (trans. Everett K. Wilson and Herman Schnurer) (Glencoe, IL: Free Press, 1961).

DURKHEIM, EMILE *The Evolution of Educational Thought* (trans. Peter Collins) (London: Routledge, 1977).

DWORKIN, ANTHONY GARY *When Teachers Give Up: Teacher Burnout, Teacher Turnover and Their Impact on Children* (Austin, TX: University of Texas, 1985).

DWORKIN, ANTHONY GARY "Perspectives on Teacher Burnout and School Reform," *International Education Journal*, Vol. 2, No. 2, 2001, pp. 69–78.

DWORKIN, ANTHONY GARY "School Reform and Teacher Burnout: Issues of Gender and Gender Tokenism," in Barbara Bank, Sara Delamont, and Catherine Marshall (eds.), *Gender and Education: An Encyclopedia* (New York: Greenwood Press, 2007).

DWORKIN, ANTHONY GARY, and ALLEN HANEY C. "Fear, Victimization, and Stress Among Urban Public School Teachers," *Journal of Organizational Behavior*, Vol. 9, 1988, pp. 159–171.

DWORKIN, ANTHONY GARY, LAWRENCE J. SAHA, and ANTWANETTE N. HILL "Teacher Burnout and Perceptions of a Democratic School Environment," *International Education Journal*, Vol. 4, No. 2, 2003, pp. 108–120.

DWORKIN, ANTHONY GARY, and MERRIC LEE TOWNSEND "Teacher Burnout in the Face of Reform: Some Caveats in Breaking the Mold," in Bruce Anthony Jones and Kathryn M. Borman (eds.), *Breaking the Mold: Alternative Structures for American Schools* (Norwood, NJ: Ablex, 1993).

DWORKIN, ANTHONY GARY, and PAMELA F. TOBE "Teacher Burnout in Light of School Safety, Student Misbehavior, and Changing Accountability Standards," in Jeanne Ballantine and Joan Spade (eds.), *Schools and Society* (Thousand Oaks: Sage/Pine Forge, 2012).

DYE, THOMAS R., and HARMON ZEIGLER *The Irony of Democracy: An Uncommon Introduction to American Politics*, 10th ed. (Belmont, CA: Wadsworth, 1997).

DYKEMA, RAVI "How Schools Fail Kids and How They Could Be Better," *Nexus*, May/June 2002.

EARLY, DIANE M., ET AL. "Teachers' Education, Classroom Quality, and Young Children's Academic Skills: Results from Seven Studies of Preschool Programs," *Child Development*, Vol. 78, No. 2, March/April 2007, pp. 558–580.

EARTHMAN, GLEN I., and LINDA LEMASTERS "Review of Research on the Relationship Between School Buildings, Student Achievement, and Student Behavior," paper presented at the annual meeting of the Council of Educational Facilities Planners, International, Tarpon Springs, FL, October 8, 1996.

EASTON, DAVID *A Systems Analysis of Political Life* (New York: Wiley, 1965).

EATON, DANICE K., ET AL. "Youth Risk Behavior Surveillance—United States, 2005," *Morbidity and Mortality Weekly Report*, Vol. 55, No. SS-5 (Washington, DC: Department of Health and Human Services. Centers for Disease Control and Prevention, June 9, 2006).

EATON, JUDITH S. "Minorities, Transfer, and Higher Education," *Peabody Journal of Education*, Vol. 66, No. 1, Fall 1990, pp. 58–70.

ECKERT, PENELOPE *Jocks and Burnouts: Social Categories and Identity in High School* (New York: Teachers College Press, 1989).

ECKHOLM, ERIK "Recession Raises Poverty Rate to a 15-Year High," *The New York Times*, September 17, 2010.

EDER, DONNA "The Cycle of Popularity: Interpersonal Relations Among Female Adolescents," *Sociology of Education*, Vol. 58, No. 3, 1985, pp. 154–165.

EDER, DONNA, ET AL. (eds.) *School Talk: Gender and Adolescent Culture* (New Brunswick, NJ: Rutgers University Press, 1995).

Education Commission of the States, "School Choice," *The Progress of Education Reform 1999–2001*, May 1999.

Education in Britain (London: Foreign and Commonwealth Office, 1995).

Education Reform, "At a Glance," Copyright 2007. Available: http://planipolis.iiep.unesco.org/upload/Ghana/Ghana_education_reform_2007.pdf (Retrieved October 3, 2010).

Effective School Practices: A Research Synthesis, 1990 (Portland, OR: Northwest Regional Educational Laboratory, 1990).

"Effective Schools: What Makes a Public School Work Well?" *Our Children*, Vol. 24, No. 1, August–September 1998, pp. 8–12.

EGERTON, JOHN "Back to Basics," *The Progressive*, September 1976, pp. 21–24.

ELIZABETH, COVAY, and WILLIAM CARBONARO "After the Bell: Participation in Extracurricular Activities," *Sociology of Education*, Vol. 83, No. 1, 2010, pp. 20–45.

ELKIND, DAVID "Educational Reform: Modern and Post-modern," *Holistic Education Review*, 1994, pp. 5–13.

ELLIOTT, MARTA "School Finance and Opportunities to Learn: Does Money Well Spent Enhance Students' Achievement?" *Sociology of Education*, Vol. 71, No. 3, July 1998, pp. 223–245.

"Enforcing the ADA, Fifth Anniversary Status Report" (Washington, DC: Department of Justice, July 26, 1995).

ENTWISLE, DORIS R., and KARL L. ALEXANDER "A Parent's Economic Shadow: Family Structure vs. Family Resources as Influences on Early School Achievement," *Journal of Marriage and the Family*, Vol. 57, No. 2, May 1995, pp. 399–409.

EPSTEIN, JOYCE L. "Target: An Examination of Parallel School and Family Structures That Promote Student Motivation and Achievement," Report 6, Johns Hopkins University, Center for Research on Elementary and Middle Schools, Baltimore, MD, January 1987a.

EPSTEIN, JOYCE L. "Toward a Theory of Family-School Connections: Teacher Practices and Parent Involvement Across the School Years," in Klaus Hurrelmann and Franz-Xavier Kaufman (eds.), *The Limits and Potential of Social Intervention* (Berlin/New York: Aldine de Gruyter, 1987b).

EPSTEIN, JOYCE L. "Effects on Student Achievement of Teachers' Practices of Parent Involvement," in S. Silvem (ed.), *Literacy Through Family, Community, and School Interaction* (Greenwich, CT: JAI Press, 1988).

EPSTEIN, JOYCE L. "School/Family/Community Partnerships," *Phi Delta Kappan*, Vol. 76, May 1995, pp. 701–712.

EPSTEIN, JOYCE L., and SUSAN L. DAUBER "School Programs and Teacher Practices of Parent Involvement in Inner-City Elementary and Middle Schools," *The Elementary School Journal*, Vol. 91, No. 3, 1991, p. 289.

ESTRICH, SUSAN "Single-sex Education Deserves a Real Chance," *USA Today*, September 15, 1994, p. A11.

EVALDSSON, ANN CARITA, and WILLIAM A. CORSARO "Play and Games in the Peer Cultures of Preschool and Preadolescent Children: An Interpretative Approach," *Childhood: A Global Journal of Child Research*, Vol. 5, No. 4, November 1998, pp. 377–402.

EWEN, LYNDA ANN "Turning Around the American Dream: The Social Implications of the Changes in Education," paper presented at American Sociological Association meetings, Washington, DC, August 1990.

Exploring Constitutional Conflicts, "The Evolution Controversy," 2006. Available: http://www.law.umkc.edu/faculty/projects/ftrials/conlaw/evolution.htm (Retrieved August 26, 2010).

FAIRWEATHER, J. S. "Faculty Reward Structures: Toward Institutional and Professional Homogenization," *Research in Higher Education*, Vol. 34, No. 5, 1993, pp. 603–623.

FALLON, DANIEL "Teacher Quality and Our Responsibility," Talk to the New York Association of Colleges for Teacher Education and the New York Association of Teacher Educators. Copyright November 2, 2000. Available: http://www.youtube.com/watch?v=KUl1vhVWlr8 (Retrieved April 3, 2011).

FARKAS, STEVE, JEAN JOHNSON, and ANN DUFFETT *Rolling Up Their Sleeves: Superintendents and Principals Talk About What's Needed to Fix Public Schools* (New York: Public Agenda, 2003), ERIC # ED482266.

FARNUM, RICHARD "Elite College Discrimination and the Limits of Conflict Theory," *Harvard Educational Review*, Vol. 67, No. 3, Fall 1997, pp. 507–530.

Federal Interagency Forum on Child and Family Statistics, *America's Children: Key National Indicators of Well-Being* (Washington, DC: U.S. Government Printing Office, 2007a).

Federal Interagency Forum on Child and Family Statistics (Washington, DC: U.S. Government Printing Office, 2007b). Available: http://childstats.gov (Retrieved April 3, 2011).

FELDMAN-JACOBS, CHARLOTTE "An Education in Making Schools Safe," *Interagency Gender Working Group*. Copyright 2006. Available: http://www.igwg.org/articles/safeschools.htm (Retrieved July 23, 2007).

FEN, H. Q. "Quanqiuhua haishi bentuhua:Gaodeng jiaoyu jianchi minzu wenhua zhuti diwei de sikao" ("Globalization or Localization?: Thinking About Higher Education's Maintaining Cultural Subjectivity of the Chinese Nation") *Heilongjiang Research on Higher Education* (Chinese Journal), No. 11, 2005, pp. 7–9.

FINKELSTEIN, BARBARA *Governing the Young. Teacher Behavior in Popular Primary Schools in 19th Century United States* (New York: Falmer Press, 1989).

FINKELSTEIN, MARTIN "The Morphing of the American Academic Profession," *Liberal Education*, Vol. 89, 2003, pp. 6–15.

FINKELSTEIN, MARTIN J., JACK H. SCHUSTER, and ROBERT K. SEAL "The American Faculty in Transition: A First Look at the New Academic Generation,"

National Center for Education Statistics (Washington, DC: U.S. Department of Education, 1995).

First Amendment Rights Center, "Religious Liberty in Public Schools: School Prayer," Copyright February 11, 2010. Available: www.firstamendmentcentr.org/rel_liberty/publicsch-ools/topic.aspx?topic=school_prayer (Retrieved September 25, 2010).

FISCHEL, WILLIAM A. *Making the Grade: The Economic Evolution of American School Districts* (Chicago, IL: Chicago University Press, 2009).

FISHER, GEORGE M. C. "World-Class Corporate Expectations of Higher Education," *Educational Record*, Fall 1990, pp. 19–21.

FISKE, EDWARD B. "Gender Issues in the College Classroom," in Paula S. Rothenberg (ed.), *Race, Class, and Gender in the United States*, 2nd ed. (New York: St. Martin's Press, 1992), pp. 52–53.

FITZGERALD, ROBERT A. *College Quality and the Earnings of Recent College Graduates* (Washington, DC: Office of Education Research Improvement, U.S. Department of Education, 2000), NCES2000–043.

FLETCHER, J. D. "Evidence for Learning from Technology-Assisted Instruction," in H. F. O'Neil, Jr. and R Perez (eds.), *Technical Applications in Education: A Learning View* (Hillsdale, NJ: Lawrence Erlbaum Associates, 2003), pp. 79–99.

FLOUD, JEAN, and A. H. HALSEY "The Sociology of Education: A Trend Report and Bibliography," *Current Sociology*, Vol. 7, 1958, pp. 165–235.

FODERARO, LISA W. "Yale, With $150 million Deficit, Plans Staff and Research Cuts," *The New York Times*, February 4, 2010.

FOGG, PIPER "The 24/7 Professor," *The Chronicle of Higher Education*, February 1, 2008.

FOLEY, E., and S. B. MCCONNAUGHY *Towards School Improvement: Lessons from Alternative High Schools* (New York: Public Education Association, 1981).

FONTAINE, DEBORAH C. "Black Women: Double Solos in the Workplace," *Western Journal of Black Studies*, Vol. 17, No. 3, Fall 1993, pp. 121–125.

"Forcing Beijing University Students to Serve a Year in the Military," *The Chronical of Higher Education*, Vol. 38, No. 8, October 16, 1991, p. A51.

FORDHAM, SIGNITHIA *Blacked Out: Dilemmas of Race, Identity, and Success at Capital High* (Chicago, IL: University of Chicago Press, 1996).

FORDHAM, Signithia, and JOHN U. OGBU "Black Students' School Success: Coping with the 'Burden of Acting White,'" *The Urban Review*, Vol. 18, 1986, pp. 176–206.

FORRESTER, GILLIAN "All in a Day's Work: Primary Teachers 'Performing' and 'Caring,'" *Gender and Education*, Vol. 17, No. 3, August 2005, pp. 271–287.

Foundation for Individual Rights in Education, *Spotlight on Speech Codes 2006: The State of Free Speech on Our Nation's Campuses* (Philadelphia, PA: Author, 2006).

FRANKENBERG, E., and C. LEE *Race in American Public Schools: Rapidly Resegregating School Districts* (Cambridge, MA: The Civil Rights Project, Harvard University, 2002), Eric ED 468 063.

FRASER, STEVEN (ed.) *Bell Curve Wars: Race, Intelligence, and the Future of America* (New York: Basic Books, 1995).

FREEDMAN, SAMUEL *Small Victories* (New York: Harper, 1990).

Freeman v. Pitts, 1992. Available: http://www.law.cornell.edu/supct/html/89-1080.ZD.html

Free Press—Reform Media, "FCC Chairman to Outline Benefits to Children and Families of National Broadband Plan with Sesame Street's Elmo," Copyright March 12, 2010. Available: http://www.freepress.net/node/77406 (Retrieved August 24, 2010).

FREIRE, PAULO *Pedagogy of the Oppressed* (New York: Herder & Herder, 1970).

FREIRE, PAULO *Education for Critical Consciousness* (New York: Herder & Herder, 1973).

FREIRE, PAULO *A Pedagogy for Liberation: Dialogues on Transforming Education* (South Hadley, MA: Bergin & Garvey, 1987).

FRIDELL, MAX, REBECCA NEWCOM BELCHER, and PHILLIP E. MESSNER "Discriminate Analysis Gender Public School Principal Servant Leadership Differences," *Leadership and Organization Development Journal*, Vol. 30, No. 8, 2009, pp. 722–736.

FRIEDMAN, ISAAC A. "High- and Low-Burnout Schools: School Culture Aspects of Teacher Burnout," *Journal of Educational Research*, Vol. 84, No. 6, July/August 1991, pp. 325–331.

FRY, R. *Hispanic Youth Dropping Out of U.S. Schools: Measuring the Challenge* (Washington, DC: Pew Hispanic Center, 2003). Available: http://www.pewhispanic.org (Retrieved April 3, 2011).

FRYER, R. G., JR., and P. TORELLI "An Empirical Analysis of 'Acting White,'" *National Bureau of Economic Research Working Paper Series*. Copyright 2005. Available: www.nber.org/papers/w11334 (Retrieved April 3, 2011).

FU, TENG MARGARET "Unequal Primary Educational Opportunity in Rural and Urban China," *China Perspective*. Copyright 2005. Available: http://chinaperspectives.revues.org/index500.html (Retrieved October 2, 2010).

FUCHS, DOUGLAS, and LYNN S. FUCHS "Introduction to Response to Intervention: What, Why, and How Valid is it?" *Reading Research Quarterly*, Vol. 41, No. 1, January/ February 2006, pp. 93–99.

FULLER, BRUCE "Is Primary School Quality Eroding in the Third World?" *Comparative Education Review*, Vol. 30, No. 4, 1986, pp. 491–508.

FULLER, BRUCE, RICHARD F. ELMORE, and GARY ORFIELD (eds.) *Who Chooses? Who Loses? Culture, Institutions, and the Unequal Effects of School Choice* (New York: Teachers College Press, 1996).

FULLER, BRUCE, SUSANNA LOEB, ANNELIE STRATH, and BIDEMI ABIOSEH CARROL "State Formation of the Child Care Sector: Family Demand and Policy Action," *Sociology of Education*, Vol. 77, No. 4, October 2004, pp. 337–358.

FULTON, MARY, and DAVID LONG *School Financial Litigation: A Historical Summary* (Denver, CO: Education Commission of the States, April 1993).

FURSTENBERG, FRANK, JR., F. SHEELA KENNEDY, VONNIE. C. MCCLOYD, ROBEN G. RUMBAUT, and RICHARD A. SETTERSTEN "Growing Up is Harder to Do," *Contexts*, Vol. 3, No. 3, 2004, pp. 33–41.

GALLAGHER, MARK "A Public Choice Theory of Budgets: Implications for Education in Less Developed Countries," *Comparative Education Review*, Vol. 37, No. 2, May 1993, pp. 90–106.

GALLEGO, M. A., G. Z. DURAN, and E. I. REYES "It Depends: A Sociohistorical Account of the Definition and Methods of Identification of Learning Disabilities," *Teachers College Record*, Vol. 108, No. 11, 2006, pp. 2195–2219.

GALTON, MAURICE "Class Size and Pupil Achievement," *International Journal of Educational Research*, Vol. 29, No. 8, Theme Issue, 1998, pp. 687–818.

GAMBETTA, DIEGO *Were They Pushed or Did They Jump: Individual Decision Making Mechanisms in Education* (Cambridge: Cambridge University Press, 2009).

GAMORAN, ADAM, and MATTHEW WEINSTEIN "Differentiation and Opportunity in Restructured Schools" *American Journal of Education*, Vol. 106, May, 1998, pp. 385–415.

GAMORAN, ADAM, and ROBERT DREEBAN "Coupling and Control in Educational Organizations," in Jeanne H. Ballantine (ed.), *Schools and Society: A Unified Reader*, 2nd ed. (Mountain View, CA: Mayfield, 1989), pp. 119–138.

GAMORAN, ADAM, ET AL. "An Organizational Analysis of the Effects of Ability Grouping," *American Educational Research Journal*, Vol. 32, No. 4, Winter 1995, pp. 687–715.

GARCIA, ANITA, and CYNTHIA MORGAN "A 50–State Survey of Requirements for the Education of Language Minority Children," *Research and Policy Brief* (Amherst, MA: Institute for Research in English Acquisition and Development, November 1997). Available: http://www.eric.ed.gov/ERICWebPortal/search/detailmini.jsp?_nfpb=true&_&ERICExtSearch_SearchValue_0=ED422747&ERICExtSearch_SearchType_0=no&accno=ED422747 (Retrieved April 3, 2011).

GARCIA, EUGENE E. "Language, Culture and Education," in Linda Darling-Hammond (ed.), *Review of Research in Education* (Washington, DC: American Educational Research Association, 1993).

GARDNER, HOWARD "The Theory of Multiple Intelligences," *Annual Dyslexia*, Vol. 37, 1987, pp. 19–35.

GARDNER, HOWARD *Intelligence Reframed: Multiple Intelligences for the 21st Century* (New York: Basic Books, 1999).

GARDNER, JOHN W. *Excellence* (New York: Harper & Row, 1984).

GARNER, CATHERINE L., and STEPHEN W. RAUDENBUSH "Neighborhood Effects on Educational Attainment: A Multilevel Analysis," *Sociology of Education*, Vol. 64, No. 4, October 1991, pp. 251–262.

GARNIER, MAURICE, and MARK SCHAFER "Educational Model and Expansion of Enrollments in Sub-Saharan Africa," *Sociology of Education*, Vol. 79, No. 2, April 2006, pp. 153–175.

GAVIN, MARY L., and STEVE DOWSHEN "How TV Affects Your Child," 2005. Nemours Foundation. Available: http://www.google.com/#hl=en&sa=X&ei=tt6YTdv0GsbLgQeJ3ICuCA&sqi=2&ved=0CBMQBSgA&q=GAVIN,+MARY+L.,+and+STEVEN+DOWSHEN+%E2%80%9CHow+TV+Affects+Your+Child,%E2%80%9D+2005.+Nemours+Foundation&spell=1&bav=on.2,or.r_gc.r_pw.&fp=c4f9bf7f64efb33f (Retrieved April 3, 2011).

GAVORA, JESSICA, and KIMBERLY SCHULD "Title IX Didn't Score the Winning Goal," *The Wall Street Journal*, July 15, 1999.

General Accounting Office, *School Vouchers: Publicly Funded Programs in Cleveland and Milwaukee* (Washington, DC: Author, 2001), GAO-01-914.

GENZEN, HOLLY "The Changing/Challenging Roles of the Principal," *The AASA Professor*, Vol. 23, No. 2, Winter 2000.

GERALD, D., and K. HAYCOCK *Engines of Inequality: Diminishing Equity at the Nations' Premier Public Universities* (Washington, DC: The Education Trust, 2006).

GERTH, H. H., and C. WRIGHT MILLS (eds.) *From Max Weber: Essays in Sociology* (New York: Oxford University Press, 1946).

GEWANDE, ATUL "When Doctors Make Mistakes," in J. Gleick (ed.), *The Best American Science Writing, 2000* (New York: Ecco Press, 2000).

GEWIRTZ, SHARON, STEPHEN J. BALL, and RICHARD BOWE *Markets, Choice and Equity in Education* (Buckingham, England: Open University Press, 1995).

Ghana Home Page: Education in Ghana, 2007. Available: http://www.ghanaweb.com/GhanaHomePage/education/ (Retrieved October 3, 2010).

GIACQUINTA, J. B., J. A. BAUER, and J. LEVIN *Beyond Technology's Promise: An Examination of Children's Educational Computing at Home* (New York: Cambridge University Press, 1993).

GILLIGAN, CAROL "Women's Place in Man's Life Cycle," *Harvard Educational Review*, Vol. 49, 1979, pp. 431–446.

GILLIGAN, CAROL, NONA P. LYONS, and TRUDY J. HANMER (eds.) *Making Connections* (Cambridge, MA: Harvard University Press, 1990), p. 26.

GILMORE, MICHAEL J., and JOSEPH MURPHY "Understanding Classroom Environments: An Organizational Sense making Approach," *Educational Administration Quarterly*, Vol. 27, No. 3, August 1991, pp. 392–429.

GIROUX, HENRY A. *Teachers as Intellectuals: Toward a Critical Pedagogy of Learning* (Hadley, MA: Bergin and Garvey, 1981).

GIROUX, HENRY A. *Postmodernism, Feminism, and Cultural Politics: Redrawing Educational Boundaries* (Albany, NY: State University of New York Press, 1991).

GIROUX, HENRY A. "Educational Reform and the Politics of Teacher Empowerment," in Joseph Kretovics and Edward J. Nussel (eds.), *Transforming Urban Education* (Boston, MA: Allyn & Bacon, 1994).

GLASS, THOMAS E., LARS BJORK, and C. CRYSS BRUNNER *The Study of the American School Superintendency* (Arlington, VA: American Association of School Administrators, 2000).

GLENN, CHARLES L. "Personal Reflections," *Choice of Schools in Six Nations* (Washington, DC: U.S. Department of Education, December 1989).

GLENN, DAVID "A Measure of Education is Put to the Test," *The Chronicle of Higher Education*, Copyright September 19, 2010. Avaialble: http://chronicle.com/article/A-Measure-of-Learning-Is-Put/124519/ (Retrieved April 3, 2011).

GLUCKMAN, IVAN B. *Dress Codes and Gang Activity* (Reston, VA: National Association of Secondary School Principals, March 1996).

Goals 2000: Educate America Act (Washington, DC: U.S. Department of Education, 1994).

GOE, LAURA, and LESLIE M. STICKLER "Teacher Quality and Student Achievement: Making the most of Recent Research," March 2008. Available: http://www.tqsource.org/publications/March2008Brief.pdf (Retrieved September 21, 2010).

GOFFMAN, ERVING *Interaction Ritual* (Garden City, NY: Doubleday, 1967).

GOLAN, SHARI, and DANA PETERSON "Promoting Involvement of Recent Immigrant Families in their Children's Education," March 2002. Harvard Family Research Project. Available: http://www.greharvard.edu/hfrp/projects/fine/resources/research/golan.html (Retrieved March 22, 2008).

GOLDEN, CLAUDIA, LAWRENCE F. KATZ, and ILYANA KUZIEKO "The Homecoming of American College Women: The Reversal of the College Gender Gap," *Journal of Economic Perspectives*, Vol. 20, No. 4, 2006, pp. 133–56.

GONZALEZ, JENNIFER "Obama Praises Community Colleges Amid Doubts About His Commitment," Copyright October, 10, 2010. Available: http://chronicle.com/article/Obama-Praises-Community/124869/ (Retrieved October 11, 2010).

GOOD, T. L., H. L. BURROSS, and M. M. MCCASLIN "Comprehensive School Reform: A Longitudinal Study of School Improvement in One State," *Teachers College Record*, Vol. 107, No. 10, 2005, pp. 2205–2226.

GOODLAD, JOHN I. *A Place Called School* (New York: McGraw-Hill, 1984).

GOODLAD, JOHN I. *Educational Renewal: Better Teachers, Better Schools* (San Francisco, CA: Jossey-Bass, 1998).

GOODLAD, JOHN I. *A Place Called School* (New York: McGraw-Hill, 2004a).

GOODLAD, JOHN I. "Corinne Mantle-Bromley, and Stephen John Goodlad," *Education for Everyone* (New York: Jossey-Bass, 2004b).

GOODMAN, JOHN L. "Reading Toward Womanhood: The Baby-Sitters Club Books and Our Daughters," *Tikkun*, Vol. 8, No. 6, 1993, pp. 7–11.

GOSE, BEN "A 'First' for Scholarships," *The Chronicle of Higher Education*, Vol. 41, No. 24, February 24, 1995, pp. A37–A38.

GOSE, BEN "Efforts to End Fraternity Hazing Have Largely Failed, Critics Charge," *The Chronicle of Higher Education*, Vol. 43, No. 32, April 18, 1997, pp. A37–A38.

GOSLIN, DAVID A. *The School in Contemporary Society* (Glenview, IL: Scott, Foresman, 1965).

GOTTFREDSON, DENISE C. *School Size and School Disorder*, Vol. 21, No. 2 (Washington, DC: National Institute of Education, February 1986).

GOULDNER, ALVIN W. "Cosmopolitans and Locals: Toward an Analysis of Latent Social Roles, I," *Administrative Science Quarterly*, Vol. 2, 1957, pp. 281–306.

GOULDNER, ALVIN W. *The Coming Crisis of Western Sociology* (New York: Avon Books, 1971).

GOULDNER, HELEN R. *Teacher's Pets, Troublemakers and Nobodies: Black Children in Elementary School* (Westport, CT: Greenwood Press, 1978).

GOYETTE, KIMBERLY, and YU XIE "Educational Expectations of Asian American Youths: Determinants and Ethnic Differences," *Sociology of Education*, Vol. 72, No. 1, 1999, pp. 22–36.

GRACEY, HARRY L. "Learning the Student Role: Kindergarten as Academic Boot Camp," in Dennis Wrong and Harry L. Gracey (eds.), *Readings in Introductory Sociology* (New York: Macmillan, 1967).

GRADY, S., and S. BIELICK "Trends in the Use of School Choice, 1993–2007," 2010. NCES 2010-004. http://nces.ed.gov/pubs2010/2010004.pdf (Retrieved April 3, 2011).

GRANT, GERALD *Hope and Despair in the American City: Why There Are No Bad Schools in Raleigh* (Cambridge, MA: Harvard University Press, 2009).

GRASHA, ANTHONY F. "Grasha-Reichmann Student Learning Styles Questionnaire," *Faculty Resource Center* (Cincinnati, OH: University of Cincinnati, 1975).

GREENWALD, STEPHEN R., and DAVID J. ROSNER "Are We Distance Educating Our Students to Death? Some Reflections on the Educational Assumptions of Distance Learning," *Radical Pedagogy*, Vol. 5, No. 1, 2003. Available: http://radicalpedagogy.icaap.org/content/issue5_1/04_greenwald-rosner.html (Retrieved April 3, 2011).

GREENWOOD, GORDON E., and CATHERINE W. HICKMAN "Research and Practice in Parent Involvement: Implications for Teacher Education," *The Elementary School Journal*, Vol. 91, No. 3, 1991, p. 287.

GRIFFITH, JAMES "An Empirical Examination of a Model of Social Climate in Elementary Schools," *Basic and Applied Psychology*, Vol. 17, Nos. 1–2, August 1995, pp. 97–117.

GRIFFITHS, D. "Systems Theory and School Districts," *Ontario Journal of Educational Research*, Vol. 8, 1965, p. 24.

GRODSKY, ERIC, JOHN ROBERRT WARREN, and ERIKA FELTS "Testing and Social Stratification in American Education," *Annual Review of Sociology*, Vol. 34, 2008, pp. 385–404.

GRUBAUGH, STEVE, and RICHARD HOUSTON "Establishing a Classroom Environment That Promotes Interaction and Improved Student Behavior," *Clearing House*, Vol. 63, April 1990, pp. 375–378.

GRUBB, W. NORTON "The Decline of Community College Transfer Rates: Evidence from National Longitudinal Surveys," *Journal of Higher Education*, Vol. 62, No. 2, March/April 1991, pp. 194–217.

GRUTTER V BOLLINGER, Copyright 2003. Available: http://www.law.cornell.edu/supct/html/02-241.ZS.html (Retrieved April 3, 2011).

GUESS, A. "Enrollment Surge for Women," Copyright August 7, 2007. Available: http://inside highered.com/news/2007/08/07/enrollment (Retrieved August 7, 2007).

GURIAN, MICHAEL, and KATHY STEVENS *The Minds of Boys: Saving our Sons from Falling Behind in School and Life* (San Francisco, CA: Jossey Bass, 2005).

GWERTZ, CATHERINE "Pathways to a Diploma," *Education Week*, Vol. 26, No. 32, 2007, pp. 29–31.

HABERMAS, JURGEN *Knowledge and Human Interests*, 2nd rev. ed. (London: Heinemann, 1978).

HACKER, ANDREW (emeritus professor at Queens College in New York) with Claudia Dreifus, *Higher Education? How Colleges Are Wasting Our Money and Failing Our Kids—And What We Can Do About It* (New York: Times Books, 2010).

HALLINAN, MAUREEN T. "Friendship Patterns in Open and Traditional Classrooms," *Sociology of Education*, Vol. 49, 1976, pp. 254–265.

HALLINAN, MAUREEN T. "Structural Effects on Children's Friendship and Cliques," *Social Psychological Quarterly*, Vol. 42, 1979, pp. 43–54.

HALLINAN, MAUREEN T. "The Effects of Ability Grouping in Secondary Schools: A Response to Slavin's Best-Evidence Synthesis," *Review of Educational Research*, Vol. 60, No. 3, Fall 1990, pp. 501–504.

HALLINAN, MAUREEN T. "Tracking: From Theory to Practice," *Sociology of Education*, Vol. 67, No. 2, 1994, pp. 79–91.

HALLINAN, MAUREEN T., and RICHARD A. WILLIAMS "Students' Characteristics and the Peer-Influence Process," *Sociology of Education*, Vol. 63, No. 2, April 1990, pp. 122–132.

HAMILTON, LAURA S., BRIAN M. STECHER, JULIE A. MARSH, JENNIFER S. MCCOMBS, ABBY ROBYN, JENNIFER L. RUSSELL, SCOTT NAFTEL, and HEATHER BARNEY *Standards-based Accountability Under No Child Left Behind: Experiences of Teachers and Administrators in Three States* (Santa Monica, CA: RAND Corporation, 2007).

HAMMACK, FLOYD M. "From Grade to Grade: Promotion Policies and At-Risk Youth," in J. M. Lakebrink (ed.), *Children at Risk* (Springfield, IL: Charles C. Thomas, 1989).

HAMMACK, FLOYD M. "From Grade to Grade: Promotion Policies and At-Risk Youth," in Joan Lakebrink (ed.), *Children at Risk* (Springfield, IL: Charles C. Thomas, 1990).

HAMMACK, FLOYD M. "What Should Be Common and What Should Not?: James Bryant Conant and U.S. High School Reform," in F. M. Hammack (ed.), *The Comprehensive High School Today* (New York: Teachers College Press, 2004).

HAMMACK, FLOYD M. "Off the record—Something Old, Something New, Something Borrowed, Something Blue: Observations on the Small Schools Movement," *Teachers College Record*, Vol. 110, September 9, 2008, pp. 2067–2072.

HAMMACK, FLOYD M. "Schools for Social Mobility: What it takes for Poor Kids to Succeed in High Achieving Schools," paper presented at the Department of Humanities and the Social Sciences, New York University, 2010a.

HAMMACK, FLOYD M. "Schools for Social Mobility: What it takes for Poor Kids to Succeed in High Achieving Schools," paper presented at the Eastern Sociological Society annual meeting, Boston, April 2010b.

HAMMERSLEY, MARTYN, and GLENN TURNER "Conformist Pupils?" in Peter Woods (ed.), *Pupil Strategies: Explorations in the Sociology of the School* (London: Croom Helm, 1980), pp. 24–49.

HAMMERSLEY, MARTYN, and PETER WOODS *Teacher Perspectives* (Milton Keynes, England: Open University Press, 1977), p. 37.

HANNUM, EMILY "Political Change and the Urban-Rural Gap in Basic Education in China, 1949–1990," *Comparative Education Review*, Vol. 43, No. 2, May 1999, pp. 193–211.

HANUSHEK, ERIC A. "The Trade-Off Between Child Quantity and Quality," *Journal of Political Economy*, Vol. 100, No. 1, February 1992, pp. 84–117.

HARDY, LARENCE "A Private Solution," *American School Board Journal*, Vol. 186, No. 4, April 1999, pp. 46–48.

HARGREAVES, DAVID H. *Social Relations in a Secondary School* (London: Routledge, 1967).

HARGREAVES, DAVID H. "Power and the Paracurriculum," in C. Richards (ed.), *Power and the Curriculum: Issues in Curriculum Studies* (London: Driffields Nafferton Books, 1977), pp. 126–137.

HARRIS, ANGEL L. "I (Don't) Hate School: Revisiting Oppositional Culture Theory of Black's Resistance to Schooling," *Social Forces*, Vol. 85, No. 2, 2006, pp. 797–834.

HARRY, BETH, and JANETTE KLINGER "Discarding the Deficit Model," *Educational Leadership*, Vol. 64, No. 5, 2007, pp. 16–21.

HART, BETTY, and TODD R. RISLEY "The Early Catastrophe: The 30 Million Word Gap," *American Educator*, Vol. 27, No. 1, 2003, pp. 4–9. Available: http://www.nccp.org/downloads/ResearchCaseSept08.pdf (Retrieved October 6, 2010).

HART, HAROLD H. *Summerhill: For and Against* (New York: Hart, 1970).

HASTINGS, NIGEL "Seats of Learning?" *Support for Learning*, Vol. 10, No. 1, February 1995, pp. 8–11.

HATCHER, RICHARD "Class Differentiation in Education: Rational Choices?" *British Journal of Sociology of Education*, Vol. 19, No. 1, 1998, pp. 5–24.

HAUSER, MARY, CURTIS FAWSON, and GLENN LATHAM "Chinese Education: A System in Transition," *Principal*, January 1990, pp. 44–45.

HAUSER, ROBERT M. "Symposium," *Contemporary Sociology*, Vol. 24, No. 2, March 1995, pp. 149–161.

HAUSER, ROBERT M., and DAVID L. FEATHERMAN *The Process of Stratification: Trends and Analysis* (New York: Academic Press, 1976).

HAWES, HUGH *Curriculum and Reality in African Primary Schools* (Harlow, Essex, England: Longman, 1979), p. 163.

HAYHOE, RUTH (ed.) *Education and Modernization: The Chinese Experience* (Oxford: Pergamon Press, 1992).

HAYHOE, RUTH "An Asian Multiversity? Comparative Reflections on the Transition to Mass Higher Education in East Asia," *Comparative Education Review*, Vol. 39, No. 3, August 1995, pp. 299–321.

HAYWARD, PAMELA A. "When Novelty Isn't Enough: A Case Study of Students' Reactions to Technology in the Classroom," *College Student Journal*, Vol. 28, No. 3, September 1994, pp. 320–325.

HEALY, PATRICK "Affirmative Action Survives at Colleges in Some States Covered by Hopwood Ruling," *The Chronicle of Higher Education*, Vol. 44, No. 33, April 24, 1998, pp. A42–A43.

HEGGER, SUSAN C. "Lawmakers Pushing Gender Equity Say 'Glass Ceiling' Starts in Schools," *The St. Louis Post-Dispatch*, September 16, 1993, p. A5.

HEILMAN, MADELINE E. "Description and Prescription: How Gender Stereotypes Prevent Women's Ascent Up the Organizational Ladder," *Journal of Social Issues*, Vol. 57, No. 4, 2001, pp. 657–674.

HEIMBUCH, JAYMI "Worldreader to boost literacy in Ghana with Kindle e-Readers," 2010. Available: http://planetgreen.discovery.com/tech-transport/worldreader-to-boost-literacy-in-ghana-with-kindle-e-readers.html (Retrieved October 2, 2010).

HELD, DAVID, and ANTHONY McGREW *Globalization Theory: Approaches and Controversies* (Cambridge, MA: Polity Press, 2007).

HEMPHILL, CLARA, and KIM NAUER *Managing by the Numbers: Empowerment and Accountability in New York City's Schools* (New York: Center for New York City Affairs, Milano The New School pf management and urban Policy, 2010).

HENRY, JULES *Culture Against Man* (New York: Vintage Books, 1963).

HENTOFF, NAT "The Great Consumer Fraud," *Current*, March 1978, pp. 3–8.

HERNANDEZ, DEBRA GERSH "Supreme Court Orders Funding of Religion-oriented Student Publication," *Editor and Publisher*, Vol. 128, No. 28, July 15, 1995, pp. 18–19, 39.

HERRNSTEIN, RICHARD J. "In Defense of Intelligence Tests," *Commentary*, February 1980, pp. 40–51.

HERRNSTEIN, RICHARD J., and CHARLES MURRAY *The Bell Curve: Intelligence and Class Structure in American Life* (New York: Free Press, 1994).

HERTZ, TOM. *Understanding Mobility in America* (Washington, DC. Center for American Progress, 2006).

HESS, FREDERICK M. *School Boards at the Dawn of the 21st Century: Conditions and Challenges of District Governance* (Alexandria, VA: National School Board Association, 2002), ERIC# ED469432.

HEYNEMAN, STEPHEN P. "Quantity, Quality, and Source," *Comparative Education Review*, Vol. 37, No. 4, November 1993, pp. 372–388.

HEYNS, B. *Summer Learning and the Effects of Schooling* (New York: Academic Press, 1978).

HIBBARD, DAVID R., and DUANE BUHRMESTER "The Role of Peers in the Socialization of Gender-Related Social Interaction Styles," *Sex Roles: A Journal of Research*, Vol. 29, Nos. 3–4, August 1998, pp. 185–202.

HIEMSTRA, ROGER, and JANET POLEY "Lessons Pertinent for Teaching with Computers," *The Clearing House*, Vol. 80, No. 3, January/February, 2007, pp. 144–148 (American Distance Education Consortium in Lincoln, Nebraska. Heldref Publications, 2007).

HILL, CATHERINE, CHRISTIANNE CORETT, and ANDRESSE ST. ROSE *Why So Few? Women in Science, Technology, Engineering and Mathematics* (Washington, DC: American Association of University Women, 2010).

HILL, J. "Documentation for the NCES Common Core of Date National Public Education Financial Survey (NPEFS), School Year 2003–04 (Fiscal Year 2004) (NCES 2006–443)," National Center for Education Statistics, U.S. Department of Education, Washington, DC, 2006.

HINDMAN, NATHANIEL CAHNERS "The 10 Poorest Countries in the World: Oxford University-United Nations," Copyright August 6, 2010. Available: http://www.HuffingtonPost.com/2010/08/03/ the-10-poorest-countries_n_668537.html#s122149 (Retrieved October 12, 2010).

HIRSCH, E. D. *Cultural Literacy: What Every American Needs to Know* (Boston, MA: Houghton Mifflin, 1987).

HIRSHFIELD, PAUL "Another Way Out: The Impact of Juvenile Arrests on High School Dropout," *Sociology of Education*, Vol. 82, No. 4, October 2009, pp. 368–393.

"Hispanic Education Fact Sheet" (Washington, DC: National Council of La Raza, February 1999).

History of Miami County, 1880 (Chicago, IL: W. H. Beers; reproduction by Unigraphic, Inc., Evansville, IN, 1973).

HOFFER, THOMAS, ANDREW GREELEY, and JAMES COLEMAN "Catholic High Schools Effects on Achievement Growth," Institute for Research on Educational Finance and Governance, Stanford University, 1985.

HOFFER, THOMAS B., and DAVID H. KAMENS "Tracking and Inequality Revisited: Secondary School Course Sequences and the Effects of Social Class on Educational Opportunities," paper presented at American Sociological Association, Pittsburgh, PA, August 1992.

HOLLINGSHEAD, A. B. *Elmtown Revisited* (New York: Wiley, 1975).

HOLSINGER, D., and R. COWELL *Positioning Secondary School Education in Developoing Countries* (Paris: IIEP-UNESCO, 2000).

HOLT, JOHN *How Children Fail* (New York: Perseus Books, 1995).

HomePage Ghana, "Education in Ghana," 2007. Available: http://www.ghanaweb.com/GhanaHomePage/education/ (Retrieved July 23, 2007).

HONIG, MEREDITH I. "No Small Thing: School District Central Office Bureaucracies and the Implementation of New Small Autonomous School Initiatives," *American Educational Research Journal*, Vol. 46, No. 2, June 2009, pp. 387–422.

HOOKS, BELL, and CORNEL WEST *Breaking Bread: Insurgent Black Intellectual Life* (Boston, MA: South End Press, 1991), Chapter 9.

HORN, C., and M. KURLAENDER *The End of Keyes—Resegregation Trends and Achievement in Denver Public Schools*, Copyright 2006. Available: http://civilrightsproject.ucla.edu/research/k-12-education/testing-and-assessment/the-end-of-keyes2014resegregation-trends-and-achievement-in-denver-public-schools/horn-the-end-of-keyes-resegregation-2006.pdf (Retrieved April 3, 2011).

HOUSE, J. DANIEL "The Relationship between Self-Beliefs, Academic Background and Achievement of

Adolescent Asian-American Students," *Child Study Journal*, Vol. 27, No. 2, 1997, pp. 95–110.

HOWARD, A. *Learning Privilege: Lessons of Power and Identity in Affluent Schooling* (New York: Routledge, 2007).

HU, WINNIE "To Close Gaps, Schools Focus on Black Boys," *The New York Times*, 2007, p. A1.

HU, WINNIE, and FORD FESSENDEN "Data Show Wide Differences in New Jersey School Spending," *The New York Times*, March 24, 2007, p. 5.

HUBBARD, LEA, and AMANDA DATNOW "Do Single-sex Schools Improve the Education of Low Income and Minority Students: An Investigation of California's Public Single-gender Academies," *Anthropology and Education Quarterly*, Vol. 36, No. 2, 2005, pp. 115–131.

HUDLEY, CYNTHIA, BRENDA BRITSCH, WILLIAM D. WAKEFIELD, TARA SMITH, MARLENE DEMORAT, and SU-JE CHO "An Attribution Retraining Program to Reduce Aggression in Elementary School Students," *Psychology in the Schools*, Vol. 35, No. 3, 1998, pp. 271–282.

Human Development Report, "China Literacy Rates," 2009. Available: http://hdrstats.undp.org/en/indicators/99/html (Retrieved September 30, 2010).

HUNTER, FIONA "Bologna Beyond 2010: Looking Backward, Looking Forward," *International Education*, Vol. 19, No. 2, March/April 2010, pp. 60–64.

HUPE, PETER, and MICHAEL HILL "Street-Level Bureaucracy and Public Accountability," *Public Administration*, Vol. 85, No. 2, 2007, pp. 279–299.

HURADO, SYLVIA, and DEBORAH FAYE CARTER "Effects of College Transition and Perceptions of the College Racial Climate on Latino College Students' Sense of Belonging," *Sociology of Education*, Vol. 70, No. 4, October 1997, pp. 324–345.

HURN, CHRISTOPHER J. *The Limits and Possibilities of Schooling: An Introduction to Sociology of Education*, 3rd ed. (Boston, MA: Allyn & Bacon, 1993).

HURN, CHRISTOPHER J. "Conflict Theory," in David L. Levinson, Peter W. Cookson, Jr., and Alan R. Sadovnik (eds.), *Education and Sociology: An Encyclopedia* (New York: Routledge/Falmer Press, 2002), pp. 111–114.

HURST, DAVID, DANA KELLY, and DANIEL PRINCIOTTA "Educational Attainment of High School Dropouts 8 Years Later," *Educational Statistics Quarterly*, Vol. 6, No. 4, 2005. Available: http://nces.ed.gov/programs/quarterly/vol_6/6_4/8_2.asp (Retrieved April 3, 2011).

HURTADO, SYLVIA, ET AL. *Findings from the 2005 Administration of Your First College Year: National Aggregates* (Los Angeles, CA: Higher Educational Research Institute, UCLA, 2007).

HYMOWITZ, KAY S. "Who Killed School Discipline?" *City Journal* (New York: The Manhattan Institute, Spring 2000).

IANNELI, VINCENT "Parenting Styles," Copyright 2004. Available: http://www.pediatrics.about.com/od/infantparentingtips/a/04_pntg_styles.htm (Retrieved September 20, 2010).

IATAROLA, PATRICE, AMY ELLEN SCHWARTZ, LEANNA STIEFEL, and COLIN CHELLMAN "Small Schools: Large Districts: Schall-School Reform and New York City's Students," *Teachers College Record*, Vol. 110, No. 9, 2008, pp. 1837–1878.

IBARRA, R. A. *Beyond Affirmative Action: Reframing the Context of Higher Education* (Madison, WI: University of Wisconsin Press, 2001).

Idea, 1997. Available: www.ed.gov/offices/OSERS. Policy.IDEA/OVERVIEW.HTML (Retrieved April 3, 2011).

ILLICH, IVAN *Deschooling Society* (New York: Harper & Row, 1971).

ILLINGWORTH, JAMES "Britain's Public Education Under Attack," Copyright 2010. Available: http://socialist-worker.org/2010/07/07/british-schools-under-attack (Retrieved September 29, 2010).

"In Beijing, Big Brother Is the Anchorman," *U.S. News & World Report*, June 26, 1989, p. 37.

Infoplease.com "World's 50 Most Populous Countries: 2007," 2007. Available: http://www.infoplease.com/ipa/A0004391.html (Retrieved July 22, 2007).

INGERSOLL, RICHARD M. "Organizational Control in Secondary Schools," *Harvard Educational Review*, Vol. 64, No. 2, Summer 1994, pp. 150–172.

INGERSOLL, RICHARD M. "Teacher Turnover and Teacher Quality: The Recurring Myth of Teacher Shortages," *Teachers College Record*, Vol. 99, No. 1, Fall 1997, pp. 41–44.

INGERSOLL, RICHARD M., and ANN MERRILL "The Status of Teaching as a Profession," in Jeanne Ballantine and Joan Z. Spade (eds.), *Schools and Society* (Thousand Oaks, CA: Sage/Pine Forge Press, 2012a).

INGERSOLL, RICHARD M., and DAVID PERDA "The Status of Teaching as a Profession," in Jeanne H. Ballantine and Joan Z. Spade (eds.), *Schools and Society: A Sociological Approach to Education*, 3rd ed. (Thousand Oaks, CA: Pine Forge Press, 2008), pp. 106–118.

INGERSOLL, RICHARD M., and ELIZABETH MERRILL "The Status of Teaching as a Profession," in Jeanne H. Ballantine and Joan Z. Spade (eds.), *Schools and Society: A Sociological Approach to Education*, 4th ed. (Thousand Oaks, CA: Sage/Pine Forge Press, 2012b), pp. 185–198.

INGERSOLL, RICHARD M., and THOMAS M. SMITH "The Wrong Solution to the Teacher Shortage," *Educational Leadership*, May 2003, pp. 30–33.

INKELES, ALEX "National Differences in Scholastic Performance," in Philip G. Altbach, Robert R. Arnove, and Gail P. Kelly (eds.), *Comparative Education* (New York: Macmillan, 1982), pp. 210–231 (esp. p. 228).

INKELES, ALEX, and DAVID H. SMITH *Becoming Modern: Individual Change in Six Developing Countries* (Cambridge MA: Harvard University Press, 1974), pp. 19–32.

IRWIN, ELIZABETH, and LEWIS MARKS *Fitting the School to the Child* (New York: Macmillan, 1924).

Inside Higher Education, "Doctorate Production Continues to Grow," Copyright 2008. Available: http://www.insidehighered.com/news/2008/11/24/ doctorates (Retrieved October 13, 2010).

Institute for International Education, "Record Numbers of International Students in U.S. Higher Education," Copyright 2009a. Available: http://www.iie.org/en/ Who-We-Are/News-and-Events/Press-Center/ Press-Releases/2009/2009-11-16-Open-Doors- 2009-International-Students-in-the-US (Retrieved October 13, 2010).

Institute of International Education, "Americans Study Abroad in Increasing Numbers," Copyright 2009b. Available: http://www.iie.org/en/ Who-We-Are/News-and-Events/Press-Center/ Press-Releases/2009/ (Retrieved October 13, 2010).

International Baccalaureate, "What is the International Baccalaureate?" 2005–2007. Available: http://www.ibo.org/who/index.cfm (Retrieved July 10, 2007).

JACKSON, PHILIP W. *Life in Classrooms* (New York: Holt, Rinehart and Winston, 1968).

JACKSON, PHILIP W., ROBERT E. BOOSTROM, and DAVID T. HANSEN *The Moral Life of Schools* (San Francisco, CA: Jossey-Bass, 1993).

JACOBOWITZ, ROBIN, MERYLE G. WEINSTEIN, CINDY MAGUIRE, MICHAEL LUEKENS, and NORM FRUCHTER *The Effectiveness of Small High Schools, 1994–95 to 2003–04* (New York: Institute for Education and Social Policy, New York University, 2007).

JACOBS, JERRY A. "Gender Inequality and Higher Education," *Annual Review of Sociology* (Palo Alto, CA: Annual Reviews, 1996), pp. 153–185.

JACOBSON, LINDA "Polls Find Growing Support for Publicly Funded Vouchers," *Education Week*, Vol. 22, September 4, 2002, p. 7.

JASCHIK, SCOTT "Surge in Distance Education at Community Colleges," *Inside Higher Education*, April 16, 2007. Available: http://www. insidehighered.com/news/2007/04/16/aacc (Retrieved April 3, 2011).

JENCKS, CHRISTOPHER, and DAVID RIESMAN *The Academic Revolution* (Garden City, NY: Doubleday, 1968).

JENCKS, CHRISTOPHER, and MEREDITH PHILLIPS (eds.) *The Black-White Test Score Gap* (Washington, DC: Brooking Institution Press, 1998).

JENCKS, CHRISTOPHER, ET AL. *Inequality: A Reassessment of the Effects of Family and Schooling in America* (New York: Basic Books, 1972).

JENCKS, CHRISTOPHER, ET AL. *Who Gets Ahead? The Determinants of Economic Success in America* (New York: Basic Books, 1979).

JENNINGS, JENNIFER "School Choice or Schools' Choice: Managing in an Era of Accountability," *Sociology of Education*, Vol. 83, No. 3, 2010, pp. 227–247.

JENKINS, MELVIN "Factors Which Influence the Success or Failure of American Indian/Native American College Students," *Research and Teaching in Developmental Education*, Vol. 15, No. 2, Spring 1999, pp. 49–53.

JENSEN, ARTHUR R. "How Much Can We Boost IQ and Scholastic Achievement?" *Harvard Educational Review*, Vol. 30, 1969, pp. 1–123.

JIBRIL, MUNZALI "Country Higher Education Profile: Nigeria," Copyright 2004. Available: http://www.bc. edu/bc_org/avp/soe/cihe/inhea/profiles/Nigeria.htm (Retrieved July 10, 2007).

JOHNSON, D. "Gambling Helps Tribe Invest in Education and the Future," *The New York Times*, February 21, 1995, pp. A1, A12.

JOHNSON, JULIA OVERTURF *Who's Minding the Kids? Child Care Arrangements: Winter 2002* (Washington, DC: U.S. Census Bureau, October 2005).

JOHNSON, WILLIAM L., ANABEL M. JOHNSON, DOUGLAS A. KRANCH, and KURT J. ZIMMERMAN "The Development of a University Version of the Charles F. Kettering Climate Scale," *Educational and Psychological Measurement*, Vol. 59, No. 2, April 1999, pp. 336–350.

JOHNSTON, JEROME "Channel One: The Dilemma of Teaching and Selling," *Phi Delta Kappan*, Vol. 76, February 1995, pp. 437–442.

JONES, JAMES D. "Tracking in the 1990s," paper presented at the American Sociological Association, New York, August 1996.

JONES, JAMES D., BETH E. VANFOSSEN, and MARGARET E. ENSMINGER "Individual and Organizational Predictors of High School Track Placement," *Sociology of Education*, Vol. 68, No. 4, October 1995, pp. 287–300.

JONES, STEVEN P., and KARLA J. SMART "Humanness Under Assault: An Essay Questioning Technology in the Classroom," *Bulletin of Science, Technology, and Society*, Vol. 18, No. 2, May 1998, pp. 87–95.

JORDON, ELLEN "Fighting Boys and Fantasy Play: The Construction of Masculinity in the Early Years of School," *Gender and Education*, Vol. 7, No. 1, March 1995, pp. 69–86.

JUNE, AUDREY WILLIAMS "Administrators' Pay Rises 4%, Beating Inflation for the 10th Consecutive Year," *The Chronicle of Higher Education*, Vol. 53, No. 26, March 2, 2007, p. A30.

KAFKA, JUDITH "Thinking Big About Getting Small: An Ideological Genealogy of Small School Reform," *Teachers College Record*, Vol. 110, No. 9, 2008, pp. 1802–1836.

KAHLENBERG, RICHARD D. *All Together Now: Creating Middle-Class Schools Through Public School Choice* (Washington, DC: Brookings Institution Press, 2001).

KAHNE, JOSEPH E., SUSAN E. SPORTE, MARISA DE LA TORRE, and JOHN Q. EASTON "Small High Schools on a Large Scale: The Impact of School Conversions in Chicago," *Educational Evaluation and Policy Analysis*, Vol. 30, No. 3, September 2006, pp. 281–315.

KALEKIN-FISHMAN, DEVORAH "Latent Messages: The Acoustical Environments of Kindergartens in Israel and West Germany," *Sociology of Education*, Vol. 64, No. 3, July 1991, pp. 209–222.

KALMIJN M., and GERBERT KRAAYKAMP "Race, Cultural Capital, and Schooling: An Analysis of Trends in the United States," *Sociology of Education*, Vol. 69, No. 1, January 1996, pp. 22–34.

KAMENS, DAVID H., JOHN W. MEYER, and AARON BENAVOT "Worldwide Patterns in Academic Secondary Education Curricula, 1920–1990," *Comparative Education Review*, Vol. 40, May 1996, pp. 106–120, 824.

KANE, THOMAS J., and CECILIA E. ROUSE "The Community College: Educating Students at the Margin Between College and Work," *Journal of Economic Perspectives*, Vol. 13, No. 1, 1999, pp. 63–84.

KANTOR, HARVEY "In Retrospect: David Tyack's The One Best System," *Reviews in American History*, Vol. 29, No. 2, June 2001, pp. 319–327.

KARABEL, JEROME, and ALBERT H. HALSEY *Power and Ideology in Education* (New York: Oxford University Press, 1977).

KAREN, DAVID "Toward a Political-Organizational Model of Gate Keeping: The Case of Elite Colleges," *Sociology of Education*, Vol. 63, No. 4, October 1990, pp. 227–240.

KAREN, DAVID "Achievement and Ascription in Admission to an Elite College: A Political-Organizational Analysis," *Sociological Forum*, Vol. 6, No. 2, June 1991, pp. 349–380.

KAREN, DAVID, and KEVIN J. DOUGHERTY "Necessary but Not Sufficient: Higher Education as a Strategy of Social Mobility," in Gary Orfield, Patricia Marin, and Catherine L. Horn (eds.), *Higher Education and the Color Line* (Cambridge, MA: Harvard University Press, 2005).

KASTL, TAMARA "Upward Bound Experience: Water, Wind and Wisdom," *Winds of Change*, Vol. 12, No. 4, Autumn 1997, pp. 71–72.

KATE PHILLIPPO "Teachers Providing Social and Emotional Support: A Study of Advisor Role Enactment in Small High Schools," *Teachers College Record*, Vol. 112, No. 8, August 2010, pp. 2258–2293.

KATI, HAYCOCK, MARY LYNCH, and JENNIFER ENGLE *Opportunity Adrift: Our Flagship Universities are Straying from Their Public Mission* (Washington, DC.: The Education Trust, 2010).

KATZ, SUSAN ROBERTA "Presumed Guilty: How Schools Criminalize Latino Youth," *Social Justice*, Vol. 24, No. 4, 1997, pp. 77–95.

KEIFER, A. K., and D. SEKAQUAPTEWA "Implicit Stereotypes, Gender Identification, and Math-Related Outcomes: A Prospective Study of Female College Students," *Psychological Science*, Vol. 18, No. 1, 2007, pp. 13–18.

KEISTER, L. A., and S. MOLLER "Wealth Inequality in the U.S.," *Annual Review of Sociology*, Vol. 26, 2000, pp. 63–81.

KELLER, B. "Philadelphia Launches Campaign to Diversify Staffs," *Education Week*, Vol. 25, No. 33, April 26, 2006, p. 15.

KERBO, HAROLD R. *Social Stratification and Inequality: Class Conflict in Historical, Comparative, and Global Perspective* (Boston, MA: McGraw-Hill, 2000).

KERCKHOFF, ALAN C. "Education and Social Stratification Processes in Comparative Perspective," *Sociology of Education*, Vol. 74, 2001, pp. 3–18 (Extra Issue: Current of Thought: Sociology of Education at the Dawn of the 21st Century).

KERCKHOFF, ALAN C., RICHARD T. CAMPBELL, JERRY M. TROTT, and VERED KRAUS "The Transmission of Socioeconomic Status and Prestige in Great Britain and the United States," *Sociological Forum*, Vol. 4, No. 2, 1989, pp. 155–177.

KEVAN, SIMON M., and JOHN D. HOWES "Climatic Conditions in Classrooms," *Educational Review*, Vol. 32, No. 3, 1980, pp. 514–525.

"Key Issues: Improving the Working Environment of Teachers," 2008. Available: http://www.tqsource.org/strategies/artist/Environment.pdf (Retrieved March 13, 2008).

KILGORE, SALLY B. "The Organizational Context of Tracking in Schools," *American Sociological Review*, Vol. 56, No. 2, April 1991, pp. 201–202.

KING, EDITH W. *Teaching Ethnic and Gender Awareness,* 2nd ed. (Dubuque, IA: Kendall/Hunt, 1990).

KING, EDITH W. *Looking into the Lives of Children: A Worldwide View* (Albert Park, Australia: James Nicholas Publishers, 1999).

KING, EDMUND J. *Other Schools and Ours: Comparative Studies for Today,* 5th ed. (London: Holt, Rinehart and Winston, 1979).

KINNEY, DAVID A. "From Nerds to Normals: The Recovery of Identity Among Adolescents from Middle School to High School," *Sociology of Education,* Vol. 66, No. 1, January 1993, pp. 21–40.

KIRBY, DOUGLAS "Making Condoms Available in Schools," *Western Journal of Medicine,* Vol. 172, No. 3, March 2000, pp. 149–151.

KIRP, D. L. *Shakespeare, Einstein, and the Bottom Line: The Marketplace of Higher Education* (Cambridge, MA: Harvard University Press, 2003).

KITSANTAS, ANASTASIA, HERBERT W. WARE, and ROSARIO MARTINEZ-ARIAS "Students' Perceptions of School Safety: Effects by Community, School Environment, and Substance Use Variables," *The Journal of Early Adolescence,* Vol. 24, No. 4, 2004, pp. 412–430.

KLEINER, ANNE, and LAURIE LEWIS *Internet Access in U.S. Public Schools and Classrooms: 1994–2002.* NCES 2004-011. U.S. Department of Education Statistics (Washington, DC: National Center for Education Statistics, 2003).

KLINGNER, JANETTE K., ALFREDO J. ARTILES, ELIZABETH KOZLESKI, BETH HARRY, SHELLEY ZION, WILLIAM TATE, GRACE ZAMORA DURÁN, and DAVID RILEY "Addressing the Disproportionate Representation of Culturally and Linguistically Diverse Students in Special Education Through Culturally Responsive Educational Systems," *Education Policy Analysis Archives,* Vol. 13, No. 38, 2005. Available: http://epaa.asu.edu/epaa/v13n38/ (Retrieved April 3, 2011).

KOHLRAUSCH, BETTINA, and MEIKE BAAS. "Unintended Outcomes of Vocational Training in Germany," papers presented at the International Sociological Association World Congress of Sociology, Sweden, July 2010.

KOMOSKI, KEN "21st Century Teachers and Learners: Prosumers in a Bi-literate Knowledge-Driven World," paper presented at AACE-SITE 2007Annual Conference, San Antonio, TX, 2007, March 25, 2007.

KORB, LAWRENCE *Sensible Budget Priorities for America's Children* (Washington, DC: General Accounting Office, Center for Defense Information, 2001).

KOZOL, JONATHAN *Savage Inequalities: Children in America's Schools* (New York: Crown Publishers, 1991), pp. 65–66, 88–89.

KRAATZ, MATTHEW S., and EDWARD J. ZAJAC "Exploring the Limits of the New Institutionalism: The Causes and Consequences of Illegitimate Organizational Change," *American Sociological Review,* Vol. 61, No. 5, 1996, pp. 812–836.

KRAFT, CHRISTINE L. "What Makes a Successful Black Student on a Predominantly White Campus?" *American Educational Research Journal,* Vol. 28, No. 2, Summer 1991, pp. 423–443.

KRAFT, RICHARD, JEANNE BALLANTINE, and DANIEL E. GARVEY "Study Abroad or International Travel? The Case of Semester at Sea," *Phi Beta Delta International Review,* Vol. 4, Fall 1993/Spring 1994, pp. 23–62.

KREIDER, ROSE M., and DIANA B. ELLIOTT *American's Families and Living Arrangements, 2007* (Washington DC: U. S. Census, P20–561, 2009).

KUH, G. D., J. KINZIE, J. A. BUCKLEY, and B. K. BRIDGES *Piecing Together the Student Success Puzzle* (San Francisco, CA: Jossey-Bass and ASHE Higher Education Report Series, 2007).

KULIS, STEPHEN "Gender Segregation Among College and University Employees," *Sociology of Education,* Vol. 70, No. 2, April 1997, pp. 151–173.

KWONG, JULIA "The Reemergence of Private Schools in Socialist China," *Comparative Education Review,* Vol. 43, No. 3, August 1997, pp. 244–259.

LABAREE, DAVID F. "Public Goods, Private Goods: The American Struggle Over Educational Goals," *American Educational Research Journal,* Vol. 34, No. 1, 1997, pp. 39–81.

LAGEMANN, ELLEN CONDLIFFE, and LEE S. SHULMAN *Issues in Education Research: Problems and Prospects* (San Francisco, CA: Jossy-Bass, 1999).

LAIRD, JENNIFER, GREGORY KIENZI, MATTHEW DEBELL, and CHRIS CHAPMAN *Dropout Rates in the United States: 2005* (Washington, DC: National Center for Educational Statistics, 2007), NCES 2007–059.

LAKE, ROBERT "An Indian Father's Plea," *Teacher Magazine,* Vol. 2, September 1990, pp. 48–53.

LAM, SHI FONG *How the Family Influences Children's Academic Achievement* (New York: Garland Publishing, Inc., 1997). ERIC # ED411095.

LAREAU, ANNETTE *Home Advantage: Social Class and Parental Intervention in Education,* 2nd ed. (Lanham, MD: Rowman Littlefield, 2000).

LAREAU, ANNETTE *Unequal Childhoods: Class, Race and Family Life* (Berkeley, CA: University of California Press, 2003).

LAREAU, ANNETTE, and ERIN MCNAMARA HORVAT "Moments of Social Inclusion and Exclusion: Race, Class, and Cultural Capital in Family-School

Relations," *Sociology of Education*, Vol. 72, No. 1, January 1999, pp. 37–53.

LARSON, EDWARD J. *Evolution: The Remarkable History of a Scientific Theory* (New York: Modern Library Chronicles, 2004).

LAUEN, DOUGLAS LEE "Contextual Explanations of School Choice," *Sociology of Education*, Vol. 80, No. 3, 2007, pp. 179–209.

LAZEAR, DAVID G. *Seven Ways of Knowing: Teaching for Multiple Intelligences* (Bloomington, IN: Phi Delta Kappa Educational Foundation, 1992).

LEAL, DAVID L., VALERIE MARTINEZ-EBERS, and KENNETH J. MEIER "The Politics of Latino Education: The Biases of At-Large Elections," *The Journal of Politics*, Vol. 66, No. 4, 2004, pp. 1224–1244.

Learning to Fail: Case Studies of Students at Risk (Bloomington, IN: Phi Delta Kappan, 1991).

LEATHERMAN, COURTNEY "Despite Their Gripes, Professors Are Generally Pleased with Careers, Poll Finds," *The Chronicle of Higher Education*, Vol. 46, March 3, 2000, p. A19.

LEE, STACEY J. *Unraveling the "Model Minority" Stereotype: Listening to Asian Youth* (New York: Teachers College Press, 1996).

LEE, STACEY J. *Up Against Whiteness: Race, School, and Immigrant Youth* (New York: Teachers College Press, 2005).

LEE, VALERIE E. "Effects of High School Restructuring and Size on Early Gains in Achievement and Engagement," *Sociology of Education*, Vol. 68, No. 4, October 1995, pp. 241–270.

LEE, VALERIE E., and DAVID T. BURKAM *Inequality at the Starting Gate: Social Background Differences in Achievement as Children Begin School* (Washington, DC: Economic Policy Institute, 2002).

LEE, VALERIE E., and DOUGLAS D. READY *Schools Within Schools: Possibilities and Pitfalls of High School Reform* (New York: Teachers College Press, 2007).

LEE, VALERIE. E., and HELEN M. MARKS "Who Goes Where? Choice of Single-Sex and Coeducational Independent Secondary Schools," *Sociology of Education*, Vol. 65, July 1992, pp. 226–253.

LEE, VALERIE E., ROBERT R. DEDRICK, and JULIA B. SMITH "The Effect of the Social Organization of Schools on Teachers' Efficacy and Satisfaction," *Sociology of Education*, Vol. 64, No. 3, July 1991, pp. 190–208.

LEE, VALERIE E., and SUSANNA. LOEB "School Size in Chicago Elementary Schools: Effects on Teachers' Attitudes and Students' Achievement," *American Educational Research Journal*, Vol. 37, No. 1, 2000, pp. 3–31.

LEES, LYNN HOLLEN "Educational Inequality and Academic Achievement in England and France,"

Comparative Education Review, Vol. 38, No. 1, February 1994, p. 86.

LEMANN, NICHOLAS *The Big Test: The Secret History of the American Meritocracy* (New York: Farrar, Strauss and Giroux, 1999).

LEMPERT, TED "School Matters: California Must Raise Latino Student Achievement," Copyright January 22, 2010. Available: http://news.newamericamedia.org/news/view_article.html?article_id=35e7746bf85a81504955d2383c5fd4cc (Retrieved October 10, 2010).

LEVERITT, MARA "School Prayer and Football Games: Don't Sideline the U.S. Constitution," *Church and State*, Vol. 53, January 2000.

LEVIN, HENRY "The Dilemma of Secondary School Comprehensive Reforms in Western Europe," *Comparative Education Review*, Vol. 22, No. 3, 1978, pp. 434–451.

LEVINE, ARTHUR *Beating the Odds: How the Poor Get to College* (San Francisco, CA: Jossey-Bass, 1995).

LEVINE, DANIEL U., and ALLAN C. ORNSTEIN "School Effectiveness and National Reform," *Journal of Teacher Education*, November/December 1993, pp. 335–345.

LEVINE, DANIEL U., and JOYCE STARK "Instructional and Organizational Arrangements That Improve Achievement in Inner City Schools," *Educational Leadership*, Vol. 40, December 1983, pp. 41–46.

LEVINE, DANIEL U., and RAYNA F. LEVINE *Society and Education*, 9th ed. (Boston, MA: Allyn & Bacon, 1996).

LEVINSON, DAVID L. "Human Capital Theory," in David L. Levinson, Peter W. Cookson, Jr., and Alan R. Sadovnik (eds.), *Education and Sociology* (New York: Routledge/Falmer, 2002), pp. 377–380.

LEVITAS, MAURICE *Marxist Perspectives in the Sociology of Education* (London: Routledge, 1974), p. 165.

LEWIN, TAMAR "College Board Tries to Police Use of 'Advance Placement' Label," *New York Times*, July 18, 2007a, p. B7.

LEWIN, TAMAR "States Found to Vary Widely on Education," *The New York Times*, June 8, 2007b. Available: http://www.nytimes.com/2007/06/08/education/08scores.html (Retrieved June 9, 2007).

LEWIN, TAMAR "China is Sending More Students to U.S.," Copyright November 16, 2009. Available: http://www.nytimes.com/2009/11/16/education/16i (Retrieved September 30, 2010).

LI, CHUNLING P. *Duanlie yu suipian: dangdai zhongguo shehui jieceng fenghua shizheng fenxi* (Rupture and Fragment: Positive Analysis on Current China's Social Stratification) (Beijing: Social Sciences Publishing House, 2005a).

LI, CHUNLING P. "Social and Political Changes and Inequality in Educational Opportunities: On the

Impact of Family Background and Institutional Factors on Educational Attainment (1940–2001)," *Social Sciences in China* (English Version) No. 3, 2005b, pp. 62–79.

LINDJORD, DENISE "Smaller Class Size: Raising the Academic Performance of Children from Low- and Moderate-Income Families," *Journal of Early Education and Family Review*, Vol. 6, No. 2, November/December 1998, pp. 6–7.

LINDSAY, GEOFF "Educational Psychology and the Effectiveness of Inclusive Education/ Mainstreaming," *British Journal of Educational Psychology*, Vol. 77, No. 1, 2007, pp. 1–24.

LI, QING "Teachers' Beliefs and Gender Differences in Mathematics: A Review," *Educational Research*, Vol. 41, No. 1, Spring 1999, pp. 63–76.

LI, SHI, and CHUNBING XING "China's Higher Education Expansion and Its Labor Market Consequences," *Discussion Paper No. 4974. May. IZA, Bonn, Germany,* 2010. Available: http://ftp.iza.org/dp4974. pdf (Retrieved October 15, 2010).

LITTLETON, ROOSEVELT *Developmental Education: Are Community Colleges the Solution?* (East Lansing, MI: National Center for Research on Teacher Learning, 1998). ERIC: ED414982.

LIU, XIAOFENG STEVEN, and J. PATRICK MAYER "Teacher's Perceptions of Their Jobs: A Multilevel Analysis of the Teacher Follow-Up Survey for 1994–95," *Teachers College Record*, Vol. 107, 2005, pp. 985–1003.

LLOYD, JANICE "Home Schooling Grows," *USA Today.* Copyright January 4, 2009. Available: http://www. usatoday.com/news/éducation/2009-01-04-home-schooling_N.htm (Retrieved September 25, 2010).

LOMPERIS, ANA MARIA TURNER "Are Women Changing the Nature of the Academic Profession?" *Journal of Higher Education*, Vol. 61, No. 6, November/ December 1990, p. 643.

LOPEZ, SHANE, and SANGEETA AGRAWAL "Teachers Score Higher than Other Professionals in Wellbeing," 2009. Available: http://www.gallup.com/poll/ 124778/teachers-score-higher-professionals.aspx (Retrieved September 21, 2010).

LORTIE, DAN C. *School Principal: Managing in Public* (Chicago, IL: University of Chicago Press, 2009).

LOUGHREY, BERNADETTE "Condoms Do Not Promote Sex in Schools," *ABC Science Online*, 2003. Available: http://www.abc.net.au/science/news/stories/ s866400.htm (Retrieved April 17, 2007).

"Louisiana Creationism Law: A 'Religious Purpose,'" *Education Week*, August 4, 1987, p. 23.

LOVELESS, TOM *The Tracking Wars: State Reform Meets School Policy* (Washington, DC: Brookings Institution Press, 1999).

LRU First Reading (for Legislative Research Unit), "Moment of Silence Laws are Common—and Controversial," Vol. 21, No. 2, January 2008. Available: www.ilga.gov/commission/lru/ Jan2008FristRdg.pdf (Retrieved March 24, 2011).

LUBECK, SALLY "Kinship and Classrooms: An Ethnographic Perspective on Education as Cultural Transmission," *Sociology of Education*, October 1984, p. 230.

LUBECK, SALLY *Sandbox Society: Early Education in Black and White America* (London: Falmer Press, 1985).

LUCAS, SAMUEL R. "Secondary School Track Rigidity in the United States: Existence, Extension, and Equity," paper presented at the American Sociological Association meetings, Pittsburgh, PA, August 1992.

LUCAS, SAMUEL R. *Tracking Inequality: Stratification and Mobility in American High Schools* (New York: Teachers College Press, 1999).

LUO, Y. "The Socialist State and Global Capital: Educational Retrenchment and Crisis in China," *Chinese Education and Society*, Vol. 40, No. 1, 2007, pp. 9–21.

LYND, ROBERT S., and HELEN M. LYND *Middletown: A Study of American Culture* (New York: Harcourt Brace & World, 1929).

LYONS, JAMES E. "How School Principals Perceive Their Roles, Rewards, and Challenges," *ERS Spectrum*, Vol. 17, No. 1, Winter 1999, pp. 18–23.

LYOTARD, J. F. *The Postmodern Condition* (trans. G. Bennington and B. Massumi) (Minneapolis, MN: University of Minnesota Press, 1984).

MACFARLANE, ANN G. "Racial Education Values," *America*, Vol. 17, No. 9, October 1, 1994, pp. 10–12.

MACIONIS, JOHN J. *Society: The Basics*, 5th ed. (Upper Saddle River, NJ: Prentice Hall, 2000), p. 46.

MACLEOD, JAY *Ain't No Makin' It: Aspirations and Attainment in a Low-Income Neighborhood* (Boulder, CO: Westview, 1996).

MACSWAN, J., and K. ROLSTAD "How Language Proficiency Tests Mislead Us About Ability: Implications for English Language Learner Placement in Special Education," *Teachers College Record*, Vol. 108, No. 11, 2006, pp. 2304–2328.

MAEROFF, GENE I. "School Boards in America: Flawed, But Still Significant," *Phi Delta Kappan*, Vol. 91, No. 6, 2010, pp. 31–34.

MAGNER, DENISE K. "Wellesley Rethinks Its Multicultural Requirement," *The Chronicle of Higher Education*, Vol. 41, No. 33, April 28, 1995, pp. A45, 47–48.

MANN, HORACE *The Twelfth Annual Report, 1848, in Life and Works of Horace Mann*, Vol. IV (New York: C. T. Dillingham, 1891).

MANSKI, CHARLES F. "Educational Choice (Vouchers) and Social Mobility," *Institute for Research on Poverty* (Madison, WI: University of Wisconsin, June 1992).

MANZO, KENNEDY K. "Students Taking More Demanding Courses," *Education Week*, Vol. 26, No. 25, February 28, 2007, pp. 1–2.

Maps of the World, "Countries with the Lowest Percent of Children in Primary School," Copyright 2006. Available: http://www.mapsofworld.com/world-top-ten/countries-with-lowest-percentage-of-childeren-of-primary-schoolmap.html (Retrieved October 12, 2010).

MARGARY MARTIN, EDWARD FERGUS, and PEDO NOGUERA (eds.) *The Academic Characteristics of Black and Latino Boys that Matter in Achievement: An Exploratory Achievement Model of Boys in Single-Sex Schools* (New York: Metropolitan Center for Urban Education, 2010).

MARGOLIS, ERIC (ed.) *The Hidden Curriculum of Higher Education* (New York: Routledge, 2001).

MARKLEIN, MARY BETH "All U.S. College Accept ACT," *USA Today*, March 19, 2007. Life, p. 01d.

MARSCHALL, MELISSA. "Parental Involvement and Educational Outcomes for Latino Students," *The Review of Policy Research*, Vol. 23, No. 5, 2006, pp. 1053–1076.

MARTIN, MARGARY, EDWARD FERGUS, and PEDRO NOGUERA (eds.), *The Academic Characteristics of Black and Latino Boys that Matter in Achievement: An Exploratory Achievement Model of Boys in Single-Sex Schools* (New York: Metropolitan Center for Urban Education). Available: https://steinhardt.nyu.edu/scmsAdmin/uploads/006/097/Academic_Model_Final_Research_Brief.PDF (Retrieved September 20, 2010).

MARTIN, MICHEL, and CLAUDIO SANCHEZ "Religion a Big Part of the Charter School Debate," June 16, 2009. Available: www.npr.org/templates/story/story.php?storyId=105461721 (Retrieved September 25, 2010).

MARTIN, KARIN A. "Becoming a Gendered Body: Practices of Preschools," *American Sociological Review*, Vol. 63, 1998, pp. 494–511.

MARVEL, JOHN, DEANNA M. LYTER, PIA PELTOLA, GREGORY A. STRIZEK, and BETH A. MORTON *Teacher Attrition and Mobility: Results from the 2004–2005 Teacher Follow-up Survey* (Washington, DC: National Center for Education Statistics, January 2007).

MARX, ALEXANDRA, URS FUHRER, and TERRY HARTIG "Effects of Classroom Seating Arrangements on Children's Question-Asking," *Learning Environments Research*, Vol. 2, No. 1, 1999, pp. 249–263.

MARX, KARL *The Division of Labor in Society* (New York: Macmillan, 1946).

MASLACH, CHRISTINA, WILMAR B. SCHAUFELI, and MICHAEL P. LEITER "Job Burnout," *Annual Review of Psychology*, Vol. 52, February 2001, pp. 397–422.

MASLOW, ABRAHAM H *Toward a Psychology of Being* (New York: Van Nostrand Reinhold, 1962).

MAURO, TONY "Supreme Court Bans Student-led Prayer at Football Games," 2000. Available: http://www.freedomforum.org/templates/documents.asp?document ID=12727 (Retrieved May 10, 2007).

MAXWELL, LESLI A. "No Clear Edge for Charter Schools Found in 15-State Study; More Successes Seen in charter Schools Serving Disadvantaged Students," *Education Week*, Vol. 29, No. 36, July 14, 2010, p. 14.

MCANDREWS, TOBIN, and WENDELL ANDERSON "Schools within Schools," 2002. *ERIC Digest* (Ed461915). Available: http://eric.ed.gov/ERICWebPortal/custom/portlets/recordDetails/detailmini.jsp? (Retrieved April 3, 2011).

MCCABE, D. "Academic Dishonesty Among High School Students," *Adolescence*, Vol. 34, No. 136, 1999, pp. 681–687.

MCCOLLUM, PAM, ALBERT CORTEZ, OANH H. MARONEY, and FELIX MONTES *Failing Our Children: Finding Alternatives to In-Grade Retention* (San Antonio, TX: Intercultural Development Research Association, 1999).

MCDERMOTT, DANA R. "Building Better Human Connections: Parenting/Caring Education for Children and Teens in School," *Childhood Education*, Vol. 80, Winter 2003/2004. Available: http://findarticles.com/p/articles/mi_qa3614/is_200301/ai_n9226234/ (Retrieved April 3, 2011).

MCDILL, EDWARD L., ET AL. "Institutional Effects on the Academic Behavior of High School Students," *Sociology of Education*, Vol. 40, 1967, pp. 181–199.

MCDONALD, LAUREN E. "Boston Public School White Enrollment Decline: White Flight of Demographic Factors?" *Equity and Excellence in Education*, Vol. 30, No. 3, December 1997, pp. 21–30.

MCDONALD, MICHAEL "Amherst-to-Yale Funding Need Follows Harvard's Crisis Over Cash," September 23, 2010. Bloomberg.Com

MCDONOUGH, PATRICIA M. *Choosing Colleges: How Social Class and Schools Structure Opportunity* (Albany, NY: State University of New York Press, 1997).

MCENEANEY, ELIZABETH H. "The Worldwide Cachet of Scientific Literacy," *Comparative Education Review*, Vol. 47, No. 2, 2003, pp. 217–237.

MCEVOY, ALAN "Interview with Dr. Edward McDill," *School Intervention Report*, Vol. 1, No. 5, February 1988, p. 7.

MCEVOY, ALAN "Confronting Gangs," *School Intervention Report*, Vol. 3, February–March 1990, pp. 1–20.

McEvoy, Alan *When Disaster Strikes* (Holmes Beach, FL: Learning Publications, 1992).

McEvoy, Alan "The Revelance of Theory to the Safe Schools Movement," *Education and Urban Society*, Vol. 31, No. 3, May 1999, pp. 275–285.

McEvoy, Alan, and Robert Welker "Antisocial Behavior, Academic Failure, and School Climate: A Critical Review," *Journal of Emotional and Behavioral Disorders*, Vol. 8, June 2000, pp. 130–140.

McFarland, Daniel A. "Student Resistance: How the Formal and Informal Organization of Classrooms Facilitates Everyday Forms of Student Defiance," *American Journal of Sociology*, Vol. 107, No. 3, 2001, pp. 612–678.

McFarland, Daniel A. "When Tensions Mount: Conceptualizing Classroom Situations and the Condition of Student-Teacher Conflict," in M. T. Hallinan, A. Gamoran, W. Kubitschek, and T. Loveless (eds.), *Stability and Change in American Education: Process and Outcomes* (Clinton Corners, NJ: Eliot Werner Publications, 2003), pp. 127–152.

McFarland, Daniel A. "Resistance as a Social Drama: A Study of Change-Oriented Encounters," *American Journal of Sociology*, Vol. 109, No. 6, 2004, pp. 1249–1318.

McGlone, M., and J. Aronson "Stereotype Threat, Identity Salience, and Spatial Reasoning," *Journal of Applied Developmental Psychology*, Vol. 27, No. 5, 2006, pp. 486–493.

McGroarty, Mary "The Societal Context of Bilingual Education," *Educational Researcher*, Vol. 21, No. 2, 1992, pp. 7–9.

McGuire, M. E. "What Happened to Social Studies? The Disappearing Curriculum," *Phi Delta Kappan*, Vol. 88, No. 8, April 2007, pp. 620–624.

McLaren, Peter L. "Schooling and the Postmodern Body: Critical Pedagogy and the Politics of Enfleshment," in H. Giroux (ed.), *Postmodernism, Feminism, and Cultural Politics: Redrawing Educational Boundaries* (New York: Suny Press, 1991), pp. 144–173.

McLaren, Peter L. "Decentering Whiteness: In Search of a Revolutionary Multiculturalism," *Multicultural Education*, Vol. 5, No. 1, Fall 1997a, pp. 4–11.

McLaren, Peter L. "Unthinking Whiteness, Rethinking Democracy: Or Farewell to the Blonde Beast; Toward a Revoluntionary Multiculturalism," *Educational Foundations*, Vol. 11, No. 2, Spring 1997b, pp. 5–39.

McNabb, Mary, Mark Hawkes, and Ullick Rouk *Critical Issues in Evaluating the Effectiveness of Technology* (Washington, DC: U.S. Department of Education, 1999). Available: http://www.eric.ed.gov/ ERICWebPortal/search/detailmini.jsp?_nfpb=true&_ &ERICExtSearch_SearchValue_0=ED452827&ERIC ExtSearch_SearchType_0=no&accno=ED452827 (Retrieved April 3, 2011).

McNeal, Ralph B. "Are Students Being Pulled Out of High School? The Effect of Adolescent Employment on Dropping Out," *Sociology of Education*, Vol. 70, No. 3, July 1997, pp. 206–220.

McNeely, Connie L. "Prescribing National Education Policies: The Role of International Organizations," *Comparative Education Review*, Vol. 39, No. 4, November 1995, pp. 483–507.

McPartland, James M., and Edward L. McDill "Control and Differentiation in the Structure of American Education," *Sociology of Education*, Vol. 55, No. 2/3, 1982, pp. 77–78.

McPartland, James M., and Saundra Murray Nettles "Using Community Adults as Advocates or Mentors for At-Risk Middle School Students: A Two-Year Evaluation of Project RAISE," *American Journal of Education*, Vol. 99, No. 4, August 1991, pp. 568–586.

McPartland, James M., Russell L. Dawkins, Jomills H. Braddock II, Robert L. Crain, and Jack Strauss "Three Reports: Effects of Employer Job Placement Decisions, and School Desegregation on Minority and Female Hiring and Occupational Attainment," Report 359, Center for Social Organization of Schools (Baltimore, MD: Johns Hopkins University, July 1985).

McPherson, M. S., and M. O. Shapiro *College Access: Opportunity or Privilege?* (New York: Holtzbrink, 2006).

McWilliam, H. O. A., and M. A. Kwamena-Poh *The Development of Education in Ghana* (Harlow, Essex, England: Longman, 1975).

"Meeting Basic Learning Needs" (New York: World Conference on Education for All, 1990), p. ix.

Medina, Jennifer "On New York School Tests, Warning Signs Ignored," *The New York Times*, October 10, 2010.

Mehan, Hugh "Understanding Inequality in Schools: The Contribution of Interpretive Studies," in Jeanne H. Ballantine and Joan Z. Spade (eds.), *Schools and Society* (Belmont, CA: Wadsworth, 2001).

Meier, Deborah "As Though They Owned the Place: Small Schools as Membership Communities," *Phi Delta Kappan*, Vol. 87, No. 9, May 2006, pp. 657–662.

Mekosh-Rosenbaum, Victoria, Joan Z. Spade, and George P. White "Effects of Homogeneous and Heterogeneous Groupings on Classroom Environment and Achievement in Middle Schools," unpublished manuscript, 1996.

Mendick, Heather "A Beautiful Myth? The Gendering of Being/Doing 'Good at Maths,'" *Gender and Education*, Vol. 17, No. 2, 2005, pp. 203–219.

MENEHAN, KELSEY *Researchers Look at Which School-based Drug Education Programs are Most Effective* (Princeton, NJ: Robert Wood Johnson Foundation, 2007).

MERTON, ROBERT K. "Social Structure and Anomie," in Robert K. Merton (ed.), *Social Theory and Social Structure*, Revised and Enlarged Edition (New York: The Free Press, 1957), pp. 131–160.

MERTZ, N. T., and S. R. McNEELY "Women on the Job: A Study of Female High School Principals," *Educational Administrative Quarterly*, Vol. 34, 1998, pp. 196–222.

MESSERLI, JOE "Should K-12 Students Be Required to Complete State-sanctioned Minimum Skills Tests?" 2003. Available: http://www.balancedpolitics.org/school_testing.htm (Retrieved April 23, 2007).

METZ, MARY H. *Classroom and Corridors: The Crisis of Authority in Desegregated Secondary Schools* (Berkeley, CA: University of California Press, 1978).

METZ, MARY H. "Real School: A Universal Drama Amidst Disparate Experience," in Douglas E. Mitchell and Margaret E. Goertz (eds.), *Education Politics for the New Century: The 20th Anniversary Yearbook of the Politics of Education Association* (London: Falmer Press, 1990), pp. 75–92, ERIC 319140.

METZ, MARY H. "Desegregation as Necessity and Challenge," *The Journal of Negro Education*, Vol. 63, No. 1, 1994, pp. 64–76.

MEYER, JOHN W., and BRIAN ROWAN "The Structure of Educational Organizations," Chapter 4 in Marshall W. Meyer and Associates, *Environments and Organizations: Theoretical and Empirical Perspectives* (San Francisco, CA: Jossey-Bass, 1978), pp. 78–109.

MEYER, JOHN W., DAVID H. KAMENS, and AARON BENAVOT *School Knowledge for the Masses* (Cambridge, MA: American Academy of Arts and Sciences, 1992).

MEYER, JOHN W., DAVID TYACK, JOANE NAGEL, and AUDRI GORDON "Publlic Education as Nation Building in America: Enrollments and Bureaucratization in the American States, 1870–1930," *American Journal of Sociology*, Vol. 85, No. 3, 1979, pp. 591–613.

MEYER, JOHN W., ET AL. *School Knowledge for the Masses: World Models and National Primary Curricular Categories in the Twentieth Century* (Washington, DC: Falmer Press, 1992).

MEYER, JOHN W., FRANCISCO RAMIREZ, and YASMIN N. SOYSAL "World Expansion of Mass Education, 1870–1980," *Sociology of Education*, Vol. 65, 1992, pp. 128–149.

Michigan Department of Education, "What Research Says about Parent Involvement in Children's Education in Relation to Academic Achievement," 2001. Available: www.michigan.gov/ . . . /Final_Parent_Involvement_Fact_Sheet_14732_7.pdf (Retrieved September 20, 2010).

Michigan Department of Education: Decision Making Yardstick 2001. "What Research Says About Parent Involvement in Children's Education," Copyright 2002. Available: http://pili.wiki.educ.msu.edu/TIB+-+FEP+-+TFK+-+Parent+Communication (Retrieved April 3, 2011).

Michigan Department of Education, "What Research Says on Parent Involvement in Children's Education," 2007. Available: www.education.com/reference/article/Ref_What_Research_Says/ (Retrieved September 25, 2010).

MICKELSON, ROSLYN ARLIN "Gender, Bourdieu, and the Anomaly of Women's Achievement Redux," *Sociology of Education*, Vol. 76, No. 4, 2003, pp. 373–375.

MICKELSON, ROSLYN ARLIN, and ANNE E. VELASCO "Mothers and Daughters Go to Work: The Relationship of Mothers' Occupations to Daughters' Career Aspirations," paper presented at the annual meeting of the American Educational Research Association, San Diego, California, 1998.

MILLER, CLAIRE CAIN, and GERALDINE FABRIKANT "Beyond the Ivied Halls, Endowments Suffer," *The New York Times*, November 26, 2008.

MILLER, C. M. L., and M. PARLETT "Cue-Consciousness," in Martyn Hammersley and Peter Woods (eds.), *The Process of Schooling: A Sociological Reader* (London: Routledge, 1976), pp. 143–149.

MILLS, C. WRIGHT *The Sociological Imagination* (New York: Grove Press, 1959).

Ministry of Education China, 2008. Available: www.moe.edu.cn/english/ministry-f.htm (Retrieved March 28, 2008).

Ministry of Education of PRC, "2005 nian quanguo jiaoyu shiye fashan tongji gongbao" ("The 2005 Educational Development Statistics Bulletin of the People's Republic of China"), 2006. Available: http://www.moe.gov.cn/edoas/website18/info29052.htm (Retrieved July 20, 2007).

Ministry of Education of PRC, "The 11th Five-Year Plan for China's Educational Development Outline," 2007. Available: http://www.moe.gov.cn/edoas/website18/info28667.htm (Retrieved July 20, 2007).

Ministry of Education of PRC, "The 9th 5-year Plan for China's Educational Development and the Development Outline by 2010," 2010. Available: 202.205.177.9/edoas/website18/en/planning_n.htm (Retrieved March 28, 2011).

Ministry of Education of the PRC and UNESCO, "China's Quiet Educaton Revolution," 2010. Available: www.moe.edu.cn/edoas.en/ (Retrieved October 2, 2010).

Miniwatts Marketing Group, "Internet World Stats," 2008. Available: http://www.internetworldstats.com/stats.htm (Retrieved July 7, 2008).

"Monitoring the Future Study, 1999" (University of Michigan, Survey Research Center, Institute for Social Research, 1999). Available: http://www.hunter.cuny.edu/socwork/nrcfcpp/downloads/ip-ppdaf.pdf (Retrieved April 3, 2011).

MONK-TURNER, ELIZABETH "Factors Shaping the Probability of Community vs. Four-Year College Entrance and Acquisition of the B.A. Degree," unpublished manuscript, 1992a.

MONK-TURNER, ELIZABETH "Is Going to a Community College Better than Not Going to College at All?" unpublished manuscript, 1992b.

MOONEY, CAROLYN J. "Academic Group Fighting the 'Politically Correct Left' Gains Momentum," *The Chronicle of Higher Education*, December 12, 1990, p. A13.

MOORE, DAVID W. *Americans Support Teaching Creationism as well as Evolution in Public Schools* (Princeton, NJ: Gallup News Service, August 30, 1999).

MOORE, JOAN, and RAQUEL PINDERHUGHES (eds.) *In the Barrios: Latinos and the Underclass Debate* (New York: Russell Sage Foundation, 1993).

MOORE, ROB, and JOHN TRENWITH "The Intergenerational Dimension of Credentialisation and Its Implications for Vocational Change in Education," *Journal of Education and Work*, Vol. 10, No. 1, March 1997, pp. 59–71.

MORENO, JOSE F., DARYL G. SMITH, SHARON PARKER, ALMA R. CLAYTON-PEDERSON, and DANIEL HIROYUKI *Multiple Lenses: An Examination of the Economic and Racial/Ethnic Diversity of College Students* (San Francisco, CA: The James Irvine Foundation, 2006).

MORGAN, NEVILLE N. "Race and Gender Differences in Support of Collective Bargaining by College and University Faculty," *Dissertation Abstracts International*, Vol. 52, No. 7–A, January 1992, pp. 2719–2720.

MORGAN, WILLIAM R., and J. MICHAEL ARMER "Islamic and Western Educational Expansion in a West African Society: A Cohort Comparison Analysis," paper presented at American Sociological Association meetings, Chicago, August 1987.

MORNA, COLLEEN LOWE "Africa's Campuses Lead Pro-Democracy Drives," *The Chronicle of Higher Education*, Vol. 37, No. 13, November 28, 1990, pp. A1, A40.

MORSE, JODIE, ANN BLACKMAN, DAN CRAY, MITCH FRANK, and MAGGIE SIEGER "Is That Your Final Answer?" *Time*, Vol. 155, No. 25, June 19, 2000. Available: http://web.ebscohost.com.exproxy.libraries.wright.edu:2048/ehost/detail?vid= 5&hid=120 (Retrieved April 23, 2007).

MORTENSON, TOM G. "Segregation of Higher Education Enrollment by Family Income and Race/Ethnicity," *Postsecondary Education Opportunity*, Vol. 160, 2005a, pp. 1–16.

MORTENSON, TOM G. "Family Income and Higher Education Opportunity 1970 to 2003," *Postsecondary Education Opportunity*, No. 162, 2005b, pp. 1–7.

MORTIMORE, PETER, ET AL. *School Matters* (Berkeley, CA: University of California Press, 1988).

MULKEY, LYNN M., ROBERT L. CRAIN, and ALEXANDER J. C. HARRINGTON "One-Parent Households and Achievement: Economic and Behavioral Explanations of a Small Effect," *Sociology of Education*, Vol. 65, No. 1, 1992.

MULLER, CHANDRA "Maternal Employment, Parent Involvement, and Academic Achievement: An Analysis of Family Resources Available to the Child," in *Resources and Actions: Parents, Their Children and Schools*, Report to the National Science Foundation and National Center for Education Statistics, Washington, DC, August 1991.

MULLER, CHANDRA "Gender Differences in Parental Involvement and Adolescents Mathematics Achievement," *Sociology of Education*, Vol. 71, No. 4, 1998, pp. 336–356.

MUNITZ, BARRY "California State University System and First Amendment Rights to Free Speech," *Education*, Vol. 112, No. 1, Fall 1991, p. 4.

MUOLA, J. M. "A Study of the Relationship Between Academic Achievement Motivation and Home Environment Among Standard Eight Pupils," 2010. Available: www.academicjournals.org/ERR2 (Retrieved September 20, 2010).

MYERS, KEN "Denial of Scholarship Case Leaves Some Officials Wondering," *National Law Journal*, Vol. 17, No. 41, June 12, 1995, p. A13.

NAEHCY (National Association for the Education of Homeless Children and Youth), "Facts about Homeless Education," 2009. Available: www.naehcy.org/facts.html (Retrieved September 26, 2010).

NAEP, "Top Mathematics Story for Urban Districts," May 26, 2009. Available: http://namtionsreportcard.gov/math_2009/ (Retrieved October 12, 2010).

NASON, R. BETH "Retaining Children: Is It the Right Decision?" *Childhood Education*, Annual Theme 1991, pp. 300–304.

National Assessment of Adult Literacy (NAAL), "Adults with Below Basic Prose Literacy," 2003. Available: http://nces.ed.gov/naal/kf_demographics.asp (Retrieved July 21, 2007).

National Center for Education Information, "Profile of Teachers in the United States 2005," 2005. Available: www.ncei.com/index.html (Retrieved September 9, 2010).

National Center for Science Education, "Still Trying to Get Creationism in Science Classes," 2010. Available: http://ncse.com (Retrieved August 26, 2010).

National Center on Addiction and Substance Abuse, "27% of Public School Students Report Gangs and Drugs on Campus," August 24, 2010. Available: www.campussafetymagazine.com/Channel/School-Safety/News/2010/08/24/27-of-Public-School-Students-Report-Gangs-and-Drugs-on-Campus.aspx (Retrieved August 26, 2010).

National Commission on Excellence in Education, *A Nation at Risk: The Imperative for Educational Reform: A Report to the Nation and the Secretary of Education, United States Department of Education* (Washington, DC: The Commission, 1983).

National Commission on Teaching and America's Future. *What Matters Most: Teaching for America's Future,* Copyright 1996. Available: http://www.eric.ed.gov/ERICWebPortal/search/detailmini.jsp?_nfpb=true&_&ERICExtSearch_SearchValue_0=ED395931&ERICExtSearch_SearchType_0=no&accno=ED3959 (Retrieved April 3, 2011).

National Education Association, "Tomorrow's Teachers: Help Wanted: Minority Teachers," 2002. Available: http://www.nea.org/tomorrowsteachers/2002/healpwanted.html (Retrieved May 14, 2007).

National Education Association, "Getting Involved in Your Child's Education," 2007. Available: http://www.nea.org/parents/index.html (Retrieved May 10, 2007).

National Endowment for the Arts, "Literary Reading in Dramatic Decline, According to National Endowment for the Arts Survey," 2004. Available: http://www.nea.gov/news/news04/ReadingAtRisk.html (Retrieved April 12, 2007).

National Head Start Association, "Head Start Research," 2007. Available: http://www.nhsa.org/research/research_re_bites_detail.htm (Retrieved April 27, 2007).

National Institute of Health (NIDA), "NIDA InfoFacts: Nationwide Trends 2009," January 2010. Available: www.drugabuse.gov/infofacts/nationtrends.html (Retrieved March 16, 2011).

National Institute on Drug Abuse, "NIDA InfoFacts: High School and Youth Trends," August 2010. Available: www.drugabuse.gov/infofacts/hsy-outhtrends.html (Retrieved August 26, 2010).

National Research Council, *From Neurons to Neighborhoods: The Science of Early Childhood Development* (New York: Carnegie Foundation of New York, 2000).

National Research Council and the Institute of Medicine, *Engaging Schools: Fostering High School Students' Engagement and Motivation to Learn.* Board on Children, Youth, and, Families, Division of Behavioral and Social Sciences and Education (Washington, DC: The National Academies Press, 2004).

National School Board Foundation, *Leadership Matters: Transforming Urban School Boards* (Alexandria, VA: Author, 1999).

National School Safety Center, "Report on School Associated Violent Deaths," Cited in "Violence and Safety," 2002. Available: http://www.schoolsafety.us/media-resources/school-associated-violent-deaths (Retrieved April 3, 2011).

National Science Foundation, *America's Academic Future,* January 1992, pp. 1–4. Available: www.nsf.gov/pubsys/ods/getpub.cfm?nsf91150 (Retrieved April 3, 2011).

National Statistics, "Local Education Authorities (LEAs)/Education and Library Boards," 2009. Available: www.statistics.gov.uk/geography/lea.asp (Retrieved September 29, 2010).

National Survey of Family Growth William and Flora Hewlett Foundation, March 2006. Available: http://www.childtrends.org/file/Facts_2005.pdf (Retrieved April 29, 2007).

National Survey of Student Engagement, 2007. Available: http://www.womenscolleges.org/perspective/nsse-study (Retrieved May 7, 2011).

National Youth Gang Center, "National Youth Gang Survey Analysis," 2007. Available: http://www.iir.com/nygc/nygsa/ (Retrieved February 2, 2008).

Nationmaster.com, "Ghanaian Education Statistics," 2010. Available: www.nationmaster.com/country/gh-ghana/edu-education (Retrieved October 2, 2010).

NATRIELLO, GARY "Failing Grades for Retention," *School Administrator,* Vol. 5, No. 7, August 1998, pp. 14–17.

NATRIELLO, GARY, and EDWARD L. MCDILL "Performance Standards, Student Effort on Homework, and Academic Achievement," *Sociology of Education,* Vol. 59, January 1986, pp. 18–31.

NCES, *National Dropout Statistics Field Test Evaluation* (Washington, DC: U.S. Department of Education, January 1992), p. xi.

NCES, *Student Victimization at School,* p. 4; and *Student Strategies to Avoid Harm at School* (Washington, DC: U.S. Department of Education, October 1995), NCES 95–203 and 95–204.

NCES, "Sources of Supply of Newly Hired Teachers," *The Condition of Education,* 1996. Indicator 56.

NCES, *Digest Educational Statistics*, "Selected Characteristics of Public School Teachers: Spring 1961 to Spring 1996," October 1997, p. 80.

NCES, *Indicators of School Crime and Safety* (Washington, DC: National Center for Education Statistics, 1998), pp. 34–35.

NCES, "Subsequent Educational Attainment of High School Dropouts," *NCES 98–085*, June 1998. Available: http://nces.ed.gov/pubs98/98085.pdf (Retrieved April 3, 2011).

NCES, *Projections of Educational Statistics to 2009*, 1999, pp. ix, 67. Available: http://nces.ed.gov/pubsearch/pubsinfo.asp?pubid=1999038 (Retrieved April 3, 2011).

NCES, "Remedial Education in Higher Education Institutions," *The Condition of Education* (Washington, DC: U.S. Department of Education, 1999), p. 85.

NCES, "Selected Characteristics of Public School Teachers: Spring 1961 to Spring 1996," *Digest of Education Statistics* (Washington, DC: Department of Education, 1999), p. 80, Table 70.

NCES, *Statistics of State School Systems; Revenues and Expenditures for Public Elementary and Secondary Education, and Common Core of Data Surveys* (Washington, DC: U.S. Department of Education, 1999).

NCES, "Elementary and Secondary School Enrollments," May 2000. Available: http://nces.ed.gov/pubs2000/2000008.pdf (Retrieved September 25, 2010).

NCES, "Public Alternative Schools and Programs for Students At Risk of Education Failure: 2000–01," 2000–2001. Available: nces.ed.gov/surveys/frss/publications/2002004/index.asp?sectionID=2 (Retrieved April 20, 2007).

NCES, "Nonfatal Student Victimization-Student Reports," 2001. *Indicators of School Crime and Safety, 2001.* Available: nces.ed.gov/pubs2002/crime2001/2.asp (Retrieved April 20, 2007).

NCES, "Distance Education at Degree-Granting Postsecondary Institutions: 2000–2001," July 2003. U.S. Department of Education, Washington, DC. Available: http://nces.ed.gov/surveys/peqis/publications/2003017/ (Retrieved July 17, 2007).

NCES, *Overview of Public Elementary and Secondary Schools and Districts, 2001–2002* (Washington, DC: U.S. Department of Education, 2003), NCES 2003–411.

NCES, *The Condition of Education 2004* (Washington, DC: U.S. Government Printing Office, 2004), NCES 2004–077.

NCES, "Average ACT Scores by Subject and Race/Ethnicity: 1997 to 2004," August 2005. U.S. Department of Education, Washington, DC.

Available: http://nces.ed.gov/pubs2005/nativetrends/ShowTable.asp?table=tables/table_4_9b.asp (Retrieved July 17, 2007).

NCES, Common Core of Data, "National Public Education Financial Survey" (Washington, DC: U.S. Department of Education, 2005).

NCES, *Digest of Educational Statistics* (Washington, DC: U.S. Department of Education, 2005), NCES 2006030.

NCES, *Status and Trends in the Education of American Indians and Alaska Natives* (Washington, DC: U.S. Department of Education, 2005), NCES 2005–108.

NCES, "Students' Reports of Gangs at School," *Indicators of School Crime and Safety: 2005*, 2005. Available: http://nces.ed.gov/programs/crimeindicators/crimeindicators2005/Indicators.asp?PubPage (Retrieved April 20, 2007).

NCES, "The Condition of Education 2005." U.S. Department of Education, Washington, DC, 2005. Available: http://nces.ed.gov/programs/quarterly/vol_7/1_2/9_1.asp (Retrieved April 13, 2007).

NCES, *Trends in Educational Equity of Girls and Women* (Washington, DC: U.S. Department of Education, 2005), NCES 2005–016.

NCES, *Youth Indicators, 2005* (Washington, DC: U.S. Department of Education, 2005), NCES 2005–050.

NCES, "Indicators of School Crime and Safety: 2006," *National Center for Educational Statistics, U.S. Department of Education, NCES 2007–003.* Copyright 2006. Available: http://nces.ed.gov/pubsearch/pubsinfo.asp?pubid=2007003 (Retrieved April 3, 2011).

NCES, *Projections of Educational Statistics to 2015* (Washington, DC: U.S. Department of Education, 2006), NCES 2006b–084.

NCES, "SAT Score Averages of College-bound Seniors, by Race/Ethnicity," *Digest of Education Statistics: 2005*, June 2006. U.S. Department of Education, Washington, DC. Available: http://nces.ed.gov/programs/digest/d05/tables/dt05_126.asp (Retrieved July 17, 2007).

NCES, "Students Carrying Weapons on School Property and Anywhere," *Indicators of School Crime and Safety: 2006*, 2006. Available: http://nces.ed.gov/programs/crimeindicators/ind_13.asp (Retrieved April 20, 2007).

NCES, The Condition of Education, "Contexts of Elementary and Secondary Education," Indicator 44. Changes in Sources of Public School Revenue, 2006. Available: http://nces.ed.gov/programs/coe/2006/section4/indicator44.asp (Retrieved May 10, 2007).

NCES, "Common Core of Data 2006," 2007. Available: http://nces.ed.gov/ccd/ccddata.asp (Retrieved June 20, 2007).

NCES, "Elementary and Secondary School Enrollment," *Education Statistics Quarterly*, 2007. Available: http://nces.ed.gov/programs/quarterly/vol_2/2_2/q3–3.asp (Retrieved May 11, 2007).

NCES, Encouraging Girls in Math and Science," 2007. Available: http://ies.ed.gov/ncee/wwc/pdf/practiceguides/20072003/pdf (Retrieved May 7, 2011).

NCES, "Trends in International Mathematics and Science Study," 2007. Available: www.nces.ed.gov/timss/results07.asp (Retrieved August 24, 2010).

NCES, "High School Coursetaking: Findings from the Condition of Education," *NCES 2007–065*. 2007. Available: http://nces.ed.gov/pubs2007/2007065.pdf (Retrieved April 3, 2011).

NCES, Institute for Education Sciences, "Overview of Public Elementary and Secondary Students, Staff, Schools, School Districts, Revenues, and Expenditures: School Year 2004–5 and Fiscal Year 2004," 2007. U.S. Department of Education 2007–309 (Washington, DC: U.S. Department of Education, 2007).

NCES, "Projections of Education Statistics to 2010: Elementary and Secondary Teachers," 2007. Available: http://nces.ed.gov/programs/quarterly/Vol_2/2_3/feature_pes2010.asp (Retrieved April 13, 2007).

NCES, *The Condition of Education, 2007* (Washington, DC: U.S. Department of Education, 2007).

NCES, "ACT Test Scores," 2009. Available: http://nces.ed.gov/programs/digest/d09/tables/dt09_147.asp (Retrieved August 27, 2010).

NCES, "Conditions of Education: Special Analysis 2009: International Assessments." Available: http://nces.ed.gov/programs/coe/2009/analysis (Retrieved October 11, 2010).

NCES, *Digest of Educational Statistics, 2009* (Washington, DC: U.S. Department of Education, 2009).

NCES, "Fast Facts: SAT Mean Scores of College-bound Seniors," 2009. Available: http://nces.ed.gov/fastfacts/display.asp?id=171 (Retrieved March 16, 2011).

NCES, "Financing schools," Ch. 2, Table 172. *Digest of Education Statistics*, 2009. Available: www.edreform.com/Fast_Facts/K12_Facts/ (Retrieved September 25, 2010).

NCES, "Number and Percentage of Degree-granting Institutions: SAT and ACT Scores of Enrollees". *Digest of Education Statistics*. Ch. 3, Postsecondary education, Table 329, 2009. Available: http://nces.ed.gov/pgrograms/digest/2009menu_tables.asp (Retrieved March 16, 2011).

NCES, *Projections of Educational Statistics to 2018*, 2009-062 (Washington, DC: U.S. Department of Education). Available: http://nces.ed.gov/programs/projections/projections2018/tables/table_03.asp?referrer=list

NCES, "SAT Test Scores," 2009. Available: http://nces.ed.gov/fastfacts/display.asp?id=171 (Retrieved August 27, 2010).

NCES, "Schools and Staffing Survey (SASS) "Public School Principal Questionnaire," Table 85 Number, highest degree, experience, and salaries of principals in public and private elementary and secondary schools, by selected characteristics, October 2009.

NCES, "Current Expenditure Per Pupil in Fall Enrollment in Public Elementary and Secondary Schools, 2006–2007." *Digest of Education Statistics* 2009, 2010. Available: http://nces.ed.gov/fastfacts/display.asp?id=66 (Retrived August 8, 2010).

NCES, "Elementary and Secondary Schools: Table 245" (Teacher numbers), *Digest of Education Statistics*. Available: www.edreform.com/Fast_Facts/k12_Facts/ (Retrieved September 14, 2010).

NCES, "Fast Facts: Public School Enrollment," 2010. Available: http://nces.ed.gov/programs/coe/2010/section1/table-encl-1.asp (Retrieved September 25, 2010).

NCES, Fast Facts 2010–13. *Digest of Education Statistics*. Available: http://nces.ed.gov/fastfacts/display.asp?id=28 (Retrieved September 21, 2010).

NCES, "Indicators of School Crime and Safety: 2009." Available: http://nces.ed.gov/programs/crimeindicators/crimeindicators2009/key.asp (Retrieved September 13, 2010).

NCES, "Teacher Follow-up Survey: 2008–09: Teacher Attrition and Mobility (Table 246)," 2010. Available: http://nces.ed.gov/surveys/sass/ovrv_whatstfs.asp (Retrieved September 21, 2010).

NCES, *The Condition of Education*, 2010 (Washington, DC: U.S. Department of Education, Table A-19-1, 2010).

NCES, "The Nation's Report Card," 2010. Available: http://nces.ed.gov/nationsreportcard/science/ (Retrieved October 12, 2010).

NEA, "Teaching in America: The Lives of Today's Public School Teachers: Teachers' Attitudes Toward Teaching," May 5, 2010. Available: http://education-portal.com/articles/Teaching_in_America_The_Lives_of_Todays_Public_School_Teachers.html (Retrieved March 23, 2011).

NEE DAULTA, MEENA SIWACH "Impact of Home Environment on the Scholastic Achievement of Children," *Journal of Human Ecology*, Vol. 23, No. 1, 2008, pp. 75–77.

NEILL, A. S. *Summerhill: A Radical Approach to Child Rearing* (New York: Hart, 1960).

NELSON, F. HOWARD *The Impact of Collective Bargaining on Teacher Transfer Rates in Urban High-Poverty*

Schools (Washington, DC: American Federation of Teachers, October 2006).

NEPPL, TRICIA K., and ANN D. MURRY "Social Dominance and Play Patterns among Preschoolers: Gender Comparison," *Sex Roles: A Journal of Research*, Vol. 36, Nos. 5–6, March 1997, pp. 381–393.

NEWPORT, FRANK "Media Portrayals of Violence Seen by Many as Causes of Real-life Violence," The Gallup Organization, May 10, 1999a. Available: http://www.gallup.com/.../media-portrayals-violence-seen-many-causes-reallife-violence.aspx (Retrieved April 3, 2011).

NEWPORT, FRANK "Television Remains Americans' Top Choice for Evening Recreation," 1999b. Gallup Poll. Available: www.gallup.com/pollreleases/pr990301a.asp/2000a (Retrieved April 3, 2011).

New York City Department of Education, 2007. Available: http://schools.nyc.gov (Retrieved April 3, 2011).

NICHD Early Child Care Research Network, "Early Child Care and Children's Development in the Primary Grades: Follow-up Results from the NICHD Study of Early Child Care," *American Educational Research Journal*, Vol. 42, 2005, pp. 537–570.

NOGUERA, PEDRO A. "Preventing and Producing Violence: A Critical Analysis of Responses to School Violence," *Harvard Educational Review*, Vol. 65, No. 2, Summer 1995, pp. 189–212.

NOHARA, DAVID "A Comparison of the NAEP-the 3rd International Mathematics and Science Study Repeat (TIMSS-R) and the Programme for International Student Assessment (PISA)," 2001. Available: www.nces.ed.gov/pubsearch/pubsinfo.asp?pubid+200107 (Retrieved March 22, 2008).

Number of Colleges Offering Specific Academic Programs and Awards, 2004–2005. *The Chronicle of Higher Education Almanac, 2006–7*. Available: http://chronicle.com/weekly/alamnac/2006/nation/0103603.htm

NUWER, HAND *Broken Pledges: The Deadly Rite of Hazing* (Marietta, GA: Longstreet Press, 1990).

NYE, B. A., C. M. ACHILLES, J. BOYD-ZAHARIAS, B. D. FULTON, and M. P. WALLENHORST "Small Is Far Better," *Better Research in the Schools*, Vol. 1, No. 1, Spring 1994, pp. 9–20.

OAKES, JEANNIE "Tracking, Inequality, and the Rhetoric of Reform: Why Schools Don't Change," *Journal of Education*, Vol. 168, No. 1, 1986, pp. 60–80.

OAKES, JEANNIE *Multiplying Inequalities: The Effects of Race, Social Class, and Tracking on Opportunities to Learn Mathematics and Science* (Santa Monica, CA: The Rand Corporation, 1990).

OAKES, JEANNIE "Two Cities' Tracking and Within-school Segregation," *Teachers College Record*, Vol. 96, No. 4, Summer 1995, pp. 681–690.

OAKES, JEANNIE, and AMY STUART WELLS "The Comprehensive High School, Detracking and the Persistence of Social Stratification," in F. M. Hammack (ed.), *The Comprehensive High School Today* (New York: Teachers College Press, 2004), pp. 87–113.

OCHILTREE, GAY "Effects of Child Care on Young Children: Forty Years of Research," Childhood Study Paper No. 5, Australian Institute of Family Studies, Melbourne, 1994.

O'CONNOR, CARLA "Dispositions Toward (Collective) Struggle and Educational Resilience in the Inner City," *American Educational Research Journal*, Vol. 34, 1997, pp. 593–629.

O'CONNOR, CARLA "Comment: Making Sense of the Complexity of Social Identity in Relation to Achievement: A Sociological Challenge in the New Millennium," *Sociology of Education*, Extra Issue, 2001, pp. 159–168.

O'CONNOR, NOGA, FLOYD M. HAMMACK, and MARC A. SCOTT "Social Capital, Financial Knowledge, and Hispanic Student College Choices," *Research in Higher Education*, Vol. 51, No. 3, May 2010, pp. 195–219.

O'DONNELL, BEN "What's Right With Fraternities," *Chronicle of Higher Education*, December 6, 2009.

OECD, "Education at a Glance," 2003. Available: www.oecd.org/document/52/0,3343,en_2649 (Retrieved March 1, 2008).

OECD, *OECD Factbook: Economic, Environmental and Social Statistics*, 2005. Available: http://www.oecd.org/document/15/0,3746,en_2649_33715_33912015_1_1_1_1,00.html

Office of Bilingual Education and Minority Affairs, *General Questions on Bilingual Education* (Washington, DC: Government Printing Office, 1996).

OGBU, JOHN U. "Immigrant and Involuntary Minorities in Comparative Perspective," in M. A. Gibson and J. U. Ogbu (eds.), *Minority Status and Schooling: A Comparative Study of Immigrant and Involuntary Minorities* (New York: Garland, 1991), pp. 3–33.

OGBU, JOHN U. "Racial Stratification in the United States," *Teachers College Record*, Vol. 96, 1994, pp. 264–298.

OGBU, J. U., and H. D. SIMONS "Voluntary and Involuntary Minorities: A Cultural-ecological Theory of School Performance with Some Implications for Education," *Anthropology and Education Quarterly*, Vol. 29, No. 2, 1998, pp. 155–188.

Ohio Revised Code 3345.27, Amended Senate Bill 497 Available: www.legislature.state.oh.us/BillText128/128_SB_191_I_Y.html (Retrieved April 6, 2011).

OLSEN, KRISTEN *Despite Increases, Women and Minorities Still Underrepresented in Undergraduate and Graduate Science and Engineering Education* (Washington, DC: National Science Foundation, January 15, 1999).

OLSEN, MARVIN E. *The Process of Social Organization: Power in Social Systems*, 2nd ed. (New York: Holt, Rinehart and Winston, 1978).

OLSON, LYNN "In More States, It's Now ACT or SAT for All," *Education Week*, Vol. 26, No. 3, September 13, 2006, pp. 1–25, p. 3.

OLSON, LYNN "School Accountability Systems Seen as Unlikely to Face Major Overhaul," *Education Week*, January 29, 2007. Available: www.edweek.org/ew/contributors/lynn.olsen.html (Retrieved August 14, 2010).

OLSON, LYNN "Scholars Suggest Policies to Bolster Teacher Quality," *Education Week*, Vol. 26, No. 32, April 5, 2007, p. 9.

OPIE, IONA *The People in the Playground* (Oxford: Oxford University Press, 1993), p. 7.

ORFIELD, GARY A. *Public School Desegregation in the United States, 1968–1980*, U.S. Department of Education (Washington, DC: Joint Center for Political Studies, 1983), p. 4.

ORFIELD, GARY A. (ed.) *Dropouts in America: Confronting the Graduation Rate Crisis* (Cambridge, MA: Harvard Education Press, 2004).

ORFIELD, GARY A. *Reviving the Goal of an Integrated Society: A 21st Century Challenge* (Los Angeles, CA: The Civil Rights Project/Proyecto Derechos Civiles at UCLA, 2009).

ORFIELD, GARY A., ET AL. "Status of School Desegregation: The Next Generation," Report to the National School Board Association (Alexandria, VA: National School Board Association, 1992).

ORFIELD, GARY A., MARK D. BACHMEIER, DAVID R. JAMES, and TAMELA EITLE "Deepening Segregation in American Public Schools: A Special Report from the Harvard Project on School Desegration," *Equity and Excellence in Education*, Vol. 30, No. 2, September 1997, pp. 5–24.

ORNSTEIN, ALLAN C. "Enrollment Trends in Big-City Schools," *Peabody Journal of Education*, Vol. 66, No. 4, Summer 1991, pp. 65–67.

ORNSTEIN, ALLAN C., and DANIEL U. LEVINE *An Introduction to the Foundations of Education*, 3rd ed. (Boston, MA: Houghton Mifflin, 1985).

OROMANER, MARK "The Cooling Out Function and Beyond: Some Applications of Sociological Analysis to the Community College," in *ASA Resource Materials for Teaching* (Washington, DC: American Sociological Association, 1995).

O'SHAUGHNESSY, LYNN "The Best and Worst College Degrees by Salary," 2009. Available: http://money-watch.bnet.com/saving-money/blog/college-solution/the-best-and-worst-college-degrees-by-salary/577/ (Retrieved September 21, 2010).

OSTRANDER, KENNETH H., and KATHERINE OSTROM "Attitudes Underlying the Politics of Parent Involvement," *National Forum of Applied Educational Research Journal*, Vol. 3, No. 2, 1991, p. 37.

OTTERMAN, SHARON "Lauded Harlem Schools Have Their Own Problems," *The New York Times*, October 12, 2010.

OUCHI, WILLIAM *Making Schools Work: A Revolutionary Plan to Get Your Children the Education They Need* (New York: Simon and Schuster, 2003).

PAGE, ANN L., and DONALD A. CLELLAND "The Kanawha County Textbook Controversy: A Study of the Politics of Life Style Concern," *Social Forces*, Vol. 57, 1978, pp. 265–281.

PALEY, V. *Boys and Girls: Superheroes in the Doll Corner* (Chicago, IL: University of Chicago Press, 1984).

PALLAS, AARON M. "The Changing Nature of the Disadvantaged Population: Current Dimensions and Future Trends," *Educational Researcher*, June/July 1989, pp. 16–22.

PALLAS, AARON M., ET AL. "Ability-Group Effects: Instructional, Social, or Institutional?" *Sociology of Education*, Vol. 67, January 1994, pp. 27–46.

Parents Involved in Community Schools v. Seattle School District No. 1, 2007. Available: http://www.law.cornell.edu/supct/html/05-908.ZS.html

PARRY, MARC "Colleges See Seventeen Percent Increase in Online Enrollment," January 26, 2010. Available: http://chronicle, com/blogPost/Colleges-See-17-Percent-Inc/20820/ (Retrieved August 27, 2010).

PARSAD, B., and J. JONES "Internet Access in U.S. Public Schools and Classrooms: 1994–2003," *Education Statistics Quarterly*, Vol. 7, Nos. 1 and 2, 2005, NCES 2005–015.

PARSONS, TALCOTT *The Structure of Social Action* (New York: McGraw-Hill, 1937).

PARSONS, TALCOTT "The School Class as a Social System: Some of Its Functions in American Society," *Harvard Educational Review*, Vol. 29, No. 4, 1959, pp. 297–318.

PARSONS, TALCOTT "Equality and Inequality in Modern Society, or Social Stratification Revisited," in Edward O. Lauman (ed.), *Social Stratification* (New York: Bobbs-Merrill, 1970), pp. 13–72.

PASCARELLA, ERNEST T., MARCIA EDISON, AMAURY NORA., PATRICK T. TERENZINI, and LINDA SERRA HAGEDORN

"Does Community College Verses Four-Year College Attendance Influence Students' Education Plans?" *Journal of College Student Development,* Vol. 39, 1998, pp. 179–193.

PASCARELLA, ERNEST T., and PATRICK T. TERENZINI *How College Affects Students: A Third Decade of Research* (San Francisco, CA: Jossey-Bass, 2005).

PASHAL, ROSANNE A., ET AL. "The Effects of Homework on Learning: A Quantitative Synthesis," *Journal of Educational Research,* Vol. 78, No. 2, 1984, pp. 97–104.

PASSOW, A. HARRY, ET AL. *The National Case Study: An Empirical Comparative Study of Twenty-One Educational Systems* (New York: Wiley, 1976).

PATERNOSTER, R., S. BUSHWAY, R. BRAME, and R. APEL "The Effect of Teenage Employment on Delinquency and Problem Behavior," *Social Forces,* Vol. 82, No. 1, 2003, pp. 297–335.

PATRICIA, SULLIVAN "Is Smaller Better? Schools Move to Reduce Class Size in Grades K-3," *Our Children,* Vol. 23, No. 7, April 1998, pp. 34–35.

PAULSTON, ROLLAND G. "Mapping Comparative Education After Postmodernity," *Comparative Education Review,* Vol. 43, No. 4, November 1999, pp. 438–463.

PEDERSEN, DARHL M. "Privacy Preferences and Classroom Seat Selection," *Social Behavior and Personality,* Vol. 22, No. 4, 1994, pp. 393–398.

PEG TYRE *The Trouble with Boys* (New York, Crown Publishers).

PENA, ROBERT A. "Cultural Differences and the Construction of Meaning: Implications for the Leadership and Organizational Context of Schools," *Educational Policy Analysis Archives,* Vol. 5, No. 10, April 8, 1997.

PENNINGTON, BILL "Small Colleges, Short on Men, Embrace Football," *The New York Times,* July 10, 2006, pp. A1, A14.

PENNINGTON, ELISABETH "A Political History of School Finance Reform in the Metropolitan Hartford Region, 1945–2005," Unpublished Senior Research Project, Educational Studies Program, Trinity College, Hartford, CT, December 2006.

People for the American Way, "Most Frequently Challenged Books, 1982–1987," *Education Week,* September 16, 1987, p. 3.

People for the American Way, "Evolution and Creationism in Public Education: An in-depth Reading of Public Opinion," Copyright 2000. Available: www.pfaw.org/issues/education/creationism-poll.pdf (Retrieved March 24, 2011).

PERKINS, JAMES A. (ed.) "Missions and Organizations: A Redefinition," *The University as an Organization: A Report for The Carnegie Commission on Higher Education* (New York: McGraw-Hill, 1973), p. 258.

PERRY, P. *Shades of White: White Kids and Racial Identities in High School* (Durham, NC: Duke University Press, 2002).

PERSELL, CAROLINE HODGES, and PETER W. COOKSON, JR. "Chartering and Bartering: Elite Education and Social Reproduction," *Social Problems,* Vol. 33, No. 2, December 1985.

PERSELL, CAROLINE HODGES, SOPHIA CATSAMBIS, and PETER W. COOKSON, JR. "Differential Asset Conversion: Class and Gender Pathways to Selective Colleges," *Sociology of Education,* Vol. 65, No. 3, July 1992, pp. 208–225.

PESCOSOLIDO, BERNICE A., and RONALD AMINZADE (eds.) *The Social Worlds of Higher Education* (Thousand Oaks, CA: Pine Forge Press, 1999).

PESHKIN, ALAN *God's Choice: The Total World of a Fundamentalist Christian School* (Chicago, IL: University of Chicago Press, 1986).

PESHKIN, ALAN *Permissible Advantage? The Moral Consequences of Elite Schooling* (Mahwah, NJ: Lawrence Erlbaum Associates, 2001).

PETERS, LAURENCE "A Look at the Digital Divide in the Mid-Atlantic Region: Some Research and Data Challenges," *EDTECH Review. Series No. 1* (Washington, DC: U.S. Department of Education, 2002).

PETERS, WILLIAM *A Class Divided* (New York: Doubleday, 1971).

PHILLIPS, MARIAN B., and AMOS J. HATCH "Why Teach? Prospective Teachers' Reasons for Entering the Profession," paper presented at the 8th Reconceptualizing Early Childhood Education Conference, Columbus, June 27, 1999.

PHILLIPS, MEREDITH E. "What Makes Schools Effective? A Comparison of the Relationship of Communitarian Climate and Academic Climate to Mathematics Achievement and Attendance During Middle School," *American Educational Research Journal,* Vol. 34, 1997, pp. 633–662.

PINCUS, FRED L. "Customized Contract Training in Community Colleges: Who Really Benefits?" paper presented at American Sociological Association meetings, Washington, DC, August 1985.

PINCUS, FRED L. "The Contradictory Effects of Customized Contract Training in Community Colleges," *Critical Sociology,* Vol. 16, Spring 1989, pp. 77–93.

PINCUS, FRED L. "How Critics View the Community College's Role in the Twenty-first Century," in George A. Baker III (ed.), *A Handbook on the Community College in America: Its History, Mission, and Management* (Westport, CO: Greenwood Press, 1994).

"Poll: Origin Theories Find Support for Schools," The Associated Press, March 11, 2000.

Pong, Suet-ling, Jaap Dronkers, and Gillian Hampden-Thompson "Family Policies and Children's School Achievement in Single- Versus Two-Parent Families," *Journal of Marriage and Family,* Vol. 65, No. 3, August 2003, pp. 681–699.

POPKEWITZ, THOMAS S., and FAZAL RIZVI (eds.) *Globalization and the Study of Education, Part II.* Yearbook of the National Society for the Study of Education (Malden, MA: Wiley-Blackwell, 2009).

POPPEN, JULIE "Area Schools Weigh Whether to Give Condoms to Students," *Rocky Mountain News,* May 16, 2005.

PORTES, ALENJANDRO, and LINGXIN HAO "Epluribus Unum: Bilingualism and Loss of Language in the Second Generation," *Sociology of Education,* Vol. 71, No. 4, October 1998, pp. 269–294.

PORTES, ALENJANDRO, and RUBEN G. RUMBAUT *Ethnicities: Children of Immigrants in America* (Berkeley, CA: University of California Press, 2001).

POST, DAVID, and SUETLING PONG "Employment During Middle School: The Effects on Academic Achievement in the U.S.A. and Abroad," *Educational Evaluation and Policy Analysis,* Vol. 22, No. 3, 2000, pp. 273–298.

POSTIGLIONE, GERARD A. *Education and Social Change in China: Inequality in a Market Economy* (Armonk, NY: M.E. Sharpe, East Gate Books, 2006).

POSTLEWAITE, CHARLOTTE C. "School Choice Gains Momentum," State Government News, June 2003.

POWELL, ARTHUR G., ELEANOR FARRAR, and DAVID K. COHEN *The Shopping Mall High School: Winners and Losers in the Educational Marketplace* (Boston, MA: Houghton Mifflin, 1985).

POWELL, JASON L., and MARGARET EDWARDS "Surveillance and Morality: Revisiting the Education Reform Act (1988) in the United Kingdom," *Surveillance and Society,* Vol. 3, No. 1, 2005, pp. 96–106.

POWERS, E. "Evaluating Title IX," June 20, 2007. Available: http://www.insidehighered.com/news/2007/06/20/titleix (Retrieved August 14, 2007).

PROVENZO, EUGENE F. *Religious Fundamentalism and American Education: The Battle for the Public Schools* (Albany, NY: State University of New York Press, 1990).

PURCELL, P., and L. STEWARD "Dick and Jane in 1989," *Sex Roles,* Vol. 22, 1990, pp. 177–185.

RABKIN, JEREMY "The Curious Case of Kiryas Joel," *Commentary,* Vol. 98, No. 5, November 1994, pp. 58–60.

RADIN, NORMA "Working Moms Are Positive Role Models," *USA Today: The Magazine of the American Scene,* August 1990, p. 5.

RAMIREZ, FRANCISCO O., and JOHN BOLI-BENNETT "The Political Construction of Mass Schooling: European Origins and Worldwide Institutionalization," paper presented at American Sociological Association meetings, Chicago, August 1987.

RAVITCH, DIANE "Multiculturalism Yes, Particularism No," *The Chronicle of Higher Education,* October 24, 1990, p. A44.

RAVITCH, DIANE "Why Public Schools Need Democratic Governance," *Phi Delta Kappan,* Vol. 91, No. 6, 2010, pp. 24–27.

RAYWID, MARY ANNE "Separate Classes for the Gifted? A Skeptical Look," *Educational Perspectives,* Vol. 26, No. 1, 1989, pp. 48–55.

RAYWID, MARY ANNE "Current Literature on Small Schools" (Charleston, WV: ERIC Clearinghouse on Rural Education and Small Schools, January 1999), p. 4.

RAYWID, MARY ANNE "Themes That Serve Schools Well," *Phi Delta Kappan,* Vol. 87, No. 9, May 2006, pp. 654–656.

READY, DOUGLAS D., and VALERIE E. LEE "Choice, Equity and the Schools-Within-Schools Reform," *Teachers College Record,* Vol. 110, No. 9, September 2008, pp. 1930–1958.

READY, DOUGLAS D., VALERIE E. LEE, and KEVIN G. WELNER "Educational Equity and School Structure: School Size, Overcrowding, and Schools-within-Schools," *Teachers College Record,* Vol. 106, No. 10, October 2004, pp. 1989–2014.

REARDON, SEAN F., JOHN T. YUN, and MICHAL KURLAENDER "Implications of Income-Based School Assignment Policies for Racial School Segregation," *Educational Evaluation and Policy Analysis,* Vol. 28, No. 1, 2006, pp. 49–75.

REBELL, MICHAEL A. "Adequacy Litigation: A New Path to Equity," in J. Petrovich and A. S. Wells (eds.), *Bringing Equity Back: Research for a New Era in American Educational Policy* (New York: Teachers College Press, 2006).

REDOVICH, DENNIS W. "The Education and Financial Systems of the World and the Big Con," 1991. Part One—World Education and Educational Reform in Europe. Report 10Update. ERIC ED4326074.

REES, NINA S., and KIRK JOHNSON "A Lesson in Smaller Class Sizes," *Heritage Views,* May 30, 2000. Available: www.heritage.org/views/2000/ed053000.html (Retrived July 10, 2010).

REICH, ROBERT B. "Jobs: Skills Before Credentials," *The Wall Street Journal,* February 2, 1994, p. A16.

REIN, ANDREW S. *The State of Municipal Services in the 1990s: Crowding, Building Conditions and Staffing in New York City Public Schools* (New York: Citizens Budget Commission, September 1997).

Religion and Ethics Newsweekly "Texas Textbook Controversy," April 30, 2010. Available: www.pbs.

org/wnet/religionandethics/episodes/april-30-2010/texas-textbook-controversy/6187/ (Retrieved August 26, 2010).

Report of the Board of Indian Commissions to the Secretary of the Interior (Meriam Report), 1928, pp. ii and 41. Available: http://www.nps.gov/history/history/online_books/laro/adhi/adhi4.htm

Retirement Living Information Center, "Taxes by State," 2007. Available: http://www.retirementliving.com/RLtaxes.html (Retrieved May 11, 2007).

RETTIG, MICHAEL D., and ROBERT LYNN CANADY "The Effects of Block Scheduling," *School Administrator*, Vol. 56, No. 3, March 1999, pp. 14–20.

REYES, AUGUSTINA H., and GLORIA M RODRIQUEZ "School Finance: Raising Questions for Urban Schools," *Education and Urban Society*, Vol. 37, No. 1, 2004, pp. 3–21.

REYES, PEDRO, and DONALD J. McCARTY "Factors Related to the Power of Lower Participants in Educational Organizations: Multiple Perspectives," *Sociological Focus*, Vol. 23, No. 1, February 1990, pp. 17–30.

REYHNER, JON, and JEANNE EDER *American Indian Education: A History* (Norman, OK: University of Oklahoma Press, 2004).

RHOADES, GARY, and SHEILA SLAUGHTER "Professors, Administrators, and Patents: The Negotiation of Technology Transfer," *Sociology of Education*, Vol. 64, April 1991, pp. 65–77.

RICHMOND-ABBOTT, MARIE *Masculine and Feminine: Gender Roles over the Life Cycle*, 2nd ed. (New York: McGraw-Hill, 1992).

RIEHL, CAROLYN, GARY NATRIELLO, and AARON M. PALLAS "Losing Track: The Dynamics of Student Assignment Processes in High School," paper presented at American Sociological Association meeting, Pittsburgh, PA, August 1992.

RIORDAN, CORNELIUS *Girls and Boys in School: Together or Separate?* (New York: Teachers College Press, 1990).

RIORDAN, CORNELIUS "What Do We Know about the Effects of Single-Sex Schools in the Private Sector? Implications for Public Schools," in A. Datnow and L. Hubbard (eds.), *Gender in Policy and Practice: Perspective on Single-Sex and Coeducational Schooling* (New York: Routledge/Falmer Press, 2002), pp. 10–30.

RIST, RAY "Student Social Class and Teacher Expectations: The Self-fulfilling Prophesy in Ghetto Education," *Harvard Education Review*, Vol. 40, 1970, pp. 411–451.

RIST, RAY "On Understanding the Processes of Schooling: The Contributions of Labeling Theory," in J. Karabel, and A. H. Halsey (eds.), *Power and Ideology in Education* (New York: Oxford University Press, 1977), pp. 292–305.

RIST, RAY "On Understanding the Processes of Schooling: The Contributions of Labeling Theory," in A. R Sadovnik (ed.), *Sociology of Education: A Critical Reader* (New York: Routledge, 2007), pp. 71–82.

ROBINSON, JEAN C. "Stumbling on Two Legs: Education and Reform in China," *Comparative Education Review*, Vol. 35, No. 1, 1991, pp. 177–189.

ROBBINS, LIZ "Lost in the School Choice Maze." *The New York Times*, May 8, 2011, p. MB1.

RODERICK, MELISSA "Grade Retention and School Dropout: Investigating the Association," *American Educational Research Journal*, Vol. 31, No. 4, Winter 1994, pp. 729–759.

RODERICK, MELISSA "Grade Retention and School Dropout: Policy Debate and Research Questions," *Phi Delta Kappan Research Bulletin*, Vol. 15, No. 8, December 1995, pp. 1–6.

RODRIGUEZ, LUIS. J. *Always Running: La Vida Loca, Gang Days in L.A.* (New York: Simon & Schuster, 1993).

ROFES, ERIC, and LISA STULBERG (eds.) *The Emancipatory Promise of Charter Schools: Toward a Progressive Politics of School Choice* (Albany, NY: State University of New York Press, 2004).

ROGER GARFIELD "Confessions of a DC Teacher," *Mother Jones*, September 6, 2010. Available: http://motherjones.com/politics/2010/09/back-to-school-dc (Revrieved August 2, 2010.

ROGERS, DAVID *110 Livingston Street: Politics and Bureaucracy in the New York City School System* (New York: Vintage Books, 1969).

ROSE, LOWELL C., and ALEC M. GALLUP "The 31st Annual Phi Delta Kappan/Gallup Poll of the Public's Attitudes Toward the Public Schools," *Phi Delta Kappan*, September 1999, pp. 41–56.

ROSE, LOWELL C., and ALEC M. GALLUP "The 36th Annual Phi Delta Kappa/Gallup Poll of the Public's Attitudes Toward the Public Schools," 2006a. Available: http://www.pdkintl.org/kappan/k0409pol.htm (Retrived July 7, 2010).

ROSE, LOWELL C., and ALEC M. GALLUP "The 38th Annual Phi Delta Kappa/Gallup Poll of the Public's Attitudes Toward the Public Schools," *Phi Delta Kappan*, Vol. 88, No. 1, 2006b, pp. 41–57.

ROSENBAUM, JAMES E. "College for All: Do Students Understand What College Demands?" *Social Psychology of Education*, Vol. 2, 1998, pp 50–85.

ROSENBAUM, JAMES E. "If Tracking is Bad, Is Detracking Better?" *American Teacher*, Winter 1999–2000, pp. 1–7.

ROSENBAUM, JAMES E. *Beyond College for All: Career Paths for the Forgotten Half* (New York: Russell Sage Foundation, 2001).

ROSENBAUM, JAMES E., and AMY BINDER "Do Employers Really Need More Educated Youths?" *Sociology of Education*, Vol. 73, No. 1, January 1997, pp. 68–85.

ROSENBAUM, JAMES E., and ANN E. PERSON "Beyond College for All: Policies and Practices to Improve Transitions into College and Jobs," *Professional School Counseling*, April 2003.

ROSENBAUM, JAMES E., ET AL. "Gatekeeping in an Era of More Open Gates: High School Counselors View of Their Influence on Students' College Plans," *American Journal of Education*, Vol. 104, No. 4, August 1996, pp. 257–279.

ROSENBERG, MATT "China Population: The Population Growth of the World's Largest Country," 2010. Available: http://geography.about.com/od/populationgeography/a/chinapopulation.htm (Retrieved September 30, 2010).

ROSENTHAL, ROBERT, and LENORE JACOBSON *Pygmalion in the Classroom* (New York: Holt, Rinehart and Winston, 1968).

ROSENWEIG, MARK R. "Are There Increase Returns to the Intergenerational Production of Human Capital? Maternal Schooling and Child Intellectual Achievement," *Journal of Human Resources*, Vol. 29, No. 2, Spring 1994, pp. 670–693.

ROSIER, KATHERINE BROWN "Competent Parents, Complex Lives: Managing Parenthood in Poverty," *Journal of Contemporary Ethnography*, Vol. 22, No. 2, July 1993, pp. 171–204.

ROSSIDES, DANIEL W. *Social Stratification: The American Class System in Comparative Perspective* (Englewood Cliffs, NJ: Prentice Hall, 1990), pp. 406–408.

ROTBERG, IRIS C. "Assessment around the World," *Educational Leadership*, Vol. 64, No. 3, November 2006.

ROTHENBERG, PAULA S. *Race, Class and Gender in the United States*, 3rd ed. (New York: St. Martin's Press, 1995, 4th ed., 1998).

ROTHSTEIN, RICHARD *Class and Schools: Using Social, Economic, and Educational Reform to Close the Black-White Achievement Gap* (Washington, DC: Economic Policy Institute, 2004).

ROUSE, C. E. "Do Two-Year Colleges Increase Overall Educational Attainment? Evidence from the States," *Journal of Policy Analysis and Management*, Vol. 17, 1998, pp. 595–620.

ROUTMAN, REGIE *Literacy at the Crossroads: Crucial Talk About Reading, Writing and Other Teaching Dilemmas* (Portsmouth, NH: Heinemann, 1996).

ROYKO, T. "The 'New' Foreigners and the Social Reconstruction of Difference: The Cultural Diversification of Japanese Education," *Comparative Education*, Vol. 40, No. 1, 2004, pp. 55–81.

RUBINSON, RICHARD "Class Formation, Politics, and Institutions: Schooling in the United States," *American Journal of Sociology*, Vol. 92, No. 3, 1986, pp. 519–548.

RUMBAUT, RUBEN G. "The Crucible Within: Ethnic Identity, Self-Esteem, and Segmented Assimilation Among Children of Immigrants," *International Migration Review*, Vol. 28, No. 4, 1994, pp. 748–793.

RUMBAUT, RUBEN G. "The New Immigration," *Contemporary Sociology*, Vol. 24, No. 4, July 1995, pp. 307–311.

RUMBAUT, RUBEN G. "Ties That Bind: Immigration and Immigrant Families in the United States," in Alan Booth, Ann C. Crouter, and Nancy S. Landale (eds.), *Immigration and the Family: Research and Policy on U.S. Immigrants* (Hillsdale, NJ: Lawrence Erlbaum Associates, 1996).

RUMBAUT, RUBEN G., and KENJI IMA "The Adaptation of Southeast Asian Refugee Youth: A Comparative Study," Office of Refugee Settlement, U.S. Department of Health and Human Services, December 1987.

RUMBERGER, RUSSELL W. "Family Influences on Dropout Behavior in One California High School," *Sociology of Education*, Vol. 63, October 1990, pp. 283–299.

RUMBERGER, RUSSELL W., and KATHARINE A. LARSON "Toward Explaining Differences in Educational Achievement Among Mexican American Language-Minority Students," *Sociology of Education*, Vol. 71, No. 1, 1998, pp. 69–92.

RURY, JOHN L. "Who Became Teachers? The Social Characteristics of Teachers in American History," in D. Warren (ed.), *American Teachers: Histories of a Profession at Work* (New York: Macmillan, 1989).

RURY, JOHN L. *Education and Social Change: Contours in the History of American Education*, 3rd ed. (New York: Routledge, 2008).

RUSSELL, ALENE "Pell Institute for the Study of Opportunity in Higher Education," Reported in *The Chronicle of Higher Education* June 16, 2008. Available: http://www.aascu.org/media/pm/pdf/pmaug08.pdf (Retrieved October 10, 2010).

RUST, VAL D., AMINATA SOUMARE, OCTAVIO PESCADOR, and MEGUMI SHIBUYA "Research Strategies in Comparative Education," *Comparative Education Review*, Vol. 43, No. 1, February 1999, pp. 86–109.

RUTTER, MICHAEL, ET AL. *Fifteen Thousand Hours: Secondary Schools and Their Effects on Children* (Cambridge, MA: Harvard University Press, 1979).

RYAN, A. M. "The Peer Group as a Context for the Development of Young Adolescents Motivation and Achievement," *Child Development*, Vol. 72, No. 4, 2001, pp. 1135–1150.

SACKS, PETER *Tearing Down the Gates: Confronting the Class Divide in American Education* (Berkeley: University of California Press, 2007).

SADKER, MYRA, and DAVID SADKER *Failing at Fairness: How our Schools Cheat Girls* (New York: Simon and Schuster, 1994).

SADOVNIK, ALAN R. "Theories in the Sociology of Education," in Jeanne H. Ballantine and Joan Z. Spade (eds.), *Schools and Society* (Belmont, CA: Wadsworth, 2004[2001]).

SADOVNIK, ALAN. R., and SUSAN. F. SEMEL *Founding Mothers and Others: Women Educational Leaders During the Progressive Era* (New York: Palgrave, 2002).

SALOMONE, ROSEMARY *Same, Different, Equal: Rethinking Single-Sex Schooling* (New Haven, CT: Yale University Press, 2003).

SALOMONE, ROSEMARY "A Place for Women's Colleges," *The Chronicle of Higher Education*, Vol. 53, No. 24, February 16, 2007, p. B20.

SALTZMAN, GREGORY. M. "Higher Education Collective Bargaining and the Law," in H. W. Wechsler (ed.), *The NEA 2001 Almanac of Higher Education* (Washington, DC: National Education Association, 2001), pp. 45–58.

SALZMAN, HAL, and LINDSAY LOWELL "Into the Eye of the Storm: Assessing the Evidence on Science and Engineering Education, Quality, and Workforce Demand," Copyright 2007. Available: http://www.urbanorg/expert.cfm?ID=Blindsaylowell (Retrieved March 22, 2008).

SAMOFF, JOEL "The Reconstruction of Schooling in Africa," *Comparative Education Review*, Vol. 37, No. 2, May 1993.

SAMOFF, JOEL, and BIDEMI CARROL "From Manpower Planning to the Knowledge Era: World Bank Policies on Higher Education in Africa," UNESCO Forum on Higher Education, Research, and Knowledge, July 2003.

SAMPSON, RANA "Bullying in Schools: Guide #12," Copyright May. 2009. Available: http://www.cops.usdoj.gov/files/ric/publications/e07063414-guide.pdf (Retrieved August 26, 2010).

SAMUELSEN, SHELBY "Student Testing: The Stakes Are Rising," *State Legislatures*, Vol. 27, No. 8, September 2001.

SANDAY, PEGGY REEVES *Fraternity Gang Rape: Sex, Brotherhood, and Privilege on Campus* (New York: New York University Press, 1990).

SANDERS, IRWIN T. "The University as a Community," in James A. Perkins (eds.), *The University as an Organization: A Report for The Carnegie Commission on Higher Education* (New York: McGraw-Hill, 1973), p. 57.

SANDLER, BERNICE RESNICK "The Chilly Classroom Climate: A Guide to Improve the Education of Women," National Association for Women in Education, Washington, DC, 1996. http://www.eric.ed.gov/ERICWebPortal/search/detai-lmini.jsp?_nfpb=true&_&ERICExtSearch_SearchValue_0=ED396984&ERICExtSearch_SearchType_0=no&accno=ED396984 (Retrieved April 3, 2011).

SAN MIGUEL, GUADALUPE, JR. *Contested Policy: The Rise and Fall of Federal Bilingual Education in the Untied States, 1960–2001* (Denton, TX: University of North Texas Press, 2004).

SAPORITO, S., and D. SOHONI "Coloring Outside the Lines: Racial Segregation in Public Schools and their Attendance Boundaries," *Sociology of Education*, Vol. 79, No. 2, 2006, pp. 81–105.

SAUTMAN, BARRY "Politicalization, Hyperpoliticization, and Depoliticization of Chinese Education," *Comparative Education Review*, Vol. 35, No. 4, November 1991, pp. 669–689.

SAWCHUK, STEPHEN "Merit Pay Found to Have Litte Effect on Achievement," *Education Week*, September 21, 2010. Avaialble: www.edweek.org/ew/contributors/stephen.sawchuk.html

SAWYER, AKILAGPA "Challenges Facing African Universities," UNESCO Forum on Higher Education, Research, and Knowledge, July 2003.

SAXENIAN, ANNALEE "From Brain Drain to Brain Circulation: Transnational Communities and Regional Upgrading in India and China," *Studies in Comparative International Development*, Vol. 40, No. 2, June 2005, pp. 35–61.

SAX, L. J., A. W. ASTIN, W. S. KORN, and K. M. MAHONEY *The American Freshman: National Norms for Fall 1999* (Los Angeles, CA: Higher Education Research Institute, 1999).

SCHAEFFER, ADAM B. "They Spend WHAT? The Real Cost of Public Schools," Copyright March 10, 2010. Available: http://www.cato.org/pub_display.php?pub_id=11432 (Retrieved September 25, 2010).

SCHEMO, DIANA JEAN "Change in Federal Rules Backs Single-Sex Public Education," *The New York Times*, October 25, 2006, p. A1.

SCHEMO, DIANA JEAN "Failing Schools See a Solution in Longer Day," [Electronic version], *The New York Times*, March 26, 2007.

SCHEURICH, JAMES JOSEPH, and MICHAEL IMBER "Educational Reforms Can Reproduce Societal Inequalities: A Case Study," *Educational Administration Quarterly*, Vol. 27, No. 3, 1991, pp. 297–320.

SCHILLER, KATHRYN S., and DAVID STEVENSON "Sequences of Opportunities for Learning Mathematics," paper presented at American Sociological Association meetings, Pittsburgh, PA, August 1992.

SCHMIDT, PETER "Department to Reconsider Controversial Bilingual-Ed Rules," *Education Week*, February 5, 1992, p. 21.

SCHNEIDER, BARBARA, ADAM E. WYSSE, and VANESSA KEESLER "Small Schools Analysis of Education Longitudinal Study of 2002," paper presented at Brookings Institute Conference, May 22, 2006.

SCHNEIDER, BARBARA, ET AL. "Public School Choice: Some Evidence from the National Education Longitudinal Study of 1988," *Education Evaluation and Policy Analysis*, Vol. 18, No. 1, Spring 1996, pp. 19–29.

SCHOENHALS, MARK, MARTA TIENDA, and BARBARA SCHNEIDER "The Educational and Personal Consequences of Adolescent Employment," *Social Forms*, Vol. 77, No. 2, December 1998, pp. 723–761.

SCHOFER, EVAN, and JOHN W. MEYER "The Worldwide Expansion of Higher Education in the Twentieth Century," *American Sociological Review*, Vol. 70, December 2005, pp. 898–920.

SCHOFIELD, JANET WARD "Review of Research on School Desegregation's Impact on Elementary and Secondary School Students," in *Handbook of Research on Multicultural Education* (New York: Macmillan, 1995), pp. 597–616.

School Matters, *Helping All Students Learn: Identifying School Districts Across the U.S. That Are Significantly Narrowing Achievement Gaps* (New York: Standard and Poor's, 2006).

School Mental Health Project, "School Staff Burnout," *Addressing Barriers to Learning*, Vol. 7, No. 2, Spring 2002, pp. 1–6.

SCHWEINHART, LAWRENCE J. "Child-Initiated Learning Activities for Young Children Living in Poverty," *ERIC Digest* (Washington, DC: Office of Educational Research and Improvement, October 1997).

Science Study, "Girls Need More Lab Work to Close Gender Gap," *Detroit News*, May 1, 1995, p. E2.

SCOTCHMER, MARION, DANIEL McGRATH, and ELLINOR CODER *Characteristics of Public School Teachers' Professional Development Activities: 1999–2000* (Washington, DC: National Center for Education Statistics, 2005).

SCOTT, JANELLE T. *School Choice and Diversity: What the Evidence Says* (New York: Teachers College Press, 2005).

SCOTT-JONES, DIANE "Educational Levels of Adolescent Childbearers at First and Second Births," *American Journal of Education*, August 1991, p. 461.

SCOTT, W. RICHARD, and JOHN W. MEYER *Environmental Linkages and Organizational Complexity: Public and Private Schools*, Project Report 84–A16, Institute for Research on Educational Finance and Governance (Stanford, CA: Stanford University, July 1984).

SEDLAK, M., C. WHEELER, D. PULLIN, and P. CUSICK *Selling Students Short: Classroom Bargains and Academic Reform in the American High School* (New York: Teachers College Press, 1986).

SEMEL, SUSAN F., and ALAN R. SADOVNIK "The Contemporary Small-School Movement: Lessons from the History of Progressive Education," *Teachers College Record*, Vol. 110, No. 9, 2008, pp. 1744–1771.

SENDOR, BENJAMIN "Religious Clubs Gain 'Equal Access' to Schools," *The American School Board Journal*, September 1990, p. 15.

"Sex Education in America: An NPR/Kaiser?Kennedy School Poll," Copyright February 24, 2004. Available: http://www.npr.org/templates/story/story.php?story-Id=1622610 (Retrieved March 16, 2011).

SEXTON, PATRICIA CAYO *The Feminized Male: Classrooms, White Collars, and the Decline of Manliness* (New York: Random House, 1969).

SHEAR, LINDA, BARBARA MEANS, KAREN MITCHELL, ANN HOUSE, TORIE GORGES, AASHA JOSHI, BECKY SMERDON, and JAMIE SHKOLNIK "Contrasting Paths to Small School Reform: Results of a 5-year Evaluation of the Bill and Melinda Gates Foundation's national High Schools Initiative," *Teachers College Record*, Vol. 110, No. 9, 2008, pp. 1986–2039.

Sheff v. O'Neill, 1996. Available: http://www.jud.ct.gov/external/news/sheff.htm

SILBERMAN, CHARLES *Crisis in the Classroom* (New York: Random House, 1970).

SIMON, SIDNEY B. *Values Clarification: A Handbook of Practical Strategies for Teachers and Students* (New York: Hart, 1972).

SIZER, THEODORE R. *Horace's Compromise: The Dilemma of the American High School* (Boston, MA: Houghton Mifflin, 1985).

SIZER, THEODORE R. *Horace's School: Redesigning the American High School* (Boston, MA: Houghton Mifflin, 1992).

SIZER, THEODORE R., and NANCY FAUST SIZER *The Students Are Watching: Schools and the Moral Contract* (Boston, MA: Beacon Press, 1999).

SLABY, RONALD G. "Closing the Education Gap on TV's 'Entertainment' Violence," *The Chronicle of Higher Education*, January 5, 1994, pp. B1–B2.

SLAVIN, ROBERT *Cooperative Learning* (New York: Longman, 1983).

SLAVIN, ROBERT "Achievement Effects of Ability Grouping in Secondary Schools: A Best-Evidence Synthesis," *Review of Educational Research*, Vol. 60, No. 3, Fall 1990, pp. 471–499.

SLAVIN, ROBERT "Cooperative Learning and Intergroup Relations," in James A. Banks and Cheryl A. Banks (eds.), *Handbook of Research on Multicultural Education* (New York: Macmillan, 1995).

SLOMCZYNSKI, KAZIMIERZ M., and TADEUSZ K. KRAUZE "The Meritocratic Relationship Between Formal Education and Occupational Status: A Cross-National Analysis," paper presented for 10th World Congress of Sociology, New Delhi, August 1986.

Small School Reform Plans, "Rethinking Schools," (title of an on line journal) Vol. 19, No. 4, Summer 2005. Available: http://www.rethinkingschools.org/archive/19_04/ques194.shtml (Retrieved March 15, 2008).

SMELZER, NEIL J. *Theory of Collective Behavior* (New York: Free Press, 1962).

SMITH, DARYL G. "Women's Colleges and Coed Colleges: Is There a Difference for Women?" *Journal of Higher Education*, Vol. 61, No. 2, March/April 1990.

SMITH, MARILYN E. *Television Violence and Behavior: A Research Summary* (Washington, DC: Office of Educational Research and Improvement, 1993).

SMITH, WILMA F. "Leadership for Educational Renewal," *Phi Delta Kappan*, Vol. 80, No. 8, 1999, pp. 602–605.

SMOCK, PAMELA J., and FRANKLIN D. WILSON "Desegregation and the Stability of White Enrollments: A School-Level Analysis, 1968–1984," *Sociology of Education*, Vol. 64, October 1991, pp. 278–292.

SMREKAR, CLAIRE, and ELLEN GOLDRING *School Choice in Urban America: Magnet Schools and the Pursuit of Equity* (New York: Teachers College Press, 1999).

SNELL, LISA "The Agony of American Education," *Reason*, Vol. 37, April 2006, p. 11. Available: http://reason.com/archives/2006/04/01/the-agony-of-american-education (Retrieved May 11, 2007).

SNYDER, BENSON R. *The Hidden Curriculum* (New York: Alfred A. Knopf, 1971).

SNYDER, ELDON E., and ELMER SPREITZER "Social Psychological Concomitants of Adolescents' Role Identities as Scholars and Athletes: A Longitudinal Analysis," *Youth and Society*, Vol. 23, No. 4, June 1992, pp. 507–522.

SNYDER, T. D., S. A. DILLOW and C. M. HOFFMAN "Indicators of School Crime and Safety: 2009," Copyright 2010. Available: nces.ed.gov/programs/crimeindicators2009/

SOARES, JOSEPH *The Power of Privilege: Yale and America's Elite Colleges* (Stanford, CA: Stanford University Press, 2007).

SOBEHART, HELEN C. *Women Leading Education across the Continents: Sharing the spirit, fanning the flames* (Lanham, MD: Rowman and Littlefield, 2009).

SOMMERFELD, MEG "Asked to 'Dream,' Student Beat the Odds," *Education Week*, April 8, 1992, p. 1.

SOMMERS, CHRISTINA HOFF "The War Against Boys," *The Atlantic Monthly*, May 2000, pp. 59–74.

SOUTO-MANNING, MARIANA, and KEVIN J. SWICK "Teachers' Beliefs About Parent and Family Involvement: Rethinking our Family Involvement Paradigm," *Early Childhood Education*, Vol. 34, No. 2, October 2006, pp. 187–193.

SOWELL, THOMAS *Race and Culture* (New York: Basic Books, 1994).

SPADE, JOAN Z. "To Group or Not to Group, Is That the Question?" final report, U.S. Department of Education, Washington, DC, September 30, 1994.

SPADE, JOAN Z., LYNN COLUMBIA, and BETH E. VANFOSSEN "Tracking in Mathematics and Science: Courses and Course Selection Procedures," *Sociology of Education*, Vol. 70, 1997, pp. 108–127.

SPENCER, DIANE "Tool Kit to Fix Family Illiteracy," *The Times Educational Supplement*, No. 4066, June 3, 1994, p. 5f.

SPENCER, STEVEN J., CLAUDE M. STEELE, and DIANE M. QUINN, "Stereotype threat and Woman's Math Performance," *Journal of Experimental Social Psychology*, Vol. 35, Nos. 4–28, 1999.

SPILLANE, JAMES, and PATRICIA BURCH "The Institutional Environment and Instructional Practice: Changing Patterns of Guidance and Control in Public Schools," in H. Mier and B. Rowan (eds.), *The New Institutionalism in Education* (Albany, NY: SUNY Press, 2006).

SPRING, JOEL "Research on Globalization and Education," *Review of Educational Research*, Vol. 78, No.2, June 2008,pp. 330–363.

STANTON-SALAZAR, RICARDO D., and SANFORD M. DORNBUSCH "Social Capital and the Reproduction of Inequality: Information Networks Among Mexican-Origin High School Students," *Sociology of Education*, April 1995, p. 116.

"State Aid to Schools: A Primer" (New York: The State Education Department, December 2005).

"State Sales Tax Rates" Copyright January 1, 2007. Available: http://www.taxadmin.org/fta/rate/sales.pdf (Retrieved May 11, 2007).

STEARNS, E., S. MOLLER, J. BLAU, and S. POTOCHNICK "Staying Back and Dropping Out: The Relationship Between Grade Retention and School Dropout," *Sociology of Education*, Vol. 80, No. 3, 2007, pp. 210–240.

STEDRON, JENNIFER "A New Day for Learning," *State Legislatures*, Vol. 33, No. 3, March 2007.

STEELE, CLAUDE M. "Race and the Schooling of Black Americans," *The Atlantic Monthly*, April 1992, pp. 68–78.

STEELMAN, LALA CARR, and BRIAN POWELL "Sponsoring the Next Generation: Parental Willingness to Pay for Higher Education,"

American Journal of Sociology, Vol. 96, No. 6, May 1991, pp. 1505–1529.

STEINBERG, STEPHEN *Turning Back: The Retreat from Racial Justice in American Thought and Policy* (Boston, MA: Beason Press, 1995).

STEPHENS, JESSICA E. "Wanted: Minority Educators for U.S. Schools," *School Business Affairs*, Vol. 65, No. 5, May 1999, pp. 37–42.

STEVENS, MITCHELL L. *The Kingdom of Children: Culture and Controversy in the Homeschooling Movement* (Princeton, NJ: Princeton University Press, 2001).

STEVENS, MITCHELL L. *Kingdom of Children: Culture and Controversy in the Homeschooling Movement* (Princeton, NJ: Princeton University Press, 2003).

STEVENS, MITCHELL L. *Creating a Class: College Admissions and the Education of Elites* (Cambridge, MA: Harvard University Press, 2007).

STEVENSON, DAVID L. "Deviant Students as a Collective Resource in Classroom Control," *Sociology of Education*, Vol. 64, No. 2, April 1991, pp. 127–133.

STEVENSON, DAVID L., and DAVID P. BAKER "The Family-School Relation and the Child's School Performance," *Child Development*, Vol. 58, 1987, pp. 1348–1357.

STEVENSON, KENNETH R. *Educational Trends Shaping School Planning and Design: 2007* (Washington, DC: National Clearinghouse for Educational Facilities, 2007).

STEWART, DAVID W. *Immigration and Education: The Crisis and the Opportunities* (New York: The Free Press/Macmillan, 1992).

STEWART, KELLY AMIS *Tests Reveal Students Unprepared for College* (Chicago, IL: The Heartland Institute, February 2004). Available: http://www. Heartland.org/ (Retrieved April 16, 2007).

STIRES, LLOYD "Classroom Seating Location, Student Grades, and Attitudes: Environment or Self-Selection?" *Environment and Behavior*, Vol. 12, 1980, pp. 241–254.

STITES, REGIE, and LADISLAUS SEMALI "Adult Literacy for Equality or Economic Growth? Changing Agendas for Mass Literacy in China and Tanzania," *Comparative Education Review*, Vol. 35, No. 1, February 1991, pp. 44–75.

STROMQUIST, NELLY P. "Romancing the State: Gender and Power in Education," *Comparative Education Review*, November 1995, p. 423.

SUGGS, W. *A Place on the Team: The Triumph and Tragedy of Title IX* (Princeton, NJ: Princeton University Press, 2005).

SUN, FENGSHOU, and ARMANDO BARRIENTOS "The Equity Challenge in China's Higher Education Finance Policy," *Higher Education Policy*, Vol. 22, No. 2, 2009,

pp. 191–207. Available: http://www.palgrave-journals.com/hep/journal/v22/n2/full/hep200827a. html (Retrieved October 2, 2010).

"Supreme Court Lets Stand Ruling Against-Race-Based Scholarship at University of Maryland," *Jet*, Vol. 88, No. 5, June 12, 1995, p. 22.

Survey of Earned Doctorates, "Fact Sheet," 2007. Available: http://www.norc.uchicago.edu/NR/rdon-lyres/B40E56EC-9A4F-4892-B871-E330BB689CD9/ 0/SEDFactSheet.pdf (Retrieved October 13, 2010).

SUTER, LARRY "International Assessments: Overview," Copyright 2001. Available: http://www.nces.ed.gov/ surveys/SurveyGroups.asp? (Retrieved March 22, 2008).

SWIDLER, A. *Organization Without Authority: Dilemmas of Social Control in Free Schools* (Cambridge, MA: Harvard University Press, 1979).

SWIFT, DAVID W. (ed.) *Ideology and Change in the Public Schools: Latest Functions of Progressive Education* (Columbus, OH: Merrill, 1971).

SZABO, LIZ "More than 1 in 5 Kids Live in Poverty," *USA Today.* Copyright June 8, 2010. Available: http:// www.usatoday.com/news/health/2010-06-08-1Achild08_ST_N.htm (Retrieved August 8, 2010).

TALAN, JAMIE "After 40 Years, Black Kids Still Lack Strong Racial Identity," *Dayton Daily News*, September 6, 1987, p. E11.

TALBERT, JOAN E. "Primary and Promise of Professional Development in the Nation's Education Reform Agenda: Sociological Views," unpublished paper, January1995.

Talk of the Nation, "Job Pool for 2010 Grads Crowded with 2009 Grads," Copyright May 24, 2010. Available: http://www.npr.org/templates/ story.php?storyId=127092817 (Retrieved October 10, 2010).

TARIS, TOON W., and BOK, INGE A. "Parenting Environment and Scholastic Achievement During Adolescence: A Retrospective Study," *Early Child Development and Care*, Vol. 121, July 1996, pp. 67–83.

TASHMAN, BILLY "Hyping District 4," *The New Republic*, Vol. 207, No. 24, December 7, 1992, pp. 14–16.

TAVRIS, CAROL "Boys Trample Girls' Turf," *Los Angeles Times*, May 7, 1990, p. B5.

TAYLOR, BARBARA M. *Characteristics of Teachers Who Are Effective in Teaching All Children to Read* (Washington, DC: National Education Association, June 2004).

TAYLOR, HUMPHREY "Scientists, Doctors, Teachers, and Military Officers Top the List of Prestigious Occupations," *The Harris Poll*, October 16, 2002. Available: http://Harrisinteractive.com/ harris_poll/index.asp?Pollyear=2002 (Retrieved August 22, 2006).

Teaching Tolerance, "Helping the Homeless in School and Out," No. 38, Fall 2010. Available: www.tolerance.org/magazine/number-38-fall-2010/helping-homeless-school-and-out (Retrieved March 24, 2011).

Teen Pregnancy State and Federal Efforts to Implement Prevention Programs and Measure Their Effectiveness (Washington, DC: General Accounting Office, 1998).

TENENBAUM, H. R., and M. D. RUCK "Are Teacher Expectations Different for Racial Minority Than for European American Students? A Meta-analysis," *Journal of Educational Psychology*, Vol. 99, No. 2, 2007, pp. 253–273.

"Ten Years Later: Berkeley After the FSM," *Christian Century*, December 4, 1974, p. 1149.

TEPPER, CLARY A., and KIMBERLY WRIGHT CASSIDY "Gender Differences in Emotional Language in Children's Picture Books," *Sex Roles: A Journal of Research*, Vol. 40, Nos. 3–4, February 1999, pp. 265–280.

"Texas Textbook Debate Inflames Passions on All Sides," May 22, 2010. Available: http://www.cbsnews.com/8301-503544_162-20005647-503544.html (Retrieved August 26, 2010).

"The American Research University," *Daedalus*, Fall 1993.

The Carnegie Corporation, "Education That Works: An Action Plan for the Education of Minorities," 1990.

The Center for Comprehensive School Reform and Improvement, "School Reform and Improvement Database," Copyright 2005. Available: http://www.csrclearinghouse.org (Retrieved June 21, 2010).

The Chronicle of Higher Education Almanac, Copyright 2006–2007. Available: http://chronicle.com/weekly/almanac/2006/nation/0102201.htm (Retrieved May 20, 2010).

The Chronicle of Higher Education Almanac, Copyright 2010a. Available: http://chronicle.com/article/Percentage-of-Faculty-Members/123927/ (Retrieved October 6, 2010).

The Chronicle of Higher Education Almanac, Copyright 2010b. Available: http://chronicle.com/article/Graphic-Increasingly-Faculty/124091/ (Retrieved October 6, 2010).

The College Board, "Hottest Careers for College Graduates: Occupations with the most Job Openings," 2010. Available: http://www.collegeboard.com/student/csearch/majors_careers/236.html (Retrieved September 8, 2010).

"The Disabled ADA: How a Narrowing ADA Threatens to Exclude the Cognitively Disabled," *Brigham Young University Law Review: 1333–1352*, 2006.

"The Educational Progress of Hispanic Students," *The Condition of Education*, 1995, U.S. Department of Education, Washington, DC, NCES 95–767.

The Education Trust, *Stalled in Secondary* (Washington, DC: The Education Trust, 2005).

The Gallup Poll, "Evolution, Creationism, Intelligent Design," 2009. Available: http://www.galluppoll.com/content/default/aspx?ci=21814 (Retrieved June 15, 2010).

The General Social Surveys, 1972–1988: Cumulative Codebook (Chicago, IL: National Opinion Research Center, 1998), pp. 123–141, 1223–1241.

The Hudson Institute, *The State of the American Dream.* Copyright 1997. Available: http://www.amazon.com/American-Hudson-Institute-executive-briefing/dp/B0006R6NYO (Retrieved June 7, 2010).

The Huffington Post, "6.7% of World has College Degree," Copyright July 19, 2010. Available: http://www.huffingtonpost.com/2010/05/19/percent-of-world-with-col_n_581807.html (Retrieved August 8, 2010).

The Institute for Diversity and Ethics in Sport, *Keeping Score When It Counts* (Orlando, FL: University of Central Florida, 2006).

The News Hour, "Charter Schools," June 11, 2007, Public Broadcasting System.

The Open University, "OU Basics: What is the OU?" 2007. Available: http://www8.open.ac.uk/about/main/the-ou-explained

The Rand Corporation, "Grades Still Pending on Vouchers and Charter Schools," 2007. Available: http://www.rand.org/publication/randreview/issues/rr.04.02/news.html (Retrieved May 10, 2007).

"The Widening Gap in Higher Education," *The Chronicle of Higher Education*, June 14, 1996, p. A10+.

The World's Women 1995: Trends and Statistics. New York: United Nations. Available: www.worldcat.org/title/worlds-women-1995-trends-and-statistics/oclc/o33126367 "after" "The Widening Gap in Higher Education," *The Chronicle of Higher Education*, June 14, 1996,p. A10+.

THOMAS, SANDRA P. "School Connectedness, Anger Behaviors, and Relationships of Violent and Nonviolent American Youth," *Perspectives in Pediatric Care*, October–December 2004. Available: findarticles.com/p/articles/mi_qa3804/is_200410/ai_n9484280 (Retrieved April 20, 2007).

THOMPSON, LYNN "School Size: Is Small Really Better?" *The Seattle Times*, October 26, 2005. Available http://community.seattletimes.nwsource.com/archive/?date=20051026&slug=smallschools26n (Retrieved August 27, 2007).

THORNBERRY, TERENCE P., and JAMES H. BURCH II "Gang Members and Delinquent Behavior," *Juvenile Justice Bulletin*, June 1997.

THORNE, BARRIE *Gender Play: Girls and Boys in School* (New Brunswick, NJ: Rutgers University Press, 1993).

THORNE, BARRIE *Gender Play: Girls and Boys in School* (New Brunswick, NJ: Rutgers University Press, 1999).

THURSTON, LINDA P., and LORI NAVARRETT "A Tough Row to Hoe: Research on Education and Rural Poor Families," in *Rural Goals 2000: Building Programs that Work*. 1996. ERIC @ED394771.

TIROZZI, GERALD N. "The Artistry of Leadership: The Evolving Role of the Secondary School Principal," *Phi Delta Kappan*, Vol. 82, No. 6, February 2001, pp. 434–439.

TOPOLNICKI, DENISE M. "Why Private Schools Are Rarely Worth the Money," *Money*, Vol. 23, No. 10, October 1994, pp. 98–112.

TORRES, CARLOS ALBERTO "Paulo Freire as Secretary of Education in the Municipality of Sao Paulo," *Comparative Education Review*, Vol. 38, No. 2, May 1994, pp. 181–214.

TREMAIN, DONALD *Occupational Prestige in Comparative Perspective* (New York: Academic Press, 1977).

TRENT, WILLIAM L. "Outcomes of School Desegregation: Findings from Longitudinal Research," *Journal of Negro Education*, Vol. 66, No. 3, Summer 1997, pp. 255–257.

TROTTER, A. "Studies Fault Results of Retention in Chicago," *Education Week*, Vol. 23, No. 31, April 14, 2004, p. 18.

TROW, MARTIN "Comparative Perspectives on British and American Higher Education," paper presented at American Sociological Association meetings, Chicago, August 1987.

TULSHYAN, RUCHIKA "Top 10 College Majors for Women," March 2, 2010. Available: http://www.forbes.com/2010/03/02/top-10-college-majors-women-forbes-women-leadership-education.html (Retrieved September 21, 2010).

TURNER, RALPH "Sponsored and Contest Mobility," *American Sociological Review*, Vol. 25, 1960, pp. 855–867.

TYACK, DAVID B. *The One Best System: A History of American Urban Education* (Cambridge, MA: Harvard University Press, 1974).

TYACK, DAVID B., and ELISABETH HANSOT *Learning Together: A History of Coeducation in American Schools* (New Haven, CT: Yale University Press, 1990).

TYSON, KAROLYN "Weighing In: Elementary-Age Students and the Debate on Attitudes Toward School Among Black Students," *Social Forces*, Vol. 80, No. 4, 2002, pp. 1157–1189.

TYSON, KAROLYN, WILLIAM DARITY, JR., and DOMINI CASTELLINO "It's Not 'A Black Thing:' Understanding the Burden of Acting White and Other Dilemmas of High Achievement," *American Sociological Review*, Vol. 70, No. 4, 2005, pp. 582–605.

UCLA, Higher Education Research Institute, *Research Brief: The American Freshman, National Norms for 2009.* Available: http://www.heri.ucla.edu/cirpoverview.php

UMEMOTO, K. *The Truce: Lessons from an L.A. Gang War* (Ithaca, NY: Cornell University Press, 2006).

UN Development Programme Report 2005. Available: www.undp.org/annualreports (Retrieved May 25, 2010).

UNDP, Human Development Report, Table 1 (New York: United Nations, 2007–2008). Available: http://hdr.undp.org/xmlsearch/reportSearch?y=2007&c=*&t=*&lang=en&k=&orderby=year

UNESCO, *Education for All Global Monitoring Report: Is the World on Track?* (Montreal: UNESCO Institute for Statistics, 2003).

UNESCO, *Children Out of School: Measuring Exclusion from Primary School* (Montreal: UNESCO Institute for Statistics, 2005).

UNESCO, "Education in China," *Statistics in Brief* (Montreal, Canada: UNESCO Institute for Statistics, 2007). Available: http://stats.uis.unesco.org/unesco/TableViewer/document.aspx (Retrieved May 20, 2010).

UNESCO, "Education for All Global Monitoring Project," 2009. Available: www.unesco.org/education/gmr2009/press/Factsheet_SSA.pdf (Retrieved October 2, 2010).

UNESCO Institute for Statistics 2010, Table 1: "Population of Primary and Lower Secondary School Age by Region (million), 2007," p. 10. International Education Statistics: Children of primary and Secondary School Age Out of School, Mar 28, 2010. Available: http://huebler.blogspot.com/2010/03/coos.html.

UNESCO Press, "Statistics Show Slow Progress Toward Universal Literacy, and More Literate Women Than Ever Before," Press Release No. 2002–55, United Nations, New York, 2002. Available: http://www.unesco.org/bpi/eng/unescopress/2002/02–59e.shtml (Retrieved April 20, 2007).

UNICEF, *Country Statistics-Nepal* (New York: United Nations). Available: www.unicef.org/statis/country (Retrieved May 21, 2010).

UNICEF, *State of the World's Children: 2000*, Table 4: Education. 2006. Available: www.unicef.org/sowc00/stat6 (Retrieved May 21, 2010).

UNICEF, *The State of the World's Children* (New York: UNICEF, 2007). Available: http://www.unicef.org/sowc07/ (Reteieved May 19, 2010).

United Nations, *Human Development Report*, 1999. Available: www.unicef.org/statis/country (Reteieved May 25, 2010).

UNICEF. United Nations Children Fund, "*China Statistics*," November 27, 2009. Available: http://www.unicef.org/infobycountry/china_statistics.html#67 (Retrieved April 6, 2011).

UNICEF, *Country Statistics-Nepal* (New York: United Nations). Available: http://www.unicef.org/infobycountry/nepal_nepal_statistics.html (Retrieved June 7, 2010).

U.S. Bureau of Labor Statistics, Department of Labor, 2006–2007. *Occupational Outlook Handbook 2006–7 Edition*. Teachers—Preschool, Kindergarten, Elementary, Middle and Secondary. Available: http://www.bls.gov/oco/ocos069.htm (Retrieve Date: May 14, 2007).

U.S. Census Bureau, *Population Division, Population Projections Program* (Washington, DC: Government Printing Office, 2000).

U.S. Census Bureau, "Percent of Americans with College Degree." *American Community Survey* (Washington, DC: U.S. Census Bureau, 2002).

U.S. Census Bureau, "Percent of High School and College Graduates," 2003. Available: www.census.gov/population/socdemo/education/cps2003/tab01a-o1.pdf (Reteieved May 30, 2010).

U.S. Census Bureau, "Children Below Poverty Level, by Race and Hispanic Origin: 1970–1996," *Current Population Reports*, 2004. No 757, pp. 60–198.

U.S. Census Bureau, "American Factfinder," 2007. Available: http://factfinder.census.gov/servlet/SAFFFacts?geo_id=&_geoContext+&_street=&_country (Retrieved April 13, 2007).

U.S. Census Bureau, "Custodial Mothers and Fathers and their Child Support: 2007," 2007. Available: http://singleparents.about.com/od/legalissues/p/portrait.htm (Retrieved August 8, 2010).

U.S. Census Bureau, "Hispanic Americans by the Numbers," July 1, 2008. Available: www.infoplease.com/ spot/hhmcensus1.html (Retrieved August 8, 2010).

U.S. Census Bureau, "Percent Distribution of Total Public Elementary-Secondary School System Revenue: 2007–2008." *Public Education Finances 2008*, Issued June 2010. Available: www2.census.gov/govs/school/08f33pub.pdf (Retrieved August 8, 2010).

U.S. Census Bureau, "Teachers, Enrollment, and Pupil-Teacher Ratio," 2010. Available: www.census.gov/compendia/statab/2010/tables/10s0245.pdf (Retrieved September 14, 2010).

U.S. Department of Commerce, Current Population Reports: Population Projections of the United States by Age, Sex, Race and Hispanic Origin: 1991 to 2050, P25–1130, Bureau of the census, Washington, DC, 1996.

U.S. Department of Education, *Digest of Educational Statistics* (Washington, DC: U.S. Department of Education, 2005).

U.S. Department of Education, "Overview: No Child Left Behind: Expanding the Promise," March 2005. Available: http://www.ed.gov/about/overview/budget/budget06/nclb/index.html (Retrieve Date: April 13, 2007).

U.S. Department of Education, *A Test of Leadership: Charting the Future of U.S. Higher Education* (Washington, DC: Author, 2006).

U.S. Department of Health and Human Services, Administration for Children and Families, Office of Head Start, *Head Start Program Fact Sheet, Fiscal Year 2006*, 2006. Available: http://www.acf.hhs.gov/programs/hsb/research/2006.htm (Retrieved July 31, 2006).

U.S. Department of Labor, Bureau of Labor Statistics, "Teachers—Preschool, Kindergarten, Elementary, Middle, and Secondary," 2007. Available: www.bls.gov/oco/ocos069.htm (Retrieved January 24, 2008).

USEEM, ELIZABETH L. "Social Class and Ability Group Placement in Mathematics in the Transition to Seventh Grade: The Role of Parental Involvement," paper presented at American Educational Research Association meetings, Boston, April 1990.

USEEM, ELIZABETH L. "Student Selection into Course Sequences in Mathematics: The Impact of Parental Involvement and School Policies," *The Journal of Research on Adolescence*, Vol. 1, No. 3, 1991, pp. 231–250.

USEEM, ELIZABETH L. *Renewing Schools: A Report on the Cluster Initiative in Philadelphia* (Philadelphia, PA: PATHS/PRISM, Spring 1994).

VAIL, KATHLEEN "Women at the Top," *American School Board Journal*, December 1999.

VAISEY, STEPHEN "Education and Its Discontents: Over Qualification in America, 1972–2002," *Social Forces*, Vol. 85, No. 2, 2006, pp. 835–864.

VALDEZ, AVELARDO *Mexican American Girls and Gang Violence* (New York: Palgrave Macmillan, 2007).

VAN HOUTTE, MIEKE, and DIMITRI VAN MAELE "Students' Sense of Belonging in Technical/Vocational Schools Versus Academic Schools," papers presented at the International Sociological Association World Congress of Sociology, Sweden, July 2010.

VANDELL, DEBORAH LOWE, and SHERI E. HEMBREE "Peer Social Status and Friendship: Independent Contributors to Children's Social and Academic Adjustment," *Merrill-Palmer Quarterly*, Vol. 40, No. 4, 1994, pp. 461–475.

VAN TASSEL-BASKA, JOYCE "A Content Analysis of Evaluation Findings Across 20 Gifted Programs," *Gifted Child Quarterly,* Vol. 50, No. 3, 2006, pp. 199–215.

VAUGHAN, GEORGE B. "Institutions on the Edge: America's Community Colleges," *Educational Record,* Vol. 72, No. 2, Spring 1991, pp. 30–33.

Vedantam, Shankar "Psych-Out Sexism: The Innocent, Unconscious Bias that Discourages Girls from Math and Science," *Slate,* March 1, 2011. Available: www.slate.com/id/2286671/pagenum/all/ (Retrieved May 7, 2011).

VELEZ, WILLIAM "Why Hispanic Students Fail: Factors Affecting Attrition in High Schools," in Leonard Cargan and Jeanne H. Ballantine (eds.), *Sociological Footprints,* 6th ed. (Belmont, CA: Wadsworth, 1994), pp. 261–267.

VELEZ, WILLIAM, and RAJSHEKHAR G. JAVALGI "Factors Affecting the Probabilities of Transferring from a Two-Year College to a Four-Year College," unpublished paper, 1994.

VERDUGO, RICHARD R., and JEFFREY M. SCHNEIDER "Quality Schools, Safe Schools: A Theoretical and Empirical Discussion," *Education and Urban Society,* Vol. 31, No. 3, May 1999, pp. 286–307.

VIADERO, DEBRA "A School of Choice," *Education Week,* Vol. 15, No. 10, November 8, 1995, pp. 31–33.

VIADERO, DEBRA "Smaller Not Necessarily Better, School-Size Study Concludes," *Education Week,* May 23, 2006.

"Violence and Safety," *Education Week,* 2004. Available: www.cdph.ca.gov/HealthInfo/injviosaf/.../ SVinventory-EPIC.pdf (Retrieved April 6, 2011).

VOELKI, K. E. "Academic Achievement and Expectations Among African-American Students," *Journal of Research and Development in Education,* Vol. 27, No. 1, Fall 1993, pp. 42–55.

VOGEL, D. L., S. R. WESTER, M. HEESACKER, and S. MADON "Confirming Gender Stereotypes: A Social Role Perspective," *Sex Roles: A Journal of Research,* Vol. 48, Nos. 11/12, 2003, pp. 519–528.

VOSSEKUIL, BRYAN, ROBERT A. FEIN, MARISA REDDY, RANDY BORUM, and WILLIAM MODZELESKI *The Final Report and Findings of the Safe School Initiative: Implications for the Prevention of School Attacks in the United States* (Washington, DC: United States Secret Service and United States Department of Education, 2002).

WAGMILLER, ROBERT L., ELIZABETH GERSHOFF, PHILIP VELIZ, and MARGARET CLEMENTS "Does Children's Academic Achievement Improve when Single Mothers Marry?" *Sociology of Education,* Vol. 83, No. 3, 2010, pp. 201–226.

WAGNER, ALAN *Measuring up Internationally: Developing Skills and Knowledge for the Global Knowledge Economy* (San Jose, CA: National Center for Public Policy and Higher Education, September 2006).

WALDEN, TEDRA, ELIZABETH LEMERISE, and MAUREEN C. SMITH "Friendship and Popularity in Preschool Classrooms," *Early Education and Development,* Vol. 10, No. 3, July 1999, pp. 351–371.

WALKER, DAVID "Britain's Campuses Expect to Face a Rush of Students," *The Chronicle of Higher Education,* Vol. 38, No. 8, October 16, 1991, p. A51.

WALLER, WILLARD *The Sociology of Teaching* (New York: Wiley, 1932/1965), pp. 120–133.

WALLERSTEIN, IMMANUAL *The Modern World System* (New York: Academic Press, 1974).

WALLERSTEIN, IMMANUEL *World-Systems Analysis: An Intoduction* (Durham, NC: Duke, 2004).

WALPOLE, MARYBETH "Socioeconomic Status and College: How SES Affects College Experiences and Outcomes," *Review of Higher Education,* Vol. 27, No. 1, Fall, 2003, pp. 45–73.

WALSH, MARK "Justices Weigh Allowing Prayers at Graduation," *Education Week,* November 13, 1991a, p. 1.

WALSH, MARK "Students at Private Schools for Blacks Post Above-Average Scores, Study Finds," *Education Week,* October 16, 1991b.

WALSH, MARK "Justices Settle Case, Nettle Policy Debate," *Education Week,* Vol. 21, July 10, 2002, pp. 1, 18–21.

WAN, YINMEI "Expansion of Chinese Higher Education Since 1998: Its Causes and Outcomes," *Asia Pacific Education Review,* Vol. 7, No. 1, 2006, pp. 19–31.

WANG, MIN QI, ET AL. "Family and Peer Influences on Smoking Behavior Among American Adolescents: An Age Trend," *Journal of Adolescent Health,* Vol. 16, No. 3, March 1995, pp. 200–203.

WARNER, W. LLOYD, ROBERT J. HAVIGHURST, and MARTIN R. LOEB *Who Shall Be Educated?* (New York: Harper & Row, 1944).

WARR, MARK "Parents, Peers, and Delinquency," *Social Forces,* Vol. 72, No. 1, September 1993, pp. 247–264.

WARREN, JOHN ROBERT, and ERIC GRODSKY "Exit Exams Harm Students Who Fail Them—and Don't Benefit Students Who Pass Them," *Phi Delta Kappan* May 2009, pp. 645–649.

WARREN, JOHN ROBERT, PAUL C. LEPORE, and ROBERT D. MARE "Employment During High School: Consequences for Students' Grades in Academic Courses," *American Educational Research Journal,* Vol. 37, No. 4, 2000, pp. 943–969.

WEBB, JOHN A., ET AL. "Relationship Among Social and Intrapersonal Risk, Alcohol Expectancies, and

Alcohol Usage Among Early Adolescents," *Addictive Behaviors,* Vol. 18, No. 2, March–April 1993, pp. 127–134.

WEBER, B. J., and L. M. OMOTANI "The Power of Believing," *Executive Educator,* Vol. 6, No. 9, September 1994, pp. 35–38.

WEBER, MAX *The Theory of Social and Economic Organization* (ed. Talcott Parsons; trans. A. M. Henderson and Talcott Parsons) (Glencoe, IL: Free Press, 1947).

WEBER, MAX "The Chinese Literati," in H. H. Gerth and C. Wright Mills (eds. and trans.), *From Max Weber: Essays in Sociology* (New York: Oxford University Press, 1958), pp. 422–433.

WEBER, MAX "The Three Types of Legitimate Rule," in Amitai Etzioni (ed.), *Complex Organizations: A Sociological Reader* (New York: Holt, Rinehart and Winston, 1961).

Webster's New Collegiate Dictionary (Springfield, Massachusetts: G. C. Merriam, 1974).

WEDGEWORTH, ROBERT "The Number of Functionally Illiterate Adults in U.S. Is Growing," 2003. National Assessment of Adult Literacy. ProLiteracy Worldwide. Available: www.tnliteracy.org/Statistics_B20E.html (Retrieved April 6, 2011).

WEDGWOOD, RUTH "Education and Poverty Reduction in Tanzania," *International Journal of Educational Development,* Vol. 27, 2007, pp. 383–396.

WEICK, KARL E. "Educational Organizations as Loosely Coupled Systems," *Administrative Science Quarterly,* Vol. 31, No. 4, December 1976, pp. 612–632.

WELCH, ANTHONY "Knowledge and Legitimation in Comparative Education," *Comparative Education Review,* Vol. 35, No. 3, 1991, pp. 508–531.

WELLS, AMY STUART, ALEJANDRA LOPEZ, JANELLE SCOTT, and JENNIFER JILLISON HOLME "Charter Schools as Postmodern Paradox: Rethinking Social Stratification in an Age of Deregulated School Choice," *Harvard Educational Review,* Vol. 69, No. 2, Summer 1999, pp. 172–204.

Wessmann v. Gittens, 1998. Available: http://lw.bna.com/lw/19981201/981657.htm

WEXLER, PHILIP *Social Analysis of Education: After the New Sociology* (London: Routledge & Kegan Paul, 1987).

WEXLER, PHILIP "New Sociology of Education," in David L. Levinson, Peter W. Cookson, Jr., and Alan R. Sadovnik (eds.), *Education and Society: An Encyclopedia* (New York: Routledge/Falmer Press, 2002), pp. 593–597.

WEXLER, PHILIP, WARREN CRICHLOW, JUNE KERN, and REBECCA MARTUSEWICZ *Becoming Somebody: Toward a Social Psychology of School* (Washington, DC: Falmer Press, 1992).

"What Matters Most: Teaching for America's Future" (New York: Report of the National Commission on Teacher and America's Future, 1996), p. 54.

"What We Know About Science Teaching and Learning" (Washington, DC: Council for Educational Developmental and Research, 1993).

WHELAN, DEBRA LAU "Librarians Respond to Decline in Reading," *School Library Journal,* 2004. Available: http://www.schoollibraryjournal.com/article/CA447790.html (Retrieved April 12, 2007).

WHITMAN, DAVID (ed.) *Sweating the Small Stuff: Inner-City Schools and the New Paternalism* (Washington DC: Thomas B. Fordham Institute, 2008).

WHIPPS, HEATHER "Census: U.S. Household Size Shrinking," September 21, 2006. Available: www.msnbc.msn.com/id/14942047/ (Retrieved August 8, 2010).

WHITAKER, JOSEPH *Whitaker Almanac* (London: J. Whitaker & Sons Ltd., 1996, 1999, 2000).

WHITEHURST, GROVER J., and MICHELLE CROFT "The Harlem Children's Zone, Promise Neighborhoods, and the Broader, Bolder Approach to Education," Brown Center on Education Policy at Brookings Institution, Washington, DC, 2010.

WIE, FANG, and SEN QI "Longitudinal Effects of Parenting on Children's Academic Achievement in African American Families," *The Journal of Negro Education,* Vol. 75, No. 3, Summer 2006, pp. 415–429.

WILKINSON, DORIS Y. "The American University and the Rhetoric of Neoconservatism," *Contemporary Sociology,* Vol. 20, No. 4, 1991, pp. 550–553.

WILKINSON, IAN A. G. "Introduction: Peer Influences on Learning: Where Are They?" *International Journal of Educational Research,* Vol. 37, No. 5, 2003, pp. 395–401.

WILLIAMS, EDITH "Paternal Involvement, Maternal Employment, and Adolescents' Academic Achievement: An 11–Year Follow-Up," *American Journal of Orthopsychiatry,* Vol. 63, No. 2, April 1993, pp. 306–312.

WILLIAMS, ROBIN *American Society: A Sociological Interpretation* (New York: Alfred A. Knopf, 1970).

WILLIAMSON, BILL *Education, Social Structure and Development* (London: Macmillan, 1979).

WILLIS, PAUL E. *Learning to Labor: How Working Class Kids Get Working Class Jobs* (New York: Columbia University Press, 1977).

WILLIS, PAUL E. *Learning to Labor: How Working Class Kids Get Working Class Jobs* (New York: Columbia University Press, 1981).

WILSON, FRANKLIN D. "The Impact of School Desegregation Programs on White Public School

Enrollment, 1968–1976," *Sociology of Education,* Vol. 58, July 1985, pp. 137–153.

WILSON, KENNETH L., and JANET P. BOLDIZAR "Gender Segregation in Higher Education: Effects of Aspirations, Mathematics Achievement, and Income," *Sociology of Education,* Vol. 63, No. 1, January 1990, pp. 62–74.

WILSON, ROBIN "Downturn Threatens the Faculty's Role in Running Colleges," *The Chronicle of Higher Education,* February 8, 2009.

WILSON, ROBIN "For-Profit Colleges Change Higher Education Landscape," *Chronicle of Higher education,* February 7, 2010.

WILSON, WILLIAM JULIUS *The Truly Disadvantaged: The Inner City, the Underclass, and Public Policy* (Chicago, IL: University of Chicago Press, 1987).

WILSON, WILLIAM JULIUS *When Work Disappears: The World of the New Urban Poor* (New York: Knopf, 1996).

WINCE-SMITH, DEBORAH L. "The Creativity Imperative: A National Perspective," *Peer Review,* No. 2, Spring 2006. Available: www.aacu.org/peerreview/pr.sp06/pr-sp06 (Retrieved January 31, 2008).

WINERIP, MICHAEL "A Popular Principal, Wounded by Government's Good Intentions," *The New York Times,* July 18, 2010a, p. A1.

WINERIP, MICHAEL "Equity of Test is Debated as Children Compete for Gifted Kindergarten," *The New York Times,* July 25, 2010b.

WINKLER, KAREN J. "Researcher's Examination of California's Poor Latino Population Prompts Debate Over the Traditional Definitions of the Underclass," *The Chronicle of Higher Education,* October 10, 1990, p. A5.

Women's Sports Foundation, "Title ix Q & A." May 26, 2005. Available: www.womenssportsfoundation.org/Content/Articles/Issues/Title%20IX/T (Retrieved May 7, 2011).

WOODHALL, MAUREEN "Sharing Costs of Higher Education: An International Analysis," *Educational Record,* Fall 1991, p. 30.

WOODS, PETER (ed.) *Pupil Strategies: Explorations in the Sociology of the School* (London: Croom Helm, 1980).

XIAOFEND, LIU S., and J. PATRICK MEYER "Teachers Perceptions of Their Jobs: A Multi-Level Analysis of the Teacher Follow Up Survey for 1994–95," *Teachers College Record,* Vol. 107, 2005, pp. 985–1003.

YANG, DONG P. "Gaodeng jiaoyu ruxue jihui: kuda zhi zhong de jieceng chaju" ("Access to Higher Education: Widening Social Class Disparities"), *Tsinghua Journal of Education* (Chinese Journal), Vol. 27, No. 1, 2006, pp. 19–25.

YOGEV, ABREHAMG, and HANNA AYALON "Vocational Education and Social Reproduction: Students' Allocation to Curricular Program in Israeli Vocational High Schools," paper presented at American Sociological Association meetings, Chicago, IL, August 1987.

YONEZAWA, SUSAN, AMY S. WELLS, and IRENE SERNA "Choosing Tracks: Freedom of Choice in Detracked Schools," *American Educational Research Journal,* Vol. 39, No. 1, 2002, pp. 37–67.

YONEZAWA, SUSAN, and MAKEBA JONES "Students Perspectives on Tracking and Detracking," *Theory into Practice,* Vol. 45, No. 1, 2006, pp. 15–23.

YOUNG, BETH A. *Characteristics of the 100 Largest Public Elementary and Secondary School Districts in the U.S., 2000–01* (Washington, DC: National Center for Educational Statistics, U.S. Department of Education, 2002), NCES 2002–351.

YOUNG, MICHAEL F. D. (ed.) *Knowledge and Control: New Directions for the Sociology of Education* (London: Collier-Macmillan, 1971).

YOUNG, ROBERT E. *A Critical Theory of Education: Habermas and Our Children's Future* (New York: Teachers College Press, 1990).

ZEHR, MARY ANN "Catholic Schools' Mission to Serve Needs Children Jeopardized by Closings," *Education Week,* Vol. 24, No. 26, March 9, 2005, p. 1.

ZHAO, LITAO, and SHENG SIXIN "Fast and Furious: Problems of China's Higher Education Expansion," EAI Background Brief No. 395. Available: www. eai. nus.edu.sg/BB395.pdf (Retrieved October 15, 2010).

ZHOU, XUEGUANG, PHYLLIS MOEN, and NANCY BRANDON TUMA "Educational Stratification in Urban China 1949–94," *Sociology of Education,* Vol. 71, No. 3, July 1998, pp. 199–222.

ZIMMERMAN, JONATHAN *Whose America? Culture Wars in the Public Schools* (Cambridge, MA: Harvard University Press, 2002).

ZIRKEL, PERRY A. "The 'N' Word," *Phi Delta Kappan,* Vol. 80, No. 9, May 1999, pp. 713–714.

ZIRKEL, PERRY A. "School Law All Stars: Two Successive Constellations," *Phi Delta Kappan,* Vol. 90, 2009. Available: www.pdkintl.org/kappan/k_v90/k0906zir.htm (Retrieved June 1, 2010).

INDEX